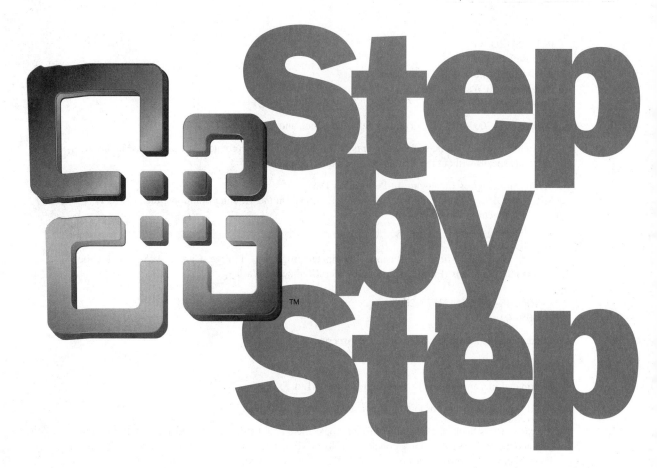

Step by Step

Microsoft®
Office System
2003 EDITION

Online Training Solutions, Inc., and Curtis Frye

PUBLISHED BY
Microsoft Press
A Division of Microsoft Corporation
One Microsoft Way
Redmond, Washington 98052-6399

Library of Congress Cataloging-in-Publication Data
Microsoft Office System Step by Step—2003 Edition / Online Training Solutions, Inc., Curtis Frye.
      p. cm. -- (Step by Step)
   Includes index.
   ISBN 0-7356-1520-9
   1. Microsoft Office. 2. Business--Computer programs. I. Frye, Curtis, 1968- II. Online Training Solutions (Firm). III. Step by step (Redmond, Wash.)

   HF5548.4.M525M5357   2003
   005.369--dc22   2003058070

Printed and bound in the United States of America.

8 9   QWT   8 7 6

Distributed in Canada by H.B. Fenn and Company Ltd.

A CIP catalogue record for this book is available from the British Library.

Microsoft Press books are available through booksellers and distributors worldwide. For further information about international editions, contact your local Microsoft Corporation office or contact Microsoft Press International directly at fax (425) 936-7329. Visit our Web site at www.microsoft.com/mspress. Send comments to *mspinput@microsoft.com*.

Acquisitions Editor: Alex Blanton
Project Editor: Aileen Wrothwell

Body Part No. X09-71449

Contents

I Microsoft Office Word 2003

1 Working with Documents   2

2 Editing and Proofreading Documents   26

Contents

III   Microsoft Office Access 2003

IV   Microsoft Office PowerPoint 2003

VI Microsoft Office FrontPage 2003

25 Enhancing Your Web Site with Graphics   632

VII   Microsoft Office Publisher 2003

26 Creating and Printing Publications   664

27 Creating Web Sites and E-mail Messages   690

VIII Microsoft Office OneNote 2003

IX Microsoft Office InfoPath 2003

What's New in The Microsoft Office System 2003

You'll notice some changes as soon as you start one of the programs that is part of The Microsoft Office System 2003. Many of the familiar program elements have been reorganized to give you better access to the features you use most, and many new features have been added to make it easier to access the tools you use most often.

Some of the features that are new or improved in The Microsoft Office System 2003 won't be apparent to you until you start using the programs. To help you quickly identify features that are new or improved with this version, this book uses the icon in the margin whenever those features are discussed or shown.

While many new features of The Microsoft Office System are discussed in this book, many other new features are covered only in the *Step by Step* books that pertain to the individual applications.

The following table lists the new features that you might be interested in, as well as the chapters in which those features are discussed.

To learn how to	Using this feature	See
View and read the document as it will appear on paper without needing to print it	Reading Layout view	Chapter 1
View small images of each page in the document	Thumbnails	Chapter 1
Display a menu of options for performing common tasks	Smart Tags	Chapter 2
Locate supporting information in local reference materials or on the Internet	Research service	Chapter 2
Track types of data, such as dates, names, and addresses, that can be used in multiple ways	Smart Tags	Chapter 9
Change your display theme	Support for Windows XP Theming	Chapter 10
Quickly update input mask options	Property Update Options	Chapter 12
Choose words that suit your presentation and your audience and research information on the Web	Thesaurus and Research task pane	Chapter 15

To learn how to	Using this feature	See
Deliver a presentation on a computer on which PowerPoint is not installed	Updated PowerPoint Viewer program	Chapter 16
Mark up slides during a presentation	Improved ink annotations	Chapter 16
Move smoothly from slide to slide when delivering an electronic slide show	New slide show navigation tools	Chapter 16
Make sure you include all the files you need when you transfer a presentation to a CD	Package for CD	Chapter 16
Quickly access your mail, calendar, contacts, tasks, and other Outlook items	Navigation Pane	Chapter 17
Open attachments without opening the item	Reading Pane	Chapter 17
Access Word's e-mail-related toolbar buttons from one convenient location	Word as your e-mail editor simplifications	Chapter 17
Read and respond to an e-mail message without closing other applications	Desktop Alerts	Chapter 17
Post attachments for group input	Live Attachments	Chapter 17
View your messages in any of 13 pre-defined views	Arrangements	Chapter 18
Quickly mark messages for follow-up	Quick Flags	Chapter 18
Assign a different signature to each Outlook account	Unique signature per account	Chapter 18
View your messages in a new way	Arrange by Conversation	Chapter 18
Collect and automatically update related information in virtual folders	Search Folders	Chapter 19
Create and organize rules in an easier way	Rules	Chapter 19
View your Calendar and the Date Navigator in a new, streamlined format	Calendar View	Chapter 20
View multiple calendars at the same time	Side-by-side calendars	Chapter 20
Easily publish entire Web sites or specific files to a local folder or Web server	Remote Web Site view	Chapter 22
Reduce the size of a page file when publishing it, by removing extraneous white space and unnecessary formatting	Optimize HTML	Chapter 22
Switch between page views and site views	Web Site tab	Chapter 22

To learn how to	Using this feature	See
Work with Web pages in Design view, Code view, Split view, and Preview view	Web page views	Chapter 22
Simultaneously view the layout and HTML code of your Web page	Split view	Chapter 22
Check your Web site against standard guidelines for accessibility	Accessibility checking	Chapter 23
See how your Web site will look in different Web browsers or at various screen resolutions	Browser and resolution reconciliation	Chapter 23
Allow multiple people to work with the same version of a document	Document workspace	Chapter 32
Centralize meeting information in one location through the Internet or an intranet	Meeting workspace	Chapter 33

Other New Features in The Microsoft Office System 2003

Microsoft OneNote

New in Office 2003, Microsoft OneNote helps you document, organize, and use information gathered during meetings, brainstorming sessions, interviews, and more. The notes you create can include text, drawings, images, and audio recordings. OneNote uses a freeform page layout, so you can place and move information wherever you want.

Microsoft InfoPath

Microsoft InfoPath, a new program in Office 2003, helps you collect and work with data by using dynamic, online forms that have a familiar Office interface. Based on the Extensible Markup Language (XML), InfoPath makes it easy to create and use robust forms to more effectively gather and share information throughout your organization.

Collaboration with The Microsoft Office System 2003

With a document workspace, you can store and edit your documents in a shared, central location, along with related tasks, documents, links, and a list of team members. When you collaborate in a meeting workspace, you can share agendas, reference information, attendee lists, and notes. You can also track action items, related documents, and more.

Getting Help

Every effort has been made to ensure the accuracy of this book and the contents of its CD-ROM. If you do run into problems, please contact the appropriate source for help and assistance.

Getting Help with This Book and Its CD-ROM

If your question or issue concerns the content of this book or its companion CD-ROM, please first search the online Microsoft Press Knowledge Base, which provides support information for known errors in or corrections to this book, at the following Web site:

www.microsoft.com/mspress/support/search.asp

If you do not find your answer at the online Knowledge Base, send your comments or questions to Microsoft Press Technical Support at:

mspinput@microsoft.com

Getting Help with The Microsoft Office System 2003

If your question is about one of the programs included in The Microsoft Office System 2003, and not about the content of this Microsoft Press book, your first recourse is that program's Help system. This system is a combination of help tools and files stored on your computer when you installed The Microsoft Office System 2003 and, if your computer is connected to the Internet, help files available from Office Online.

To find out about different items on the screen, you can display a *ScreenTip*. To display a ScreenTip for a toolbar button, for example, point to the button without clicking it. Its ScreenTip appears, telling you its name. In some dialog boxes, you can click a question mark icon to the left of the Close button in the title bar to display the program's Help window with information related to the dialog box.

When you have a question about using a program, you can type it in the "Type a question for help" box at the right end of the program window's menu bar. Then press Enter to display a list of Help topics from which you can select the one that most closely relates to your question.

Another way to get help is to display the Office Assistant, which provides help as you work in the form of helpful information or a tip. If the Office Assistant is hidden when a tip is available, a light bulb appears. Clicking the light bulb displays the tip, and provides other options.

If you want to practice getting help, you can work through this exercise, which demonstrates two ways to get help. This exercise uses Microsoft Word as an example, but you can follow the same steps to get help in any of the programs that are part of The Microsoft Office System 2003.

BE SURE TO start Word before beginning this exercise.

1 At the right end of the menu bar, click the **Type a question for help** box.

2 Type **How do I get help?**, and press [Enter].

A list of topics that relate to your question appears in the Search Results task pane.

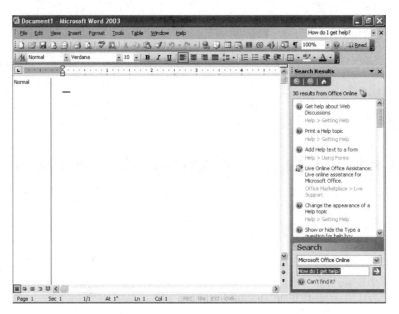

You can click any of the help topics to get more information or instructions.

3 In the **Search Results** task pane, scroll down the results list, and click **About getting help while you work**.

The Microsoft Office Word Help window opens, displaying information about that topic.

Maximize

4 At the right end of the Microsoft Office Word Help window's title bar, click the **Maximize** button, and then click **Show All**.

The topic content expands to provide in-depth information about getting help while you work.

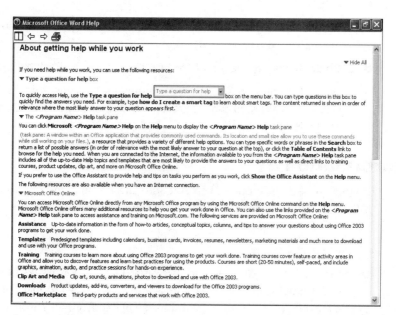

Close

5 At the right end of the Microsoft Office Word Help window's title bar, click the **Close** button, to close the window.

6 On the **Help** menu, click **Microsoft Office Word Help**.

The Word Help task pane opens.

7 In the task pane, click **Table of Contents**.

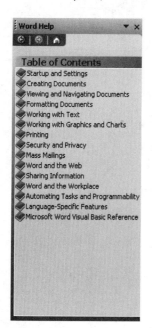

The task pane now displays a list of help topics organized by category, like the table of contents in a book.

Back

8 On the toolbar at the top of the task pane, click the **Back** button.

Notice the categories of information that are available from the Microsoft Office Online Web site. You can also reach this Web site by clicking Microsoft Office Online on the Help menu.

More Information

If your question is about a Microsoft software product and not about the content of this Microsoft Press book, please search the appropriate product support center or the Microsoft Knowledge Base at:

support.microsoft.com

In the United States, Microsoft software product support issues not covered by the Microsoft Knowledge Base are addressed by Microsoft Product Support Services. The Microsoft software support options available from Microsoft Product Support Services are listed at:

support.microsoft.com

Outside the United States, for support information specific to your location, please refer to the Worldwide Support menu on the Microsoft Product Support Services Web site for the site specific to your country:

support.microsoft.com

Using the Book's CD-ROM

The CD-ROM included with this book contains all the practice files you'll use as you work through the exercises in this book. By using practice files, you won't waste time creating sample content with which to experiment—instead, you can jump right in and concentrate on learning how to use The Microsoft Office System 2003.

What's on the CD-ROM?

In addition to the practice files, the CD-ROM contains some exciting resources that will really enhance your ability to get the most out of using this book and The Microsoft Office System, including the following:

- *Microsoft Office System 2003 Step by Step* in e-book format.

- *Insider's Guide to Microsoft Office OneNote 2003* in e-book format.

- *Microsoft Office System Quick Reference* in e-book format.

- *Introducing the Tablet PC* in e-book format.

- *Microsoft Computer Dictionary, Fifth Edition* in e-book format.

- 25 business-oriented templates for use with programs in The Microsoft Office System.

- 100 pieces of clip art.

Important The CD-ROM for this book does not contain The Microsoft Office System 2003 software. You should purchase and install that program before using this book.

Minimum System Requirements

To use this book, you will need:

- **Computer/Processor**

  Computer with a Pentium 133-megahertz (MHz) or higher processor

- **Memory**

  64 MB of RAM (128 MB recommended) plus an additional 8 MB of RAM for each program in The Microsoft Office System (such as Word) running simultaneously

■ **Hard Disk**

   ■ 245 MB of available hard disk space with 115 MB on the hard disk where the operating system is installed

   ■ An additional 32 MB of hard disk space is required for installing the practice files.

   Hard disk requirements will vary depending on configuration; custom installation choices may require more or less hard disk space

■ **Operating System**

   Microsoft Windows 2000 with Service Pack 3 (SP3) or Microsoft Windows XP or later

■ **Drive**

   CD-ROM drive

■ **Display**

   Super VGA (800 × 600) or higher-resolution monitor with 256 colors

■ **Peripherals**

   Microsoft Mouse, Microsoft IntelliMouse, or compatible pointing device

■ **Software**

   Microsoft Office Word 2003, Microsoft Office Excel 2003, Microsoft Office Access 2003, Microsoft Office PowerPoint 2003, Microsoft Office Outlook 2003, Microsoft Office FrontPage 2003, Microsoft Office Publisher 2003, Microsoft Office OneNote 2003, Microsoft Office InfoPath 2003, and Microsoft Internet Explorer 5 or later

Important   In order to complete some of the Access exercises in this book, you will need to install the Jet 4.0 Service Pack 7, which you can obtain from the Windows Update Web site at *windowsupdate.microsoft.com*.

Installing the Practice Files

You need to install the practice files on your hard disk before you can open them in Outlook for use in the chapters' exercises. Follow these steps to copy the CD's files to your computer:

1   Insert the CD-ROM into the CD-ROM drive of your computer.

   The Step by Step Companion CD End User License Agreement appears. Follow the on-screen directions. It is necessary to accept the terms of the license agreement in order to use the practice files. After you accept the license agreement, a menu screen appears.

Important If the menu screen does not appear, start Windows Explorer. In the left pane, locate the icon for your CD-ROM drive and click this icon. In the right pane, double-click the StartCD executable file.

2   Click **Install Practice Files**.

3   Click **Next** on the first screen, and then click **Yes** to accept the license agreement on the next screen.

4   If you want to install the practice files to a location other than the default folder (*My Documents\Microsoft Press\Office 2003 SBS*), click the **Browse** button, select the new drive and path, and then click **OK**.

5   Click **Next** on the **Choose Destination Location** screen, click **Next** on the **Select Features** screen, and then click **Next** on the **Start Copying Files** screen to install the selected practice files.

6   After the practice files have been installed, click **Finish**.

Within the installation folder are subfolders for each chapter in the book.

7   Close the Step by Step Companion CD window, remove the CD-ROM from the CD-ROM drive, and return it to the envelope inside the book.

Opening the Practice Data Files in Outlook

Chapters 17 through 21 each have an accompanying Outlook data file containing the practice files pertinent to that chapter. You need to open the chapter's data file in Outlook before you can use the practice files. Follow these steps prior to beginning each chapter:

1   Start Outlook.

2   On the **File** menu, point to **Open**, and then click **Outlook Data File**.

The Open Outlook Data File dialog box appears.

3   On the **Places** bar, click **My Documents**.

4   In the folder list, double-click **Microsoft Press, Office 2003 SBS**, and then the appropriate chapter folder and subfolder (if applicable).

Tip See "Using the Practice Files," below, for the list of chapter folders, subfolders, and practice files.

5   Click the Outlook data file, and then click **OK**.

The data file opens in Outlook and is visible at the bottom of the Navigation Pane.

Using the Practice Files

Each exercise is preceded by a paragraph or paragraphs that list the files needed for that exercise and explains any file preparation you need to take care of before you start working through the exercise, as shown here:

BE SURE TO start Word before beginning this exercise.
USE the TrackChange document in the practice file folder for this topic. This practice file is located in the My Documents\Microsoft Press\Office 2003 *SBS\Collaborating\Tracking* folder and can also be accessed by clicking *Start/All Programs/Microsoft Press/Microsoft Office System 2003 Step by Step*.
OPEN the TrackChange document.

Usually you will be instructed to open the practice files from within the application in which you are working. However, you can also access the files directly from Windows by clicking the Start menu items indicated. Locate the file in the chapter subfolder and then double-click the file to open it.

The following table lists each chapter's practice files.

Chapter	Folder	Subfolder	Files
Chapter 1: Working with Documents	WorkingDoc	OpeningDoc DecidingView	ExistDoc OpenDoc ViewDoc
Chapter 2: Editing and Proofreading Documents	EditingProof	EditingDoc UsingShort FindingWord UsingOutline FindingText CheckingSpell	EditDoc EntryAuto Thesaurus OutlineText ReplaceText SpellCheck
Chapter 3: Changing the Appearance of Text	ChangingText	ChangingChar ChangingPara CreatingList AutoFormatting ChangingStyle	FormatText FormatPara CreateList FormatAuto FormatStyle
Chapter 4: Presenting Information in Tables and Columns	PresentingInfo	PresentingTable FormattingTable WorkingData PresentingColumn	CreateTable FormatTable DataTable InsertTable CreateColumn
Chapter 5: Setting up a Workbook	SettingUpWorkbook		Easier DataRead AddPicture

Chapter	Folder	Subfolder	Files
Chapter 6: Performing Calculations on Data	PerformingCalculations		NameRange Formula FindErrors
Chapter 7: Changing Document Appearance	ChangingDocAppearance		Formats CreateNew EasyRead Conditional Follow Margins
Chapter 8: Focusing on Specific Data Using Filters	UsingFilters		Filter Calculations Validate
Chapter 9: Creating a New Database	CreateNew	CheckDB Refine Manipulate	Contacts GardenCo GardenCo
Chapter 10: Simplifying Data Entry with Forms	Forms	FormByWiz Properties Layout Controls Events AutoForm Subform	GardenCo GardenCo tgc_bkgrnd GardenCo GardenCo tgc_logo2 GardenCo AftUpdate GardenCo GardenCo
Chapter 11: Locating Specific Information	Queries	Sort FilterDS FilterForm AdvFilter QueryDes QueryWiz Aggregate	GardenCo GardenCo GardenCo GardenCo GardenCo GardenCo GardenCo
Chapter 12: Keeping Your Information Accurate	Accurate	FieldSize InputMask ValRules Lookup QueryUp QueryDel	FieldTest FieldTest FieldTest FieldTest GardenCo GardenCo

Chapter	Folder	Subfolder	Files
Chapter 30: Recording and Viewing Information	InfoForms		TimeCard AssetList PhoneList Fleet TimeCard2
Chapter 31: Collecting and Storing Information	Design		CustRequest
Chapter 32: Working in a Document Workspace	Document		TGCMktgPlan
Chapter 33: Teaming Up in a Meeting Workspace	Meeting		ReleaseSched PressRelease MeetingNotes RevisedRelease

Uninstalling the Practice Files

After you finish working through this book, you should uninstall the practice files to free up hard disk space.

1 On the Windows taskbar, click the **Start** button, and then click **Control Panel**.

2 In Control Panel, click **Add or Remove Programs**.

3 In the list of installed programs, click **Microsoft Office System 2003 Step By Step**, and then click the **Remove** or **Change/Remove** button.

4 In the **Uninstall** dialog box, click **OK**.

5 After the files are uninstalled, click **Finish**, and then close the Add or Remove Programs window and Control Panel.

Important If you need additional help installing or uninstalling the practice files, please see "Getting Help" earlier in this book. Microsoft Product Support Services does not provide support for this book or its CD-ROM.

Quick Reference

54   To clear text formatting

1   Select the text whose formatting you want to clear.

2   In the **Reveal Formatting** task pane, point to the **Selected text** box at the top of the task pane, click the down arrow that appears to its right, and then click **Clear Formatting**.

54   To select all text that has the same formatting

1   Select one instance of the formatted text.

2   In the **Reveal Formatting** task pane, point to the **Selected text** box, click the down arrow to its right, and then click **Select All Text With Similar Formatting**.

59   To add an animation effect

1   Select the text you want to animate.

2   On the **Format** menu, click **Font**.

3   Click the **Text Effects** tab.

4   In the **Animations** box, select the animation effect that you want to add to the selected text, and click **OK**.

60   To align paragraphs

1   Select the text you want to align.

2   On the Formatting toolbar, click the **Align Left**, **Center**, **Align Right**, or **Justify** button.

60   To set a tab stop

●   Click the **Tab** button until it displays the type of tab you want, and then click the horizontal ruler where you want to set the tab stop.

60   To format paragraphs

1   Click the paragraph you want to format.

2   On the **Format** menu, click **Paragraph**.

3   Select the formatting options you want to apply, and click **OK**.

60   To copy one paragraph's formatting to another paragraph

1   Select the paragraph whose formatting you want to copy.

2   On the Standard toolbar, click the **Format Painter** button.

3   Select the paragraph that you want to format.

60   To show or hide formatting marks

●   On the Standard toolbar, click the **Show/Hide ¶** button.

74 **To specify AutoFormat options**

1 On the **Tools** menu, click **AutoCorrect Options**.

2 Click the **AutoFormat As You Type** tab.

3 Select or clear AutoFormat rule check boxes, and click **OK**.

76 **To create a custom style**

1 Select the text for which you want to create a custom style.

2 In the **Styles and Formatting** task pane, click **New Style**.

3 In the **Name** box, type a name for the style.

4 In the **Formatting** area, define the style, and click **OK**.

Chapter 4 Presenting Information in Tables and Columns

Page 84 **To insert a table**

1 Click where you want to position the table.

2 On the **Table** menu, point to **Insert**, and then click **Table**.

3 Enter the dimensions of the table in the **Number of columns** and **Number of rows** boxes, and click **OK**.

84 **To merge table cells**

1 Select the cells you want to merge.

2 On the **Table** menu, click **Merge Cells**.

84 **To convert text to a table**

1 Select the text you want to convert.

2 On the **Table** menu, point to **Convert**, and then click **Text to Table**.

3 Enter the dimensions of the table, and click **OK**.

84 **To sort a table**

1 Click anywhere in the table you want to sort.

2 On the **Table** menu, click **Sort**.

3 Click the down arrow to the right of the **Sort by** box, click the column by which you want to sort, select the option to sort in descending or ascending order, and click **OK**.

90 **To apply a Table AutoFormat**

1 Click anywhere in the table you want to format.

2 On the **Table** menu, click **Table AutoFormat**.

3 Scroll down the **Table styles** list, click the table style you want to apply, and then click **Apply**.

95 **To use a formula to total a column of values in a table**

1 Click the cell where you want the result of the formula to appear.

2 On the **Table** menu, click **Formula** to open the **Formula** dialog box.

3 Click **OK** to total the values.

95 **To insert a file created in another program into a document**

1 Click the location where you want to insert the file.

2 On the **Insert** menu, click **Object** to open the **Object** dialog box, and then click the **Create from File** tab.

3 Click **Browse**, navigate to the file you want to insert, and double-click it.

4 Click **OK**.

97 **To embed a new object in a document**

1 Click in the location where you want to insert the embedded object.

2 On the **Insert** menu, click **Object** to open the **Object** dialog box, and then click the **Create New** tab.

3 In the **Object type** list, click the type of object you want to embed.

4 Select the **Display as icon** check box if you want the embedded object to appear in the document as an icon.

5 Click **OK**.

6 Create the new object, and then click a blank area of the document to deselect it.

100 **To format text in multiple columns**

1 Click anywhere in the document to format all the text, or select the part of the document you want to format in columns.

2 On the **Format** menu, click **Columns**.

3 Choose the number and style of columns you want, and then click **OK**.

Chapter 5 **Setting Up a Workbook**

Page 107 **To name a worksheet**

1 In the lower left corner of the workbook window, right-click the desired sheet tab.

2 From the shortcut menu that appears, click **Rename**.

3 Type the new name for the worksheet, and press Enter.

3   Select the **Lock aspect ratio** check box if you want to maintain the relationship between the image's height and its width.

4   Type the percentage value you would like the new image to be in the **Height** box.

5   Click **OK**.

Chapter 6   **Performing Calculations on Data**

Page 124   **To name a range of cells**

1   Select the cells to be included in the range.

2   Click in the **Name Box**.

3   Type the name of the range, and press [Enter].

126   **To write a formula**

1   Click the cell into which the formula will be written.

2   Type an equal sign, and then type the remainder of the formula.

126   **To enter a range into a formula**

1   Click the cell into which the formula will be written.

2   Type an equal sign, and then type the first part of the formula.

3   Select the cells to be used in the formula.

4   Finish typing the formula.

126   **To create a formula with a function**

1   Click the cell where you want to create the formula.

2   On the **Insert** menu, click **Function**.

3   Click the function you want to use, and then click **OK**.

4   Type the arguments for the function in the argument boxes, and then click **OK**.

126   **To create a formula with a conditional function**

1   Click the cell where you want to create the formula.

2   On the **Insert** menu, click **Function**.

3   In the **Select a function** list, click **IF**, and then click **OK**.

4   In the **Logical_test** box, type the test to use.

5   In the **Value_if_true** box, type the value to be printed if the logical test evaluates to true. (Enclose a text string in quotes.)

6   In the **Value_if_false** box, type the value to be printed if the logical test evaluates to false. (Enclose a text string in quotes.)

3 Click the down arrow, and then click (**Custom...**) in the list.

4 In the upper left box of the **Custom AutoFilter** dialog box, click the down arrow, and from the list that appears, click a comparison operator.

5 Type the arguments for the comparison in the boxes at the upper right, and click **OK**.

166 **To remove a filter**

● On the **Data** menu, point to **Filter** and then click **AutoFilter**.

166 **To filter for a specific value**

1 Click the top cell in the column to filter.

2 On the **Data** menu, point to **Filter** and then click **AutoFilter**.

3 Click the down arrow, and then, from the list of unique column values that appears, click the value for which you want to filter.

171 **To find a total**

● Select the cells with the values to be summed. The total appears on the status bar, in the lower right corner of the Excel window.

171 **To edit a function**

1 Click the cell with the function to be edited.

2 On the **Insert** menu, click **Function**.

3 Edit the function in the **Function Arguments** dialog box.

171 **To allow only numeric values in a cell**

1 Click the cell to be modified.

2 On the **Data** menu, click **Validation**.

3 Click the **Settings** tab.

4 In the **Allow** box, click the down arrow, and from the list that appears, click **Whole number**.

5 Click **OK**.

Chapter 9 **Creating a New Database**

Page 173 **To create a new database by using the Database wizard**

1 If the **New File** task pane is not displayed, open it by clicking the **New** button on the toolbar.

2 In the **Templates** area of the task pane, click **On my computer**, and then click the **Databases** tab to display the available templates.

3 Double-click the template you want to use.

4 Follow the steps of the **Database Wizard**, and click **Finish** to complete the process.

To edit the property settings of a table

1 Display the table in Design view.

2 Click in the **Data Type** cell of the field you want to edit, click the down arrow, and then click the **Data Type** you want to set for the field.

3 In the **Field Properties** area, click the **General** or the **Lookup** tab, click the property you want to edit, and enter the property, or select the property from the drop-down list of options.

To hide a column

● Click in the column, and then on the **Format** menu, click **Hide Columns**.

To freeze columns

● With the columns selected, on the **Format** menu, click **Freeze Columns**.

Chapter 10 **Simplifying Data Entry with Forms**

To create a form by using a wizard

1 On the **Objects** bar, click **Forms**.

2 Double-click **Create form by using wizard** to display the first page of the **Form Wizard**.

3 Follow the instructions of the **Form Wizard**, and then click **Finish**.

To change the properties in a form

1 Display the form in Design view.

2 Use the buttons and boxes on the Formatting toolbar to change the formatting of labels and controls.

3 To change the properties of a control, in the form, right-click the control you want to change, and click **Properties** from the shortcut menu.

4 Click the appropriate tab, click the property you want to change, and then change the property setting.

To add a graphic and a caption to a form

1 Display the form in Design view.

2 Click the **Image** control in the Toolbox, and then drag a rectangle in the location where you will add the graphic.

3 Navigate to the folder that contains the graphic, and double-click the graphic file.

4   To add a caption, click the **Label** control in the Toolbox, and then drag another rectangle in the location where you will add the caption.

5   Type the caption, and press [Enter].

228   **To create a form by using AutoForm**

1   On the **Objects** bar, click **Forms**.

2   On the database window's toolbar, click the **New** button.

3   Click the AutoForm format that you want from the list, click the **Table/Query** down arrow, select the table or query on which you want to base the form, and then click **OK**.

4   Click the **Save** button, enter a name for the form in the **Save As** dialog box, and then click **OK**.

230   **To add a subform to a form**

1   Make sure the tables on which you want to base your main form and the subform have a relationship.

2   Open the main form in Design view and if necessary, open the Toolbox and make sure the **Control Wizards** button is active (is orange).

3   On the Toolbox, click the **Subform/Subreport** button, and drag a rectangle to the location on your main form where you want to insert a subform.

4   Follow the instructions on the **Subform Wizard**, and click **Finish** on the wizard's last page to complete the process.

5   Adjust the size and location of the objects on your form as necessary.

238   **To create a form and subform by using a wizard**

1   To create the form in your database, on the **Objects** bar, click **Forms**, and then click the **New** button on the database window's toolbar.

2   Click **Form Wizard**, select the form's base table from the list at the bottom of the page, and then click **OK**.

3   Verify that the table you selected is shown in the **Table/Queries** list and then double-click each field that you want to include in the new form to move it to the **Fields in my new table** list.

4   To create the subform, display the **Tables/Queries** list, and select the table on which you want to base the subform.

5   Double-click each field you want to add to the subform, and then click **Next**.

6   Follow the instructions on the wizard, and then click **Finish** to create the form and subform.

4 To include a field in the query, drag it from the field list at the top of the window to consecutive columns in the design grid. To copy all fields to the grid, double-click the title bar above the field list to select the entire list, and then drag the selection over the grid.

5 Click the **Run** button to run the query and display the results in Datasheet view.

253 **To add an expression to a query**

1 Open the query in Design view.

2 Right-click the appropriate cell in the design grid, and then click **Build** on the shortcut menu.

3 In the **Expression Builder** dialog box, double-click the **Functions** folder in the first column of the elements area, and then click **Built-in Functions**.

4 Build your expression, and then click **OK**.

5 Press ⌈Enter⌋ to move the insertion point out of the field, which completes the entry of the expression.

6 To rename the expression, double-click **Expr1**, and then type the name you want.

7 Click the **Run** button to run the query and see the results in Datasheet view.

264 **To perform a calculation in a query**

1 Open the query in which you want to perform a calculation.

2 Click in the field in which you want to perform the calculation, and then click the **Totals** button on the toolbar.

3 In the new **Totals** cell for the field, click the down arrow, and then click the calculation you want to perform from the drop-down list.

Chapter 12 **Keeping Your Information Accurate**

Page 270 **To specify data type settings**

1 Display the table in Design view.

2 Click in the **Data Type** cell of the field you want to change, click the down arrow, and then click the data type you want.

274 **To set a field's size property**

1 Display the table in Design view.

2 Click in the field you want to change, and then in the **Field Properties** area, click in the **Field Size** box, click the down arrow, and change the setting to what you want.

276 **To create a custom input mask**

1 Display the table in Design view.

2 Select the field for which you want to set an input mask, and in the **Field Properties** area, click **Input Mask**.

3 Click the ... button to start the **Input Mask Wizard**. (Click **Yes** if you are prompted to first save the table or install this feature.)

4 Select an input mask from the options, or enter your own input mask in the **Try It** box, and then click **Next**.

5 Specify whether you want to store the symbols with the data, and then click **Finish**.

6 Press [Enter] to accept the mask.

281 **To set a field validation rule**

1 Display the table in Design view.

2 Select the field you want to add a rule to, and in the **Field Properties** area, click the **Validation Rule** box,

3 Click the ... button at the right end of the **Validation Rule** box to open the Expression Builder, or type an expression and press [Enter].

4 In the **Validation Text** box, type a description of the rule.

5 Click in the **Caption** box, and indicate the type of entry that can be made in the field, for example, **Phone Number**.

6 Save and close the table.

284 **To use a Lookup List to restrict data**

1 Display the table in Design view.

2 Click the **Data Type** cell for the field in which you want to use a Lookup List, click the down arrow, and then click **Lookup Wizard**.

3 Select the option to either look up the values in a table or query, or to type in the values that you want, and click **Next**.

4 Follow the wizard's instructions (which will be determined by your choice in step 3), and then click **Finish**.

290 **To create and run an update query**

1 Create a query that displays the information you want and then open the query in Design view.

2 On the **Query** menu, click **Update Query**.

3 In the **Update To** row of the field you want to update, type the text you want, or create an expression.

4 Click the **Run** button, click **Yes** when Access warns you that you are about to update records, and save and close the query.

294 **To create and run a delete query**

1 Create a query that displays the information you want and then open the query in Design view.

2 On the **Query** menu, click **Delete Query**.

3 Type the text you want in the **Criteria** row under the appropriate field.

4 Click the **Run** button to run the delete query and click **Yes** when Access warns you that you are about to delete records.

5 Save and close the query.

Chapter 13 Creating Presentations

Page 302 **To view the presentation in a particular view**

● In the lower-left corner of the window, click the button for the view you want.

302 **To hide the formatting of a slide in Slide Sorter view**

● Hold down the Alt key and the mouse button while pointing to a slide.

302 **To advance to the next slide in a slide show**

● Without moving your mouse, click the mouse button.

314 **To start a new presentation with a design template**

1 In the **New Presentation** task pane, click **From Design Template**.

2 In the **Slide Design** task pane, click the slide design you want.

3 In the **Slide Design** task pane, click the **Other Task Panes** down arrow to display a list of the task panes, and then click **Slide Layout**.

4 In the **Slide Layout** task pane, click a slide layout.

Chapter 14 Working with Slides

Page 323 **To apply a new format to a slide**

1 Select the slide you want to reformat.

2 In the **Slide Layout** task pane, scroll down until you see the layout you want to apply, and then click it.

1   Select the slide you want to format.

2   On the **Format** menu, click **Slide Layout**.

3   Click the down arrow to the right of the selected slide layout.

4   On the menu, click **Reapply Layout**.

1   In the open presentation, click where you want to insert the slide.

2   On the **Insert** menu, click **Slides from Files**.

3   Click the **Find Presentation** tab, if necessary, and then click **Browse**.

4   Navigate to the location of the file to insert, select it, and then click **Open**.

5   Click the slides that you want to insert.

6   Click **Insert**.

1   Click the **Slide Sorter View** button.

2   Drag the slide you want to move to a different location.

1   Click the text placeholder.

2   In the **Notes** pane, click the **Click to add notes** placeholder and type your notes.

●   On the **View** menu, click **Notes Page**.

Working with Slide Text

1   On the Drawing toolbar, click the **Text Box** button, and position the pointer where you want to place the text label.

2   Click the slide.

1   On the Drawing toolbar, click the **Text Box** button.

2   Position the upside-down T-pointer where you want the word processing box to appear, and then drag the pointer to create a box that is roughly the size you want.

3   Release the mouse button.

Chapter 16   Setting Up and Delivering Slide Shows

367 **To mark up a slide using the pen tool**

1 Click a slide, and then click the **Slide Show** button.

2 Right-click anywhere on the screen, click **Pointer Options** on the shortcut menu, click **Felt Tip Pen**, and then make your mark.

367 **To remove marks on a slide**

● Right-click anywhere on the screen, click **Pointer Options**, and then click **Erase All Ink on Slide**.

371 **To deliver a slide show on one monitor and use Presenter view on another**

1 Open the PowerPoint presentation you want to set up.

2 On the **Slide Show** menu, click **Set Up Show**.

3 In the **Set Up Show** dialog box's **Multiple monitors** area, click the down arrow to the right of the **Display slide show on** box, and click the name of the monitor you want to use to project the slide show.

4 Select the **Show Presenter View** check box, and click **OK**.

5 Click **Slide Show** button to start the slide show, using the navigation tools in Presenter view to deliver the presentation.

372 **To change the order of slides in a list**

● Select a slide, and in the **Define Custom Show** dialog box click the up arrow or the down arrow to the right of the **Slides in custom show** box.

372 **To hide a slide**

● In Slide Sorter view, select a slide and then click the **Hide Slide** button on the Slide Sorter toolbar.

376 **To manually set slide timings**

1 Click the **Slide Sorter View** button, and then click a slide.

2 On the **Slide Show** menu, click **Slide Transition**.

3 In the **Advance slide** area, select the **Automatically after** check box, and then click the up arrow twice to the timing you want.

4 Click **Slide Show**.

5 At the bottom of the **Slide Transition** task pane, click the **Apply to All Slides** button.

380 **To set up a self-running slide show**

1 Open the presentation, and then on the **Slide Show** menu, click **Set Up Show**.

2 In the **Set Up Show** dialog box's **Show type** area, select the **Browsed at a kiosk (full screen)** option.

3   Click **OK**.

4   To test the show, move to Slide 1, and click the **Slide Show** button.

5   Press [Esc] to stop the slide show.

6   On the **File** menu, click **Save As** and navigate to the folder where you want to store the self-running presentation.

7   Click the down arrow to the right of the **Save as type** box, and click **PowerPoint Show** in the drop-down list.

8   In the **File name** box, assign a name to the self-running version of the show, and click **Save**.

Chapter 17   Working with Outlook

Page 396   **To toggle AutoPreview on and off**

   ●   On the **View** menu, click **AutoPreview**.

396   **To display the Reading Pane**

   ●   On the **View** menu, click **Reading Pane** and then **Right** or **Bottom**.

396   **To open a message**

   ●   In the Inbox or other message folder, double-click the message you want to open.

396   **To open an attachment**

1   Open the message containing the attachment.

2   In the message header or body, double-click the attachment.

396   **To open an attachment without opening the message**

1   With the Reading Pane visible, click the message containing the attachment.

2   In the Reading Pane, double-click the attachment.

402   **To display the All Mail Folders list**

   ●   On the Navigation Pane, click the **Mail** icon.

406   **To add an entry to the Address Book**

1   On the **Tools** menu, click **Address Book**.

2   Click the **New Entry** button.

3   In the **New Entry** dialog box, click **New Contact**.

4   In the **Put this entry** drop-down list, click the address book to which you want to add the contact, and then click **OK**.

5   In the **Untitled – Contact** dialog box, type the information you want to save for this contact, and then click **Save and Close**.

406 **To create a distribution list**

1 On the **Tools** menu, click **Address Book**.

2 Click the **New Entry** button.

3 In the **New Entry** dialog box, click **New Distribution List**.

4 In the **Put this entry** drop-down list, click the address book to which you want to add the distribution list, and then click **OK**.

5 In the **Untitled – Distribution List** dialog box, in the **Name** box, type the name of the distribution list.

6 To add distribution list members from an existing address book, click the **Select Members** button. In the **Select Members** dialog box, select the contacts you want to add to the distribution list, and then click **OK**.

7 To add new distribution list members, click the **Add New** button. In the **Add New Member** dialog box, type the display name and e-mail address of the new contact, select the **Add to Contacts** check box if you want, and then click **OK**.

8 Click **Save and Close**.

410 **To attach a file to a message**

1 With the message open, on the toolbar, click the **Insert File** button.

2 In the **Insert File** dialog box, browse to the file you want to attach, click the file, and then click the **Insert** button.

416 **To send an instant message from an e-mail message**

1 Open a message to or from your instant messaging contact.

2 In the message header, click the **Person Names Smart Tag** next to the contact's name, and then on the shortcut menu click **Send Instant Message**.

Chapter 18 Managing E-mail Messages

Page 421 **To select the message format**

● On the Message form's toolbar, click the down arrow to the right of the **Message format** box, and click **HTML**, **Rich Text**, or **Plain Text**.

421 **To format messages by using stationery**

1 On the **Tools** menu, click **Options**.

2 In the **Options** dialog box, click the **Mail Format** tab.

3 In the **Use this stationery by default** list, select the stationery you want.

4 Click **OK**.

To customize message stationery

1   On the **Tools** menu, click **Options**.

2   In the **Options** dialog box, click the **Mail Format** tab.

3   Click the **Stationery Picker** button.

4   In the Stationery Picker dialog box, click the stationery you want to customize, and then click the **Edit** button.

5   Apply the formatting you want, and click **OK** in each of the open dialog boxes.

To respond to voting buttons in a message

1   Preview the message in the Reading Pane or open the message.

2   Click the **Infobar**, click the voting option you want, and then click **OK**.

To set message delivery options

1   Compose a new e-mail message.

2   On the Message form's toolbar, click the **Options** button.

3   In the **Delivery options** area of the **Message Options** dialog box, select the check boxes for the options you want.

4   Click **Close**.

To set the importance of a message

1   Compose a new e-mail message.

2   On the Message form's toolbar, click the **Options** button.

3   In the **Message settings** area of the **Message Options** dialog box, click the down arrow to the right of the **Importance** box, and then click **Low**, **Normal**, or **High**.

4   Click **Close**.

To sort messages

●   Click the heading of the column by which you'd like to sort messages.

To group messages

●   On the **View** menu, point to **Arrange By**, and then click the field by which you'd like to group messages.

To color-code messages

1   On the **Tools** menu, click **Organize**.

2   In the **Ways to Organize** pane, click **Using Colors**.

3   Select the type of messages you want to color-code and the color you want them to be, and then click the **Apply Color** button.

3   In the **Create a New View** dialog box, type the name of the new view, select the type of view, select the folders on which the view can be used, and then click **OK**.

4   In the **Customize View** dialog box, click the button of the element you want to customize.

5   In the resulting dialog box, make the changes you want, and then click **OK**.

6   Repeat Steps 4 and 5 for each element you want to change.

7   Click **OK** to close the **Customize View** dialog box and save your changes.

8   Click **Apply View**, and then click **Close**.

465   **To create a rule to filter messages**

1   On the **Tools** menu, click **Rules and Alerts**.

2   In the **Rules and Alerts** dialog box, click **New Rule**.

3   In the Rules Wizard, follow the instructions to create the new rule.

4   When you are done, click **Finish**, and then click **OK**.

470   **To filter junk or adult-content messages**

1   On the **Actions** menu, point to **Junk E-mail**, and then click **Junk E-mail Options**.

2   Select a level of protection, and then click **OK**.

471   **To create a folder**

1   On the **File** menu, point to **New**, and then click **Folder**.

2   In the **Create New Folder** dialog box, in the **Name** box, type the name of the folder.

3   In the **Folder contains** list, click the kind of items you want to store in the folder.

4   In the **Select where to place the folder** list, click the mailbox or folder in which you want to create the new folder.

5   Click **OK**.

471   **To move a message to a folder**

1   Right-click the message, and on the shortcut menu, click **Move to Folder**.

2   In the **Move Items** dialog box, click the folder to which you want to move the message, and then click **OK**.

474   **To share a folder**

1   In the **Folder List**, right-click the folder, and on the shortcut menu, click **Sharing**.

2   Click the **Add** button.

3 Select the person with whom you want to share your folder, and then click **OK**.

4 Click **Apply**, and then click **OK**.

475 To make someone a delegate

1 On the **Tools** menu, click **Options**.

2 On the **Delegates** tab, click **Add**.

3 In the **Type Name or Select from List** box, select the person you want to make a delegate, and click **OK**.

4 In the **Delegate Permissions** dialog box, select the permissions you want to grant the delegate, and then click **OK**.

5 Click **OK** to close the **Options** dialog box.

480 To save a message as an HTML file

1 Select the message, and on the **File** menu, click **Save As**.

2 In the **Save As** dialog box, browse to the location where you want to save the file.

3 In the **Save as type** drop-down list, click **HTML**.

4 Click the **Save** button.

483 To specify global archive settings

1 On the **Tools** menu, click **Options**.

2 In the **Options** dialog box, click the **Other** tab, and then click the **AutoArchive** button.

3 In the **AutoArchive** dialog box, choose the global archive settings you want, and click **OK** to close each of the open the dialog boxes.

483 To specify archive settings for a folder

1 In the **Folder List**, click the folder you want to archive.

2 On the **File** menu, point to **Folder**, and then click **Properties**.

3 In the **Properties** dialog box, click the **AutoArchive** tab.

4 Select the settings with which you want to archive the folder, and click **OK**.

Chapter 20 Managing Your Calendar

Page 490 To select a calendar view

● On the **View** menu, point to **Arrange By**, point to **Current View**, and then click the view you want.

3 In the **Calendar work week** area of the **Calendar Options** dialog box, select the check boxes for your work days.

4 Click **OK** in each of the open dialog boxes.

507 To change your time zone

1 On the **Tools** menu, click **Options**.

2 On the **Preferences** tab of the **Options** dialog box, click the **Calendar Options** button.

3 In the **Calendar Options** dialog box, click the **Time Zone** button.

4 In the **Time Zone** dialog box, click the time zone you want, and then click **OK** in each of the open dialog boxes.

511 To manually label an appointment

1 Double-click the appointment.

2 In the **Appointment** form, click the down arrow to the right of the **Label** box, and then click a label.

3 Click **Save and Close**.

511 To label appointments by using a rule

1 On the toolbar, click the **Calendar Coloring** button, and then click **Automatic Formatting**.

2 In the **Automatic Formatting** dialog box, click the **Add** button.

3 In the **Name** box, type a name for .the rule.

4 In the **Label** list, click a label.

5 Click the **Condition** button, enter the filtering conditions, and then click **OK** in each of the open dialog boxes.

512 To print your calendar

1 Make sure the Calendar is displayed, but no appointment is open.

2 On the toolbar, click the **Print** button.

3 In the **Print** dialog box, select a print style, and click the **Print** button.

Chapter 21 **Scheduling and Managing Meetings**

Page 520 To plan a meeting

1 On the **Actions** menu, click **Plan a Meeting**.

2 In the **Plan a Meeting** dialog box, click the **Add Others** button and then click **Add from Address Book**.

3   In the **Select Attendees and Resources** dialog box, select the Required and Optional attendees and the Resources, and then click **OK**.

4   In the Free/Busy area, drag the red and green bars to set the meeting time, and then click the **Make Meeting** button.

5   In the resulting meeting form, complete any additional information, and then click **Send**.

520   **To set or remove a reminder**

1   In the meeting form, select or clear the **Reminder** check box.

2   If setting a reminder, select the amount of time before the meeting that you want to be reminded.

3   Close the meeting form and save your changes.

520   **To invite others to a meeting**

1   In the meeting form, click the **Scheduling** tab, and then click the **Add Others** button.

2   Click the contacts you want to add, click the **Required** or **Optional** button, and then click **OK**.

527   **To schedule an online meeting**

1   On the toolbar, click the down arrow to the right of the **New** button, and then click **Meeting Request**.

2   On the **Meeting** form, select the **This is an online meeting using** check box.

3   Complete the remaining meeting information, and then click **Send**.

528   **To accept a meeting request**

1   In the open meeting request or in the Reading Pane, click **Accept**.

2   Choose whether to edit and send a response, and then click **OK**.

528   **To decline a meeting request**

1   In the open meeting request or in the Reading Pane, click **Decline**.

2   Choose whether to edit and send a response, and then click **OK**.

528   **To propose a new meeting time**

1   In the open meeting request or in the Reading Pane, click the **Propose New Time** button.

2   In the Free/Busy area, select the preferred time, and click the **Propose Time** button.

528   **To automatically respond to meeting requests**

1   On the **Tools** menu, click **Options**.

2   On the **Preferences** tab of the **Options** dialog box, click the **Calendar Options** button.

3 In the **Calendar Options** dialog box, click the **Resource Scheduling** button.

4 In the **Resource Scheduling** dialog box, select the check boxes for the automatic response options you want, and then click **OK** in the open dialog boxes.

528 **To reschedule a meeting**

1 Open the meeting, and click the **Scheduling** tab.

2 In the Free/Busy area, select new start and end dates and times.

3 Click the **Send Update** button.

533 **To cancel a meeting**

1 Open the meeting, and on the **Actions** menu, click **Cancel Meeting**.

2 Choose whether to send a cancellation notice to the attendees, and then click **OK**.

536 **To create a group schedule**

1 Make sure the Calendar is displayed.

2 On the toolbar, click the **View Group Schedules** button.

3 In the **View Group Schedules** dialog box, click the **New** button.

4 In the **Create New Group Schedule** dialog box, type a name for the group schedule, and then click **OK**.

5 Add the group members you want, and then click **Save and Close**.

539 **To open another person's calendar directly**

1 On the **File** menu, point to **Open**, and click **Other User's Folder**.

2 Click the **Name** button, click the name of the person whose folder you want to open, and then click **OK**.

3 Make sure Calendar appears in the **Folder** box, and then click **OK**.

540 **To save your Calendar as a Web page**

1 On the **File** menu, click **Save as Web Page**.

2 In the **Duration** area, enter the start and end dates for which you want to save the calendar.

3 In the **File Name** box, type the name and path with which you want to save the Web page.

4 Click **Save**.

542 **To publish your free and busy times**

1 On the **Tools** menu, click **Options**.

2 In the **Calendar** area of the **Options** dialog box, click the **Calendar Options** button.

3   In the **Advanced options** area of the **Calendar Options** dialog box, click the **Free/Busy Options** button.

4   Select the **Publish at my location** check box, and in the **Publish at my location** box, type the server location and file name.

5   Close each of the open dialog boxes.

6   On the **Tools** menu, point to **Send/Receive**, and then click **Free/Busy Information** to publish your free/busy information to your server.

7   To view your published free/busy information, open your Web browser, and in the **Address** box, type the URL of the file on the server.

Chapter 22   Understanding How FrontPage Works

Page 555   **To open an existing FrontPage-based Web site**

1   On the **File** menu, click **Open Site**.

2   In the **Open Site** dialog box, browse to the folder where your Web site is stored.

3   Click the name of the Web site you want, and then click **Open**.

Chapter 23   Creating a Web Site to Promote Yourself or Your Company

Page 572   **To create a Web site by using a template**

1   In the **New Web site** area of the **New** task pane, click **More Web site templates**.

2   In the **Web Site Templates** dialog box, click the icon for the type of Web site you want to create, and click **OK**.

582   **To insert existing text into a Web page**

1   Open the page into which you want to insert text in the Page view editing window.

2   Position the insertion point where you want the text to appear.

3   On the **Insert** menu, click **File**.

4   Browse to the folder that contains the text you want to insert.

5   Click the file that contains the text in the list of available files, and then click **Open** to insert the full text of the document in your Web page.

596   **To insert a hyperlink**

1   Open the page, and move the insertion point to the location where you want to insert a hyperlink.

2   Type or select the text you want to hyperlink.

3 On the **Insert** menu, click **Hyperlink**.

4 In the **Insert Hyperlink** dialog box, click the **Browse for File** button, browse to the folder that contains the file you want to link to, click the file, and click **OK** twice.

598 **To preview a Web site**

1 Open the page in Design view.

2 At the bottom of the Page view editing window, click the **Show Preview View** button to switch to the Preview pane.

3 On the Standard toolbar, click the **Preview in Browser** button to see how the site looks in your default Web browser.

4 Click each of the navigation links to view the different pages of the site.

602 **To delete a Web site**

1 In the **Folder List**, right-click the top-level folder of the site you want to delete, and click **Delete** on the shortcut menu to open the **Confirm Delete** dialog box.

2 Select the **Delete this Web site entirely** option, and then click **OK** to delete the Web site.

Chapter 24 **Presenting Information in Lists and Tables**

Page 610 **To create a table**

● Position the insertion point where you want to insert the table, and on the Standard toolbar, click the **Insert Table** button.

● On the **Table** menu, point to **Insert**, and then click **Table**.

● On the **Table** menu, click **Draw Table**.

617 **To add information to a table**

● Position the insertion point in a cell, and then type the information.

617 **To add a header row to a table**

● Click in the first row in the table, and on the Tables toolbar, click the **Insert Rows** button.

620 **To edit a table**

● To delete a row or column, click in the row or column, point to **Select** on the **Table** menu, and click **Column** or **Row**. Then on the Tables toolbar, click the **Delete Cells** button.

● To adjust the size of the columns in a table, point to the right border of the column you want to adjust, and drag or double-click the border.

- To size the cells of a table to fit their contents, click anywhere in the table, and on the Tables toolbar, click the **AutoFit to Contents** button.

- To edit the structure of a table through the **Table Properties** dialog box, right-click anywhere in the table, click **Table Properties** on the shortcut menu, enter your table specifications, and then click **OK**.

- To make all the columns the same width, select the columns, and on the Tables toolbar, click the **Distribute Columns Evenly** button.

625 **To manually format a table**

1 Select the cells you want to format.

2 Right-click the selection, and click **Cell Properties** on the shortcut menu.

3 In the **Cell Properties** dialog box, enter your table format specifications, and then click **OK**.

625 **To apply a ready-made format to a table**

1 Click anywhere in the table.

2 On the Tables toolbar, click the **Table AutoFormat** button.

3 In the **Table AutoFormat** dialog box, use the Down Arrow key to scroll through the **Formats** list on the left.

4 Select the format you want to apply, and click **OK**.

629 **To split a table into two or more tables**

1 Click in the row where you want to split the table.

2 On the **Table** menu, click **Split Table**.

Chapter 25 **Enhancing Your Web Site with Graphics**

Page 634 **To insert clip art**

1 On the **Insert** menu, point to **Picture**, and then click **Clip Art**.

2 Use the Clip Art task pane's search feature to find items that you want, then click an image to insert it into your Web page.

634 **To insert a picture**

1 On the **Insert** menu, point to **Picture**, and then click **From File** to display the **Picture** dialog box.

2 In the **Picture** dialog box, browse to the folder that contains the picture you want to insert.

3 Select the image you want, and then click **Insert** to insert the graphic in the Web page at the insertion point.

638 **To size a picture**

1 Double-click the picture to display the **Picture Properties** dialog box.

2 On the **Appearance** tab, select the **Specify size** check box, and set the **Width** to the desired number of pixels. (To prevent distortion, ensure that the **Keep aspect ratio** check box is selected.)

638 **To crop a picture**

1 Click the picture to select it, and on the Pictures toolbar, click the **Crop** button.

2 Drag the handles of the dashed-line crop box to redefine the size as you like.

3 Click the **Crop** button again or press [Enter] to crop the picture to the specified shape and size.

638 **To rotate a shape**

● Click the shape, and drag its rotate handle (the green dot).

638 **To move a shape out from behind another shape**

● Right-click the shape, and on the shortcut menu, point to **Order**, and then click **Bring to Front**.

638 **To format an AutoShape**

1 Right-click the shape, and click **Format AutoShape**.

2 In the **Format AutoShape** dialog box, click the appropriate tab, and choose from among the available setting options.

3 Click **OK** to close the dialog box and apply your settings.

643 **To create and test a thumbnail of a picture**

1 Click the picture to select it and open the Pictures toolbar.

2 On the Pictures toolbar, click the **Auto Thumbnail** button.

3 On the Standard toolbar, click **Preview in Browser**. Save the page and embedded graphics if prompted to do so.

4 When your Web page opens in your browser, click the thumbnail to display the full-size graphic, and then click the browser's **Back** button to return to the thumbnail.

645 **To insert a pre-defined shape**

1 On the **Insert** menu, point to **Picture**, and then click **New Drawing**.

2 On the Drawing toolbar, click **AutoShapes** to see the menus of available shapes.

3 Click the shape category, and then click the shape you want to insert.

4 Repeat Step 3 and move the shapes as needed until you have completed your drawing.

654 **To create a photo gallery in your open Web site**

1. On the **Insert** menu, click **Web Component**, and then select **Photo Gallery**.
2. In the **Choose a Photo Gallery Option** box, select the layout option you want, and click **Finish**.
3. In the **Photo Gallery Properties** dialog box, click **Add**, and then click **Pictures from Files**.
4. Browse to the folder that contains your picture files.
5. Select all the files at once by clicking the first file, holding down the Shift key, and clicking the last file. Then click **Open** to import them into the photo gallery.
6. Click **OK** to close the **Photo Gallery Properties** dialog box and generate the photo gallery.

Chapter 26 Creating and Printing Publications

Page 670 **To create a print publication using a design set**

1. In the **New Publication** task pane, click **Design Sets**.
2. In the list that appears, click the type of design you want, and in the preview pane, click the type of publication you want.
3. Edit the contents of the publication as you wish.
4. On the **File** menu, click **Close**, and when prompted to save the file, click **Yes**.
5. In the **Save as** dialog box, browse to the folder where you want to save the file.
6. In the **File name** box, type a name for your publication, and then click **Save**.

677 **To create a print publication from a blank page**

1. In the **New Publication** task pane, click **Blank Print Publication**.
2. Insert text and images as you wish.
3. On the **File** menu, click **Close**, and when prompted to save the file, click **Yes**.
4. In the **Save as** dialog box, browse to the folder where you want to save the file.
5. In the **File name** box, type a name for your publication, and then click **Save**.

677 **To create a print publication from a Publisher template**

1. In the **New Publication** task pane, click **Publications for Print**.
2. In the list that appears, click the type of publication you want, and in the preview pane, click the sample publication you want.
3. Edit the contents of the publication as you wish.

4   On the **File** menu, click **Close**, and when prompted to save the file, click **Yes**.

5   In the **Save as** dialog box, browse to the folder where you want to save the file.

6   In the **File name** box, type a name for your publication, and then click **Save**.

680   To preview and print a publication

1   On the Standard toolbar, click the **Print Preview** button.

2   Move the magnifying pointer over the publication, and click to zoom in on any area you want to examine more closely. Then click again to zoom back out

3   If necessary, on the Print Preview toolbar, click **Close** to return to the publication and make adjustments.

4   On either the Print Preview toolbar or the Standard toolbar, click the **Print** button to display the Print dialog box.

5   In the **Name** box, check the name of the printer that will be used, and if necessary click the down arrow and select a different printer.

6   Set the print range and the number of copies, and then click **OK**.

682   To create a publication based on a template

1   In the **New Publication** task pane, click **Templates**.

2   In the preview pane, click the template you want.

3   Edit the contents of the publication as you wish.

4   On the **File** menu, click **Close**, and when prompted to save the file, click **Yes**.

5   In the **Save as** dialog box, browse to the folder where you want to save the file.

6   In the **File name** box, type a name for your publication, and then click **Save**.

682   To prepare a publication for commercial printing using spot-color processing

1   Open the publication.

2   On the **Tools** menu, point to **Commercial Printing Tools**, and then click **Color Printing**.

3   In the Color Printing dialog box in the **Print all colors as** area, click the **Spot color(s)** option.

4   If a message box appears at this point, read the message, and click **OK**.

5   Change or add inks or colors as needed, and when finished, click **OK**.

682   To prepare a publication for commercial printing using process-color printing

1   Open the publication.

2   On the **Tools** menu, point to **Commercial Printing Tools**, and then click **Color Printing**.

3   In the Color Printing dialog box in the **Print all colors as** area, click the **Process Colors (CMYK)** option.

4   If a message box appears at this point, read the message, and click **OK**.

5   Change or add inks or colors as needed, and when finished, click **OK**.

Chapter 27   **Creating Web Sites and E-mail Messages**

Page 693   **To send a publication as e-mail**

1   Open the publication you want to send as e-mail.

2   On the **File** menu, point to **Send E-Mail**, and click **E-mail Preview**.

3   Verify that the publication appears as you wish, and in the upper-right corner of the preview window, click the **Close** button.

4   On the **File** menu, point to **Send E-mail**, and click **Send This Page as Message**.

5   Type the e-mail addresses of the recipients in the **To** box.

6   Type the e-mail addresses of people who should receive a copy of the message in the **Cc** box.

7   Type a subject line in the **Subject** box.

8   On the e-mail toolbar, click **Send**.

702   **To create a Web site from an existing publication**

1   Open the publication.

2   On the **File** menu, click **Convert to Web Publication**.

3   Choose whether to save your print publication before converting it to a Web publication, and then click **Next**.

4   On the next screen, indicate whether you want to add a navigation bar to your Web publication, and then click **Finish**.

5   Edit the contents of the publication as necessary. If you added a navigation bar, be sure to position it as you want and edit the labels and properties as necessary.

6   On the Web Tools toolbar, click the **Web Page Preview** button.

7   Verify that your site appears and functions as it should in the Web browser, and then close the Web browser.

8   On the Web Tools toolbar, click the **Publish to the Web** button.

9   In the **Publish to the Web** dialog box, browse to the location where you want to publish the site, and click **Save**.

713   **To convert a Web publication to a print publication**

1   Open the publication from which the Web site was created.

2   On the **File** menu, click **Convert to Print Publication**.

3   Choose whether to save your Web publication before converting it to a print publication, and then click **Finish**.

Chapter 28   Taking Notes

Page 716 **To get started with OneNote**

1   Open OneNote.

2   Click the **Title** box at the top of the first page, and type the title you want.

3   Click in the body of the page, and beginning typing your notes.

4   When finished, on the **File** menu, click **Exit**.

716 **To insert an image into your notes**

1   Open OneNote.

2   Click where you want to insert the image.

3   On the **Insert** menu, click **Picture**.

4   Browse to the folder in which the image is stored, select the image, and click **Insert**.

721 **To add a drawing to your notes**

1   Open OneNote.

2   On the standard toolbar, click the down arrow to the right of the **Pen** button.

3   In the drop-down list, click the type and color of pen you want.

4   Drag your mouse over the note page to create your drawing.

722 **To find and insert Web clippings**

1   Open OneNote.

2   On the **Tools** menu, click **Research**.

3   In the **Search for** box, type the words you want to search for.

4   In the drop-down list, select the references in which you want to search, and then click the **Start searching** button.

5   In the **Search Results** list, click the item you want.

6   When the item opens in the browser window, locate the content you want (text or images), and then drag your mouse to select it.

7   On the **Edit** menu, click **Copy**.

8   Switch to OneNote, and click on the page where you want to insert the Web clipping.

9   On the **Edit** menu, click **Paste**.

3 Type the section name, and press `Enter`.

4 Right-click the new section tab, point to **Section Color** on the shortcut menu, and select the color you want.

728 **To move a section to a folder**

1 Open OneNote.

2 Right-click the section tab, and click **Move** on the shortcut menu.

3 In the **Move section to** list, select the folder, and click **Move**.

Chapter 29 **Working with Notes**

Page 733 **To take Quick Notes**

1 In the system tray on the Windows task bar (near the clock), click the **Microsoft OneNote** icon.

2 Type the notes you want in the **Mini OneNote** window.

3 To add a new page, click the **New Page** button.

4 To move through the pages, click the **Next Page** or **Previous Page** button.

5 Click the **Close** button.

736 **To mark notes with Note Flags**

1 Open OneNote.

2 Click on the note page where you want the flag to appear.

3 On the standard toolbar, click the down arrow next to the **Note Flags** button, and click flag you want.

736 **To customize Note Flags**

1 Open OneNote.

2 On the standard toolbar, click the down arrow next to the **Note Flags** button, and click **Customize My Note Flags**.

3 In the task pane, click the flag you want to modify or click an *Unidentified* flag to create a new one.

736 **To see a summary of the Note Flags in your notebook**

1 Open OneNote.

2 On the **View** menu, click **Note Flags Summary**.

3 In the **Search in** list near the bottom of the pane, select the part of your notebook you want.

741 To search notes

1   Open OneNote.

2   In the **Search** box, type the word(s) you want to find, and then click the **Find** button.

3   To move through the search results, click the Next Match or the **Previous Match** button.

4   To see a list of all the pages containing matches, click the number of search results – for example, *2 of 2.*

743 To send notes in e-mail

1   Open OneNote.

2   Select the page tab(s) for the page(s) you want to send.

3   On the standard toolbar, click the **E-mail** button.

4   In the **To** box, Type the e-mail addresses for the recipients.

5   In the **Cc** box, type the e-mail addresses for the people who should receive a copy of the message.

6   In the **Subject** box, type the subject you want.

7   In the **Introduction** box, type the text you want to lead into your notes.

8   On the E-mail toolbar, click the **Send a Copy** button.

Chapter 30   Working with InfoPath Forms

Page 751 To fill out an InfoPath form

1   In the **Fill Out a Form** task pane, click **More Forms**.

2   In the **Forms** dialog box, click the tab you want, click the form you want, and then click **OK**.

3   Enter information into the form as needed.

4   On the **File** menu, click **Close**.

5   When prompted to save the file, click **Yes**.

6   Browse to the location where you want to save the form, in the **File name** box, type a name, and click **Save**.

757 To update a completed form

1   In the **Fill Out a Form** task pane, under **Open a form**, click **On My Computer**.

2   Browse to the location where the form is saved, click the file you want, and then click **Open**.

3   Edit the information in form as needed.

4 On the **File** menu, click **Close**.

5 When prompted to save the file, click **Yes**.

760 **To change views in a form**

● On the **View** menu, click the view you want.

762 **To import data into a form from another form**

1 In the **Fill Out a Form** task pane, under **Open a form**, click **On My Computer**.

2 Browse to the location where the form is saved, click the file you want, and then click **Open**.

3 On the **File** menu, click **Merge Forms**.

4 Browse to the location where the form containing the data you want is stored, select the files you need, and then click **Merge**.

762 **To export form data**

1 In the **Fill Out a Form** task pane, under **Open a form**, click **On My Computer**.

2 Browse to the location where the form is saved, click the file you want, and then click **Open**.

3 On the **File** menu, point to **Export To**, and then click **Microsoft Excel**.

4 In the **Export to Excel Wizard**, select the options you want and the fields you want to export.

5 Click **Finish**.

765 **To send a form as e-mail**

1 In the **Fill Out a Form** task pane, under **Open a form**, click **On My Computer**.

2 Browse to the location where the form is saved, click the file you want, and then click **Open**.

3 On the **File** menu, click **Send to Mail Recipient**.

4 In the **To** box, type the recipient's e-mail address.

5 In the **Cc** box, type the e-mail addresses of the people who should receive a copy of the message, if any.

6 On the E-mail toolbar, click the **Send** button.

765 **To publish a form to the Web**

1 In the **Fill Out a Form** task pane, under **Open a form**, click **On My Computer**.

2 Browse to the location where the form is saved, click the file you want, and then click **Open**.

3 On the **File** menu, point to **Export To**, and then click **Web**.

4 Browse to the location where you want to save the Web files, in the **File name** box, type a name for your Web form, and then click **Export**.

Chapter 31 **Designing InfoPath Forms**

Page 771 To customize a sample form

1 In the **Fill Out a Form** task pane, click **Design a Form**, and then click **Customize a sample**.

2 Click the form you want, and then click **OK**.

3 In the task pane, click the aspect of the form you want to modify.

4 Modify the form as needed.

5 On the **File** menu, click **Close**.

6 When prompted to save the file, click **Yes**.

7 Browse to the location where you want to save the form, in the **File name** box, type a name, and click **Save**.

771 To design a new form

1 In the **Fill Out a Form** task pane, click **Design a Form**, and then click **New blank form**.

2 Using the task pane to guide you, create a layout for your form, add controls, define the data source, and specify views.

3 On the **File** menu, click **Close**.

4 When prompted to save the file, click **Yes**.

5 Browse to the location where you want to save the form, in the **File name** box, type a name, and click **Save**.

771 To add a table or section

1 In the **Design Tasks** task pane, click **Layout**.

2 Place your mouse pointer in the form where you want to add the table or section, and in the task pane, click the type of table or section you want.

771 To add a control

1 In the **Design Tasks** task pane, click **Controls**.

2 Place your mouse pointer in the form where you want to add the control, and in the task pane, click the type of control you want.

3 In the **Shared Workspace** task pane, click the **Members** tab.

4 Click the down arrow to the right of the **Location for new workspace** box, select a location for your workspace site, and then click **Create**. If no locations appear in the list, type the URL to the SharePoint Services Web site where you have permission to create document workspaces, and then click **Create**.

796 **To create a document workspace by sending a shared attachment**

1 Open a new e-mail message.

2 In the **To** box, type the e-mail addresses of the message recipients.

3 In the **Cc** box, type the e-mail addresses of the people who should receive a copy of the message.

4 In the **Subject** box, type a phrase introducing your message.

5 On the Standard toolbar, click the **Insert File** button.

6 Navigate to the Office document for which you want to create a document workspace, select it, and click **Insert**.

7 In the message header, click **Attachment Options**.

8 In the **Attachment Options** task pane, click **Shared attachments**.

9 Click the down arrow to the right of the **Create Document Workspace at** box, and select a location for your workspace site. If no locations appear in the list, type the URL to the SharePoint Services Web site where you have permission to create document workspaces.

10 On the Standard toolbar, click the **Send** button.

796 **To add members to a workspace**

1 In the **Shared Workspace** task pane, click the **Members** tab.

2 Near the bottom of the task pane, click **Add New Members**.

3 On the **Add Users** page, enter the e-mail addresses of the new members, separated by semi-colons.

4 Select the group to which the users belong, and click **Next**.

5 Enter a display name for each user, and then indicate whether the users will receive e-mail notification regarding their membership in the workspace.

6 If users will receive an e-mail notice that they have been added to the workspace, specify a subject line and body text for the message.

7 Click **Finish**.

801 **To create a task in a document workspace**

1. In the **Shared Workspace** task pane, click the **Tasks** tab.
2. Near the bottom of the task pane, click **Add New Task.**

806 **To update a workspace document directly**

1. Point your Web browser to the document workspace site.
2. In the **Shared Documents** list, point to the document you want to update, and then click the down arrow that appears to the right of it.
3. In the drop-down list, click **Edit in Microsoft Word** or the equivalent for other Office documents.
4. Edit the document as needed, and then on the **File** menu, click **Close.**
5. When prompted to save the changes, click **Yes.**

810 **To start a discussion in a document workspace**

1. In the **Shared Workspace** task pane, click **Open Site in Browser.**
2. In the left navigation column, click **Discussions.**
3. Click the discussion board you want, and then click **New Discussion.**

Chapter 33 Teaming Up in a Meeting Workspace

Page 819 **To create a meeting workspace**

1. Open a meeting request, or open an appointment and on the Standard toolbar, click **Invite Attendees.**
2. Click the **Meeting Workspace** button, and in the **Meeting Workspace** task pane, click **Change Settings** if desired.
3. Click **Create.**

819 **To view a meeting workspace**

1. Open the meeting for which the workspace was created.
2. In the **Meeting Workspace** task pane, click **Go to workspace**, or in the body of the meeting request, click the name of the workspace.

819 **To add or remove attendees**

1. Open the meeting workspace.
2. In the **Attendees** area, click **Manage Attendees.**

I
Microsoft Office Word 2003

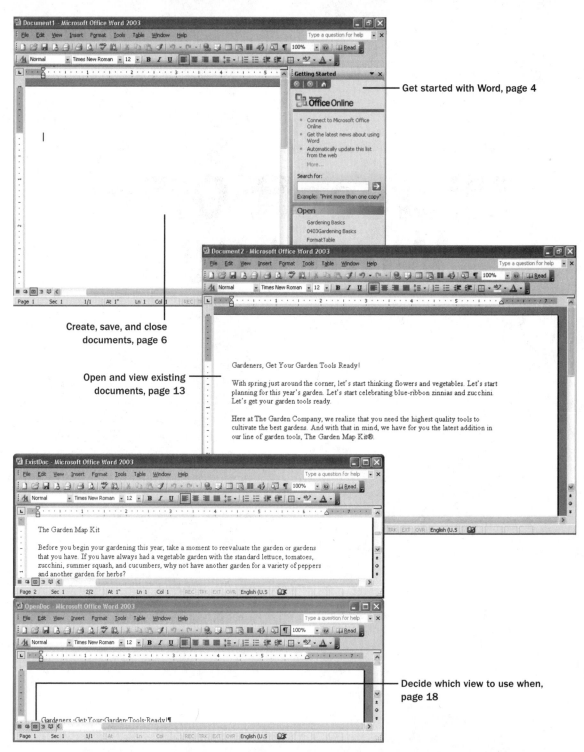

Get started with Word, page 4

Create, save, and close documents, page 6

Open and view existing documents, page 13

Decide which view to use when, page 18

Chapter 1 at a Glance

1 Working with Documents

In this chapter you will learn to:

✔ Get started with Word.

✔ Create, save, and close documents.

✔ Open and view existing documents.

✔ Decide which view to use when.

When you use a computer program to create, edit, and produce text documents, you are *word processing*. Word-processing programs help you create professional-quality documents because you can type and format text, correct errors, and preview your work before you print or distribute a document.

Microsoft Office Word 2003 is one of the most sophisticated word-processing programs available today. You can use Word to compose and update a wide range of business and personal documents. In addition, Word includes many *desktop publishing* features that you can use to enhance the appearance of documents so that they are appealing and easy to read. Whether you need to create a letter, memo, fax, annual report, or newsletter, Word has the power and flexibility to produce professional documents quickly and easily.

In this chapter, you'll start by entering text to create a document, and then you'll save the document as a *file*. While saving the document, you'll create a *folder* in which to store it. You'll also open other documents so that you can see how to move around in them and switch between them. Finally, you'll explore the different ways you can view documents in Word.

See Also Do you need only a quick refresher on the topics in this chapter? See the Quick Reference entries on page xxxiii.

 On the CD Before you can use the practice files in this chapter, you need to install them from the book's companion CD to their default location. See "Using the Book's CD-ROM" on page xxi for more information.

Getting Started with Word

When you first start Word, the Word *program window* opens. This window includes many of the menus, tools, and other features found in every Microsoft Office System program window, as well as some that are unique to Office 2003 and some that are unique to Word.

Title bar

Menu bar   Document window   Formatting toolbar

Insertion point   Ruler   Standard toolbar

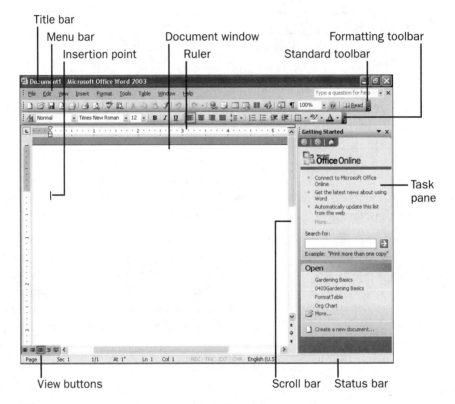

Task pane

View buttons   Scroll bar   Status bar

Tip What you see on your screen might not match the graphics in this book exactly. The screens in this book were captured on a monitor set to 800 x 600 resolution with 24-bit color and the Windows XP Standard color scheme. By default, the Standard and Formatting toolbars share one row, which prevents you from seeing all their buttons. To make it easier for you to find buttons, the Standard and Formatting toolbars in the graphics in this book appear on two rows. If you want to change your setting to match the screens in this book, click Customize on the Tools menu. On the Options tab, select the "Show Standard and Formatting toolbars on two rows" check box, and then click Close.

You enter and edit text in the *document window*, which is part of the Word program window. The *insertion point*, the blinking vertical line that appears in the document window, indicates where the text will appear when you begin to type.

Word organizes commands for common tasks in the *task pane*, a small window next to your document that opens when you are most likely to need it. For example, when you start Word, you see the Getting Started task pane, which includes commands for opening and creating documents. You can use the Getting Started task pane to open a saved or blank document, to create a document based on an existing one, or to create a document from a *template*, a file containing structure and style settings that help you create a specific type of document, such as a memo or résumé. You can show or hide a task pane whenever you like by clicking Task Pane on the View menu. Clicking the command hides the task pane if it is currently displayed or shows it if it is currently hidden. (This type of on/off command is called a *toggle*.) If you want to use a task pane other than the one that is currently displayed, you can select the one you want from the Other Task Panes menu on the task pane's title bar. If you no longer need the task pane, you can hide it. The document window then expands to fill the width of the program window.

Tip The Getting Started task pane opens each time you start Word. If you do not want the task pane to appear when you start Word, click Options on the Tools menu, click the View tab, clear the Startup Task Pane check box, and click OK.

In this exercise, you will start Word and then explore and close the task pane.

BE SURE TO start your computer, but don't start Word before beginning this exercise.

1   On the taskbar, click **Start**, point to **All Programs**, point to **Microsoft Office**, and then click **Microsoft Office Word 2003**.

The Word program window opens with a blank document in the document window and the Getting Started task pane displayed.

Tip You can also start Word by creating a shortcut icon on the Windows desktop. Simply double-click a shortcut icon to start its associated program. To create a shortcut, click the Start button, point to All Programs, point to Microsoft Office, right-click Microsoft Office Word 2003, point to Send To, and then click "Desktop (create shortcut)."

2   At the right end of the title bar of the **Getting Started** task pane, click the **Other Task Panes** down arrow.

The Other Task Panes menu opens.

3 Press the `Esc` key, or click an empty place in the document.

Word closes the Other Task Panes menu.

Close

4 At the right end of the **Getting Started** task pane title bar, click the **Close** button.

The Getting Started task pane closes, and the document window expands to fill the width of the program window.

5 On the **View** menu, click **Task Pane** to open the task pane again.

Troubleshooting If you don't see the Task Pane command on the View menu, it is hidden. Word personalizes your menus and toolbars to reduce the number of menu commands and toolbar buttons you see on the screen. When you click a menu name on the View menu, a short menu appears, containing only the commands you use most often. To make the complete menu appear, you can leave the pointer over the menu name for a second or two (called *hovering*), double-click the menu name, or point to the chevrons (the double arrows) at the bottom of the short menu.

Creating, Saving, and Closing Documents

Creating a Word document is as simple as typing text. The insertion point indicates where the text will appear in the document. When the text you're typing goes beyond the right margin, Word "wraps" the text to the next line. Because of this *word wrap* feature, which is common in word-processing and desktop-publishing programs, you press `Enter` only to start a new paragraph, not a new line.

The text you type appears in the document window and is stored by the computer, but only temporarily. If you want to keep a copy of the text, you must save the document as a file. Specifying a name and location for the file ensures that you can retrieve the file later.

To save a new document in Word, you click the Save button on the Standard toolbar or click the Save As command on the File menu. Either action displays the Save As dialog box, where you can name the file and indicate where you want to save it.

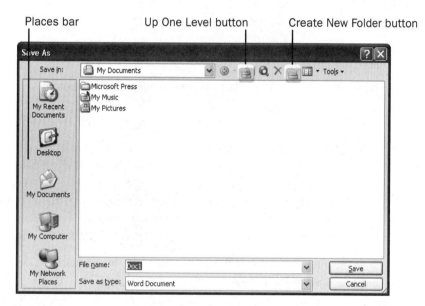

To help you locate the disk and folder where you want to store a new file, you can click the Up One Level button to move up one folder level, or you can use the Places bar on the left side of the dialog box to move to another location on your computer. The Places bar provides quick access to locations commonly used for storing files. For example, to save a file on a floppy disk, you click the My Computer icon on the Places bar, and then double-click 3½ Floppy (A:).

To keep your documents organized and easily accessible, you can store related documents in a folder. You can create folders ahead of time in Windows, or you can create them in Word by clicking the Create New Folder button in the Save As dialog box.

After you save a document once using the Save As dialog box, you can save subsequent changes by clicking the Save button on the Standard toolbar. Each time you do, the new version overwrites the previous version. To keep the new version without overwriting the original, you click the Save As command on the File menu and save the new version either in the same folder with a different name or in a different folder. You cannot store two documents with the same name in the same folder.

Tip   You can tell Word to periodically save a document you are working on in case the program stops responding or you lose power. Word saves the changes in a recovery file according to the time interval specified in the AutoRecover option. To turn on the AutoRecover option and specify a time interval for automatic saving, click Options on the Tools menu, click the Save tab, select the "Save AutoRecover info every" check box, specify the period of time, and then click OK. If your power fails or if Word stops responding while you have documents open, the next time you start Word, the Document Recovery task pane appears with a list of recovered documents. From there you can open a document, view any repairs, and compare recovered versions.

In this exercise, you'll enter text in a new document, add a symbol, save your new document, and then close it.

New Blank
Document

1   On the Standard toolbar, click the **New Blank Document** button.

A new document window opens.

Toolbar Options

Troubleshooting   If a button mentioned in this book doesn't appear on the specified toolbar on your screen, it is probably hidden. You can display the rest of that toolbar's buttons by clicking the Toolbar Options button at the right end of the toolbar, pointing to Add or Remove Buttons, then pointing to the toolbar's name and clicking the button you want. You can also double-click the move handle (the four vertical dots) at the left end of a toolbar to quickly expand it.

2   With the insertion point at the beginning of the new document, type Gardeners, Get Your Garden Tools Ready!, and then press ⌈Enter⌉.

The text appears in the new document.

3   Press ⌈Enter⌉ again to insert a blank line below the heading.

4   Type With spring just around the corner, let's start thinking flowers and vegetables. Let's start planning for this year's garden. Let's start celebrating blue-ribbon zinnias and zucchini. Let's get your garden tools ready.

Notice that you did not need to press ⌈Enter⌉ when the insertion point reached the right margin because the text wrapped to the next line.

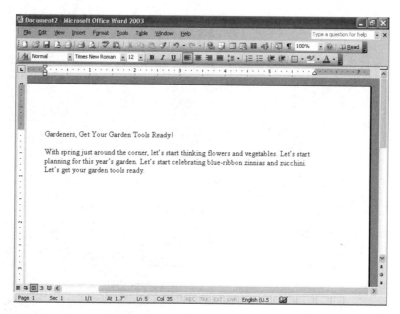

Important   If a colored wavy line appears under a word or phrase, Word is flagging a possible error: red indicates spelling, green indicates grammar, and blue indicates inconsistent formatting. A dotted purple line indicates a Smart Tag, which recognizes certain types of text as data that you can use with other programs. For example, Word tags a person's name as data that you can add to an electronic address book. For now, ignore any errors.

5   Press Enter two times to insert a blank line between paragraphs, and then type **Here at The Garden Company, we realize that you need the highest quality tools to cultivate the best gardens. And with that in mind, we have for you the latest addition in our line of garden tools, The Garden Map Kit.**

6   Press the ← key to move the insertion point one character to the left, between the letter *t* and the period.

7   On the **Insert** menu, click **Symbol**.

Word displays the Symbol dialog box.

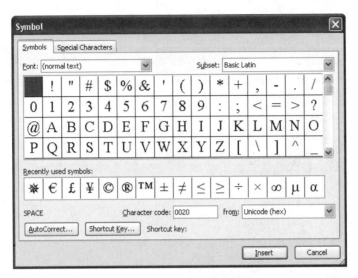

8 In the **Recently used symbols** area of the **Symbols** tab, click ® (the registered sign); or scroll through the list of symbols until you find this sign, and then click it.

9 Click the **Insert** button, and then click the **Close** button.

Word places the registered sign before the period in your document.

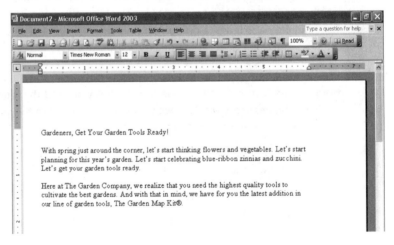

Tip You can insert some common symbols either by using the Symbol dialog box or by typing characters that Word recognizes as representing the symbol. For example, if you type two consecutive dashes followed by a word and a space, Word changes the two dashes to a professional-looking em-dash—like this one. (This symbol gets its name from the fact that it was originally the width of the character *m*.)

Save

10 On the Standard toolbar, click the **Save** button.

The Save As dialog box appears, displaying the contents of the My Documents folder.

11 In the list of the folder and file names stored in your *My Documents* folder, double-click the *Microsoft Press* folder, double-click the *Office 2003 SBS* folder, and then double-click the *WorkingDoc* folder.

The contents of the folder for this chapter appear in the Save As dialog box.

12 Click the New Folder icon on the toolbar. Name this new folder "CreatingDoc" and press Enter. Double-click the new *CreatingDoc* folder.

You can see that the CreatingDoc folder is currently empty. Word has entered the word *Gardeners*, the first word in the document, in the "File name" box as a suggested name for this file.

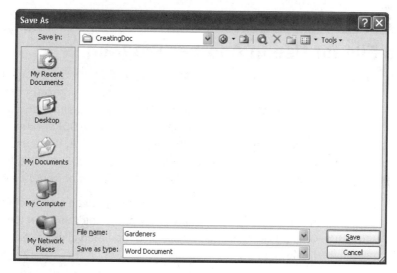

Tip Word uses the first few characters (or words) in the document to suggest a file name. You can accept this suggested name or type a new one. Depending on your Windows setup, file names might appear with an *extension*, which is a period followed by a three-letter program identifier. For Word, the extension is *.doc*. You don't have to type the extension after the file name in the Save As dialog box.

Create New
Folder

13 On the toolbar to the right of the **Save in** box, click the **Create New Folder** button.

The New Folder dialog box appears so that you can create a new folder within the CreatingDoc folder.

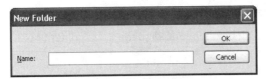

14 Type **NewFolder**, and click **OK**.

NewFolder becomes the current folder.

15 In the **File name** box, double-click *Gardeners*, type **FirstSave**, and click the **Save** button.

The Save As dialog box closes, and the name of the document, FirstSave, appears in the program window's title bar.

16 At the right end of the menu bar (not the title bar), click the **Close Window** button.

Close Window

The FirstSave document closes.

Saving a File for Use in Another Program

You can save a document in a *file format* other than the Word document format. A file format is the way that a program stores a file so that the program can open the file later. Saving a document in another format is important if you share documents with people who use previous versions of Word (such as Word 6.0/95) or other programs that have a different file format (such as WordPerfect). For example, if you use Word 6.0 on your home computer, you can create a document in Word 2003 at the office, save it in the Word 6.0 format, and then open and edit the document on your home computer.

If you are not sure of the format of a document, you can use the Properties dialog box to display the document's format information, including the version, type, and creator of the file. On the File menu, click Properties, and then click the General tab to display the document format information.

To save a document in another file format:

1 On the **File** menu, click **Save As**.

The Save As dialog box appears.

2 In the **File name** box, type a new name for the document.

3 Click the down arrow to the right of the **Save as type** box, and click the file format you want to use.

4 Click **Save**.

Opening and Viewing Existing Documents

After you save a document as a file, you can open the document again at any time. To open an existing document, you can use the Getting Started task pane. To create a new document based on an existing one, you can use the New Document task pane. This is useful when you want to take existing text and use it in a new document without changing the original document.

You can also open a document by clicking the Open button on the Standard toolbar.

When you open a document, a program button with the Word program icon and the document's name appears on the taskbar. You can have many documents open at the same time, but only one is the current or active document. The program button of the active document is darker than the others. To move between open documents, click the program buttons on the taskbar, or use the Window menu, which lists all open documents and indicates the active document with a check mark to the left of its name.

You can use the vertical and horizontal scroll bars to move around the active document. Using the scroll bars does not move the insertion point—it changes only your view of the document in the window. For example, if you drag the vertical scroll box down to the bottom of the scroll bar, the end of the document comes into view, but the insertion point does not move. Here are some other ways to use the scroll bars:

- Click the up or down scroll arrow on the vertical scroll bar to move the document window up or down one line of text.

- Click above or below the scroll box to move up or down one windowful.

- Click the left or right scroll arrow on the horizontal scroll bar to move the document window to the left or right several characters at a time.

- Click to the left or right of the scroll box to move left or right one windowful.

You can also move around a document by moving the insertion point. You can click to place the insertion point at a particular location, or you can press a key or a *key combination* on the keyboard to move the insertion point. For example, pressing the End key moves the insertion point to the right end of a line of text, whereas pressing the Ctrl and End keys at the same time moves the insertion point to the end of the document. To use a key combination, you hold down the first key (for example, Ctrl) and then press the second key (for example, End). After the action takes place, you release both keys.

Tip   The program window's status bar shows the location of the insertion point (by page, section, inch, line, and column).

The following table shows the keys and key combinations you can use to move the insertion point quickly.

Pressing this key	Moves the insertion point
←	Left one character at a time
→	Right one character at a time
↓	Down one line at a time
↑	Up one line at a time
Ctrl + ←	Left one word at a time
Ctrl + →	Right one word at a time
Home	To the beginning of the current line
End	To the end of the current line
Ctrl + Home	To the start of the document
Ctrl + End	To the end of the document
Ctrl + Page Up	To the beginning of the previous page
Ctrl + Page Down	To the beginning of the next page
Page Down	Up one screen
Page Up	Down one screen

If you create longer documents, you can use the Select Browse Object palette at the bottom of the vertical scroll bar to move quickly through a document. When you click the Select Browse Object button, a palette appears with browsing options, such as Browse by Page, Browse by Comment, and Browse by Graphic.

In this exercise, you will move around a document, switch between open documents, view nonprinting characters and text, and view documents in more than one window at the same time.

USE the *ExistDoc* and *OpenDoc* documents in the practice file folder for this topic. These practice files are located in the *My Documents\Microsoft Press\Office 2003 SBS\WorkingDoc\OpeningDoc* folder and can also be accessed by clicking *Start/All Programs/Microsoft Press/Microsoft Office System 2003 Step by Step.*

Open

1 On the Standard toolbar, click the **Open** button.

The Open dialog box appears, showing the contents of the folder you used for your last open or save action.

2   On the Places bar, click the **My Documents** icon to display the contents of that folder.

3   Double-click the *Microsoft Press* folder, double-click the *Office 2003 SBS* folder, double-click the *WorkingDoc* folder, and then double-click the *OpeningDoc* folder.

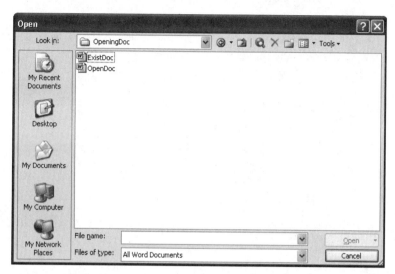

4   Click the *ExistDoc* file, and then click the **Open** button.

The ExistDoc document opens in the Word program window.

Troubleshooting   If you work on a network, documents might be stored in a common location so that more than one person can access them. If you try to open a document that is already open on another person's computer, Word gives you three options. You can open a Read Only copy that allows you to view the document but not save any changes in the same file, you can create and edit a copy of the document on your computer and merge your changes later, or you can ask to receive notification when the original copy becomes available.

5   In the greeting, click after the colon (:) to position the insertion point.

6   Press the [Home] key to move the insertion point to the beginning of the line.

7   Press the [→] key five times to move the insertion point to the beginning of the word *Garden* in the greeting.

8   Press the [End] key to move the insertion point to the end of the line.

9   Press [Ctrl]+[End] to move the insertion point to the end of the document.

10   Press [Ctrl]+[Home] to move the insertion point to the beginning of the document.

11   Drag the vertical scroll box to the bottom of the vertical scroll bar.

The end of the document comes into view. Note that the location of the insertion point has not changed—just the view of the document.

12   Click above the vertical scroll box to change the view of the document by one screen.

13   In the horizontal scroll bar, click the right scroll arrow twice so that the left side of the document scrolls out of view.

14   Drag the horizontal scroll box all the way to the left.

Select Browse
Object

15   At the bottom of the vertical scroll bar, click the **Select Browse Object** button.

A palette of objects appears.

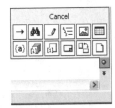

16   Move the pointer over the palette of objects.

The name of each object appears at the top of the palette as you point to it.

Browse by
Page

17   Click the **Browse by Page** button.

The insertion point moves from the beginning of page 1 to the beginning of page 2.

18   On the Standard toolbar, click the **Open** button, and when the **Open** dialog box appears, double-click the *OpenDoc* file.

Troubleshooting   If a document becomes corrupted and won't open, you can try to repair it. On the Standard toolbar, click the Open button, and click (don't double-click) the file you want to open. Then click the down arrow to the right of the Open button, and click Open and Repair on the menu of options.

The OpenDoc document opens in its own document window. If your taskbar is visible, it shows two program buttons, each with the name of an open document. The darker button indicates the active document, which is currently the OpenDoc document.

Tip   If you have hidden your Windows taskbar to reduce screen clutter, you can display it at any time by pointing to the bottom of your screen. If you work with several open programs, you can reduce crowding on the taskbar by setting Word to show only one program button. On the Tools menu, click Options, and in the Show area of the View tab, clear the Windows in Taskbar check box, and click OK. You can then use the Window menu to switch between open documents.

¶
Show/Hide ¶

19 On the Standard toolbar, click the **Show/Hide ¶** button.

The document changes to reveal formatting and hidden text.

Paragraph mark

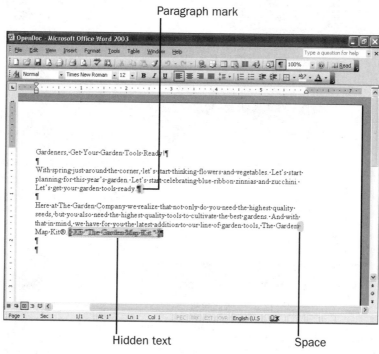

Hidden text　　　　　　　　　　　　Space

20 On the taskbar, click the **ExistDoc** program button to make its document active.

If your taskbar is hidden, first point to the bottom of the screen to display it.

21 On the menu bar, click **Window**.

The two open files are listed at the bottom of the Window menu.

22 On the **Window** menu, click **Arrange All**.

The two document windows are sized and stacked one on top of the other. Each window has a menu bar, toolbar, and scroll bars, so you can work on each document independently.

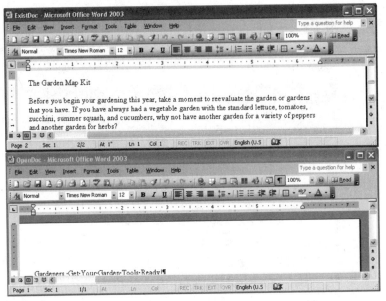

Maximize

23 At the right end of the ExistDoc window's title bar, click the **Maximize** button.

The document window expands to fill the program window.

24 On the **Window** menu, click **OpenDoc**, and then maximize its window.

CLOSE the *ExistDoc* and *OpenDoc* documents.

Close

Troubleshooting If you click the Close button at the end of the title bar instead of clicking the Close Window button at the end of the menu bar, you will close any open Word documents and quit the Word program. To continue working, start Word again.

Deciding Which View to Use When

In Word, you can view a document in a variety of ways:

- *Print Layout view* displays a document on the screen the way it will look when printed. You can see elements such as margins, page breaks, headers and footers, and watermarks.

- *Normal view* displays the content of a document with a simplified layout so that you can type and edit quickly. Page breaks are indicated only as dotted lines, and you cannot see layout elements such as headers and footers.

- *Web Layout view* displays a document on the screen the way it will look when viewed in a Web browser. You can see backgrounds, AutoShapes, and other effects. You can also see how text wraps to fit the window and how graphics are positioned.

- *Outline view* displays the structure of a document as nested levels of headings and body text, and provides tools for viewing and changing its hierarchy.

See Also   For information about outlining, see "Using an Outline to Rearrange Paragraphs" in Chapter 2.

New in Office 2003

Reading Layout view and thumbnails

- *Reading Layout view* (which is new in Word 2003) as much of the content of the document as will fit in the screen at a size that is comfortable for viewing. In this view, you have access to the Reading Layout and Reviewing toolbars, which you can use to adjust the view, display page thumbnails, search the document, and suggest changes.

- *Document Map* displays a list of your document's headings in a separate pane so that you can see the structure of the document while viewing and editing its text.

In this exercise, you explore Word's views so that you have an idea of which one is most appropriate for which task. After opening a document you switch between views, noticing the differences. You also zoom in and out, open up the Document Map, and work with thumbnails.

USE the *ViewDoc* document in the practice file folder for this topic. This practice file is located in the *My Documents\Microsoft Press\Microsoft Office System 2003 SBS\WorkingDoc\DecidingView* folder and can also be accessed by clicking *Start/All Programs/Microsoft Press/Microsoft Office System 2003 Step by Step*. OPEN the *ViewDoc* document.

Normal View

1   If the Normal View button in the lower-left corner of the window is not already active, click the **Normal View** button, or on the **View** menu, click **Normal**.

2   Scroll through the document.

     You can see the basic content of the document without any extraneous elements. The active area on the ruler indicates the width of the text column, dotted lines indicate page breaks, and scrolling is quick and easy.

The ruler indicates the width of the text column.

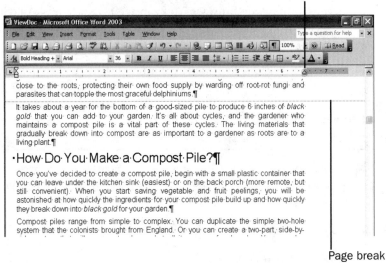

Page break

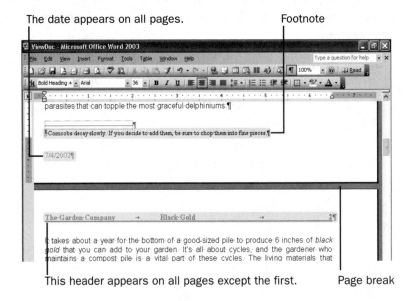

3 Press Ctrl+Home, and click the **Web Layout View** button in the lower-left corner of the window, or on the **View** menu, click **Web Layout**.

Web Layout View

4 Scroll through the document.

In a Web browser, the text column fills the window and has no page breaks.

5 Press Ctrl+Home, and click the **Print Layout View** button in the lower-left corner of the window, or on the **View** menu, click **Print Layout**.

Print Layout View

6 Scroll through the document.

The date appears on all pages.

Footnote

This header appears on all pages except the first.

Page break

As you can see, when printed the document will have footnotes, the date will be printed at the bottom of each page, and a header will appear on all pages except the first.

7 On the **Tools** menu, click **Options**. Then on the **View** tab, clear the **White space between pages** check box, and click **OK**.

The white space at the top and bottom of each page and the gray space between pages is hidden.

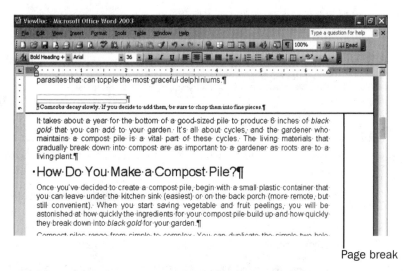

Page break

8 Restore the white space by clicking **Options** on the **Tools** menu, selecting the **White space between pages** check box, and clicking **OK**.

Tip You can also show or hide the white space by pointing between the pages until the Show White Space pointer or Hide White Space pointer appears, and then clicking.

Outline View

9 Press Ctrl+Home, and click the **Outline View** button in the lower-left corner of the window, or on the **View** menu, click **Outline**.

The screen changes to show the document's hierarchical structure, and the Outlining toolbar appears.

10 On the Outlining toolbar, click the down arrow to the right of the **Show All Levels** box, and click **Show Level 2**.

The document collapses to display only the Level 1 and Level 2 headings.

Outlining toolbar

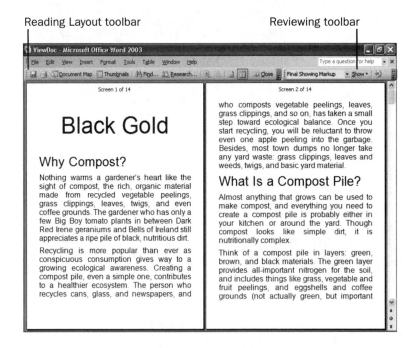

Reading Layout

11 In the lower-left corner of the window, click the **Reading Layout** button, or on the **View** menu, click **Reading Layout**. (You can also click the **Read** button on the Standard toolbar.)

The screen changes to display the document in Reading Layout view, and the Reading Layout and Reviewing toolbars appear.

Reading Layout toolbar   Reviewing toolbar

Allow
Multiple Pages

Troubleshooting If your screen doesn't look like ours, click all active buttons on the Reading Layout toolbar to toggle them off, and then click the Allow Multiple Pages button.

12 On the Reading Layout toolbar, click the **Allow Multiple Pages** button to toggle it off, and then click the **Thumbnails** button.

A pane opens on the left side of the screen showing each page of the document as a *thumbnail* image. You can use these thumbnails to quickly move around the document.

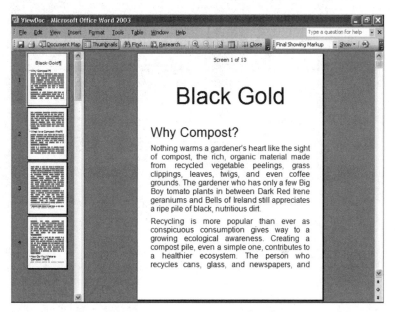

13 In the left pane, click the scroll bar below the scroll box, and then click thumbnail **8**.

The eighth page appears on the screen.

Actual Page

14 On the Reading Layout toolbar, click the **Actual Page** button.

The screen changes to show the same section of text as it will look when printed. The thumbnails still appear in the left pane, but they have changed to reflect the number of pages in the document in Print Layout view.

15 On the Reading Layout toolbar, click the **Document Map** button.

In the pane on the left side of the screen, an outline of the headings in the document replaces the thumbnails, and the first heading on the active page is highlighted.

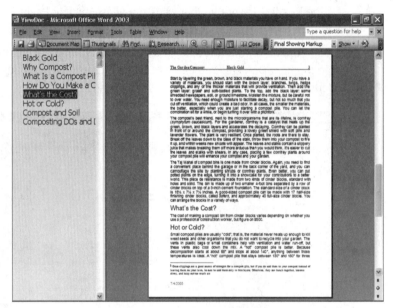

16 In the Document Map, click the *Black Gold* heading.

The page containing that heading is now displayed.

17 On the Reading Mode toolbar, click the **Document Map** button again to toggle it off, and then click the **Close** button.

18 In the lower-left corner of the window, click the **Print Layout View** button.

19 On the Standard toolbar, click the down arrow to the right of the **Zoom** box, and click **50%**.

The screen changes to display the text of the document at half its size.

20 Click the **Zoom** box, type 40, and press Enter.

The first two pages of the document are now displayed.

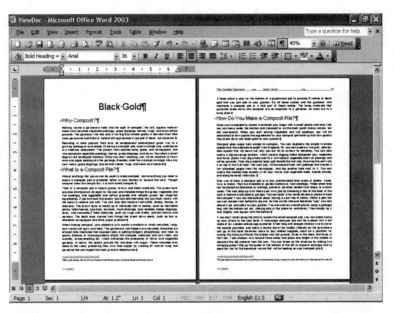

Next Page

21   On the right side of the window, click the **Next Page** button until the third and fourth pages of the document are displayed.

22   In the lower-left corner of the window, click the **Normal View** button.

Note that Normal view is still displayed at 100%. You can change the magnification in each view independently.

23   On the **View** menu, click **Print Layout**, and then return the **Zoom** setting to **100%**.

CLOSE the *ViewDoc* document, and if you are not continuing on to the next chapter, quit Word.

Key Points

■   You can open more than one Word document, and you can view more than one document at a time, but only one document can be active at a time.

■   You create Word documents by entering text and symbols at the insertion point, and you can move the insertion point to any location by clicking the document or by pressing keys and key combinations.

■   When you save a Word document, you can specify its name, location, and file format in the Save As dialog box.

■   You can view a document in a variety of ways, depending on your needs as you create the document and on the purpose for which you are creating it.

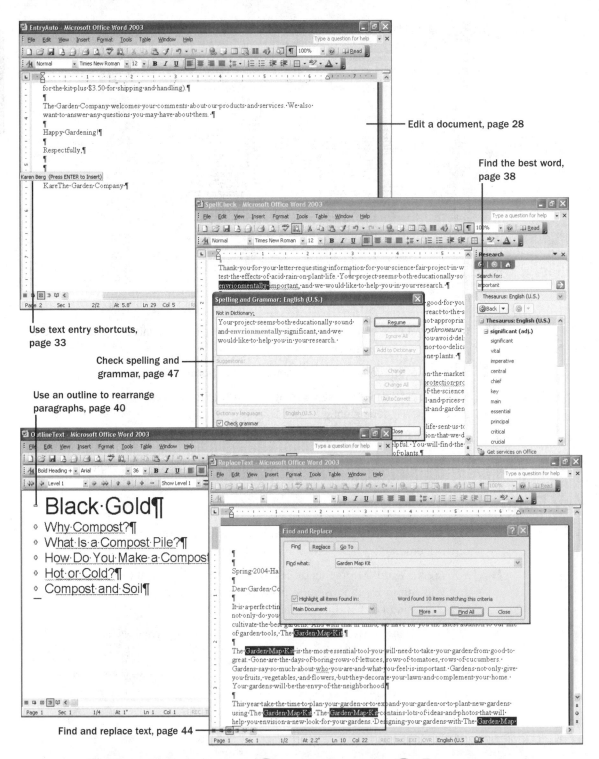

Edit a document, page 28

Find the best word, page 38

Use text entry shortcuts, page 33

Check spelling and grammar, page 47

Use an outline to rearrange paragraphs, page 40

Find and replace text, page 44

Chapter 2 at a Glance

2 Editing and Proofreading Documents

In this chapter you will learn to:

✔ Edit a document.

✔ Use text entry shortcuts.

✔ Find the best word.

✔ Use an outline to rearrange paragraphs.

✔ Find and replace text.

✔ Check spelling and grammar.

Unless the documents you create are intended for no one's eyes but your own, you need to be able to ensure that they are correct, logical, and persuasive. Whether you are a novice or an experienced writer, Microsoft Office Word 2003 has several tools that make creating professional documents easy and efficient:

- Editing tools provide quick-selection techniques and drag-and-drop editing to make it easy to move and copy text anywhere you want it.

- Shortcuts for handling often-used text enable you to save and recall specialized terms or proper names with the press of a key.

- Reference and research tools include a thesaurus that makes it easy to track down synonyms and a research service that provides access to a variety of Internet reference materials.

- Outlining tools allow easy rearranging of headings and text to ensure that your argument is logical.

- Search tools can be used to locate and replace words and phrases, either one at a time or throughout a document.

- Spelling and grammar features make it easy to correct typos and grammatical errors before you share the document with others.

In this chapter, you'll work with the text of a document to get it ready for distribution. You'll explore editing techniques, create and enter AutoText entries, ensure that the document is organized logically, and check that the language is precise and correct.

See Also Do you need only a quick refresher on the topics in this chapter? See the Quick Reference entries on page xxxiii.

Important Before you can use the practice files in this chapter, you need to install them from the book's companion CD to their default location. See "Using the Book's CD-ROM" on page xxi for more information.

Editing a Document

You will rarely write a perfect document that doesn't require any editing. You can edit a document as you create it, or you can write it first and then revise it. Or you might want to edit a document created for one purpose to create another document for a different purpose. For example, a marketing letter from last year might be edited to create a new letter for this year's marketing campaign. Editing encompasses many tasks, such as inserting and deleting words and phrases, correcting errors, and moving and copying text to different places in the document.

Inserting text is easy; you click to position the insertion point and simply begin typing. When you insert text, existing text moves to the right to accommodate the text that you are inserting, and the text that reaches the right margin wraps to the next line, if necessary.

Troubleshooting If you have Word set to Overtype mode, existing text will not move to the right when you type new text. Instead, each character you type will replace an existing character. To determine whether Word is in Overtype mode or Insert mode, check the letters OVR in the status bar. If they are gray, Word is in Insert mode. If they are black, Word is in Overtype mode. To toggle between these modes, you can either double-click the letters OVR in the status bar or press the [Insert] key.

Deleting text is equally easy, but it helps to know how to *select* it. Selected text appears highlighted on the screen. You can select specific items as follows:

- To select a word, double-click it. The word and the space following it are selected. Punctuation following a word is not selected.

- To select a sentence, click anywhere in the sentence while holding down the [Ctrl] key. The first character in the sentence through the space following the ending punctuation mark are selected.

- To select a paragraph, triple-click it.

You can select adjacent words, lines, or paragraphs by positioning the insertion point at the beginning of the text you want to select, holding down the [Shift] key, and then pressing an arrow key or clicking at the end of the text that you want to select. To select blocks of text that are not adjacent in a document, you select the first block, hold down the [Ctrl] key, and then click to select the next block.

To select a block of text quickly, you can use the *selection area*, a blank strip to the left of the document's text column. When the pointer is in the selection area, it changes from an I-beam to a right-pointing arrow.

You can use the selection area to quickly select these items:

- To select a line, click the selection area to the left of the line.

- To select a paragraph, double-click the selection area to the left of the paragraph.

- To select an entire document, triple-click the selection area.

Selection area

To deselect text, click anywhere in the document window except the selection area.

After selecting the text you want to work with, deleting it is an easy task: press the `Backspace` or `Del` key. If you want to delete only one or a few characters, you don't have to make a selection first: you can simply position the insertion point and then press `Backspace` or `Del` until the characters are all gone. Pressing `Backspace` deletes the character to the left of the insertion point. Pressing `Del` deletes the character to the right of the insertion point.

As you edit a document, Word keeps track of the changes you make so that you can easily reverse a change and restore your original text. This is useful when you make a mistake, such as inadvertently deleting a word. To undo the last action that you performed, click the Undo button on the Standard toolbar. To display the last five or six actions you have performed, click the down arrow to the right of the Undo button. To undo an action and all subsequent actions, click that action in the list.

If you undo an action, you can restore, or redo, the action by clicking the Redo button. You can click the down arrow to the right of the Redo button to restore multiple undone actions.

Tip Selecting an action from the Undo or Redo button's list undoes or redoes that action and all editing actions you performed after that one. You cannot undo or redo any single action except the last one you performed.

After selecting text, you can move it in one of the following ways:

■ Use the Cut and Paste commands or buttons. Cut text disappears from the document but is temporarily stored in an area of your computer's memory called the *Office Clipboard*. After cutting the text, you reposition the insertion point and paste the text in a new location somewhere in the same document or in a different document.

■ Use the Copy and Paste commands or buttons. Text that is copied rather than cut is also stored on the Office Clipboard but remains in its original location after it is pasted in the new location.

■ Use *drag-and-drop editing*, which does not involve the Office Clipboard, when you need to move or copy text within a paragraph or line. To move selected text, you point to it, hold down the mouse button, drag the text to another place, and then release the mouse button. To copy selected text, you hold down the [Ctrl] key as you drag.

The Office Clipboard is useful for moving and copying information between pages and documents or for moving text in long documents. You can use the Office Clipboard to store items of information from one or more sources in one storage area that can be accessed by all Office programs.

In this exercise, you will edit text in the existing document. You'll insert and delete text, undo the deletion, copy and paste a phrase, and move a paragraph.

BE SURE TO start Word before beginning this exercise.
USE the *EditDoc* document in the practice file folder for this topic. This practice file is located in the *My Documents\Microsoft Press\Office 2003 SBS\EditingProof\EditingDoc* folder and can also be accessed by clicking *Start/All Programs/Microsoft Press/Microsoft Office System 2003 Step by Step*.
OPEN the *EditDoc* document.

1 Double-click the word *Early* at the top of the document to select it, and then press [Enter] to delete the word and replace it with a new blank paragraph.

2   Press ⌊End⌋ to move the insertion point to the end of the line, press ⌊Space⎯⎯⎯⌋, and then type **Has Arrived!**

The text appears at the end of the line.

3   Press the ⌊↓⌋ key four times, hold down ⌊Ctrl⌋, and then click anywhere in the first sentence of the first paragraph to select it.

4   Press ⌊Del⌋ to delete the sentence.

Undo

5   On the Standard toolbar, click the **Undo** button to restore the deleted text.

6   Click the down scroll arrow until the phrase *Happy Gardening!* appears, position the mouse pointer in the selection area to the left of the phrase, and click once to select the entire line of text.

Copy

7   On the Standard toolbar, click the **Copy** button.

The text is copied to the Clipboard.

Paste

8   Press ⌊Ctrl⌋+⌊Home⌋ to move to the beginning of the document, and on the Standard toolbar, click the **Paste** button.

Paste Options

Tip   If a Paste Options button appears next to the pasted selection, you can ignore it for now. Clicking the Paste Options button displays a list of options that determine how the information is pasted into your document.

Cut

9   Select the new line of text, and on the Standard toolbar, click the **Cut** button.

The Clipboard task pane appears, displaying the current items in the Office Clipboard.

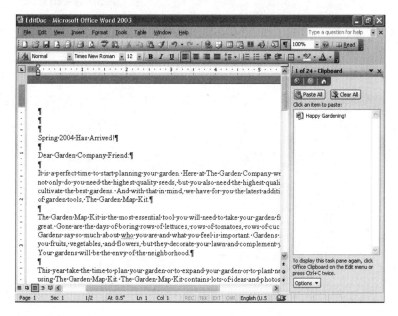

Clipboard icon

Tip You can paste the items listed in the Clipboard task pane into any Office program, either individually or all at once. You can choose not to have the Clipboard task pane appear when you cut or copy multiple items. You can also choose to display the Clipboard icon in the status area of the taskbar when the Office Clipboard is turned on. To access these options, click Options at the bottom of the Clipboard task pane. If the Clipboard task pane is turned off, you can open it by clicking Office Clipboard on the Edit menu.

10 Press ⌃Ctrl+End to move the insertion point to the end of the document, and then press Enter to insert a blank line.

11 In the **Clipboard** task pane, click the *Happy Gardening!* box to paste the text from the Clipboard in the document.

12 At the right end of the **Clipboard** task pane's title bar, click the **Close** button.

Close

13 If necessary, scroll up to the paragraph that begins *The Garden Company welcomes your comments*, and triple-click anywhere in the paragraph to select it.

14 Hold down the Shift key and press the ↓ key.

The blank paragraph is added to the selection.

15 Point to the selection, hold down the mouse button, and drag the paragraph down to the left of *Happy Gardening!*.

When you release the mouse, the text appears in its new location.

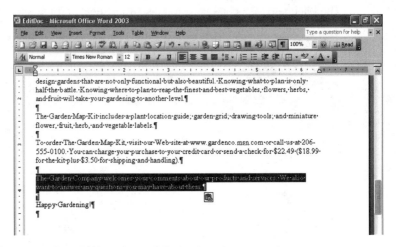

Save

16 On the Standard toolbar, click the **Save** button.

Word saves your changes to the document.

CLOSE: the *EditDoc* document.

Using Text Entry Shortcuts

Word provides several quick and easy ways to enter frequently used text in a document, including the following:

- *AutoCorrect* corrects commonly misspelled words so that you don't have to correct them yourself. You can also use this feature to insert text when you type an abbreviation.

- *AutoText* is similar to AutoCorrect but works only when you want it to, rather than automatically.

- *Date and time fields* supply the date and time from your computer's internal calendar and clock, so you don't have to look them up.

Have you noticed that Word automatically corrects some misspellings as you type them? For example, if you type *teh*, Word changes it to *the* as soon as you press `Space`. This is a feature of AutoCorrect. Besides relying on it to correct misspelled words, you can also use AutoCorrect to insert a phrase when you type an abbreviation. For example, you can set AutoCorrect to insert the words *The Garden Company* when you type the abbreviation *gc*. To accomplish this, you enter the abbreviation and the phrase in the AutoCorrect dialog box. You can also use this dialog box to check AutoCorrect options or to change or modify an AutoCorrect setting.

If you don't want Word to automatically change a misspelling or an abbreviation, you can reverse the change by clicking the Undo button before you type anything else, or you can turn off AutoCorrect options by pointing to the change and clicking the AutoCorrect Options button that appears below it. The AutoCorrect Options button first appears as a small blue box near the changed text and then becomes a button.

If you prefer to read and approve Word's changes before it automatically inserts them, you can use the AutoText feature to save time and create consistency in your documents. Word comes with built-in AutoText entries for commonly used items, such as the salutations and closings for letters, and you can create your own AutoText entries for the words and phrases you use repeatedly, such as your name, address, company, and job title.

To insert a built-in AutoText entry—for example, the closing of a letter—you click AutoText on the Insert menu, point to the category—for example, Closing—and then click the closing you want to insert in your document (for example, Respectfully yours,). To insert an AutoText entry you have created (for example, the name and address of Karen Berg, the owner of The Garden Company), you type the first four letters of the entry to display a ScreenTip of the full entry, press [Enter] to insert the entry in the document, and continue typing. If you are typing a different word with the same first four letters as the AutoText entry and you don't want to insert the entry, you just continue typing.

Besides commonly used words and phrases, you can also insert the date and the time, either as text entries or as date and time fields. If you insert a field, you can choose to have Word update the date and time whenever you open the document or whenever you print the document. Word uses your computer's internal calendar and clock as its source.

When you type certain information, such as the date and time, names, street addresses, telephone numbers, or the names of recent Microsoft Outlook e-mail message recipients, Word recognizes the information and displays a dotted line under the text to indicate that it has been flagged with a *Smart Tag*. Pointing to the underlined text displays the Smart Tag Actions button. You can click this button to display a menu of options for performing common tasks associated with that type of information. For example, if you type a name and address, Word flags it as a Smart Tag, and you can then add it to your Contacts list in Outlook.

In this exercise, you'll use AutoCorrect and change its settings. You will then insert a built-in AutoText entry and create and insert a custom AutoText entry. You'll also insert the date and examine actions you can perform using Smart Tags.

USE the *EntryAuto* document in the practice file folder for this topic. This practice file is located in the *My Documents\Microsoft Press\Office 2003 SBS\EditingProof\UsingShort* folder and can also be accessed by clicking *Start/All Programs/Microsoft Press/Microsoft Office System 2003 Step by Step*.
OPEN the *EntryAuto* document.

1 On the **Tools** menu, click **AutoCorrect Options**.

The AutoCorrect dialog box appears, displaying the AutoCorrect tab.

2 Clear the **Capitalize first letter of sentences** check box so that Word will not capitalize a lowercase letter or word that follows a period.

3 Click the **Replace** text box, and type gc.

4 Press the [Tab] key to move the insertion point to the **With** text box.

5 Type The Garden Company.

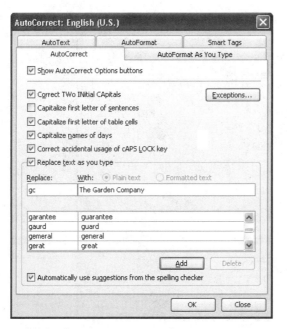

6   Click **Add** to add the entry to the correction list.

The text for the new AutoCorrect entry will now be inserted in a document each time you type its abbreviation and press `Space`.

7   Click **OK** to close the **AutoCorrect** dialog box.

8   Press `Ctrl`+`End` to place the insertion point at the end of the document.

9   Type *gc*, and then press `Space`.

The text *gc* changes to *The Garden Company*.

10   Press `Home` to move to the beginning of the line, and press `Enter` to start a new paragraph.

11   On the **Insert** menu, point to **AutoText**, point to **Closing**, and then click **Respectfully,**.

Word inserts this standard closing text at the location of the insertion point.

12   Press `Enter` four times to leave space for a signature.

13   On the **Insert** menu, point to **AutoText**, and then click **AutoText** on the submenu.

The AutoCorrect dialog box appears with the AutoText tab active.

14   In the **Enter AutoText entries here** text box, type Karen Berg.

15 Click **Add**, and then click **OK**.

The AutoCorrect dialog box closes.

16 Type **Kare**.

A ScreenTip displays *Karen Berg (Press ENTER to Insert)*.

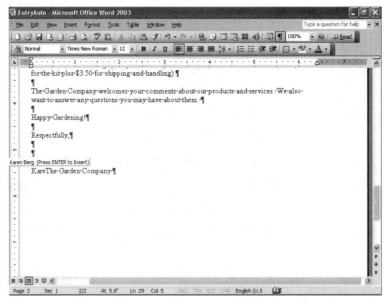

17 Press ⎡Enter⎤ to insert the full name, and then press ⎡Enter⎤ again.

18   Press <kbd>Ctrl</kbd>+<kbd>Home</kbd> to move to the top of the document.

19   On the **Insert** menu, click **Date and Time**.

The Date and Time dialog box appears.

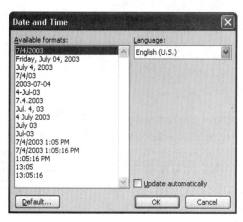

20   Click today's date with the **month dd yyyy** format, such as July 4, 2003, and click **OK**.

Word enters the current date in the document.

Smart Tag
Actions

21   Point to the date, and when the **Smart Tag Actions** button appears, click it.

22   On the button's menu, click **Smart Tag Options**.

The AutoCorrect dialog box appears, displaying the Smart Tags tab.

You can use this dialog box to turn the Smart Tags feature on and off. Do not turn off the feature at this time.

23   Click **OK** to close the **AutoCorrect** dialog box.

24   On the Standard toolbar, click the **Save** button.

Save

Word saves your changes to the document.

CLOSE the *EntryAuto* document.

Finding the Best Word

Language is often contextual—the language you use in a letter to a friend is different from the language you use in business correspondence. To make sure you are using words that best convey your meaning in any given context, you can use Word's *Thesaurus* to look up alternative words or synonyms for a selected word. To use the Thesaurus, you select the word that you want to look up, and on the Tools menu, click Language and then Thesaurus. The Research task pane appears, displaying a list of synonyms with equivalent meanings.

In this exercise, you'll use the Thesaurus to replace one word with another.

USE the *Thesaurus* document in the practice file folder for this topic. This practice file is located in the *My Documents\Microsoft Press\Office 2003 SBS\EditingProof\FindingWord* folder and can also be accessed by clicking *Start/All Programs/Microsoft Press/Microsoft Office System 2003 Step by Step.*
OPEN the *Thesaurus* document.

1   Double-click the word **important** in the last line of the first paragraph.

2   On the **Tools** menu, click **Language**, and then click **Thesaurus**.

The Research task pane appears, listing synonyms for the word *important*.

3   Click the minus sign to the left of *significant*.

Word hides the list of synonyms under *significant*, bringing the synonym *valuable* and its own list of synonyms into view.

4   Click the plus sign to the left of *significant*, and then point to the word **significant** in the **Meanings** area just below it.

Word surrounds the meaning with a box containing a down arrow.

5   Click the down arrow to the right of the word *significant* (don't click the word itself), and click **Insert** on the drop-down menu.

Word replaces *important* with *significant*.

6   Close the **Research** task pane.

7   On the Standard toolbar, click the **Save** button.

Save

Word saves your changes to the document.

CLOSE the *Thesaurus* document.

Translating Text

Word provides a basic multi-language dictionary and translation feature so that you can look up text in the dictionary of a different language and translate words and phrases.

To translate text or look up words in another language:

1   If you want to translate a word or phrase, select it. If you want to look up a word or phrase, make sure nothing is selected.

2   On the **Tools** menu, point to **Language**, and then click **Translate**.

If you are prompted to install the feature, click Yes.

3   If you want to look up a word or phrase, type it in the **Search for** box, and click

Start searching

the adjacent **Start searching** button.

If you are translating a selection, the word or phrase already appears in the "Search for" box.

4   In the **Translation** area of the **Research** task pane, change the dictionary settings in the **From** and **To** boxes as necessary.

The translated text appears in the bottom part of the pane.

Researching Information

**New in
Office 2003**

Research
Service

In addition to the Thesaurus, the Research task pane provides access to a variety
of informational resources, collectively known as the *Research service*, from within Word.
You can enter a topic in the "Search for" text box and specify in the box below which
resource Word should use to look for information regarding that topic. By clicking
"Research options" at the bottom of the Research task pane, you can specify which of a
predefined list of reference materials, such as Encarta and various Internet resources, will
be available from a drop-down list, and you can add your own reference-material sources.

To use the Research service:

1   Display the **Research** task pane by clicking **Research** on the **Tools** menu.

2   In the **Search for** text box, type the topic you are interested in researching.

        For example, you might type *deer-proof plants*.

3   Click the down arrow to the right of the text box below, and select the resource
you want to use to search for information.

        For example, you might click MSN Search.

4   Click the **Start searching** button.

Start searching

        The search results are displayed in the task pane.

5   Click the plus sign to the left of topics that interest you.

        You can click a hyperlink to a Web address to go to the Web to track down further
information. You can also select part of a topic, right-click to display a shortcut
menu, click Copy, and then paste the selection into your document. Or you can
click Look Up on the shortcut menu to research information about the selection.

Using an Outline to Rearrange Paragraphs

Word provides a variety of ways in which to view a document. If you are creating a
document that contains headings, you can format it with built-in heading styles that
include outline levels. Then it is easy to view and organize the document by using
Outline view. This view enables you to see only the headings of a document, level by
level, and to rearrange the document as needed without scrolling through all the pages.

See Also   For more information about formatting with styles, see the topic "Changing
the Look of Characters and Paragraphs with Styles" in Chapter 3.

To view a document in Outline view, click the Outline View button in the lower-left corner of the window. The screen displays the document and the Outlining toolbar. This toolbar includes buttons you can click to display a specific heading level, to *promote* or *demote* headings or body text to change their level, and to move headings and their text up or down in the document. The indentations and symbols in Outline view indicate the level of a heading or paragraph in the document's structure and do not appear in the document when you print it.

In this exercise, you'll switch to Outline view, promote and demote headings, move headings, and expand and collapse the outline.

USE the *OutlineText* document in the practice file folder for this topic. This practice file is located in the *My Documents\Microsoft Press\Office 2003 SBS\EditingProof\UsingOutline* folder and can also be accessed by clicking *Start/All Programs/Microsoft Press/Microsoft Office System 2003 Step by Step*.
OPEN the *OutlineText* document.

Outline View

1 In the lower-left corner of the window, click the **Outline View** button.

The screen changes to display the document in Outline view, and the Outlining toolbar appears.

Show Level

2 On the Outlining toolbar, click the down arrow to the right of the **Show Level** box, and click **Show Level 1**.

The document collapses to display only level 1 headings.

3 Click the *Hot or Cold?* heading.

4 On the Outlining toolbar, click the **Demote** button.

Demote

The *Hot or Cold?* heading changes to a level 2 heading.

5   On the Outlining toolbar, click the down arrow to the right of the **Show Level** box, and click **Show All Levels**.

The document expands to show the headings and their text. Note that the *Hot or Cold?* heading appears in a smaller font, and the body text under the heading is indented. When you restructure a heading in Outline view, the paragraphs below that heading are also restructured.

6   Press [Ctrl]+[Home] to move the insertion point to the beginning of the document.

7   On the Outlining toolbar, click the down arrow to the right of the **Show Level** box, and click **Show Level 2**.

The outline collapses to show all the first and second level headings.

Move Up

8   Click anywhere in the *Composting DOs and DON'Ts* heading, and then on the Outlining toolbar, click the **Move Up** button.

The heading moves above the *Compost and Soil* heading.

9   On the Outlining toolbar, click the down arrow to the right of the **Show Level** box, and click **Show All Levels**.

The document expands to show the *Composting DOs and DON'Ts* heading and its related paragraph, which is now above the *Compost and Soil* heading.

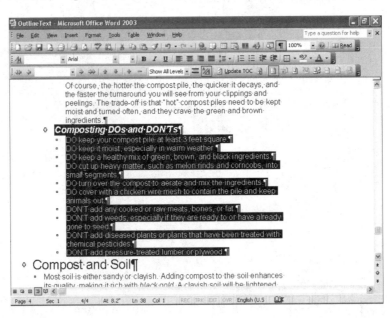

10 Press [Ctrl]+[Home] to move the insertion point to the beginning of the document. Then on the Outlining toolbar, click the down arrow to the right of the **Show Level** box, and click **Show Level 2**.

11 Click anywhere in the *Hot or Cold?* heading, and on the Outlining toolbar, click the **Promote** button.

Promote

The heading changes to level 1.

12 On the Outlining toolbar, click the **Expand** button.

Expand

The paragraphs and headings under level 1 *Hot or Cold?* heading are now visible.

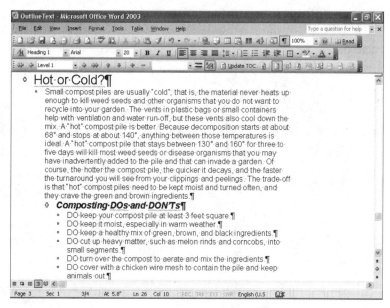

13 On the Outlining toolbar, click the **Collapse** button.

Collapse

14 On the **View** menu, click **Print Layout**.

The Outlining toolbar disappears, and you can now scroll through the document to see the effects of the reorganization.

CLOSE the *OutlineText* document without saving it.

Finding and Replacing Text

One way to ensure that the text in your documents is consistent and accurate is to use Word's Find command to search for every instance of a particular word or phrase. For example, the marketing director of The Garden Company might search for every instance of *The Garden Map Kit* to check that the capitalization is correct. If you know that you want to substitute one word or phrase for another, you can use the Replace command to find each occurrence of the text you want to change and replace it with different text.

Clicking the Find command on the Edit menu displays the Find tab of the Find and Replace dialog box, and clicking the Replace command displays the Replace tab, which is similar to the Find tab but has more options. After you enter the text you want to find in the "Find what" text box, you can click the Find Next button to locate the next occurrence of that text. On the Replace tab, you can then use the following buttons:

- ■ Click the Replace button to replace the selected occurrence with the text in the "Replace with" box and move to the next occurrence.

- ■ Click the Replace All button to replace all occurrences with the text in the "Replace with" box.

- ■ Click the Find Next button to leave the selected occurrence as it is and locate the next one.

You can use other options in the Find and Replace dialog box to carry out more complicated searches. Clicking the More button expands the box to make these additional options available.

Clicking the Less button hides the additional search options.

Using the options in the Search drop-down list, you can guide the direction of the search. You can select the "Match case" check box to match capitalization and select the "Find whole words only" check box to find only whole-word occurrences of the "Find what" text. If you want to check that your usage of two similar words, such as *effect* and *affect*, is correct, you can select the "Use wildcards" check box and then enter one of Word's *wildcard characters* in the "Find what" text box to locate variable information. The two most common wildcard characters are:

- The ? wildcard stands for any single character in this location in the "Find what" text.

- The * wildcard stands for any number of characters in this location in the "Find what" text.

Tip   To see a list of the other available wildcards, use Help to search for *wildcards*.

Selecting the "Sounds like" check box finds occurrences of the search text that sound the same but are spelled differently, such as *there* and *their*. Selecting the "Find all word forms" check box finds occurrences of a particular word in any form, such as *plant*, *planted*, and *planting*. Finally, you can locate formatting, such as bold, or special characters, such as tabs, by selecting them from the Format or Special drop-down list.

In this exercise, you will find a phrase and replace some instances of it, and then you'll replace one phrase with another one throughout the entire document.

USE the *ReplaceText* document in the practice file folder for this topic. This practice file is located in the *My Documents\Microsoft Press\Office 2003 SBS\EditingProof\FindingText* folder and can also be accessed by clicking *Start/All Programs/Microsoft Press/Microsoft Office System 2003 Step by Step*.
OPEN the *ReplaceText* document.

1   With the insertion point at the beginning of the document, click **Find** on the **Edit** menu.

The Find and Replace dialog box appears with the Find tab displayed.

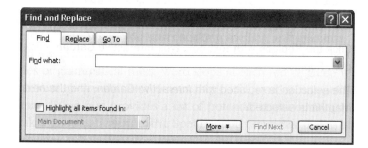

The options displayed in the Spelling and Grammar dialog box depend on the type of error Word encounters. The following table describes these options.

Button or Option	Function
Ignore Once	Leaves the highlighted error unchanged and finds the next spelling or grammar error. If you click the document to edit it, this button changes to Resume. After you finish editing, click Resume to continue checking the document.
Ignore All	Leaves all occurrences of the highlighted spelling error unchanged throughout the document and continues checking the document. Word ignores the spelling of this word in this document and in all documents whose spelling is checked during the current Word session.
Ignore Rule	Leaves all occurrences of the highlighted grammar error unchanged throughout the document and continues checking the document. Word ignores the grammar rule in this document and in all documents whose spelling and grammar is checked during the current Word session.
Next Sentence	Transfers to the document the corrections you've typed within the Spelling and Grammar dialog box and continues checking the document. This enables you to correct grammatical errors without having to switch between the Spelling and Grammar dialog box and the document window.
Add to Dictionary	Adds the selected word in the "Not in dictionary" text box to the custom dictionary. The custom dictionary contains the words you specify.
Change	Changes the highlighted error to the word you select in the Suggestions box.
Change All	Changes all occurrences of the highlighted error to the word you select in the Suggestions box and continues checking the document.
Explain	Provides more information about the grammar error.
AutoCorrect	Adds the spelling error and its correction to the AutoCorrect list so that Word corrects it automatically the next time you type it.
Undo	Undoes the last spelling or grammar action you performed.
Options	Opens the Spelling and Grammar options dialog box. Use this dialog box to open a different custom dictionary or to change the rules that Word uses to check spelling and grammar.

In this exercise, you'll check the spelling in the document and add common terms that are not already in the online dictionary. Then you will find, review, and correct a grammar error.

USE the *SpellCheck* document in the practice file folder for this topic. This practice file is located in the *My Documents\Microsoft Press\Office 2003 SBS\EditingProof\CheckingSpell* folder and can also be accessed by clicking *Start/All Programs/Microsoft Press/Microsoft Office System 2003 Step by Step*. OPEN the *SpellCheck* document.

1 Right-click *bot*, the first word with a red wavy underline.

The shortcut menu lists possible correct spellings for this word, as well as actions you might want to carry out.

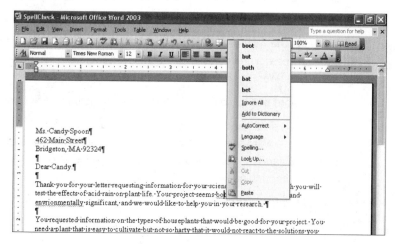

2 On the shortcut menu, click **both**.

Word removes the red wavy underline and inserts the correction.

Spelling and Grammar

3 Press Ctrl+Home to move to the beginning of the document, and on the Standard toolbar, click the **Spelling and Grammar** button.

The Spelling and Grammar dialog box appears, highlighting *envrionmentally*, the first word that Word does not recognize.

Troubleshooting If the spelling and grammar checker doesn't find the errors in this document, you need to reset the spelling and grammar checker. On the Tools menu, click Options, click the Spelling & Grammar tab, click Recheck Document, and then click Yes to recheck words and grammar that were previously checked or that you chose to ignore.

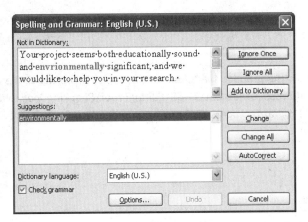

4 With *environmentally* selected in the **Suggestions** box, click **AutoCorrect**.

Word adds the misspelling and its correction to the AutoCorrect list, so the next time you type *envrionmentally* by mistake, the spelling will be corrected for you as you type. Word then flags *harty* as the next possible misspelling.

5 With the word *hearty* selected in the **Suggestions** box, click **Change All**.

Word changes this and a subsequent occurrence of *harty* to *hearty*. It then flags *crassula* as a word that it doesn't recognize. *Crassula*, a type of plant, is spelled correctly. By adding words like this one to the custom dictionary, you can prevent Word from continuing to flag them.

6 Click **Add to Dictionary**.

7 Click **Ignore All** for each of the three Latin plant names.

Word then flags a possible grammar error and indicates that this text could be a sentence fragment, meaning, in this case, that the sentence is missing a verb.

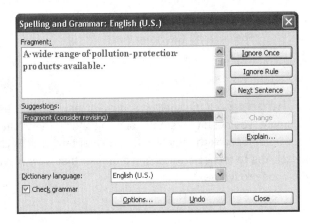

8 In the **Fragment** box, click before the word *available*, type are, press `Space`, and then click **Change**.

Word displays a message, indicating that it has finished checking the spelling and grammar of the document.

9 Click **OK** to close the message box.

10 On the Standard toolbar, click the **Save** button.

Save

Word saves your changes to the document.

CLOSE the *SpellCheck* document, and if you are not continuing on to the next chapter, quit Word.

Key Points

■ You can undo and redo a single action or the last several actions you performed, by using the Undo and Redo buttons.

■ You can cut or copy text and paste it elsewhere. Cut and copied text is stored on the Office Clipboard.

■ You can create text for repeated use with Word's AutoCorrect and AutoText features. You can also insert fields that display the date and time.

■ You can use the Thesaurus to look up alternative words or synonyms for a selected word, and use the Research service to access specialized reference materials and online resources.

■ You can outline a document and use the outline to rearrange the document.

■ You can find each occurrence of a word or phrase and replace it with another.

■ You can correct individual spelling and grammar errors as you type, or you can check an entire document for errors.

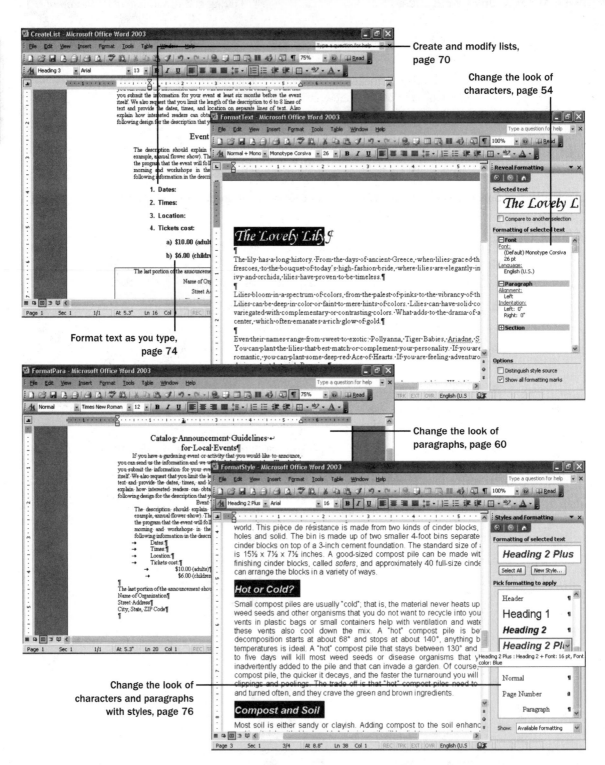

Create and modify lists, page 70

Change the look of characters, page 54

Format text as you type, page 74

Change the look of paragraphs, page 60

Change the look of characters and paragraphs with styles, page 76

Chapter 3 at a Glance

3 Changing the Appearance of Text

In this chapter you will learn to:

✔ Change the look of characters.

✔ Change the look of paragraphs.

✔ Create and modify lists.

✔ Format text as you type.

✔ Change the look of characters and paragraphs with styles.

The way your documents look helps them convey their message. You want the documents you create with Microsoft Office Word 2003 to look professional—well designed and polished—and you want the appearance of your text to reflect its contents. The format of your paragraphs and pages influences the appeal of your documents and helps draw the reader's attention to important information. To enhance the appearance of your documents, you can format the text so that key points stand out and your arguments are easy to grasp.

In this chapter, you'll improve the appearance of the text in a document by changing text characteristics. You'll also change the appearance of the paragraphs in a document by indenting them and changing their alignment, and by setting tab stops for lines within paragraphs. You'll also create and modify bulleted and numbered lists. Finally, you'll see how to use Word features that format text as you type and that apply sets of formatting with a few mouse clicks.

See Also   Do you need only a quick refresher on the topics in this chapter? See the Quick Reference entries on page xxxiii.

 Important   Before you can use the practice files in this chapter, you need to install them from the book's companion CD to their default location. See "Using the Book's CD-ROM" on page xxi for more information.

Changing the Look of Characters

The text you type in a document is displayed in a particular font. A *font* is a complete set of characters that all have the same design. The fonts that are available vary from one computer to another. Common fonts include Times New Roman, Courier, and Arial.

You can vary a font's basic design by changing the following *attributes*:

- Almost every font comes in a range of *font sizes*. The font size is measured in *points*, from the top of letters that have parts that stick up (ascenders), such as *b*, to the bottom of letters that have parts that drop down (descenders), such as *p*. Each point is equal to about 1/72 of an inch.

- Almost every font comes in a range of *font styles*. The most common are regular (or plain), italic, bold, and bold italic.

- Fonts can be enhanced by applying *font effects*, such as underlining, small capital letters, or shadows.

- A range of *font colors* is available in a standard palette, but you can also specify custom colors.

- You can alter *character spacing* by pushing characters apart or squeezing them together to achieve a desired effect.

After you have selected an appropriate font for each element of a document, you can use these sets of attributes to achieve different effects. Although some attributes might cancel each other out, they are usually cumulative. For example, The Garden Company might use a bold font in various sizes and various shades of green to make different heading levels stand out in a newsletter. Collectively, the font and the attributes used to vary its look are called *character formatting*.

Tip   The way you use attributes in a document can influence its visual impact on your readers. Used judiciously, attributes can make a plain document look attractive and professional, but excessive use can make it look amateurish and detract from the message. For example, using too many different fonts within the same document is the mark of inexperience, so the rule of thumb is to not use more than two or three. Also, because lowercase letters tend to recede, using all uppercase (capitals) letters can be useful for titles and headings or for certain kinds of emphasis. However, large blocks of uppercase letters are tiring to the eye. (Where do the terms *uppercase* and *lowercase* come from? Until the advent of computers, individual letter blocks were assembled to form the words that would appear on a printed page. The blocks were stored alphabetically in cases, with the capital letters in the upper case and the small letters in the lower case.)

When you are formatting a document, you can open the Reveal Formatting task pane to display the formatting of selected text, such as its font and font effects. In this task pane you can display, change, or clear the formatting for the selected text. You can also use the Reveal Formatting task pane to select text based on formatting, which enables you to compare the formatting used in the selected text with formatting used in other parts of the document.

In this exercise, you will format the text in a document by changing its font, font size, font color, and character spacing.

BE SURE TO start Word before beginning this exercise.
USE the *FormatText* document in the practice file folder for this topic. This practice file is located in the *My Documents\Microsoft Press\Office 2003 SBS\ChangingText\ChangingChar* folder and can also be accessed by clicking *Start/All Programs/Microsoft Press/Microsoft Office System 2003 Step by Step*.
OPEN the *FormatText* document.

1   Select *The Lovely Lily*, the title at the top of the document.

Font

2   On the Formatting toolbar, click the down arrow to the right of the **Font** box, scroll the list of available fonts, and click **Monotype Corsiva**.

Troubleshooting   If Monotype Corsiva is not available, select a similar script-style font, such as Brush Script MT.

The title at the top of the document now appears in the new font.

Font Size

3   On the Formatting toolbar, click the down arrow to the right of the **Font Size** box, and click **26** in the list.

The size of the title text increases to 26 points.

4   On the **Format** menu, click **Reveal Formatting**.

The Reveal Formatting task pane appears, displaying the formatting of the selected text.

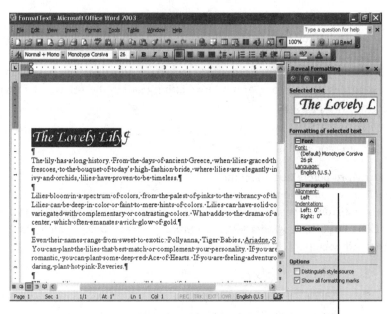

Formatting summary for the selected text

5 In the **Font** area of the **Reveal Formatting** task pane, click the **Font** link (the blue underlined word) to display the **Font** dialog box.

6 In the **Effects** area of the Font dialog box, select the **Outline** check box.

In the Preview box, the text changes to show how it will look with this effect applied.

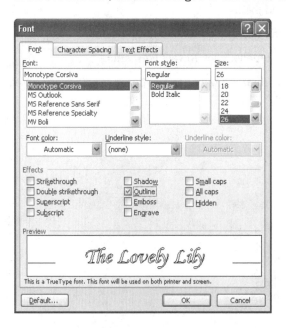

7 Click the **Character Spacing** tab.

8 Click the down arrow to the right of the **Spacing** box, and click **Expanded**.

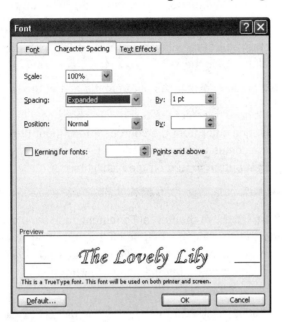

9 Click the up arrow to the right of the adjacent **By** box until the spacing is expanded by **2 pt** (points), and then click **OK**.

The selected text appears with an outline effect and with the spacing between the characters expanded by 2 points. Both of these effects are now listed in the Font area of the Reveal Formatting task pane.

10 At the top of the **Reveal Formatting** task pane, point to the **Selected text** box, and when a down arrow appears, click the arrow, and then click **Clear Formatting**.

The formatting of the selected text is removed.

Undo

11 On the Standard toolbar, click the **Undo** button.

The formatting of the selected text is restored.

12 Select the word *pinks* in the first sentence of the second paragraph.

Font Color

13 On the Formatting toolbar, click the down arrow to the right of the **Font Color** button, and then on the color palette, click the **Pink** box in the first column of the fourth row.

The color of the selected word is now pink. (You'll need to deselect it in order to see the color.) Its formatting is listed in the Font area of the Reveal Formatting task pane.

Tip   To apply the most recently selected color to other text, select the word or phrase, and then click the Font Color button (not the down arrow). The color that appears on the Font Color button is applied to the selected text.

Highlight

14   Select the phrase *rich glow of gold* at the end of the second paragraph, click the down arrow to the right of the **Highlight** button on the Formatting toolbar, and then on the color palette, click the **Yellow** box in the first column of the first row.

The highlighted phrase now stands out from the rest of the text.

Tip   You don't have to select the text before choosing a highlighting color. If you select a highlighting color from the color palette without first selecting text, the mouse pointer becomes a highlighter, and you can drag across text to highlight it. Click the Highlight button to turn off the highlighter.

15   Select the text *Pollyanna, Tiger Babies, Ariadne, Scheharazade* in the third paragraph.

Troubleshooting   If the Reveal Formatting task pane overlays some of the text in the document, you can either scroll the horizontal scroll bar or make the task pane narrower. Point to the left border of the task pane, and when the pointer changes to a double arrow, drag the border toward the right so that more of the document's text is visible.

16   On the **Format** menu, click **Font** to open the **Font** dialog box, select the **Small caps** check box, and click **OK**.

The lowercase letters in the names of the lilies now appear in small capital letters, making those names easy to find in the text.

17   In the same paragraph, select *Ace of Hearts*, hold down the ⌘ key, and double-click *Reveries* in the last line of the paragraph to add that word to the selection.

18   Press the F4 key.

These two lily names now appear in small caps. When you press F4, your last editing or formatting action is applied to the selected text.

19   In the **Reveal Formatting** task pane, point to the **Selected text** box, click the down arrow, and then click **Select All Text With Similar Formatting**.

All the flower names that have been formatted in small caps are selected.

Bold

20   On the Formatting toolbar, click the **Bold** button.

The flower names are now both small caps and bold.

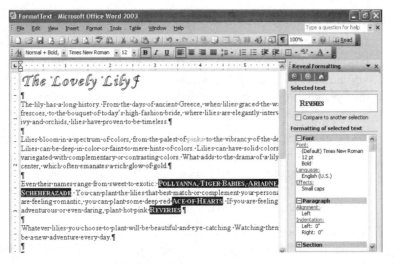

Close

21 In the **Reveal Formatting** task pane, click the **Close** button.

The Reveal Formatting task pane closes.

Save

22 On the Standard toolbar, click the **Save** button.

Word saves your changes to the document.

CLOSE the *FormatText* document.

Animating Text

If someone will be reading your document on a computer, you can apply effects that will make your text vibrant and visually alive. For example, you can add flashing lights or a marquee that will draw your reader's attention to specific words and phrases. To create these special effects, you apply an animation effect to selected text.

To apply an animation effect:

1 Select the text that you want to animate.

2 On the **Format** menu, click **Font**.

The Font dialog box appears.

3 Click the **Text Effects** tab.

4 In the **Animations** box, select the animation effect you want to apply to the selected text.

5 Click **OK**.

Changing the Look of Paragraphs

You can enhance the appearance of a paragraph by changing the way text is aligned, modifying the spacing between paragraphs, and adding borders and shading around text. In Word, a *paragraph* is any amount of text that ends when you press the [Enter] key. A paragraph can include a single sentence consisting of one or more words, or several sentences.

You control the width of paragraphs by setting the left and right margins, and you control the length of pages by setting the top and bottom margins. The margin size controls the amount of white space that surrounds your text. You can use the options in the Page Setup dialog box to control the margins of the entire document and of specific sections of the document.

After you've set up a document's margins, you can control the position of the text within the margins. In Word, you can align lines of text in different locations along the horizontal ruler using tab stops. You can also indent paragraphs, controlling where the first line of text begins, where the second and subsequent lines begin, and where paragraph text wraps at the right margin.

Finding and Replacing Formatting

In addition to searching for words and phrases, you can use the Find and Replace dialog box to search for a specific format and replace it with a different format.

To search for a specific format and replace it with a different format:

1   On the **Edit** menu, click **Replace**.

     The Find and Replace dialog box appears, displaying the Replace tab.

2   Click the **More** button to expand the dialog box, click the **Format** button, and then click **Font** or **Paragraph**.

     The Find Font or Find Paragraph dialog box appears. (You can also click Style to search for paragraph styles or character styles.)

3   In the dialog box, click the format you want to find, and then click **OK**.

4   Click the **Replace With** text box, click **Format**, click **Font** or **Paragraph**, click the format you want to use, and then click **OK**.

5   Click **Find Next** to search for the next occurrence of the format, and then click **Replace** to replace that one instance or **Replace All** to replace every instance.

While you are adjusting the appearance of paragraphs in a document, it is a good idea to work in Print Layout view, which shows two rulers: the horizontal ruler at the top and the vertical ruler along the left side of the document window.

You can use Word's horizontal ruler to set *tab stops*. Tab stops are locations across the page that you can use to align text. By default, left-aligned tab stops are set every half-inch, as indicated by gray marks below the ruler. To set a tab stop using the ruler, you click the Tab button located at the left end of the ruler until the type of tab stop you want appears. This table shows the Tab button options.

Tab	Symbol	Action
Left Tab	└	Aligns the left end of the text with the stop.
Center tab	┴	Aligns the center of the text with the stop.
Right Tab	┘	Aligns the right end of the text with the stop.
Decimal Tab	┸	Aligns the decimal point in the text with the stop.
Bar Tab	I	Draws a vertical bar the length of the paragraph containing the insertion point.

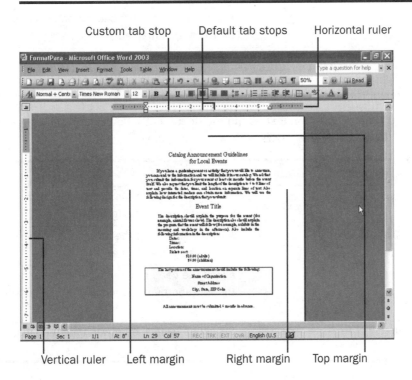

Custom tab stop   Default tab stops   Horizontal ruler

Vertical ruler   Left margin   Right margin   Top margin

After selecting the type of tab stop, you click the ruler where you want to set the tab stop. Word then removes any default tab stops to the left of the one you set. To remove a tab stop, you drag it down and away from the ruler.

To move the text to the right of the insertion point to the next tab stop, you press the [Tab] key. The text is then aligned on the tab stop according to its type. For example, if you set a center tab stop, pressing [Tab] moves the text so that its center is aligned with the tab stop.

Tip   When you want to fine-tune the position of tab stops, you can click Tabs on the Format menu to display the Tabs dialog box. You might also open this dialog box if you want to use *tab leaders*—visible marks such as dots or dashes connecting the text before the tab with the text after it. For example, tab leaders are useful in a table of contents to carry the eye from the text to the page number.

In addition to tab stops, the horizontal ruler also displays *indent markers* that use to control how text wraps on the left or right side of a document. You use these markers to indent text from the left or right margins as shown in this table.

Indent	Symbol	Action
First Line Indent	▽	Begins a paragraph's first line of text at this marker.
Hanging Indent	△	Begins a paragraph's second and subsequent lines of text at this marker.
Left Indent	▢	Indents the text to this marker.
Right Indent	△	Wraps the text when it reaches this marker.

You can also position text within the document's margin using the alignment buttons on the Formatting toolbar, as shown in this table.

Alignment	Button	Action
Align Left	≣	Aligns each line of the paragraph at the left margin, with a ragged right edge.
Align Right	≣	Aligns each line of the paragraph at the right margin, with a ragged left edge.
Center	≣	Aligns the center of each line in the paragraph between the left and right margins, with ragged left and right edges.
Justify	▤	Stretches each line between the margins, creating even left and right edges.

To add space between paragraphs, you can press the ⌨Enter key to insert a blank line, or for more precise control, you can adjust the spacing before and after paragraphs. For example, instead of indicating a new paragraph by indenting the first line, you could add 12 points of blank space before a new paragraph. You use the Paragraph dialog box to adjust the paragraph spacing.

You also use the Paragraph dialog box to adjust line spacing. You can select Single, 1.5 lines, or Double spacing; or you can enter a specific spacing in points.

To set off a paragraph from the rest of the document, you can add borders and shading. For example, if The Garden Company is sending a letter to customers advertising a spring sale, they might put a border around the paragraph they want customers to pay the most attention to. Alternatively, they might shade the background of the paragraph to create a subtler effect.

Collectively, the settings used to vary the look of paragraphs are called *paragraph formatting*. After you indent, align, space, border, or shade one paragraph, you can press ⌨Enter to apply the same formatting to the next paragraph that you type. To apply the formatting to an existing paragraph, you can use the Format Painter button to quickly copy the formatting of one paragraph to another.

In this exercise, you'll set margins, change text alignment, insert and modify tab stops, modify line spacing, and add borders and shading around text to change the appearance of the paragraphs in the document.

USE the *FormatPara* document in the practice file folder for this topic. This practice file is located in the *My Documents\Microsoft Press\Office 2003 SBS\ChangingText\ChangingPara* folder and can also be accessed by clicking *Start/All Programs/Microsoft Press/Microsoft Office System 2003 Step by Step*. OPEN the *FormatPara* document.

Print Layout View

1 In the lower-left corner of the document window, click the **Print Layout View** button. Then zoom the page to **75%**.

You can now see how the text column is aligned between the left and right margins. In addition to the horizontal ruler at the top of the document window, a vertical ruler appears on the left side of the document window.

2 On the **File** menu, click **Page Setup**.

The Page Setup dialog box appears, displaying the Margins tab with the value in the Top text box selected in the Margins area,

3 Type 1.5". Then select the value in the **Bottom** text box, and type 1.5".

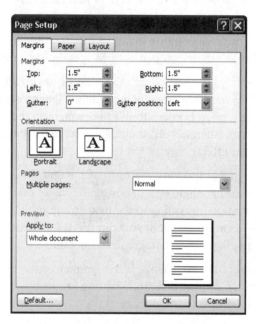

4 Click **OK** to close the **Page Setup** dialog box.

The amount of blank space at the top and bottom of each page increases from 1 inch to 1.5 inches.

Tip The standard size of a page is 8.5 inches by 11 inches. With margins of 1.5 inches on each side, you are left with a work area that is 5.5 inches wide.

Center

5 Click immediately to the left of the word *for* in the title, hold down the [Shift] key, press the [Enter] key, and then on the Formatting toolbar, click the **Center** button.

You have broken the title so that it wraps to a second line without starting a new paragraph. Word indicates this *text wrapping break* or *line break* with a bent arrow and centers the two lines of the title, making it appear more balanced.

Tip When you apply paragraph formatting to a line of text that ends with a line break, the formatting is applied to the entire paragraph, not just that line.

Line break

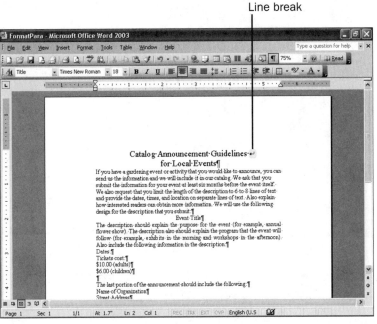

Justify

6 Click anywhere in the first paragraph, and then on the Formatting toolbar, click the **Justify** button.

The edges of the paragraph are now flush against both the left and right margins.

First Line Indent

7 On the horizontal ruler, drag the **First Line Indent** marker to the 0.5-inch mark.

The first line of text is indented a half inch from the left margin.

Left Indent

8 Click anywhere in the paragraph that starts *The description should explain*, and on the horizontal ruler, drag the **Left Indent** marker to the 0.5-inch mark.

The First Line Indent and Hanging Indent markers move with the Left Indent marker, and the entire paragraph is now indented a half inch from the left margin.

Right Indent

9 Drag the **Right Indent** marker to the 5-inch mark.

The paragraph is now indented from the right margin as well.

Tip Left and right margin indents are often used to draw attention to special paragraphs, such as quotations.

Left indent   First-line indent   Right indent

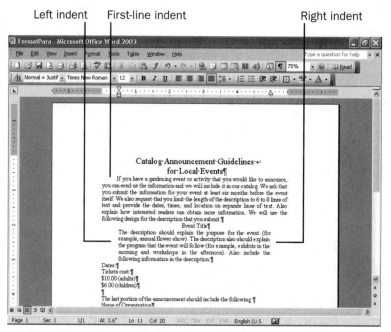

10 Scroll down the page, select the *Dates:* and *Tickets cost:* paragraphs, make sure the **Left Tab** button is active, and click the ruler at the 1-inch mark to set a left tab stop.

11 Click to the left of the word *Dates:* to position the insertion point there, and then press the [Tab] key.

Word left-aligns the text at the new tab stop.

12 Press [End] to move the insertion point to the end of the line, and press [Enter] to create a new paragraph. Press [Tab], and then type **Times:**.

13 Press [Enter] to create a new paragraph, press [Tab], type **Location:**, press the [→] key to move the insertion point to the beginning of the next paragraph, and then press [Tab].

14 Drag through any part of the two paragraphs that start with *$10.00* and *$6.00*, click the **Tab** button three times to activate the **Decimal Tab** button, and then click the ruler at the 2.5-inch mark to set a decimal tab.

Tip   When applying paragraph formatting, you don't have to select the entire paragraph.

15   Click to the left of *$10.00*, press `Tab`, click to the left of *$6.00*, and press `Tab` again.

The dollar amounts are now aligned on their decimal points.

16   Drag again through any part of the two paragraphs with dollar amounts, and on the horizontal ruler, drag the decimal tab stop from the 2.5-inch mark to the 2.0-inch mark. Then press the `Home` key to see the results.

Left-aligned tabs

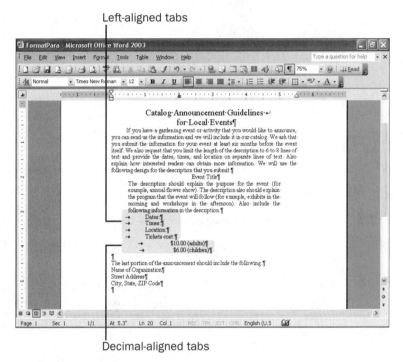

Decimal-aligned tabs

17   Press `Ctrl`+`Home` to move the insertion point to the top of the document, and on the **Format** menu, click **Paragraph**.

The Paragraph dialog box appears.

Tip   When you want to make several adjustments to the alignment, indentation, and spacing of selected paragraphs, it is sometimes quicker to use the Paragraph dialog box than to click buttons and drag markers.

18   In the **Spacing** area, click the up arrow to the right of the **After** text box until the setting is **12 pt**.

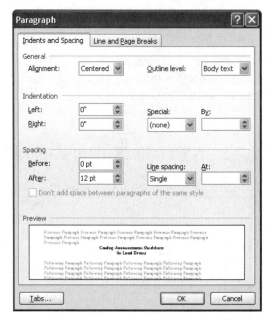

19 Click **OK** to close the **Paragraph** dialog box.

The paragraph below the title moves down, setting the title off from the rest of the document.

Format Painter

20 On the Standard toolbar, click the **Format Painter** button, point to the *Event Title* paragraph, and click to copy the formatting from the title paragraph.

Word changes the font size of the paragraph to 18 points and adds space between the title paragraph and the following one.

21 On the **Format** menu, click **Paragraph**, and in the **Spacing** area of the **Paragraph** dialog box, click the up arrow to the right of the **Before** text box until the setting is **12 pt**. Then click **OK**.

Word adds space between the *Event Title* paragraph and the one before it.

Center

22 Scroll to the bottom of the document, drag through any part of the last four paragraphs, and then on the Formatting toolbar, click the **Center** button.

Word centers the paragraphs.

23   On the **Format** menu, click **Paragraph,** click the down arrow to the right of the **Line Spacing** text box, click **1.5 lines,** and click **OK.**

24   On the **Format** menu, click **Borders and Shading.**

The Borders and Shading dialog box appears, displaying the Borders tab.

25   In the **Setting** area, click the **Shadow** icon to select that border style.

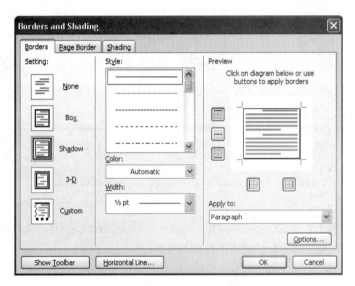

Tip   You can change the settings in the Style, Color, and Width boxes to create the kind of border you want. If you want only one, two, or three sides of the paragraph to have a border, click the buttons surrounding the image in the Preview area.

26   Click the **Shading** tab, click the **Light Yellow** box in the third column of the last row of the color palette, and then click **OK.**

A border with a shadow surrounds the text, and the background color is light yellow.

27   Move the pointer to the center of the page about two lines below the yellow shaded box.

The pointer's shape changes to indicate that double-clicking will center whatever text you type next. You can use this *Click and Type* feature to create appropriately aligned text wihtout pressing the ⌈Enter⌋ key.

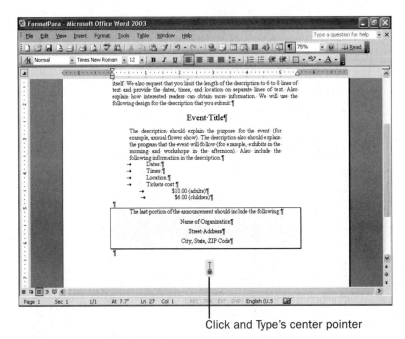

Click and Type's center pointer

28 Double-click to position the insertion point, and then type **All announcements must be submitted 6 months in advance.**

The newly inserted text appears centered in the document.

¶
Show/Hide ¶

29 On the Formatting toolbar, click the **Show/Hide ¶** button to hide the formatting marks.

Word hides the non-printing characters.

Save

30 On the Standard toolbar, click the **Save** button.

Word saves your changes to the document.

CLOSE the *FormatPara* document.

Creating and Modifying Lists

To organize lists in a document, such as lists of events, names, numbers, or procedures, you can format the information in a bulleted or numbered list. A *bullet* is a small graphic, such as a dot, that introduces an item in a list. Where the order of items is not important, use bullets. Use numbers instead of bullets when you want to emphasize sequence, as in a series of steps. If you move, insert, or delete items in a numbered list, Word renumbers the list for you. If the items in a list are out of order, alphabetically or numerically, you can sort the items in ascending or descending order using the Sort command on the Table menu.

For emphasis, you can change any bullet or number style to one of Word's predefined formats. For example, you can switch round bullets to check boxes, or change the letters in Roman numerals from uppercase to lowercase. You can also customize the list style or insert a picture as a bullet. Use the Bullets and Numbering dialog box to modify, format, and customize your list.

Word makes it easy to start a bulleted or numbered list, like this:

■ To create a bulleted list, type * (an asterisk) at the beginning of a paragraph, and then press [Space] or [Tab].

■ To create a numbered list, type 1. (the numeral 1 followed by a period) at the beginning of a paragraph, and then press [Space] or [Tab].

Then type the first item in the list and press [Enter]. The next bullet or number in the list appears, and Word changes the formatting to a list. You can type the next item in the list or press [Enter] or [Backspace] to end the list.

You can change a bulleted or numbered list into an outline consisting of main headings and subheadings. To create an outline from scratch, type I. at the beginning of a line, press [Tab], type a main heading, and then press [Enter]. You can type another main heading or press [Tab] to add a subheading under the main heading.

See Also   For another way to create outlines, see "Using an Outline to Rearrange Paragraphs" in Chapter 2.

In this exercise, you will create a bulleted and numbered list, modify them by adjusting their indents, and then apply outline numbering.

USE the *CreateList* document in the practice file folder for this topic. This practice file is located in the *My Documents\Microsoft Press\Office 2003 SBS\ChangingText\CreatingList* folder and can also be accessed by clicking *Start/All Programs/Microsoft Press/Microsoft Office System 2003 Step by Step*. OPEN the *CreateList* document.

1   Scroll down the document, and drag through any part of the four paragraphs aligned with *Dates:*.

Numbering

2   On the Formatting toolbar, click the **Numbering** button.

The selected paragraphs are reformatted as a numbered list.

3   On the **Format** menu, click **Bullets and Numbering**.

The Bullets and Numbering dialog box appears, displaying the Numbered tab.

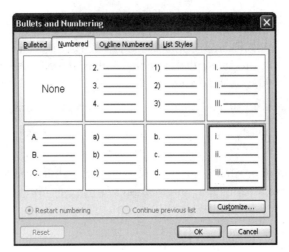

4 Click the **A. B. C.** box in the first column of the second row, and click **OK**.

The numbers change to capital letters.

5 On the **Table** menu, click **Sort**.

The Sort Text dialog box appears.

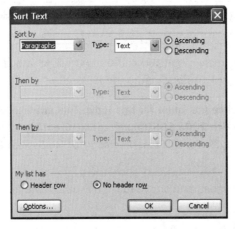

6 With the **Ascending** option selected, click **OK**.

The list changes to reflect the new sort order. Because the prices of tickets are not included in the sorting, the list now makes no sense.

7 On the Standard toolbar, click the **Undo** button.

The list returns to its unsorted state.

Undo

8   Drag through any part of the two paragraphs that start with *$10.00* and *$6.00*.

Bullets

9   On the Formatting toolbar, click the **Bullets** button.

The selected paragraphs appear as a bulleted list.

ʹDecrease
Indent

10   On the Formatting toolbar, click the **Decrease Indent** button.

The bulleted list merges with the numbered list because the two lists are now indented at the same level.

Increase
Indent

11   On the Formatting toolbar, click the **Increase Indent** button.

The selected items move back to the right and become a bulleted list again.

12   On the **Format** menu, click **Bullets and Numbering**.

The Bullets and Numbering dialog box appears, displaying the Bulleted tab.

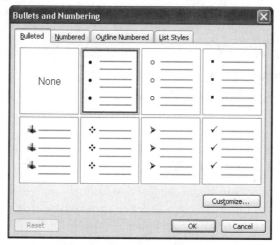

13   Click the color bullet box in the first column of the second row, and then click **OK**.

The bullet character changes from circles to colors.

14   Drag through any part of all the paragraphs in the numbered and bulleted lists.

15   On the **Format** menu, click **Bullets and Numbering**, and then click the **Outline Numbered** tab.

16   Click the box in the third column of the second row, click **OK**, and then press Home.

The lettered list changes from letters to numbers and the bulleted list changes to letters.

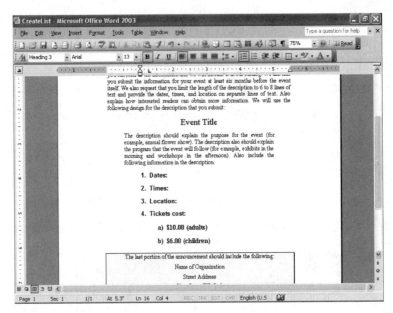

Save

17   On the Standard toolbar, click the **Save** button.

           Word saves your changes to the document.

CLOSE the *CreateList* document.

Formatting Text as You Type

Word's list formatting capabilities are just one example of its ability to intuit how you are going to want to format an element based on what you type. For example, instead of manually creating a line by typing underscores (_) across the length of a page, you can type three consecutive hyphens (-) and press [Enter] to have Word's AutoFormat feature draw a single line across the page. Or you can type three consecutive equal signs (=) and press [Enter] to have Word draw a double line.

In this exercise, you will add a double border using an AutoFormat shortcut. You'll also inspect the AutoFormat As You Type tab of the AutoCorrect dialog box to see what items Word can automatically format for you.

USE the *FormatAuto* document in the practice file folder for this topic. This practice file is located in the *My Documents\Microsoft Press\Office 2003 SBS\ChangingText\AutoFormatting* folder and can also be accessed by clicking *Start/All Programs/Microsoft Press/Microsoft Office System 2003 Step by Step*. OPEN the *FormatAuto* document.

1   Press [Ctrl]+[End] to move the insertion point to the end of the document, and then press [Enter].

2　Press ⌈:⌉ three times, and press ⌈Enter⌉.

AutoCorrect
Options

Word draws a double line across the page and displays the AutoCorrect Options button.

Tip　Clicking the AutoCorrect Options button displays a menu of options related to the line you just drew. You can remove the line, disable (turn off) the AutoCorrect border lines options, or open the AutoCorrect dialog box, where you can make further modifications to this feature.

3　Type: Color:, and press ⌈Enter⌉.

4　Type 1., and press ⌈Tab⌉. Then type Palest pink to deepest red, and press ⌈Enter⌉.

Word assumes you want to continue the list and indents both list items.

5　Type Solid or variegated, and press ⌈Enter⌉ twice.

Word continues the list the first time you press ⌈Enter⌉, but ends the list and creates a normal paragraph when you press ⌈Enter⌉ the second time.

6　Type Names:, and press ⌈Enter⌉.

7　On the **Tools** menu, click **AutoCorrect Options**, and then click the **AutoFormat As You Type** tab.

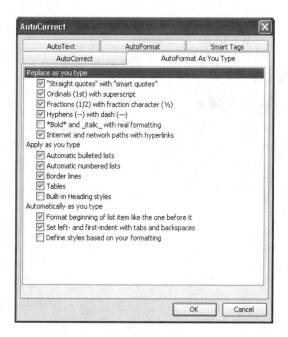

Tip   You can automatically format a document as you type using the options in the AutoFormat As You Type tab in the AutoCorrect dialog box, or you can format a document after you type using the AutoFormat command on the Format menu. In the AutoFormat dialog box, select the "AutoFormat now" option or the "AutoFormat and review each change" option, and then click OK.

8   In the **Apply as you type** area, clear the **Automatic numbered lists** check box, and click **OK**.

9   Type 1., press the [Tab] key, type **Pollyanna**, and press [Enter].

Instead of setting up the numbered list, Word starts a normal paragraph.

10   On the **Tools** menu, click **AutoCorrect Options**, and click the **AutoFormat As You Type** tab.

11   In the **Apply as you type** area, select the **Automatic numbered lists** check box, and click **OK**.

12   Press the [Backspace] key to move back to the previous paragraph, and then press [Enter] again.

Word assumes you want to continue the list and indents both list items.

13   Click the **AutoCorrect Options** button to view the commands available, and then click away from the menu to close it without making a selection.

CLOSE the *FormatAuto* document without saving your changes.

Changing the Look of Characters and Paragraphs with Styles

As you change the appearance of the text in your documents, you might find that you have created a look, or style, of your own. In Word, a *style* is a collection of character and paragraph formatting that can be saved. Then instead of applying each format individually, you can apply all of them at once by using a style.

Styles come in two varieties:

■   You use *character styles* to format selected characters. You can apply character styles to a single letter, a word, a paragraph, or the entire document. This type of style consists of collections of attributes. For example, a character style might specify that the selected text should be 18-point, bold, underlined, and red.

■   You use *paragraph styles* to format entire paragraphs. This type of style consists of indents, alignment, paragraph and line spacing, bullets or numbering, and tabs as well as character attributes to be applied to the entire paragraph. For example, a paragraph style might specify that the paragraph containing the insertion point should be centered, with a border and a hanging indent, as well as 18-point, bold, underlined, and red.

Styles are stored in *templates*, and Word's default template is called the *Normal template*. Unless you specify otherwise, the documents you create are all based on the Normal template, which contains a set of predefined styles. The most basic of these predefined styles, *Normal style*, is used for all regular paragraphs, formatting them as 12-point, regular Times New Roman text that is left-aligned and single-spaced, with no extra space above and below it.

All the text you type in documents based on the Normal template uses the Normal style until you apply another style. For example, you might apply the predefined Heading 1 style to text you want to serve as a document's title. To apply another style, you can click the down arrow to the right of the Style box on the Formatting toolbar and make a selection from the drop-down list, or you can use the Styles and Formatting task pane.

Tip   If a wavy blue line appears under a word or phrase as you type, Word detects inconsistent formatting. To remove the wavy blue line without making any change, right-click the word or phrase, and then click Ignore Once to bypass that instance of the inconsistency, or Ignore All to bypass that and all upcoming instances of the inconsistency. To turn off the formatting options, click Options on the Tools menu, click the Edit tab, clear the "Keep track of formatting" check box, clear the "Mark formatting inconsistencies" check box, and click OK.

When Word's predefined styles don't meet your needs, you can create new ones in several ways:

- You can modify an existing style. You can redefine the style for just this document or for all documents based on this template. The formatting of any text to which you have already applied the style will be updated to reflect the new definition.

- You can create a style by example. You can format text the way you want it and then create a style that reflects the look of the text.

- You can define a style from scratch. You can click New Style in the Style and Formatting task pane and then use the New Style dialog box to specify the character formatting and paragraph formatting for the style.

Tip   If you want to define a style for a bulleted or numbered list, click Bullets and Numbering on the Format menu. Then click the List Styles tab, click Add, define the style, and click OK.

In this exercise, you will apply, modify, and delete a style using the Styles and Formatting task pane.

USE the *FormatStyle* document in the practice file folder for this topic. This practice file is located in the *My Documents\Microsoft Press\Office 2003 SBS\ChangingText\ChangingStyle* folder and can also be accessed by clicking *Start/All Programs/Microsoft Press/Microsoft Office System 2003 Step by Step.* OPEN the *FormatStyle* document.

1　If necessary, change the **Zoom** setting to **100%**, and then select the *Why Compost?* paragraph.

2　On the **Format** menu, click **Styles and Formatting**.

The Styles and Formatting task pane appears.

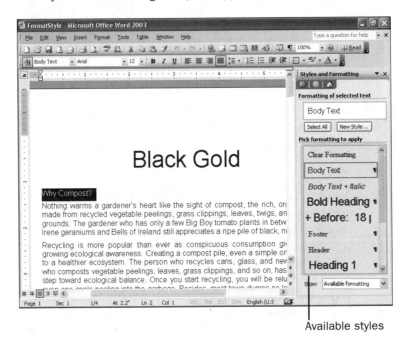

Available styles

3　In the **Styles and Formatting** task pane, point to the **Formatting of selected text** box.

A ScreenTip appears, listing the formatting of the style applied to the selected text. In this case, the style is Body Text.

4　Scroll down the **Pick formatting to apply** list, and click the **Heading 2** style.

The selected text changes to reflect the formatting assigned to the Heading 2 style.

5　Scroll down the document, and select the *What Is a Compost Pile?* paragraph. Then scroll until you can see *How Do You Make a Compost Pile?*, hold down the Ctrl key, and select that paragraph. Then add the *Hot or Cold?* and *Compost and Soil* paragraphs to the selection.

6 In the **Styles and Formatting** task pane, click the **Heading 2** style to apply the style to the selected paragraphs.

7 Scroll to the top of the document, click anywhere in the *Why Compost?* paragraph, and in the **Styles and Formatting** task pane, click **Select All**.

Word selects all the text formatted with the style of the selected text, which is Heading 2.

8 In the **Styles and Formatting** task pane, click **New Style**.

The New Style dialog box appears.

9 In the **Name** text box, type Heading 2 Plus to create a new style of that name.

10 In the **Formatting** area, click the down arrow to the right of the **Font Size** box, and click **16**. Then click the down arrow to the right of the **Font Color** box, and click the **Blue** box in the sixth column of the second row.

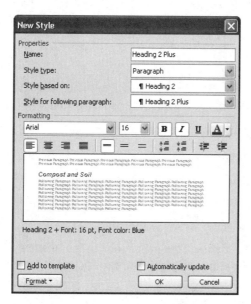

11 Click **OK** to close the **New Style** dialog box.

The Heading 2 Plus style appears in the Styles and Formatting task pane.

12 In the **Styles and Formatting** task pane, click the **Heading 2 Plus** style.

Word applies the new style to all the selected paragraphs. A ScreenTip tells you the main characteristics of this style.

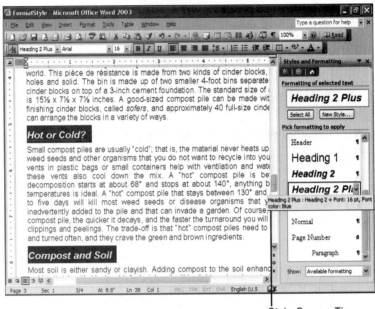

Style Screen Tip

13 In the **Styles and Formatting** task pane, point to the **Heading 2 Plus** style, click the down arrow that appears to its right, and click **Modify**.

The Modify Style dialog box appears.

I

Italic

14 In the **Formatting** area, click the **Italic** button to deselect that attribute, and click **OK**.

The Heading 2 Plus style is updated, along with all text to which the style is applied.

15 In the **Styles and Formatting** task pane, click the **Heading 2 style**.

The selected text changes to reflect that style.

16 In the **Styles and Formatting** task pane, point to the **Heading 2 Plus** style, click the down arrow that appears to its right, and click **Delete**.

A message asks whether you want to delete the style.

17 Click **Yes** to delete the **Heading 2 Plus** style.

18 At the bottom of the **Styles and Formatting** task pane, click the down arrow to the right of the **Show** text box, and then click **Formatting in use**.

The task pane now lists only the styles actually used in the document.

19 Close the **Styles and Formatting** task pane.

20 On the Standard toolbar, click the **Save** button.

Save

Word saves your changes to the document.

CLOSE the *FormatStyle* document, and if you are not continuing to the next chapter, quit Word.

Key Points

- You can change the look of characters by changing the font, size, style, and effect.

- You can change the look of paragraphs by varying their indentation, spacing, and alignment and by setting tab stops.

- You can create and modify bulleted and numbered lists by using the buttons on the Formatting toolbar and the Bullets and Numbering dialog box.

- You can use the AutoFormat feature to automatically format text as you type.

- You can apply character styles and paragraph styles to selected text to change several formats at once.

- You can use the Reveal Formatting task pane to display, change, or clear the formatting for the selected text. You can also use this task pane to select text with the same formatting throughout a document.

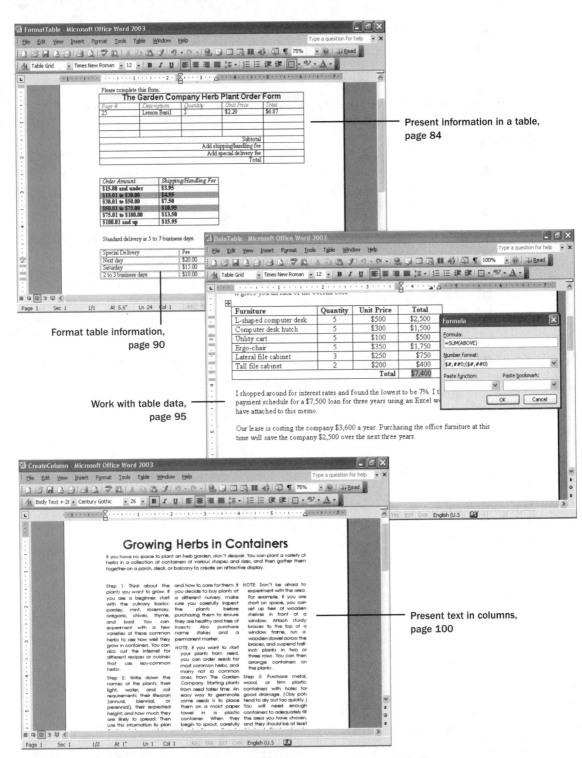

Present information in a table, page 84

Format table information, page 90

Work with table data, page 95

Present text in columns, page 100

Chapter 4 at a Glance

4 Presenting Information in Tables and Columns

In this chapter you will learn to:

✔ Present information in a table.

✔ Format table information.

✔ Work with table data.

✔ Present text in columns.

You can use a table to make information in a document concise, consistent, and easy to read. A table organizes information neatly into rows and columns. The intersection of a row and column is called a *cell*. With Microsoft Office Word 2003, you can create a uniform table with standard-sized cells, draw a custom table with various-sized cells, or you can create a table from existing text. After you create your table, you can enter text, numbers, and graphics into cells. At any time, you can change the table's size; insert and delete columns, rows, and cells; and format individual entries or the entire table. To help readers interpret the information in your table, you can sort the information in a logical order. To perform standard mathematical calculations on numbers in a table—for example, to total the values in a column or row—you can use the Formula command on the Table menu. To perform more complex calculations or statistical analysis, you can create a Microsoft Office Excel worksheet and insert it into your document.

To group and organize information in a document, you can use columns of text. Dividing text into columns is useful when you are creating a newsletter or brochure. In Word, you can define the number of columns you want on a page and then allow text to flow from the bottom of one column to the top of the next, as in newspapers. You can also manually end one column and move subsequent text to the next column.

In this chapter, you will create and format tables, and work with table data. You will also format text that currently appears in one column into four columns.

See Also Do you need only a quick refresher on the topics in this chapter? See the Quick Reference entries on page xxxiii.

Important Before you can use the practice files in this chapter, you need to install them from the book's companion CD to their default location. See "Using the Book's CD-ROM" on page xxi for more information.

Presenting Information in a Table

To add a simple table to a document, you can use the Insert Table button on the Standard toolbar and then select the number of rows and columns you want from the grid that appears. If you want to set the size of the table along with other options, such as table formatting, you use the Insert command on the Table menu to open the Insert Table dialog box. You can also convert existing plain text into a table.

After you create a table, you can type text or numbers into cells and press the ⟦Tab⟧ key to move the insertion point from cell to cell. If the insertion point is positioned in the rightmost cell in the last row of the table, pressing ⟦Tab⟧ adds another row to the bottom of the table. In addition to the ⟦Tab⟧ key, you can use the arrow keys or you can simply click a cell to position the insertion point there.

You can modify a table's structure at any time. To change the structure, you often need to select the entire table or specific rows or columns, using the following methods:

- To select the entire table, click the Select Table button that appears above and to the left of the first cell in the table whenever you point to the table. Or on the Table menu, point to Select, and then click Table.

- To select a column or row, point to the top border of the column or the left border of the row, and when the pointer changes to an arrow, click once.

- To select a cell, triple-click the cell.

- To select multiple cells, click the first cell, hold down the ⟦Shift⟧ key, and press the arrow keys to select adjacent cells in a column or row.

   Tip The document must be in Print Layout view for you to use the Select Table button at the upper-left of the table or the table resize handle at the lower right of the table.

After you've learned the fundamentals of working with tables, you can efficiently organize large amounts and various types of information. The basic methods for manipulating tables are as follows:

- Insert a row or column. Click anywhere in a row or column adjacent to where you want to make the insertion. Then on the Table menu, point to Insert, and click Rows Above, Rows Below, Columns to the Right, or Columns to the Left. If you select more than one row or column and use an Insert command, Word inserts that number of rows or columns in the table.

■ Delete a row or column. Click anywhere in the row or column, and on the Table menu, point to Delete, and then click Rows or Columns.

■ Size an entire table. To size a table quickly, drag the table resize handle in the lower-right corner of the table in Print Layout view.

■ Size a single column or row. Change the width of a column or row by pointing to its right or bottom border and dragging it.

■ Merge cells. Create cells that span columns by selecting the cells you want to merge and clicking Merge Cells on the Table menu. For example, to center a title in the first row of a table, you can create one merged cell that spans the table's width.

■ Split cells. If you need to divide a merged cell into its component cells, split it by clicking Split Cells on the Table menu.

■ Move a table. Select the table, and drag it to a new location. Or use the Cut and Paste commands to move the table.

■ Sort information. Use the Sort command on the Table menu to sort the rows in ascending or descending order by the data in any column. For example, you can sort a table that has the column headings Name, Address, ZIP Code, and Phone Number on any one of those columns to arrange the information in alphabetical or numerical order.

In this exercise, you will work with three tables. First you'll create a table, enter text, add rows, and merge cells. Then you'll create a second table by converting existing tabbed text. Finally, you'll sort information in a third table.

BE SURE TO start Word before beginning this exercise.
USE the *CreateTable* document in the practice file folder for this topic. This practice file is located in the *My Documents\Microsoft Press\Office 2003 SBS\PresentingInfo\PresentingTable* folder and can also be accessed by clicking *Start/All Programs/Microsoft Press/Microsoft Office System 2003 Step by Step.*
OPEN the *CreateTable* document.

1 Press the ⬇ key to position the insertion point in the blank line below the *Please complete this form* paragraph.

2 On the **Table** menu, point to **Insert**, and then click **Table**.

The Insert Table dialog box appears.

3   Be sure that the **Number of columns** box displays **5**, click the **Number of rows** up arrow to display **5**, and then click **OK**.

A blank table with five columns and five rows appears. The insertion point is located in the first cell.

4   In the selection area, point to the first row, and click to select the row.

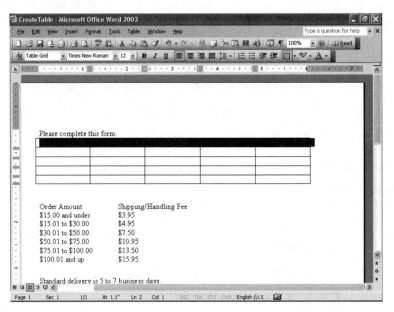

5   On the **Table** menu, click **Merge Cells** to combine the cells in the first row into one cell.

6   Type **The Garden Company Herb Plant Order Form**.

The text appears in the first row.

7   Click the first cell in the second row, type **Page #**, and press ⌨Tab.

8   Type **Description**, and press ⌨Tab. Then, pressing ⌨Tab after each entry to move the insertion point to the next column, type **Quantity** (⌨Tab), **Unit Price** (⌨Tab), and **Total** (⌨Tab).

The insertion point is now in the first column of the third row.

9   Type **25**, press ⌨Tab, and then type **Lemon basil** (⌨Tab), **3** (⌨Tab), **$2.29**, (⌨Tab), and **$6.87**.

10 In the selection area, point to the fourth row, hold down the mouse button, and drag downward to select the last two rows.

11 On the **Table** menu, point to **Insert**, and then click **Rows Below**.

Word adds two new rows and selects them.

12 In the last row, click the first cell, hold down ⌨Shift, and then press ⌨→ four times to select the first four cells in the row.

13 On the **Table** menu, click **Merge Cells**.

Word combines the selected cells in the last row into one cell.

14 Type **Subtotal**, and press ⌨Tab twice.

Word adds a new row to the bottom of the table. Note that the new row has the same structure as the preceding row.

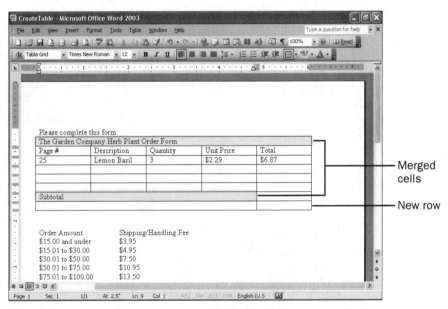

15 Type **Add shipping/handling fee**, press ⌨Tab twice to add a new row, and then type **Add special delivery fee**.

16 Press ⟨Tab⟩ twice to add a new row, and then type Total.

17 Below the table, select the paragraphs that begin with *Order Amount* and end with *$15.95*.

18 On the **Table** menu, point to **Convert**, and then click **Text to Table**.

The Convert Text to Table dialog box appears.

19 Make sure that the **Number of columns** box displays **2**, and then click **OK**.

The selected text appears in a table with two columns and seven rows.

20 Click the table to deselect the cells, and point to the right border of the table. When the pointer changes to two opposing arrows, double-click the right border to make the right column just wide enough to hold its longest line of text.

21 Scroll down, click anywhere in the special delivery table, and on the **Table** menu, click **Sort**.

The Sort dialog box appears.

22 Click the down arrow to the right of the **Sort by** box, and click **Fee**.

23 Select the **Descending** option. Then make sure the **Header row** option in the **My list has** area is selected, and click **OK**.

Word sorts the table in descending order based on the Fee column.

24 Point to the selected special delivery table.

Word displays a Select Table button and a table resize handle.

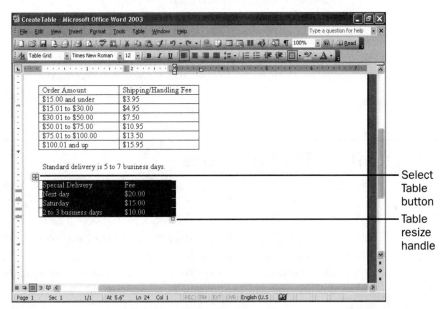

Select Table button

Table resize handle

25 With the special delivery table still selected, drag the table resize handle in the lower-right corner to the right, releasing the mouse button when the right edges of the special delivery and shipping and handling fees tables are aligned.

Tip To make finer adjustments, hold down the Alt key while you drag, but be careful not to click the mouse button. [Alt]+click opens the Research task pane.

26 On the Standard toolbar, click the **Save** button.

Save

Word saves your changes to the document.

CLOSE the *CreateTable* document.

Formatting Table Information

To enhance the appearance of a table, you can format its text by using the buttons on the Formatting toolbar, just as you would to format any text in a Word document. You can apply character formatting such as font styles and font effects, and you can apply paragraph formatting such as alignment and indenting.

You can also format the table's structure by adding borders and shading. Clicking the Borders and Shading command on the Format menu opens the Borders and Shading dialog box, where you can specify options to best delineate the relationships within your table.

To quickly apply predefined sets of formatting to a table, you can choose a *table autoformat*. Clicking the Table AutoFormat command on the Table menu displays the Table AutoFormat dialog box, which offers formats that include a variety of borders, colors, and attributes to give your tables a professional look.

Working with Table Properties

You can control many aspects of a table by clicking Table Properties on the Table menu and setting options on the tabs of the Table Properties dialog box. On the Table tab, you can specify the preferred width of the entire table, as well as the way it interacts with the surrounding text. On the Row tab, you can specify the height of each row, whether a row is allowed to break across pages, and whether a row of column headings should be repeated at the top of each page. On the Column tab, you can set the width of each column, and on the Cell tab, you can set the preferred width of cells and the vertical alignment of text within them.

To adjust table properties:

1   On the **Table** menu, click **Table Properties**.

The Table Properties dialog box appears.

2   Click the tab of the table element whose properties you want to adjust.

3   Make adjustments to the properties as necessary.

4   Click **OK** to close the **Table Properties** dialog box.

Creating Styles for Tables

If none of the table autoformats meets your needs, you can create formatting styles for table text in much the same way you create styles for regular paragraph text.

To create a style for text in a table:

1   On the **Format** menu, click **Styles and Formatting**.

     The Styles and Formatting task pane appears.

2   In the **Styles and Formatting** task pane, click **New Style**.

     The New Style dialog box appears.

3   Type a name for the new style, click the down arrow to the right of the **Style type** box, and click **Table**.

4   Click the down arrow to the right of the **Apply formatting to** box, and select which text the new style should be applied to.

5   Select the formatting options you want, and click **OK**.

6   Select the text you want to format with the new style, and in the **Pick formatting to apply** list, click the style.

Many of the table formatting tools are available on the Tables and Borders toolbar. You can turn on this toolbar either by clicking Toolbars on the View menu and then clicking Tables and Borders, or by clicking the Tables and Borders button on the Standard toolbar.

In this exercise, you will format the text in a table and add shading to a cell. You'll also apply an autoformat and add a border to a table.

USE the *FormatTable* document in the practice file folder for this topic. This practice file is located in the *My Documents\Microsoft Press\Office 2003 SBS\PresentingInfo\FormattingTable* folder and can also be accessed by clicking *Start/All Programs/Microsoft Press/Microsoft Office System 2003 Step by Step*. OPEN the *FormatTable* document.

1   In the selection area, point to the first row in the order-form table, and click to select the first row.

2   On the Formatting toolbar, click the down arrow to the right of the **Font** box, and click **Arial**. Then click the down arrow to the right of the **Font Size** box, and click **16**.

Bold

Center

3 On the Formatting toolbar, click the **Bold** button.

The bold font style is applied to the text.

4 On the Formatting toolbar, click the **Center** button.

The text appears in the center of the cell.

5 On the **Format** menu, click **Borders and Shading**.

The Borders and Shading dialog box appears.

6 Click the **Shading** tab.

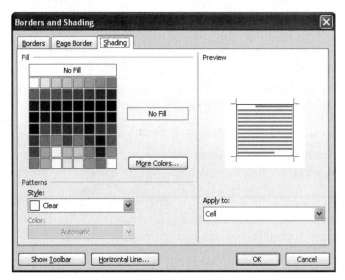

7 In the third column of the seventh row in the color palette, click the **Yellow** box, and then click **OK**.

Word shades the background of the first row in light yellow.

8 Select the second row of the table.

Italic

9 On the Formatting toolbar, click the **Bold** button, and then click the **Italic** button.

The headings in the second row are now italic.

Font Color

10 On the Formatting toolbar, click the down arrow to the right of the **Font Color** button, and then in the first column of the third row of the color palette, click the **Red** box.

11 Select the last four rows in the order-form table.

Align Right

12 On the Formatting toolbar, click the **Align Right** button.

Word aligns the text in the last four rows at the right margin.

Tip To change the direction of text in a cell—for example, to rotate column headings so that they read vertically instead of from left to right—select the cell(s), click Text Direction on the Format menu, and then make adjustments in the Text Direction – Table Cell dialog box.

13 Zoom the document to **75%**.

14 Click anywhere in the shipping and handling fees table, and on the **Table** menu, click **Table AutoFormat**.

The Table AutoFormat dialog box appears.

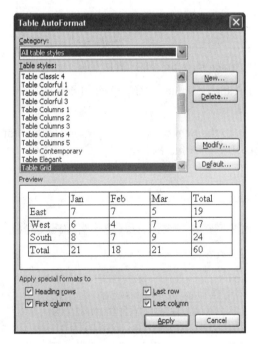

15 Scroll through the **Table styles** list, click **Table List 8**, and then click **Apply**.

Word formats the table in yellow and red.

16 Click anywhere in the special delivery table, and on the **Format** menu, click **Borders and Shading**. Then click the **Borders** tab.

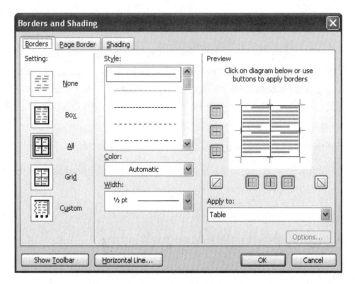

17 In the **Setting** area, make sure the **All** icon is selected.

18 In the **Style** list, click the down scroll arrow (not the scroll bar) twice, and then click the double-line style.

19 Click the down arrow to the right of the **Color** box, and in the first column of the third row of the color palette, click the **Red** box.

20 Click **OK**.

Word adds a red double border to the entire table.

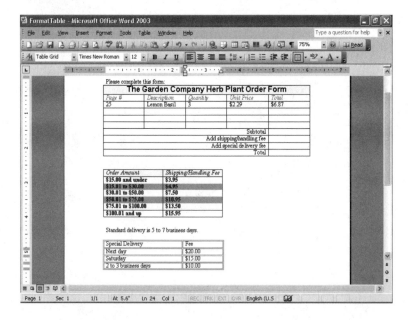

Save

21   On the Standard toolbar, click the **Save** button.

Word saves your changes to the document.

CLOSE the *FormatTable* document.

Working with Table Data

You can perform certain calculations on numbers in a Word table using one of Word's built-in formulas. A *formula* is a mathematical expression that performs calculations, such as adding or averaging values. To construct a formula, you use the Formula dialog box, which you can access by clicking Formula on the Table menu . A formula consists of an equal sign followed by a function name, such as SUM, followed by the location of the cells on which you want to perform the calculation.

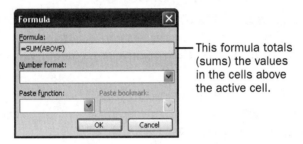

This formula totals (sums) the values in the cells above the active cell.

To use a function other than SUM in the Formula dialog box, click the down arrow to the right of the "Paste function" box, and click the function you want in the drop-down list. Word has several built-in functions, including functions to count (COUNT) the number of values in a column or row or to find the maximum (MAX) or minimum (MIN) value in a series of cells.

Although many Word formulas refer to the cells above or to the left of the active cell, you can also use the contents of specified cells or constant values in formulas. To reference a particular cell in a formula, you type the *cell address* in parentheses after the function name. The cell address is a combination of the column letter and the row number, as in *a1* for the cell at the intersection of the first column and the first row. For example, the formula =SUM(b2,b3) totals the values in cells b2 and b3.

When Word's functions don't meet your needs, you can insert a Microsoft Excel worksheet in a Word document. Part of The Microsoft Office System, Excel is an electronic spreadsheet program that provides extensive mathematical and accounting capabilities. For example, you can use an Excel worksheet to determine a payment schedule for a loan.

There are three ways to insert Excel worksheet data into a Word document:

■ **By copying and pasting.** You can open the Excel worksheet, copy the data you want to use, and paste it as a table in a Word document.

■ **By linking.** You can use the Object command on the Insert menu to create a link between the source worksheet and the Word document.

■ **By embedding.** You can also use the Object command on the Insert menu to embed a worksheet in a Word document. The worksheet then exists as an Excel object in the document rather than as a separate file, and you can continue to manipulate it using Excel.

Deciding How to Insert an Excel Worksheet

To decide how to insert an Excel worksheet in a Word document, you need to understand how Microsoft Office System programs integrate data from outside sources. This understanding will enable you to decide how to use information created in any other program, not just Excel.

If you need to maintain a connection with the source Excel worksheet or you need to be able to manipulate the data in Excel after it is included in the Word document, you can use Microsoft's *OLE Linking and Embedding* technology. This technology enables you to insert an *object* (a file or part of a file) created in one program into a file created in another program. The object is sometimes called the *source file*, and the file into which you are inserting the information is called the *destination file*. The difference between linking and embedding is the type of connection that is maintained between the source and destination files.

A *linked object* maintains a direct connection (or link) to the source file, and its data is stored there, not in the destination file. The destination file displays only a representation of the linked data. If you want to update the data, you do it in the source file. Then when you open the destination file, the linked object is updated.

An *embedded object* becomes part of the destination file. Its data is stored as well as displayed there and is no longer connected to the source file. If you want to update the data, you do it in the destination file using the source program, but the source file does not change.

Whether an object should be linked or embedded depends on whether the information in the destination file must be synchronized with the information in the source file.

If you do not need to maintain a connection between the source file and the destination file, you can copy and paste information between programs using the Copy and Paste buttons on the Standard toolbar. If you use this method, the source files and the destination files are not connected. The pasted information becomes part of the destination file, and you use the tools in the destination program to edit the pasted information.

Embedding a New Object

You can embed a variety of objects into a Word document including worksheets, charts, graphics, and sound or video clips. You can use existing files, or you can create new ones on the fly while you are working on a Word document.

To embed a new object in a Word document:

1   Click the document where you want to place the object.

2   On the **Insert** menu, click **Object**.

The Object dialog box appears.

3   If necessary, click the **Create New** tab, and in the **Object type** list, click the type of object you want to embed.

4   Select the **Display as icon** check box if you want the embedded object to appear in the document as an icon.

5   Click **OK**.

Word opens the windows and tools you need to create the object. These vary greatly, depending on which object you chose to insert.

6   Create the new object, and then click a blank area of the document to deselect your object.

Tip   After you have copied the worksheet data in Excel, you can use the Paste Special command on Word's Edit menu to link or embed the worksheet data. Paste Special enables you to copy information from one location and paste it in another location using a different format, such as Microsoft Excel Object, Picture, or HTML Format.

To update a linked or embedded worksheet, you double-click it in the Word document. If the worksheet is linked, the source worksheet opens in Excel. When you change the source worksheet, the linked worksheet in the Word document is also updated. If the worksheet is embedded, the Excel row and column headers appear and Excel's menus and toolbars replace Word's so that you can make changes to the worksheet object. The source worksheet remains unchanged.

Tip   If you change a value in a Word table, you must recalculate formulas manually. If you change a value in an Excel worksheet, the formulas are automatically recalculated.

In this exercise, you will calculate data in a table. Then you'll embed an Excel worksheet in a Word document and change the worksheet data.

USE the *DataTable* document and the *InsertTable* workbook in the practice file folder for this topic. These practice files are located in the *My Documents\Microsoft Press\Office 2003 SBS\PresentingInfo \WorkingData* folder and can also be accessed by clicking *Start/All Programs/Microsoft Press /Microsoft Office System 2003 Step by Step*.
OPEN the *DataTable* document.

1 Click the lower-right cell of the furniture table (to the right of the cell containing *Total*).

2 On the **Table** menu, click **Formula** to open the **Formula** dialog box.

The Formula box shows the formula =*SUM(ABOVE)*, meaning that the formula will add the numbers in the cells above the current (active) cell.

3 Click the down arrow to the right of the **Number format** box, and click **$#,##0.00;($#,##0.00)**, which specifies the format for positive and negative currency values.

4 In the **Number format** box, delete **.00** from both the positive and negative portions of the format.

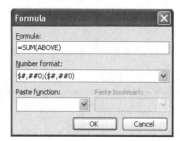

5 Click **OK** to display the total cost of the furniture in the cell.

AutoSum

Tip To quickly total a column or row of numbers, click the last cell in a column or row of values, and then click the AutoSum button on the Tables and Borders toolbar.

6 Press ⌃Ctrl+End to move to the end of the document, and press Enter.

7 On the **Insert** menu, click **Object** to open the **Object** dialog box, and then click the **Create from File** tab.

8 Click **Browse**, navigate to the *Microsoft Press\Office 2003 SBS\PresentingInfo \WorkingData* folder, and then double-click the *InsertTable* file.

The InsertTable file appears in the "File name" box.

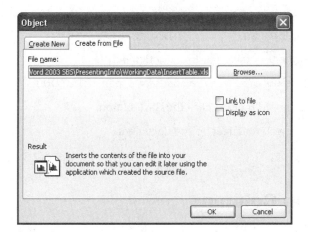

9   Make sure the **Link to file** and **Display as** icon options are not selected, and then click **OK**.

The Excel worksheet appears in the document.

10   Scroll up to see the beginning of the inserted worksheet, and double-click anywhere in the worksheet.

The Excel row and column headers appear above and to the left of the table, and Excel's menus and toolbars replace Word's.

11   Click cell **B4**, type 10000, and then press the Enter key.

New loan amount

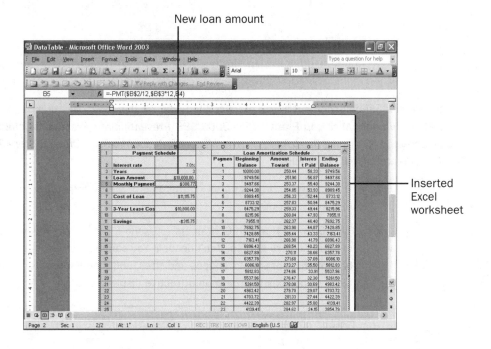

Inserted Excel worksheet

Excel recalculates the data in the table to show the payment schedule for a $10,000 loan.

12   Click anywhere outside the Excel worksheet.

The table is updated with the costs for a loan of $10,000.

Save

13   On the Standard toolbar, click the **Save** button.

Word saves your changes to the document.

CLOSE the *DataTable* document.

Presenting Text in Columns

By default, Word displays text in one column, but you can specify that text be displayed in two, three, or more columns to create layouts like those used in newsletters and brochures. In Word, a *column* is a block of text that has its own margins. When you create multiple columns, the text flows, or "snakes", from the bottom of one column to the top of the next. You can insert a column break to force subsequent text to move to the next column.

You can create a multi-column format by using the Columns command on the Format menu or the Columns button on the Standard toolbar. No matter how you set up the columns, you can change their width in the Columns dialog box, and you can format text in columns as you would any other text. For example, you can change the indentation or the alignment of text in a column using the horizontal ruler or buttons on the Formatting toolbar.

In this exercise, you will format text into four columns, reduce the amount of space between the columns, and indent column text. You'll also break the columns at specific locations instead of allowing the text to flow naturally from one column to the next.

USE the *CreateColumn* document in the practice file folder for this topic. This practice file is located in the *My Documents\Microsoft Press\Office 2003 SBS\PresentingInfo\PresentingColumn* folder and can also be accessed by clicking *Start/All Programs/Microsoft Press/Microsoft Office System 2003 Step by Step*. OPEN the *CreateColumn* document.

1   Press `Enter`, and then press `↑` to position the insertion point at the beginning of the document.

2   Type Growing Herbs in Containers, press `Enter`, then type If you have no space to plant an herb garden, don't despair. You can plant a variety of herbs in a collection of containers of various shapes and sizes, and then gather them together on a porch, deck, or balcony to create an attractive display., and press `Enter`.

3   Change the first paragraph of the document to 26-point, bold text so that this title stands out.

4   Click just to the left of the paragraph that begins *Step 1* (do not click in the selection area). Then double-click the letters *EXT* in the status bar to turn on Word's Extend Selection mode, and press [Ctrl]+[End].

Word selects the text from the *Step 1* paragraph through the end of the document.

Tip   If you want to format an entire document with the same number of columns, you can simply click anywhere in the document—you don't have to select the text.

5   On the **Format** menu, click **Columns**.

The Columns dialog box appears.

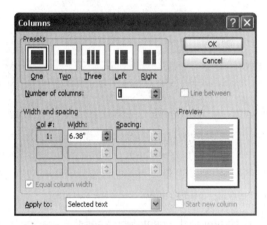

6   Click the up arrow to the right of the **Number of columns** box until the setting is **3**, and click **OK**.

Word inserts a section break above the selection. It then formats the text after the section break in three columns.

7   On the **Edit** menu, click **Select All** to select all the text in the document.

Justify

8   On the Formatting toolbar, click the **Justify** button.

All the paragraphs now align at their left and right margins.

Center

9   Press [Ctrl]+[Home] to deselect the text and move to the first paragraph of the document, and then on the Formatting toolbar, click the **Center** button to center the title.

100% ▼
Zoom

10   On the Standard toolbar, click the down arrow to the right of the **Zoom** button, and click **75%**.

More of the document is now displayed in the document window.

11   Click anywhere in the first column.

On the horizontal ruler, Word indicates the margins of the columns.

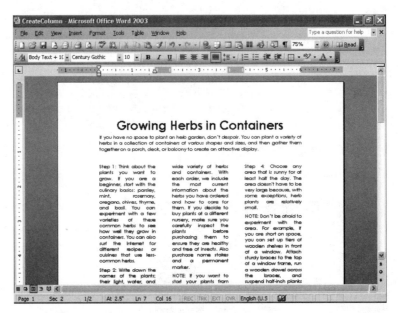

12   On the horizontal ruler, point to the **Right Margin** marker for the second column (the white bar to the right of the 4-inch mark), and when the pointer changes to a double-headed arrow, drag the indicator $^1/_8$ inch (one tick mark) to the right.

Word widens all the columns to reflect the new setting.

Tip   Dragging the pointer to the right decreases the spacing between the columns, which decreases the amount of white space on the page. Dragging to the left increases the spacing, which increases the amount of white space.

13   Click anywhere in the *NOTE* paragraph toward the top of the second column.

Hanging Indent

14   On the horizontal ruler, drag the **Hanging Indent** marker $^1/_8$ inch (one tick mark) to the right.

All the lines in the *NOTE* paragraph except the first are now indented, offsetting the note from the step.

15   Click anywhere in the *NOTE* paragraph at the top of the third paragraph, and press the [F4] key to apply the same formatting to this paragraph.

16   Scroll to the second page, click just to the left of *Step 8*, click **Break** on the **Insert** menu to open the **Break** dialog box, select the **Column break** option, and then click **OK**.

The text that follows the column break moves to the top of the next column.

17   Click just to the left of *Step 10*, and press [F4].

The columns are now more evenly balanced on the page.

Print Preview

18 On the Standard toolbar, click the **Print Preview** button to view the document formatted in columns.

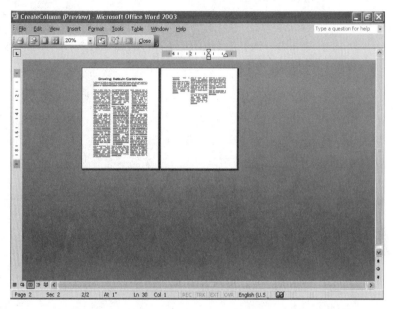

19 On the Print Preview toolbar, click the **Close** button to close the print preview window.

Save

20 On the Standard toolbar, click the **Save** button.

Word saves your changes to the document.

CLOSE the *CreateColumn* document, and if you are not continuing on to the next chapter, quit Word.

Key Points

■ You can create a table and format it to make information concise, consistent, and easy to read.

■ You can format text in a table using the buttons on the Formatting toolbar, and you can add borders and shading. You can also format a table and its text quickly by applying a table autoformat.

■ You can perform calculations on the values in a table using one of Word's built-in formulas. For complex calculations or analyses, you can insert an Excel worksheet in a Word document.

■ To vary the layout of a document, you can create two, three, or more columns and format column text as you would any other text.

II
Microsoft Office
Excel 2003

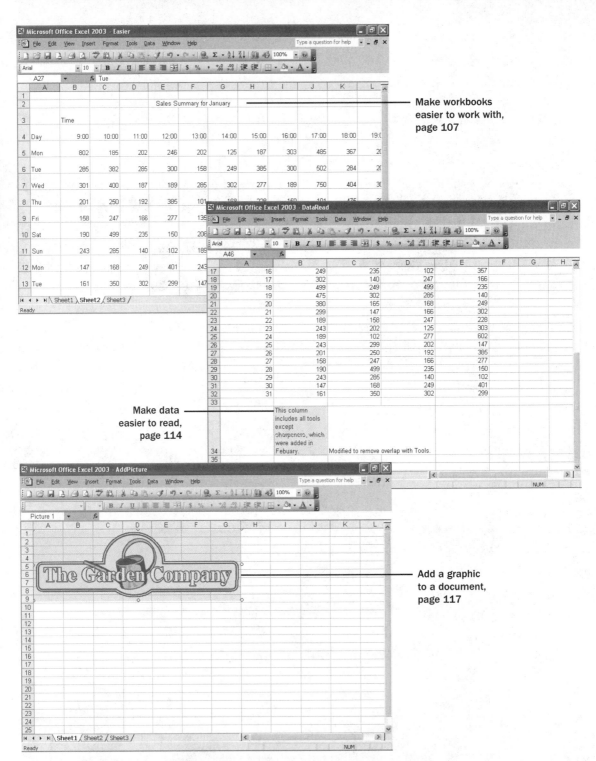

Make workbooks easier to work with, page 107

Make data easier to read, page 114

Add a graphic to a document, page 117

Chapter 5 at a Glance

5 Setting Up a Workbook

In this chapter you will learn to:

✔ Make workbooks easier to work with.

✔ Make data easier to read.

✔ Add a graphic to a document.

One of the real strengths of Microsoft Excel is that the program helps you manage large quantities of data with ease. Part of the reason managing large data collections is so easy with Excel is that you can change how Excel displays your data within a worksheet. If you want more space between the rows or columns of a worksheet, want to temporarily limit which data is shown on the screen, or even just want to add descriptions that make it easier for you and your colleagues to understand the data that's stored in a worksheet, you can do so quickly. You can also change how those descriptions appear in a cell, setting them apart from the data in the worksheet.

Another way you can customize your worksheets is to add graphics, such as your company's logo or the image of a product, to a worksheet. Adding graphics to worksheets promotes awareness of your company, identifies the data as belonging to your company, and, in the case of a product image, gives viewers valuable information they need to make a purchase decision.

In this chapter, you'll learn how to make workbooks easier to work with, make data easier to read, and add a graphic to a document.

See Also   Do you need only a quick refresher on the topics in this chapter? See the quick reference entries on page xxxiii.

Important   Before you can use the practice files in this chapter, you need to install them from the book's companion CD to their default location. See "Using the Book's CD-ROM" on page xxi for more information.

Making Workbooks Easier to Work With

An important component of making workbooks easy to work with is to give users an idea of where to find the data they're looking for. Excel provides several ways to set up signposts directing users toward the data they want. The first method is to give each workbook a descriptive name. Once users have opened the proper workbook, you can guide them to a specific worksheet by giving each worksheet a name; the names are displayed on the sheet tabs in the lower-left corner of the workbook window. To change a worksheet's name, you right-click the sheet tab of the worksheet you want and, from the shortcut menu that appears, choose Rename. Choosing Rename opens the worksheet name for editing. You can also change the order of worksheets in a workbook by dragging the sheet tab of a worksheet to the desired position on the navigation bar, bringing the most popular worksheets to the front of the list.

If you need more than three worksheets in most of the workbooks you create, you can change the default number of worksheets in your new workbooks. To change the default number of worksheets, on the Tools menu, click Options. In the Options dialog box, click the General tab, and, in the Sheets In New Workbook box, type the number of worksheets you want in your new workbooks, and click OK.

After you have put up the signposts that make your data easy to find, you can take other steps to make the data in your workbooks easier to work with. For instance, you can change the width of a column or the height of a row in a worksheet by dragging the column or row's border to the desired position. Increasing a column's width or a row's height increases the space between cell contents, making it easier to select a cell's data without inadvertently selecting data from other cells as well.

Tip   You can apply the same change to more than one row or column by selecting the rows or columns you want to change and then dragging the border of one of the selected rows or columns to the desired location. When you release the mouse button, all of the selected rows or columns will change to the new height or width.

Modifying column width and row height can make a workbook's contents easier to work with, but you can also insert a row or column between the edge of a worksheet and the cells that contain the data to accomplish this as well. Adding space between the edge of a worksheet and cells, or perhaps between a label and the data to which it refers, makes the workbook's contents less crowded and easier to work with. You insert rows by clicking a cell and then, on the Insert menu, clicking Rows. Excel inserts a row above the active cell. You insert a column in much the same way by clicking Columns on the Insert menu. When you do this, Excel inserts a column to the left of the active cell.

Likewise, you can insert individual cells into a worksheet. To insert a cell, click the cell that is currently in the position where you want the new cell to appear, and on the Insert menu, click Cells to display the Insert dialog box. In the Insert dialog box, you can choose whether to shift the cells surrounding the inserted cell down (if your data is arranged as a column) or to the right (if your data is arranged as a row). When you click OK, the new cell appears, and the contents of affected cells shift down or to the right, as appropriate. In a similar vein, if you want to delete a block of cells, select the cells, and on the Edit menu, click Delete to display the Delete dialog box, complete with option buttons that let you choose how to shift the position of the cells around the deleted cells.

Tip   The Insert dialog box also includes option buttons you can select to insert a new row or column; the Delete dialog box has similar buttons that let you delete an entire row or column.

In some cases, the values you want to put in the new cells might already exist in your worksheet. For example, Catherine Turner might have typed some sales data into a blank worksheet in anticipation of modifying the sheet once the rest of the data was entered. You can move cells from another part of your worksheet, rather than just copy or cut the values from the cells and paste them into other cells, by using a variation of the standard cut-and-paste operation. After you select the cells and click the Cut toolbar button on the Standard toolbar, on the Insert menu, click Cut Cells. The Insert Paste dialog box will appear, allowing you to choose how to shift the cells surrounding the cells you're inserting.

Tip   If you click the Copy toolbar button instead of the Cut toolbar button, the menu item on the Insert menu will be Copy Cells instead of Cut Cells.

Merge and
Center

Sometimes adding cells or even changing a row's height or a column's width isn't the best way to improve your workbook's usability. For instance, even though a column label might not fit within a single cell, increasing that cell's width (or every cell's width) might throw off the worksheet's design. While you can type individual words in cells so that the label fits in the worksheet, another alternative is to merge two or more cells. Merging cells tells Excel to treat a group of cells as a single cell as far as content and formatting go. To merge cells into a single cell, you click the Merge and Center toolbar button. As the name of the button implies, Excel centers the contents of the merged cell.

Tip   Clicking a merged cell and then clicking the Merge and Center toolbar button removes the merge.

If you want to delete a row or column, you right-click the row or column head and then, from the shortcut menu that appears, click Delete. You can temporarily hide a number of rows or columns by selecting those rows or columns and then, on the Format menu, pointing to Row or Column and then clicking Hide. The rows or columns you selected disappear, but they aren't gone for good, as they would be if you'd used Delete. Instead, they have just been removed from the display until you call them back; to return the hidden rows to the display, on the Format menu, point to Row or Column and then click Unhide.

When you insert a row, column, or cell in a worksheet with existing formatting, the Insert Options button appears. As with the Paste Options button and the Auto Fill Options button, clicking the Insert Options button displays a list of choices you can make about how the inserted row or column should be formatted. The options are summarized in the following table:

Option	Action
Format Same as Above	Apply to the inserted row the formatting of the row above it.
Format Same as Below	Apply to the inserted row the formatting of the row below it.
Format Same as Left	Apply to the inserted column the formatting of the column to its left.
Format Same as Right	Apply to the inserted column the formatting of the column to its right.
Clear Formatting	Apply the default format to the new row or column.

In this exercise, you make the worksheet containing last January's sales data easier to read. First you name the worksheet and bring it to the front of the list of worksheets in its workbook. Next you increase the column width and row height of the cells holding the sales data. In addition, you merge and center the worksheet's title and then add a row between the title and the row that holds the times for which The Garden Company recorded sales. Then you add a column to the left of the first column of data and then hide rows containing data for all but the first week of the month.

BE SURE TO start Excel before beginning this exercise.
USE the *Easier.xls* document in the practice file folder for this topic. This practice file is located in the *My Documents\Microsoft Press\Office 2003 SBS\SettingUpWorkbook* folder, and can also be accessed by clicking *Start/All Programs/Microsoft Press/Microsoft Office System 2003 Step by Step*.
OPEN the *Easier.xls* document.

Cut

1   Select cells C1 to D3 and, on the **Standard** toolbar, click the **Cut** button.

2   Select cells B5 to C7.

3   On the **Insert** menu, click **Cut Cells**.

The Insert Paste dialog box appears.

4   If necessary, select the **Shift Cells Right** option, and click **OK**.

The cut cells appear in cells B5 to C7, pushing the existing cells to the right. The values in cells C5 to C7 are repeated incorrectly in cells D5 to D7.

5   Select cells D5 to D7 and, on the **Edit** menu, click **Delete**.

The Delete dialog box appears.

6   If necessary, select the **Shift Cells Left** option, and click **OK**.

Cells D5 to D7 are deleted.

7   In the lower-left corner of the workbook window, right-click the **Sheet2** sheet tab.

8   From the shortcut menu that appears, click **Rename**.

Sheet2 is highlighted.

9   Type **January**, and press Enter.

The name of the worksheet changes from *Sheet2* to *January*.

20	Tue	202	102	277	187	187
21	Wed	300	401	150	125	385
22	Thu	189	299	102	283	277
23	Fri	101	166	401	166	201
24	Sat	135	235	299	202	125
25	Sun	206	140	382	243	444

Sheet1 \ **January** / Sheet3 /

Ready

10   Click the **January** sheet tab, and drag it to the left of the **Sheet1** sheet tab.

The January sheet tab moves to the left of the Sheet1 sheet tab. As the sheet tab moves, an inverted black triangle marks the sheet's location in the workbook.

11   Click the column head for column A, and drag to column M.

Columns A through M are highlighted.

12   Position the mouse pointer over the right edge of column A, and drag the edge to the right until the ScreenTip reads *Width: 10.00 (75 pixels)*.

The width of the selected columns changes.

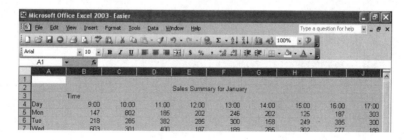

13 Select rows 3 through 35.

Rows 3 through 35 are highlighted.

14 Position the mouse pointer over the bottom edge of row 3, and drag the edge down until the ScreenTip says *Height: 25.50 (34 pixels)*.

The height of the selected rows changes.

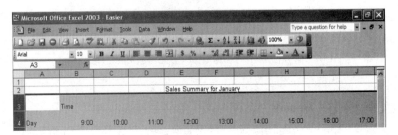

15 Click cell E2, and drag to cell G2.

Merge and
Center

16 On the Formatting toolbar, click the **Merge and Center** toolbar button.

Important Depending on the screen resolution you have set on your computer and which toolbar buttons you use most often, it's possible that not every button on every toolbar will appear on your Excel toolbars. If a button mentioned in this book doesn't appear on a toolbar, click the Toolbar Options down arrow on that toolbar to display the rest of the buttons available on that toolbar.

Cells E2, F2, and G2 are merged into a single cell, and the new cell's contents are centered.

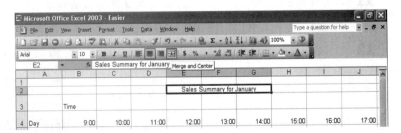

17 Click cell A3.

18 On the **Insert** menu, click **Rows**.

A new row, labeled row 3, appears above the row previously labeled row 3.

You can also make your worksheet data easier to read by ensuring that the data labels at the top of a column *freeze*, or remain on the screen regardless of how far down in the document you scroll. For instance, Catherine Turner, the owner of The Garden Company, might not remember which data is kept in which column in a worksheet. Freezing the data labels at the top of the column would let her scroll to the last row of the worksheet and still have the labels visible as a reference. Excel marks the division between frozen and unfrozen cells with a *split bar*.

Split bar

Troubleshooting   When you tell Excel to freeze rows in your worksheet, Excel freezes the rows above the active cell and the columns to the left of the active cell. So, if you want to freeze the top three rows of your worksheet, click the first cell in the fourth row (cell A4) and then turn on the freeze. If you wanted to freeze the top three rows and the first column, you would click the second cell in the fourth row (cell B4).

In this exercise, you prevent the text in a cell from spilling over into adjoining cells, allowing you to enter comments in those adjoining cells without obscuring the contents of the first cell. You then change the alignment of the cells containing the data labels for the columns in your worksheet and then freeze those data labels so that they remain at the top of the page as you scroll down through the worksheet.

USE the *DataRead.xls* document in the practice file folder for this topic. This practice file is located in the *My Documents\Microsoft Press\Office 2003 SBS\SettingUpWorkbook* folder, and can also be accessed by clicking *Start/All Programs/Microsoft Press/Microsoft Office System 2003 Step by Step*.
OPEN the *DataRead.xls* document.

1   If necessary, click the **SalesbyCategory** sheet tab.

2   Click cell B34.

3   On the **Format** menu, click **Cells**.

The Format Cells dialog box appears.

4   If necessary, click the **Alignment** tab.

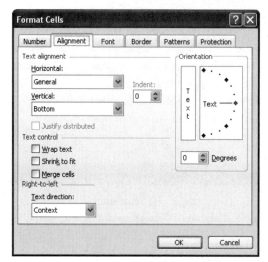

5   If necessary, select the **Wrap text** check box, and click **OK**.

The text in cell B34 wraps to fit within the original borders of the cell.

6   Click cell B1, and drag to cell E1.

7   On the Formatting toolbar, click the **Center** button.

Center

The contents of the selected cells are centered within those cells.

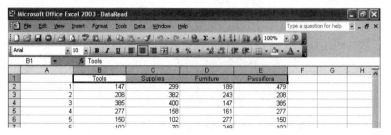

8   Click cell A2.

9   On the **Window** menu, click **Freeze Panes**.

A split bar appears between row 1 and row 2.

10   On the vertical scroll bar, click the down arrow.

Row 1 stays in place while the remaining rows scroll normally.

11   On the **Window** menu, click **Unfreeze Panes**.

The split bar disappears, and all rows scroll normally.

Save

12 On the Standard toolbar, click the **Save** button.

Excel saves your changes.

CLOSE the *DataRead.xls* document.

Adding a Graphic to a Document

An important part of establishing a strong business is creating a memorable corporate identity. Setting aside the obvious need for sound management, two important physical attributes of a strong retail business are a well-conceived shop space and an eye-catching, easy-to-remember logo. Once you or your graphic artist has created a logo, you should add the logo to all of your documents, especially any that might be seen by your customers. Not only does the logo mark the documents as coming from your company, it also serves as an advertisement, encouraging anyone who sees your worksheets to call or visit your company.

One way to add a picture to a worksheet is to go through the Insert menu and click the Picture item. Clicking Picture shows a submenu that lists several sources from which you can choose a picture to add; in this case, where you're adding a logo you've saved as a graphics file, you can click the From File item to open a dialog box that lets you locate the picture you want to add from your hard disk.

Tip When you insert a picture, the Picture toolbar might appear. The Picture toolbar contains buttons that let you change the picture's contrast, brightness, and so on. You can use those buttons to change your picture's appearance, but you don't get as much control as when you use the Format Picture dialog box, presented later in this section.

Once you've added the picture to your worksheet, you can change the picture's location on the worksheet by dragging it to the desired spot. You can also change the appearance of the picture by opening the Format menu and choosing Picture. Then, in the Format Picture dialog box, you can modify the image's size or brightness, rotate the image on the page, or crop away any portion of the image that you don't want to show.

You can also resize a picture by clicking it and then dragging one of the handles that appears on the graphic. Using the Format Picture dialog box helps ensure that the *aspect ratio*, or relationship between the picture's height and width, doesn't change. If you do accidentally resize a graphic by dragging a handle, just click the Undo button to remove your change.

If you'd like to generate a repeating image in the background of a worksheet, forming a tiled pattern behind your worksheet's data, you can open the Format menu, point to Sheet, and click Background. In the Sheet Background dialog box, click the image that you want to serve as the background pattern for your worksheet, and click OK.

Tip To remove a background image from a worksheet, open the Format menu, point to Sheet, and click Delete Background.

In this exercise, you add the new logo for The Garden Company to an existing worksheet, change the graphic's location on the worksheet, reduce the size of the graphic, change the image's brightness and contrast, rotate and crop the image, delete the image, and then set the image as a repeating background for the worksheet.

USE the *AddPicture.xls* document in the practice file folder for this topic. This practice file is located in the *My Documents\Microsoft Press\Office 2003 SBS\SettingUpWorkbook* folder, and can also be accessed by clicking *Start/All Programs/Microsoft Press/Microsoft Office System 2003 Step by Step.*
OPEN the *AddPicture.xls* document.

1 Click cell A1.

2 On the **Insert** menu, point to **Picture**, and then click **From File**.

The Insert Picture dialog box appears.

3 If necessary, navigate to the SettingUpWorkbook folder and then double-click **tgc_logo.gif**.

The chosen graphic appears in the AddPicture.xls file.

4 Right-click the graphic, and from the shortcut menu that appears, click **Format Picture**.

The Format Picture dialog box appears.

5　Click the **Size** tab.

The Size tab page appears. Notice that the Lock aspect ratio check box is selected.

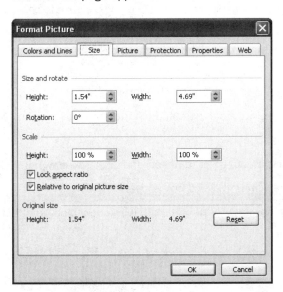

6　In the **Scale** section of the tab page, clear the contents of the **Height** box, and type 50%.

7　In the **Size and Rotate** section of the tab page, clear the contents of the **Rotation** box, type 180, and click **OK**.

The picture is resized, maintaining the original aspect ratio, and rotated.

8　Click the center of the graphic, and drag it so that it is centered horizontally on the screen and the top of the graphic is just below row 1.

The graphic moves with your mouse pointer.

Troubleshooting　Remember that dragging one of the handles at the edge of the graphic will resize the graphic. If you accidentally resize the logo instead of moving it, click the Undo button.

9　On the **Format** menu, click **Picture**.

The Format Picture dialog box appears.

10　Click the **Picture** tab.

The Picture tab page appears.

11 In the **Image Control** section of the dialog box, clear the contents of the **Brightness** box, and type 40.

12 In the **Image Control** section of the dialog box, clear the contents of the **Contrast** box, and type 40.

13 In the **Crop From** section of the dialog box, clear the contents of the **Top** box, type .5, and click **OK**.

The image changes to reflect the properties you set.

14 If necessary, select the image, and, on the **Standard** toolbar, click the **Cut** button.

The image disappears.

15 On the **Format** menu, point to **Sheet**, and click **Background**.

The Sheet Background dialog box appears.

16 If necessary, navigate to the SettingUpWorkbook folder and then double-click **tgc_logo.gif**.

The image repeats in the background of the active worksheet.

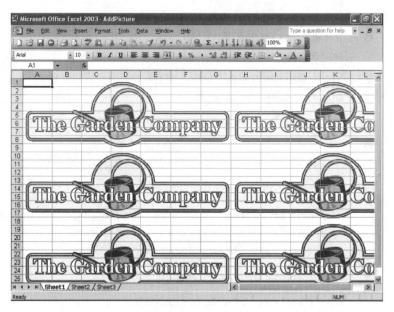

Save

17 On the Standard toolbar, click the **Save** button.

Excel saves your changes.

CLOSE the *AddPicture.xls* document.

Key Points

- You can control how many worksheets appear in new workbooks you create. If you always use workbooks where each worksheet represents a month of the year, change the default number of worksheets to 12!

- Making sure your data is easily readable is one of the best things you can do for your colleagues. Be sure your worksheet columns and rows are roomy enough to accommodate your data.

- Remember that you can add or delete individual cells from a worksheet. Rather than go through a lengthy cut-and-paste routine when you forgot to type a cell value, just add a cell where you need it.

- If you add a graphic to your worksheet, you can change the graphic's size and appearance using the Format Picture dialog box.

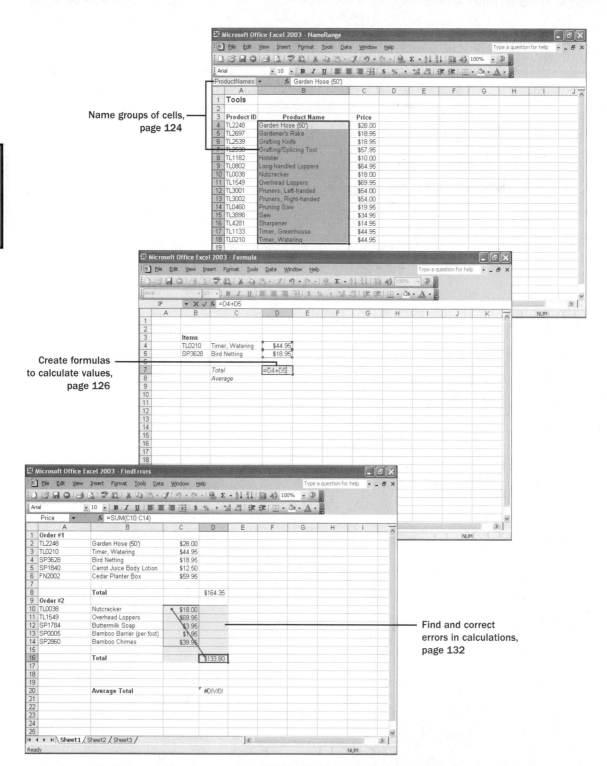

Name groups of cells,
page 124

Create formulas
to calculate values,
page 126

Find and correct
errors in calculations,
page 132

Chapter 6 at a Glance

6 Performing Calculations on Data

In this chapter you will learn to:

✔   Name groups of cells.

✔   Create formulas to calculate values.

✔   Find and correct errors in calculations.

Microsoft Excel workbooks give you a handy place to store and organize your data, but you can also do a lot more with your data in Excel. One important task you can perform in Excel is to calculate totals for the values in a series of related cells. You can also use Excel to find out other information about the data you select, such as the maximum or minimum value in a group of cells. Finding the maximum or minimum value in a group can let you identify your best salesperson, product categories you might need to pay more attention to, or suppliers that consistently give you the best deal. Regardless of your bookkeeping needs, Excel gives you the ability to find the information you want. And if you should make an error, you can find the cause and correct it quickly.

Many times you can't access the information you want without referencing more than one cell, and it's also often true that you'll use the data in the same group of cells for more than one calculation. Excel makes it easy to reference a number of cells at once, letting you define your calculations quickly.

In this chapter, you'll learn how to streamline references to groups of data in your worksheets and how to create and correct formulas that summarize the sales and product data from The Garden Company.

See Also   Do you need only a quick refresher on the topics in this chapter? See the quick reference entries on pages xxxiii.

 Important   Before you can use the practice files in this chapter, you need to install them from the book's companion CD to their default location. See "Using the Book's CD-ROM" on page xxi for more information.

Naming Groups of Data

When you work with large amounts of data, it's easier to identify groups of cells that contain related data. In the following graphic, for example, cells C2 through C6 hold the prices of items from a customer's order.

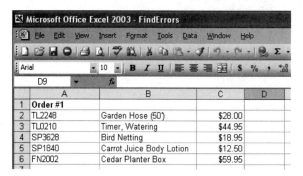

Rather than specify the cells individually every time you want to use the data they contain, you can define those cells as a *range* (also called a *named range*). For instance, you could group the items from the previous graphic into a range named *OrderItems1*. Whenever you want to use the contents of that range in a calculation, you can simply use the name of the range instead of specifying each cell individually.

You can create a named range in a number of ways, two of which you can access through the Insert menu. The first method works well if you have a column of data with a label at the head of the column, as in the following graphic.

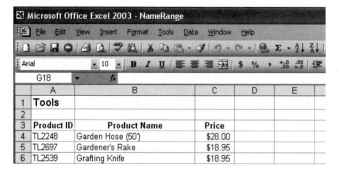

In this case, you access the Create Names dialog box by pointing to Name on the Insert menu and clicking Create. In the Create Names dialog box, you can define a named range by having Excel use the label in the top cell as the range's name. You can also create and delete named ranges through the Define Name dialog box, which you access by pointing to Define on the Insert menu and clicking Name.

A final way to create a named range is to select the cells you want in the range, click in the Name box next to the formula bar, and then type the name for the range. You can display the ranges available in a workbook by clicking the Name box's down arrow.

Important   Every range in a workbook must have a unique name. Assigning the name of an existing range to a new range removes the original reference, likely affecting how your worksheet behaves.

In this exercise, you will create named ranges to streamline references to groups of cells.

USE the *NameRange.xls* document in the practice file folder for this topic. This practice file is located in the *My Documents\Microsoft Press\Office 2003 SBS\PerformingCalculations* folder, and can also be accessed by clicking *Start/All Programs/Microsoft Press/Microsoft Office System 2003 Step by Step*.
OPEN the *NameRange.xls* document.

1   If necessary, click the **Tools** sheet tab.

2   Click cell C3 and drag to cell C18.

The selected cells are highlighted.

3   On the **Insert** menu, point to **Name**, and then click **Create**.

The Create Names dialog box appears.

4   If necessary, select the **Top row** check box.

5   Click **OK**.

Excel assigns the name *Price* to the cell range.

6   In the lower left corner of the workbook window, click the **Supplies** sheet tab.

The Supplies worksheet appears.

7   Click cell C4 and drag to cell C29.

8   On the **Insert** menu, point to **Name**, and then click **Define**.

The Define Name dialog box appears.

9   In the **Names in Workbook** box, type **SuppliesPrice** and then click **OK**.

Excel assigns the name *SuppliesPrice* to the cell range, and the Define Name dialog box disappears.

10   In the lower-left corner of the workbook window, click the **Furniture** sheet tab.

The Furniture worksheet appears.

11   Click cell C4 and drag to cell C18.

12   Click in the Name box.

The contents of the Name box are highlighted.

13   Type **FurniturePrice**, and press [Enter].

Excel assigns the name *FurniturePrice* to the cell range.

14   On the **Insert** menu, point to **Name**, and then click **Define**.

The Define Name dialog box appears.

15   In the **Names in workbook** list of the **Define Name** dialog box, click **Price**.

Price appears in the Names in workbook box.

16   In the **Names in workbook** box, delete *Price*, type **ToolsPrice**, and then click **OK**.

The Define Name dialog box disappears.

17   On the Standard toolbar, click the **Save** button.

Save

CLOSE the *NameRange.xls* document.

Creating Formulas to Calculate Values

Once you've added your data to a worksheet and defined ranges to simplify data references, you can create a *formula*, or an expression that performs calculations on your data. For example, you can calculate the total cost of a customer's order, figure the average sales for all Wednesdays in the month of January, or find the highest and lowest daily sales for a week, month, or year.

To write an Excel formula, you begin the cell's contents with an equal sign—when Excel sees it, it knows that the expression following it should be interpreted as a calculation and not text. After the equal sign, you type the formula. For instance, you can find the sum of the numbers in cells C2 and C3 using the formula *=C2+C3*. After you have entered a formula into a cell, you can revise it by clicking the cell and then editing the formula in the formula bar. For example, you can change the preceding formula to *=C3-C2*, which calculates the difference between the contents of cells C2 and C3.

Troubleshooting If Excel treats your formula as text, make sure you haven't accidentally put a space before the equal sign. Remember, the equal sign must be the first character!

Typing the cell references for 15 or 20 cells in a calculation would be tedious, but Excel makes it easy to handle complex calculations. To create a new calculation, you click Function on the Insert menu. The Insert Function dialog box appears, with a list of *functions*, or predefined formulas, from which you can choose.

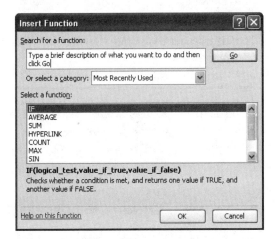

The most useful functions in the list are described in the following table:

Item	Description
SUM	Returns the sum of the numbers in the specified cells
AVERAGE	Finds the average of the numbers in the specified cells
COUNT	Finds the number of entries in the specified cells
MAX	Finds the largest value in the specified cells
MIN	Finds the smallest value in the specified cells

Two other functions you might use are the NOW() and PMT() functions. The NOW() function returns the time the workbook was last opened, so the value will change every time the workbook is opened. The proper form for this function is *=NOW()*; to update the value to the current date and time, just save your work, close the workbook, and then reopen it. The PMT() function is a bit more complex. It calculates payments due on a loan, assuming a constant interest rate and constant payments. To perform its calculations, the PMT() function requires an interest rate, the number of months of payments, and the starting balance. The elements to be entered into the function are called *arguments* and must be entered in a certain order. That order is written *PMT(rate, nper, pv, fv, type)*. The following table summarizes the arguments in the PMT() function:

Argument	Description
rate	The interest rate, to be divided by 12 for a loan with monthly payments
nper	The total number of payments for the loan
pv	The amount loaned (pv is short for present value, or principal)
fv	The amount to be left over at the end of the payment cycle (usually left blank, which indicates 0)
type	0 or 1, indicating whether payments are made at the beginning or at the end of the month (usually left blank, which indicates 0, or the end of the month)

If you wanted to borrow $20,000 at an 8 percent interest rate and pay the loan back over 24 months, you could use the PMT() function to figure out the monthly payments. In this case, the function would be written *=PMT(8%/12, 24, 20000)*, which calculates a monthly payment of $904.55.

You can also add the names of any ranges you've defined to a formula. For example, if the named range *Order1* refers to cells C2 through C6, you can calculate the average of cells C2 through C6 with the formula *=AVERAGE(Order1)*. If you want to include a series of contiguous cells in a formula but you haven't defined the cells as a named range, you can click the first cell in the range and drag to the last cell. If the cells aren't contiguous, hold down the [Ctrl] key and click the cells to be included. In both cases, when you release the mouse button, the references of the cells you selected appear in the formula.

Another use for formulas is to display messages when certain conditions are met. For instance, Catherine Turner, the owner of The Garden Company, might provide a free copy of a gardening magazine to customers making purchases worth more than $150. This kind of formula is called a *conditional formula,* and it uses the IF function. To create a conditional formula, you click the cell to hold the formula and open the Insert Function dialog box. From within the dialog box, you select **IF** from the list of available functions and then click OK. The Function Arguments dialog box appears.

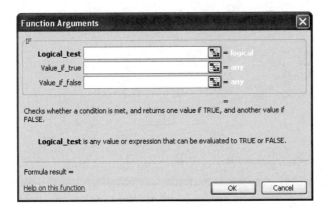

When you work with an IF function, the Function Arguments dialog box will have three boxes: Logical_test, Value_if_true, and Value_if_false. The Logical_test box holds the condition you want to check. To check whether the total for an order is greater than $150, the expression would be *SUM(Order1)>150*.

Now you need to have Excel display messages indicating whether the customer should receive a free magazine. To have Excel print a message from an IF function, you enclose the message in quotes in the Value_if_true or Value_if_false box. In this case, you would type *"Qualifies for a free magazine!"* in the Value_if_true box and *"Thanks for your order!"* in the Value_if_false box.

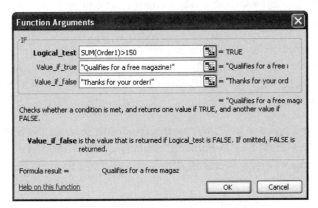

Once you've created a formula, you can copy it and paste it into another cell. When you do, Excel will try to change the formula so that it works in the new cells. For instance, in the following graphic, cell D8 contains the formula *=SUM(C2:C6)*.

Clicking cell D8, copying the cell's contents, and then pasting the result into cell D16 writes =*SUM(C10:C14)* into cell D16. Excel has reinterpreted the formula so that it fits the surrounding cells! Excel knows it can reinterpret the cells used in the formula because the formula uses a *relative reference*, or a reference that can change if the formula is copied to another cell. Relative references are written with just the cell row and column (for example, *C14*). If you want a cell reference to remain constant when the formula using it is copied to another cell, you can use an absolute reference. To write a cell reference as an absolute reference, you type *$* before the row name and the column number. If you wanted the formula in cell D16 to show the sum of values in cells C10 through C14 regardless of the cell into which it is pasted, you would write the formula as =*SUM($C$10:$C$14)*.

Tip   If you copy a formula from the formula bar, use absolute references, or use only named ranges in your formula. Excel won't change the cell references when you copy your formula to another cell.

In this exercise, you create a formula to find the total cost of an order, copy that formula to another cell, and then create a formula to find the average cost of items in the order. The cells with the cost of products in this order are stored in the named range *OrderItems*.

USE the *Formula.xls* document in the practice file folder for this topic. This practice file is located in the *My Documents\Microsoft Press\Office 2003 SBS\PerformingCalculations* folder, and can also be accessed by clicking *Start/All Programs/Microsoft Press/Microsoft Office System 2003 Step by Step*.
OPEN the *Formula.xls* document.

1   Click cell D7.

D7 becomes the active cell.

2   In the formula bar, type =SUM, drag from cell D4 to D5, and press [Enter].

The value $63.90 appears in cell D7.

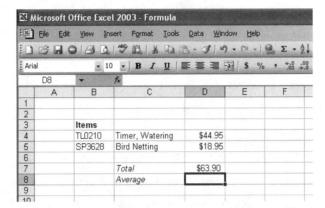

Copy

3 Click cell D7, and then, on the Standard toolbar, click the **Copy** button.

Excel copies the formula in cell D7 to the Clipboard.

Paste

4 Click cell D8, and then, on the Standard toolbar, click the **Paste** button.

The value *$18.95* appears in cell D8, and *=SUM(D5:D6)* appears in the formula bar.

5 Press [Del].

The formula in cell D8 disappears.

6 On the **Insert** menu, click **Function**.

The Insert Function dialog box appears.

7 Click **AVERAGE**, and then click **OK**.

The Function Arguments dialog box appears, with the contents of the Number 1 box highlighted.

8 Type **OrderItems**, and then click **OK**.

The Function Arguments dialog box disappears, and *$31.95* appears in cell D8.

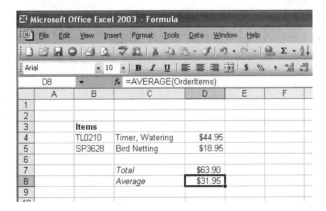

9   Click cell C10.

10   On the **Insert** menu, click **Function**.

       The Insert Function dialog box appears.

11   In the **Select a function** list, click **IF** and then click **OK**.

       The Function Arguments dialog box appears.

12   In the **Logical_test** box, type **D7>50**.

13   In the **Value_if_true** box, type **"5% discount"**.

14   In the **Value_if_false** box, type **"No discount"** and then click **OK**.

       The Function Arguments dialog box disappears, and *5% discount* appears in cell C10.

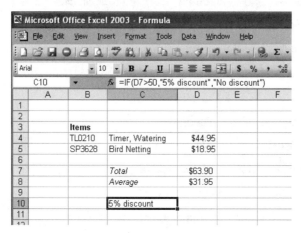

Save

15   On the Standard toolbar, click the **Save** button.

       Excel saves your changes.

CLOSE the *Formula.xls* document.

Finding and Correcting Errors in Calculations

Including calculations in a worksheet gives you valuable answers to questions about your data. As is always true, however, it is possible for errors to creep into your formulas. Excel makes it easy to find the source of errors in your formulas by identifying the cells used in a given calculation and describing any errors that have occurred. The process of examining a worksheet for errors in formulas is referred to as *auditing*.

Excel identifies errors in several ways. The first way is to fill the cell holding the formula generating the error with an *error code*. In the following graphic, cell D8 has the error code *#NAME?*.

When a cell with an erroneous formula is the active cell, an Error button appears next to it. You can click the button's down arrow to display a menu with options that provide information about the error and offer to help you fix it.

The following table lists the most common error codes and what they mean:

Error Code	Description
#####	The column isn't wide enough to display the value.
#VALUE!	The formula has the wrong type of argument (such as text where a TRUE or FALSE value is required).
#NAME?	The formula contains text that Excel doesn't recognize (such as an unknown named range).
#REF!	The formula refers to a cell that doesn't exist (which can happen whenever cells are deleted).
#DIV/0!	The formula attempts to divide by zero.

Another technique you can use to find the source of formula errors is to ensure that the appropriate cells are providing values for the formula. For example, you might want to calculate the total sales for a product category, but say you accidentally create a formula referring to the products' names, not their prices. You can identify that kind of error by having Excel trace a cell's *precedents*, which are the cells with values used in the active cell's formula. Excel identifies a cell's precedents by drawing a blue tracer arrow from the precedent to the active cell.

You can also audit your worksheet by identifying cells with formulas that use a value from a given cell. For example, you might have the total cost of a single order used in a formula that calculates the average cost of all orders placed on a given day. Cells that use another cell's value in their calculations are known as *dependents*, meaning that they depend on the value in the other cell to derive their own value.

As with tracing precedents, you can point to Formula Auditing on the Tools menu and then click Trace Dependents to have Excel draw blue arrows from the active cell to those cells that have calculations based on that value.

If the cells identified by the tracer arrows aren't the correct cells, you can hide the arrows and correct the formula. To hide the tracer arrows on a worksheet, you point to Formula Auditing on the Tools menu and click Remove All Arrows.

If you prefer to have the elements of a formula error presented as text in a dialog box, you can use the Error Checking dialog box (which you display by clicking Error Checking on the Tools menu) to view the error and the formula in the cell where the error occurs. You can also use the controls in the Error Checking dialog box to move through the formula one step at a time, to choose to ignore the error, or to move to the next or the previous error. If you click the Options button, you can also use the controls in the Options dialog box to change how Excel determines what is an error and what isn't.

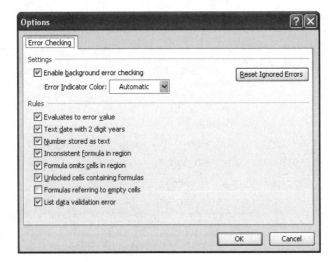

Tip   One change worth noting is that you can have the Error Checking tool ignore formulas that don't use every cell in a region (such as a row or column). If you clear the Formula Omits Cells In Region check box, you can create formulas that don't add up every value in a row or column (or rectangle) without Excel marking them as an error.

For times when you just want to display the results of each step of a formula and don't need the full power of the Error Checking tool, you can use the Evaluate Formula dialog box to move through each element of the formula. To display the Evaluate Formula dialog box, you point to Formula Auditing on the Tools menu and click Evaluate Formula. The Evaluate Formula dialog box is much more useful for examining formulas that don't produce an error but aren't generating the result you expect.

Finally, you can monitor the value in a cell regardless of where in your workbook you are by opening a watch window that displays the value in the cell. For example, if one of your formulas uses values from cells in other worksheets, or even other workbooks, you can set a watch on the cell that contains the formula and then change the values in the other cells. To set a watch, click the cell you want to monitor, point to Formula Auditing on the Tools menu, and then click Show Watch Window. Click Add Watch to have Excel monitor the selected cell.

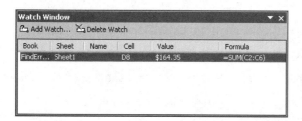

As soon as you type in the new value, the watch window displays the new result of the formula. When you're done watching the formula, select the watch, click Delete Watch, and close the watch window.

In this exercise, you use the formula auditing capabilities in Excel to identify and correct errors in a formula.

USE the *FindErrors.xls* document in the practice file folder for this topic. This practice file is located in the *My Documents\Microsoft Press\Office 2003 SBS\PerformingCalculations* folder, and can also be accessed by clicking *Start/All Programs/Microsoft Press/Microsoft Office System 2003 Step by Step*.
OPEN the *FindErrors.xls* document.

1 Click cell D20.

2 On the **Tools** menu, point to **Formula Auditing**, and then click **Show Watch Window**.

3 Click **Add Watch**, and then click **Add** in the **Add Watch** dialog box.

Cell D20 appears in the watch window.

4 Click cell D8.

=SUM(C2:C6) appears in the formula bar.

5 On the **Tools** menu, point to **Formula Auditing**, and then click **Trace Precedents**.

A blue arrow appears between cell D8 and the group of cells from C2 to C6, indicating that cells in the C2:C6 range are precedents of the value in cell D8.

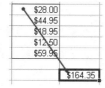

6   On the **Tools** menu, point to **Formula Auditing**, and then click **Remove All Arrows**.

     The arrow disappears.

7   Click cell A1.

8   On the **Tools** menu, click **Error Checking**.

     The Error Checking dialog box appears.

9   Click **Next**.

     The error in cell D8 appears in the **Error Checking** dialog box.

10   Click the **Close** button to close the **Error Checking** dialog box.

11   On the **Tools** menu, point to **Formula Auditing**, and then click **Trace Error**.

     Blue arrows appear, pointing to cell D20 from cells D7 and D15. These arrows indicate that using the values (or lack of values, in this case) in the indicated cells is generating the error in cell D20.

12   On the **Tools** menu, point to **Formula Auditing**, and then click **Remove All Arrows**.

     The arrows disappear.

13   In the formula bar, delete the existing formula, type =AVERAGE(D8,D16), and press Enter.

     The value $149.08 appears in cell D20.

14   Click cell D20.

15   On the **Tools** menu, point to **Formula Auditing**, and then click **Evaluate Formula**.

     The Evaluate Formula dialog box appears, with the formula from cell D20 displayed.

16 Click **Evaluate**.

The result of the formula in cell D20 appears.

17 Click **Close**.

18 In the watch window, click the watch in the list.

19 Click **Delete Watch**.

The watch disappears.

20 On the **Tools** menu, point to **Formula Auditing**, and then click **Hide Watch Window**.

The watch window disappears.

Save

21 On the Standard toolbar, click the **Save** button.

Excel saves your changes.

CLOSE the *FindErrors.xls* document.

Key Points

■ You can add a group of cells to a formula by typing the formula and then, at the spot in the formula where you want to name the cells, selecting the cells using the mouse.

■ Creating named ranges lets you refer to entire blocks of cells with a single term, saving you lots of time and effort.

■ When you write a formula, be sure you use absolute referencing ($A$1) if you want the formula to remain the same when it's copied from one cell to another, or relative referencing (A1) if you want the formula to change to reflect its new position in the worksheet.

■ Rather than type in a formula from scratch, you can use the Insert Function dialog box to help you on your way.

■ You can monitor how the value in a cell changes by adding a watch to the watch window.

■ To see which formulas refer to the values in the selected cell, use Trace Dependents; if you want to see which cells provide values for the formula in the active cell, use Trace Precedents.

■ You can step through the calculations of a formula in the Evaluate Formula dialog box, or go through a more rigorous error-checking procedure using the Error Checking tool.

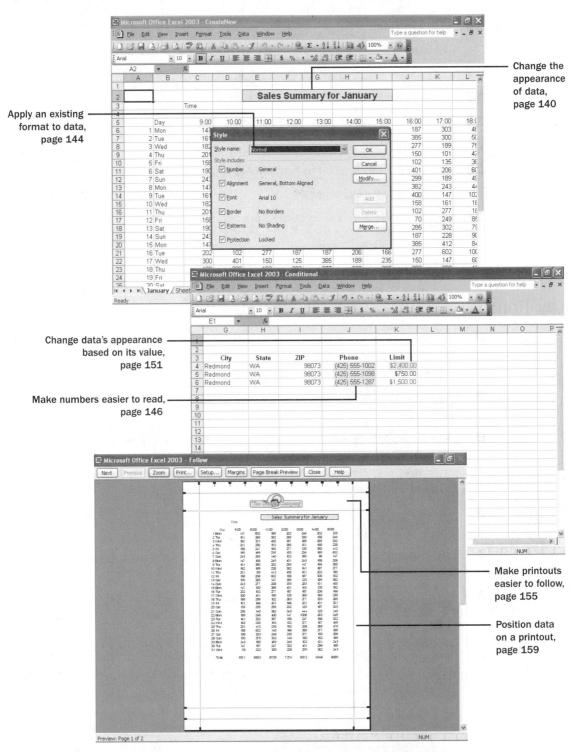

Change the appearance of data, page 140

Apply an existing format to data, page 144

Change data's appearance based on its value, page 151

Make numbers easier to read, page 146

Make printouts easier to follow, page 155

Position data on a printout, page 159

Chapter 7 at a Glance

7 Changing Document Appearance

In this chapter you will learn to:

- ✔ Change the appearance of data.
- ✔ Apply an existing format to data.
- ✔ Make numbers easier to read.
- ✔ Change data's appearance based on its value.
- ✔ Make printouts easier to follow.
- ✔ Position data on a printout.

An important aspect of working with data entered into a workbook is ensuring that the data is easy to read. Microsoft Excel gives you a wide variety of ways to make your data easier to understand; for example, you can change the font, letter size, or color used to present a cell's contents. You can also change how your data appears on the printed page, such as by changing your printer's margins or adding information at the top or bottom of every page.

Changing how data appears on a worksheet helps set the contents of a cell apart from the contents of surrounding cells. The simplest example is that of a data label. If a column on your worksheet has a list of days, you can set a label—for example, *Day*—apart easily by presenting it in bold type that's noticeably larger than the type used to present the data to which it refers. To save time, you can define a number of custom formats and then apply them quickly to the desired cells.

You might also want to specially format a cell's contents to reflect the value in that cell. For instance, Catherine Turner, the owner of The Garden Company, might grant some credit to The Garden Company's better customers, use Excel to track each customer's purchases, and use that information to determine which customers are nearing their credit limit. A quick way to distinguish when a customer is close to his or her credit limit is to change how their outstanding balance is presented in its cell. Catherine might, for example, change the color of the font from the standard black to blue when a customer is within 10 percent of his or her limit.

In addition to changing how data appears in the cells of your worksheet, you can also use headers and footers to add page numbers, current data, or graphics to the top and bottom of every printed page.

In this chapter, you'll learn how to change the appearance of data, apply existing formats to data, make numbers easier to read, change data's appearance based on its value, make printouts easier to follow, and position your data on the printed page.

See Also   Do you need only a quick refresher on the topics in this chapter? See the quick reference entries on page xxxiii.

 Important   Before you can use the practice files in this chapter, you need to install them from the book's companion CD to their default location. See "Using the Book's CD-ROM" on page xxi for more information.

Changing the Appearance of Data

Excel spreadsheets can hold and process lots of data, but when you manage numerous spreadsheets it can be hard to remember from a worksheet's title exactly what data is kept in that worksheet. Data labels give you and your colleagues information about data in a worksheet, but it's important to format the labels so that they stand out visually. To make your data labels or any other data stand out, you can change the format of the cells in which the data is stored.

Time			
Day	9:00	10:00	11:00
1 Mon	147	802	185
2 Tue	161	285	382
3 Wed	182	301	400
4 Thu	201	250	192

Most of the tools you need to change a cell's format can be found on the Formatting toolbar.

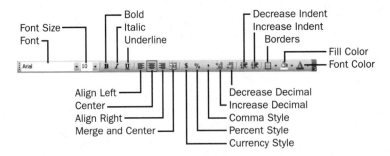

Important   Depending on the screen resolution you have set on your computer and which toolbar buttons you use most often, it's possible that not every button on every toolbar will appear on your Excel toolbars. If a button mentioned in this book doesn't appear on a toolbar, click the Toolbar Options button he small arrow at the right end of a toolbar to display the rest of its buttons.

B
Bold

You can apply the formatting represented by a toolbar button by selecting the cells you want to apply the style to and then clicking the appropriate button. If you want to set your data labels apart by making them appear bold, click the Bold button. If you have already made a cell's contents bold, selecting the cell and clicking the Bold button will remove the formatting.

Tip   Deleting a cell's contents doesn't delete the cell's formatting. To delete a cell's formatting, select the cell and then, on the Edit menu, point to Clear and click Formats.

Items on the Formatting toolbar that give you choices, such as the Font Color control, have a down arrow at the right edge of the control. Clicking the down arrow displays a list of options accessible for that control, such as the fonts available on your system or the colors you can assign to a cell.

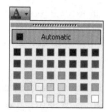

Borders

Another way you can make a cell stand apart from its neighbors is to add a border around the cell. In versions of Excel prior to Excel 2002, you could select the cell or cells to which you wanted to add the border and use the options available under the Formatting toolbar's Borders button to assign a border to the cells. For example, you could select a group of cells and then choose the border type you wanted. That method of adding borders is still available in Excel, but it has some limitations. The most important limitation is that, while creating a simple border around a group of cells is easy, creating complex borders makes you select different groups of cells and apply different types of borders to them. The current version of Excel makes creating complex borders easy by letting you draw borders directly on the worksheet.

To use the new border-drawing capabilities, display the Borders toolbar.

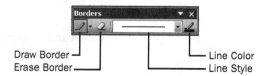

Draw Border
Erase Border
Line Color
Line Style

To draw a border around a group of cells, click the mouse pointer at one corner of the group and drag it to the diagonal corner. You will see your border expand as you move the mouse pointer. If you want to add a border in a vertical or horizontal line, drag the mouse pointer along the target grid line—Excel will add the line without expanding it to include the surrounding cells. You can also change the characteristics of the border you draw by using the options on the Borders toolbar.

Another way you can make a group of cells stand apart from its neighbors is to change their shading, or the color that fills the cells. On a worksheet with monthly sales data for The Garden Company, for example, owner Catherine Turner could change the fill color of the cells holding her data labels to make the labels stand out even more than by changing the formatting of the text used to display the labels.

If you want to change the attributes of every cell in a row or column, you can click the header of the row or column you want to format and select your desired format.

One task you can't perform using the tools on the Formatting toolbar is to change the standard font for a workbook, which is used in the Name box and in the formula bar. The standard font when you install Excel is Arial, a simple font that is easy to read on a computer screen and on the printed page. If you want to choose another font, click Options on the Tools menu, which displays the General tab page, and use the Standard Font and Size controls to set the new default for your workbook.

Important   The new standard font won't take effect until you quit Excel and restart the program.

In this exercise, you emphasize a worksheet's title by changing the format of cell data, adding a border to a cell, and then changing a cell's fill color. After those tasks are complete, you change the default font for the workbook.

BE SURE TO start Excel before beginning this exercise.
USE the *Formats.xls* document in the practice file folder for this topic. This practice file is located in the *My Documents\Microsoft Press\Office 2003 SBS\ChangingDocAppearance* folder, and can also be accessed by clicking *Start/All Programs/Microsoft Press/Microsoft Office System 2003 Step by Step*.
OPEN the *Formats.xls* document.

1   If necessary, click the **January** sheet tab.

2   Click cell E2.

      Cell E2 is highlighted.

3   On the Formatting toolbar, click the **Font Size** down arrow and, from the list that appears, click **14**.

      The text in cell E2 changes to 14-point type, and row 2 expands vertically to accommodate the text.

Bold

4   On the Formatting toolbar, click the **Bold** button.

      The text in cell E2 appears bold.

5   Click the row head for row 5.

      Row 5 is highlighted.

Center

6   On the Formatting toolbar, click the **Center** button.

      The contents of the cells in row 5 are centered.

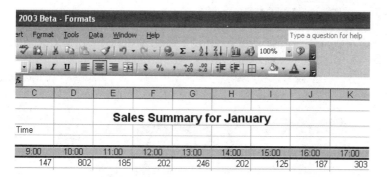

7   Click cell E2.

Cell E2 is highlighted.

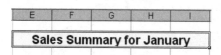
Borders

8   On the Formatting toolbar, click the down arrow at the right of the **Borders** button and then, from the list that appears, click **Draw Borders**.

The Borders toolbar appears, and the mouse pointer changes to a pencil.

9   Click the left edge of cell E2 and drag to the right edge.

A border appears around cell E2.

10   On the **Borders** toolbar, click the **Close** button.

The Borders toolbar disappears.

Fill Color

11   On the Formatting toolbar, click the **Fill Color** down arrow.

The Fill Color color palette appears.

12   In the **Fill Color** color palette, click the yellow square.

Cell G2 fills with a yellow background.

E	F	G	H	I
Sales Summary for January				

13   On the **Tools** menu, click **Options**.

The Options dialog box appears.

14   If necessary, click the **General** tab. Click the **Standard Font** down arrow and select **Courier New**.

15   Click the **Size** down arrow, select **9**, and click **OK**.

16   Click **OK** to clear the dialog box that appears.

Save

17   On the Standard toolbar, click the **Save** button.

Excel saves your changes.

CLOSE the *Formats.xls* document.

Applying an Existing Format to Data

As you work with Excel, you will probably develop preferred formats for data labels, titles, and other worksheet elements. Rather than add the format's characteristics one element at a time to the target cells, you can have Excel store the format and recall it as needed. You can find the predefined formats available to you in the Style dialog box.

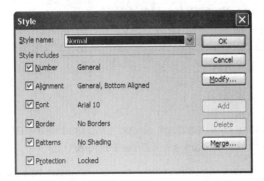

You can apply an existing style to a cell from within the Style dialog box. If none of the existing styles are what you want, you can create your own by typing the name of your new style in the Style name box and then clicking Modify. The Format Cells dialog box appears.

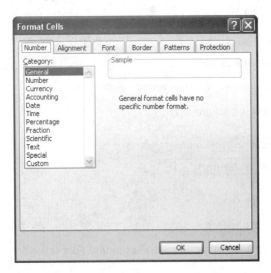

Once you've set the characteristics of your new style, click OK to make your style available permanently.

The Style dialog box is quite versatile, but it's overkill if all you want to do is apply formatting changes you made to a cell to the contents of another cell. To do so, you can use the Standard toolbar's Format Painter button; just click the cell with the format you want to copy, click the Format Painter button, and select the target cells.

Of course, if you want to change the formatting of an entire worksheet, the Format Painter and the Style dialog box are not the most efficient tools available to you. Instead, Excel lets you apply *AutoFormats*, which are pre-defined format patterns for a group of cells (as opposed to styles, which are pre-defined formats for individual cells). To apply an AutoFormat, you select the cells you want to format and click AutoFormat on the Format menu. In the AutoFormat dialog box, select the AutoFormat you want to apply and click OK.

In this exercise, you create a style, apply the new style to a data label, and then use the Format Painter to apply the style to the contents of another cell. Finally you assign an AutoFormat.

USE the *CreateNew.xls* document in the practice file folder for this topic. This practice file is located in the *My Documents\Microsoft Press\Office 2003 SBS\ChangingDocAppearance* folder, and can also be accessed by clicking *Start/All Programs/Microsoft Press/Microsoft Office System 2003 Step by Step.*
OPEN the *CreateNew.xls* document.

1　If necessary, click the **January** sheet tab.

2　Click cell C3.

3　On the **Format** menu, click **Style**.

　　The Style dialog box appears, with *Normal* in the Style name box.

4　In the **Style name** box, delete the existing value and then type **Emphasis**.

　　The Add button is activated.

5　Click **Modify**.

　　The Format Cells dialog box appears.

6　If necessary, click the **Font** tab.

　　The Font tab page appears.

7　In the **Font style** box, click **Bold Italic**.

　　The text in the Preview pane, in the lower-right corner of the dialog box, changes to reflect your choice.

8　Click the **Alignment** tab.

　　The Alignment tab page appears.

9   In the **Horizontal** box, click the down arrow and, from the list that appears, click **Center**.

10 Click **OK**.

The Format Cells dialog box disappears.

11 Click **OK**.

The Style dialog box disappears, and the text in cell C3 takes on the chosen style.

Format Painter

12 On the Standard toolbar, click the **Format Painter** button.

The mouse pointer changes to a white cross with a paintbrush icon next to it.

13 Click cell B5.

Cell B5 takes on the format of cell C3.

Microsoft Office Excel 2003 - CreateNew				
File Edit View Insert Format Tools Data Window				
Arial	10	**B** *I* U		
B5		*fx* Day		
A	B	C	D	E
1				
2				**Sale**
3		*Time*		
4				
5	*Day*	9:00	10:00	11:00
6	1 Mon	147	802	185

14 Select cells A3 to P38.

15 On the **Format** menu, click **AutoFormat**.

The AutoFormat dialog box appears.

16 Scroll the list, click the **List 3** AutoFormat, and click **OK**.

The AutoFormat dialog box disappears, and the cells take on the selected AutoFormat.

Save

17 On the Standard toolbar, click the **Save** button.

Excel saves your changes.

CLOSE the *CreateNew.xls* document.

Making Numbers Easier to Read

Changing the format of the cells in your worksheet can make your data much easier to read, both by setting data labels apart from the actual data and by adding borders to define the boundaries between labels and data even more clearly. Of course, using formatting options to change the font and appearance of a cell's contents doesn't help with idiosyncratic data types such as dates, phone numbers, or currency.

For example, consider U.S. phone numbers. These numbers are 10 digits long and have a three-digit area code, a three-digit exchange, and a four-digit line number written in the form *(###) ###-####*. While it's certainly possible to type a phone number with the expected formatting in a cell, it's much simpler to type a sequence of 10 digits and have Excel change the data's appearance.

You can tell Excel to expect a phone number in a cell by opening the Format Cells dialog box to the Number tab and displaying the formats available under the Special category.

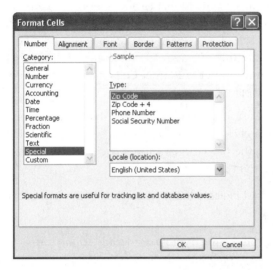

Clicking Phone Number from the Type list tells Excel to format 10-digit numbers in the standard phone number format. As you can see by comparing the contents of the active cell and the contents of the formula bar in the next graphic, the underlying data isn't changed, just its appearance in the cell.

Troubleshooting   If you type a nine-digit number in a field that expects a phone number, you won't see an error message; instead, you'll see a two-digit area code. For example, the number *4255550122* would be displayed as *(425) 555-0122*. An 11-digit number would be displayed with a four-digit area code.

Just as you can instruct Excel to expect a phone number in a cell, you can also have it expect a date or a currency amount. You can make those changes from the Format Cells dialog box by choosing either the Date category or the Currency category. The Date category lets you pick the format for the date (and determine whether the date's appearance changes due to the Locale setting of the operating system on the computer viewing the workbook). In a similar vein, selecting the Currency category displays controls to set the number of places after the decimal point, the currency symbol to use, and the way in which Excel should display negative numbers.

You can also create a custom numeric format to add a word or phrase to a number in a cell. For example, you can add the phrase *per month* to a cell with a formula that calculates average monthly sales for a year to ensure that you and your colleagues will recognize the figure as a monthly average. To create a custom number format, click Cells on the Format menu to open the Format Cells dialog box. Then, if necessary, click the Number tab to display the Number tab page.

In the Category list, click Custom to display the available custom number formats in the Type list. You can then click the base format you want and modify it in the Type box. For example, clicking the *0.00* format causes Excel to format any number in a cell with two digits to the right of the decimal point.

Tip The zeros in the format indicate that that position in the format can accept any number as a valid value.

To customize the format, click in the Type box and add to the format any symbols or text you want. For example, typing a dollar sign to the left of the existing format and then typing *"per month"* to the right of the existing format causes the number 1500 to be displayed as *$1500.00 per month*.

Important You need to enclose any text in quotes so that Excel recognizes the text as a string to be displayed in the cell.

In this exercise, you assign date, phone number, and currency formats to ranges of cells in your worksheet. After you assign the formats, you test them by entering customer data.

USE the *EasyRead.xls* document in the practice file folder for this topic. This practice file is located in the *My Documents\Microsoft Press\Office 2003 SBS\ChangingDocAppearance* folder, and can also be accessed by clicking *Start/All Programs/Microsoft Press/Microsoft Office System 2003 Step by Step*.
OPEN the *EasyRead.xls* document.

1 Click cell B4.

2 On the **Format** menu, click **Cells**.

The Format Cells dialog box appears.

3   If necessary, click the **Number** tab.

4   In the **Category** list, click **Date**.

The Type list appears with a list of date formats.

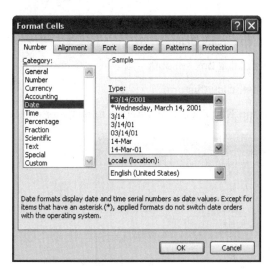

5   In the **Type** list, click ***3/14/01**.

6   Click **OK**.

Excel assigns the chosen format to the cell.

7   On the Standard toolbar, click the **Format Painter** button.

Cell B4 is highlighted with a marquee outline.

Format Painter

8   Click cell B5 and drag to cell B23.

Excel assigns the format from cell B4 to cells B5:B23.

9   Click cell J4.

10   On the **Format** menu, click **Cells**.

The Format Cells dialog box appears.

11   In the **Category** list, click **Special**.

The Type list appears with a list of special formats.

12   In the **Type** list, click **Phone Number** and then click **OK**.

The Format Cells dialog box disappears.

13 On the Standard toolbar, click the **Format Painter** button.

Cell J4 is highlighted with a marquee outline.

14 Click cell J5 and drag to cell J23.

Excel assigns the format from cell J4 to cells J5:J23.

15 Click cell K4.

16 On the **Format** menu, click **Cells**.

The Format Cells dialog box appears.

17 In the **Category** list, click **Custom**.

The contents of the Type list are updated to reflect your choice.

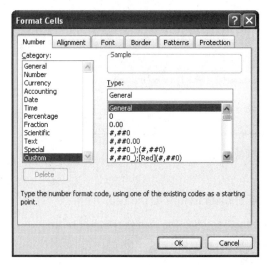

18 In the **Type** list, click the **#,##0.00** item.

#,##0.00 appears in the Type box.

19 In the **Type** box, click to the left of the existing format and type $, and then click to the right of the format and type "total".

20 Click **OK**.

The Format Cells dialog box disappears.

21 On the Standard toolbar, click the **Format Painter** button.

Cell K4 is highlighted with a marquee outline.

22 Click cell K5 and drag to cell K23.

Excel assigns the format from cell K4 to cells K5:K23.

23 In cell B4, type January 25, 2004 and press [Enter].

The contents of cell B4 change to *1/25/04*, matching the format you set earlier.

24 Type the following text in the indicated cells:

Cell	Type this:
C4	C100001
D4	Steven
E4	Levy
F4	6789 Elm Street
G4	Redmond
H4	WA
I4	87063
J4	4255550102
K4	2400

Notice that the phone number and the currency amount change to match the formats that you created earlier.

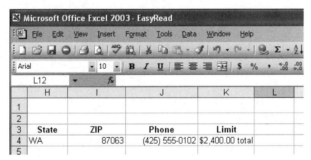

25 On the Standard toolbar, click **Save** to save your changes.

CLOSE the *EasyRead.xls* document.

Changing Data's Appearance Based on Its Value

Recording sales, credit limits, and other business data in a worksheet lets you make important decisions about your operations. And as you saw earlier in this chapter, you can change the appearance of data labels and the worksheet itself to make interpreting your data easier.

Another way you can make your data easier to interpret is to have Excel change the appearance of your data based on its value. These formats are called *conditional formats* because the data must meet certain conditions to have a format applied to it. For instance, if owner Catherine Turner wanted to highlight any Saturdays on which daily sales at The Garden Company were over $4,000, she could define a conditional format that tests the value in the cell recording total sales, and that will change the format of the cell's contents when the condition is met.

To create a conditional format, you click the cells to which you want to apply the format, open the Format menu, and click Conditional Formatting to open the Conditional Formatting dialog box. The default configuration of the Conditional Formatting dialog box appears in the following graphic.

The first list box lets you choose whether you want the condition that follows to look at the cell's contents or the formula in the cell. In almost every circumstance, you will use the contents of the cell as the test value for the condition.

Tip   The only time you would want to set a formula as the basis for the condition would be to format a certain result, such as a grand total, the same way every time it appeared in a worksheet.

The second list box in the Conditional Formatting dialog box lets you select the comparison to be made. Depending on the comparison you choose, the dialog box will have either one or two boxes in which you enter values to be used in the comparison. The default comparison *between* requires two values, whereas comparisons such as *less than* require one.

After you have created a condition, you need to define the format to be applied to data that meets that condition. You do that in the Format Cells dialog box. From within this dialog box, you can set the characteristics of the text used to print the value in the cell. When you're done, a preview of the format you defined appears in the Conditional Formatting dialog box.

You're not limited to creating one condition per cell. If you like, you can create additional conditions by clicking the Add button in the Conditional Formatting dialog box. When you click the Add button, a second condition section appears.

Important   Excel doesn't check to make sure your conditions are logically consistent, so you need to be sure you enter your conditions correctly.

Excel evaluates the conditions in the order you entered them in the Conditional Formatting dialog box and, upon finding a condition the data meets, stops its comparisons. For example, suppose Catherine wanted to visually separate the credit limits of The Garden Company's customers into two different categories: those with limits under $1,500 and those with limits from $1,500 to $2,500. She could display her customers' credit limits with a conditional format using the conditions in the following graphic.

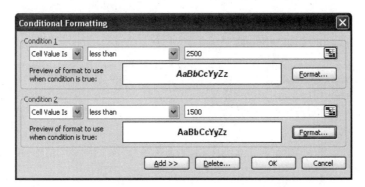

In this case, Excel would compare the value *1250* with the first condition, *<2500*, and assign that formatting to the cell containing the value. That the second condition, *<1500*, is "closer" is irrelevant—once Excel finds a condition the data meets, it stops comparing.

Tip   You should always enter the most restrictive condition first. In the preceding example, setting the first condition to *<1500* and the second to *<2500* would result in the proper format.

In this exercise, you create a series of conditional formats to change the appearance of data in worksheet cells displaying the credit limit of The Garden Company's customers.

USE the *Conditional.xls* document in the practice file folder for this topic. This practice file is located in the *My Documents\Microsoft Press\Office 2003 SBS\ChangingDocAppeance* folder, and can also be accessed by clicking *Start/All Programs/Microsoft Press/Microsoft Office System 2003 Step by Step*.
OPEN the *Conditional.xls* document.

1   If necessary, click cell K4.

2   On the **Format** menu, click **Conditional Formatting**.

The Conditional Formatting dialog box appears.

3   In the second list box, click the down arrow and then, from the list that appears, click **between**.

The word *between* appears in the second list box.

4   In the first argument box, type **1000**.

5   In the second argument box, type **2000**.

6   Click the **Format** button.

The Format Cells dialog box appears.

7   If necessary, click the **Font** tab.

The Font tab page appears.

8   In the **Color** box, click the down arrow and then, from the color palette that appears, click the blue square.

The color palette disappears, and the text in the Preview pane changes to blue.

9   Click **OK**.

The Format Cells dialog box disappears.

10   Click the **Add** button.

The Condition 2 section of the dialog box appears.

11   In the second list box, click the down arrow and then, from the list that appears, click **between**.

The word *between* appears in the second list box.

12   In the first argument box, type **2000**.

13   In the second argument box, type **2500**.

14   Click the **Format** button.

The Format Cells dialog box appears.

15   In the **Color** box, click the down arrow and then, from the color palette that appears, click the green square.

The color palette disappears, and the text in the Preview pane changes to green.

16   Click **OK**.

The Format Cells dialog box disappears.

17   Click **OK**.

The Conditional Formatting dialog box disappears.

18   In cell K4, click the fill handle, and drag it to cell K6.

The contents of cells K5 and K6 change to *$2,400.00*, and the Auto Fill Options button appears.

Auto Fill
Options

19   Click the **Auto Fill Options** button, and from the list that appears, click **Fill Formatting Only**.

The contents of cells K5 and K6 revert to their previous values, and Excel applies the conditional formats to the selected cells.

ZIP	Phone	Limit
98073	(425) 555-1002	$2,400.00
98073	(425) 555-1098	$750.00
98073	(425) 555-1287	$1,500.00

20   On the Standard toolbar, click the **Save** toolbar button to save your changes.

CLOSE the *Conditional.xls* document.

Making Printouts Easier to Follow

Changing how your data appears in the body of your worksheets can make your data much easier to understand, but it doesn't communicate when the worksheet was last opened or whom it belongs to. You could always add that information to the top of every printed page, but you would need to change the current date every time you opened the document; and if you wanted the same information to appear at the top of every printed page, any changes to the body of your worksheets could mean you would need to edit your workbook so that the information appeared in the proper place.

If you want to ensure that the same information appears at the top or bottom of every printed page, you can do so using headers or footers. A header is a section that appears at the top of every printed page, while a footer is a section that appears at the bottom of every printed page. To create a header or footer in Excel, you open the Page Setup dialog box to the Header/Footer tab.

Important   Everything you will learn about creating headers in this section applies to creating footers as well. Also, you can have both headers and footers in the same document.

The list boxes on the Header/Footer tab page will hold a number of standard headers and footers, such as page numbers by themselves or followed by the name of the workbook. You can create your own headers by opening the Header dialog box.

In the Header dialog box, you can add your own text or use the box's buttons to change the appearance of the text in the header or to insert a date, time, or page number. Beginning with Excel 2002, you have had the option of adding a graphic to a header or footer. Adding a graphic such as a company logo to a worksheet lets you identify the worksheet as referring to your company and helps reinforce your company's identity if you include the worksheet in a printed report distributed outside your company. After you insert a graphic into a header or footer, the Format Picture button will become available. Clicking that button will open a dialog box with tools to edit your graphic.

In this exercise, you create a custom header and a custom footer for a workbook. You add a graphic to the footer and then edit the graphic using the Format Picture dialog box.

USE the *Follow.xls* document in the practice file folder for this topic. This practice file is located in the *My Documents\Microsoft Press\Office 2003 SBS\ChangingDocAppearance* folder, and can also be accessed by clicking *Start/All Programs/Microsoft Press/Microsoft Office System 2003 Step by Step*.
OPEN the *Follow.xls* document.

1 On the **View** menu, click **Header and Footer**.

The Page Setup dialog box appears, opened to the Header/Footer tab page.

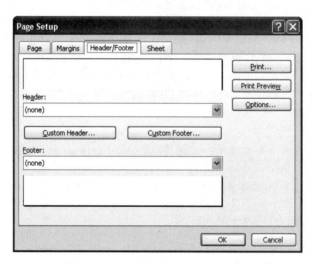

2 Click the **Custom Footer** button.

The Footer dialog box appears.

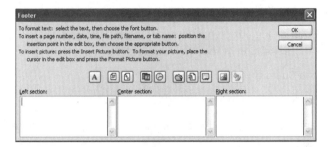

Insert Picture

3   Click anywhere in the **Center section** box, and then click the **Insert Picture** button.

The Insert Picture dialog box appears.

4   Navigate to the ChangingDocAppearance folder, and then double-click the *tgc_logo.gif* file.

The Insert Picture dialog box disappears, and *&[Picture]* appears in the Center section box.

Format Picture

5   Click the **Format Picture** button.

The Format Picture dialog box appears.

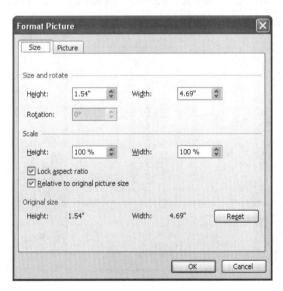

6   If necessary, select the **Lock aspect ratio** check box.

7   In the **Height** box, type 50% and then click **OK**.

The Format Picture dialog box disappears.

8   In the **Footer** dialog box, click **OK**.

The Footer dialog box disappears, and part of the graphic you added appears in the footer section of the Page Setup dialog box.

9   Click the **Custom Header** button.

The Header dialog box appears.

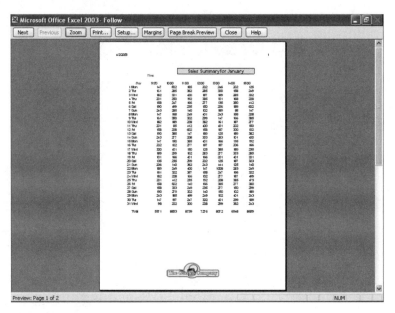

10   Click anywhere in the **Left section** box, and then click the **Date** button.

&[Date] appears in the Left section box.

Date

11   Click anywhere in the **Right section** box, and then click the **Page Number** button.

&[Page] appears in the Right section box.

Page Number

12   Click **OK**.

The Header dialog box disappears.

13   Click the **Print Preview** button.

The Print Preview window appears.

14   Click **Close**.

The Print Preview window and the **Page Setup** dialog box disappear.

15   Click cell E2.

16 On the **Edit** menu, point to **Clear**, and then click **All**.

The contents of the merged cell disappear, and the cells are unmerged.

Save

17 On the Standard toolbar, click the **Save** button to save your changes.

CLOSE the *Follow.xls* document.

Positioning Data on a Printout

Once you have your data and any headers or footers in your workbook, you can change your workbook's properties to ensure that your worksheets display all of your information and that printing is centered on the page.

One of the workbook properties you can change is its margins, or the boundaries between different sections of the printed page. You can view a document's margins and where the contents of the header, footer, and body appear in relation to those margins in the Print Preview window.

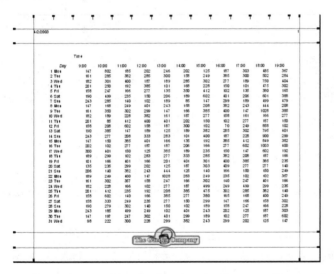

In the above graphic, the logo in the footer spills over the top margin of the footer. To remove the overlap, you can move the footer's top margin up, increasing the amount of space devoted to the footer. Increasing the size of the footer reduces the size of the worksheet body, meaning fewer rows can be printed on a page.

Another issue with printing worksheets is that the data in worksheets tends to be wider horizontally than a standard sheet of paper. For example, the data in the worksheet in the previous graphic is several columns wider than a standard piece of paper. You can use the controls in the Page Setup dialog box to change the alignment of the rows and columns on the page. When the columns follow the long edge of a piece of paper, the page is laid out in *portrait mode*; when the columns follow the short edge of a piece of paper, it is in *landscape mode*. The following graphic displays the contents of the previous worksheet laid out in landscape mode.

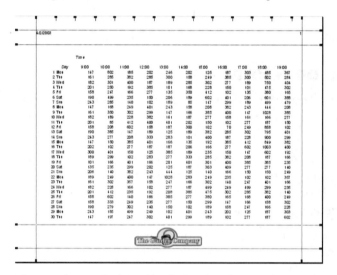

This is a better fit, but not all the data fits on the printed page. Once again, the Page Setup dialog box comes to the rescue. From within that dialog box, you can have Excel reduce the size of the worksheet's contents until the entire worksheet can be printed on a single page and also have Excel center the printed matter on the page so that there is an even margin around the printing.

In this exercise, you change the margins in a workbook to stop the graphic in the footer from overlapping with the data in the body of the worksheet. You then change the alignment of the workbook so that its contents are laid out in landscape mode and centered on the printed page.

USE the *Margins.xls* document in the practice file folder for this topic. This practice file is located in the *My Documents\Microsoft Press\Office 2003 SBS\ChangingDocAppearance* folder, and can also be accessed by clicking *Start/All Programs/Microsoft Press/Microsoft Office System 2003 Step by Step*.
OPEN the *Margins.xls* document.

Print Preview

1 On the Standard toolbar, click the **Print Preview** button.

The Print Preview window opens.

2   Click **Margins**.

Margin lines appear.

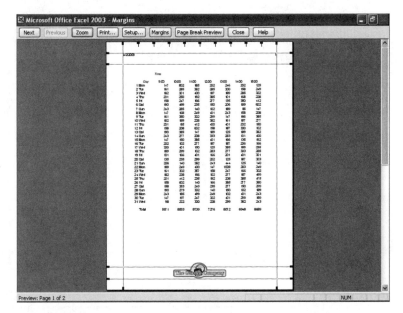

3   Drag the second margin line from the bottom of the page up until it clears the graphic.

The top edge of the footer moves above the graphic.

4   Click **Setup**.

The Page Setup dialog box appears.

5   If necessary, click the **Page** tab.

6   Select the **Landscape** option button.

7   Select the **Fit to** option button and set to 1 page wide by 1 page tall.

8   Click the **Margins** tab.

The Margins tab page appears.

9   In the **Center on page** section of the tab page, select both the **Horizontally** check box and the **Vertically** check box.

10 Click **OK**.

The Page Setup dialog box disappears. The document view in the Print Preview window changes to reflect the new settings.

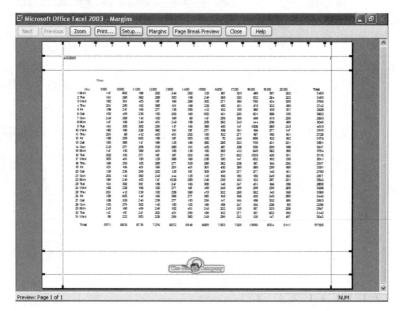

11 Click **Close**.

The Print Preview window disappears.

Save

12 On the Standard toolbar, click the **Save** button to save your changes.

CLOSE the *Margins.xls* document.

Key Points

■ If you don't like the default font in which Excel displays your data, you can change it.

■ You can use cell formatting, including borders, alignment, and fill colors, to emphasize certain cells in your worksheets. This emphasis is particularly useful for making column and row labels stand out from the data.

■ Excel comes with a number of existing styles that let you change the appearance of individual cells.

- If you want to apply the formatting from one cell to another cell, use the Format Painter to copy the format quickly.

- There are quite a few AutoFormats you can apply to groups of cells. If you see one you like, use it and save yourself lots of formatting time.

- Conditional formats let you set rules so that Excel will change the appearance of a cell's contents based on its value.

- Pay careful attention to how your worksheets appear when printed. Use header, footer, graphic, alignment, and margin settings to make your data look great on the page.

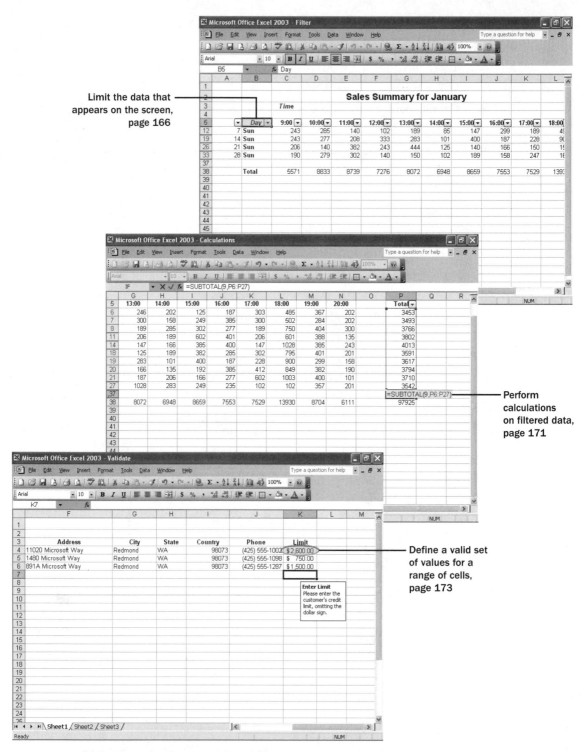

Limit the data that appears on the screen, page 166

Perform calculations on filtered data, page 171

Define a valid set of values for a range of cells, page 173

Chapter 8 at a Glance

8 Focusing on Specific Data Using Filters

In this chapter you will learn to:
✔   Limit the data that appears on the screen.
✔   Perform calculations on filtered data.
✔   Define a valid set of values for a range of cells.

An important aspect of working with large amounts of data is the ability to zero in on the most important data in a worksheet, whether that data represents the best 10 days of sales in a month or slow-selling product lines that you might need to reevaluate. In Microsoft Office Excel 2003, you have a number of powerful, flexible tools with which you can limit the data displayed in your worksheet. Once your worksheet displays the subset of the data you need to make a decision, you can perform calculations on that data. You can discover what percentage of monthly sales were made up by the 10 best days in the month, find your total sales for particular days of the week, or locate the slowest business day of the month.

Just as you can limit the data displayed by your worksheets, you can limit the data entered into them as well. Setting rules for data entered into cells lets you catch many of the most common data entry errors, such as entering values that are too small or too large, or attempting to enter a word in a cell that requires a number. Should you add a validation rule to worksheet cells after data has been entered into them, you can circle any invalid data so that you know what to correct.

In this chapter, you'll learn how to limit the data that appears in your worksheets, perform calculations on the remaining data, and limit the data that can be entered into specific cells.

See Also   Do you need only a quick refresher on the topics in this chapter? See the quick reference entries on page xxxiii.

 Important   Before you can use the practice files in this chapter, you need to install them from the book's companion CD to their default location. See "Using the Book's CD-ROM" on page xxi for more information.

Limiting the Data That Appears on the Screen

Excel spreadsheets can hold as much data as you need them to, but you might not want to work with all of the data in a worksheet at the same time. For example, you might want to see the sales figures for your company during the first third, second third, and final third of a month. You can limit the data shown in a worksheet by creating a *filter*, which is a rule that selects rows to be shown in a worksheet.

To create a filter, you click the cell in the group you want to filter and use the Data menu to turn on *AutoFilter*. When you turn on AutoFilter, which is a built-in set of filtering capabilities, a down arrow button appears in the cell that Excel recognizes as the column's label.

Important When you turn on filtering, Excel treats the cells in the active cell's column as a range. To ensure that the filtering works properly, you should always add a label to the column you want to filter.

Clicking the down arrow displays a list of values and options. The first few items in the list are filtering options, such as whether you want to display the top 10 values in the column, create a custom filter, or display all values in the column (that is, remove the filter). The rest of the items in the list are the unique values in the column—clicking one of those values displays the row or rows containing that value.

Choosing the Top 10 option from the list doesn't just limit the display to the top 10 values. Instead, it opens the Top 10 AutoFilter dialog box. From within this dialog box, you can choose whether to show values from the top or bottom of the list, define the number of items you want to see, and choose whether the number in the middle box indicates the number of items or the percentage of items to be shown when the filter is applied. Using the Top 10 AutoFilter dialog box, you can find your top 10 salespeople or identify the top five percent of your customers.

When you choose Custom from the AutoFilter list, you can define a rule that Excel uses to decide which rows to show after the filter is applied. For instance, you can create a rule that only days with total sales of less than $2,500 should be shown in your worksheet. With those results in front of you, you might be able to determine whether the weather or another factor resulted in slower business on those days.

Two related things you can do in Excel are to choose rows at random from a list and to display the unique values in a column in the worksheet (not in the down arrow's list, which you can't normally work with). Generating a list of unique values in a column can give you important information, such as from which states you have customers or which categories of products sold in an hour.

Selecting rows randomly is useful for selecting customers to receive a special offer, deciding which days of the month to audit, or picking prize winners at an employee party. To choose rows, you can use the RAND function, which generates a random value between 0 and 1 and compares it with a test value included in the statement. A statement that returns a TRUE value 30 percent of the time would be *RAND()<=30%*; that is, whenever the random value was between 0 and .3, the result would be TRUE. You could use this statement to select each row in a list with a probability of 30 percent.

In this exercise, you create a filter to show the top five sales days in January, show sales figures for Mondays during the same month, display the days with sales of at least $3,000, pick random days from the month to audit, and then generate a list of unique values in one of the worksheet's columns.

USE the *Filter.xls* document in the practice file folder for this topic. This practice file is located in the *My Documents\Microsoft Press\Office 2003 SBS\UsingFilters* folder, and can also be accessed by clicking *Start/All Programs/Microsoft Press/Microsoft Office System 2003 Step by Step*.
OPEN the *Filter.xls* document.

1   If necessary, click the **January** sheet tab.

2   Click cell P5.

3   On the **Data** menu, point to **Filter**, and then click **AutoFilter**.

A down arrow appears in cell P5.

4   In cell P5, click the down arrow and, from the list that appears, click (**Top 10...**).

The Top 10 AutoFilter dialog box appears.

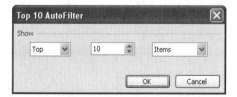

5   Click in the middle box, delete *10*, type 5, and click **OK**.

Only the rows containing the five largest values in column P are shown.

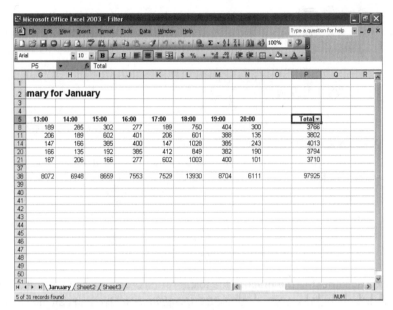

6   On the **Data** menu, point to **Filter**, and then click **AutoFilter**.

The filtered rows reappear.

7   Click cell B5.

8   On the **Data** menu, point to **Filter**, and then click **AutoFilter**.

A down arrow appears in cell B5.

9   In cell B5, click the down arrow and, from the list of unique column values that appears, click **Mon**.

Only rows with *Mon* in column B are shown in the worksheet.

10   On the **Data** menu, point to **Filter**, and then click **AutoFilter**.

The filtered rows reappear.

11   Click cell P5, and then, on the **Data** menu, point to **Filter**, and then click **AutoFilter**.

A down arrow appears in cell P5.

12   In cell P5, click the down arrow and then, from the list that appears, click (**Custom...**).

The Custom AutoFilter dialog box appears.

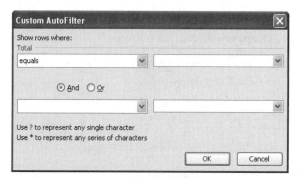

13   In the upper-left box, click the down arrow and, from the list that appears, click **is greater than or equal to**.

14   In the upper-right box, type **3000** and then click **OK**.

Only rows with totals of at least 3000 are shown in the worksheet.

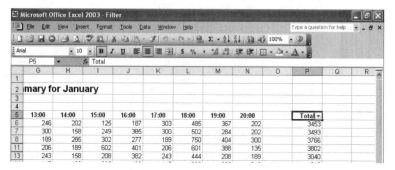

15   On the **Data** menu, point to **Filter**, and then click **AutoFilter**.

The filtered rows reappear.

16   On the **Data** menu, point to **Filter**, and then click **AutoFilter**.

A down arrow appears in cell P5.

17   In cell P5, click the down arrow and then, from the list of unique column values that appears, click **2236**.

All rows except the row containing *2236* in column P disappear.

18   On the **Data** menu, point to **Filter**, and then click **AutoFilter**.

The filtered rows reappear.

19   In cell Q5, type **Audit**.

20   In cell Q6, type **=RAND()<17%**.

If the result of the RAND function is less than *17%*, cell Q6 will display *TRUE*; otherwise, cell Q6 will display *FALSE*.

21   Drag the **AutoFill** handle from cell Q6 to cell Q36.

TRUE and *FALSE* values appear in the cells from Q6 to Q36 with a frequency of approximately 16 percent and 84 percent, respectively.

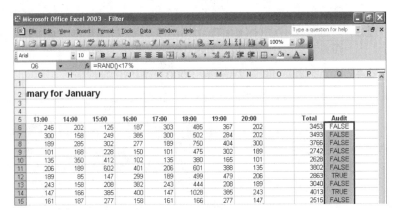

22   On the **Data** menu, point to **Filter**, and then click **Advanced Filter**.

The Advanced Filter dialog box appears.

23   Clear the **List Range** box, and then click cell B5 and drag to cell B36.

$B$5:$B$36 appears in the List Range box.

24   Select the **Unique records only** check box, and then click **OK**.

Rows with the first occurrence of a value are displayed in the worksheet.

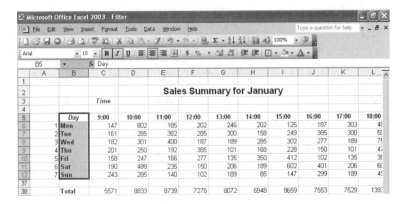

25   On the **Data** menu, point to **Filter**, and then click **Show All**.

The filtered rows reappear.

Save

26   On the **Standard** toolbar, click the **Save** button.

Excel saves your changes.

CLOSE the *Filter.xls* document.

Performing Calculations on Filtered Data

When you filter your worksheet, you limit the data that appears. The ability to focus on the data that's most vital to your current needs is important, but there are a few limitations. One limitation is that any formulas you have created don't change their calculations, even if some of the rows used in the formula are hidden by the filter.

There are two ways you can find the total of a group of filtered cells. The first method is to use AutoCalculate. To use AutoCalculate, you select the cells you want to find the total for. When you do, the total for the cells appears on the status bar, at the lower edge of the Excel window.

When you use AutoCalculate, you aren't limited to finding the sum of the selected cells. To display the other functions you can use, you right-click the AutoCalculate pane and select the function you want from the shortcut menu that appears.

AutoCalculate is great for finding a quick total or average for filtered cells, but it doesn't make the result available in the worksheet. To make the value available in your worksheet, you can create a SUBTOTAL function. As with AutoCalculate, you can choose the type of calculation the function performs.

In this exercise, you use AutoCalculate to find the total of a group of cells in a filtered worksheet, create a SUBTOTAL function to make the same value available in the worksheet, and then edit the SUBTOTAL function so that it calculates an average instead of a sum.

USE the *Calculations.xls* document in the practice file folder for this topic. This practice file is located in the *My Documents\Microsoft Press\Office 2003 SBS\UsingFilters* folder, and can also be accessed by clicking *Start/All Programs/Microsoft Press/Microsoft Office System 2003 Step by Step*.
OPEN the *Calculations.xls* document.

1   If necessary, click the **January** sheet tab.

2   Click cell P5.

3   On the **Data** menu, point to **Filter**, and then click **AutoFilter**.

A down arrow button appears in cell P5.

4   In cell P5, click the down arrow button and then, from the list that appears, click (**Top 10...**).

The Top 10 AutoFilter dialog box appears.

5   Click **OK**.

Tip   Clicking OK here accepts the default setting of the Top 10 AutoFilter dialog box, which is to show the top 10 values in the selected cells.

The **Top 10 AutoFilter** dialog box disappears, and the rows with the 10 highest values in column P are displayed.

6   Click cell P6 and drag to cell P27.

The cells are selected, and on the status bar, in the lower right corner of the Excel window, *SUM=36781* appears in the AutoCalculate pane.

7   Click cell P37, and then, on the **Standard** toolbar, click the **AutoSum** button.

Σ
AutoSum

The formula *=SUBTOTAL(9,P6:P36)* appears in the formula bar.

8   Press ⌈Enter⌉.

The value *36781* appears in cell P37. The value in cell P38 also changes to *134706*, but that calculation includes the subtotal of the filtered cells in the column.

9   Click cell P37, and then, in the formula bar, edit the formula so that it reads *=SUBTOTAL(1,P6:P36)* and then press ⌈Enter⌉.

By changing the 9 to a 1 in the SUBTOTAL function, the function now calculates an average instead of a sum. The average of the top 10 values in cells P6 through P36, *3678.1* appears in cell P37. The value in cell P38 also changes to *101603.1*, but that calculation includes the average of the filtered cells in the column.

10   If necessary, click cell P37 and then press ⌈Del⌉.

Excel deletes the SUBTOTAL formula from cell P37, and the total in cell P38 changes to *97925*.

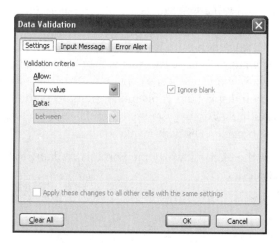
Save

11   On the Standard toolbar, click the **Save** button.

Excel saves your changes.

CLOSE the *Calculations.xls* document.

Defining a Valid Set of Values for a Range of Cells

Part of creating efficient and easy-to-use worksheets is to do what you can to ensure that the data entered into your worksheets is as accurate as possible. While it isn't possible to catch every typographical or transcription error, you can set up a validation rule to make sure the data entered into a cell meets certain standards.

To create a validation rule, you open the Data Validation dialog box.

You can use the Data Validation dialog box to define the type of data that Excel should allow in the cell and then, depending on the data type you choose, to set the conditions data must meet to be accepted in the cell. In the following graphic, Excel knows to look for a whole number value between 1000 and 2000.

Setting accurate validation rules can help you and your colleagues avoid entering a customer's name in the cell designated to hold their phone number or setting a credit limit above a certain level. To require a user to enter a numeric value in a cell, display the Settings page of the Data Validation dialog box, click the Allow down arrow, and depending on your needs, choose either Whole number or Decimal from the list that appears.

If you want to set the same validation rule for a group of cells, you can do so by selecting the cells to which you want to apply the rule (such as a column where you enter the credit limit of customers of The Garden Company) and setting the rule using the Data Validation dialog box. One important fact you should keep in mind is that Excel lets you create validation rules for cells where you have already entered data. Excel doesn't tell you if any cells have data that violate your rule, but you can find out by having Excel circle any worksheet cells containing data that violates the cell's validation rule. To do so, you display the Tools menu, point to Formula Auditing, and click Show Formula Auditing Toolbar. On the Formula Auditing toolbar, click the Circle Invalid Data button to circle cells with invalid data.

When you're ready to hide the circles, display the Formula Auditing toolbar and click the Clear Validation Circles button.

Of course, it's frustrating if you want to enter data into a cell and, when a message box appears, telling you the data you tried to enter isn't acceptable, you aren't given the rules you need to follow. Excel lets you create messages that tell the user what values are expected before the data is entered and then, if the conditions aren't met, reiterate the conditions in a custom error message.

You can turn off data validation in a cell by displaying the Settings page of the Data Validation dialog box and clicking the Clear All button in the lower left corner of the dialog box.

In this exercise, you create a data validation rule limiting the credit line of The Garden Company customers to $2,500, add an input message mentioning the limitation, and then create an error message should someone enter a value greater than $2,500. After you've created your rule and messages, you test them.

USE the *Validate.xls* document in the practice file folder for this topic. This practice file is located in the *My Documents\Microsoft Press\Office 2003 SBS\UsingFilters* folder, and can also be accessed by clicking *Start/All Programs/Microsoft Press/Microsoft Office System 2003 Step by Step*.
OPEN the *Validate.xls* document.

1   Select cells K4 through K7.

2   On the **Data** menu, click **Validation**.

The Data Validation dialog box appears with the Settings tab page in front.

3   In the **Allow** box, click the down arrow and, from the list that appears, click **Whole Number**.

Boxes labeled Minimum and Maximum appear below the Data box.

4   In the **Data** box, click the down arrow and, from the list that appears, click **less than or equal to**.

The Minimum box disappears.

5   In the **Maximum** box, type 2500.

6   Clear the **Ignore blank** check box.

7   Click the **Input Message** tab.

The Input Message tab page appears.

8   In the **Title** box, type Enter Limit.

9   In the **Input Message** box, type Please enter the customer's credit limit, omitting the dollar sign.

10   Click the **Error Alert** tab page.

      The Error Alert tab page appears.

11   In the **Style** box, click the down arrow and, from the list that appears, choose **Stop**.

      The icon that will appear in your message box changes to the **Stop** icon.

12   In the **Title** box, type Error, and then click **OK**.

13   Click cell K7.

      A ScreenTip with the title *Enter Limit* and the text *Please enter the customer's credit limit, omitting the dollar sign* appears near cell K7.

14   Type 2501, and press Enter.

      A stop box with the title Error and default text appears.

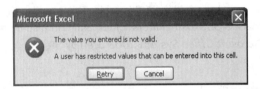

Tip   Leaving the Error message box blank causes Excel to use its default message: *The value you entered is not valid. A user has restricted values that can be entered into this cell.*

15   Click **Cancel**.

      The error box disappears.

Important   Clicking Retry lets you edit the bad value, while clicking Cancel deletes the entry.

16   Click cell K7.

      Cell K7 becomes the active cell, and the ScreenTip reappears.

17   Type 2500, and press Enter.

      Excel accepts your input.

18   On the **Tools** menu, point to **Formula Auditing**, and click **Show Formula Auditing Toolbar**.

      The Formula Auditing toolbar appears.

Circle
Invalid Data

19   On the **Formula Auditing** toolbar, click the **Circle Invalid Data** button.

A red circle appears around the value in cell K4.

Clear
Validation
Circles

20   On the **Formula Auditing** toolbar, click the **Clear Validation Circles** button.

The red circle around the value in cell K4 disappears.

21   On the **Formula Auditing** toolbar, click the **Close** box.

The Formula Auditing toolbar disappears.

22   On the Standard toolbar, click the **Save** button.

Save

CLOSE the *Validate.xls* document.

Key Points

- A number of filters are defined in Excel—you may find the one you want already in place.

- Filtering an Excel worksheet based on values in a single column is easy to do, but you can create a custom filter to limit your data based on the values in more than one column as well.

- Don't forget that you can get a running total (or average, or any one of several other summary operations) for the values in a group of cells. Just select the cells and look on the status bar: the result will be there.

- Functions aren't set in stone when you create them. You can use the controls in the Function box to edit your functions.

- Use data validation techniques to improve the accuracy of data entered into your worksheets, and to identify data that doesn't meet the guidelines you set.

III
Microsoft Office Access 2003

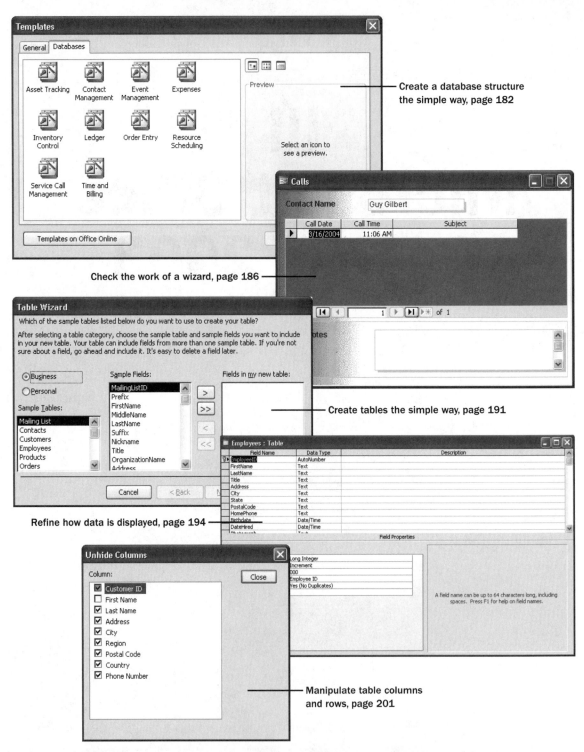

Create a database structure
the simple way, page 182

Check the work of a wizard, page 186

Create tables the simple way, page 191

Refine how data is displayed, page 194

Manipulate table columns
and rows, page 201

Chapter 9 at a Glance

9 Creating a New Database

In this chapter you will learn to:

✔ Create a database structure the simple way.

✔ Check the work of a wizard.

✔ Create tables the simple way.

✔ Refine how data is displayed.

✔ Manipulate table columns and rows.

Creating the structure for a database is easy. But an empty database is no more useful than an empty Microsoft Office Word document or an empty Microsoft Office Excel worksheet. It is only when you fill, or *populate*, a database with data in tables that it starts to serve a purpose. As you add queries, forms, and reports, it becomes easier to use. If you customize it with a switchboard and your tools, it moves into the realm of being a *database application*.

Not every database has to be refined to the point that it can be classified as an application. Databases that only you or a few experienced database users will work with can remain fairly rough-hewn. But if you expect an administrative assistant to enter data or your company's executives to generate their own reports, spending a little extra time in the beginning to create a solid database application will save a lot of work later. Otherwise, you'll find yourself continually repairing damaged files or walking people through seemingly easy tasks.

As a member of The Microsoft Office System 2003, Access 2003 takes a lot of the difficult and mundane work out of creating and customizing a database by providing *wizards* that you can use to create entire databases or individual tables, forms, queries, and other objects. It is generally easier to use a wizard to create something that is similar to what you need and then modify it than it is to create the same thing by hand.

In this chapter, you'll create a couple of databases from scratch, first by using a wizard to rapidly create the structure for a sophisticated contact management database, complete with tables, queries, forms, and reports. After exploring this database and entering a few records to get an idea of what a wizard can provide in the way of a starting point, you will discard this database and start working on a simpler contacts database for The Garden Company. By the end of this chapter, you will have a GardenCo database containing three tables that will serve as the foundation for many of the exercises in this book.

See Also   Do you need only a quick refresher on the topics in this chapter? See the Quick Reference entries on page xxxiii.

Important   Before you can use the practice files in this chapter, you need to install them from the book's companion CD to their default location. See "Using the Book's CD-ROM" on page xxi for more information.

Creating a Database Structure the Simple Way

A few years ago (the distant past in computer time), creating a database structure from scratch involved first analyzing your needs and then laying out the database design on paper. You would decide what information you needed to track and how to store it in the database. Creating the database structure could be a lot of work, and after you had created it and entered data, making changes could be difficult. Wizards have changed this process. Committing yourself to a particular database structure is no longer the big decision it once was. By using the Database Wizard, you can create a dozen database applications in less time than it used to take to sketch the design of one on paper. Access wizards might not create exactly the database application you want, but they can quickly create something very close.

In this exercise, you will use the Database Wizard to create a new database structure. The new database, in this case, will contain the structure for a contact management database.

BE SURE TO start Access before beginning this exercise.

New

1   If the **New File** task pane is not displayed, open it by clicking the **New** button on the Database toolbar.

2   In the **Templates** area of the task pane, click **On my computer,** and then click the **Databases** tab to display the available templates.

Tip　The Database Wizard uses predefined *templates* to create fairly sophisti-cated database applications. In addition to the templates provided with Access, if you are connected to the Internet, you will find additional templates and other resources by following the link to "Templates on Microsoft.com" that is on the New File task pane.

3　Double-click **Contact Management.**

The File New Database dialog box appears so that you can provide a name for your new database and specify where to store it.

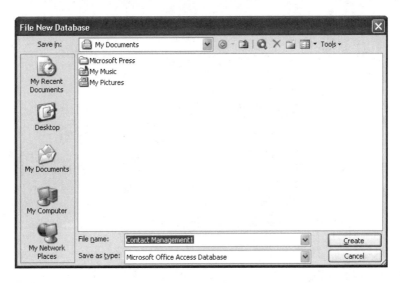

Tip   The default folder for storing Access database files is My Documents. You can change this default to any other folder by clicking Options on the Tools menu when a database file is open, entering a new path in the Default database folder box on the General tab, and clicking OK.

4   Navigate to the *My Documents\Microsoft Press\Office System 2003 SBS\CreateNew* folder, in the **File name** box, replace *Contact Management1* with **Contacts**, and then click **Create**.

Tip   Naming conventions for Access database files follow those for Microsoft Windows files. A file name can contain up to 215 characters including spaces, but creating a file name that long is not recommended. File names cannot contain the following characters: \ / : * ? " < > |. The extension for an Access database file is *.mdb*.

The database window is displayed, and then you see the first page of the Database Wizard, which tells you the type of information that will be stored in this database.

5   This page requires no input from you, so click **Next** to move to the second page of the **Database Wizard**.

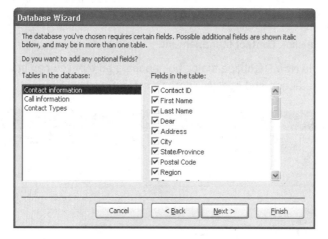

This page lists the three tables that will be included in the Contacts database. The box on the right lists the fields you might want to include in the table selected in the box on the left. Required fields have a check mark in their check boxes. Optional fields are italic. You can select the check box of an optional field to include it in the selected table.

6   Click each table name, and browse through its list of fields, just to see what is available.

7   Indicate that you want to include all the selected fields in the three tables by clicking **Next** to move to the next page of the wizard.

The next page of the wizard appears, displaying a list of predefined styles that determine what the elements of the database will look like.

Tip   Whenever the Back button is active (not gray) at the bottom of a wizard's page, you can click it to move back through previous pages and change your selections. If the Finish button is active, you can click it at any time to tell a wizard to do its job with no further input from you. Most of the options set by a wizard can be modified later, so clicking Finish does not mean that whatever the wizard creates is cast in stone.

8   Click each of the styles to see what they look like.

9   Click **Blends,** and click **Next**.

10   Click each of the report styles to see what they look like.

11   Click **Bold,** and click **Next**.

12   Change the proposed database name to Contacts, leave the **Yes, I'd like to include a picture** check box cleared, and click **Next**.

The Next button is unavailable on this page, indicating that this is the wizard's last page. By default, the "Yes, start the database" check box is selected, and the "Display Help on using a database" check box is cleared.

13   Leave the default settings as they are, and click **Finish**.

The process of creating a database can take from several seconds to several minutes. While the wizard creates the database, an alert box tells you what is happening and how much of the process is complete. When the wizard finishes its work, it opens the newly created Contacts database with the switchboard displayed.

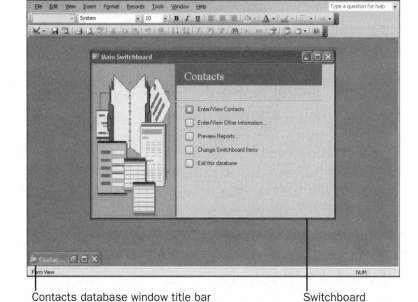

Contacts database window title bar   Switchboard

The switchboard opens, and the Contacts database window is minimized. (You can see its title bar in the lower left corner of the Access window.)

Close

14 At the right end of the Main Switchboard window's title bar, click the **Close** button.

15 At the right end of the Contacts database window title bar, click the **Close** button to close the database.

Checking the Work of a Wizard

Using a wizard to create a database is quick and painless, but just what do you end up with? The Database Wizard creates a database application, complete with a switchboard, several tables, and some other objects. In many cases, all you have to do to have a working database application is add the data. If the wizard's work doesn't quite suit your needs, you can modify any of the database objects or use another type of wizard to add more objects.

For example, if you tell the Database Wizard to create a contact management database, it creates three tables. It doesn't create any queries for this type of database, but it does for some of the other types. It creates forms that you can use to enter or view data, and two reports that you can use to list contacts or summarize the calls made or received during the week. Finally, it creates a switchboard so that users can quickly access the parts of the database needed to perform specific tasks.

In this exercise, you'll use the switchboard to take a quick tour of the Contacts database that the Database Wizard has created. You can't check out some of the objects unless the database contains data, so along the way, you will enter information in several of the tables.

USE the *Contacts* database in the practice file folder for this topic. This practice file is located in the
My Documents\Microsoft Press\Office 2003 SBS\CreateNew\CheckDB folder and can also be accessed
by clicking *Start/All Programs/Microsoft Press/Microsoft Office System 2003 Step by Step*.
OPEN the *Contacts* database and acknowledge the safety warning, if necessary.

1 In the switchboard, click the **Enter/View Other Information** button to display the Forms Switchboard window.

This switchboard has two buttons: the first opens a form you can use to enter or view contact types, and the second returns you to the Main Switchboard window.

2 Click **Enter/View Contact Types** to display the **Contact Types** form.

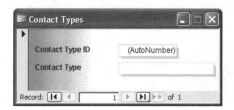

If the underlying Contact Types table contained any records, you could use this form to view them. The only action you can take now is to add a new record.

3 In the **Contact Type** box, type Supplier and press the [Enter] key.

Access supplies the entry for the Contact Type ID field. Access keeps track of this number and enters the next available number in this field whenever you add a new record.

4 Repeat the previous step to enter records for Customer and Shipper.

Close

5 Use the *Navigation buttons* at the bottom of the form to scroll through the records in the **Contact Types** table. Then click the **Close** button to close the form.

Important With most computer programs, *saving* your work often is important to avoid losing it if your computer crashes or the power goes out. With Access, it is not only *not* important to save your data, it is *not possible* to manually save it. When you move the insertion point out of a record after entering or editing information, Access saves that record. This mixed blessing means that you don't have to worry about losing your changes, but you do have to remember that any data entry changes you make are permanent and can be undone only by editing the record again.

6 Click **Return to Main Switchboard.**

7 Click **Enter/View Contacts.**

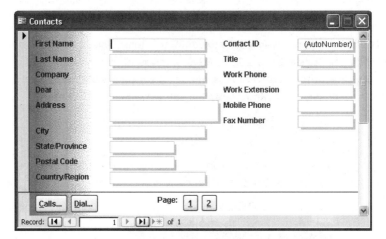

The Contacts form is displayed. You use this two-page form to enter records in the underlying Contacts table or to view records that are already there. The form has buttons at the bottom to switch between pages and to open other forms from which you can place calls (Dial) or where you can record information about communications you've had with the contact (Calls).

8 Enter some information on this form—your own first and last name will do—and notice that when you enter your name, Access provides a contact ID.

9 At the bottom of the form, click the **2** button to move to page 2, and then expand the list of contact types.

The list displays the three types you just entered in the Contact Types table through the Contact Types form.

10 Click one of the contact types.

11 Return to the first page, click in the **Work Phone** box to place the insertion point there, type 555-0100, and press [Enter].

12 Click in the **Work Phone** box again, and click **Dial.**

The AutoDialer dialog box appears, with the contents of the box that is currently selected on the form displayed as a potential number to dial.

Tip   This dialog box is not part of Access; it is a Windows utility. When you click the Dial button, VBA code attached to the button calls the utility. If you were to click Setup, the Windows Phone And Modem Options dialog box would be displayed. (If you don't have a modem installed, the Install New Modem dialog box appears instead.)

13 Click **Cancel** to close the **AutoDialer** dialog box, and then click the **Calls** button.

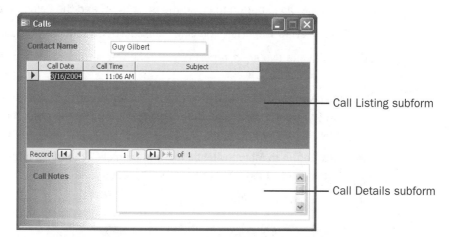
Call Listing subform

Call Details subform

The Calls form is displayed. This form includes the Call Listing subform, which lists any previous calls you have recorded, and the Call Details subform, which displays details of the selected call. You can record information about communications (phone calls, e-mail exchanges, and so on) that you've had with this contact.

14 Click in the **Subject** cell of the new record, and enter Order information as the subject.

Access adds a New Record line, where the Call Date and Call Time fields default to the current date and time.

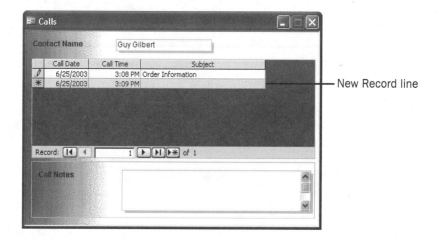
New Record line

15 Click in the **Call Notes** box, and type a short note.

16 Click the **Close** button to close the **Calls** form, and then close the **Contacts** form.

17 Click **Preview Reports** to display the Reports Switchboard window.

18 Preview the two short reports by clicking the button for each one, reading it, and then closing it.

When you preview the Weekly Call Summary report, you can enter a range of dates that you want included on the report. If you accept the default range of the current week, the summary of the call you just added is included in the report.

19 Click **Return to Main Switchboard**, and then click the **Close** button to close the Main Switchboard window without closing the database.

20 Double-click the database window's title bar to restore the window.

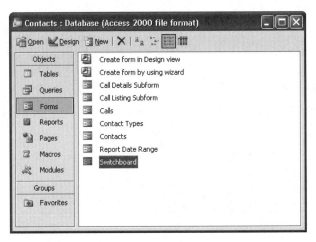

21 Explore all the objects in the database by clicking each type on the **Objects** bar and then opening the individual tables, forms, and reports.

You won't be able to open the Report Date Range form directly, because it is designed to be opened by VBA code that supplies the information that the form needs.

CLOSE the *Contacts* database.

9 Accept **Customers** as the table na
click **Next**.

The wizard suggests *CustomerID* a
and asks what type of data the fie

10 Click **Numbers and/or letters I ent**

The last page of the wizard is disp
option buttons on this page to det
view or in Datasheet view, or whe
you can enter data.

11 Accept the default selection, **Ente**
to create and open the **Customers**

12 Scroll horizontally through the tab
based on your selections on its fi

The Customers table appears in t

13 Start the **Table Wizard** again, this
wizard in the database window.

14 Select the Business option, click
fields to the **Fields in my new tal**
Fields list and clicking the > butt

EmployeeID
FirstName
LastName
Title
Address
City
StateOrProvince
PostalCode
HomePhone
Birthdate
DateHired
Photograph
Notes

Creating Tables the Simple Way

When you use the Database Wizard to create a contact management database, the database has all the *components* needed to store basic information about people. But suppose The Garden Company needs to store different types of information for different types of contacts. For example, it might want to maintain different types of information about employees, customers, and suppliers. In addition to the standard information—such as names, addresses, and phone numbers—the company might want to track these other kinds of information:

- Employee Social Security number, date of hire, marital status, deductions, and pay rate

- Customer order and account status

- Supplier contact, current order status, and discounts

While building the database, you could add a lot of extra fields to the Contacts table and then fill in just the ones it needs for each contact type, but cramming all this information into one table would soon get pretty messy. It's better to create a database with one table for each contact type: employee, customer, and supplier.

The Database Wizard doesn't offer exactly this combination of tables, so in this exercise, you will create a GardenCo database with an empty structure. You will then add several tables to the database by using the Table Wizard.

1 On the toolbar, click the **New** button to display the **New File** task pane.

New

2 In the **New** area of the **New File** task pane, click **Blank database**.

3 Navigate to the *My Documents\Microsoft Press\Office System 2003 SBS\CreateNew \CreateGrdn* folder, in the **File name** box, replace *db1* with **GardenCo**, and then click **Create**.

Access displays a database window that contains no tables, queries, forms, or other database objects. (You can confirm that the database is empty by clicking each of the object types on the Objects bar.)

4 On the database window's toolbar, click the **New** button to display the **New Table** dialog box.

Tip   Instead of clicking the New button, on the Database toolbar, you can click the down arrow to the right of the New Object button, and then click Table; or you can click Tables on the Objects bar, and then double-click "Create table by using wizard"; or you can click Table on the Insert menu, and then double-click Table Wizard.

5 Double-click **Table Wizard**.

The wizard's first page appear[s]
personal tables. Although the
or personal use, depending c
might find the sample table y

6 Take a few minutes to browse
option to see those sample t

Each category contains a list
Tables list, the Sample Field:
(If you need more fields, you c
in the Sample Fields list and
to the "Fields in my new table
the "Fields in my new table" l
your new table list.

7 Select the **Business** option, a

8 Click the **>>** button to copy a
and then click **Next**.

The next page of the wizard
new table and specify wheth
primary key consists of one

Primary

View

Close

Another interesting property is Validation Rule. None of the wizard-generated tables use *validation rules*, because the rules are too specific to the data being entered to anticipate, but let's take a quick look at how they work.

10 Click in the **Validation Rule** box, and enter <Now(). Then click in the **Validation Text** box and type "Date entered must be today or earlier."

A rule is created stating that the date entered must be before (less than) the current instant in time, as determined by the system clock of the computer where the database is stored. If you enter a date in the future, Access will not accept it and will display the validation text in an alert box.

Important   The Format, Input Mask, and Validation Rule properties seem like great ways to be sure that only valid information is entered in your tables. But if you aren't careful, you can make data entry difficult and frustrating. Test your properties carefully before releasing your database for others to use.

11 Click the **View** button to return to Datasheet view, clicking **Yes** when prompted to save the table.

Tip   When you try to switch from Design view to Datasheet view after making changes (and sometimes even if you haven't made any changes), you are presented with an alert box stating that you must save the table. If you click No, you remain in Design view. If you click Yes, Access saves your changes and switches to Datasheet view. If you want to switch views without saving changes that you have made inadvertently, click No, and then click the table's Close button. When Access displays another alert box, click No to close the table without saving any changes.

12 Enter a future date in both the **Birthdate** and **Date Hired** fields.

The Birthdate field, which has no validation rule, accepts any date, but the Date Hired field won't accept a date beyond the one set on your computer.

13 Click **OK** to close the alert box, change the **Date Hired** value to a date in the past, and then click the **Close** button to close the **Employees** table.

14 In the database window, click **Suppliers**, and click the **Design** button to open the table in Design view.

15 Delete the **Country/Region**, **PaymentTerms**, **EmailAddress**, and **Notes** fields by clicking in the row selector and pressing the ⌦ key.

Tip   Access alerts you that deleting the EmailAddress field requires deleting the field and all its indexes. Click Yes. (You will see this alert again in step 17; click Yes each time to delete the fields.)

16　Close the **Suppliers** table, clicking **Yes** to save your changes.

17　Open the **Customers** table in Design view, and delete the following fields: CompanyName, CompanyOrDepartment, ContactTitle, Extension, FaxNumber, EmailAddress, and Notes.

18　Click in the **CustomerID** field, and change the **Field Size** property from 4 to 5.

19　Change the following fields and their captions (note that there is no space in the first two new field names, but there is a space between the words in their captions):

Original field name	New field name	New caption
ContactFirstName	FirstName	First Name
ContactLastName	LastName	Last Name
BillingAddress	Address	Address
StateOrProvince	Region	Region
Country/Region	Country	Country

20　Close the **Customers** table, clicking **Yes** to save it.

CLOSE the *GardenCo* database.

Manipulating Table Columns and Rows

When you refine a table's structure by adding fields and changing field properties in Design view, you are affecting the data that is stored in the table. But sometimes you will want to adjust the table itself to get a better view of the data. If you want to look up a phone number, for example, but the names and phone numbers are several columns apart, you will have to scroll the table window to get the information you need. You might want to rearrange columns or hide a few columns to be able to see the fields you are interested in at the same time.

You can manipulate the columns and rows of an Access table without in any way affecting the underlying data. You can size both rows and columns, and you can also hide, move, and freeze columns. You can save your table formatting so that the table will look the same the next time you open it, or you can discard your table adjustments without saving them.

In this exercise, you will open a table and manipulate its columns and rows. To make the value of table formatting more apparent, you will work with a version of the GardenCo database that has several tables containing many records.

USE the *GardenCo* database in the practice file folder for this topic. This practice file is located in the
My Documents\Microsoft Press\Office 2003 SBS\CreateNew\Manipulate folder and can also be accessed
by clicking *Start/All Programs/Microsoft Press/Microsoft Office System 2003 Step by Step*.
OPEN the *GardenCo* database and acknowledge the safety warning, if necessary.

1   On the **Objects** bar, click **Tables**.

2   Double-click the **Customers** table to open it in Datasheet view.

3   Drag the vertical bar at the right edge of the **Address** column header to the left
until the column is about a half inch wide.

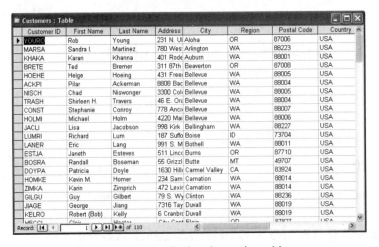

The column is too narrow to display the entire address.

4   Point to the vertical bar between the **Address** and **City** column headers, and double-
click.

The column to the left of the vertical bar is the minimum width that will display all
the text in that field in all records. This technique is particularly useful in a large
table where you can't easily determine the length of a field's longest entry.

5   On the left side of the datasheet, drag the horizontal bar between any two record
selectors downward to increase the height of all rows in the table.

6 On the **Format** menu, click **Row Height** to display the **Row Height** dialog box.

7 Select the **Standard Height** check box, and then click **OK**.

The height of all rows is returned to the default setting. (You can also set the rows to any other height in this dialog box.)

8 Click in the **First Name** column, and then on the **Format** menu, click **Hide Columns**.

The First Name column disappears, and the columns to its right shift to the left. If you select several columns before clicking Hide Columns, they all disappear.

Tip You can select adjacent columns by clicking in the header of one, holding down the Shift key, and then clicking in the header of another. The two columns and any columns in between are selected.

9 To restore the hidden field, on the **Format** menu, click **Unhide Columns** to display the **Unhide Columns** dialog box.

10   Select the **First Name** check box, and then click **Close**.

Access redisplays the First Name column.

11   Drag the right side of the database window to the left to reduce its size so that you cannot see all fields in the table.

12   Point to the **Customer ID** column header, hold down the mouse button, and drag through the **First Name** and **Last Name** column headers. Then with the three columns selected, on the **Format** menu, click **Freeze Columns**.

The first three columns will remain in view when you scroll the window horizontally to view columns that are off the screen to the right.

13   On the **Format** menu, click **Unfreeze All Columns** to restore the columns to their normal condition.

14   Close the table without saving your changes.

CLOSE the *GardenCo* database.

Smart Tags

New in Office 2003
Smart Tags

A smart tag appears as a shortcut menu that displays options pertinent to a specific word, field, or type of content. For example, if Word determines that several words you typed might be a person's name, it will place a purple dotted line beneath them. If you move the mouse pointer over the underlined words, Word displays a Smart Tag Actions button. When you click this button Word displays a list of possible actions that includes sending e-mail, scheduling a meeting, and adding to contacts.

Smart tags were introduced as part of Windows XP and were supported in some Office XP programs. With The Microsoft Office System 2003 they have been extended to Access.

When you create a table in Access, you can apply one or more smart tags to each field. When information from that field is displayed in a table, form, or query, and the mouse pointer is moved over the text, the Smart Tag Action button is displayed and some action can be taken that is appropriate for the kind of information.

There are not currently a lot of smart tags available for use in Access, but they are being created by third-party developers and made available on the Web.

For more information about smart tags, see *www.officesmarttags.com*.

Key Points

- Microsoft Office Access 2003 includes wizards to help you quickly and easily create databases and their objects, such as tables, queries, forms and reports.

- In Design view, you can modify any object you created with a wizard.

- Rather than storing all information in one table, you can create several different tables for each specific type of information, such as employee contact information, customer contact information, and supplier contact information.

- Properties determine what data can be entered in a field, and how the data will look on the screen. In Design view, you can change some properties without affecting the data stored in the table; but changing some might affect the data, so you must exercise caution when modifying properties.

- You can adjust the structure of a table—by manipulating or hiding columns and rows—without affecting the data stored in the table.

- When you create a table in Access, you can apply one or more smart tags to each field. When information from that field is displayed in a table, form, or query, and the mouse pointer is moved over the text, the Smart Tag Action button is displayed and some action can be taken that is appropriate for the kind of information.

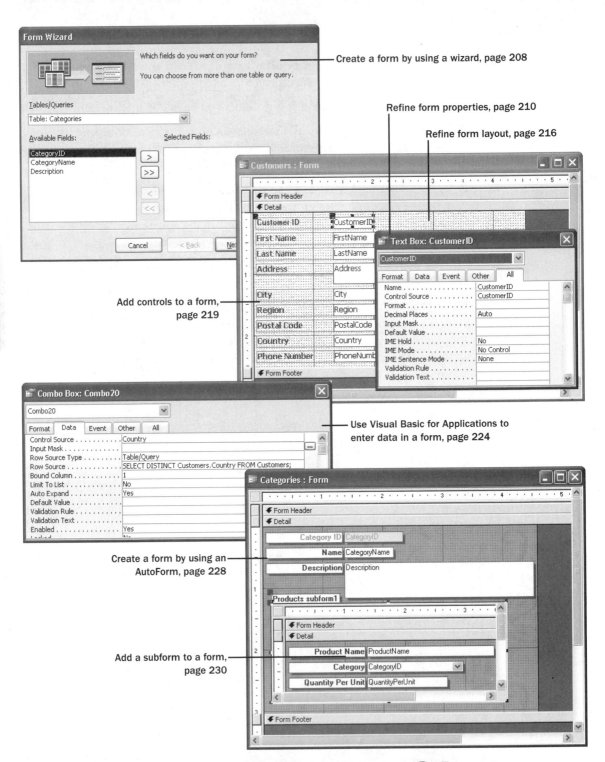

Create a form by using a wizard, page 208

Refine form properties, page 210

Refine form layout, page 216

Add controls to a form, page 219

Use Visual Basic for Applications to enter data in a form, page 224

Create a form by using an AutoForm, page 228

Add a subform to a form, page 230

10 Simplifying Data Entry with Forms

In this chapter you will learn to:

✔   Create a form by using a wizard.

✔   Refine form properties.

✔   Refine form layout.

✔   Add controls to a form.

✔   Use Visual Basic for Applications to enter data in a form.

✔   Create a form by using an AutoForm.

✔   Add a subform to a form.

A database that contains the day-to-day records of an active company is useful only if it can be kept up to date and if particular items of information can be found quickly. Although Microsoft Office Access 2003 is fairly easy to use, entering, editing, and retrieving information in Datasheet view is not a task you would want to assign to someone who's not familiar with Access. Not only would these tasks be tedious and inefficient, but working in Datasheet view leaves far too much room for error, especially if details of complex transactions have to be entered into several related tables. The solution to this problem, and the first step in the conversion of this database to a *database application*, is to create and use forms.

A form is an organized and formatted view of some or all of the fields from one or more tables or queries. Forms work interactively with the tables in a database. You use *controls* in the form to enter new information, to edit or remove existing information, or to locate information. Like printed forms, Access forms can include *label controls* that tell users what type of information they are expected to enter, as well as *text box controls* in which they can enter the information. Unlike printed forms, Access forms can also include a variety of other controls, such as *option buttons* and *command buttons* that transform Access forms into something very much like a Microsoft Windows dialog box or one page of a wizard.

Tip   Some forms are used to navigate among the features and functions of a data-base application and have little or no connection with its actual data. A *switchboard* is an example of this type of form.

As with other Access objects, you can create forms by hand or with the help of a wizard. Navigational and housekeeping forms, such as switchboards, are best created by hand in Design view. Forms that are based on tables, on the other hand, should always be created with a wizard and then refined by hand—not because it is difficult to drag the necessary text box controls onto a form, but because there is simply no point in doing it by hand.

In this chapter, you will create some forms to hide the complexity of the GardenCo database from the people who will be entering and working with its information. First you will discover how easy it is to let the Form Wizard create forms that you can then modify to suit your needs. You'll learn about the controls you can place in a form, and the properties that control its function and appearance. After you have created a form containing controls, you will learn how to tell Access what to do when a user performs some action in a control, such as clicking or entering text. You will also take a quick look at subforms (forms within a form).

See Also   Do you need only a quick refresher on the topics in this chapter? See the Quick Reference entries on pages xxxiii.

Important   Before you can use the practice files in this chapter, you need to install them from the book's companion CD to their default location. See "Using the Book's CD-ROM" on page xxi for more information.

Creating a Form by Using a Wizard

Before you begin creating a form, you need to know what table it will be based on and have an idea of how the form will be used. Having made these decisions, you can use the Form Wizard to help create the basic form. Remember though, that like almost any other object in Access, after the form is created you can always go into Design view to customize the form if it does not quite meet your needs.

In this exercise, you'll create a form that will be used to add new customer records to the Customers table of The Garden Company's database.

USE the *GardenCo* database and the *tgc_bkgrnd* graphic in the practice file folder for this topic. These practice files are located in the *My Documents\Microsoft Press\Office 2003 SBS\Forms\Properties* folder and can also be accessed by clicking *Start/All Programs/Microsoft Press/Microsoft Office System 2003 Step by Step*. OPEN the *GardenCo* database and acknowledge the safety warning, if necessary.

1   With **Forms** selected on the **Objects** bar, click **Customers** in the list of forms, and click the **Design** button to open the form in Design view.

Label control   Text control

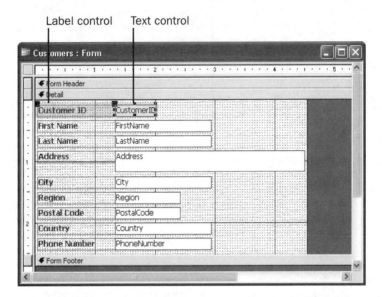

When a form is created, some of its properties are inherited from the table on which it is based. In this example, the names assigned to the text boxes (*FirstName*, *LastName*, and so on) are the field names from the Customers table, and the labels to the left of each text box reflect the Caption property of each field. The size of each text box is determined by the Field Size property.

Tip   After a form has been created, its properties are not bound to their source. In previous versions of Access, changing the table's field properties had no impact on the corresponding form property, and vice versa. Now in Access 2003, when you modify an inherited field property in Table Design view, you can choose to update the property in all or some controls that are bound to the field.

2   Click the **Customer ID** label (not its text box). Then on the Formatting toolbar, click the down arrow to the right of the **Font** button, and click **Microsoft Sans Serif**. (If you don't see Microsoft Sans Serif, click **MS Sans Serif**.)

3   With the label still selected, click the down arrow to the right of the **Font Size** box, and click **8** to make the font slightly smaller.

4   Right-click the **CustomerID** text box (not its label), and click **Properties** on the shortcut menu to display the **Properties** dialog box for the **CustomerID** text box.

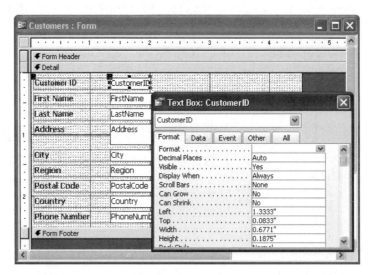

All the settings available on the toolbar (plus a few more) are also available in a Properties dialog box that is associated with each control. You can use this dialog box to display the properties of any object in the form, including the form itself: simply click the down arrow to the right of the box at the top of the dialog box, and click the object whose properties you want to display.

You can display related types of properties by clicking the appropriate tab: Format, Data, Event, or Other. You can also display all properties by clicking the All tab.

5   Click the **Format** tab, scroll to the **Font Name** property, and change it to **Microsoft Sans Serif** (or **MS Sans Serif**). Then set **Font Size** to **8**, and set **Font Weight** to **Bold**.

On the form behind the dialog box, you can see how these changes affect the CustomerID text in the text box (you might have to move the dialog box).

Tip   When you are working in Design view with the Properties dialog box open, you can drag the dialog box by its title bar to the side of the screen so that you can see the changes you're making to the form.

6   Click the down arrow to the right of the box at the top of the **Properties** dialog box, and click **FirstName_Label** box to select the label to the left of the **FirstName** text box.

7   Repeat step 5 to change the font settings for this control.

These different ways of selecting a control and changing its properties provide some flexibility and convenience, but you can see that it would be a bit tedious to apply any of them to a few dozen controls in a form. The next two steps provide a faster method.

8   Click anywhere in the form, and then press `Ctrl`+`A` to select all the controls in the **Detail** section of the form.

> **Tip**   You can also select all the controls in a form by opening the Edit menu and clicking Select All, or by dragging a rectangle over some portion of all the controls.

Small black handles appear around all the controls to indicate that they are selected. The title bar of the Properties dialog box now displays *Multiple selection*, and the Objects list is blank. Only the Format settings that have the same settings for all the selected controls are displayed. Because the changes you made in the previous steps are not shared by all the selected controls, the Font Name, Font Size, and Font Weight settings are now blank.

9   To apply the settings to all the selected controls, set the **Font Name**, **Font Size**, and **Font Weight** properties as you did in step 5.

10   With all controls still selected, on the **Format** tab, click **Back Style**, and set it to **Normal**.

The background of the labels will no longer be transparent.

11   Click **Back Color**, and then click the **...** button at the right end of the box to display the **Color** dialog box.

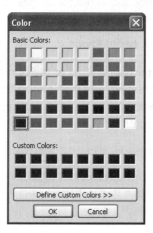

12   Click pale yellow (the second option in the top row), click **OK**, and then press `Enter` to accept the change.

The background of all the controls changes to pale yellow.

Tip If you don't see a color you want to use, click Define Custom Colors, work with the various settings until you have specified the desired color, and then click Add to Custom Colors.

13 Set **Special Effect** to **Shadowed**, and set **Border Color** to a shade of green.

You can either click the **...** button and make a selection, or type a color value such as **32768** in the Border Color box.

14 Click the **Detail** section in the form to deselect all the controls.

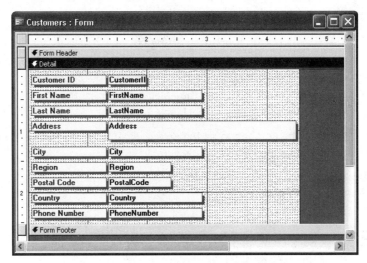

15 Click the label to the left of **FirstName**, and in the **Properties** dialog box, scroll up to the **Caption** box and change *First Name* to **Name**.

16 Repeat step 15 to change *Phone Number* to **Phone**.

Tip You can edit the Caption property of a label or the Control Source property of a text box by selecting it, clicking its text, and then editing the text as you would in any other Windows program. However, take care when editing the Control Source property, which defines where the content of the text box comes from.

17 Remove the label to the left of **LastName** by clicking it and then pressing the ⌈Del⌉ key.

18 Select all the labels, but not their corresponding text boxes, by holding down the ⌈Shift⌉ key as you click each of them. Then in the **Properties** dialog box, scroll down and set the **Text Align** property to **Right**.

19 On the **Format** menu, point to **Size**, click **To Fit** to size the labels to fit their contents, and then click anywhere in the form, but outside the controls, to deselect them.

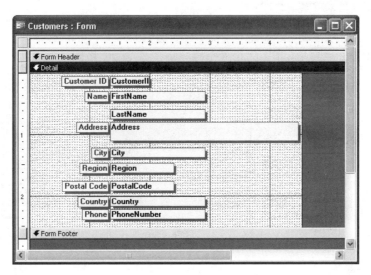

Tip   The order in which you make formatting changes, such as the ones you just made, can have an impact on the results. If you don't see the expected results, click the Undo button or press Ctrl+Z to step back through your changes, and then try again.

20 Hold down the Shift key while clicking each text box to select all the text boxes but not their corresponding labels, and in the **Properties** dialog box, change the **Left** setting to **1.5"** to insert a little space between the labels and the text boxes.

21 Change the **Font Weight** property to **Normal**, and then click anywhere in the form, but outside the controls, to deselect them.

22 To change the background to one that better represents The Garden Company, click the down arrow to the right of the box at the top of the **Properties** dialog box, click **Form**, click the **Picture** property—which shows *(bitmap)*—and then click the ... button to open the **Insert Picture** dialog box.

23 Navigate to the *My Documents\Microsoft Press\Office System 2003 SBS\Forms \Properties* folder, and double-click **tgc_bkgrnd**. (If you don't see this file listed, change the **Files of type** setting to **Graphics Files**.)

The form's background changes, and the path to the graphic used for the new background is displayed in the Picture property box.

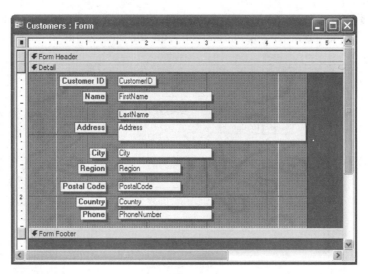

Save

24 Click the **Save** button to save the design of your **Customers** form.

25 Close the form. (The **Properties** dialog box closes when you close the form.)

CLOSE the *GardenCo* database.

Refining Form Layout

The forms created by a wizard are functional, not fancy. However, it's fairly easy to customize the layout to suit your needs. You can add and delete labels, move both labels and text controls around the form, add logos and other graphics, and otherwise improve the layout of the form to make it attractive and easy to use.

As you work with a form's layout, it is important to pay attention to the shape of the pointer, which changes to indicate the manner in which you can change the selected item. Because a text box and its label sometimes act as a unit, you have to be careful to notice the pointer's shape before making any change. This table explains what action each shape indicates:

Pointer	Shape	Action
🖑	Hand	Drag to move both controls together, as one.
🖕	Pointing finger	Drag to move just the control.
⇕	Vertical arrows	Drag the top or bottom border to change the height.

Pointer	Shape	Action
↔	Horizontal arrows	Drag the right or left border to change the width.
↘	Diagonal arrows	Drag the corner to change both the height and width.

In this exercise, you will rearrange the label and text box controls in the Customers form to make them more closely fit the way people will work with them.

USE the *GardenCo* database in the practice file folder for this topic. This practice file is located in the *My Documents\Microsoft Press\Office 2003 SBS\Forms\Layout* folder and can also be accessed by clicking *Start/All Programs/Microsoft Press/Microsoft Office System 2003 Step by Step.*
OPEN the *GardenCo* database and acknowledge the safety warning, if necessary.

1   Open the **Customers** form in Design view.

2   If necessary, drag the lower-right corner of the Form window down and to the right until you can see the form footer at the bottom of the form and have an inch or so of blank area to the right of the background.

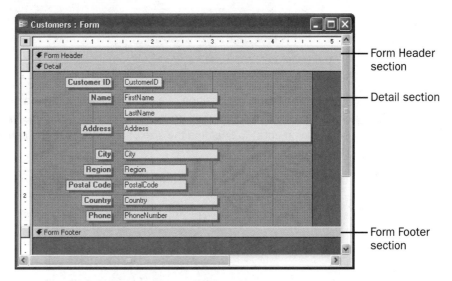

The form is divided into three sections: Form Header, Detail, and Form Footer. Only the Detail section currently has anything in it.

3   Point to the right edge of the **Detail** background, and when the pointer changes to a two-way arrow, drag the edge of the background to the right until you can see about five full grid sections.

4 Click the **LastName** text box, and then slowly move the pointer around its border, from black handle to black handle, noticing how it changes shape.

5 Move the pointer over the **LastName** text box and when it changes to a hand, drag it up and to the right of the **FirstName** text box.

6 One by one, select each control, resize it, and move it to the location shown in the following graphic. (Don't worry if you don't get everything aligned exactly as shown here.)

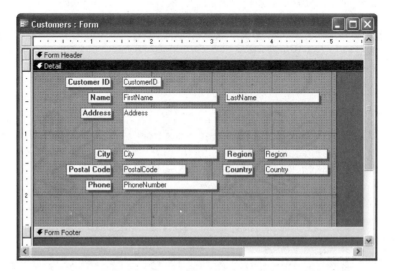

Tip To fine-tune the position of a control, click it and then hold down the Ctrl key while pressing the appropriate arrow key—←, ↓, ↑, or →—to move the control in small increments. To fine-tune the size of a control, use the same process but hold down the Shift key.

7 On the **Format** menu, click **AutoFormat** to display the **AutoFormat** dialog box.

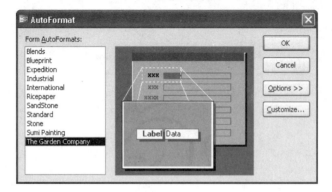

8   Click the **Customize** button to display the **Customize AutoFormat** dialog box.

9   Click **Create a new AutoFormat based on the Form 'Customers'**, and then click **OK**.

Tip   Form controls inherit whatever theme is set in the operating system. To change the theme, open the Control Panel, click Display, click the Themes tab, select a new theme, and then click OK.

10   In the **New Style Name** dialog box, type **The Garden Company** as the name of the new style, and then click **OK**.

Back in the AutoFormat database, the new style appears in the Form AutoFormats list. From now on, this style will be available in any database you open on this computer.

11   Click **OK** to close the **AutoFormat** dialog box.

Tip   Access saves data automatically as you enter it, but layout changes to any object must be manually saved.

Save

12   Click the **Save** button.

13   Close the form.

CLOSE the *GardenCo* database.

Adding Controls to a Form

Every form has three basic sections: Form Header, Detail, and Form Footer. When you use a wizard to create a form, the wizard adds a set of controls for each field that you select from the underlying table to the Detail section and leaves the Form Header and Form Footer sections blank. Because these sections are empty, Access collapses them, but you can size all the sections by dragging their *selectors*. Although labels and text box controls are perhaps the most common controls found in forms, you can also enhance your forms with many other types of controls. For example, you can add groups of option buttons, check boxes, and list boxes to present people with choices instead of making them type entries in text boxes.

The most popular controls are stored in the Toolbox. Clicking the More Controls button displays a list of all the other controls on your computer. The controls displayed when you click the More Controls button are not necessarily associated with Access or even with another Microsoft Office program. The list includes every control that any program has installed and registered on your computer.

Important   Some controls, such as the Calendar Control, can be very useful. Others might do nothing when you add them to a form, or might do something unexpected and not entirely pleasant. If you feel like experimenting, don't do so in an important database.

In this exercise, you will add a graphic and a caption to the Form Header section of the Customers form from the GardenCo database. You will also replace the Country text box control in the Detail section with a combo box control.

USE the *GardenCo* database in the practice file folder for this topic. This practice file is located in the *My Documents\Microsoft Press\Office 2003 SBS\Forms\Controls* folder and can also be accessed by clicking *Start/All Programs/Microsoft Press/Microsoft Office System 2003 Step by Step*. OPEN the *GardenCo* database and acknowledge the safety warning, if necessary.

1   Open the **Customers** form in Design view.

2   Point to the horizontal line between the **Form Header** section selector and the **Detail** section selector, and when the pointer changes to a double-headed arrow, drag the **Detail** section selector down a little over an inch.

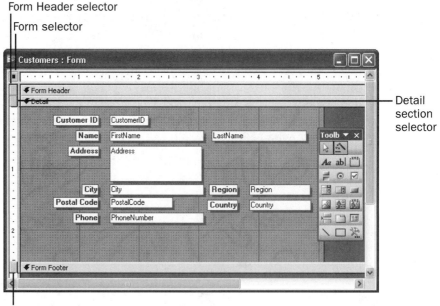

Toolbox

3 If the Toolbox isn't displayed, click the **Toolbox** button on the Form Design toolbar.

You can also open the View menu and select the Toolbox check box. To keep the Toolbox open but out of the way, you can drag it off to the side, and dock it on one edge of the screen.

4 To get an idea of the controls that are available, move the pointer over the buttons in the Toolbox, pausing just long enough to display each button's ScreenTip.

Image

5 Click the **Image** control in the Toolbox, and then drag a rectangle about 1 inch high and 3 inches wide at the left end of the **Form Header** section.

When you release the mouse button, Access displays the Insert Picture dialog box, in which you can select an image to insert in the control.

6 Navigate to the *My Documents\Microsoft Press\Office System 2003 SBS\Forms \Controls* folder, and double-click **tgc_logo2**. (If you don't see this file listed, change the **Files of type** setting to **Graphics Files**.)

The Garden Company logo appears inside the image control.

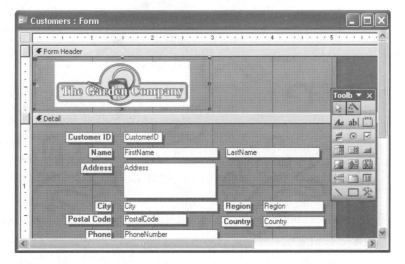

Tip If the control isn't large enough, the image is cropped. You can enlarge the control to display the entire image. (You might also have to enlarge the Form Header section.)

Label

7 To add a caption to the header, click the **Label** control in the Toolbox, and then drag another rectangle in the header section.

Access inserts a label control containing the insertion point, ready for you to enter a caption.

8 Type the caption **Customers**, and press Enter .

The Customers label takes on the formatting of the other labels.

9 With the **Customers** label selected, press the F4 key to display the **Properties** dialog box.

10 Change the **Font Size** property to **18**, and change the **Text Align** property to **Center**. Then close the **Properties** dialog box.

11 On the **Format** menu, point to **Size**, and then click **To Fit**.

12 Adjust the size and position of the two controls you added so that they are side-by-side.

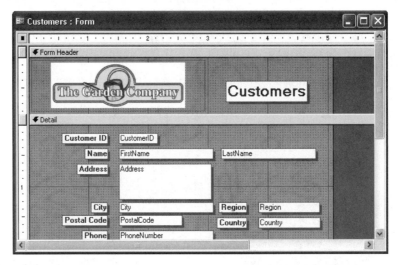

Control Wizards

13 If the **Control Wizards** button is active (orange) in the toolbox, click it to deactivate it.

With the Control Wizards button turned off, you can create a control with all the default settings without having to work through the wizard's pages.

Combo Box

14 Insert a combo box in the **Details** section by clicking the **Combo Box** control in the Toolbox and then dragging a rectangle just below the current **Country** text box.

When you release the mouse button, Access displays a combo box control, which is *unbound* (not attached to a field in the Customers table).

Troubleshooting Access provides a number for each control as it is created, so don't be concerned if the number displayed in your control is different from what you see in the graphics in this book.

Format Painter

15 Copy the formatting of the **Country** text box to the new combo box control by clicking the **Country** text box, clicking the **Format Painter** button on the Form Design toolbar, and then clicking the combo box control.

Both the combo box control and its label take on the new formatting.

16 Right-click the combo box and click **Properties** on the shortcut menu to display the **Properties** dialog box.

17 Click the **Data** tab, set the **Control Source** property to **Country**, and then type the following in the **Row Source** box:

```
SELECT DISTINCT Customers.Country FROM Customers;
```

(Note that there is no space between *Customers* and *Country*; there is only a period. There is also a semi-colon at the end of the text.)

This line is a query that extracts one example of every country in the Country field of the Customers table and displays the results as a list when you click the box's down arrow.

(You might have to widen the Properties dialog box to display the whole query.)

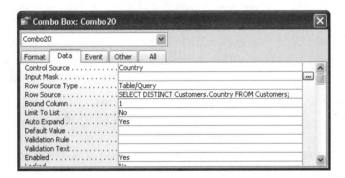

Tip   If you need to add a new customer from a country that is not in the list, you can type the new country's name in the combo box. After the record is added to the database, that country shows up when the combo box list is displayed.

18 If necessary, set the **Row Source Type** to **Table/Query**.

19 Click the label to the left of the combo box (if necessary, drag the **Properties** dialog box to see the combo box label). Then click the dialog box's **Format** tab, change the caption to **Country**, and close the dialog box.

20 Delete the original **Country** text box and its label, and move the new combo box and label into their place, resizing them as needed.

21 Click the **View** button to see your form.

View

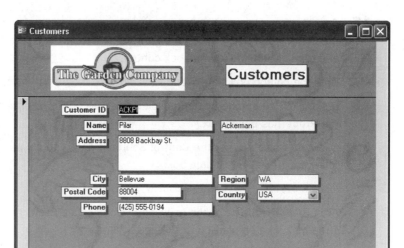

22   Scroll through a couple of records, and display the combo box's list to see how you can select a country.

23   You don't need the *record selector*—the gray bar along the left edge of the form— so return to Design view, and display the **Properties** dialog box for the entire form by clicking the **Form** selector (the box at the junction of the horizontal and vertical rulers) and pressing ⬚. Then on the **Format** tab, change **Record Selectors** to **No**. While you're at it, change **Scroll Bars** to **Neither**. Then close the **Properties** dialog box.

24   Save the form's new design, and switch to Form view for a final look.

25   Close the form.

CLOSE the *GardenCo* database.

Using Visual Basic for Applications to Enter Data in a Form

As you might have suspected by now, almost everything in Access, including the Access program itself, is an object. One of the characteristics of objects is that they can recognize and respond to *events*, which are essentially actions. Different objects recognize different events. The basic events, recognized by almost all objects, are Click, Double Click, Mouse Down, Mouse Move, and Mouse Up. Most objects recognize quite a few other events. A text control, for example, recognizes about 17 different events; a form recognizes more than 50.

Tip   You can see the list of events recognized by an object by looking at the Event tab on the object's Properties dialog box.

While you use a form, objects are signaling events, or *firing events*, almost constantly. However, unless you attach a *macro* or *Microsoft Visual Basic for Applications (VBA) procedure* to an event, the object is really just firing blanks. By default, Access doesn't do anything obvious when it recognizes most events. So without interfering with the program's normal behavior, you can use an event to specify what action should happen. You can even use an event to trigger the running of a macro or a VBA procedure that performs a set of actions.

Sound complicated? Well, it's true that events are not things most casual Access users tend to worry about. But because knowing how to handle events can greatly increase the efficiency of objects such as forms, you should take a glimpse at what they're all about while you have a form open.

For example, while looking at customer records in the GardenCo database, you might have noticed that the CustomerID is composed of the first three letters of the customer's last name and the first two letters of his or her first name, all in capital letters. This technique will usually generate a unique ID for a new customer. If you try to enter an ID that is already in use, Access won't accept the new entry, and you'll have to add a number or change the ID in some other way to make it unique. Performing trivial tasks, such as combining parts of two words and then converting the results to capital letters, is something a computer excels at. So rather than typing the ID for each new customer record that is added to The Garden Company's database, you can let VBA do it instead.

In this exercise, you will write a few lines of VBA code, and attach the code to the After Update event in the LastName text box in the Customers form. When you change the content of the text box and attempt to move somewhere else in the form, the Before Update event is fired. In response to that event, Access updates the record in the source table, and then the After Update event is fired. This is the event you are going to work with. This is by no means an in-depth treatment of VBA, but this exercise will give you a taste of VBA's power.

USE the *GardenCo* database and the *AftUpdate* text file in the practice file folder for this topic. This practice file is located in the *My Documents\Microsoft Press\Office 2003 SBS\Forms\Events* folder and can also be accessed by clicking *Start/All Programs/Microsoft Press/Microsoft Office System 2003 Step by Step*. OPEN the *GardenCo* database and acknowledge the safety warning, if necessary.

1 With **Forms** selected on the **Objects** bar, click **Customers** in the list of forms, and click the **Design** button.

2 Click the **LastName** text box to select it, and if necessary, press F4 to open the **Properties** dialog box.

3   Click the **Event** tab to see the options.

This tab lists the events to which the LastName text box control can respond to.

4   Click **After Update** in the list, and then click the **...** button.

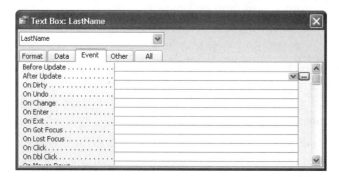

The Choose Builder dialog box appears, offering you the options of building an expression, a macro, or VBA code.

5   Click **Code Builder**, and then click **OK** to open the VBA Editor.

Project Explorer   Sub statement

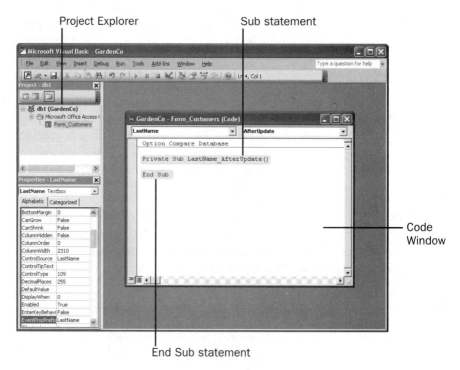

End Sub statement

Code Window

The Project Explorer pane lists any objects you have created to which you can attach code; in this case, only the Customers form (Form_Customers) is listed. As you create more forms and reports, they will appear here.

The Code window displays a placeholder for the procedure that Access will use to handle the After Update event for the LastName text control. This procedure is named *Private Sub LastName_AfterUpdate()*, and at the moment it contains only the Sub and End Sub statements that mark the beginning and end of any procedure.

6 Launch a text editor, such as Microsoft Notepad, navigate to the *My Documents \Microsoft Press\Office System 2003 SBS\Forms\Events* folder, open the *AftUpdate* practice file, and copy the following lines of text to the Clipboard. Then [Alt]+[Tab] back to the Code window and paste the text between the Private Sub LastName_AfterUpdate() and End Sub statements:

```
'Create variables to hold first and last names
' and customer ID
Dim fName As String
Dim lName As String
Dim cID As String

'Assign the text in the LastName text box to
' the lName variable.
lName = Forms!customers!LastName.Text

'You must set the focus to a text box before
' you can read its contents.
Forms!customers!FirstName.SetFocus
fName = Forms!customers!FirstName.Text

'Combine portions of the last and first names
' to create the customer ID.
cID = UCase(Left(lName, 3) & Left(fName, 2))

'Don't store the ID unless it is 5 characters long
' (which indicates both names filled in).
If Len(cID) = 5 Then
   Forms!customers!CustomerID.SetFocus

   'Don't change the ID if it has already been
   ' entered; perhaps it was changed manually.
   If Forms!customers!CustomerID.Text = "" Then
      Forms!customers!CustomerID = cID
   End If
End If

'Set the focus where it would have gone naturally.
Forms!customers!Address.SetFocus
```

Important   When a line of text is preceded by an apostrophe, the text is a comment that explains the purpose of the next line of code. In the VBA Editor, comments are displayed in green.

View Microsoft
Access

7   Save the file, click the **View Microsoft Access** button to return to the Access window, and then close the **Properties** dialog box.

New Record

8   Switch to Form view and size the window as necessary. Then on the **Navigation** bar, click the **New Record** button to create a new record.

9   Press the ⎇Tab key to move the insertion point to the text box for the *FirstName* field, type John, press ⎇Tab to move to the text box for the *LastName* field, type Coake, and then press ⎇Tab again.

If you entered the VBA code correctly, *COAJO* appears in the CustomerID text box.

10   Change the first and last name to something else and notice that the **CustomerID** text box doesn't change even if the names from which it was derived do change.

11   Press the ⎋Esc key to remove your entry, and then try entering the last name first, followed by the first name.

Access does not create a Customer ID. The code does what it was written to do but not necessarily what you want it to do, which is to create an ID regardless of the order in which the names are entered. There are several ways to fix this problem. You could write a similar procedure to handle the After Update event in the FirstName text box, or you could write one procedure to handle both events and then jump to it when either event occurs. You won't do either in these exercises, but if you are interested, you can look at the code in the database file for the next exercise to see the second solution.

12   Press ⎋Esc to clear your entries, and then close the **Customers** form.

13   Press ⎇Alt+⎇Tab to switch to the VBA Editor, which is still open, and close the editor.

CLOSE the *GardenCo* database.

Creating a Form by Using an AutoForm

Although a form doesn't have to include all the fields from a table, when it is used as the primary method of creating new records, it usually does include all of them. The quickest way to create a form that includes all the fields from one table is to use an *AutoForm*. And as with the forms created by a wizard, you can easily customize these forms.

In this exercise, you will create an AutoForm that displays information about each of the products carried by The Garden Company.

USE the *GardenCo* database in the practice file folder for this topic. This practice file is located in the *My Documents\Microsoft Press\Office 2003 SBS\Forms\AutoForm* folder and can also be accessed by clicking *Start/All Programs/Microsoft Press/Microsoft Office System 2003 Step by Step*. OPEN the *GardenCo* database and acknowledge the safety warning, if necessary.

1   On the **Objects** bar, click **Forms**.

2   On the database window's toolbar, click the **New** button to display this **New Form** dialog box, which lists all the ways you can create a form.

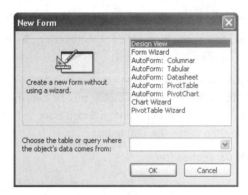

3   Click **AutoForm: Columnar** in the list of choices, click the down arrow to the right of the box at the bottom of the dialog box, click **Categories**, and then click **OK**.

The dialog box closes, and after a moment a new Categories form is displayed in Form view.

Save

4   Click the **Save** button, accept the default name of *Categories* in the **Save As** dialog box, and click **OK** to view the form.

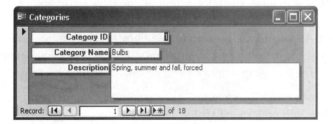

Tip   When AutoForm creates a form, Access applies the background style you selected the last time you used the Form Wizard (or the default style, if you haven't used the wizard). If your form doesn't look like this one, switch to Design view, and on the Format menu, click AutoFormat. You can then select The Garden Company style from the list displayed.

5 This form looks pretty good as it is, but switch to Design view so that you can make a few minor changes.

6 Delete the word *Category* from the **Category Name** label.

7 The **CategoryID** value is provided by Access and should never be changed, so you need to disable that text box control. Click the control and if necessary, press F4 to display the control's **Properties** dialog box.

8 On the **Data** tab, change **Enabled** to **No**, and close the dialog box.

 Disabling the CategoryID text box changes it, and the label text, to gray.

9 Switch to Form view, and scroll through a few categories. Try to edit entries in the **Category ID** field to confirm that you can't.

10 You don't need scroll bars or a record selector in this form, so return to Design view, and display the form's **Properties** dialog box by clicking the **Form** selector and pressing F4. On the **Format** tab, change **Scroll Bars** to **Neither** and **Record Selectors** to **No**, and then close the dialog box.

11 Save and close the **Categories** form.

CLOSE the *GardenCo* database.

Adding a Subform to a Form

A form can display information (fields) from one or more tables or queries. If you want to display fields from several tables or queries in one form, you have to give some thought to the *relationships* that must exist between those objects.

In Access, a relationship is an association between common fields in two tables, and you can use it to relate the information in one table to the information in another table. For example, in the GardenCo database a relationship can be established between the Categories table and the Products table because both tables have a CategoryID field. Each product is in only one category, but each category can contain many products, so this type of relationship—the most common—is known as a *one-to-many relationship*.

As you create forms and queries, Access might recognize some relationships between the fields in the underlying tables. However, it probably won't recognize all of them without a little help from you.

Other Types of Relationships

In addition to one-to-many relationships, you can create *one-to-one relationships* and *many-to-many relationships*, but they are not as common.

In a one-to-one relationship, each record in one table can have one and only one related record in the other table. This type of relationship isn't commonly used because it is easier to put all the fields in one table. However, you might use two related tables instead of one to break up a table with many fields, or to track information that applies to only some of the records in the first table.

A many-to-many relationship is really two one-to-many relationships tied together through a third table. For example, the GardenCo database contains Products, Orders, and Order Details tables. The Products table has one record for each product sold by The Garden Company, and each product has a unique ProductID. The Orders table has one record for each order placed with The Garden Company, and each record in it has a unique OrderID. However, the Orders table doesn't specify which products were included in each order; that information is in the Order Details table, which is the table in the middle that ties the other two tables together. Products and Orders each have a one-to-many relationship with Order Details. Products and Orders therefore have a many-to-many relationship with each other. In plain language, this means that every product can appear in many orders, and every order can include many products.

In this exercise, you will first define the relationship between the Categories and Products tables in the GardenCo database. You will then add a *subform* to a form. For each category displayed in the main form, this subform will display all the products in that category.

USE the *GardenCo* database in the practice file folder for this topic. This practice file is located in the *My Documents\Microsoft Press\Office 2003 SBS\Forms\Subform* folder and can also be accessed by clicking *Start/All Programs/Microsoft Press/Microsoft Office System 2003 Step by Step.*
OPEN the *GardenCo* database and acknowledge the safety warning, if necessary.

Relationships

1 On the Database toolbar, click the **Relationships** button to open the Relationships window.

Show Table

2 If the **Show Table** dialog box isn't displayed, on the toolbar, click the **Show Table** button. Then double-click **Categories** and **Products** in the list displayed. Close the **Show Table** dialog box to view the Relationships window.

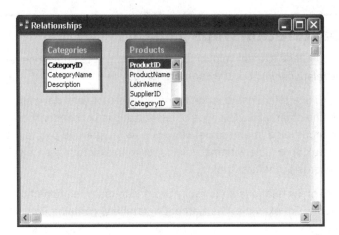

3 Click **CategoryID** in one table, and drag it on top of **CategoryID** in the other table.

Access displays the Edit Relationships dialog box, which lists the fields you have chosen to relate and offers several options.

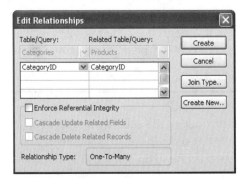

4 Select the **Enforce Referential Integrity** check box, select the other two check boxes, and then click **Create**.

Tip Access uses a system of rules called *referential integrity* to ensure that relationships between records in related tables are valid, and that you don't accidentally delete or change related data. When the Cascade Update Related Fields check box is selected, changing a primary key value in the primary table automatically updates the matching value in all related records. When the Cascade Delete Related Records check box is selected, deleting a record in the primary table deletes any related records in the related table.

Access draws a line representing the one-to-many relationship between the CategoryID fields in each of the tables.

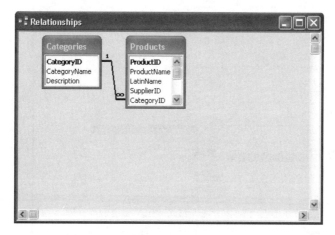

Tip   You can edit or delete a relationship by right-clicking the line and clicking the appropriate command on the shortcut menu.

5   Close the Relationships window, and click **Yes** when prompted to save the window's layout.

6   Open the **Categories** form in Design view.

7   Enlarge the Form window, and drag the **Form Footer** section selector down about 1 inch to give yourself some room to work.

Toolbox

8   If the Toolbox isn't displayed, click the **Toolbox** button.

Control Wizards

9   Make sure the **Control Wizards** button in the Toolbox is active (orange).

Subform/
Subreport

10   Click the **Subform/Subreport** button, and drag a rectangle in the lower portion of the **Details** section.

A white object appears in the form, and the first page of the Subform Wizard opens.

Tip   If prompted, follow the instructions to install this wizard.

11   Leave **Use existing Tables and Queries** selected, and click **Next**.

12   In the **Tables/Queries** list, click **Table: Products**.

13   Add the **ProductName, CategoryID, QuantityPerUnit, UnitPrice,** and **UnitsInStock** fields
to the **Selected Fields** list by clicking each one and then clicking the **>** button.

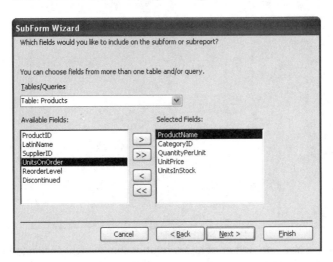

14   Click **Next** to display the third page of the wizard.

Because the Category ID field in the subform is related to the Category ID field
in the main form, the wizard selects "Show Products for each record in Categories
using CategoryID" as the "Choose from a list" option.

Tip   If the wizard can't figure out which fields are related, it selects the
"Define my own" option and displays list boxes in which you can specify the fields
to be related.

15   Click **Next** to accept the default selection, and then click **Finish**, to accept the default
name for the subform and complete the process.

Access displays the Categories form in Design view, with an embedded Products
subform. The size and location of the subform is determined by the original rectangle
you dragged in the form.

16   Adjust the size and location of the objects in your form as needed to view
the entire subform.

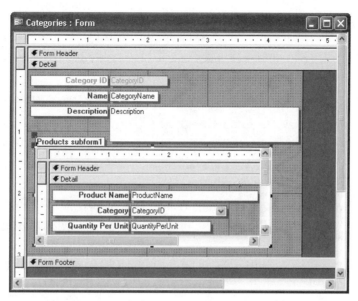

17 Notice the layout of the subform in Design view, and then click **View** to switch to Form view.

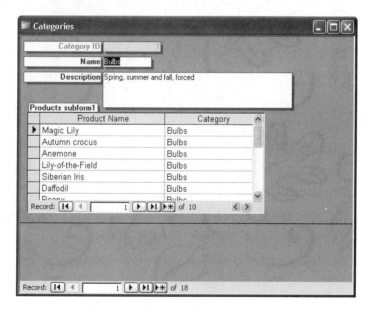

The format of the subform has totally changed. In Design view, it looks like a simple form, but in Form view, it looks like a datasheet.

18 Switch back to Design view, make any necessary size adjustments, and if necessary, open the **Properties** dialog box.

19 Click the **Form** selector in the upper-left corner of the subform twice.

The first click selects the Products subform control, and the second click selects the form. A small black square appears on the selector.

20 On the **Format** tab of the **Properties** dialog box, change both **Record Selectors** and **Navigation Buttons** to **No**.

While on this tab, notice the Default View property, which is set to Datasheet. You might want to return to this property and try the other options after finishing this exercise.

21 Close the **Properties** dialog box, switch back to Form view, and drag the dividers between column headers until you can see all the fields.

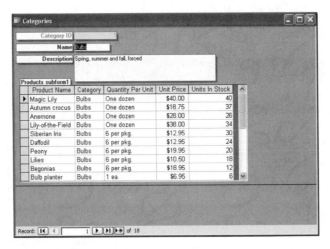

Tip   You can quickly adjust the width of columns to fit their data by double-clicking the double arrow between column headings.

First Record

22 Click the navigation buttons to scroll through several categories. When you are finished, click the **First Record** button to return to the first category (Bulbs).

As each category is displayed at the top of the form, the products in that category are listed in the datasheet in the subform.

23 Click the category name to the right of the first product.

The arrow at the right end of the box indicates that this is a combo box.

24 Click the arrow to display the list of categories, and change the category to **Cacti**.

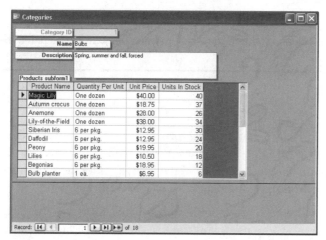
Next Record

25 Click the **Next Record** navigation button to move to the next category (Cacti).

You can see that the first product is now included in this category.

26 Display the list of categories, and then restore the first product to the **Bulbs** category.

27 You don't want people to be able to change a product's category, so return to Design view. Then in the subform, click the **CategoryID** text box control, and press ⌦.

The CategoryID text box and its label are deleted.

Important   You included the CategoryID field when the wizard created this subform because it is the field that relates the Categories and Products tables. The underlying Products table uses a combo box to display the name of the category instead of its ID number, so that combo box also appears in the subform.

28 Save the form, switch back to Form view, and then adjust the width of the subform columns and the size of the Form window until you can clearly see the fields.

Product Name	Quantity Per Unit	Unit Price	Units In Stock
Magic Lily	One dozen	$40.00	40
Autumn crocus	One dozen	$18.75	37
Anemone	One dozen	$28.00	26
Lily-of-the-Field	One dozen	$38.00	34
Siberian Iris	6 per pkg.	$12.95	30
Daffodil	6 per pkg.	$12.95	24
Peony	6 per pkg.	$19.95	20
Lilies	6 per pkg.	$10.50	18
Begonias	6 per pkg.	$18.95	12
Bulb planter	1 ea.	$6.95	6

29 Close the **Categories** form, saving your changes to both the form and the subform.

CLOSE the *GardenCo* database.

Creating a Form and Subform by Using a Wizard

If you know when you create a form that you are going to add a subform, you can do the whole job with the Form Wizard, like this:

1 To create the form in your database, on the **Objects** bar, click **Forms,** and then click the **New** button on the database window's toolbar.

2 Click **Form Wizard,** select the form's base table from the list at the bottom of the page, and then click **OK.**

3 Verify that the table you selected is shown in the **Table/Queries** list, and then click the **>>** button to include all the fields in the new form.

4 To create the subform, display the **Tables/Queries** list, and click the name of the subform's base table.

5 Double-click the desired fields to add them to the list of selected fields, and then click **Next.**

6 Accept the default options, and click **Next.**

7 Accept the default **Datasheet** option, and click **Next.**

8 Click **Finish** to create the form and subform.

You can then clean up the form to suit your needs, just as you did in the previous exercise.

Key Points

■ A form is an organized and formatted view of some or all of the fields from one or more tables or queries. Forms work interactively with the tables in a database. You use controls in the form to enter new information, to edit or remove existing information, or to locate information.

■ When you know what table to base your form on, and have an idea of how the form will be used, you can use the Form Wizard to quickly create a form. You can make modifications to the form in Design view.

■ The two most common views to use in forms are Form view, in which you view or enter data, and Design view, in which you add controls, change form properties, and change the form layout.

■ In a form, each text box (the box where data is entered or viewed) is bound— or linked—to a specific field in the form's underlying table. The table is the record source and the field is the control source. Each control has a number of properties, such as font style, size and color, which you can change to improve a form's appearance.

- In Design view, you can resize any of the three basic sections of a form: the Form Header, Detail, and Form Footer. You can customize any section of your form's layout by adding and deleting labels, moving labels and text controls, and adding logos and other graphics. The most popular controls are stored in the Toolbox.

- The objects in your form can recognize and respond to events, which are essentially actions. But without a macro or VBA procedure attached to it, an event doesn't actually do anything. Knowing how to handle events can greatly increase the efficiency of objects, such as forms. For example, as you enter the first and last names of a new customer, your form could respond to one (or more) events to create an ID based on the customer's first and last name.

- The quickest way to create a form that includes all the fields from one table is to use an AutoForm, which can easily be customized later in Design view.

- If you want to display fields from several tables or queries in one form, you have to give some thought to the relationships that must exist between those objects. In Access, a relationship is an association between common fields in two tables, and you can relate the information in one table to the information in another table. There are three types of relationships that Access recognizes: one-to-one, one-to-many, and many-to-many.

- After you define a relationship between tables, you can add subforms to your forms. For example, for each category displayed in your main form, you might have a subform that displays all the products in that category.

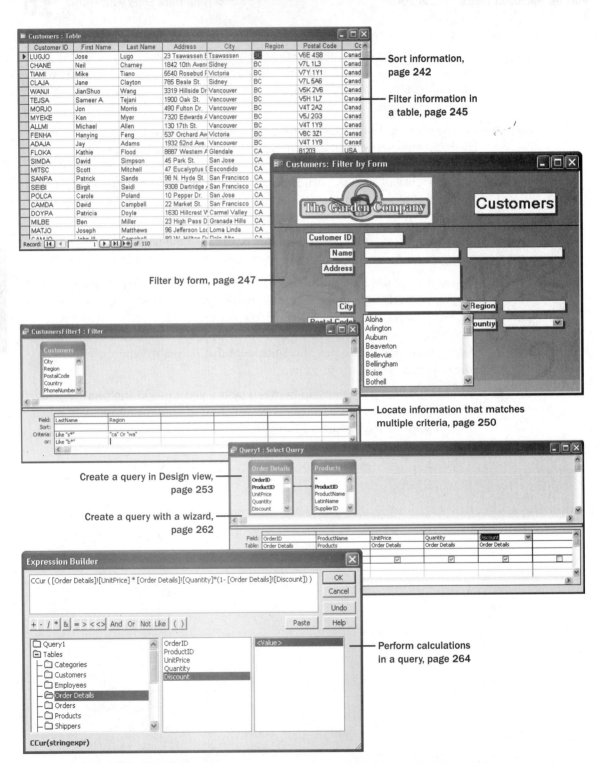

Sort information, page 242

Filter information in a table, page 245

Filter by form, page 247

Locate information that matches multiple criteria, page 250

Create a query in Design view, page 253

Create a query with a wizard, page 262

Perform calculations in a query, page 264

Chapter 11 at a Glance

11 Locating Specific Information

In this chapter you will learn to:

✔ Sort information.

✔ Filter information in a table.

✔ Filter by form.

✔ Locate information that matches multiple criteria.

✔ Create a query in Design view.

✔ Create a query with a Wizard.

✔ Perform calculations in a query.

A database is a repository for information. It might hold a few records in one table or thousands of records in many related tables. No matter how much information is stored in a database, it is useful only if you can locate the information you need when you need it. In a small database you can find information simply by scrolling through a table until you spot what you are looking for. But as a database grows in size and complexity, locating specific information becomes more difficult.

Microsoft Office Access 2003 provides a variety of tools you can use to organize the display of information in a database and to locate specific items of information. Using these tools, you can focus on just part of the information by quickly sorting a table based on any field (or combination of fields), or you can filter the table so that information containing some combination of characters is displayed (or excluded from the display). With a little more effort, you can create queries to display specific fields from specific records from one or more tables. You can even save these queries so that you can use them over and over again, as the information in the database changes.

A query can do more than simply return a list of records from a table. You can use functions in a query that perform calculations on the information in the table to produce the sum, average, count, and other mathematical values.

Working with the GardenCo database, in this chapter you will learn how to pinpoint precisely the information you need in a database using sorting and filtering tools, and queries. Note that you cannot continue with the database from the last chapter; you must use the practice files on the companion CD-ROM.

See Also Do you need only a quick refresher on the topics in this chapter? See the Quick Reference entries on pages xxxiii.

Important Before you can use the practice files in this chapter, you need to install them from the book's companion CD to their default location. See "Using the Book's CD-ROM" on page xxi for more information.

Sorting Information

Information stored in a table can be sorted in either ascending or descending order, based on the values in one or more fields in the table. You could, for example, sort a customer table alphabetically based first on the last name of each customer and then on the first name. Such a sort would result in this type of list, which resembles those found in telephone books:

Last	First
Smith	Denise
Smith	James
Smith	Jeff
Thompson	Ann
Thompson	Steve

Occasionally you might need to sort a table to group all entries of one type together. For example, to qualify for a discount on postage, The Garden Company might want to sort customer records on the postal code field to group the codes before printing mailing labels.

If a field with the Text data type contains numbers, you can sort the field numerically by padding the numbers with leading zeros so that all entries are the same length. For example, 001, 011, and 101 are sorted correctly even if the numbers are defined as text.

How Access Sorts

The concept of sorting seems pretty intuitive, but sometimes your computer's approach to such a concept is not so intuitive. Sorting numbers is a case in point. In Access, numbers can be treated as text or as numerals. Because of the spaces, hyphens, and punctuation typically used in street addresses, postal codes, and telephone numbers, the numbers in these fields are usually treated as text, and sorting them follows the logic applied to sorting all text. Numbers in a price or quantity field, on the other hand, are typically treated as numerals.

When Access sorts text, it sorts first on the first character in the selected field in every record, then on the next character, then on the next, and so on—until it runs out of characters. When Access sorts numbers, it treats the contents of each field as a single value, and sorts the records based on that value. This tactic can result in seemingly strange sort orders. For example, sorting the list in the first column of the following table as text produces the list in the second column. Sorting the same list as numerals produces the list in the third column:

Original	Sort as text	Sort as number
1	1	1
1234	11	2
23	12	3
3	1234	4
11	2	5
22	22	11
12	23	12
4	3	22
2	4	23
5	5	1234

In this exercise, you will learn several ways to sort the information in a datasheet or a form.

BE SURE TO start Access before beginning this exercise.

USE the *GardenCo* database in the practice file folder for this topic. This practice file is located in the *My Documents\Microsoft Press\Office 2003 SBS\Queries\Sort* folder and can also be accessed by clicking *Start/All Programs/Microsoft Press/Microsoft Office System 2003 Step by Step*.

OPEN the *GardenCo* database and acknowledge the safety warning, if necessary.

1   On the **Objects** bar, click **Tables**.

2   Double-click **Customers** to open the table in Datasheet view.

Sort Ascending

3   To sort by Region, click anywhere in the **Region** column, and then click the **Sort Ascending** button.

> **Tip**   You can also use the Sort Ascending or Sort Descending commands by pointing to Sort on the Records menu; or you can right-click the column in the datasheet and click either command on the shortcut menu.

The records are rearranged in order of region.

Sort Descending

4   To reverse the sort order, while still in the **Region** column, click the **Sort Descending** button.

The records for the state of Washington (WA) are now at the top of your list. In both sorts, the region was sorted alphabetically, but the City field was left in a seemingly random order. What you really want to see is the records arranged by city within each region.

> **Tip**   Access can sort on more than one field, but it sorts consecutively from left to right. So the fields you want to sort must be adjacent, and they must be arranged in the order in which you want to sort them.

5   To move the **Region** field to the left of the **City** field, click its header to select the column, and then click the header again and drag the column to the left until a dark line appears between **Address** and **City**.

6   Because **Region** is already selected, hold down the ⬚shift⬚ key and click the **City** header to extend the selection so that both the **Region** and **City** columns are selected.

7   Click the **Sort Ascending** button to arrange the records with the regions in ascending order and the city names also in ascending order within each region (or in this case, each state).

> **Tip**   You can sort records while viewing them in a form. Click the box of the field on which you want to base the sort, and then click one of the Sort buttons. However, you can't sort on multiple fields in Form view.

8 The order of the columns in the **Customers** table doesn't really matter, so close the **Customers** table without saving changes.

CLOSE the *GardenCo* database.

Filtering Information in a Table

Sorting the information in a table organizes it in a logical manner, but you still have the entire table to deal with. If your goal is to locate all records containing information in one or more fields that match a particular pattern, one of the available Filter commands will satisfy your needs. For example, you could quickly create a filter to locate every customer of The Garden Company who lives in Seattle, or everyone who placed an order on January 13, or all customers who live outside of the United States.

You can apply simple filters while viewing information in a table or a form. These filters are applied to the contents of a selected field, but you can apply another filter to the results of the first one to further refine your search.

Tip The Filter commands you will use in this exercise are available by pointing to Filter on the Records menu; by clicking buttons on the toolbar; and by looking at the shortcut menu. However, not all Filter commands are available in each of these places.

Wildcards

When you don't know or aren't sure of a character or set of characters, you can use *wildcard characters* as placeholders for those unknown characters in your search criteria. The most common wildcards are listed in this table:

Character	Description	Example
*	Match any number of characters.	*Lname = Co** returns Colman and Conroy
?	Match any single alphabetic character.	*Fname = eri?* returns Eric and Erik
#	Match any single numeric character.	*ID = 1##* returns any ID from 100 through 199

In this exercise, you will practice several methods of filtering information in a table.

USE the *GardenCo* database in the practice file folder for this topic. This practice file is located in the *My Documents\Microsoft Press\Office 2003 SBS\Queries\FilterDS* folder and can also be accessed by clicking *Start/All Programs/Microsoft Press/Microsoft Office System 2003 Step by Step*.
OPEN the *GardenCo* database and acknowledge the safety warning, if necessary.

1 Open the **Customers** table in Datasheet view.

Filter By
Selection

2 Click any instance of **Sidney** in the **City** field, and then click the **Filter By Selection** button.

The number of customers displayed in the table changes from *110* to *2,* because only two customers live in Sidney.

Important   When you filter a table, the records that don't match the filter aren't removed from the table; they are simply not displayed.

3 Click the **Remove Filter** button to redisplay the rest of the customers.

Remove Filter

4 What if you want a list of all customers who live anywhere that has a postal code starting with *V7L*? Find an example of this type of postal code in the table, select the characters **V7L**, and then click the **Filter By Selection** button again.

Only the two records with postal codes starting with *V7L* are now visible.

5 Click **Remove Filter**.

6 What if this table is enormous and you aren't sure if it contains even one *V7L*? Right-click any postal code, click **Filter For** on the shortcut menu, type V7L* in the cell, and press ⌷Enter⌷ to see the same results.

The asterisk (*) is a wildcard that tells Access to search for any entry in the postal code field that starts with *V7L*.

7 To find out how many customers live outside the United States, remove the current filter, right-click the **Country** field in any USA record, and click **Filter Excluding Selection** on the shortcut menu.

You see all customers from other countries (in this case, only Canada).

8 To experiment with one more filtering technique, remove the filter, save and close the **Customers** table, and double-click **Orders** to open the table in Datasheet view.

9 To find all orders taken by Michael Emanuel on January 23, right-click **Emanuel, Michael** in the **EmployeeID** field, and click **Filter By Selection** on the shortcut menu.

Troubleshooting   If you do not see employee names listed in the EmployeeID field, it is because you continued with the database from the previous exercise. You must use the practice database supplied for this exercise. For instructions on installing the practice files, see "Using the Book's CD-ROM" on page XXX.

10   Right-click **1/23/2003** in the **OrderDate** field, and again click **Filter By Selection** on the shortcut menu.

You now have a list of Michael's orders on the 23rd of January. You could continue to refine this list by filtering on another field, or you could sort the results by clicking in a field and then clicking one of the Sort buttons.

Tip   After you have located just the information you want and have organized it appropriately, you can display the results in a form or report. Click the New Object button on the toolbar, and follow the directions.

11   Remove the filters by clicking the **Remove Filter** button.

12   Save and close the **Orders** table.

CLOSE the *GardenCo* database.

Tip   You can use the Filter commands to filter the information in a table when you are viewing it in a form. The Filter For command is often useful with forms because you don't have to be able to see the desired selection.

Filtering By Form

The Filter By Form command provides a quick and easy way to filter a table based on the information in several fields. If you open a table and then click the Filter By Form button, what you see looks like a simple datasheet. However, each of the blank cells is a combo box with a scrollable drop-down list of all the entries in that field.

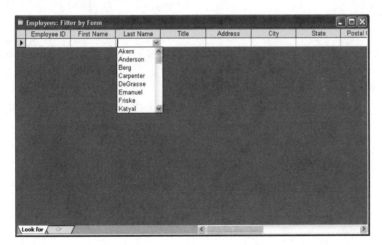

You can make a selection from the list and click the Apply Filter button to display only the records containing your selection.

Using Filter By Form on a table that has only a few fields, such as this one, is easy. But using it on a table that has a few dozen fields gets a bit cumbersome. Then it's easier to use Filter By Form in the form version of the table. If you open a form and then click Filter By Form, you see an empty form. Clicking in any box and then clicking its down arrow displays a list of all the entries in the field.

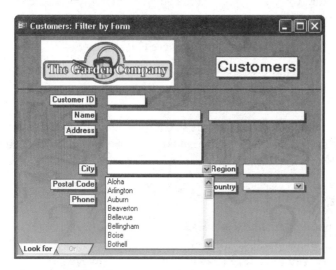

If you make a selection and click the ApplyFilter button, clicking the Next Record navigation button displays the first record that meets your selection criteria, then the next, and so on.

Tip   Filter By Form offers the same features and techniques whether you are using it in a form or a table. Because defining the filter is sometimes easier in a form and viewing the results is sometimes easier in a table, you might consider using AutoForm to quickly create a form for a table. You can then use the form with Filter By Form rather than the table, and then switch to Datasheet view to look at the results.

In this exercise, you will try to track down a customer whose last name you have forgotten. You're pretty sure the name starts with S and the customer is from California or Washington, so you're going to use Filter By Form to try to locate the customer's record.

USE the *GardenCo* database in the practice file folder for this topic. This practice file is located in the *My Documents\Microsoft Press\Office 2003 SBS\Queries\FilterForm* folder and can also be accessed by clicking *Start/All Programs/Microsoft Press/Microsoft Office System 2003 Step by Step.*
OPEN the *GardenCo* database and acknowledge the safety warning, if necessary.

1   Click **Forms** on the **Objects** bar, and double-click **Customers** to open the **Customers** form in Form view.

2   Click the **Filter By Form** button on the toolbar.

Filter By Form

The Customers form, which displays the information from one record, is replaced by its Filter By Form version, which has a blank box for each field and the "Look for" and "Or" tabs at the bottom.

3   Click the second **Name** box (last name), type s*, and press ⌷Enter⌷ to tell Access to display all last names starting with S.

Access converts your entry to the proper format, or *syntax*, for this type of expression: *Like "s*".*

4   Click the **Region** box, and click **CA** in the drop-down list.

5   Click the **Apply Filter** button to see only the customers living in California whose last names begin with S.

Apply Filter

Access replaces the filter window with the regular Customers form, and the navigation bar at the bottom of the form indicates that three filtered records are available.

6   Click the **Filter By Form** button to switch back to the filter.

Your filter criteria are still displayed. When you enter filter criteria using any method, they are saved as a form property and are available until they are replaced by other criteria.

7   To add the customers from another state, click the **Or** tab.

This tab has the same blank cells as the "Look for" tab. You can switch back and forth between the two tabs to confirm that your criteria haven't been cleared.

Tip   When you display the "Or" tab, a second "Or" tab appears so that you can include a third state if you want.

8   Type s* in the **LastName** box, type or click **WA** in the **Region** box, and then click the **Apply Filter** button.

You can scroll through the filtered Customers form to view the six matched records.

9   Close the **Customers** form.

CLOSE the *GardenCo* database.

Locating Information that Matches Multiple Criteria

Filter By Selection, Filter For <input>, and Filter By Form are quick and easy ways to hone in on the information you need, as long as your filter criteria are fairly simple. But suppose The Garden Company needs to locate all the orders shipped to Midwest states between specific dates by either of two shippers. When you need to search a single table for records that meet multiple criteria or that require complex expressions as criteria, you can use the Advanced Filter/Sort command.

You work with the Advanced Filter/Sort command in the design grid. You can use this *design grid* to work with only one table.

Table field list   Design grid

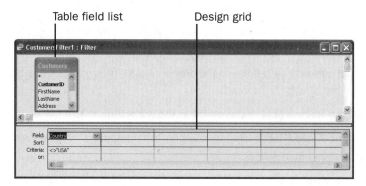

Tip   If you create a simple query in the filter window that you think you might like to use again, you can save it as a query. Either click Save As Query on the File menu; click the Save As Query button on the toolbar; or right-click in the filter window, and then on the shortcut menu, click Save As Query.

In this exercise, you will create a filter to locate customers in two states using the Advanced Filter/Sort command. After locating the customers, you will experiment a bit with the design grid to get a better understanding of its filtering capabilities.

USE the *GardenCo* database in the practice file folder for this topic. This practice file is located in the *My Documents\Microsoft Press\Office 2003 SBS\Queries\AdvFilter* folder and can also be accessed by clicking *Start/All Programs/Microsoft Press/Microsoft Office System 2003 Step by Step*.
OPEN the *GardenCo* database and acknowledge the safety warning, if necessary.

1   Click **Tables** on the **Objects** bar, and double-click **Customers** to open the **Customers** table in Datasheet view.

2   On the **Records** menu, point to **Filter**, and then click **Advanced Filter/Sort**.

Tip   Remember, if you don't see the command on the menu, you can hover over a short menu to display the long menu, or click the double-chevrons at the bottom of the menu.

Access opens the filter window with the Customers field list in the top area.

3   If the design grid is not blank, on the **Edit** menu, click **Clear Grid**.

4   Double-click **LastName** to copy it to the **Field** cell in the first column of the design grid.

5   Click in the **Criteria** cell under **LastName**, type s*, and press ⏎Enter.

Access changes the criterion to *"Like "s*"*".

6   Scroll to the bottom of the **Customers** field list, and double-click **Region** to copy it to the next available column of the design grid.

7   Click in the **Criteria** cell under **Region**, type ca or wa, and press ⏎Enter.

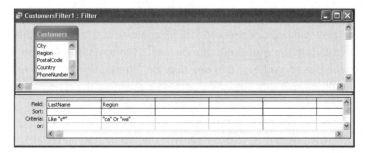

Your entry has changed to *"ca" Or "wa"*. The filter will now match customers with a last name beginning with s who live in California or Washington.

8   On the **Filter** menu, click **Apply Filter/Sort** to view the records that match the criteria.

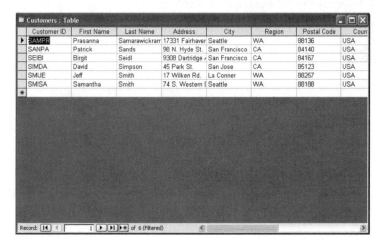

Tip   You can keep an eye on both the filter window and the table window if you reduce both in size.

9   On the **Records** menu, click **Filter** and then **Advanced Filter/Sort** to return to the filter window.

10   Click in the **or** cell in the **LastName** column, type b*, and press Enter.

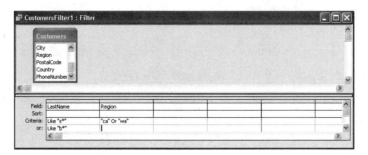

11   On the **Filter** menu, click **Apply Filter/Sort**.

The result includes records for all customers with last names that begin with s or b, but some of the b names live in Montana and Oregon. If you look again at the design grid, you can see that the filter is formed by combining the fields in the Criteria row with the *And* operator, combining the fields in the "Or" row with the *And* operator, and then using the *Or* operator to combine the two rows. So the filter is searching for customers with names beginning with s who live in California or Washington, or customers with names beginning with b, regardless of where they live.

12   Return to the filter window, type ca or wa in the **or** cell under **Region**, and press Enter.

13   Apply the filter again to see only customers from California and Washington.

14   Close the **Customers** table without saving your changes.

CLOSE the *GardenCo* database.

Expressions

The word *expressions*, as used in Access, is synonymous with *formulas*. An expression is a combination of *operators*, *constants*, *functions*, and *control properties* that evaluates to a single value. Access builds formulas using the format *a=b+c*, where *a* is the result and *=b+c* is the expression. An expression can be used to assign properties to tables or forms, to determine values in fields or reports, as part of queries, and in many other places.

The expressions you use in Access combine multiple *criteria* to define a set of conditions that a record must meet before Access will select it as the result of a filter or query. Multiple criteria are combined using logical, comparison, and arithmetic operators. Different types of expressions use different operators.

The most common *logical operators* are *And*, *Or*, and *Not*. When criteria are combined using the *And* operator, a record is selected only if it meets them all. When criteria are combined using the *Or* operator, a record is selected if it meets any one of them. The *Not* operator selects all records that don't match its criterion.

Common *comparison operators* include < (less than), > (greater than), and = (equal). These basic operators can be combined to form <= (less than or equal to), >= (greater than or equal to), and <> (not equal to). The *Like* operator is sometimes grouped with the comparison operators and is used to test whether or not text matches a pattern.

The common *arithmetic operators* are + (add), - (subtract), * (multiply), and / (divide), which are used with numerals. A related operator, & (a text form of +) is used to concatenate—or put together—two text strings.

Creating a Query in Design View

When you want to work with more than one table, you need to move beyond filters and into the realm of queries. The most common type of query selects records that meet specific conditions, but there are several other types, as follows:

- A *select query* retrieves data from one or more tables and displays the results in a datasheet. You can also use a select query to group records and calculate sums, counts, averages, and other types of totals. You can work with the results of a select query in Datasheet view to update records in one or more related tables at the same time.

  - A *duplicate query* is a form of select query that locates records that have the same information in one or more fields that you specify. The Find Duplicates Query Wizard guides you through the process of specifying the table and fields to use in the query.

- An *unmatched query* is a form of select query that locates records in one table that don't have related records in another table. For example, you could use this to locate people in the customer table who don't have an order in the order table. The Find Unmatched Query Wizard guides you through the process of specifying the tables and fields to use in the query.

- A *parameter query* prompts you for information to be used in the query—for example, a range of dates. This type of query is particularly useful if the query is the basis for a report that is run periodically.

- A *crosstab query* calculates and restructures data for easier analysis. It can calculate a sum, average, count, or other type of total for data that is grouped by two types of information—one down the left side of the datasheet and one across the top. The cell at the junction of each row and column displays the results of the query's calculation.

- An *action query* updates or makes changes to multiple records in one operation. It is essentially a select query that performs an action on the results of the selection process. Four types of actions are available: *delete queries*, which delete records from one or more tables; *update queries*, which make changes to records in one or more tables; *append queries*, which add records from one or more tables to the end of one or more other tables; and *make-table queries*, which create a new table from all or part of the data in one or more tables.

Tip Access also includes SQL queries, but you won't be working with this type of query in this book.

Filters and Sorts vs. Queries

The major differences between using filtering or sorting and using a query are:

- The Filter and Sort commands are usually faster to implement than queries.

- The Filter and Sort commands are not saved, or are saved only temporarily. A query can be saved permanently and run again at any time.

- The Filter and Sort commands are applied only to the table or form that is currently open. A query can be based on multiple tables and other queries, which don't have to be open.

You can create a query by hand or by using a wizard. Regardless of how you create the query, what you create is a statement that describes the conditions that must be met for records to be matched in one or more tables. When you run the query, the matching records appear in a datasheet in Datasheet view.

In this exercise, you will create an order entry form that salespeople can fill in as they take orders over the phone. The form will be based on a select query that combines information from the Order Details table and the Products table. The query will create a datasheet listing all products ordered with the unit price, quantity ordered, discount, and extended price. Because the extended price isn't stored in the database, you will calculate this amount directly in the query.

USE the *GardenCo* database in the practice file folder for this topic. This practice file is located in the *My Documents\Microsoft Press\Office 2003 SBS\Queries\QueryDes* folder and can also be accessed by clicking *Start/All Programs/Microsoft Press/Microsoft Office System 2003 Step by Step*.
OPEN the *GardenCo* database and acknowledge the safety warning, if necessary.

1　On the **Objects** bar, click **Queries**.

2　Double-click **Create query in Design view**.

　　Access opens the query window in Design view and then opens the Show Table dialog box.

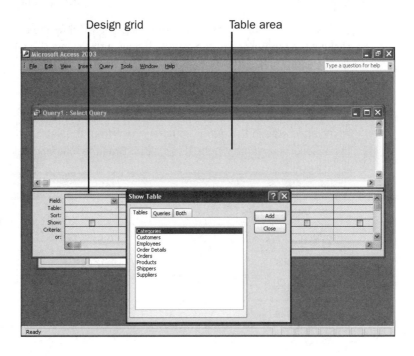

Design grid　　　　　　　　Table area

You can use the Show Table dialog box to specify which tables and saved queries to include in the current query.

3   With the **Tables** tab active, double-click **Order Details** and **Products** to add both tables to the query window. Then close the dialog box.

Each table you added is represented in the top portion of the window by a small field list window with the name of the table—in this case, Order Details and Products—in its title bar.

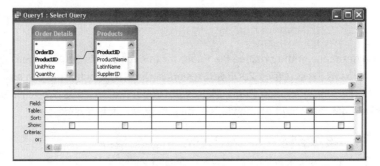

At the top of each list is an asterisk, which represents all the fields in the list. Primary key fields in each list are bold. The line from ProductID in the Order Details table to ProductID in the Products table indicates that these two fields are related.

Tip   To add more tables to a query, reopen the Show Tables dialog box by right-clicking the top portion of the query window and clicking Show Table on the shortcut menu; or by clicking the Show Table button on the toolbar.

The lower area of the query window is taken up by a design grid where you will build the query's criteria.

4   To include fields in the query, you drag them from the lists at the top of the window to consecutive columns in the design grid. Drag the following fields from the two lists:

From table	Field
Order Details	OrderID
Products	ProductName
Order Details	UnitPrice
Order Details	Quantity
Order Details	Discount

Tip You can quickly copy a field to the next open column in the design grid by double-clicking the field. To copy all fields to the grid, double-click the title bar above the field list to select the entire list, and then drag the selection over the grid. When you release the mouse button, Access adds the fields to the columns in order. You can drag the asterisk to a column in the grid to include all the fields in the query, but you also have to drag individual fields to the grid if you want to sort on those fields or add conditions to them.

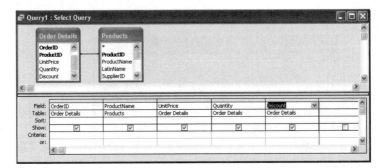

Run

5 Click the **Run** button to run the query and display the results in Datasheet view.

The results show that the query is working so far. There are two things left to do: sort the results on the OrderID field and add a field for calculating the extended price, which is the unit price times the quantity sold minus any discount.

View

6 Click the **View** button to return to Design view.

The third row in the design grid is labeled Sort. If you click in the Sort cell in any column, you can specify whether to sort in ascending order, descending order, or not at all.

7   Click in the **Sort** cell in the **OrderID** column, click the down arrow, and click **Ascending**.

Neither of the tables includes an extended price field. There is no point in entering this information in a table, because you will use the Expression Builder to insert an expression in the design grid that computes this price from existing information.

8   Right-click the **Field** row of the first blank column in the design grid (the sixth column), and on the shortcut menu, click **Build** to open the **Expression Builder** dialog box.

Operator buttons   Expression box

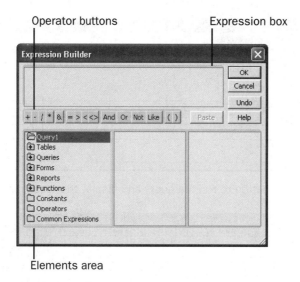

Elements area

Here is the expression you will build:

```
<CCur([Order Details].[UnitPrice]*[Quantity]*(1-[Discount]))>
```

The only part of this expression that you probably can't figure out is the CCur function, which converts the results of the math inside its parentheses to currency format.

9   Double-click the **Functions** folder in the first column of the elements area, and then click **Built-In Functions**.

The categories of built-in functions are displayed in the second column.

10   Click **Conversion** in the second column to limit the functions in the third column to those in that category. Then double-click **Ccur** in the third column.

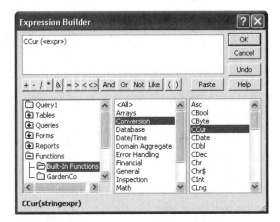

You've inserted the currency conversion function in the expression box. The <<*expr*>> inside the parentheses represents the other expressions that will eventually result in the number Access should convert to currency format.

11   Click **<<expr>>** to select it so that the next thing you enter will replace it.

12   The next element you want in the expression is the **UnitPrice** field from the Order Details table. Double-click the **Tables** object, click **Order Details**, and then double-click **UnitPrice**.

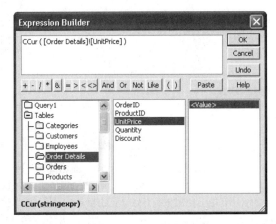

Your last action left the insertion point after UnitPrice, which is exactly where you want it.

13 Now you want to multiply the amount in the **UnitPrice** field by the amount in the **Quantity** field. Start by clicking the * (asterisk) button in the row of operator buttons below the expression box.

Access inserts the multiplication sign and another *<<Expr>>* placeholder.

14 Click **<<Expr>>** to select it, and then insert the **Quantity** field by double-clicking it in the second column.

What you have entered so far multiplies the price by the number ordered, which results in the total cost for this item. However, The Garden Company offers discounts on certain items at different times of the year. The amount of the discount is entered by the sales clerk and stored in the Order Details table. In the table, the discount is expressed as the percentage to deduct—usually 10 to 20 percent. But it is easier to compute the percentage the customer will pay—usually 80 to 90 percent of the regular price—than it is to compute the discount and then subtract it from the total cost.

15 Type *(1-, then double-click **Discount**, and type), and then widen the window to see the whole expression.

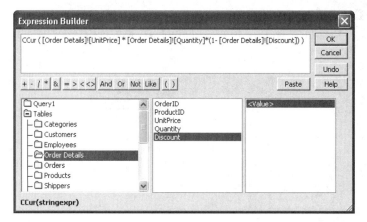

Remember that the discount is formatted in the datasheet as a percentage, but it is stored as a decimal number between 0 and 1. When you look at it you might see 10%, but what is actually stored in the database is 0.1. So if the discount is 10 percent, the result of *(1-Discount) is *.9. In other words, the formula multiplies the unit price by the quantity and then multiplies that result by 0.9.

16 Click **OK**.

Access closes the Expression Builder and copies the expression to the design grid.

17 Press ⌊Enter⌋ to move the insertion point out of the field, which completes the entry of the expression.

> **Tip** You can quickly make a column in the design grid as wide as its contents by double-clicking the line in the gray selection bar that separates the column from the column to its right.

18 Access has given the expression the name *Expr1*. This name isn't particularly meaningful, so rename it by double-clicking **Expr1** and then typing **ExtendedPrice**.

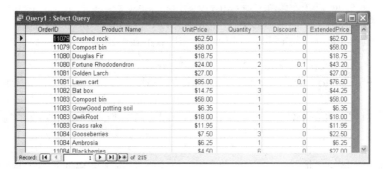

View

19 Click the **View** button to see the results in Datasheet view.

The orders are now sorted on the OrderID field, and the extended price is calculated in the last field.

20 Scroll down to see a few records with discounts.

If you check the math, you will see that the query calculates the extended price correctly.

21 Close the query window, and when prompted to save the query, click **Yes**. Type **Order Details Extended** to name the query, and click **OK** to close it.

CLOSE the *GardenCo* database.

Expression Builder

When an expression is a valid filter or query option, you can usually either type the expression or use the Expression Builder to create it. You open the Expression Builder by either clicking Build on a shortcut menu or clicking the ... button (sometimes referred to as the Build button) at the right end of a box that can accept an expression.

The Expression Builder isn't a wizard; it doesn't lead you through the process of building an expression. But it does provide a hierarchical list of most of the elements that you can include in an expression. After looking at the list, you can either type your expression in the expression box, or you can select functions, operators, and other elements to copy them to the expression box, and then click OK to transfer them to the filter or query.

Creating a Query with a Wizard

The process used to create a simple select query with the Query Wizard is almost identical to that for creating a form with the Form Wizard. With the Query Wizard, you can add one or more fields from existing tables or queries to the new query.

For Access to work effectively with multiple tables, it must understand the relationships between the fields in those tables. You have to create these relationships before using the Query Wizard, by clicking the Relationships button and then dragging a field in one table over the identical field in another table (the field names don't have to be the same in each table, but the field contents must represent the same information).

In this exercise, you will use the Query Wizard to create a new query that combines information from the Customers and Orders tables to provide information about each order. These tables are related through their common CustomerID fields. (This relationship has already been established in the GardenCo database files used in this chapter.)

USE the *GardenCo* database in the practice file folder for this topic. This practice file is located in the *My Documents\Microsoft Press\Office 2003 SBS\Queries\QueryWiz* folder and can also be accessed by clicking *Start/All Programs/Microsoft Press/Microsoft Office System 2003 Step by Step*.
OPEN the *GardenCo* database and acknowledge the safety warning, if necessary.

1 On the **Objects** bar, click **Queries,** and then double-click **Create query by using wizard.**

The first page of the Simple Query Wizard opens.

Tip You can also start the Query Wizard by clicking Query on the Insert menu or clicking the arrow to the right of the New Object button list, and then double-clicking Simple Query Wizard.

2 In the **Tables/Queries** list, click **Table: Orders.**

3 Click the **>>** button to move all available fields in the **Available Fields** list to the **Selected Fields** list.

4 Select **Table: Customers** from the **Tables/Queries** list.

5 In the **Available Fields** list, double-click the **Address, City, Region, PostalCode,** and **Country** fields to move them to the **Selected Fields** list, and then click **Next.**

Tip If the relationship between two tables hasn't already been established, you will be prompted to define it and then start the wizard again.

6 Click **Next** again to accept the default option of showing details in the results of the query.

7 Change the query title to Orders Qry, leave the **Open the query to view information** option selected, and then click **Finish**.

Access runs the query and displays the results in Datasheet view. You can scroll through the results and see that information is displayed for all the orders.

View Design

8 Click the **View** button to view the query in Design view.

Notice that the Show box is, by default, selected for each of the fields used in the query. If you want to use a field in a query—for example, to sort on, to set criteria for, or in a calculation—but don't want to see the field in the results datasheet, you can clear its Show check box.

View

9 Clear the **Show** check box for **OrderID**, **CustomerID**, and **EmployeeID**, and then click the **View** button to switch back to Datasheet view.

The three fields have been removed from the results datasheet.

10 Click the **View** button to return to Design view.

This query returns all records in the Orders table. To have this query match the records for a range of dates, you will convert it to a parameter query, which asks for the date range each time you run it.

11 In the **OrderDate** column, click in the **Criteria** cell, and type the following, exactly as shown:

Between [Type the beginning date:] And [Type the ending date:]

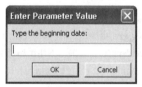

Run

12 Click the **Run** button to run the query.

13 In the dialog box displayed, type 1/1/03, and press ⏎.

14 In the second **Enter Parameter Value** dialog box, type 1/31/03, and press ⏎ again.

The datasheet is displayed again, this time listing only orders between the parameter dates.

15 Close the datasheet, clicking **Yes** to save the query.

CLOSE the *GardenCo* database.

Performing Calculations in a Query

You typically use a query to locate all the records that meet some criteria. But sometimes you are not as interested in the details of all the records as you are in summarizing them in some way. As an example, you might want to know how many orders have been placed this year or the total dollar value of all orders placed. The easiest way to get this information is to create a query that groups the necessary fields and does the math for you. To do this, you use *aggregate functions* in the query.

Access queries support the following aggregate functions:

Function	Calculates
Sum	Total of the values in a field
Avg	Average of the values in a field
Count	Number of values in a field, not counting Null (blank) values
Min	Lowest value in a field
Max	Highest value in a field
StDev	Standard deviation of the values in a field
Var	Variance of the values in a field

In this exercise, you will create a query that calculates the total number of products in The Garden Company's inventory, the average price of all the products, and the total value of the inventory.

USE the *GardenCo* database in the practice file folder for this topic. This practice file is located in the *My Documents\Microsoft Press\Office 2003 SBS\Queries\Aggregate* folder and can also be accessed by clicking *Start/All Programs/Microsoft Press/Microsoft Office System 2003 Step by Step*.
OPEN the *GardenCo* database and acknowledge the safety warning, if necessary.

1 On the **Objects** bar, click **Queries**, and then double-click **Create query in Design view**.

Access first opens the query window in Design view and then displays the Show Table dialog box.

2 In the **Show Table** dialog box, double-click **Products**, and click **Close**.

Access adds the Products table to the query window and closes the Show Table dialog box.

3   In the list of fields in the **Products** table, double-click **ProductID** and then **UnitPrice**.

Access moves both fields to the design grid.

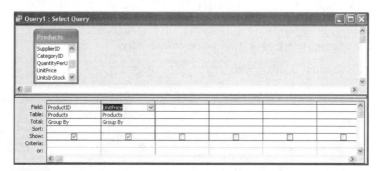
Σ
Totals

4   Click the **Totals** button on the toolbar.

A row named *Total* is added to the design grid.

5   Click in the **Total** cell of the **ProductID** column, click the down arrow, and click **Count** in the drop-down list.

Access enters the word *Count* in the Total cell. When you run the query, this function will return a count of the number of records containing a value in the ProductID field.

6   In the **UnitPrice** column, set the **Total** cell to **Avg**.

When you run the query, this function will return the average of all the UnitPrice values.

Run

7   Click the **Run** button.

The result of the query is a single record containing the count and the average price.

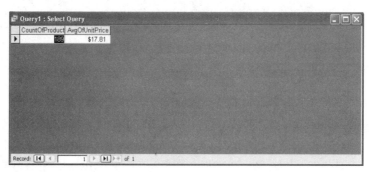

View

8 Click the **View** button to return to Design view.

9 In the **Field** cell of the third column, type **UnitPrice*UnitsInStock** and press Enter.

The text you typed is changed to *Expr1: [UnitPrice]*[UnitsInStock]*. This expression will multiply the price of each product by the number of units in stock.

10 Set the **Total** cell of the third column to **Sum** to return the sum of all the values calculated by the expression.

11 Select **Expr1:**, and type Value of Inventory:.

12 Run the query again.

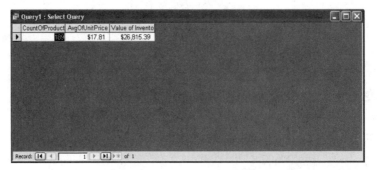

13 Close the query window, clicking **No** when prompted to save the query.

CLOSE the *GardenCo* database.

Key Points

- ■ Microsoft Office Access 2003 provides a variety of tools you can use to organize the display of information in a database and to locate specific items of information, making it easy to search through and find information in your database, even as it grows in size and complexity.

- ■ You can sort through a table in either ascending or descending order, based on the values in any field (or combination of fields). In Access, numbers can be treated as text or numerals.

- ■ You can filter a table so that information containing some combination of characters is displayed (or excluded from the display). You can apply simple filters while viewing information in a table or a form. These filters are applied to the contents of a selected field, but you can apply another filter to the results of the first one to further refine your search.

■   You can use the Filter By Form command to filter a table or form based on the information in several fields. Since defining a filter is often easier in a form and viewing the results is easier in a table, you can use AutoForm to quickly create a form for a table. You can use the form with Filter By Form, and then switch to Datasheet view to see the results.

■   When you need to search a single table for records that meet multiple criteria or that require complex expressions as criteria, you can use the Advanced Filter/Sort command.

■   You can create queries to display specific fields from specific records from one or more tables, even designing the query to perform calculations for you. You can then save your queries for later use.

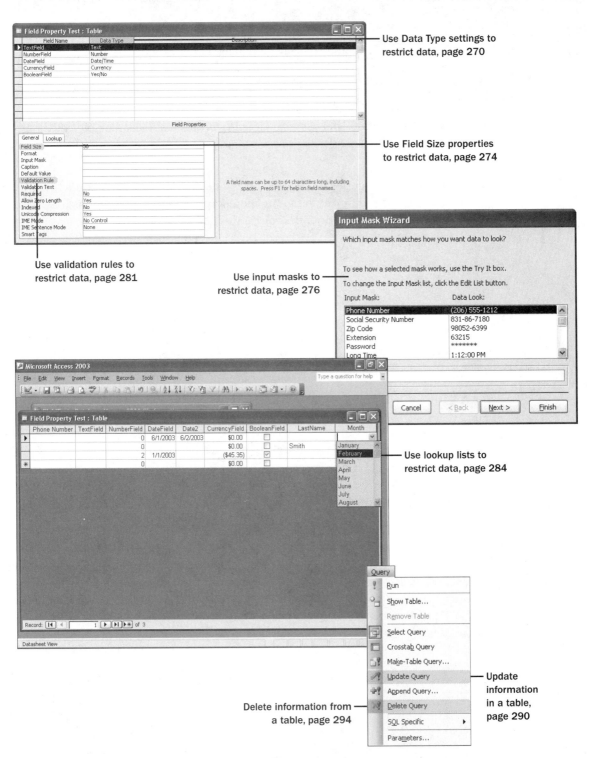

Use Data Type settings to
restrict data, page 270

Use Field Size properties
to restrict data, page 274

Use validation rules to
restrict data, page 281

Use input masks to
restrict data, page 276

Use lookup lists to
restrict data, page 284

Update
information
in a table,
page 290

Delete information from
a table, page 294

12 Keeping Your Information Accurate

In this chapter you will learn to:

✔ Use Data Type settings to restrict data.

✔ Use Field Size properties to restrict data.

✔ Use input masks to restrict data.

✔ Use validation rules to restrict data.

✔ Use lookup lists to restrict data.

✔ Update information in a table.

✔ Delete information from a table.

Depending on how much information you have and how organized you are, you might compare a database to an old shoebox or a file cabinet, into which you toss items such as photographs, bills, receipts, and a variety of other paperwork for later retrieval. However, neither a shoebox nor a file cabinet restricts what you can place in it (other than how much can fit in it) or imposes any order on its content. It is up to you to decide what you store there and to organize it properly so that you can find it when you next need it.

When you create a database with Microsoft Office Access 2003, you can set *properties* that restrict what can be entered in it, thereby keeping the database organized and useful. For example, The Garden Company wouldn't want its employees to enter text into *fields* that should contain numbers, such as price fields. Similarly, they wouldn't want to encourage employees to enter a long text description in a field when a simple "yes" or "no" answer would work best. The *field properties* that control input are: Required, Allow Zero Length, Field Size, Input Mask, and Validation Rule. The Required and Allow Zero Length properties are fairly obvious. If the Required property is set to *Yes*, the field can't be left blank. However, if Allow Zero Length is set to *Yes*, you can enter an empty *string* (two quotation marks with nothing in between), which looks like an empty field. The other properties are more complex, so you'll focus on them in the exercises in this chapter.

Tip   Each property has many options. For more information about how to use properties, search for *field property* in Access online Help.

To ensure the ongoing accuracy of a database, you can create and run *action queries* that quickly update information or delete selected records from a table. For example, The Garden Company might decide to increase the price of all products in one category, or to remove one entire product line. This type of updating is easy to do with an action query. Not only does using a query save time, but it avoids human-input errors.

The exercises in this chapter demonstrate how to use the *data type* setting and some of the field properties to restrict the data that can be entered in a table or form. It is difficult to experiment with field properties in a table that is already filled with information because changing a field's data type or properties can destroy or alter the data. For that reason, the first few exercises in this chapter use a new database that you will create just for the purpose of experimenting with data types and properties. Then you will resume working with sample GardenCo database files provided on the book's companion CD.

See Also   Do you need only a quick refresher on the topics in this chapter? See the Quick Reference entries on page xxxiii.

Important   Before you can use the practice files in this chapter, you need to install them from the book's companion CD to their default location. See "Using the Book's CD-ROM" on page xxi for more information.

Using Data Type Settings to Restrict Data

The Data Type setting restricts entries to a specific type of data: text, numbers, dates, and so on. If, for example, the data type is set to Number and you attempt to enter text, Access refuses the entry and displays a warning.

In this exercise, you will create a new blank database, add fields of the most common data types, and experiment with how the Data Type setting and Field Size property can be used to restrict the data entered into a table.

BE SURE TO start Access before beginning this exercise.

1   In the **New File** task pane, click **Blank Database** in the **New** section to display the **File New Database** dialog box.

If the New File task pane does not appear, on the toolbar, click the New button.

New

2 In the **File name** box, type FieldTest, navigate to the *My Documents\Microsoft Press \Office 2003 SBS\Accurate\DataType* folder, and then click **Create**.

Access opens the database window for the new database.

3 Double-click **Create table in Design view**.

A blank Table window opens in Design view so that you can define the fields that categorize the information in the table. You will define five fields, one for each of the data types: *Text, Number, Date/Time, Currency,* and *Yes/No.*

4 Click in the first **Field Name** cell, type TextField, and press Tab to move to the **Data Type** cell.

5 The data type defaults to **Text**, which is the type you want. Press Tab twice to accept the default data type and move the insertion point to the next row.

6 Type NumberField, and press Tab to move to the **Data Type** cell.

7 Click the down arrow to expand the list of data types, click **Number**, and then press Tab twice.

Tip Rather than displaying the list of data types and clicking one, you can type the first character of the desired type, and it will be entered in the cell.

8 Repeat steps 4 through 7 to add the following fields:

Field	Data type
DateField	Date/Time
CurrencyField	Currency
BooleanField	Yes/No

Tip The data type referred to as Yes/No in Access is more commonly called *Boolean* (in honor of George Boole, an early mathematician and logistician). This data type can hold either of two mutually exclusive values, often expressed as *yes/no, 1/0, on/off,* or *true/false.*

9 Click the **Save** button, type Field Property Test to name the table, and then click **OK**.

Save

Access displays a dialog box recommending that you create a primary key.

10   You don't need a primary key for this exercise, so click **No**.

11   Click the row selector for **TextField** to select the first row.

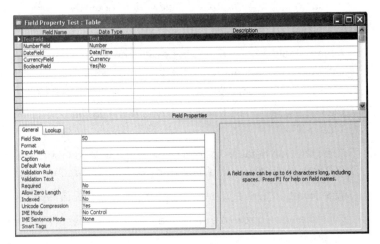

The properties of the selected field are displayed in the lower portion of the dialog box.

View

12   Click in each field and review its properties, and then click the **View** button to display the table in Datasheet view.

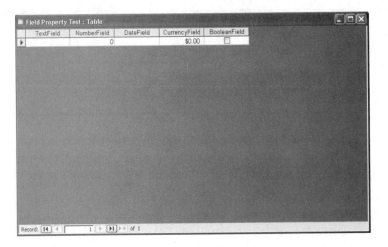

13 The insertion point should be in the first field. Type This entry is 32 characters long, and press [Tab] to move to the next field.

14 Type Five hundred, and press [Tab].

The data type for this field is Number. Access displays an alert box refusing your text entry.

15 Click **OK**, replace the text with the number 500, and press [Tab].

16 Type a number or text (anything but a date) in the date field, and press [Tab]. When Access refuses it, click **OK**, type Jan 1, and press [Tab].

The date field accepts almost any entry that can be recognized as a date, and displays it in the default date format. Depending on the format on your computer, Jan 1 might be displayed as *1/1/2003* or *1/1/03*.

Tip   If you enter a month and day but no year in a date field, Access assumes the date is in the current year. If you enter a month, day, and two-digit year from 00 through 29, Access assumes the year is 2000 through 2029. If you enter a two-digit year that is greater than 29, Access assumes you mean 1930 through 1999.

17 Type any text or a date in the currency field, and press [Tab]. When Access refuses the entry, click **OK**, type –45.3456 in the field, and press [Tab].

Access stores the number you entered but displays ($45.35), the default format for displaying negative currency numbers.

Tip   Access uses the regional settings in the Microsoft Windows Control Panel to determine the display format for date, time, currency, and other numbers. If you intend to share database files with people in other countries, you might want to create custom formats to ensure that the correct currency symbol is always displayed with your values. Otherwise, the numbers won't change, but displaying them as dollars, pounds, pesos, or euros will radically alter their value.

18 Enter text or a number in the **Boolean** field. Then click anywhere in the field to toggle the check box between **Yes** (checked) and **No** (not checked), finishing with the field in the checked state.

This field won't accept anything you type; you can only switch between two predefined values.

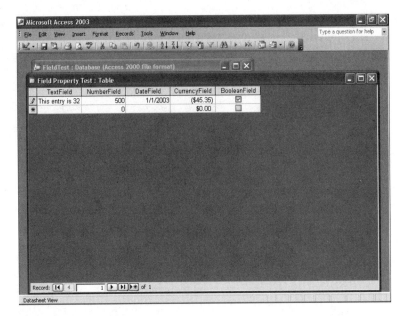

Tip In Design view, you can open the Properties dialog box, and on the Lookup tab, set the Boolean field to display as a check box, text box, or combo box. You can also set the Format property on the General tab to use True/False, Yes/No, or On/Off as the displayed values in this field (though the stored values will always be -1 and 0).

19 Close the table.

CLOSE the *FieldTest* database.

Using Field Size Properties to Restrict Data

You can set the Field Size property for the Text, Number, and AutoNumber data types. This property restricts the number of characters that you can enter in a text field and the size of numbers that can be entered in a number or AutoNumber field. For text fields, the Field Size property can be set to any number from 0 to 255. AutoNumber fields are automatically set to Long Integer. Number fields can be set to any of the following values:

Setting	Description
Byte	Stores numbers from 0 to 255 (no fractions).
Integer	Stores numbers from –32,768 to 32,767 (no fractions).
Long Integer	(The default.) Stores numbers from –2,147,483,648 to 2,147,483,647 (no fractions).

Setting	Description
Single	Stores numbers from –3.402823E38 to –1.401298E–45 for negative values and from 1.401298E–45 to 3.402823E38 for positive values.
Double	Stores numbers from –1.79769313486231E308 to –4.94065645841247E–324 for negative values and from 1.79769313486231E308 to 4.94065645841247E–324 for positive values.
Decimal	Stores numbers from -10^28 -1 through 10^28 -1.

By setting the Field Size property to a value that allows the largest valid entry, you prevent the user from entering certain types of invalid information. If you try to type more characters in a text field than the number allowed by the Field Size setting, Access beeps and refuses to accept the entry. Likewise, a value that is below or above the limits of a number field is rejected when you try to move out of the field.

In this exercise, you will change the Field Size property for several fields to see the impact this has on data already in the table and on new data that you enter.

USE the *FieldTest* database in the practice file folder for this topic. This practice file is located in the *My Documents\Microsoft Press\Office 2003 SBS\Accurate\FieldSize* folder and can also be accessed by clicking *Start/All Programs/Microsoft Press/Microsoft Office System 2003 Step by Step*.
OPEN the *FieldTest* database.

1 Open the **Field Property Test** table in Design view.

2 Click in the **TextField** row, and in the **Field Properties** area, change the **Field Size** property from *50* to *12*.

3 Click in the **NumberField** row, click the **Field Size** property, click its down arrow, and change the setting from *Long Integer* to **Byte**.

The number of characters that can be entered in the text field is restricted to 12, and the values that can be entered in the number field are restricted to the range 0 to 255.

View

4 Click the **View** button to return to Datasheet view, clicking **Yes** when prompted to save the table.

The table contains data that doesn't fit these new property settings, so Access displays a warning that some data might be lost.

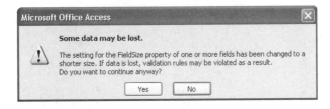

5 Click **Yes** to acknowledge the risk, and click **Yes** again to accept the deletion of the contents of one field.

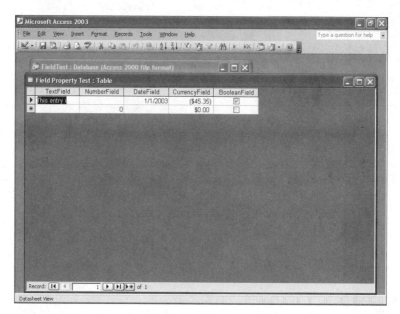

TextField now contains only 12 characters, rather than the 32 you entered. The other 20 characters have been permanently deleted. NumberField is empty because it is now limited to whole numbers from *0* through *255*, and the value of *500* that you entered was deleted.

6 Type **2.5** as the **NumberField** entry, and press $\boxed{\text{Enter}}$.

The number is rounded to the nearest whole number.

7 Close the table.

CLOSE the *FieldTest* database.

Using Input Masks to Restrict Data

When you use *masks* in tables or forms, people entering information can see at a glance the format in which they should make entries and how long they should be. You can use the InputMask property to control how data is entered in text, number, date/time, and currency fields. This property has three sections, separated by semi-colons, like the mask for a telephone number, shown here:

!\(000") "000\-0000;1;#

The first section contains characters that are used as placeholders for the information to be typed, as well as characters such as parentheses and hyphens. Together, all these characters control the appearance of the entry. The following list explains the purpose of the most common input mask characters:

Character	Description
0	Required digit (0 through 9).
9	Optional digit or space.
#	Optional digit or space; blank positions are converted to spaces; plus and minus signs are allowed.
L	Required letter (A through Z).
?	Optional letter (A through Z).
A	Required letter or digit.
a	Optional letter or digit.
&	Required character (any kind) or a space.
C	Optional character (any kind) or a space.
<	All characters that follow are converted to lowercase.
>	All characters that follow are converted to uppercase.
!	Characters typed into the mask fill it from left to right. You can include the exclamation point anywhere in the input mask.
\	Character that follows is displayed as a literal character.
Password	Creates a password entry box. Any character typed in the box is stored as the character but displayed as an asterisk (*).

Any characters not included in this list are displayed as literal characters. If you want to use one of the special characters in this list as a literal character, precede it with the \ (backslash) character.

The second and third sections of the input mask are optional. Including a 1 or leaving nothing in the second section tells Access to store only the characters entered; including a 0 tells it to store both the characters entered and the mask characters. The character in the third section is displayed in a new record as the placeholder for the characters to be typed. This placeholder defaults to an underscore if the section is omitted.

The input mask !\(000") "000\-0000;1;# creates this display in a field in both a table and a form:

(###) ###-####

In this example, you are restricting the entry to ten digits—no more and no less. Access stores just the digits entered, not the parentheses, space, and dash (though those characters could be displayed in your table, form, or report if you set the correct format property).

In this exercise, you will use the Input Mask Wizard to apply a predefined telephone input mask to a text field, forcing entered numbers into the (206) 555-0001 format. You will then create a custom mask to force the first letter of an entry to be uppercase (a capital letter).

USE the *FieldTest* database in the practice file folder for this topic. This practice file is located in the *My Documents\Microsoft Press\Office 2003 SBS\Accurate\InputMask* folder and can also be accessed by clicking *Start/All Programs/Microsoft Press/Microsoft Office System 2003 Step by Step*.
OPEN the *FieldTest* database.

1   Open the **Field Property Test** table in Design view.

2   In the first blank **Field Name** cell, type PhoneField, and leave the data type set to *Text*.

3   Click the row selector to select the row, and then drag the new field to the top of the field list so that it will appear at the left end of the table.

4   Save the table design, and with **PhoneField** still selected, click **Input Mask** in the **Field Properties** area.

5   Click the ... button to the right of the cell to start the **Input Mask Wizard** and display the first page of the wizard. (Click **Yes** if you are prompted to install this feature.)

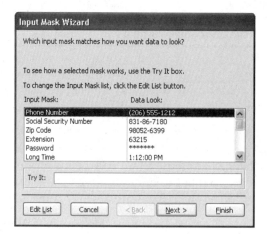

Tip   You can create an input mask by hand for text, number, date, or currency fields, or you can use this wizard to apply one of several standard masks for text and date fields.

6   With **Phone Number** selected in the **Input Mask** list, click **Next**.

The second page of the wizard displays the input mask and gives you the opportunity to change the placeholder character that will indicate what to type. The exclamation point causes Access to fill the mask from left to right with whatever is typed. The parentheses and hyphen are characters that Access will insert in the specified places. The 9s represent optional digits, and the 0s represent required digits, so you can enter a telephone number with or without an area code.

Tip   Because Access fills the mask from left to right, you would have to press the Right Arrow key to move the insertion point past the first three placeholders to enter a telephone number without an area code.

7   Change 999 to 000 to require an area code, and then change the placeholder character to #.

8   Click **Next**.

On the third page of the wizard, you specify whether you want to store the symbols with the data. If you store the symbols, the data will always be displayed in tables, forms, and reports in this format. However, the symbols take up space, meaning that your database will be larger.

9 Accept the default selection—to store data without the symbols—by clicking **Finish**.

Access closes the wizard and displays the edited mask as the Input Mask property.

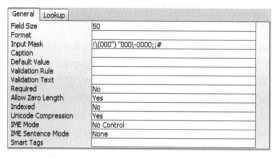

10 Press ⌨️Enter to accept the mask.

Access changes the format of the mask to *!\(000") "000\-0000;;#*. Notice the two semicolons that separate the mask into its three sections. Because you told Access to store data without the symbols, nothing is displayed in the second section of the mask.

New In Office 2003
Property
Update Options

Tip When you press ⌨️Enter, a button is added in front of the Input Mask. This is the Property Update Options button, and if you click it, a list of options is displayed. In this case, the only option is to apply the input mask everywhere PhoneField is used. This button disappears when you edit any other property or change to a different field.

View

11 Save your changes, and click the **View** button to return to Datasheet view.

12 Press the ⬇️ key to move to the new record, and type a series of at least ten digits and then some letters to see how the mask works.

Any letters you type are ignored. The first ten digits are formatted as a telephone number. If you type more than ten digits, they are also ignored. If you type fewer than ten digits and press Tab or Enter, Access warns you that your entry doesn't match the input mask.

Tip An input mask can contain more than just the placeholders for the data to be entered. If, for example, you type "The number is" in front of the telephone number in the Input Mask property, the default entry for the field is *The number is (###) ###-####*. Then if you place the insertion point to the left of *The* and start typing numbers, the numbers replace the # placeholders, not the text. The Field Size setting is not applied to the characters in the mask, so if this setting is *15*, the entry is not truncated even though the number of displayed characters (including spaces) is 28.

13　Return to Design view, and add a new field below **BooleanField**. Name it LastName. Leave the **Data Type** setting as the default **Text**.

14　Select the new field, click **Input Mask**, type >L<?????????????????? (18 question marks), and press ⌊Enter⌋.

The > forces all following text to be uppercase. The *L* requires a letter. The < forces all following text to be lowercase. Each *?* allows any letter or no letter, and there is one fewer question mark than the maximum number of letters you want to allow in the field (19, including the leading capital letter). The Field Size setting must be greater than this maximum.

15　Save your changes, return to Datasheet view, type smith in the **LastName** field of one of the records, and press ⌊Tab⌋. Try entering SMITH, and then McDonald.

As you can see, only the first letter is capitalized, no matter how you try to type the name, so this type of mask has its limitations. But it can be useful in many situations.

16　Close the table.

CLOSE the *FieldTest* database.

Using Validation Rules to Restrict Data

A *validation rule* is an *expression* that can precisely define the information that will be accepted in one or several fields in a record. You might use a validation rule in a field containing the date an employee was hired to prevent a date in the future from being entered. Or if you make deliveries to only certain local areas, you could use a validation rule on the phone field or ZIP code field to refuse entries from other areas.

You can type validation rules in by hand, or you can use the *Expression Builder* to create them. At the field level, Access uses the rule to test an entry when you attempt to leave the field. At the table level, Access uses the rule to test the content of several fields when you attempt to leave the record. If an entry doesn't satisfy the rule, Access rejects the entry and displays a message explaining why.

In this exercise, you will create and test several field validation rules and one table validation rule.

USE the *FieldTest* database in the practice file folder for this topic. This practice file is located in the *My Documents\Microsoft Press\Office 2003 SBS\Accurate\ValRules* folder and can also be accessed by clicking *Start/All Programs/Microsoft Press/Microsoft Office System 2003 Step by Step*.
OPEN the *FieldTest* database.

1　Open the **Field Property Test** table in Design view.

2   To add a validation rule to **PhoneField** that will prevent the entry of an area code other than 206 or 425, select **PhoneField**, and click in the **Validation Rule** box.

A ... button appears at the end of the Validation Rule box. You can click this button to use the Expression Builder to create an expression, or you can type an expression in the box.

3   Type the following in the **Validation Rule** box, and press Enter :

Like "206*" Or Like "425*"

Troubleshooting   Be sure to include the asterisk after the 206 and 425.

4   In the **Validation Text** box, type Area code must be 206 or 425.

A rule for the first three digits typed in the PhoneField field is set including the text that Access should display if someone attempts to enter an invalid phone number.

5   Click in the **Caption** box, and type **Phone Number**.

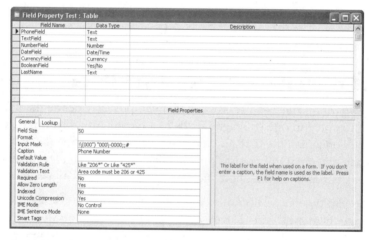

6   Save the table.

Access warns you that data integrity rules have changed. The table violates the new rule because it contains blank phone number fields.

7   Click **No** to close the message box without testing the data.

Tip   You can test the validation rules in a table at any time by right-clicking the title bar of the table and clicking Test Validation Rules on the shortcut menu.

8   Return to Datasheet view, where the caption for the first field is now *Phone Number*.

9　　Place the insertion point to the left of the first # of any **Phone Number** field, type 3605550009, and press ⌷Enter⌷.

Tip　To select the entire field, move the pointer to the left end of the Phone Number field, and when the pointer changes to a thick cross, click the field. The insertion point is then at the start of the area code when you begin typing.

The Validation Rule setting causes Access to display an alert box, warning you that the area code must be either 206 or 425.

10　Click **OK** to close the alert box, type a new phone number with one of the allowed area codes, and press ⌷Enter⌷.

11　Return to Design view, and add another date field. Type Date2 as the field name, set the data type to **Date/Time**, and drag the new field to just below **DateField**.

12　Right-click the table window, and click **Properties** on the shortcut menu to open the **Table Properties** dialog box.

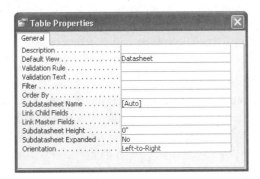

Tip　This dialog box is not the same one displayed when you right-click the table in the database window and click Properties. The only point in common between the two is the Description property, which you can enter in either dialog box.

13　Click in the **Validation Rule** box, type [DateField]<[Date2], and press ⌷Enter⌷.

14　Type Date2 must be later than DateField, and close the dialog box.

A table validation rule is added that ensures that the second date is always later than the first one.

15　Save the table (click **No** to close the data-integrity alert box), and return to Datasheet view.

16 In any record, type 6/1/03 in **DateField** and 5/1/03 in **Date2,** and then click in another record.

Access displays the Validation Text setting from the Table Properties dialog box, reminding you that Date2 must be later than DateField.

17 Click **OK,** change **Date2** to 6/2/2003, and click in another record.

18 Close the table.

CLOSE the *FieldTest* database.

Using Lookup Lists to Restrict Data

It is interesting how many different ways people can come up with to enter the same items of information in a database. Asked to enter the name of their home state, for example, residents of the state of Washington will type *Washington, Wash,* or *WA,* plus various typos and misspellings. If you ask a dozen sales clerks to enter the name of a specific product, customer, and shipper in an invoice, the probability that all of them will type the same thing is not very high. In cases like this, in which the number of correct choices is limited (to actual product name, actual customer, and actual shipper), providing the option to choose the correct answer from a list will improve your database's consistency.

Minor inconsistencies in the way data is entered might not be really important to someone who later reads the information and makes decisions. Most people know that *Arizona* and *AZ* refer to the same state. But a computer is very literal, and if you tell it to create a list so that you can send catalogs to everyone living in *AZ,* the computer won't include anyone whose state is listed in the database as *Arizona.*

You can limit the options for entering information in a database in several ways:

■ For only two options, you can use a Boolean field represented by a check box. A check in the box indicates one choice, and no check indicates the other choice.

■ For several mutually exclusive options on a form, you can use *option buttons* to gather the required information.

■ For more than a few options, a *combo box* is a good way to go. When you click the down arrow at the end of a combo box, a list of choices is displayed. Depending on the properties associated with the combo box, if you don't see the option you want, you might be able to type something else, adding your entry to the list of possible options displayed in the future.

■ For a short list of choices that won't change often, you can have the combo box look up the options in a list that you provide. Although you can create a lookup list by hand, it is a lot easier to use the *Lookup Wizard*.

In this exercise, you will use the Lookup Wizard to create a list of months from which the user can choose.

USE the *FieldTest* database in the practice file folder for this topic. This practice file is located in the *My Documents\Microsoft Press\Office 2003 SBS\Accurate\Lookup* folder and can also be accessed by clicking *Start/All Programs/Microsoft Press/Microsoft Office System 2003 Step by Step*.
OPEN the *FieldTest* database.

1 Open the **Field Property Test** table in Design view.

2 Add a new field below **LastName**. Name it **Month**, and set the data type to **Lookup Wizard**.

The first page of the Lookup Wizard appears.

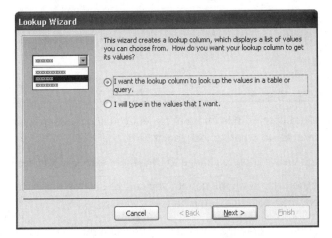

You can use this wizard to create a combo box that provides the entry for a text field. The combo box list can come from a table or query, or you can type the list in the wizard.

Tip If a field has a lot of potential entries, or if they will change often, you can link them to a table. (You might have to create a table expressly for this purpose.) If the field has only a few items and they won't change, typing the list in the wizard is easier.

3 Select the **I will type in the values that I want option**, and then click **Next**.

4 Leave the number of columns set to *1*, and click in the **Col1** box.

5 Enter the 12 months of the year (January, February, and so on), pressing ⟨Tab⟩ after each one to move to a new row. Then click **Next**.

6 Accept the Month default label, and click **Finish**.

7 In the **Field Properties** area, click the **Lookup** tab to view the Lookup information for the **Month** field.

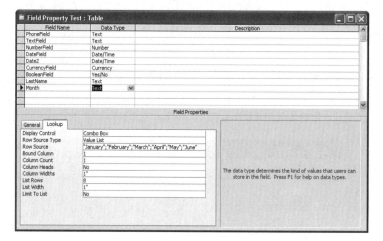

The wizard entered this information, but you could easily figure out what you would have to enter to create a lookup list by hand.

8 Click the **View** button to change to Datasheet view, clicking **Yes** to save your changes.

View

9 Adjust the column widths so that you can see all the fields, by dragging the vertical bars between columns in the header.

Tip You can drag the vertical bars between the columns to make them smaller than the text in them. You can also double-click the vertical bars to automatically size the columns to fit the text in them.

10 Click in the **Month** field of a record, and then click the down arrow to display the list.

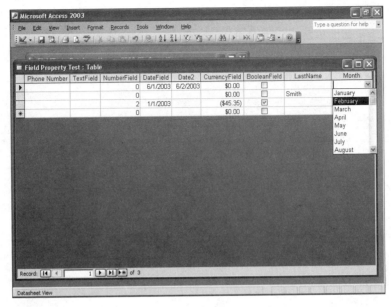

11 Click **February** to enter it in the field.

12 Click in the next **Month** field, type Jan, and press ⏎ Enter.

As soon as you type the *J*, the combo box displays *January*. If you had typed *Ju*, the combo box would have displayed *June*.

13 In the next **Month** field, type jly, and press ⏎ Enter.

Even though the entry isn't in the list, it is accepted just as you typed it. Although there might be times when you want to allow the entry of information other than the items in the list, this isn't one of those times, so you need to change the field properties to limit what can be entered.

14 Return to Design view.

The last property on the Lookup tab is "Limit To List". It is currently set to *No*, which allows people to enter information that isn't in the list.

15 Change **Limit To List** to **Yes**.

16 Save the table, return to Datasheet view, type jly in a new **Month** field, and press ⏎ Enter.

Access informs you that the text you entered is not in the list, and refuses the entry.

17 Click **OK**, and then click **July** in the list.

A list of the names of months is convenient for people, but if your computer has to deal with this information in some mathematical way, a list of the numbers associated with each month is easier for it to use. There is a solution that will work for both humans and machines.

18 Return to Design view, create a new field named Month2, and again set the data type to **Lookup Wizard**.

19 Select the **I will type in the values that I want** option, and click **Next**.

20 Type 2 to add a second column, and then click in the **Col1** box.

Access adds a second column, labeled *Col2*.

21 Enter the following numbers and months in the two columns, pressing [Tab] to move from column to column:

Number	Month	Number	Month
1	January	7	July
2	February	8	August
3	March	9	September
4	April	10	October
5	May	11	November
6	June	12	December

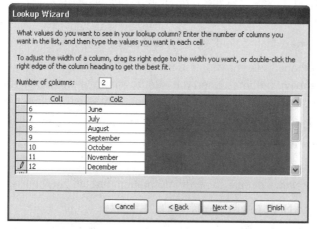

22 Click **Next** to move to the next page.

23 Accept the default selection of **Col1** as the column whose data you want to enter when a selection is made from the list, and click **Finish**.

You return to the table, and the Field Properties area displays the Lookup information.

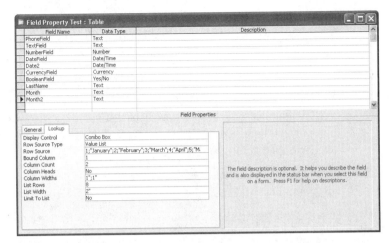

The wizard has inserted your column information into the Row Source box and set the other properties according to your specifications.

24 Change **Limit To List** to **Yes**.

25 Save your changes, switch to Datasheet view, and then click the down arrow in a **Month2** field to display the list.

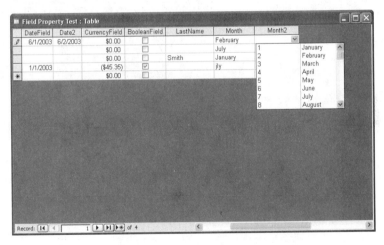

26 Click **January**.

Access displays the number *1* in the field, which is useful for the computer. However, people might be confused by the two columns and by seeing something other than what they clicked or typed.

27 Switch back to Design view, and in the **Column Widths** box—which appears as *1";1"*—change the width for the first column to **0** (you don't have to type the symbol for inches) to prevent it from being displayed.

28 Save your changes, return to Datasheet view, and as a test, in the remaining records set **Month2** to **February** in two records and to **March** in one record.

Only the name of the month is now displayed in the list, and when you click a month, that name is displayed in the field. However, Access actually stores the associated number from the list's first column.

29 Right-click in the **Month2** column, click **Filter For** on the shortcut menu, type **2** in the box, and press Enter.

Only the two records with February in the **Month2** field are now displayed.

30 Click the **Remove Filter** button, and then repeat the previous step, this time typing **3** in the box to display the one record with March in the **Month2** field.

Remove Filter

CLOSE the *FieldTest* database, saving your changes.

Updating Information in a Table

As you use a database and as it grows, you might discover that errors creep in or that some information becomes out of date. You can tediously scroll through the records looking for those that need to be changed, but it is more efficient to use a few of the tools and techniques provided by Access for that purpose.

If an employee has consistently misspelled the same word, you can use the Find and Replace commands on the Edit menu to locate each instance of the misspelled word and replace it with the correct spelling. This command works much like the same commands in Microsoft Office Word or Microsoft Office Excel.

However, if you decide to increase the price of some products or replace the content of a field only under certain circumstances, you need the power of an *update query*, which is a select query that performs an action on the query's results.

In this exercise, you will open the GardenCo database and use an update query to increase the price of all bulbs and cacti by 10 percent.

USE the *GardenCo* database in the practice file folder for this topic. This practice file is located in the *My Documents\Microsoft Press\Office 2003 SBS\Accurate\QueryUp* folder and can also be accessed by clicking *Start/All Programs/Microsoft Press/Microsoft Office System 2003 Step by Step*.
OPEN the *GardenCo* database and acknowledge the safety warning, if necessary.

1 On the **Objects** bar, click **Queries**.

2 In the **Queries** pane, double-click **Create query by using wizard**.

3　In the **Tables/Queries** list, select **Table: Categories**.

4　Double-click **CategoryName** to move it from the **Available Fields** list to the **Selected Fields** list.

5　In the **Tables/Queries** list, select **Table: Products**.

6　Double-click **ProductName** and **UnitPrice** to move them from the **Available Fields** list to the **Selected Fields** list.

7　Click **Finish** to accept all defaults and create the query.

Access displays the query results in a datasheet. Only the Category Name, Product Name, and Unit Price fields are displayed.

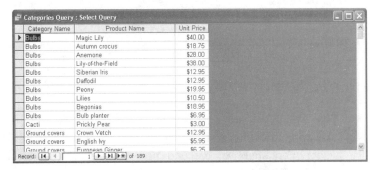

View

8　Click the **View** button to display the query in Design view.

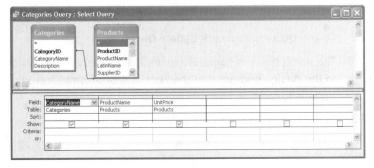

This query displays the products in all categories. You want to raise the prices of only the bulbs and cacti, so your first task is to change this query so that it selects just those categories.

9　In the **Criteria** row under **CategoryName**, type **bulbs**, and then type **cacti** in the **or** row.

10　Click the **Run** button to run the query and confirm that only bulbs and cacti are listed, and then return to Design view.

Run

A select query that selects just the records you want to change is created. But to actually make a change to the records, you have to use an update query.

11 Click the **Query** menu to display the commands that apply to a query.

The four available action queries are listed toward the middle of the menu, with exclamation points in their icons.

Tip You can't create an action query directly; you must first create a select query and then change the query to one of the action types. With an existing select query open, you can find the command to convert it to an action query either on the Query menu, in the list that appears when you click the Query Type button's arrow, or on the shortcut menu that appears when you right-click the query and point to Query Type.

12 On the **Query** menu, click **Update Query**.

The select query is converted to an update query. The only noticeable changes to the design grid are that the Sort and Show rows have been removed and an Update To row has been added.

13 In the **Update To** row under **UnitPrice**, type [UnitPrice]*1.1.

Tip   You enclose UnitPrice in brackets to indicate that it is an Access object. If you use the Expression Builder to insert this expression, it looks like this: *[Products]![UnitPrice]*1.1*. Because this description of the field includes the table in which it is found, this expression can be inserted in other tables.

When you run an update query, you make changes to the table that can't be undone. Because of this, you should create a backup copy of the table before running the query. For the purposes of this exercise, however, before running the query you will perform one simple check.

You can quickly create a backup copy of a table by displaying the Tables pane in the database window, clicking the table you want to back up, and then pressing [Ctrl]+[C] followed by [Ctrl]+[V]. In the dialog box that appears, provide a name for the backup table, and click OK.

View

14 Click the **View** button.

In a select query, clicking the View button is the same as clicking the Run button. But in an update query, clicking the View button simply displays a list of the fields that will be updated. In this case, you see a list of unit prices that matches the ones shown earlier in the select query.

15 Return to Design view, and then click the **Run** button.

Access displays a rather firm warning.

16 Click **Yes** to acknowledge the warning, and then click the **View** button again to display the **UnitPrice** field, where all the prices have been increased by 10 percent.

17 Save and close the query.

CLOSE the *GardenCo* database.

Deleting Information from a Table

Over time, some types of information in a database can become obsolete. The Products table in The Garden Company database, for example, maintains a list of all the products the company currently offers for sale or has sold in the past. When a product is no longer available for sale, a check mark is placed in the Discontinued field. Discontinued products aren't displayed in the catalog or pushed by salespeople, but they are kept in the database for a while in case it becomes practical to sell them again. A similar situation could exist with customers who haven't placed an order in a long time or who have asked to be removed from a mailing list but might still place orders.

Eventually, the time comes to clean house and discard some records. You could do this by scrolling through the tables and deleting records by hand, but if all the records to be deleted match some pattern, you can use a *delete query* to quickly get rid of all of them.

Important   Keep in mind several things when deleting records from a database. First, there is no quick recovery of deleted records. Second, the effects of a delete query can be more far-reaching than you intend. If the table in which you are deleting records has a relationship with another table, and the "Cascade Delete Related Records" option for that relationship is set, records in the second table will also be deleted. Sometimes this is what you want, but sometimes it isn't. For example, you don't want to delete the records of previous sales just because you're deleting discontinued products. There are two solutions to this problem: back up your database before deleting the records; or create a new table (perhaps named *Deleted<file name>*), and then move the records you want to delete to the new table.

In this exercise, you will create a delete query to remove all discontinued products from the Products table of the GardenCo database.

USE the *GardenCo* database in the practice file folder for this topic. This practice file is located in the *My Documents\Microsoft Press\Office 2003 SBS\Accurate\QueryDel* folder and can also be accessed by clicking *Start/All Programs/Microsoft Press/Microsoft Office System 2003 Step by Step*. OPEN the *GardenCo* database and acknowledge the safety warning, if necessary.

1   On the **Objects** bar, click **Queries**.

2   Double-click **Create query in Design view** to open both the query window and the **Show Table** dialog box.

3   Double-click **Products** to add that table to the list area of the query window, and then click **Close** to close the **Show Table** dialog box.

4   Double-click the asterisk at the top of the list of fields to include all the fields in the query.

Products.* appears in the Field row of the first column of the design grid, and *Products* appears in the Table row.

Tip   Double-clicking the asterisk in the field list is a quick way to move all the fields in the table to the query, without having each field appear in its own column. However, when you do it that way you can't set Sort, Show, and Criteria values for individual fields. To set these values, you have to add the specific fields to the design grid, thereby adding them twice. To avoid displaying the fields twice, clear the check mark in the Show row of the duplicate individual fields.

5   Scroll to the bottom of the field list, and double-click **Discontinued** to copy it to the next available column in the design grid.

6   On the **Query** menu, click **Delete Query** to convert this select query to a delete query.

Tip   You might have to hover over the short menu or click the double–chevrons to see the Delete Query command on the long menu.

In the design grid, the Sort and Show rows have disappeared, and a Delete row has been added. In the first column, which contains the reference to all fields in the Products table, the Delete row contains the word *From*, indicating that this is the table from which records will be deleted. When you add individual fields to the remaining columns, as you did with the Discontinued field, the Delete row displays *Where*, indicating that this field can include deletion criteria.

7   Type Yes in the **Criteria** row under **Discontinued**.

The Discontinued field is set to the Boolean data type, which is represented in the datasheet as a check box that has a check mark to indicate Yes and no check mark to indicate No. To locate all discontinued products, you need to identify records with the Discontinued field set to Yes.

View

8   To check the accuracy of the query, click the **View** button.

Access displays a list of 18 discontinued products that will be deleted, but it hasn't actually changed the table yet. Scroll to the right to verify that all records display a check in the Products.Discontinued field.

View

9   Click the **View** button to return to Design view.

Tip   Before actually deleting records, you might want to display the Relationships window by clicking Relationships on the Tools menu. If the table you are deleting from has a relationship with any table containing order information that shouldn't be deleted, right-click the relationship line, click Edit Relationship on the shortcut menu, and make sure that Enforce Referential Integrity is selected and Cascade Delete Related Records is *not* selected.

Run

10   Click the **Run** button to run the delete query.

Access displays a warning to remind you of the permanence of this action.

11   Click **Yes** to delete the records.

12   Click the **View** button to see that all the records were deleted.

Save

13   If you think you might run the same delete query in the future, click the **Save** button, and name the query. Then close the query.

> **Tip**   If you are concerned that someone might accidentally run a delete query and destroy records you weren't ready to destroy, change the query back to a select query before saving it. You can then open the select query in Design view and change it to a delete query when you want to run it again.

14   Close the query.

CLOSE the *GardenCo* database.

Key Points

■   When you create a database with Microsoft Office Access 2003, you can set properties that restrict what can be entered in it.

■   To ensure the ongoing accuracy of a database, you can create and run action queries that quickly update information or delete selected records from a table.

■   The Data Type setting restricts entries to a specific type of data: text, numbers, dates, and so on. For example, if the data type is set to Number and you try to enter text, Access refuses your entry and displays a warning.

■   You can set the Field Size property for the Text, Number, and AutoNumber data types. This property restricts the number of characters allowed in a text field, and the size of numbers that can be entered in a number or AutoNumber field.

■   The input mask property controls the format in which data can be entered, and restricts the number of characters that can be entered in a field. For example, the mask for a telephone number can be set to have three sections separated by semicolons, so someone entering information can see at a glance the format for ten numbers in that particular field.

■   You can use a validation rule to precisely define the information that will be accepted in one or several fields in a record. At the field level, Access uses the rule to test an entry when you attempt to leave the field, and does not accept entries that don't meet the rule. At the table level, Access uses the rule to test the content of several fields when you attempt to leave the record, rejecting an entry that doesn't satisfy the rule.

- For fields in which the number of correct entries is limited, you can use a lookup field to ensure that users enter the right information. This helps prevent inconsistencies in how data is entered and makes it easier and more efficient to sort and perform searches on your data.

- You can use an update query to quickly perform an action based on the results of a query. For example, you can search and replace the contents of a field under certain circumstances, which are defined in the update query.

- You can use a delete query to quickly delete records that have become obsolete. You should always back up your database before running a delete query, and you must exercise caution when deleting records in this way. The effects of a delete query can be far-reaching, and there is no quick recovery of deleted records.

IV
Microsoft Office
PowerPoint 2003

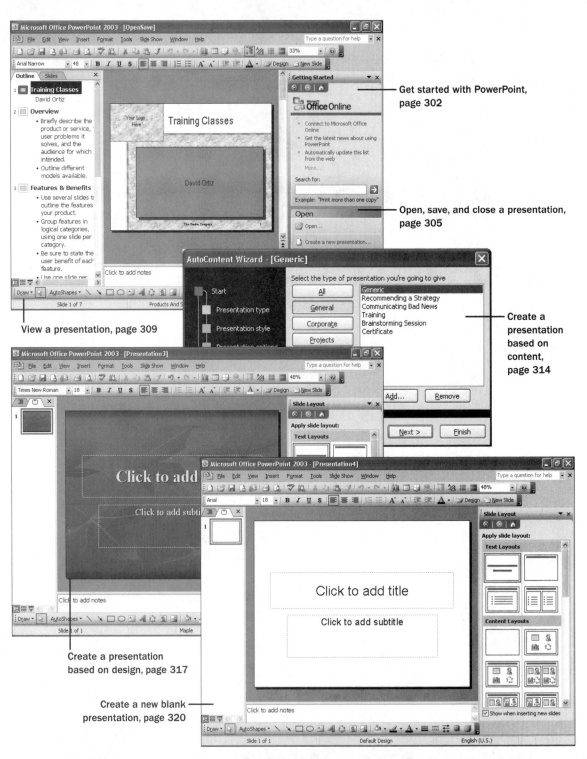

Get started with PowerPoint, page 302

Open, save, and close a presentation, page 305

View a presentation, page 309

Create a presentation based on content, page 314

Create a presentation based on design, page 317

Create a new blank presentation, page 320

13 Creating Presentations

In this chapter you will learn to:
- ✔ Get started with PowerPoint.
- ✔ Open, save, and close a presentation.
- ✔ View a presentation.
- ✔ Create a presentation based on content.
- ✔ Create a presentation based on design.
- ✔ Create a new blank presentation.

Microsoft Office PowerPoint 2003 enables you to create and organize slide shows, overhead transparencies, speaker notes, audience handouts, outlines, and more—all in a single presentation file. Whether you want to deliver training, conduct a brainstorming or business-planning session, present a progress report, manage a project, or make a marketing pitch, you can use PowerPoint's tools to help you design, create, print, share, and deliver a powerful presentation.

For example, suppose Karen Berg, the owner of a fictional business called The Garden Company, wants to improve the name recognition of her company and promote its products. As part of her promotional efforts, she wants to provide gardening classes to increase product awareness and customer skills. Karen can use PowerPoint to create a series of professional-looking slides to accomplish these purposes.

In this chapter you will familiarize yourself with PowerPoint's working environment. You will open, save, and close an existing PowerPoint presentation, and explore various ways you can view slides. Finally, you will create and save three new presentations: one from scratch, one using the help of a wizard, and one using a design template.

See Also   Do you need only a quick refresher on the topics in this chapter? See the Quick Reference entries on pages xxxiii.

Important   Before you can use the practice files in this chapter, you need to install them from the book's companion CD to their default location. See "Using the Book's CD-ROM" on page xxi for more information.

Getting Started with PowerPoint

The most common way to start PowerPoint is to use the Start button on the Windows taskbar. When you start PowerPoint, its *program window* displays the components and features common to all Microsoft Office programs, as well as some that are unique to Office 2003 and some that are unique to PowerPoint.

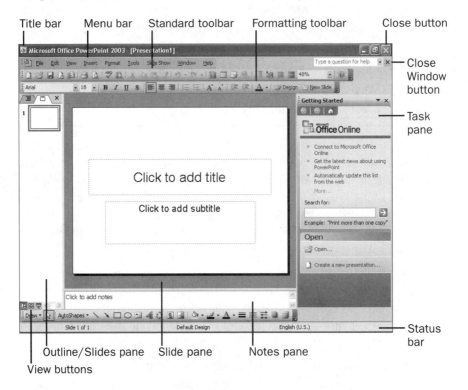

Title bar   Menu bar   Standard toolbar   Formatting toolbar   Close button

Close Window button

Task pane

Status bar

Outline/Slides pane   Slide pane   Notes pane

View buttons

Tip   What you see on your screen might not match the graphics in this book exactly. The screens in this book were captured on a monitor set to 800 x 600 resolution with 24-bit color and the Windows XP Standard color scheme. By default, the Standard and Formatting toolbars share one row, which prevents you from seeing all their buttons. To make it easier for you to find buttons, the Standard and Formatting toolbars in the graphics in this book appear on two rows. If you want to change your setting to match the screens in this book, click Customize on the Tools menu. On the Options tab, select the "Show Standard and Formatting toolbars on two rows" check box, and then click Close.

Displayed within the program window is the *presentation window*, the area in which you create slides by typing text, drawing shapes, creating graphs, and inserting objects. The *insertion point*, the blinking vertical line that appears when you click in the presentation window, indicates where text you type or an object you insert will appear.

On the right side of the program window, PowerPoint displays a *task pane* that you can use to quickly choose commands appropriate to a specific task. For example, when you first start PowerPoint, the Getting Started task pane appears with the commands you commonly use to open an existing presentation or create a new one. When you add a new slide to a presentation, the Slide Layout task pane appears, with common slide designs from which you can choose. If you want to use a task pane other than the one displayed, you can click the Other Task Panes down arrow at the right end of the task pane's title bar to display a drop-down list of the available task panes, and then click the one you want to see. You can hide the task pane to free up valuable screen space, or display it if it is hidden, by clicking Task Pane on the View menu. (This type of on/off command is called a *toggle*.) To close the task pane, click the Close button at the right end of the task pane's title bar.

Tip   The task pane opens each time you start PowerPoint. If you don't want the task pane to appear when you start the program, click Options on the Tools menu, click the View tab, clear the "Startup Task Pane" check box, and click OK.

In the lower-left corner of the presentation window are view buttons that enable you to look at a presentation in different ways. By default, PowerPoint opens in *Normal view*, the main view used to write and design presentations. This view is made up of three panes:

- The *Outline/Slides pane* shows tabs that you use to alternate between seeing an outline of your slide text (Outline tab) and seeing the slides displayed as thumbnails (Slides tab).

- The *Slide pane* shows the slide selected in the Outline/Slides pane as it will appear in the presentation.

- The *Notes pane* provides a place for entering speaker notes.

You can size any of the panes by dragging the gray bars that separate them.

As with any Microsoft Windows program, you can temporarily hide the PowerPoint window with the Minimize button, and adjust the size of the window with the Restore Down/Maximize button. You can close a presentation with the Close Window button at the right end of the menu bar; and you can quit PowerPoint with the Close button at the right end of the title bar.

To find out the name of an item on the screen, you can display its *ScreenTip*. To see the name of a toolbar button, for example, you point to the button for a few seconds (this is called *hovering*), and its ScreenTip will appear.

In this exercise, you will start PowerPoint, explore various task panes, and then close the task pane.

BE SURE TO start your computer, but don't start PowerPoint yet.

1   On the taskbar, click **Start**, point to **All Programs**, point to **Microsoft Office**, and then click **Microsoft Office PowerPoint 2003**.

Tip   You can also start PowerPoint by creating a shortcut icon on the Windows desktop. Simply double-click a shortcut icon to start its associated program. To create a shortcut, click the Start button, point to All Programs, point to Microsoft Office, right-click Microsoft Office PowerPoint 2003, point to Send To, and then click "Desktop (create shortcut)."

The PowerPoint window opens with a blank presentation in the presentation window and the Getting Started task pane displayed.

2   At the right end of the task pane's title bar, click the **Other Task Panes** down arrow.

A menu of available task panes appears.

3   Press the [Esc] key, or click an empty place in the presentation window.

PowerPoint closes the menu.

Close

4   Click the **Close** button at the right end of the task pane's title bar (not the one at the right end of the menu bar or the program window's title bar).

The Getting Started task pane closes, and the presentation window expands to fill the width of the program window.

5 On the **View** menu, click **Task Pane**.

Troubleshooting If you don't see the Task Pane command on the View menu, it is hidden. PowerPoint personalizes your menus and toolbars to reduce the number of menu commands and toolbar buttons you see on the screen. When you click a menu name on the menu bar, a short menu appears, containing only the commands you use most often. To make the complete menu appear, you can hover over the menu name for a second or two, double-click the menu name, or point to the chevrons (the double arrows) at the bottom of the short menu.

6 The Getting Started task pane opens, and the presentation window contracts to make room for it.

Opening, Saving, and Closing a Presentation

If you click Open on the File menu after you start PowerPoint for the first time, the contents of the My Documents folder are displayed by default in the Open dialog box. If the file you want to open is stored in another folder, you can use the Up One Level button to move upward in your hard disk's folder structure, or you can click the down arrow to the right of the "Look in" box and then click folders and subfolders until the one you want is displayed. You can use the *Places bar* to quickly move to another location on your computer (or network, if you are connected to one). The Places bar provides easy access to locations commonly used to store files.

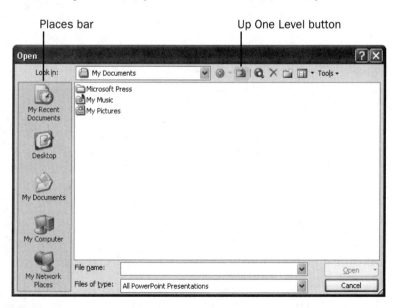

Places bar   Up One Level button

Tip If you can't locate a file but you have some information about the file, such as part of the filename, the slide title, or summary property information, you can use Power-Point's Basic Search task pane to locate the file. For more information, search on *About finding files* in Help.

When you create a new presentation, it exists only in your computer's temporary memory until you save it. To save your work, you must give the presentation a name and store it on your computer's hard disk. The first time you save a presentation, you click the Save button on the Standard toolbar or click Save As on the File menu to open the Save As dialog box, where you assign a name and storage location. If you want to create a new folder to store the file in, you can quickly do that in the Save As dialog box by clicking the Create New Folder button on the dialog box's toolbar. To save the file in a different folder or on a different hard disk, click the down arrow to the right of the "Save in" box and navigate to that folder or disk.

Create New Folder button

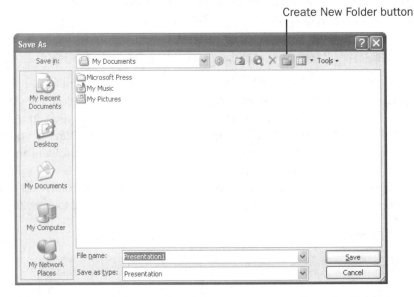

After you've saved the presentation once using the Save As dialog box, you can save new changes simply by clicking the Save button. The new version of the presentation then overwrites the previous version.

If you want to keep both the new version and the previous version, you click Save As on the File menu and use the Save As dialog box to save the new version with a different name. You can save the new file in the same folder as the old file, in a different folder (or subfolder), or on a different hard disk. (You cannot store two files with the same name in the same folder.)

In this exercise, you will start PowerPoint and open an existing presentation. You will then save the presentation with a new name in a folder that you create. Finally, you will close the presentation.

USE the *OpenSave* presentation in the practice file folder for this topic. This practice file is located in the *My Documents\Microsoft Press\Office 2003 SBS\CreatingPresent\Opening* folder and can also be accessed by clicking *Start/All Programs/Microsoft Press/Microsoft Office System 2003 Step by Step.*

1   On the **File** menu, click **Open**.

PowerPoint displays the Open dialog box, which is where you specify the name and location of the presentation you want to open.

2   If My Documents is not displayed in the **Look in** box, click **My Documents** on the Places bar.

3   Double-click the *Microsoft Press* folder, double-click the *Office System 2003 SBS* folder, the *CreatingPresent* folder, and then the *Opening* folder.

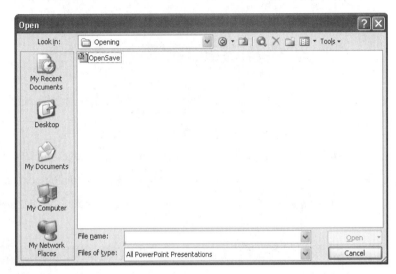

4   Click the *OpenSave* file to select it, and click **Open**.

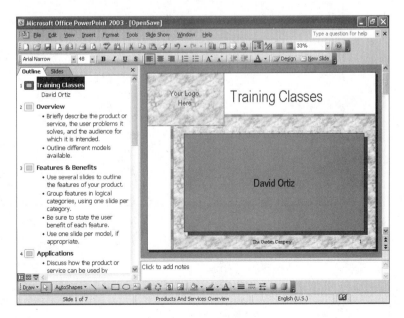

5   On the **File** menu, click **Save As**.

The Save As dialog box appears, displaying the contents of the folder you last used in the Save As or Open dialog box.

Troubleshooting   If the Opening folder is not displayed in the "Save in" box, click the My Documents icon on the Places bar, and then repeat step 3 to navigate to the Opening folder.

Create
New Folder

6   Click the **Create New Folder** button to create a subfolder of the *Opening* folder.

The New Folder dialog box appears.

7   Type **MyPresentation**, and click **OK**.

MyPresentation is now the current folder in the Save As dialog box.

8   In the **File name** box at the bottom of the **Save As** dialog box, type **NewPresentation**.

The new version of the presentation will be stored in the *MyPresentation* folder with the name *NewPresentation*.

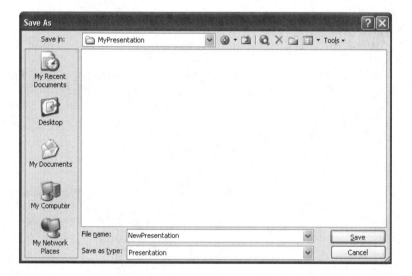

Troubleshooting   Programs that run on the Windows operating system use file name extensions to identify different types of files. For example, PowerPoint presentation files are assigned the extension *.ppt*. If you are used to typing the file name extension when you save a file, be aware that Windows XP programs do not display these extensions by default, and you shouldn't type them in the Save As dialog box. PowerPoint automatically saves the file with whatever extension is associated with the type of file selected in the "Save as type" box at the bottom of the dialog box.

9   Click **Save**.

PowerPoint saves a new version of the OpenSave presentation as NewPresentation in the MyPresentation folder. It closes the OpenSave file, which is still stored in the Opening folder, and opens the new file in the presentation window, as indicated by the NewPresentation file name in the PowerPoint title bar.

10   Close the NewPresentation file by clicking the **Close Window** button at the right end of the menu bar.

Close Window

Viewing a Presentation

Microsoft Office Specialist

PowerPoint has four views to help you create, organize, and display presentations:

■   In *Normal view*, you can work with a presentation in three ways: as a text outline or set of slide miniatures (called *thumbnails*) in the Outline/Slides pane; as a slide in the Slide pane; and as speaker notes in the Notes pane.

■   In *Slide Sorter view*, you can preview an entire presentation as thumbnails—as if you were looking at photographic slides on a light board—and easily reorder the slides. If titles are hard to read in this view, you can hide the slide formatting by holding down the ⌈Alt⌉ key and the mouse button.

■   In *Notes Page view,* you can add fancy speaker notes. Although you can add speaker notes in Normal view's Notes pane, you must be in Notes Page view if you want to add graphics to your notes.

■   In *Slide Show view*, you can display slides as an electronic presentation, with the slides filling the entire screen. At any time during the development of a presentation, you can quickly and easily review the slides for accuracy and flow as an audience will see them.

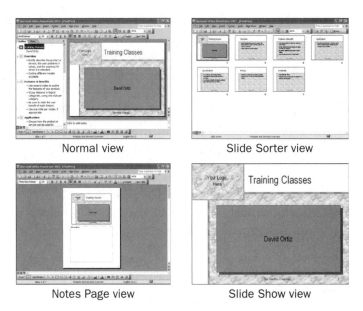

Normal view   Slide Sorter view

Notes Page view   Slide Show view

You switch from one view to another by using commands on the View menu or by clicking the view buttons in the lower-left corner of the presentation window. (There is no view button to switch to Notes Page view; you must click Notes Page on the View menu.)

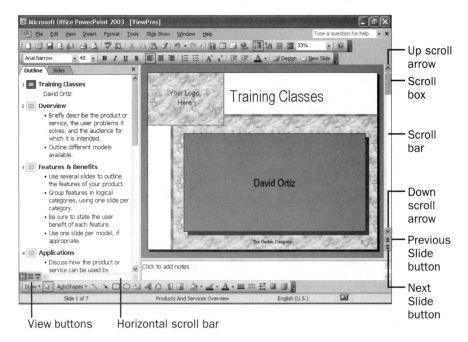

You can browse through the slides in a presentation in three ways: You can click the scroll arrows to scroll line by line, click above or below the scroll box to scroll window

by window, or drag the scroll box to move immediately to a specific slide. To view the previous and next slides in the Slide pane, you can click the Next Slide and Previous Slide buttons, which are located at the bottom of the vertical scroll bar. You can also press the Page Up or Page Down key to scroll window by window.

In this exercise, you will switch to different PowerPoint views and then display slides in a slide show. You will also browse through the presentation by using the scroll bars and the Next Slide and Previous Slide buttons to move around in the Outline/Slides pane and to move from slide to slide in the Slide pane.

USE the *ViewPres* presentation in the practice file folder for this topic. This practice file is located in the *My Documents\Microsoft Press\Office 2003 SBS\CreatingPresent\Viewing* folder and can also be accessed by clicking *Start/All Programs/Microsoft Press/Microsoft Office System 2003 Step by Step*. **OPEN** the *ViewPres* presentation.

1   In the **Outline/Slides** pane, click the slide icon adjacent to the *Features and Benefits* heading.

Slide 3 of the presentation is now shown in the adjacent Slide pane.

2   In the **Outline/Slides** pane, click the **Slides** tab.

The pane switches from showing an outline of the text of the presentation to showing thumbnails of the slides. Slide 3 is still selected in the Outline/Slides pane and is displayed in the Slide pane.

Outline tab

Slides tab

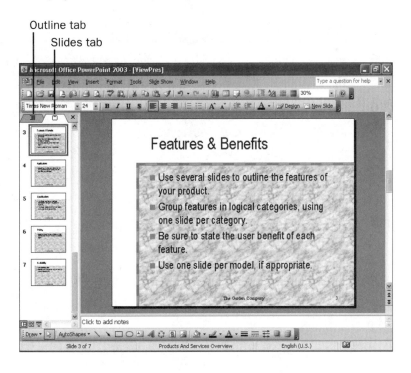

3 In the **Outline/Slides** pane, drag the scroll box to the top of the scroll bar, and click the thumbnail for the first slide.

Slide
Sorter View

4 In the lower-left corner of the presentation window, click the **Slide Sorter View** button.

The Outline/Slide and Notes panes close, the Slide pane expands, and all the slides now appear as thumbnails. Slide 1 is surrounded by a dark border, indicating that the slide is selected.

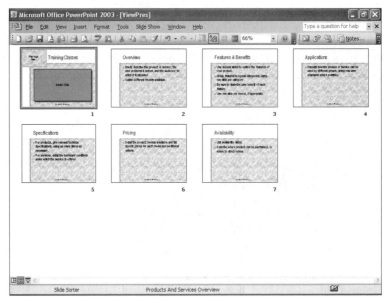

5 Hold down the [Alt] key, point to any slide, and hold down the mouse button.

The slide's formatting disappears so that the title is easier to read.

6 Release the [Alt] key and the mouse button, and then double-click **Slide 1**.

PowerPoint displays the presentation in Normal view, with Slide 1 active.

Slide Show

7 In the lower-left corner of the presentation window, click the **Slide Show** button.

The program window disappears, and the first slide in the presentation is displayed full-screen.

8 Without moving your mouse, click its button to advance to the next slide.

Tip To end a slide show before you reach the last slide, press [Esc].

9 Continue clicking your mouse button to advance through the presentation one slide at a time.

After the last slide in the presentation, PowerPoint displays a black screen.

Tip When you run a slide show, the black screen appears by default. To change this setting, click Options on the Tools menu, click the View tab, clear the "End with black slide" check box, and click OK.

10 Click the black screen to return to Normal view.

11 In the **Outline/Slides** pane, click the **Outline** tab, and then click the down scroll arrow a few times to scroll the hidden text into view.

12 In the **Outline/Slides** pane, drag the scroll box to the end of the scroll bar.

The end of the outline appears.

13 In the **Slide** pane, click below the scroll box in the scroll bar.

The next slide appears in the Slide pane, and on the Outline tab, the text moves to display that slide's title at the top of the pane.

Previous Slide

14 At the bottom of the **Slide** pane's scroll bar, click the **Previous Slide** button.

The previous slide appears in the Slide pane and the text on the Outline tab moves again.

Next Slide

15 In the **Slide** pane, click the **Next Slide** button repeatedly until you reach the end of the presentation.

16 In the **Slide** pane's scroll bar, drag the scroll box until you see *Slide 3 of 7* in the slide indicator box, but don't release the mouse button yet.

— Slide indicator box

17   The slide indicator box tells you the slide number and title of the slide to which the scroll box is pointing. In the scroll bar, the scroll box indicates the relative position of the slide in the presentation.

18   Release the mouse button.

The Slide pane displays the third slide, and the left end of the status bar indicates that you are viewing *Slide 3 of 7*.

CLOSE the *ViewPres* presentation.

Creating a Presentation Based on Content

Microsoft Office Specialist

When you want to create a new presentation, the *AutoContent Wizard* can save you time by helping you organize and write the presentation's text. The wizard takes you through a step-by-step process, prompting you for presentation information, including the general topic of the presentation you want to give, the way you will deliver it, and the content for the *title slide*, which is the first slide in the presentation. When you finish, the wizard provides a suggested outline that you can modify.

Choosing the Best Method to Start a Presentation

The New Presentation task pane provides four options for creating a new presentation:

- Click "Blank presentation" if you have content ready and a design in mind. After you click this option, the Slide Layout task pane appears with predesigned slide layouts from which you can choose a layout suitable for the slide you want to create.

- Click "From design template" if you have content ready but need help with the look of the presentation. Each template provides predefined slide colors and text styles from which you can choose. After you click this option, the Slide Design task pane appears, in which you can choose a template.

- Click "From AutoContent wizard" if you need help with both the presentation's content and its look. The AutoContent Wizard prompts you for a presentation title and information about the presentation and lets you choose a presentation style and type. PowerPoint then provides a basic outline to help you organize the content into a professional presentation.

- Click "From existing presentation" if you have an existing presentation that is close enough in either content or design that you can use it as a template for the new one. After you click this option, the New from Existing Presentation dialog box appears, so that you can browse to the file you want through the "Look in" box.

- Click "Photo Album" if you want to create an album of photographs or a portfolio of other graphics images.

In this exercise, you will use the AutoContent Wizard to create a presentation, and then you will save the results.

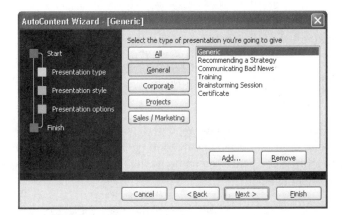

New

1   On the Standard toolbar, click the **New** button. Then if the **New Presentation** task pane is not displayed, click the **Other Task Panes** down arrow at the right end of the task pane's title bar, and click **New Presentation** in the drop-down list.

2   In the **New Presentation** task pane, click **From AutoContent wizard**.

The AutoContent Wizard displays its Start page. On the left side of the page is a "roadmap" of the pages with the active page indicated by a green box.

3   Read the introduction, and then click **Next**.

The box next to *Presentation type* turns green to indicate that this is now the current page. The second page prompts you to select a presentation type. To help you identify presentation types quickly, the wizard organizes presentations by category.

4   Click the **Sales / Marketing** button.

Presentations in the sales and marketing category appear in the list on the right side of the page.

5   In the list, click **Product/Services Overview**, and click **Next**.

The wizard prompts you to specify how you will display the presentation.

6   With the **On-screen presentation** option selected, click **Next**.

The wizard prompts you to enter information for the title slide and for footer information to be included on each slide.

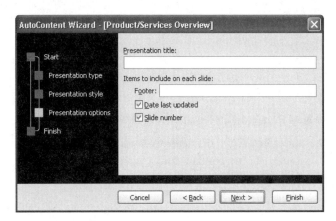

7   Click the **Presentation title** box, type Training Classes, and press the [Tab] key to move the insertion point to the Footer box.

8   In the **Footer** box, type The Garden Company.

9   Clear the **Date last updated** check box to hide the date on each slide.

10 Leave the **Slide number** check box selected so that the slide number will be displayed on each slide, and click **Next**.

11 Click **Finish**.

The PowerPoint presentation window appears in Normal view with content provided by the wizard in outline form on the Outline/Slides pane and the title slide in the Slide pane. The name on the title slide is the name of the registered PowerPoint user.

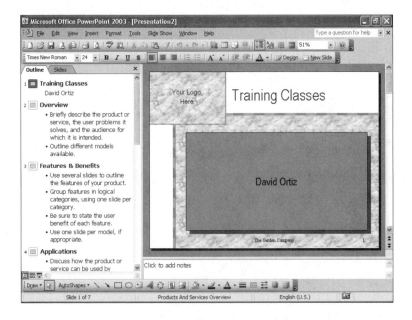

Save

12 On the Standard toolbar, click the **Save** button.

PowerPoint displays the Save As dialog box and suggests the title of the first slide as the name of the file.

13 In the **File name** box, replace the selected name with **AutoContent**.

14 On the Places bar, click **My Documents**. Then double-click the *Microsoft Press* folder, double-click the *Office System 2003 SBS* folder, and double-click the *CreatingPresent* folder.

The contents of the CreatingPresent folder are displayed.

Create
New Folder

15 Click the **Create New Folder** button, type **NewAuto** as the name of the folder, and click **OK**.

16 Click **Save**, or press the ⌈Enter⌉ key to save the AutoContent presentation in the NewAuto folder.

The title bar now displays AutoContent as the name of the current file.

CLOSE the *AutoContent* presentation.

Creating a Presentation Based on Design

When you don't need help with the content of a presentation but you do need help with its design, you can start a new presentation, without any sample text, based on a *design template*. A design template is a blank presentation with a professionally designed format and color scheme to which you can add slides. You can use one of the design templates that come with PowerPoint, or you can create your own.

After you select a design template, you can choose the layout for each slide, such as a slide with a graph, and then type the text and add any other elements you want. You select a layout by clicking it in the Slide Layout task pane.

In this exercise, you will start a new presentation with a design template and then choose a slide layout.

1 Close any open presentations, and then display the task pane by clicking **Task Pane** on the **View** menu. If the **New Presentation** task pane is not displayed, click the **Other Task Panes** down arrow to the right of the task pane's title bar, and click **New Presentation** in the drop-down list.

2 In the **New Presentation** task pane, click **From design template**.

A blank presentation opens, and the Slide Design task pane appears, with thumb-nails of a variety of design templates.

Tip The templates available in the Slide Design task pane are the same ones used by the AutoContent Wizard.

3 In the **Slide Design** task pane, point to a design template.

The name of the design template appears as a ScreenTip, and a down arrow appears on the right side of the design icon.

Troubleshooting Don't worry if your thumbnails are much larger than the ones shown here.

4 In the **Slide Design** task pane, click the down arrow to the right of the design template you are pointing to.

A menu appears with commands you can apply to the design template.

5 If **Show Large Previews** does not have a check mark beside it, click **Show Large Previews**.

The size of the design template thumbnails increases to make it easier to see the designs.

6 In the **Slide Design** task pane, drag the scroll box about half way down the vertical scroll bar until you see the Maple design, and then click **Maple**.

A title slide with the Maple design appears in the Slide pane.

7 At the right end of the task pane's title bar, click the **Other Task Panes** down arrow, and then click **Slide Layout**.

The Slide Layout task pane appears, with thumbnails of layouts you can apply to the selected slide. The default Title Slide layout is currently applied.

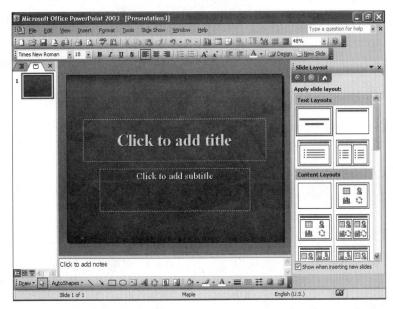

8 In the **Slide Layout** task pane, point to different slide layouts to see their ScreenTips.

9 In the **Text Layouts** area of the **Slide Layout** task pane, click the **Title Only** thumbnail.

PowerPoint applies the Title Only layout to the selected slide.

10 In the **Text Layouts** area of the **Slide Layout** task pane, click the **Title Slide** thumbnail.

PowerPoint applies the Title Slide layout to the selected slide.

Close

11 Click the **Close** button at the right end of the task pane.

The task pane closes.

Close Window

12 Click the **Close Window** button at the right end of the menu bar, and click **No** when you are asked if you want to save the file.

Creating a New Blank Presentation

If you want to create the text and design of a presentation from scratch, you can work with a new blank presentation. When you first start PowerPoint, a blank presentation appears in the presentation window. If you are already working in PowerPoint, you can click New on the File menu to display a new blank presentation.

In this exercise, you will create a blank presentation and then save it.

1   If the **New Presentation** task pane is not displayed, click the **Other Task Panes** down arrow at the right end of the task pane's title bar, and click **New Presentation** in the drop-down list.

> **Troubleshooting**   If the task pane is not open, click Task Pane on the View menu.

2   In the **New Presentation** task pane, click **Blank presentation**.

New

You can also click the New button on the Standard toolbar. PowerPoint displays a blank presentation with the default Title Slide layout. The Slide Layout task pane appears, with thumbnails of the available slide layouts.

3   On the title bar of the **Slide Layout** task pane, click the **Close** button.

Close

4   On the **File** menu, click **Save As**.

The Save As dialog box appears.

5   Browse to the *My Documents\Microsoft Press\Office 2003 SBS\CreatingPresent* folder.

Create New
Folder

6　Click the **Create New Folder** button, type NewBlank, and click **OK**.

7　In the **File name** box, type BlankPresentation, and click **Save**.

　　PowerPoint saves the presentation with the name BlankPresentation in the NewBlank folder.

CLOSE the *BlankPresentation* presentation, and if you are not continuing on to the next chapter, quit PowerPoint.

Tip　You can tell PowerPoint to periodically save a presentation you are working on in case the program stops responding or you lose electrical power. PowerPoint saves the changes in a recovery file according to the time interval specified in the AutoRecover option. To turn on the AutoRecover option and specify the time interval for automatic saving, click Options on the Tools menu, click the Save tab, select the "Save AutoRecover info every" check box, specify the period of time, and then click OK.

Key Points

■　PowerPoint has four views to help you create, organize, and display presentations: Normal, Slide Sorter, Notes Page, and Slide Show.

■　You can choose one of three ways to scroll through the slides in a presentation: by clicking the scroll arrows to scroll line by line, by clicking above or below the scroll box to scroll window by window, or by dragging the scroll box to move immediately to a specific slide.

■　You can save a presentation with a new name in an existing folder or in a new folder that you can create from within PowerPoint. You cannot store two presentations with the same name in the same folder.

■　The way you create a new presentation depends on whether you need help coming up with the content or the design. If you need help with the content, you can use the AutoContent Wizard. If you have content ready but need help with the look, you can use a design template. If you have content ready and have a design in mind, you can create a blank presentation.

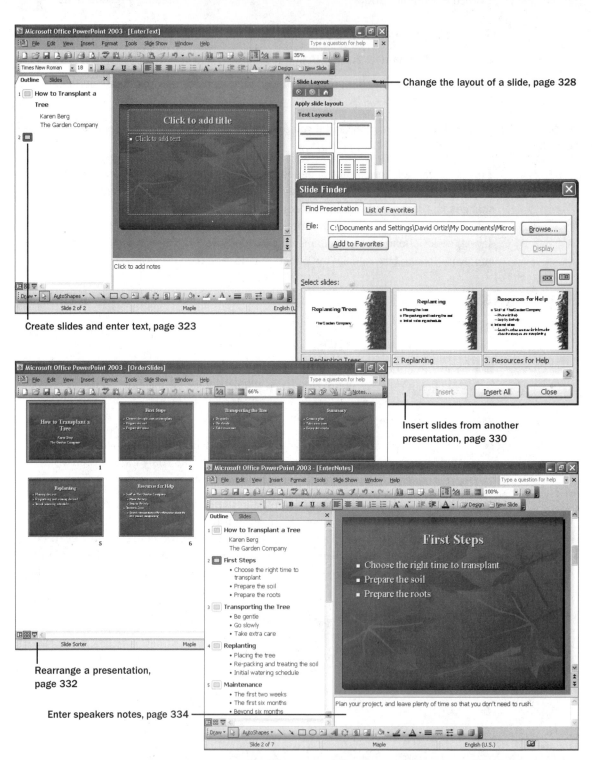

Change the layout of a slide, page 328

Create slides and enter text, page 323

Insert slides from another presentation, page 330

Rearrange a presentation, page 332

Enter speakers notes, page 334

Chapter 14 at a Glance

14 Working with Slides

In this chapter you will learn to:

✔ Create slides and enter text.

✔ Change the layout of a slide.

✔ Insert slides from another presentation.

✔ Rearrange a presentation.

✔ Enter speaker notes.

To work efficiently with Microsoft Office PowerPoint 2003, you need to know how to build a presentation by adding slides and entering text. You can add slides by using commands or simply by typing on the Outline tab of the Outline/Slides pane in Normal view. After adding a slide, you can change its layout by simply clicking a representation in the Slide Layout task pane. You can then customize the slide with your own text, using familiar word-processing techniques. After you have assembled a group of slides, you can turn your attention to their organization, and if you are planning on delivering the presentation to a live audience, you can jot down notes to guide your talk as you work, rather than waiting until the end of the development process.

In this chapter, you will enter text in a slide, create a new slide, change the slide's layout, insert slides from another presentation, rearrange slides, and enter speaker notes.

See Also   Do you need only a quick refresher on the topics in this chapter? See the Quick Reference entries on page xxxiii.

 Important   Before you can use the practice files in this chapter, you need to install them from the book's companion CD to their default location. See "Using the Book's CD-ROM" on page xxi for more information.

Creating Slides and Entering Text

There are two ways to quickly and easily add new slides to a presentation:

■ Click the New Slide button on the Formatting toolbar.

■ Click the New Slide command on the Insert menu.

When you use either of these methods, a new slide with the default layout is inserted into the presentation immediately after the current slide, and the Slide Layout task pane opens so that you can change the default layout if you want. You can also create new slides by pressing keyboard shortcuts while you are entering text on the Outline tab of the Outline/Slides pane, as follows:

- Press [Enter] if the insertion point is at the right end of a slide title.
- Press [Ctrl]+[Enter] if the insertion point is at the right end of a bulleted item.
- Press [Shift]+[Tab] if the insertion point is at the left end of a bulleted item.

When you create a slide with a layout that includes text, the slide is displayed in the Slide pane with one or more boxes called *text placeholders*. After you enter text in a placeholder, the placeholder becomes a *text object*. An *object* is a discrete element of a slide that can be positioned and sized independently of other objects. In this case, the object is a box containing text.

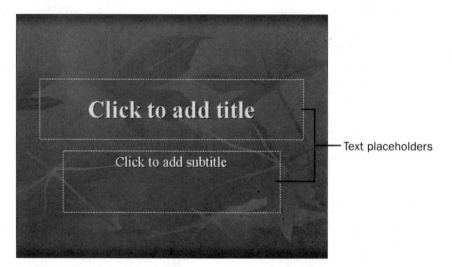

Text placeholders

You can enter and organize text either in the Slide pane or on the Outline tab of the Outline/Slides pane. As you type, the text appears in both places. On the Outline tab, a slide icon appears next to the title for each slide, and subordinate paragraphs appear below the title, indented and preceded by a bullet. In the Slide pane, how the text is displayed will depend on which layout is applied to the slide.

In this exercise, you will enter a tile and subtitle on an existing slide. You'll create a new slide and enter its title text in the Slide pane, and then you'll create more slides and enter titles and bulleted items on the Outline tab.

BE SURE TO start PowerPoint before beginning this exercise.

USE the *EnterText* presentation in the practice file folder for this topic. This practice file is located in the *My Documents\Microsoft Press\Office 2003 SBS\WorkingSlide\EnteringText* folder and can also be accessed by clicking *Start/All Programs/Microsoft Press/Microsoft Office System 2003 Step by Step*.

OPEN the *EnterText* presentation.

1　In the **Slide** pane, click the **Click to add title** text placeholder.

　　A selection box surrounds the placeholder, and a blinking insertion point appears in the center of the box, indicating that the text you type will be centered in text object.

2　Type How to Transplant a Tree.

　　Do not type a period at the end of title names or bulleted items.

　　Tip　　If you make a typing error, press Backspace to delete the mistake, and then type the correct text. For more information about editing text, see Chapter 4, "Working with Slide Text."

3　In the **Outline/Slides** pane, click the **Outline** tab and notice that the text you typed also appears there.

4　Click the **Click to add subtitle** text placeholder.

　　The title text object is deselected, and the subtitle object is selected.

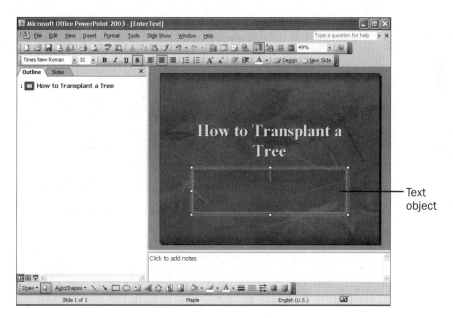

Text object

5 Type Karen Berg, and then press ⌷Enter⌷ to move the insertion to the next line.

6 Type The Garden Company.

7 On the Formatting toolbar, click the **New Slide** button.

PowerPoint creates a new slide with the default slide layout (a title and bulleted list) and opens the Slide Layout task pane. The Outline tab now displays an icon for a second slide, and the status bar displays *Slide 2 of 2*.

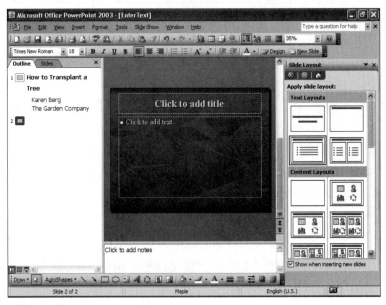

8 Without clicking anywhere, type First Steps.

Tip If you start typing on an empty slide without first having selected a place-holder, PowerPoint enters the text into the title object.

The text appears both in the Slide pane and on the Outline tab. You can work directly in either place to enter your ideas.

9 At the right end of the task pane's title bar, click the **Close** button.

Close

10 On the **Outline** tab, click to the right of Slide 2's title.

A blinking insertion point appears.

11 Press `Enter`.

PowerPoint adds a new slide icon on the Outline tab.

12 Press the `Tab` key.

On the Outline tab, the slide icon changes to a bullet on Slide 2.

13 Type **Choose the right time to transplant**, and press `Enter`.

PowerPoint adds a new bullet at the same level.

14 Type **Prepare the soil**, and press `Enter`.

15 Type **Prepare the roots**, and press `Enter`.

16 Press `Shift`+`Tab`.

This keyboard shortcut turns a bulleted item into a new slide.

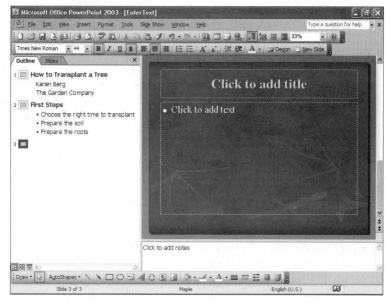

17 Type **Transporting the Tree**, press `Enter`, and then press `Tab`.

PowerPoint creates a new bullet for Slide 3.

18 Type **Be gentle**, and then press `Enter`.

A new bullet appears.

19   Type Go slowly, press ⌷Enter⌷, and then type Take extra care.

20   Press ⌷Ctrl⌷+⌷Enter⌷.

This keyboard shortcut creates a new slide instead of another bullet.

21   Type Summary, press ⌷Enter⌷, and then press ⌷Tab⌷.

22   Type Create a plan, and press ⌷Enter⌷.

23   Type Take your time, and press ⌷Enter⌷.

24   Type Enjoy the results.

25   On the Standard toolbar, click the **Save** button to save the presentation.

Save

CLOSE the *EnterText* presentation.

Changing the Layout of a Slide

You can change the layout of an existing slide by selecting the slide and clicking a different layout thumbnail in the Slide Layout task pane. If you make changes to the layout of a slide—such as sizing or moving a placeholder—but then decide you would rather use the original layout, you can reapply the layout without losing text you have already entered, by clicking a command on the layout thumbnail's drop-down list.

When you manually alter the layout or the types of items on a slide, PowerPoint uses an *automatic layout behavior* to apply a slide layout that matches your changes.

In this exercise, you will reapply a layout to a slide, and then you'll apply a different layout.

USE the *ChangeLayout* presentation in the practice file folder for this topic. This practice file is located in the *My Documents\Microsoft Press\Office 2003 SBS\WorkingSlide\Changing* folder and can also be accessed by clicking *Start/All Programs/Microsoft Press/Microsoft Office System 2003 Step by Step*. OPEN the *ChangeLayout* presentation.

1   In the vertical scroll bar to the right of the **Slide** pane, drag the scroll box to Slide 4.

2   Click anywhere in the bulleted list, and point to the text object's frame (but not to a handle). Then drag the object to the bottom of the slide.

3   On the **Format** menu, click **Slide Layout**.

The Slide Layout task pane opens with the current slide layout thumbnail selected.

4   Point to the current thumbnail, and click the down arrow that appears to its right.

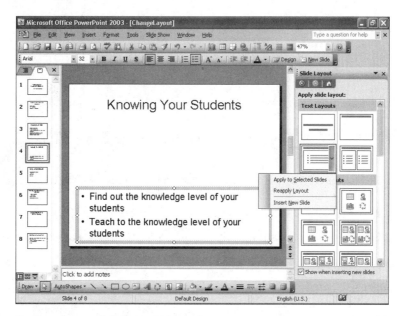

5   On the menu, click **Reapply Layout**.

PowerPoint moves the title object back to its original position on the slide.

6   In the **Slide Layout** task pane, scroll down until you reach the **Text and Content Layouts** area.

7   In the **Text and Content Layouts** area, click the **Title, Text, and Content** slide layout.

The layout of Slide 4 changes so that the bulleted list occupies the left half of the screen and a content placeholder occupies the right half. You can now insert a table, diagram or organization chart, clip art or picture, or a media clip as the content object.

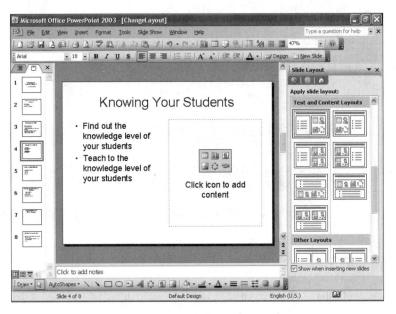

8 Close the **Slide Layout** task pane.

9 On the Standard toolbar, click the **Save** button to save the presentation.

Save

CLOSE the *ChangeLayout* presentation.

Inserting Slides from Another Presentation

You can save time while creating a presentation by using slides that you or someone else has already created. When you insert slides from one presentation into another, the slides conform to the color and design of the current presentation, so you don't have to make many changes.

In this exercise, you will insert slides from one presentation into another.

USE the *InsertSlide* and *SlideInsert* presentations in the practice file folder for this topic. These practice files are located in the *My Documents\Microsoft Press\Office 2003 SBS\WorkingSlide\Inserting* folder and can also be accessed by clicking *Start/All Programs/Microsoft Press /Microsoft Office System 2003 Step by Step*.
OPEN the *InsertSlide* presentation.

1 On the **Outline** tab, click to the right of the last bulleted item in Slide 4.

2 On the **Insert** menu, click **Slides from Files**.

Troubleshooting　　Remember, if you don't see the Slide from Files command on the short View menu, hover over the menu name, double-click the menu name, or point to the chevrons (the double arrows) at the bottom of the short menu to expand the menu.

The Slide Finder dialog box appears.

3　On the **Find Presentation** tab, click the **Browse** button.

The Browse dialog box appears.

4　Check that My Documents appears in the **Look in** box. (If it doesn't, click the **My Documents** icon on the Places bar.) Then double-click the *Microsoft Press*, *Office System 2003 SBS*, *WorkingSlide*, and *Inserting* folders.

5　Click the *SlideInsert* file, and then click **Open**.

The Slide Finder dialog box reappears.

6　Click Slide 2, click Slide 3, click the right scroll arrow, and then click Slide 4 to select the slides you want to insert.

Tip　If you use one or more slides in several presentations, you can click "Add to Favorites" to save the selected slides on the List of Favorites tab in the Slide Finder dialog box.

7　Click the **Insert** button.

PowerPoint inserts the slides after the current slide.

8 Click **Close** to close the **Slide Finder** dialog box.

The text of the inserted slides appears on the Outline tab, and the last slide inserted appears in the Slide pane.

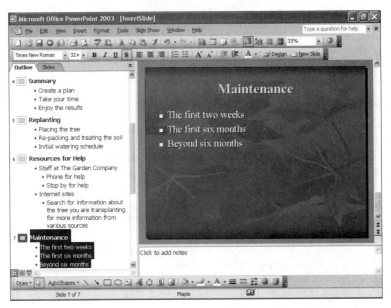

9 On the Standard toolbar, click the **Save** button to save the presentation.

Save

CLOSE the *InsertSlide* presentation.

Rearranging a Presentation

After you have created several slides, whether by adding them and entering text or by inserting them from another presentation, you might need to rearrange the order of your slides to make them most effectively communicate your message. Rearranging a presentation is best done in Slide Sorter view, where you can drag slides from one location to another.

In this exercise, you'll rearrange slides in Slide Sorter view.

USE the *OrderSlides* presentation in the practice file folder for this topic. This practice file is located in the *My Documents\Microsoft Press\Office 2003 SBS\WorkingSlide\Rearranging* folder and can also be accessed by clicking *Start/All Programs/Microsoft Press/Microsoft Office System 2003 Step by Step*. OPEN the *OrderSlides* presentation.

Slide Sorter View

1 In the lower-left corner of the **Outline/Slides** pane, click the **Slide Sorter View** button.

PowerPoint displays the presentation as a set of thumbnails and opens the Slide Sorter toolbar above the presentation window.

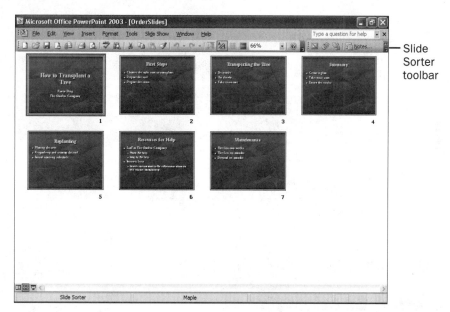

2 Drag Slide 4 ("Summary") to the empty space after Slide 7 ("Maintenance").

When you release the mouse button, Slide 4 moves to its new position, and PowerPoint repositions and renumbers the other slides in the presentation.

Tip In Slide Sorter view, you can also move slides from one open presentation to another. Open the presentations, switch to Slide Sorter view in each presentation window, and click Arrange All on the Window menu. Then drag the slides from one presentation window to another.

3 Drag Slide 5 ("Resources for Help") between Slides 6 and 7.

4 Double-click Slide 2.

PowerPoint returns to the previous view—in this case, Normal view—with Slide 2 active.

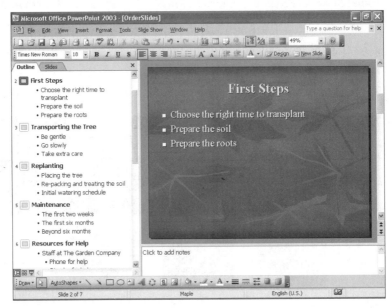

Save

5 On the Standard toolbar, click the **Save** button to save the presentation.

CLOSE the *OrderSlides* presentation.

Entering Speaker Notes

If you will be delivering your presentation before a live audience, you will probably need some speaker notes to guide you. Each slide in a PowerPoint presentation has a corresponding notes page. As you create each slide, you can enter notes that relate to the slide's content on this page. You do this in the Notes pane.

You enter and change text in the Notes pane the same way you do in the Slide pane and on the Outline tab. You simply click the Notes pane and begin typing. If you want to include something other than text in your speaker notes, you must switch to Notes Page view by clicking Notes Page on the View menu. You also switch to Notes Page view if you want to review all the notes at once.

In this exercise, you will enter text in the Notes pane, switch to Notes Page view, and move from page to page.

USE the *EnterNotes* presentation in the practice file folder for this topic. This practice file is located in the *My Documents\Microsoft Press\Office 2003 SBS\WorkingSlide\EnteringNotes* folder and can also be accessed by clicking *Start/All Programs/Microsoft Press/Microsoft Office System 2003 Step by Step.* OPEN the *EnterNotes* presentation.

Next Slide

1 At the bottom of the vertical scroll bar to the right of the Slide pane, click the **Next Slide** button.

2 In Slide 2's **Notes** pane, click the **Click to add notes** text placeholder.

The notes placeholder text disappears, and a blinking insertion point appears.

3 Type Plan your project, and leave plenty of time so that you don't need to rush.

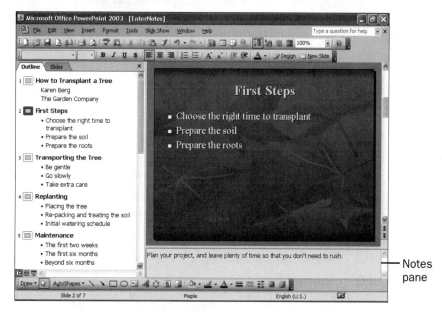

Notes pane

4 On the **View** menu, click **Notes Page**.

Slide 2 is displayed in Notes Page view, with the view percentage set so that the page will fit in the window.

Zoom

5 On the Standard toolbar, click the down arrow to the right of the **Zoom** box, and then click **75%**.

You can now read the notes more easily.

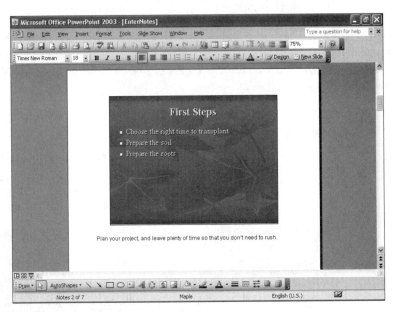

6   Click the **Next Slide** button.

The status bar displays *Notes 3 of 7*.

7   On Slide 3, click the **Click to add text** placeholder.

8   Type **It is important to have a large enough vehicle to transport the tree and the soil and other supplies you will need.**

9   On the Standard toolbar, click the down arrow to the right of the **Zoom** box, and click **Fit**.

The entire notes page appears in the window.

10   Click the **Normal View** button.

The note you entered in Notes Page view appears in the Notes pane in Normal view.

Normal View

11   On the Standard toolbar, click the **Save** button to save the presentation.

Save

CLOSE the *EnterNotes* presentation, and if you are not continuing on to the next chapter, quit PowerPoint.

Key Points

- You can enter text in either the Slide pane or on the Outline tab of the Outline/Slides pane. As you type, the text appears in both locations.

- You can quickly and easily add new slides to a presentation by either clicking the New Slide button on the Formatting toolbar or by clicking the New Slide command on the Insert menu.

- You can change the current layout of a slide by selecting a new layout from the Slide Layout task pane. You can also reapply the original slide layout without losing any slide content.

- You can insert slides from one presentation into another. The inserted slides conform to the design of the presentation into which they are inserted.

- You can rearrange a presentation in Slide Sorter view by dragging slides from one location to another.

- You can enter speaker notes that appear on separate notes pages.

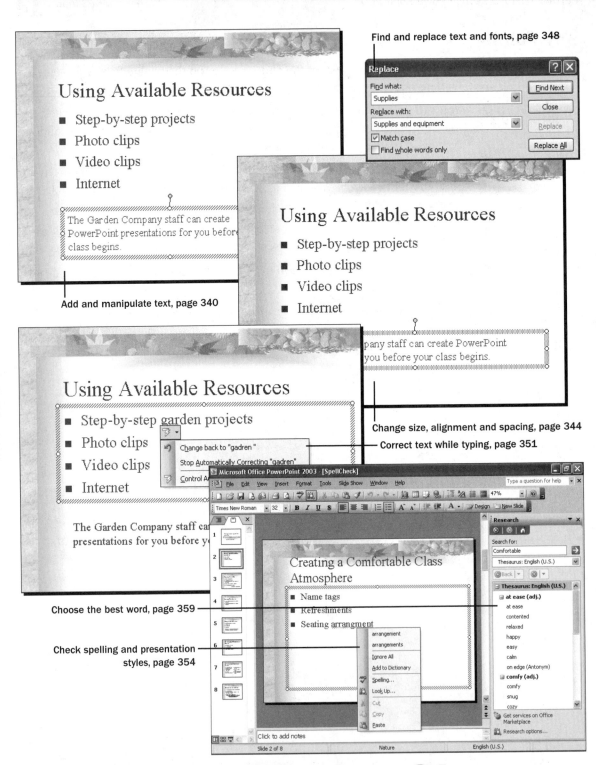

Find and replace text and fonts, page 348

Add and manipulate text, page 340

Change size, alignment and spacing, page 344

Correct text while typing, page 351

Choose the best word, page 359

Check spelling and presentation styles, page 354

Chapter 15 at a Glance

15 Working with Slide Text

In this chapter you will learn to:

✔ Add and manipulate text.

✔ Change size, alignment, and spacing.

✔ Find and replace text and fonts.

✔ Correct text while typing.

✔ Check spelling and presentation styles.

✔ Choose the best word.

In Microsoft Office PowerPoint 2003, you can add text directly to the slides of a presentation and then modify the text to fine-tune your message. You have complete control over the placement and position of slide text. With PowerPoint, you have several alternatives for placing text in *text objects* on your slides:

■ Text placeholders for entering slide titles and subtitles

■ Text labels for short notes and phrases

■ Word processing boxes for longer text

You can also place text inside objects such as circles, rectangles, or stars.

In this chapter, you will create several kinds of text objects. You will also edit text, change its appearance, find and replace words and phrases, and replace fonts. You will watch PowerPoint correct errors as you type them, check spelling, check presentation styles, and use the Thesaurus to find the word that best suits your presentation.

See Also Do you need only a quick refresher on the topics in this chapter? See the Quick Reference entries on page xxxiii.

Important Before you can use the practice files in this chapter, you need to install them from the book's companion CD to their default location. See "Using the Book's CD-ROM" on page xxi for more information.

Adding and Manipulating Text

In PowerPoint, it's easy to add and edit text from both the Slide pane and the Outline/Slides pane. In the Slide Pane, you can enter titles, bullet items, and supplemental text. To change the title or bullet items, or create new ones, you can view them without the supplemental text on the Outline tab of the Outline/Slides pane, and make changes from there as well.

Text appears on slides in objects, boxes that contain text and that are handled as a unit—for example, a title is one text object, and a bulleted list is another. Before you can manipulate a text object, you first need to select it in one of two ways:

■   Clicking anywhere in the text in the text object displays a *slanted-line selection box* around the text object. You can then edit the text—for example, you can add, delete, or correct words and punctuation.

The Garden Company —— Slanted-line selection box

■   Clicking the edge of a slanted-line selection box selects the entire object and displays a *dotted selection box* around the text object. You can then manipulate the object as a unit—for example, you can size the object, move it, or copy it as a whole.

The Garden Company —— Dotted selection box

To deselect an object, you click a blank area of the slide.

The white circles at each corner of either type of selection box are *sizing handles*, which you can use to size the object.

When a text object is surrounded by a dotted selection box, you can move or copy the text object anywhere on the slide. Dragging is the most efficient way to move a text object within a single slide, and you can copy it just as easily by holding down the Ctrl key while you drag it.

When you want to include other types of text on a slide—for example, annotations or minor points that do not belong in a list—you can create a text box using the Text Box button on the Drawing toolbar. There are two types of text boxes:

■   A *text label* is used for text that does not wrap to a second line within the text box, such as a short note or phrase. You simply click the Text Box button, click the slide where you want to place the label, and then type the text.

■   A *word processing box* is used for text that wraps within the text box, such as longer notes or sentences. You can create a word processing box by using the Text Box tool to drag a text box of the appropriate size, and then typing the text.

After you have created a text label or word processing box, you can change one into the other by changing the word-wrap and fit-text options in the Format Text Box dialog box. You can also change a text label into a word processing box by dragging one of the corner sizing handles.

In this exercise, you will select and deselect a text object, move a text object by dragging its selection box, add text in a text object, and then create a text label and a word processing box.

BE SURE TO start PowerPoint before beginning this exercise.
USE the *AddText* presentation in the practice file folder for this topic. This practice file is located in the *My Documents\Microsoft Press\Office 2003 SBS\WorkingText\Adding* folder and can also be accessed by clicking *Start/All Programs/Microsoft Press/Microsoft Office System 2003 Step by Step*.
OPEN the *AddText* presentation.

1   On Slide 1, click the subtitle.

The text within the text object is selected, as indicated by the blinking insertion point and the slanted-line selection box.

2   Point to the selection box, and when the pointer changes to a four-headed arrow, click the mouse button once.

The text object is selected as a unit, as indicated by the dotted selection box.

Tip   You can select an object as a unit with just one click. Position the pointer above or below the object until it changes to a four-headed arrow, and then click. The dotted selection box appears to show that the entire object is selected.

3   Click outside the selection box in a blank area of the slide to deselect the object.

Next Slide

4   In the **Slide** pane, click the **Next Slide** button at the bottom of the vertical scroll bar twice.

Slide 3 is now displayed.

5   Double-click *TGC* in the bulleted list, and type The Garden Company.

6   Click a blank area of the slide to deselect the object.

Text Box

7   If necessary, display the Drawing toolbar. Then click the **Text Box** button, and point below the last bullet on the slide.

The pointer appears as an upside-down T.

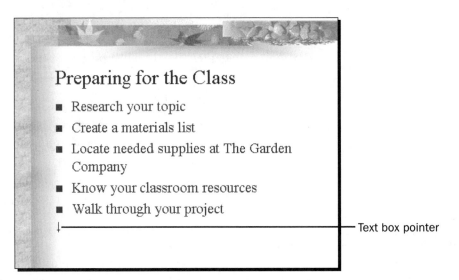

Text box pointer

8   Click the slide to create a text box.

A small, empty text box appears with a blinking insertion point inside it.

9   Type **See Slide 5 for available resources.**

If you wanted to rotate the object, you could drag the green rotating handle above the text box.

10   Click the slanted-line selection box (don't click a handle).

The slanted-line selection box changes to a dotted selection box.

11   Point to the dotted selection box (not to a handle), and drag the box to the right.

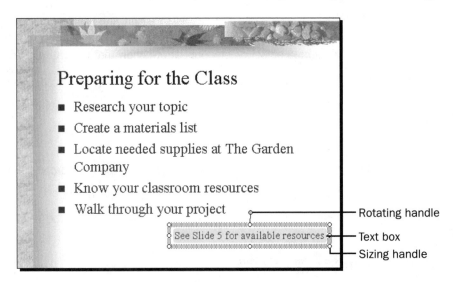

Rotating handle

Text box

Sizing handle

Tip   If you look carefully, you can see the text label in the slide's thumbnail on the Slides tab of the Outline\Slides pane. However, the text label does not appear on the Outline tab. Only text entered in a title or bullet point object appears on the Outline tab.

12   Click a blank area of the slide to deselect the text box.

13   Move to Slide 5, and on the Drawing toolbar, click the **Text Box** button.

14   Point below the last bullet, and drag to create a box that extends the width of the slide's title.

No matter what height you make the box, it snaps to a standard size when you release the mouse button. It is surrounded by a slanted-line selection box and contains a blinking insertion point.

15   Type The Garden Company staff can create PowerPoint presentations for you before your class begins.

The width of the box does not change, but as the words wrap, the box's height increases to accommodate the complete entry.

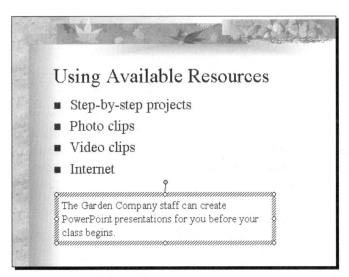

16   Click a blank area of the slide to deselect the text box.

17   On the Standard toolbar, click the **Save** button to save the presentation.

Save

CLOSE the *AddText* presentation.

Changing Size, Alignment, and Spacing

A text object can be adjusted to accommodate the text it holds, and text can be wrapped to fit within an object of a certain size.

To size an object to fit a given amount of text, you can either manually size it or you can use the "Resize AutoShape to fit text" option on the Text Box tab in the Format AutoShape dialog box.

To control the way text is aligned within an object, you can select the object and click one of the following alignment buttons on the Formatting toolbar:

■   The Align Left button aligns text evenly along the left edge of the object and is useful for paragraph text.

■   The Align Right button aligns text evenly along the right edge of the object and is useful for text labels.

■   The Center button aligns text in the middle of the object and is useful for titles and headings.

You can also select an object and adjust the space between lines of text by using the Line Spacing command on the Format menu. You can adjust the space before and after paragraphs by clicking the Increase Paragraph Spacing or Decrease Paragraph Spacing button on the Formatting toolbar.

In this exercise, you will adjust a text object and a text placeholder, change the alignment of text in a text object, decrease paragraph spacing, and adjust line spacing.

USE the *AlignText* presentation in the practice file folder for this topic. This practice file is located in the *My Documents\Microsoft Press\Office 2003 SBS\WorkingText\Aligning* folder and can also be accessed by clicking *Start/All Programs/Microsoft Press/Microsoft Office System 2003 Step by Step*.
OPEN the *AlignText* presentation.

1   On the **Slides** tab of the **Outline\Slides** pane, click Slide 5.

2   Click the text at the bottom of the slide, and then click the slanted-line selection box to select the entire text box.

The text box is surrounded by a dotted selection box.

3   Point to the right-middle handle, and when the pointer changes to a two-headed arrow, drag the handle to the right to extend the text box about an inch.

The text wraps to fit the wider text object.

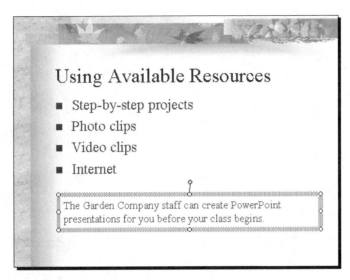

4   On the **Format** menu, click **Text Box**.

Troubleshooting   This command is available only if a text box is selected. If you don't see the command, reselect the text box at the bottom of Slide 5.

The Format Text Box dialog box appears.

5   Click the **Text Box** tab, and clear the **Word wrap text in AutoShape** check box.

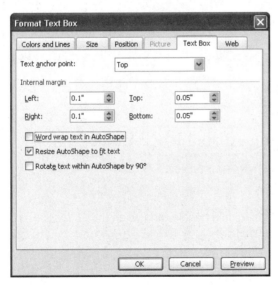

6   Click **OK**.

The word processing box changes to a text label and stretches in one long line beyond the slide boundary.

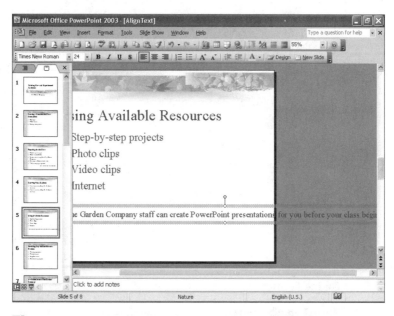

Tip   You can convert a text label to a word processing box by dragging a sizing handle to reduce the width of the text box. The text inside the box wraps to fit the new dimensions of the text box.

Undo

7   On the Standard toolbar, click the **Undo** button to restore the word processing box.

8   Point to the left of the bullet points on Slide 5, and when the pointer changes to a four-headed arrow, click to select the bullet point text object.

The dotted selection box indicates that the text object is larger than it needs to be.

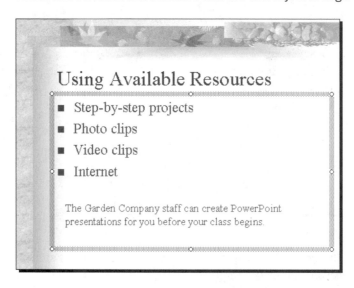

9   On the **Format** menu, click **Placeholder**.

The Format AutoShape dialog box appears.

Tip   The command on the Format menu changes depending on the type of object selected. As you saw in step 4, if a text box is selected, the command on the Format menu is Text Box, and the Format Text Box dialog box appears when you click the command.

10   Click the **Text Box** tab, select the **Resize AutoShape to fit text** check box, and click **OK**.

The object adjusts to fit the size of the text.

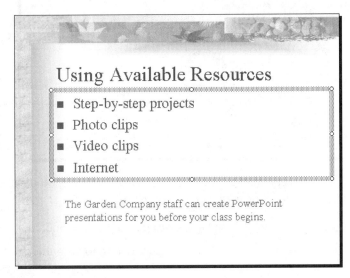

11   Click a blank area of the slide to deselect the object, and then move to Slide 8.

12   Click the text in the word processing box at the bottom of the slide, and on the Formatting toolbar, click the **Center** button.

The text in the text object is centered in the text box.

Center

13   On the **Format** menu, click **Line Spacing**.

The Line Spacing dialog box appears.

14   In the **Before paragraph** box, click the up arrow until the setting is **1**.

Tip   You can also click the Increase Paragraph Spacing button on the Formatting toolbar to increase the space before paragraphs. If this button is not available on the Formatting toolbar, click the Toolbar Options button at the right end of the toolbar, point to Add or Remove Buttons and then Formatting to display a list of additional Formatting buttons, click the Increase Paragraph Spacing button to place it on the toolbar, and then click a blank area of the slide to deselect the menu.

15 In the **Line Spacing** box, click the up arrow until the setting is **1.5**.

16 Click the **Preview** button.

The paragraph spacing and line spacing of the word processing box at the bottom of the slide have both increased.

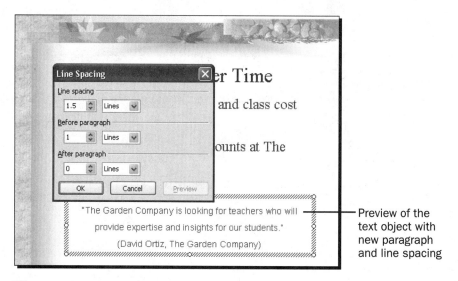

Preview of the text object with new paragraph and line spacing

Tip You can manipulate a title or bulleted list object the same way you manipulate a text label or word processing box.

17 Click **Cancel** to close the **Line Spacing** dialog box without making any changes.

18 On the Standard toolbar, click the **Save** button to save the presentation.

Save

CLOSE the *AlignText* presentation.

Finding and Replacing Text and Fonts

You can locate and change specific text in a presentation by using the Find and Replace commands on the Edit. You use the Find tab of the Find and Replace dialog box to locate each occurrence of the text you are looking for, and you use the Replace tab to locate the text and replace it with something else. You can change all occurrences of the text with the click of a button, or only specific occurrences.

The Find and Replace commands include options for more detailed searches:

■ To search for whole words, you select the "Find whole words only" check box. For example, if the text you are searching for is *plan*, PowerPoint skips over *plant*.

■   To search for a word or phrase that exactly matches the *case,* or capitalization, you specify, you select the "Match case" check box. For example, if you are searching for *IRS,* PowerPoint skips over *firs.*

In addition to finding and replacing text, you can also find and replace a font in a presentation. With the Replace Fonts command, you can replace every instance of one font with another.

In this exercise, you will use the Replace command to find and replace a word, and then you'll use the Replace Fonts command to find and replace a font.

USE the *ReplaceText* presentation in the practice file folder for this topic. This practice file is located in the *My Documents\Microsoft Press\Office 2003 SBS\WorkingText\Finding* folder and can also be accessed by clicking *Start/All Programs/Microsoft Press/Microsoft Office System 2003 Step by Step.*
OPEN the *ReplaceText* presentation.

1   On the **Edit** menu, click **Replace**.

     The Replace dialog box appears.

2   In the **Find what** box, type **Supplies**, and press ⎄Tab.

3   In the **Replace with** box, type **Supplies and equipment**.

4   Select the **Match case** check box to find the text in the **Find what** box exactly as you typed it.

5   Click **Find Next**.

     PowerPoint finds and selects the word *Supplies* on Slide 6.

     Tip   If the Replace dialog box covers up the selected text, move the dialog box out of the way by dragging its title bar.

6   Click **Replace**.

     PowerPoint replaces *Supplies* with *Supplies and equipment.* An alert box tells you that PowerPoint has finished searching the presentation.

7   Click **OK**, and then click **Close** to close the **Replace** dialog box.

8   Click a blank area of the slide to deselect the text object on Slide 6.

9   On the **Format** menu, click **Replace Fonts**.

The Replace Font dialog box appears.

10 Click the down arrow to the right of the **Replace** box, and click **Arial** in the drop-down list.

11 Click the down arrow to the right of the **With** box, scroll down the drop-down list, and click **Impact**.

12 Click **Replace**.

Throughout the presentation, the text formatted with the Arial font changes to the Impact font.

13 Click **Close** to close the **Replace Font** dialog box.

14 Move to Slide 8.

At the bottom of the slide, the note in the word processing box is now displayed in the Impact font.

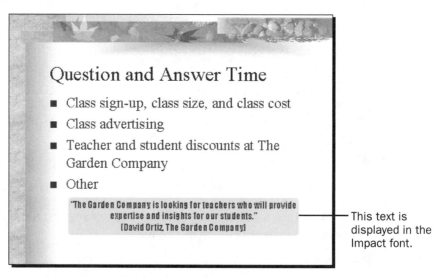

This text is displayed in the Impact font.

Save

15 On the Standard toolbar, click the **Save** button to save the presentation.

CLOSE the *ReplaceText* presentation.

Correcting Text While Typing

As you type text in a presentation, you might be aware that you have made a typographical error, but when you look at the text, the mistake isn't there. PowerPoint uses a feature called *AutoCorrect* to correct common capitalization and spelling errors as you type them. For example, if you type *teh* instead of *the* or *WHen* instead of *When*, AutoCorrect corrects the entry.

When you point to a word that AutoCorrect has changed, the AutoCorrect Options button appears, enabling you to control text correction. You can change the text back to its original spelling, or you can stop AutoCorrect from automatically making corrections. You can also display the AutoCorrect dialog box and make changes to the AutoCorrect settings.

You can customize AutoCorrect to recognize misspellings you routinely type or to ignore text you do not want AutoCorrect to change. You can also create your own AutoCorrect entries to automate the typing of frequently used text. For example, people at The Garden Company could customize AutoCorrect to enter the name of the company when they type only *tgc*.

In addition to using AutoCorrect to correct text as you type, PowerPoint uses the AutoFit feature to size text to fit its object. For example, if you type more text than will fit in a title's text object, AutoFit shrinks the font's size until it all fits. The AutoFit Options button, which appears near the text the first time its size is changed, gives you control over automatic sizing. For example, you can stop sizing text for the current text object while retaining your global AutoFit settings. You can also display the AutoCorrect dialog box and change the AutoFit settings there.

In this exercise, you will add an AutoCorrect entry, use AutoCorrect to fix a misspelled word, and then use AutoFit to make the size of text fit its object.

USE the *CorrectText* presentation in the practice file folder for this topic. This practice file is located in the *My Documents\Microsoft Press\Office 2003 SBS\WorkingText\Correcting* folder and can also be accessed by clicking *Start/All Programs/Microsoft Press/Microsoft Office System 2003 Step by Step*.
OPEN the *CorrectText* presentation.

1 On the **Tools** menu, click **AutoCorrect Options**.

 The AutoCorrect dialog box appears.

2 In the **Replace** box on the **AutoCorrect** tab, type gadren, and press ⎇.

3 In the **With** box, type garden, and then click **Add**.

When you type *gadren* in any presentation, PowerPoint will replace it with *garden*.

4 Click **OK** to close the **AutoCorrect** dialog box.

5 Move to Slide 5, click to the left of the word *projects*, type gadren, and press
Space .

PowerPoint corrects the word *gadren* to *garden*.

6 Point to *garden* to display the **AutoCorrect Options** button, and click the button.

AutoCorrect
Options

A drop-down list of options appears.

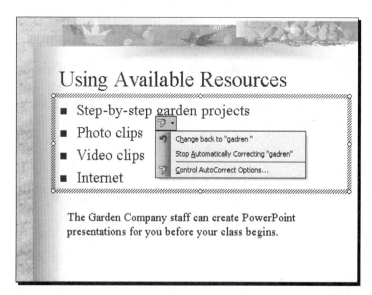

7 Click a blank area of the slide to close the **AutoCorrect Options** menu.

8 Move to Slide 7, click to the right of the word *table* in the last bullet point, and press the [Enter] key.

9 Type Installing a new lawn.

PowerPoint makes the text of the bullet points smaller so that they all fit in the text object. The AutoFit Options button appears to the left of the object.

AutoFit Options

10 Click to the **AutoFit Options** button to display a list of options.

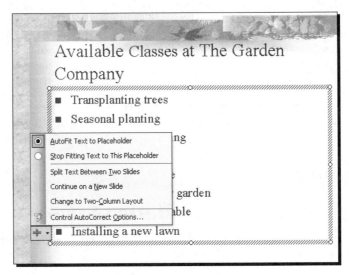

11 Click **Change to Two-Column Layout**.

Another bulleted list object appears to the right of the first one.

12 Type Installing a sprinkler system.

13 Select the *Bouquets from your garden*, *Building a potting table*, and *Installing a new lawn* bullet points in the bulleted list on the left.

14 Drag the selection to the left of *Installing a sprinkler system* in the bulleted list on the right.

All the bullet points in both lists increase in size.

15 Click a blank area of the slide to deselect the object.

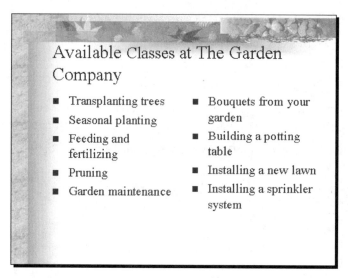

Save

16 On the Standard toolbar, click the **Save** button to save the presentation.

CLOSE the *CorrectText* presentation.

Checking Spelling and Presentation Styles

You can use two different methods to ensure that the words in your presentations are spelled correctly:

- By default, PowerPoint's spelling checker checks the spelling of the entire presentation—all slides, outlines, notes pages, and handout pages—against its built-in dictionary. To draw attention to words that are not in its dictionary and that might be misspelled, PowerPoint underlines them with a wavy red line. When you encounter a wavy red line under a word, you can right-click the word and choose the correct spelling from the shortcut menu, or tell PowerPoint to ignore the word. To turn off this feature, you can click Options on the Tools menu and clear the "Check spelling as you type" check box on the Spelling and Style tab of the Options dialog box.

- You can opt out of using the "Check spelling as you type" option and instead use the Spelling button on the Standard toolbar to check the entire presentation when you finish creating it. PowerPoint then works its way through the presentation, and if it encounters a word that is not in its dictionary, it displays a dialog box so that you can decide how to deal with the word.

PowerPoint includes built-in dictionaries in several languages, so you can check presentations that use languages other than English. (You can mark foreign words so that PowerPoint won't flag them as misspellings.) You can add words to PowerPoint's supplemental dictionary (called CUSTOM.DIC), or create custom dictionaries to check the spelling of unique words. You can also use dictionaries from other Microsoft programs.

PowerPoint's style checker works with the Office Assistant to help you keep the styles you use in your presentations consistent. That way, your audience can focus on content without being distracted by visual mistakes. When the Office Assistant is visible, the style checker reviews the presentation for typical errors—incorrect font size, too many fonts, too many words, inconsistent punctuation, and other readability problems. The style checker then suggests ways to improve the presentation.

In this exercise, you will correct a misspelled word, mark a foreign word, and check the spelling of an entire presentation. You will then set the style options and check the presentation style.

USE the *SpellCheck* presentation in the practice file folder for this topic. This practice file is located in the *My Documents\Microsoft Press\Office 2003 SBS\WorkingText\Spelling* folder and can also be accessed by clicking *Start/All Programs/Microsoft Press/Microsoft Office System 2003 Step by Step*.
OPEN the *SpellCheck* presentation.

1   Move to Slide 2, and right-click the word *arrangment*, which has a wavy red underline.

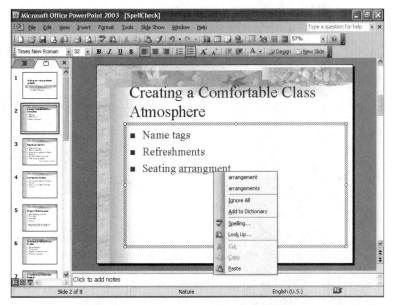

2   Click *arrangement* in the list to replace the misspelled word, and then move to Slide 8.

The French phrase *je ne sais quoi* has been flagged as a possible error.

3 Select *je ne sais quoi*, and on the **Tools** menu, click **Language**.

The Language dialog box appears.

4 Scroll down the list, click **French (France)**, click **OK**, and then click a blank area of the slide.

Behind the scenes, PowerPoint has marked the phrase as French, and the phrase no longer has wavy red underlines.

Spelling

5 Move to Slide 1, and on the Standard toolbar, click the **Spelling** button.

Troubleshooting If a message box tells you that this feature is not yet installed, click Yes to install it before proceeding.

PowerPoint begins checking the spelling in the presentation. The spelling checker stops on the word *Maintanance* and displays the Spelling dialog box.

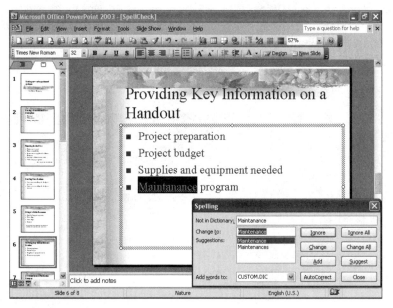

6 Click **Change**.

PowerPoint replaces *Maintanance* with the suggested *Maintenance*, and then stops on the word *Bouquays*, suggesting *Bouquets* as the correct spelling.

Tip Click the AutoCorrect button in the Spelling dialog box to add the misspelling and the correct spelling of a word to the AutoCorrect table of entries.

7　Click **Change**.

Next the spelling checker stops on *TGCGardenersOnly*. This term does not appear in the dictionary, but you know it is a proper name that is spelled correctly.

8　Click **Add**.

The term *TGCGardenersOnly* is added to the supplemental dictionary called CUSTOM.DIC. A message box tells you that PowerPoint has finished the spelling check.

Tip　If you do not want to change a word or add it to the supplemental dictionary, you can click Ignore or Ignore All. The spelling checker then ignores that word or all instances of the word in the presentation in subsequent spell checking sessions.

9　Click **OK**.

10　Move to Slide 1, and on the **Tools** menu, click **Options**.

The Options dialog box appears.

11　Click the **Spelling and Style** tab, select the **Check style** check box, and then click **Style Options**.

Troubleshooting　If PowerPoint prompts you to turn on the Office Assistant, click Enable Assistant, and then click Yes if you are prompted to install this feature.

The Style Options dialog box appears.

12　Select the **Slide title punctuation** check box. Then click the down arrow to the right of the adjacent box, and click **Paragraphs do not have punctuation**.

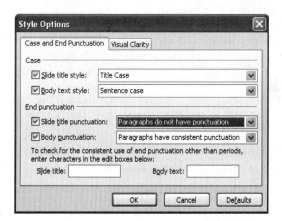

13 Click **OK** to close the **Style Options** dialog box, and then click **OK** again to close the **Options** dialog box.

14 Click the title of Slide 1, and then click the light bulb icon that appears.

The Office Assistant appears to tell you that the title of this slide does not conform to the rule that all words should have initial capital letters (title case).

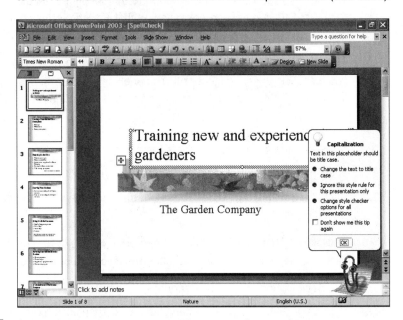

15 Select the **Change the text to title case** option.

PowerPoint capitalizes all the words of the title.

> **Tip** If you make a decision about a style tip, the Office Assistant might not display that tip again unless you reset the tips. To reset the tips, right-click the Office Assistant, click Options, click "Reset my tips," and click OK.

Save

16 On the Standard toolbar, click the **Save** button to save the presentation.

BE SURE TO click Options on the Tools menu and clear the "Check style" check box on the Spelling and Style tab if you don't want PowerPoint to continue giving style suggestions.
CLOSE the *SpellCheck* presentation.

Changing Capitalization

You can change the case of selected text by using the Change Case command on the Format menu. Options include sentence case, title case, uppercase, lowercase, or toggle case, which changes uppercase to lowercase and vice versa.

To change the text case:

1   Select the text you want to change.

2   On the **Format** menu, click **Change Case**.

The Change Case dialog box appears with the Sentence case option set as the default.

3   Click the option you want to apply to the selected text.

4   Click **OK**.

Choosing the Best Word

***New in
Office 2003***
Thesaurus
and Research
task pane

Language is often contextual—the language you use in a presentation to club members is different from the language you use in a business presentation. To make sure you are using words that best convey your meaning in any given context, you can use PowerPoint's *Thesaurus* to look up alternative words, or synonyms, for a selected word. To use the Thesaurus, you select the word you want to look up, and on the Tools menu, click Thesaurus. The Research task pane appears, displaying a list of synonyms with equivalent meanings.

In this exercise, you will access the Thesaurus and replace a word with a more appropriate one.

USE the *Thesaurus* presentation in the practice file folder for this topic. This practice file is located in the *My Documents\Microsoft Press\Office 2003 SBS\WorkingText\Choosing* folder and can also be accessed by clicking *Start/All Programs/Microsoft Press/Microsoft Office System 2003 Step by Step*.
OPEN the *Thesaurus* presentation.

1   Move to Slide 2, and double-click the word *Comfortable* in the title.

2   On the **Tools** menu, click **Thesaurus**.

The Research task pane appears, listing synonyms for the word *comfortable*.

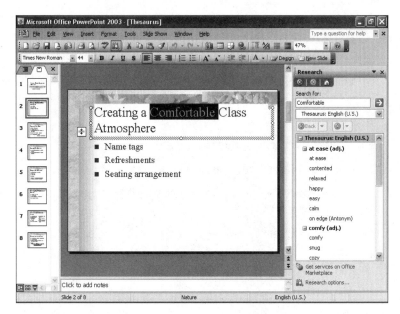

3 Click the minus sign to the left of *comfy* to bring more of the synonym list into view.

4 Point to the word *relaxed*, click the down arrow that appears to the right, and click **Insert** on the drop-down menu.

You can also simply click the word to insert it. Word replaces *Comfortable* with *Relaxed*, mirroring the existing punctuation.

Save

5 On the Standard toolbar, click the **Save** button to save the document.

CLOSE the *Thesaurus* presentation and the Research task pane, and if you are not continuing on to the next chapter, quit PowerPoint.

Key Points

- When you click the text in a text object, it is surrounded by a slanted-line selection box, which indicates that you can edit and format the text. When you click the slanted-line selection box, the text is surrounded by a dotted selection box, which indicates that you can manipulate the object as a unit.

- In addition to titles and bullet points or other paragraphs, you can create two types of text boxes: text labels, and word processing boxes. The first is a single line of text, and the second is a note that wraps in a box. You can change one into the other by changing the word-wrap and fit-text options in the Format Text Box dialog box.

- You can align text to the left or right, or you can center it in a text object. You can also adjust the text object to fit the amount of text it contains.

- You can use the Find and Replace commands on the Edit menu to locate and change text. You can also replace one font with another throughout a presentation with the Replace Font command.

- PowerPoint uses AutoCorrect to correct common capitalization and spelling errors as you type. It uses AutoFit to ensure that the text you type fits in its object. The AutoCorrect Options and AutoFit Options buttons give you control over whether text is corrected and sized.

- PowerPoint's spelling checker checks the spelling of slides, outlines, notes pages, and handout pages. You can mark foreign words and add words to a dictionary so that they don't get flagged as misspellings.

- You can use PowerPoint's Thesaurus to look up synonyms for a selected word and insert a new word into the presentation.

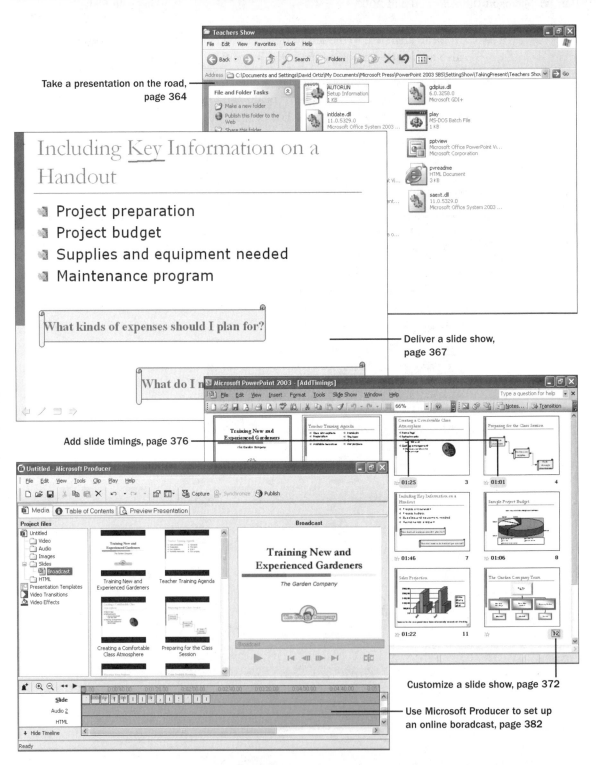

Take a presentation on the road, page 364

Deliver a slide show, page 367

Add slide timings, page 376

Customize a slide show, page 372

Use Microsoft Producer to set up an online boradcast, page 382

Chapter 16 at a Glance

16 Setting Up and Delivering Slide Shows

In this chapter you will learn to:

✔ Take a presentation on the road.

✔ Deliver a slide show.

✔ Customize a slide show.

✔ Add slide timings.

✔ Use Microsoft Producer to set up an online broadcast.

The goal of all the effort involved in creating a presentation is to be able to effectively deliver it to a specific audience. In Microsoft Office PowerPoint 2003, you can deliver a presentation as an electronic slide show in Slide Show view. In this view, instead of the slide appearing in a presentation window within the PowerPoint program window, the slide occupies the entire screen.

When you deliver an electronic slide show you navigate through the slides by clicking the mouse button. You can move forward and backward one slide at a time, and you can jump to specific slides as the needs of your audience dictate. You can hide individual slides, or if you know that you will be giving variations of the same presentation to several different audiences, you can hide sets of slides as separate presentations that you show only if appropriate. You can rehearse a presentation and add timings to slides so that you can pace your presentation. You can also use slide timings to set up a slide show to run unattended, either just once or continuously.

If your computer is on a network or if you have access to the Internet, you can give a slide show on any other computer on the network by using PowerPoint 2003's online broadcasting feature. You can also set up and deliver an online presentation via Microsoft NetMeeting. PowerPoint also includes features to help you deliver a presentation on the road.

In this chapter, you'll first use the Package for CD feature to package a presentation so that everything is available when you move it to another computer. Then you'll explore various navigation tools as you deliver a presentation. You'll see how to take notes, create custom and self-running presentations, and broadcast a presentation over a network.

See Also   Do you need only a quick refresher on the topics in this chapter? See the Quick Reference entries on page xxxiii.

Important   Before you can use the practice files in this chapter, you need to install them from the book's companion CD to their default location. See "Using the Book's CD-ROM" on page xxi for more information.

Taking a Presentation on the Road

When you develop a presentation on the computer from which you will be delivering it, you will have all the fonts, linked objects, and other components of the presentation available when the lights go down and you launch your first slide. However, if you need to transport your presentation to a different computer in order to deliver it, you need to be sure you have everything you need.

New in Office 2003

Package for CD

Microsoft Office PowerPoint 2003 provides a feature called *Package for CD* for when you have to transport your presentation. It helps to gather all the presentation components and then compress and save them to a CD, floppy disk, or other type of removable media, or to a hard disk. Linked files are included in the presentation package by default. TrueType fonts are stored with the presentation if you select the Embed TrueType Fonts option.

Tip   You can embed fonts when you package a presentation, or you can do it when you save a new presentation. In the Save As dialog box, click Tools, click Save Options, and on the Save tab select the "Embed TrueType fonts" check box. Then select the "Embed characters in use only (best for reducing file size)" option to embed only those characters used in the presentation, or select the "Embed all characters (best for editing by others)" option to embed all the characters in the font set.

New in Office 2003

Updated PowerPoint Viewer program

PowerPoint comes with a special program called the *PowerPoint Viewer*, which you can use to deliver a presentation on a computer that does not have PowerPoint installed. You can easily install the PowerPoint Viewer program on any compatible system (one that uses the Microsoft Windows operating system). When you run Package for CD, you have the option of including the PowerPoint Viewer with the packed presentation.

When you complete the Package for CD process, PowerPoint creates two files:

■   *Pngsetup* is a setup file that takes apart the presentation package and sets up the presentation for delivery.

■   *Pres0.ppz* is a compressed version of your presentation.

The Pngsetup and Pres0.ppz files need to be stored in the same folder for the slide show delivery to be successful. To unpack and deliver your presentation, simply double-click the Pngsetup file, and follow the instructions that appear.

In this exercise, you will use Package for CD to create a presentation package in a folder on your hard drive. You will then deliver the presentation using the PowerPoint Viewer.

BE SURE TO start PowerPoint before beginning this exercise.
USE the *RoadPres* presentation in the practice file folder for this topic. This practice file is located in the *My Documents\Microsoft Press\Office 2003 SBS\SettingShow\TakingPresent* folder and can also be accessed by clicking *Start/All Programs/Microsoft Press/Microsoft Office System 2003 Step by Step*.
OPEN the *RoadPres* presentation.

1   On the **File** menu, click **Package for CD**.

The Package for CD dialog box appears.

2   In the **Name the CD** box, type Teachers Show.

PowerPoint will include the open presentation, all its linked files, and the PowerPoint Viewer in the presentation package, but you need to specifically tell it to include embedded fonts.

3   Click **Options**.

The Options dialog box appears.

4   Select the **Embedded TrueType fonts** check box, and click **OK**.

Important   It is especially important to select the "Embedded TrueType fonts" check box if you are using fonts that are not typically installed by Windows. Then when you open the presentation on a computer that doesn't have these TrueType fonts installed, the presentation looks the same as it did on your computer. Be aware that including embedded fonts in a presentation package can increase the file size dramatically.

5   Click **Copy to Folder**.

The Copy to Folder dialog box appears.

6   Click **Browse**, navigate to the *My Documents\Microsoft Press\Office System 2003 SBS \SettingShow\TakingPresent* folder, and click **Select**.

7   When you return to the **Copy to Folder** dialog box, click **OK**.

PowerPoint displays a message box that reports its progress as it creates the presentation package.

8   Click **Close** to close the **Package for CD** dialog box.

Close

9   At the right end of the title bar, click the **Close** button to close the presentation and quit PowerPoint.

10   Display the taskbar, click the **Start** button, and then click **My Documents**.

The My Documents window opens.

11 Navigate to the *Microsoft Press\Office System 2003 SBS\SettingShow\TakingPresent* *\Teachers Show* folder on your hard disk.

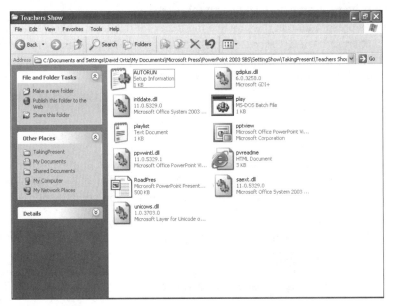

12 In the list of file and folder names, right-click the *RoadPres* file, and click **Open With** on the shortcut menu.

Troubleshooting   If clicking Open With displays a submenu that lists the Microsoft Office PowerPoint Viewer, click that option and skip steps 13 through 15. If the submenu doesn't list the viewer, click Choose Program, and continue with step 13.

13 If the **Programs** list in the **Open With** dialog box includes **Microsoft Office PowerPoint Viewer**, click that option, click **OK**, and skip steps 14 and 15. Otherwise, click **Browse**.

14 Double-click **Microsoft Office**, double-click **OFFICE11**, and then double-click **PPTVIEW**.

15 With **Microsoft Office PowerPoint Viewer** selected in the **Programs** list, click **OK**.

The PowerPoint Viewer displays the presentation's title slide, and the title and subtitle automatically fly in from the right.

16 Click the mouse button to advance to the next slide.

17 Press the ⎋ key to end the presentation.

The PowerPoint Viewer closes.

18 Close the Teachers Show window.

Delivering a Slide Show

The simplest way to advance from one slide to the next in Slide Show view is to click the mouse button. However, PowerPoint 2003 provides a popup toolbar that appears when you move the mouse while in Slide Show view to enable you to move around in other ways.

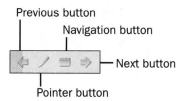

Previous button
Navigation button
Next button
Pointer button

New In Office 2003
New slide show navigation tools

You can use the following techniques to navigate through a slide show:

- To start a slide show with a particular slide, select the slide in Normal or Slide Sorter view, and then click the Slide Show button.

- To move to the next slide, press [Space] or the → key; click the Next button on the popup toolbar that appears when you move the mouse during a slide show; or right-click the screen, and click Next on the shortcut menu.

- To move to the previous slide, press the ← key; click the Previous button on the popup toolbar that appears when you move the mouse during a slide show; or right-click the screen, and click Previous on the shortcut menu.

- To jump to a slide out of sequence (even one that is hidden), click the Navigation button on the popup toolbar that appears when you move the mouse during a slide show, click Go to Slide, and then click the slide on the submenu; or right-click the screen, click Go to Slide, and then click the slide on the submenu.

See Also   For information about hiding slides, see "Customizing a Slide Show" in this chapter.

- To display the slides in a custom slide show, click the Navigation button on the popup toolbar that appears when you move the mouse during a slide show, click Custom Show, and click the show on the submenu; or right-click the screen, click Custom Show, and click the show on the submenu.

See Also   For information about custom slide shows, see "Customizing a Slide Show" in this chapter.

- To end a slide show at any time, click the Navigation button on the popup toolbar, and click End Show; right-click the screen, and click End Show on the shortcut menu; or press [Esc].

Tip   If you are in the middle of a slide show and can't remember how to move to a particular slide, click the Navigation button on the popup toolbar, and then click Help. PowerPoint displays a long list of keyboard shortcuts for carrying out slide show tasks. For example, you can press N to go to the next slide, press H to show a hidden slide, press E to erase pen annotations, or press A to show the pointer arrow.

New in
Office 2003
Improved ink
annotations

During a slide show, you can annotate slides by drawing freehand lines and shapes to emphasize a point. To do this, you click the Pointer arrow on the popup toolbar, click a pen tool, and then begin drawing. You can change the ink color at any time during the presentation by clicking the Pointer arrow, clicking Ink Color, and clicking a color in the palette that appears.

In this exercise, you will use the popup toolbar to navigate through a presentation in Slide Show view and to end a slide show. You'll also use the pen tool to mark up a slide during a slide show, and you'll change the pen color.

USE the *DeliverShow* presentation in the practice file folder for this topic. This practice file is located in the *My Documents\Microsoft Press\Office 2003 SBS\SettingShow\DeliveringShow* folder and can also be accessed by clicking *Start/All Programs/Microsoft Press/Microsoft Office System 2003 Step by Step*. OPEN the *DeliverShow* presentation.

Slide Show

1   With Slide 1 selected, click the **Slide Show** button.

PowerPoint displays the first slide in the presentation, and the title and subtitle fly in from the right.

2   Click anywhere on the screen, or press [Space].

The slide show advances to the next slide.

3   Press the ← key twice to display the previous slide, and then press the → key to display the next slide.

4   Move the mouse.

PowerPoint displays the pointer, and the popup toolbar appears in the lower-left corner of the screen.

Troubleshooting   If the popup toolbar doesn't appear, press [Esc] to end the slide show, and then on the Tools menu, click Options. On the View tab, select the "Show popup toolbar" check box, and click OK.

⇨
Next

5   On the popup toolbar, click the **Next** button.

The first bullet point on Slide 2 appears.

6   Right-click anywhere on the screen, and then on the shortcut menu, click **Previous**.

The bullet point disappears.

7 Right-click anywhere on the screen, and point to **Go to Slide**.

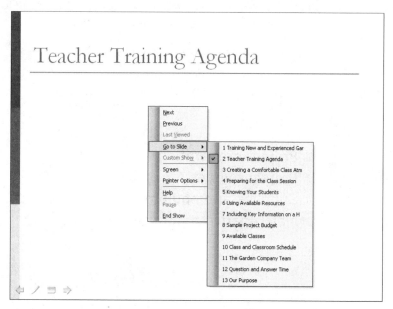

8 In the list of slide names, click **8 Sample Project Budget**.

9 Display the popup toolbar, click the **Navigation** button, and click **Next**.

A budget chart appears on Slide 8.

Navigation

10 Right-click anywhere on the screen, and click **End Show**.

Slide 8 appears in Normal view.

Tip   If you click all the way through to the end of the slide show, PowerPoint displays a black screen to indicate that the next click will return you to the previous view. If you do not want the black screen to appear at the end of a slide show, click Options on the Tools menu. Then on the View tab, clear the "End with black slide" check box, and click OK. Clicking while the last slide is displayed will then return you directly to the previous view.

11 Move to Slide 7, and click the **Slide Show** button.

PowerPoint displays the current slide in Slide Show view.

12 Right-click anywhere on the screen, point to **Pointer Options** on the shortcut menu, and then click **Felt Tip Pen**.

The pointer changes to resemble the tip of a felt tip pen.

Important   When the pen tool is active in Slide Show view, clicking the mouse does not advance the slide show to the next slide. You need to switch back to the regular pointer to advance the slide using the mouse.

13   Draw a line under the word *Key* in the title.

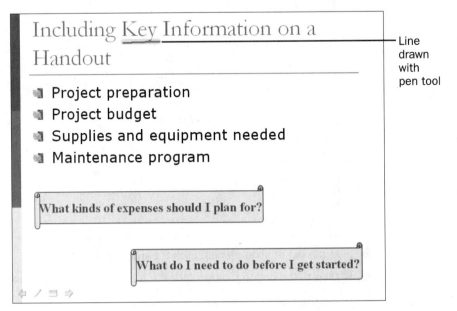

Line drawn with pen tool

Including Key Information on a Handout

- Project preparation
- Project budget
- Supplies and equipment needed
- Maintenance program

What kinds of expenses should I plan for?

What do I need to do before I get started?

14   Right-click anywhere on the screen, point to **Pointer Options**, and then click **Erase All Ink on Slide**.

The line is erased.

15   Press [Space] twice to display the Sample Project Budget slide and its chart.

16   On the popup toolbar, click the **Pointer** arrow, and then click **Ink Color**.

Pointer arrow

The Ink Color palette appears with a selection of colors.

17   On the **Ink Color** palette, click any color box.

18   Draw circles around *$500* and *Fall/Winter* in the chart's title.

19   Right-click anywhere on the screen, point to **Pointer Options**, and then click **Arrow**.

The pen tool changes back to the regular pointer, and you can now click the mouse button to advance to the next slide.

20　Press ⎡Esc⎤ to stop the slide show.

A message asks whether you want to keep your ink annotations.

21　Click **Discard**.

Slide 8 appears in Normal view.

CLOSE the *DeliverShow* presentation.

Using Presenter View with Multiple Monitors

If your computer is connected to two monitors, you can view a slide show on one monitor while you control it from the other. This is useful when you want to control a slide show and run other programs that the audience doesn't need to see.

You can set up your presentation to use multiple monitors by clicking Set Up Show on the Slide Show menu, and then in the "Multiple monitors" area of the Set Up Show dialog box, specifying which monitor the slide show should be displayed on and selecting the Show Presenter View check box. You can then control the slide show by using special presenter tools in Presenter view. You can see details about what bullet point or slide is coming next, see your speaker notes, and jump directly to any slide.

Important　Before you can use multiple monitors, you need to install the proper hardware and software. Install the secondary monitor or projecting device according to the manufacturer's instructions. Check with your computer manufacturer to find out whether integrated dual-monitor support is available so that you can utilize the Presenter view.

To deliver a slide show on one monitor and use Presenter view on another:

1　Open the PowerPoint presentation you want to set up.

2　On the **Slide Show** menu, click **Set Up Show**.

The Set Up Show dialog box appears.

3　In the **Multiple monitors** area, click the down arrow to the right of the **Display slide show on** box, and click the name of the monitor you want to use to project the slide show.

The slide show will run full-screen on the specified monitor, but will appear in Normal view on the other monitor.

4　In the **Multiple monitors** area, select the **Show Presenter View** check box, and click **OK**.

SlideShow ▾　**5**　Click **Slide Show** button to start the slide show.

6　In Presenter view, use the navigation tools to deliver the presentation.

Customizing a Slide Show

If you plan to present variations of the same slide show to different audiences, you don't have to create a separate presentation for each audience. Instead, you can select slides from the presentation that are appropriate for a particular audience and group them as a custom show. You can then run the custom show using just those slides. For example, a slide show to train The Garden Company employees in how to conduct classes for customers might include slides that are not appropriate for a training session for people hired on contract. Because the training materials are similar for the two groups, rather than creating two presentations, The Garden Company can develop the employee presentation first and then create a custom show for contractors using a subset of the slides in the employee presentation.

Sometimes you might want to be able to make an on-the-spot decision during a presentation about whether to display a particular slide. You can give yourself this flexibility by hiding the slide so that you can skip over it if its information doesn't seem useful to a particular audience. If you decide to include the slide's information in the presentation, you can display it by using the Go to Slide command and clicking that slide in a list, or you can insert an action button on a visible slide that you can click to jump to that slide.

In this exercise, you will create and edit a custom show. You will also hide a slide and use an action button to display it when necessary. Finally, you will run the slide show to see how custom shows, hidden slides, and action buttons work.

USE the *CustomShow* presentation in the practice file folder for this topic. This practice file is located in the *My Documents\Microsoft Press\Office 2003 SBS\SettingShow\CreatingCustom* folder and can also be accessed by clicking *Start/All Programs/Microsoft Press/Microsoft Office System 2003 Step by Step*. OPEN the *CustomShow* presentation.

1   On the **Slide Show** menu, click **Custom Shows**.

     The Custom Shows dialog box appears.

2   Click **New**.

     The Define Custom Show dialog box appears. The default custom show name is selected in the "Slide show name" box.

3   In the **Slide show name** box, type Contractors.

4   In the **Slides in presentation** box, click slide 8, and then click **Add**.

     Slide 8 appears as Slide 1 in the "Slides in custom show" box on the right.

5   In turn, select Slides 2 through 7, and 12 through 14 in the **Slides in presentation** list, and add them to the custom slide show.

The slides appear in sequential order in the "Slides in custom show" box on the right.

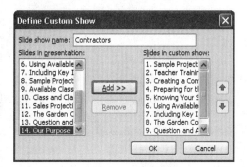

6   Click **OK**.

7   In the **Custom Shows** dialog box, click **Show** to start the custom slide show.

8   Click through all the slides, including the blank one at the end of the show.

9   In Normal view, click **Custom Shows** on the **Slide Show** menu.

10   In the **Custom shows** list, verify that **Contractors** is selected, and then click **Edit**.

The Define Custom Show dialog box appears.

11   In the **Slides in custom show** box, click Slide 8 to select the item.

12   Click **Remove**.

PowerPoint removes the slide from the custom show, but not from the main presentation.

Tip   To change the order of the list, move a slide by selecting it and clicking the up arrow or the down arrow to the right of the "Slides in custom show" box.

13   Click **OK** to close the **Define Custom Show** dialog box, and click **Close** to close the **Custom Shows** dialog box.

14   Scroll to the bottom of the **Outline/Slides** pane. Then on the **Slides** tab, right-click Slide 12, and click **Hide Slide** on the shortcut menu.

PowerPoint puts a shadow box around and a diagonal line through the number 12 to indicate that the slide is hidden.

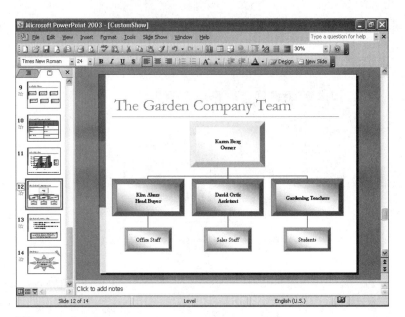

Hide Slide

Tip In Slide Sorter view, you can select a slide and then click the Hide Slide button on the Slide Sorter toolbar.

Slide Show

15 Click Slide 11, click the **Slide Show** button, and then press [Space] to move to the next slide.

Because Slide 12 is hidden, PowerPoint skips from Slide 11 to Slide 13.

16 Press the ← key to return to the previous slide, Slide 11.

17 Right-click anywhere on the screen, point to **Go To Slide**, and then click (**12**) **The Garden Company Team**.

The hidden slide appears in Slide Show view.

18 Press [Esc] to end the slide show.

Action
Button: Return

19 Move to Slide 11, and on the **Slide Show** menu, point to **Action Buttons**, and then click the **Action Button: Return** button in the lower-left corner of the menu.

20 Click the lower-right corner of the slide.

PowerPoint inserts a large action button where you clicked and displays the Action Settings dialog box.

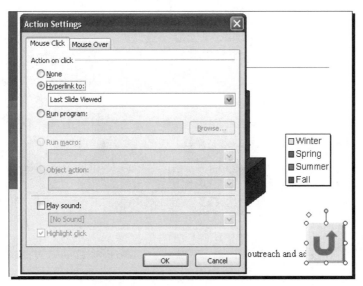

21 In the **Action on click** area, click the down arrow to the right of the box below **Hyperlink to**, and click **Slide** in the drop-down list.

The Hyperlink to Slide dialog box appears.

22 Scroll to the bottom of the **Slide title** list, and click (**12**) **The Garden Company Team**.

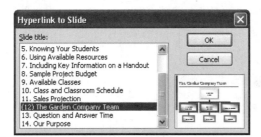

23 Click **OK** to close the **Hyperlink to Slide** dialog box, and click **OK** again to close the **Action Settings** dialog box.

24 Use the action button's sizing handles to make it smaller, and then position it in the lower-right corner of the slide.

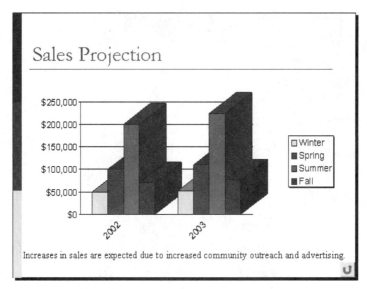

25 Click the **Slide Show** button, and then click the slide's action button.

PowerPoint displays the hidden slide.

26 Press [Esc] to end the slide show.

27 On the Standard toolbar, click the **Save** button to save the presentation.

Save

CLOSE the *CustomShow* presentation.

Adding Slide Timings

You can advance through a slide show in one of two ways:

■ Manual advance, which you control by clicking the mouse button, pressing keys, or clicking commands.

■ Automatic advance, which moves through the slide show automatically, keeping each slide on the screen for the length of time you specify.

The length of time a slide appears on the screen is controlled by its *slide timing*. You can apply a timing to a single slide, to a group of slides, or to an entire presentation by selecting the slides, clicking Slide Transition on the Slide Show menu, and in the "Advance slide" area of the Slide Transition task pane, entering the number of minutes and seconds in the "Automatically after" box.

If you are unsure how much time to allow for the slide timings of a presentation, you can rehearse the slide show while PowerPoint automatically tracks and sets the timing for you, reflecting the amount of time you spend on each slide during the rehearsal.

This technique allows you to spend more time talking about some slides than others. You set slide timings during the rehearsal by clicking Rehearse Timings on the Slide Show menu, or in Slide Sorter view, clicking the Rehearse Timings button on the Slide Sorter toolbar.

In this exercise, you will first set slide timings manually and then you will set them automatically during a slide show rehearsal.

USE the *AddTimings* presentation in the practice file folder for this topic. This practice file is located in the *My Documents\Microsoft Press\Office 2003 SBS\SettingShow\AddingTiming* folder and can also be accessed by clicking *Start/All Programs/Microsoft Press/Microsoft Office System 2003 Step by Step.* OPEN the *AddTimings* presentation.

Slide
Sorter View

1 Click the **Slide Sorter View** button, and then click Slide 3.

Slide Transition

2 On the Slide Sorter toolbar, click the **Slide Transition** button.

Troubleshooting   In Slide Sorter view, the toolbars appear on a single row. If you don't see the Slide Transition button, click the Toolbar Options button, and then click the Slide Transition button on the drop-down menu.

The Slide Transition task pane appears.

3 In the **Advance slide** area, select the **Automatically after** check box, and then click the up arrow twice to show **00:02**.

Because both check boxes in the "Advance slide" area are selected, the slide will advance either after two seconds or when you click the mouse.

Tip   When both check boxes are selected, a mouse click in Slide Show view always advances to the next bullet point or slide, even if the slide's timing has not elapsed. If you want to prevent PowerPoint from advancing to the next bullet point or slide, right-click the current slide, and click Pause on the shortcut menu.

4 Click **Slide Show**.

Slide 3 appears, its bullet points are displayed one at a time, and then PowerPoint moves to Slide 4.

Tip   Slide timings are divided equally among the animations for each slide. So if a slide has a title and four bullet points that are all animated and you assign a timing of 1 minute to the slide, the elements will appear at 12-second intervals.

5 Press [Esc] to end the show, and then in Slide Sorter view, click Slide 3.

Adjacent to the animation icon below the lower-left corner of Slide 3 is the slide timing you just applied.

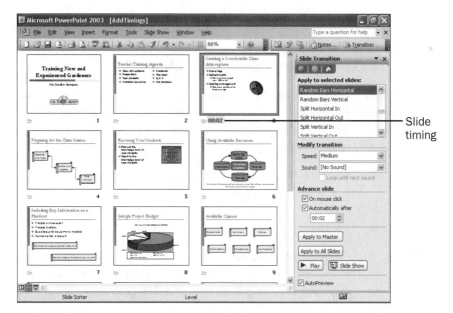

Slide timing

6 At the bottom of the **Slide Transition** task pane, click the **Apply to All Slides** button.

PowerPoint applies the current Slide Transition settings, including the slide timing, to all the slides.

Important   When you click Apply to All Slides, all the transition effects applied to the active slide are transferred to the other slides. If you have applied different transitions to different slides, those individually specified transitions are overwritten. So it's a good idea to apply all the effects that you want the slides to have in common first. Then if you want, you can select each slide and customize its effects. (Bear in mind, though, that too many effects in one presentation can distract the audience from your message.)

7 Click **Slide Show**, watch as the slides advance, and click the mouse button when the black screen is displayed.

8 In the **Advance slide** area of the **Slide Transition** task pane, clear the **Automatically after** check box, and then click **Apply to All Slides**.

The slide timings disappear from below the slides.

Important   Before you carry out the remaining steps in this exercise, read all the steps carefully so that you understand what you need to do after you begin rehearsing the presentation.

Rehearse
Timings

9   Click Slide 1, and then on the Slide Sorter toolbar, click the **Rehearse Timings** button.

PowerPoint switches to Slide Show view, starts the show, and displays the Rehearsal toolbar in the upper-left corner of the screen. A Slide Time counter is timing the length of time Slide 1 remains on the screen.

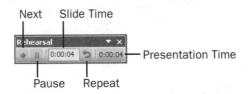

10   Wait about 10 seconds, and then click the **Next** button.

Next

11   Work your way slowly through the slide show, clicking **Next** to display each bullet point on each slide and then move to the next slide.

Repeat

12   If you want to repeat the rehearsal for a particular slide, click the **Repeat** button on the Rehearsal toolbar to reset the Slide Time for that slide to 0.00.00.

[X]

Close

Tip   If you want to start the entire rehearsal over again, click the Rehearsal toolbar's Close button, and when a message asks whether you want to keep the existing timings, click No.

When you reach the end of the slide show, a message box displays the elapsed time for the presentation and asks whether you want to apply the recorded slide timings.

13   Click **Yes**.

You return to Slide Sorter view, where the recorded timings have been added below each slide. The timing for the active slide, Slide 1, appears in the "Automatically after" box in the "Advance slide" area of the Slide Transition task pane, and you can manually adjust the timing if you want.

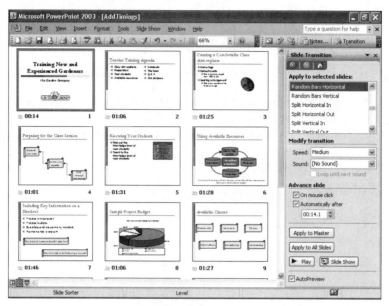

14   At the bottom of the **Slide Transition** task pane, click the **Slide Show** button.

PowerPoint runs the slide show, using the recorded timings.

15   Press [Esc] at any time to stop the slide show.

Save

16   On the Standard toolbar, click the **Save** button to save the presentation, and then close the **Slide Transition** task pane.

CLOSE the *AddTimings* presentation.

Creating a Self-Running Presentation

When slide timings have been applied to a PowerPoint presentation, the presentation can be set up to run automatically, either once or continuously. Self-running slide shows are a great way to communicate information without a presenter needing to be in attendance. You might want to set up a presentation to run unattended in a booth at a trade show or as a product demonstration in a store. A self-running show turns off all navigation tools except action buttons and other action settings available to the viewer.

To set up a self-running slide show.

1   Open the presentation, and then on the **Slide Show** menu, click **Set Up Show**.

The Set Up Show dialog box appears.

2   In the **Show type** area, select the **Browsed at a kiosk (full screen)** option.

When you select this option, PowerPoint selects the "Loop continuously until 'Esc'" check box in the "Show options" area and dims the option so that you cannot clear it. If you have attached a recorded narration to the presentation, it will play with the presentation unless you select the "Show without narration" check box.

3   Click **OK**.

4   To test the show, move to Slide 1, and click the **Slide Show** button.

Slide Show

The presentation runs continuously, using its transitions, animations, and slide timings.

5   Press [Esc] to stop the slide show.

6   On the **File** menu, click **Save As**.

The Save As dialog box appears.

7   Navigate to the folder where you want to store the self-running presentation.

8   Click the down arrow to the right of the **Save as type** box, and click **PowerPoint Show** in the drop-down list.

9   In the **File name** box, assign a name to the self-running version of the show, and click **Save**.

PowerPoint saves the presentation as a slide show.

10   Close the presentation.

11   When you are ready to run the show, click the **Start** button on the taskbar, click **My Documents**, navigate to the folder where the slide show file is stored, and double-click it.

The slide show opens in Slide Show view and begins to play.

12   Press [Esc] to stop the slide show and exit the presentation.

Using Microsoft Producer to Set Up an Online Broadcast

These days, it is not unusual for an organization to have employees or members in different cities or even in different countries. When it is not possible or desirable to gather people together for a presentation, you can prepare the presentation for broadcast over a computer network or even the Internet by using Microsoft Producer. You can also save the presentation on a Web server so that people who are not able to attend the broadcast can view it later.

Important   To broadcast a presentation, you need Microsoft Producer installed on your computer. This program is not installed by default; to install and use it, you will need to download the necessary software from the Microsoft Office Online Web site. On the Help menu, click Microsoft Office Online, and click Downloads in the left pane of the Web site's home page. Then in the Search box, type *Producer*, and click the Go button. Click the link to the PowerPoint 2003 add-in called Microsoft Producer, and follow the download instructions.

In this exercise, you will use Producer to publish a presentation for online broadcast.

BE SURE TO download Microsoft Producer for PowerPoint 2003 from the Microsoft Office Online Web site before beginning this exercise.

USE the *Broadcast* presentation in the practice file folder for this topic. This practice file is located in the *My Documents\Microsoft Press\Office 2003 SBS\SettingShow\BroadcastingPresent* folder and can also be accessed by clicking *Start/All Programs/Microsoft Press/Microsoft Office System 2003 Step by Step.*

1   Click the **Start** menu, point to **All Programs**, point to **Microsoft Office**, and then click **Microsoft Producer for PowerPoint 2003**.

If the Microsoft Producer dialog box appears asking how you want to create your presentation, click Cancel.

2   On the **File** menu, click **Import**.

The Import File dialog box appears.

3   Navigate to the *My Documents\Microsoft Press\Office 2003 SBS\SettingShow \BroadcastingPresent* folder, and double-click the *Broadcast* file.

The Import dialog box appears, showing a progress bar while Producer imports your presentation. When the process is complete, your presentation appears on Producer's Media tab.

4   In the **Project Files** pane, click the **Broadcast** presentation icon, and drag it to the **Timeline** at the bottom of the screen.

Producer adds the slides in your presentation to the Slide Track of the Timeline, using the order and duration specified in PowerPoint for each slide.

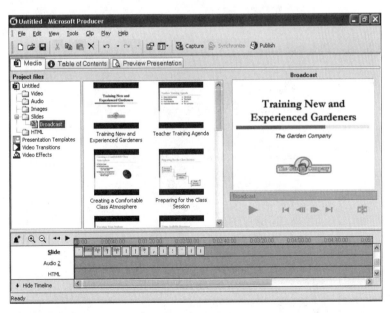

5   Click the **Table of Contents** tab. In the **Introduction** area, type Training New and Experienced Gardeners in the **Title** box, and in the **Presenter** box, type The Garden Company.

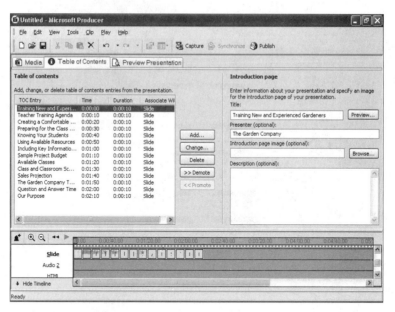

6 On the toolbar, click the **Publish** button.

The first page of the Publish Wizard appears.

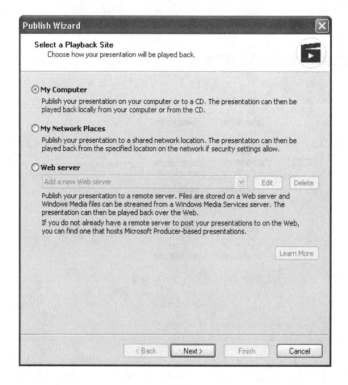

7 Click **Next** to accept My Computer as the location for publishing your presentation.

(You also have the option of publishing the presentation on a network or on a Web server.) The Publishing Destination page appears.

8 In the **File name** box, type Training1. Make sure that the **Publish files to** box specifies that the presentation will be saved in your My Documents folder, and click **Next**.

The Presentation Information page appears.

9 You already specified a title and a presenter on the Producer Table of Contents tab, so click **Next** to continue.

The Publish Setting page appears.

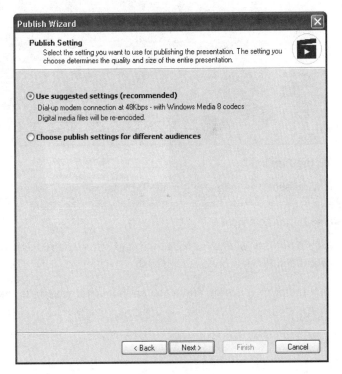

10 Click **Next** to use the suggested settings.

The Publish Your Presentation page appears.

11 Click **Next** to publish your presentation.

The Presentation Preview page appears. You could finish the publication process by clicking Finish, but this page also gives you the opportunity to preview your presentation in a Web browser.

12 In the **Preview presentation for playback in** area, click the **Internet Explorer 5.0 or later for Windows** link.

The presentation's Introduction page appears in a browser window, displaying the text you entered on the Producer Table of Contents tab.

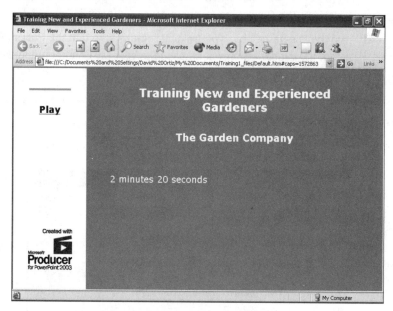

13 Click the **Play** link.

The slide show begins playing in the browser window, just as it would if you were viewing it as a remote broadcast. You can watch the entire slide show, or click the Pause button to stop it.

14 Click the browser window's **Close** button to return to Producer, and on the wizard's **Presentation Preview** page, click **Finish**.

CLOSE Producer, saving your project if you wish, and if you are not continuing on to the next chapter, quit PowerPoint.

Key Points

- You can use Package for CD to create a presentation package that you can copy to a CD or a folder on another computer. This package contains everything you need to run the presentation.

- You can include the PowerPoint Viewer in a presentation package so that you can run the presentation on a computer on which PowerPoint is not installed.

- You can use a variety of toolbar buttons, commands, and keyboard shortcuts to navigate through a presentation in Slide Show view. You can also add actions buttons to slides to assist in navigation.

- You can use different types of pen tools and different pen colors to mark up slides during a slide show, and you can save or discard these annotations.

- When the complete slide show is not desired or required for a particular audience, you can select slides from among all those available to create a custom show.

- You can hide slides and then decide to display them only if they are appropriate for a particular situation or audience.

- You can assign timings to slides manually, or you can practice the slide show and have PowerPoint record the slide timing that you use in rehearsal. You can then use these timings to automatically advance from one slide to the next.

- When you need to give a presentation to a remote audience, you can schedule and host an online broadcast. You can also participate in an online broadcast as an audience member.

V
Microsoft Office Outlook 2003

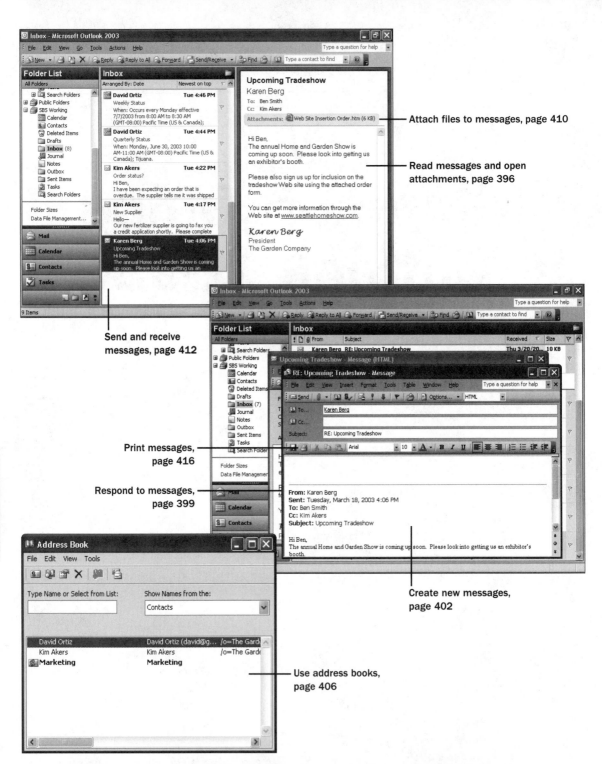

Attach files to messages, page 410

Read messages and open attachments, page 396

Send and receive messages, page 412

Print messages, page 416

Respond to messages, page 399

Create new messages, page 402

Use address books, page 406

17 Working with Outlook

In this chapter you will learn to:

✔ Start Outlook for the first time.

✔ Read messages and open attachments.

✔ Respond to messages.

✔ Create new messages.

✔ Use address books.

✔ Attach files to messages.

✔ Send and receive messages.

✔ Print messages.

✔ Create and send instant messages.

Microsoft Office Outlook 2003 is a personal information management program that helps you manage your time and information more effectively and enables you to share information and collaborate with others more easily.

Electronic mail, or *e-mail*, is an essential form of communication in today's workplace. In Outlook, you will find all the tools you need to use e-mail effectively and manage your electronic messages. With Outlook, you can:

■ Send and receive e-mail messages.

■ Attach files to your messages.

■ Create and manage an address book.

■ Organize and archive your messages.

■ Personalize your messages.

You can also use Outlook to send *instant messages* to your online contacts.

This chapter first discusses the ways Outlook can be set up and what to expect when you initially start the program. Then you'll learn how to create, read, respond to, and print messages; attach files to messages and open attachments; and create and use an address book. Finally, you will learn how to create and send instant messages from within Outlook.

See Also Do you need only a quick refresher on the topics in this chapter? See the Quick Reference entries on page xxxiii.

Important   Before you can use the practice files in this chapter, you need to install them from the book's companion CD to their default location. See "Using the Book's CD-ROM" on page xxi for more information.

Starting Outlook for the First Time

Outlook 2003 supports e-mail accounts that work with a computer running *Microsoft Exchange Server* or a computer set up as an *Internet mail* server. This topic discusses these two types of accounts and explains what you might expect to see the first time you start Outlook.

If you are connected to a *local area network (LAN)* that includes a computer running Microsoft Exchange Server, you send and receive e-mail both internally (within your organization) and externally (over the Internet) using that server. Your network or system administrator will supply the information you need to set up an Exchange e-mail account. With Outlook 2003, you can connect to your Exchange Server from anywhere you can connect to the Internet.

If you are working on a stand-alone computer or on a network that does not have its own mail server, using Internet mail requires that you have an e-mail account with an *Internet Service Provider (ISP)*. You connect to the ISP using a modem and a phone line, a high-speed connection such as DSL or cable, or through a LAN, as follows:

■   If you are using a modem, you can manually establish a connection when you need it, or you can set up *dial-up networking* to automatically connect whenever you start Outlook. Your ISP can provide the phone number, modem settings, and any other special information you need for both types of connection.

■   If you are connected to a LAN, it must be configured to provide access to your ISP from your computer. Your network or system administrator can provide you with the appropriate information to gain access to Internet mail through the LAN.

Regardless of how you connect to your ISP, to send and receive Internet mail, you will need to know the names of your incoming and outgoing e-mail servers, your account name, and your password.

Different Types of Internet Mail Accounts

Outlook 2003 supports three types of Internet mail accounts—POP3, IMAP, and HTTP.

■ *Post Office Protocol 3 (POP3)* is a type of e-mail account commonly provided by ISPs. With a POP3 account, you connect to an e-mail server, and download your messages to your local computer.

■ *Internet Message Access Protocol (IMAP)* is similar to POP3 except that your messages are stored on the e-mail server. You connect to the server to read the message headers, and select which messages you want to download to your local computer.

■ *Hypertext Transfer Protocol (HTTP)* is used whenever you access Web pages from the Internet. When HTTP is used as an e-mail protocol, messages are stored, retrieved, and displayed as individual Web pages. Hotmail is an example of an HTTP e-mail account.

When you start Outlook 2003 for the first time, what you see depends on whether you have upgraded to Outlook 2003 from a previous version or are using it on your computer for the first time:

■ Upgrading to Outlook 2003. If you have used a previous version of Outlook on your computer, you already have an Outlook *profile*. This profile is a collection of all the data necessary to access one or more e-mail accounts and address books. In this case, Outlook 2003 picks up your existing profile settings, and you don't have to re-set them.

■ Using Outlook for the first time. If this is the first time you are using Outlook on your computer, you will be asked to create a profile. To complete this step, you will need specific information about your e-mail account, including your account name, your password, and the names of the incoming and outgoing e-mail servers that handle your account. Your system administrator or ISP can provide you with this information.

If you are using Outlook for the first time on your computer, follow these steps to set up your Outlook profile.

BE SURE TO install and activate Microsoft Office Outlook 2003 before beginning this exercise.

1   Click the **Start** button, point to **All Programs**, then **Microsoft Office System 2003**, and then click **Microsoft Office Outlook 2003**.

Outlook starts and displays the Outlook 2003 Startup Wizard.

2   Click **Next**.

The Account Configuration dialog box appears with the Yes option selected.

3   Click **Next**.

The Server Type dialog box appears.

4   Select the option that corresponds to your e-mail account, and click **Next**.

An account settings dialog box appears. The content of this dialog box is determined by the type of e-mail account you selected in the Server Type dialog box.

5   Complete the wizard by entering the information provided by your system administrator or ISP.

When you finish the wizard, the Outlook program window appears.

6   If this is the first time you've started a Microsoft Office program on your computer, you are prompted to enter your full name and initials in the **User Name** dialog box. This information is used to identify and track changes that you make within Office documents. Enter the requested information, and click **OK**.

Important   If you upgraded to Outlook 2003 from an earlier version, any custom settings you made for your old version of the program carry over to the new version. As a result, as you work your way through the exercises in this book, some of the instructions might not work quite the same way for you, and your screen might not look the same as the book's graphics. The instructions and graphics are based on a default installation of Outlook on a networked computer with an Exchange e-mail account. If you are not working on a network or you have changed the default settings, don't worry. You will still be able to follow along with the exercises, but you might occasionally have to reverse a setting or skip a step. (For example, if AutoPreview is already active on your screen, you would skip the step to turn on AutoPreview.)

The Navigation Pane

New in Office 2003
Navigation Pane

The new Navigation Pane replaces the Outlook Bar from previous versions of Outlook. The Navigation Pane provides quick access to Outlook's components and folders. It can display the Mail, Calendar, Contacts, Tasks, Notes, Journal or Shortcuts pane or the Folder List, which includes Search Folders and Public Folders. The Calendar, Contacts, Tasks, Notes, and Journal panes include easy-to-use links to share your folders or open other Outlooks users' shared folders.

To hide or show the Navigation Pane:

■   On the **View** menu, click **Navigation Pane**.

To make the Navigation Pane taller or shorter:

■   Point to the top of the Navigation Pane so that the cursor becomes a double-headed arrow and drag up or down.

Navigation Pane items are displayed in order, as large buttons in the upper rows of the pane, and then as small buttons on the bottom row. Any buttons the Navigation Pane is not big enough to display are available on the "Configure buttons" button's shortcut menu.

To change which buttons the Navigation Pane displays and their order:

1   Click the **Configure buttons** button, and on the shortcut menu, click **Navigation Pane Options**.

2   To add or remove a button, select or clear its check box.

3   To change the position of a button, click its name and then click the **Move Up** or **Move Down** button until the buttons are in the order you want.

Reading Messages and Opening Attachments

When you start Outlook, any new messages on your *e-mail server* are displayed in your Inbox. With Outlook, you can view and read your messages in several ways:

- You can scan for your most important messages by using *AutoPreview*, which displays the first three lines of each message in your Inbox.

- You can read a message without opening it by viewing it in the *Reading Pane*.

- You can open the message in its own window for easier reading by double-clicking the message in the Inbox.

E-mail messages can contain many types of files as *attachments*. For example, a colleague might send a Microsoft Word document to you by attaching it to an e-mail message. You can open these files from the Reading Pane or from an open message.

The examples in this book center around a fictitious plant and garden accessories store called The Garden Company. The practice files used in this book are the messages and other items of Ben Smith, the administrative assistant for the Garden Company. In this exercise, you will preview a message, open a message, and open an attachment.

USE the *SBSWorking* data file in the practice file folder for this topic. This practice file is located in the *My Documents\Microsoft Press\Office 2003 SBS\Working* folder and can also be accessed by clicking *Start/All Programs/Microsoft Press/Microsoft Office System 2003 Step by Step.*
BE SURE TO start Outlook before beginning this exercise.
OPEN the *SBSWorking* data file from within Outlook.

Maximize

1   If the Outlook window does not fill your screen, click the **Maximize** button in the upper-right corner of the program window so you can see its contents.

Folder List

2   In the **Navigation Pane** on the left side of the window, click the **Folder List** icon.

Expand

3   In the **Folder List** click the **Expand** button next to the *SBS Working* folder and then click the Inbox in the *SBS Working* folder.

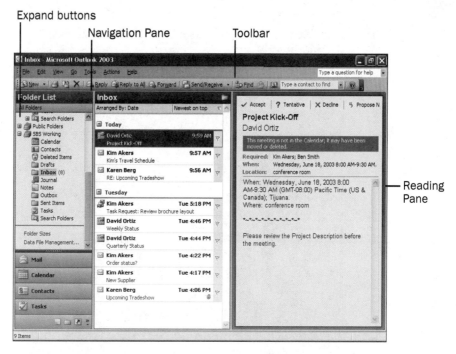

Expand buttons

Navigation Pane

Toolbar

Reading Pane

You now see the initial practice files for this course.

4   If necessary, move the vertical divider between the center and right panes so you can see the contents as shown in the graphic above.

5   On the **View** menu, click **AutoPreview**.

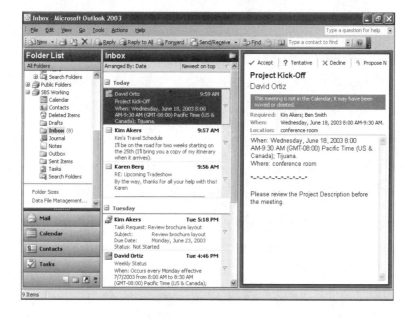

You can now see up to three lines of each of each message in your Inbox.

6 In the SBS Working Inbox, locate the original **Upcoming Tradeshow** message (not the later reply) from Karen Berg, the owner of The Garden Company. Then click the message to display it in the Reading Pane.

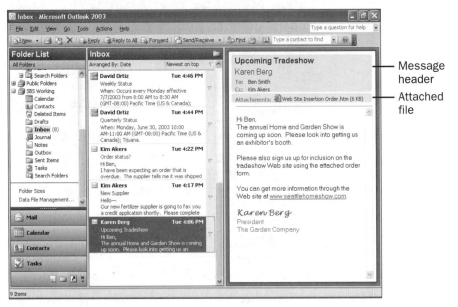

Using the scroll bar if necessary, you can see the full content of the message in the Reading Pane. Note that the Reading Pane shows the full *message header* (the information that appears at the top of the e-mail message, including the subject, sender, and recipients) and the names of any attached files.

7 In the message header, double-click **Web Site Insertion Order.htm** to open the attachment.

8 If you see a message warning you about opening attachments, click the **Open** button.

The Web Site Insertion Order form appears in your default Web browser.

9 Click the **Inbox** taskbar button to return to that folder without closing the e-mail message.

10 On the **View** menu, point to **Reading Pane** and then click **Bottom**.

The Reading Pane now appears at the bottom of the Outlook window rather than on the right side.

New in
Office 2003
Reading Pane

11 On the **View** menu, point to **Reading Pane** and then click **Off** to close the Reading Pane entirely.

You can now see more of the messages in the folder at a glance.

12 Double-click the **Upcoming Tradeshow** message to open it.

The message appears in its own Message window.

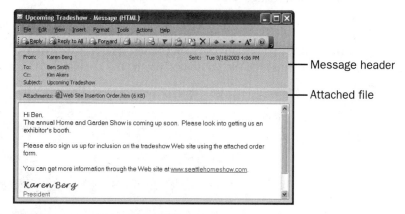 ——— Message header

——— Attached file

13 Note the message header and the attached file at the top.

Restore Down

14 Don't worry if your window is not the same size as this one. As with other windows, you can size Outlook windows to suit the way you work by using the Maximize and Restore Down buttons, or by dragging the window's frame.

Close

15 Click the **Close** button to close the Upcoming Tradeshow message window.

Responding to Messages

You can respond to e-mail messages in different ways. You can reply only to the person who sent the message, or you can reply to the person who sent the message and all the people to whom the original message was addressed. Whether you reply to only the sender or to everyone, your reply does not include any files that were attached to the original message.

You can forward a message you have received to anyone, not just the person who originally sent the message or any of the other recipients. A forwarded message includes any files that were attached to the original message.

In this exercise, you will reply to and forward messages.

USE the *SBSWorking* data file in the practice file folder for this topic. This practice file is located in the *My Documents\Microsoft Press\Office 2003 SBS\Working* folder and can also be accessed by clicking *Start/All Programs/Microsoft Press/Microsoft Office System 2003 Step by Step*.
BE SURE TO start Outlook and open the *SBSWorking* data file before beginning this exercise.
OPEN the *Upcoming Tradeshow* message in the *SBS Working* Inbox.

1 Look at the header information at the top of the Message window.

Note that this message was sent to Ben Smith, and a copy was sent to Kim Akers, the head buyer for The Garden Company. The message also includes an attachment.

2 On the Message window Standard toolbar, click the **Reply** button.

The Reply Message *form* is displayed on your screen.

Enter the primary recipients
of the message in the To box.   E-mail toolbar

Enter the recipients of courtesy copies in the Cc box.

Note that the reply will be sent only to Karen Berg and that the attachment is not included. Note also that a prefix, *RE:*, has been added to the subject line. This prefix indicates that this is a response to an earlier message.

New in Office 2003
Word as your e-mail editor simplifications

Tip   If Microsoft Word is your default e-mail editor, the Reply form displays Word's new E-mail toolbar in addition to Outlook's Standard toolbar. The E-mail toolbar groups the e-mail-related buttons from the Standard and Formatting toolbars, so you have more room to work.

3   With the insertion point in the body of the message, type What size booth would you like?

4   Click the **Send** button.

The reply is sent to Karen Berg.

Important   Because the e-mail addresses in these exercises are fictitious, any messages you send to these addresses will be returned to you as undeliverable. Simply delete any returned message by clicking it and then clicking the Delete button.

5   If the original message closes, reopen it from the practice file Inbox.

Tip   You can instruct Outlook to close an open message when you respond to it. On the Tools menu, click Options. On the Preferences tab, click the E-mail Options button. In the E-mail Options dialog box, select the "Close original message on reply or forward" check box, and then click OK in each dialog box to close it.

6   On the toolbar, click the **Reply to All** button.

The Reply Message form appears. You can see from the message header that this reply will be sent to both Karen Berg and Kim Akers. Again, the attachment is not included.

7   Type I faxed the form to the show organizers.

8   Click the **Send** button.

The reply is sent to Karen Berg and Kim Akers.

9   Reopen the original e-mail if necessary.

10   On the toolbar, click the **Forward** button.

The Forward Message form appears.

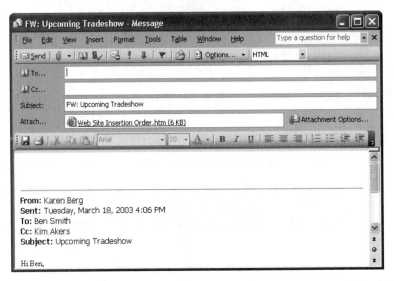

11 Note that the address lines are blank and that the attachment is included. Note also that a prefix, *FW:*, has been added to the subject line. This prefix indicates that this is a forwarded message.

12 In the **To** box, type your own e-mail address.

13 Press the ⒯ᵃᵇ key until you get to the message body, type You might be interested in this!, and then click the **Send** button.

New in
Office 2003
Desktop Alerts

14 The message is forwarded to you. When you receive the message, a small transparent notification called a *desktop alert* pops up in the lower-right corner of your screen. You can hold the mouse over the desktop alert to solidify the box and read the first few lines of the message, click the alert to open the message, or click one of the buttons in the box to flag the message for follow-up, delete it, or mark it as read.

15 When the message arrives in your Inbox, open it and examine the message header.

Note how the subject line and attachment appear.

☒
Close

16 If necessary, close the open Message window by clicking its **Close** button.

See Also   You can send instant replies to meeting requests and messages with voting buttons. For more information see "Changing Message Settings and Delivery Options" in Chapter 18, "Managing E-Mail Messages" and "Responding to Meeting Requests" in Chapter 21, "Scheduling and Managing Meetings."

Creating New Messages

With Outlook, communicating by e-mail is quick and easy. You can send messages to people in your office and at other locations. You can personalize your messages using Outlook's many formatting options; you can also embed hyperlinks in and attach files to your messages.

If you have installed Microsoft Office Word 2003, Outlook can use Word as its default e-mail editor. Many of Word's powerful text-editing capabilities, including styles, tables, and themes, are available to you as you create messages in Outlook. Word will check your spelling as you type, correcting many errors automatically. You can also have Word check the spelling of your message when you send it.

Important　The exercises in this book assume that you are using Word as your default e-mail editor.

Tip　If Word is not your default e-mail editor and you would like it to be, on the Tools menu, click Options. Click the Mail Format tab, and select the "Use Microsoft Word to edit e-mail messages" check box. To turn off Word as your default e-mail editor, make sure the check box is cleared.

In this exercise, you will compose and send a new e-mail message. You can complete this exercise from the practice file Inbox or your own.

OPEN the Inbox.

New Mail
Message

1　On the toolbar, click the **New Mail Message** button.

An Untitled Message form appears. Take a few minutes to investigate the Message window menus and commands. If you are familiar with Word, you will recognize many of them.

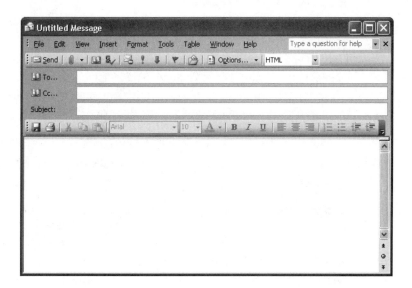

Tip By clicking the down arrow to the right of the New Mail Message button, you can choose to create other types of Outlook items such as appointments, contacts, tasks, notes, or faxes, as well as organizational items such as folders and data files.

2   In the **To** box, type Karen@gardenco.msn.com. Then type ; (a semi-colon), and type Kim@gardenco.msn.com.

Tip By default, Outlook requires that you separate multiple e-mail addresses with semicolons. If you prefer, you can instruct Outlook to accept both semicolons and commas. To do this, on the Tools menu, click Options. On the Preferences tab, click the E-mail Options button, and then click the Advanced E-mail Options button. Select the "Allow comma as address separator" check box, and then click OK to close each window.

If your recipient's address is in your *address book* or you've typed it in a message header before, Outlook automatically completes the address for you, and pressing the ⎀Tab⎀ key inserts the entry. If there are multiple matches, Outlook presents a list of items that match what you've typed so far. Use the arrow keys to select the item you want, and press the Enter key.

Tip If you are working on a network that uses Exchange Server, when you send messages to other people on your network, you can type just the part of the address that is to the left of the @ sign. The remaining part of the address identifies the server that handles the e-mail account, so within an organization, the server name is not needed.

3   Press ⎀Tab⎀, and in the **Cc** box, type your own e-mail address.

Tip If you want to send a copy of a message to a person without the other recipients being aware of it, you can send a "blind" copy. Display the Bcc box by clicking the arrow to the right of the Options button, and then clicking Bcc. Then type the person's e-mail address in the Bcc box.

4   Press the ⎀Tab⎀ key to move to the **Subject** box, and type Today's schedule.

5   Press ⎀Tab⎀ again, and type Here are the people who will be working today. Then press ⎀Enter⎀ twice.

Important After your message has been open for a period of time, Outlook saves a *draft* of it in the Drafts folder so that any work you have done is saved if you are somehow disconnected from Outlook before you send the message. If you close a message without sending it, Outlook asks you if you want to save the message in the Drafts folder. To find these messages later, click the Drafts folder under your name in the All Mail Folders list. If the All Mail Folders list is not visible, click the Mail icon on the Navigation Pane to display it.

6　On the **Table** menu, point to **Insert**, and then click **Table**.

Word's Insert Table dialog box appears.

7　Change the number of columns to **4**, and click **OK**.

A table appears in your message.

8　Fill in the cells of the table as shown here, pressing ⟦Tab⟧ to move from cell to cell.

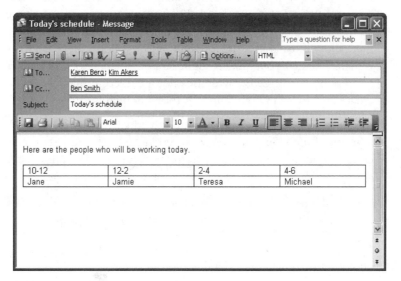

9　Click the **Send** button.

The Message form closes, and the message is sent on its way.

Recalling Messages

If you are connected to a network that uses Microsoft Exchange Server, you can recall messages you've sent. For example, if you discover an error in a message you've sent, you can recall the message so that you can correct the error and resend the message.

To recall a message:

1　In the *Sent Items* folder, open the message you want to recall.

2　On the **Actions** menu, click **Recall This Message**.

3　Select whether you want to delete unread copies of the message or delete unread copies and replace them with a new message, and then click **OK**.

You can recall or replace a message only if its recipient is logged on, using Microsoft Outlook, and has not yet read the message or moved it from the Inbox.

Using Address Books

You can store e-mail addresses along with other contact information in the Outlook address book so you don't have to type them each time you send a message. Instead, simply click the To button in the Message form, and then select recipients by name.

If you are using Outlook with Exchange Server, an Exchange address book called the *Global Address List* might already be available to you. This resource contains the e-mail addresses of all the people on your network. If a Global Address List is available, Outlook will use this as your default address book. Because the Global Address List is maintained by your system administrator, you cannot add to it; you must use another address book to create any entries not included in that list. By default, entries you create are stored in your *Contacts* folder, which is a type of address book.

Address book entries can be for an individual contact or for a *distribution list*— a group of individual addresses stored as a single entity. For example, to facilitate communication with a team, you might create a distribution list including the addresses for all the people working on a particular project.

Tip   With or without an address book, you can address messages by typing the full address into the To, Cc, or Bcc boxes in the Message form.

In this exercise, you will create address book entries, create a distribution list, and address a message from the address book.

1   On the **Tools** menu, click **Address Book**.

The Address Book window appears. If you are working on a network, the "Show Names from the" setting is *Global Address List*. Otherwise, it is *Contacts*.

2   Click the down arrow to the right of the **Show Names from the** box, and click **Contacts** (not **All Contacts**) in the drop-down list.

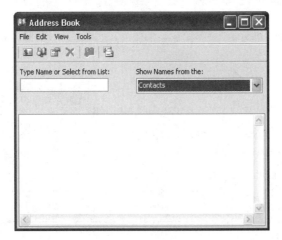

New Entry

3   On the toolbar, click the **New Entry** button.

The New Entry dialog box appears.

4   In the **Select the entry type** box, click **New Contact**, and then click **OK**.

A new Contact form appears.

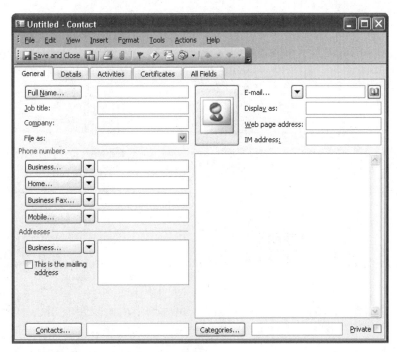

5   In the **Full Name** box, type David Ortiz.

6   In the **E-mail** box, type David@gardenco.msn.com.

7   Click the **Save and Close** button.

The Contact form closes, and the contact appears in the Address Book window.

8   Now you'll add another entry. Click the **New Entry** button, click **New Contact**, and then click **OK**.

The Contact form appears.

9   In the **Full Name** box, type Kim Akers.

10   In the **E-mail** box, type Kim@gardenco.msn.com.

11   Press the ⟨Tab⟩ key, and in the **Display as** box, delete the e-mail address and paren-theses so that the box contains only the name *Kim Akers*.

12   Click the **Save and Close** button.

The Contact form closes, and the contact appears in the Address Book window.

13   Now you'll create a distribution list. Click the **New Entry** button, click **New Distribution List**, and then click **OK**.

The Distribution List form appears.

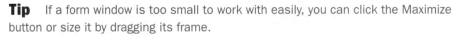
Maximize

Tip   If a form window is too small to work with easily, you can click the Maximize button or size it by dragging its frame.

14   In the **Name** box, type **Marketing**, and then click the **Select Members** button.

The Select Members dialog box appears.

15   If necessary, click the down arrow to the right of the **Show Names from the** box, and click **Contacts** in the drop-down list.

16   With David Ortiz selected in the **Name** list, click the **Members** button.

David Ortiz is added to the distribution list.

17   In the **Name** list, click **Kim Akers**, and click the **Members** button.

Kim Akers is added to the distribution list.

Tip   To add multiple names to the distribution list simultaneously, click a name in the Name list, hold down the Ctrl key, click any additional names you want to add, and then click the Members button.

18   Click **OK** to close the **Select Members** dialog box.

You return to the Distribution List form.

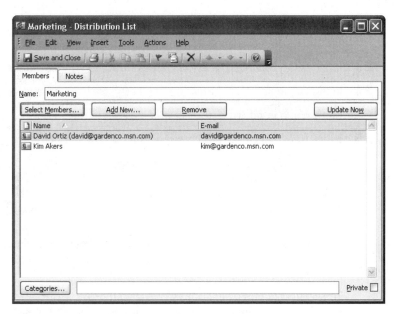

19 Click the **Save and Close** button.

The Distribution List form closes, and the Address Book window appears with the contacts and distribution list shown.

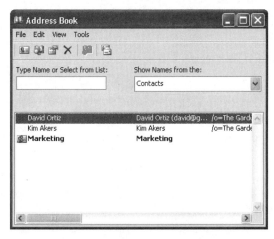

Close

20 Click the **Close** button.

The Address Book window closes.

21 On the toolbar, click the **New Mail Message** button.

New Mail
Message

A new, blank Message form opens.

22 Click the **To** button in the message header.

The Select Names dialog box appears.

23 If necessary, change the **Show Names from the** setting to **Contacts**.

24 In the **Name** list, click **Kim Akers**, and then click the **To** button.

Kim's name is added to the list of recipients in the To box.

25 In the **Name** list, click **Marketing**, and then click the **Cc** button.

The distribution list's name is added to the list of recipients in the Cc box.

Tip   You can type distribution list names in the To and Cc boxes just like any other e-mail address. Outlook will then match what you type with the name in your address book and will display the name as bold and underlined, which indicates that the name represents a distribution list rather than an individual address.

26 Click **OK**.

The Select Names dialog box closes, and the recipient names are added to the To and Cc boxes on the Message form.

27 Close the message without sending it. When prompted to save it, click **No**.

Attaching Files to Messages

A convenient way to distribute files such as Word documents or Excel spreadsheets to other people or groups of people is to attach them to an e-mail message. Outlook makes it easy to attach files to your messages.

Important   You can attach any type of file to an e-mail message, but when sending attachments, be sure that your recipients have the software required to open your file. For example, if you are attaching a Word document, your recipients must have Word installed on their computers to open your attachment.

In this exercise, you will attach a Word document to an e-mail message.

USE the *Attachment* document in the practice file folder for this topic. This practice file is located in the *My Documents\Microsoft Press\Office 2003 SBS\Working\Attach* folder and can also be accessed by clicking *Start/All Programs/Microsoft Press/Microsoft Office System 2003 Step by Step*.

New Mail
Message

1 On the toolbar, click the **New Mail Message** button.

A new, blank Message form appears.

2　In the **To** box, type your own e-mail address.

3　Click in the **Subject** box, and type First Draft.

4　Press the Tab key, and then type Here is a document for your review.

5　Press Enter to move to the next line.

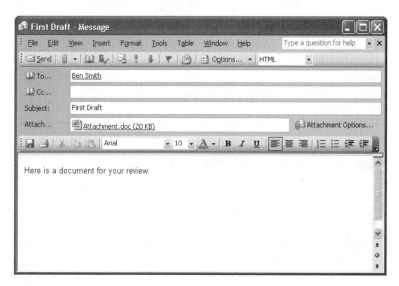

Insert File

6　On the Message form's toolbar, click the **Insert File** button (not the down arrow to the right of the button).

The Insert File dialog box appears.

Tip　You can embed a hyperlink to a Web site in an e-mail message simply by including the site's *uniform resource locator (URL)*. To embed a hyperlink, simply type the URL (for example, *www.microsoft.com*) followed by a space. Outlook formats the URL to appear as a link. Your recipients can simply click the link in the message to open the Web page.

7　Browse to the practice file folder, click the **Attachment** document, and then click the **Insert** button.

The document appears in the Attach box in the message header.

8　Close the message without sending it. If prompted to save it, click **No**.

Sending Attachments for Shared Review

When you send an e-mail attachment with the default options, it is sent as an independent file that each recipient can edit separately. If your team is running Microsoft Windows SharePoint Services, you have the option of sending Microsoft Office System documents as *shared attachments* (also known as *live attachments*). Shared attachments are saved on the SharePoint Document Workspace Web site, which is a team Web site where your group can collaborate to work on files and discuss a project. When working on shared files in a Document Workspace, multiple people can work on a single version of a file rather than sending the document back and forth for editing.

To send a shared attachment:

1   Create and address a message and attach an Office document to it.

2   In the message header, click the **Attachment Options** button.

The Attachment Options task pane opens.

3   In the **Attachments Options** task pane, select the **Shared attachments** option.

4   In the **Create Document Workspace at** box, type the URL for the Document Work-space server. You must have appropriate permissions to access this server.

If a Document Workspace site does not already exist at the specified URL, it will be created for you.

5   Send the message.

Sending and Receiving Messages

Depending on your e-mail account and network configuration, messages you send could go out instantaneously or be kept in your Outbox until you choose to send them. If you are connected to the Internet, your messages will usually go out instantaneously. If you are not connected to the Internet (for example, if you use a dial-up connection), your messages will typically be kept in your Outbox until you connect.

How you receive messages also depends on your type of e-mail account and your Outlook configuration. Outlook might check for new messages periodically and down-load them automatically. Or, you might need to manually check for new messages.

Copies of messages you send are kept in the Sent Items folder by default. To see these messages, click the Sent Items folders in your mailbox in the Mail pane or Folder List.

Tip   If you do not want to keep copies of your sent messages, on the Tools menu, click Options, click the E-mail Options button, clear the "Save copies of messages in Sent Items folder" check box, and click OK.

In this exercise, you will send a message, check for new messages, and delete a message.

BE SURE TO start this exercise in your own Inbox.

New Mail
Message

1   On the toolbar, click the **New Mail Message** button.

A new Message form appears.

2   In the **To** box, type your own e-mail address.

3   Click in the **Subject** box, and type **Sending and Receiving Test**.

4   Press the [Tab] key, and in the message body, type **This is a test**. Then click the **Send** button.

The message closes.

Mail

5   If the **Mail** pane is not open, click the **Mail** icon on the Navigation Pane.

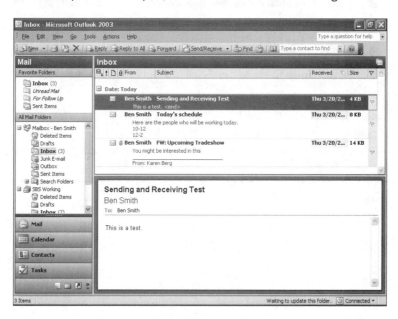

6   In the **All Mail Folders** list, click the **Outbox** folder under your own mailbox.

The contents of the Outbox are displayed. If the message you sent appears in the Outbox, you must send the message manually. If the Outbox is empty, your message was sent automatically.

7   To send any messages in your Outbox and check for new messages on your e-mail server, click the **Send/Receive** button on the toolbar.

Outlook connects to your e-mail server to send and receive messages. Depending on your setup, it might access your modem and connection line. When your message is sent, it disappears from the Outbox. When new messages are received, they appear in your Inbox.

8   In the Favorite Folders list, click **Inbox** to see your new message(s).

The contents of the Inbox are displayed.

Multiple E-Mail Accounts

With Outlook, you can get all your e-mail in one place by configuring more than one account in your profile. To add an e-mail account to your profile:

1   On the **Tools** menu, click **E-mail Accounts** to start the E-mail Accounts Wizard.

2   Select the **Add a new e-mail account** option, and then click **Next**.

3   Select the appropriate e-mail server type option, and then click **Next**.

4   Enter the required server and account settings, and then click **Next**.

5   Click **Finish** to close the E-mail Accounts Wizard.

If you have more than one e-mail account in your profile, you can send your mail from any of your accounts. On the E-mail toolbar in the Message form, click the down arrow to the right of the Accounts button, and then click the account you want in the drop-down list. The Accounts button is only visible when multiple accounts are configured.

Printing Messages

There might be occasions when you need a hard copy, or printout, of an e-mail message. For example, you might need to print the directions to an afternoon appointment or distribute copies of a message at a meeting. With Outlook, you can print your e-mail messages in much the same way you would any other document.

Depending on the format (*HTML*, *Rich Text*, or *Plain Text*) of the message you want to print, you can set a number of page setup options, including paper size, margins, and orientation. You can also use Print Preview to see how a message will appear when printed. (Print Preview is not available for messages in HTML format.)

See Also   For more information about Outlook e-mail message formats, see "Formatting Messages" in Chapter 18, "Managing E-Mail Messages."

In this exercise, you will change the page setup for a message and then print it.

USE the *SBSWorking* data file in the practice file folder for this topic. This practice file is located in the *My Documents\Microsoft Press\Office 2003 SBS\Working* folder and can also be accessed by clicking *Start/All Programs/Microsoft Press/Microsoft Office System 2003 Step by Step*.
BE SURE TO start Outlook, open the *SBSWorking* data file, and install a printer before beginning this exercise.
OPEN the *Upcoming Tradeshow* message in the *SBS Working* Inbox.

1   On the message window's **File** menu, point to **Page Setup**, and click **Memo Style**.

The Page Setup dialog box appears.

2 In the **Left** box, type 1.0 to set the left margin to 1 inch, and click **OK**.

The Page Setup dialog box closes, and your new settings are now in effect for this message.

3 On the **File** menu, click **Print**.

The message is printed with the default print options.

CLOSE the *Upcoming Tradeshow* message.

Troubleshooting   If the Save As dialog appears, you do not have a printer installed. If you are working on a network, your administrator can provide the information you need to install a printer. If you are working on a stand-alone computer, click the Start button, and then click "Printers and Faxes." Then under "Printer tasks" click "Add a printer," and follow the wizard's instructions.

Tip   You can change print options in the Print dialog box. To display the Print dialog box, on the File menu, click Print.

Creating and Sending Instant Messages

You can communicate with your contacts in real time with *instant messages*. Instant messaging is a private online chat method. After you establish a connection with someone who is online and using instant messaging, messages you send to that person appear on his or her screen instantly. Likewise, you see responses from that person instantly on your screen. Instant messaging is especially useful for brief exchanges and can be much more immediate than e-mail. By default, Outlook supports instant messaging using Microsoft MSN Messenger Service or Microsoft Exchange Instant Messaging Service. When Outlook starts, you are automatically logged on to the service you installed.

Before you can use instant messaging, you must obtain the instant messaging addresses of the people you want to communicate with, and add those addresses to the Outlook Contact forms of those people. Then they have to tell their instant messaging programs to accept messages from your address.

After this setup work is done, when you log on to your instant messaging service, you can see whether a contact is online. A contact's online status is displayed in the InfoBar on the Contact form and on any e-mail address associated with the contact. You can choose how your status appears to others. For example, if you need to step away from your desk, you can set your status to *Be Right Back* so that any contacts who are online can see that you are temporarily unavailable.

Important For this exercise, you will need the assistance of a co-worker or friend who is using MSN Messenger or Exchange Instant Messaging Service. You must have already added that person to your MSN Messenger contacts, and that person must have accepted your request to add him or her. For help with any of these tasks, refer to the MSN Messenger online Help.

In this exercise, you will create and send instant messages.

BE SURE TO have the person to whom you want to send an instant message log on to their IM account before beginning this exercise.

1   On the **Tools** menu, click **Options**.

2   In the **Options** dialog box, click the **Other** tab.

3   Under **Person Names**, select **Enable the Person Names Smart Tag** check box, and then select the **Display Messenger Status in the From field** check box.

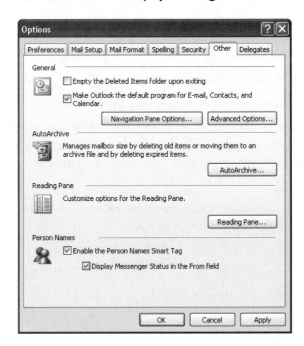

4 Click **OK**.

> **Tip** When smart tags appear next to your contacts' names in messages, the smart tags indicate their Online status.

Contacts icon

5 In the Navigation Pane, click the **Contacts** icon.

The contents of the Contacts folder are displayed.

New Contact

6 If you already have a contact entry for the person who is assisting you with this exercise, double-click that entry. If you do not have a contact entry for that person, click the **New Contact** button.

The Contact form opens.

7 If you are creating a new contact, in the **Full Name** box, type the person's name.

8 Click in the **IM address** box, and type the e-mail address the person uses for instant messaging.

Note that this address might not be the same address used for e-mail correspondence. You'll need to get this information from the person you want to contact using instant messaging.

9 Click the **Save and Close** button.

The contact information is saved.

Person Names
Smart Tag

10 In a message window or the Reading Pane, click the contact's **Person Names Smart Tag** next to their name on the **From**, **To** or **CC** line, and then on the shortcut menu click **Send Instant Message**.

The Instant Message window appears.

11 In the message box, type Hello, and click the **Send** button.

The message is sent. It appears in an Instant Message window on your contact's screen. The status bar indicates when your contact is typing a message. Wait for a reply, and when you receive it, try sending a few more messages.

CLOSE the instant messaging window.
BE SURE TO return Outlook to its default state. Turn AutoPreview off and turn the Reading Pane on, at the right side of the window. Then close the *SBS Working* data file.

Key Points

- Messages to you appear in your Inbox. You can see the first few lines of each message in AutoPreview, open a message in its own window, or preview messages in the Reading Pane.

- You can reply to the sender or to the sender and all other recipients using the Reply and Reply to All buttons. A copy of each e-mail message you send is stored in the Sent Mail folder.

- You can add attachments to your messages using the Insert File button.

- You can store e-mail addresses in an address book so that when you send a message, you can click the To button in the Message form and then select recipients by name.

- You can send instant messages to your contacts who have also added you to their contact list by using the Person Names Smart Tag.

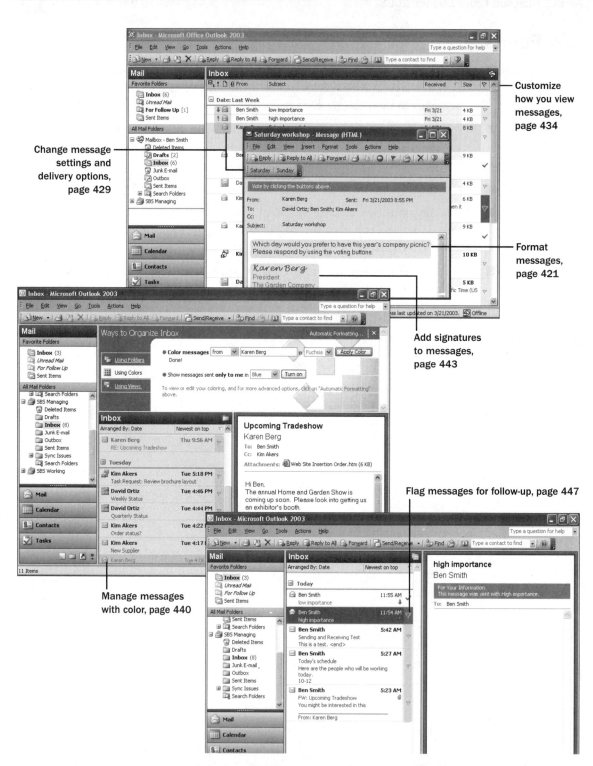

Customize
how you view
messages,
page 434

Change message
settings and
delivery options,
page 429

Format
messages,
page 421

Add signatures
to messages,
page 443

Flag messages for follow-up, page 447

Manage messages
with color, page 440

Chapter 18 at a Glance

18 Managing E-Mail Messages

In this chapter you will learn to:

✔ Format messages.

✔ Change message settings and delivery options.

✔ Customize how you view messages.

✔ Manage messages with color.

✔ Add signatures to messages.

✔ Flag messages for follow-up.

In today's business world, e-mail is an essential method of communication. But when you use your e-mail regularly and receive a large volume of messages, it can be difficult to manage them all. Microsoft Office Outlook 2003 has many features to help you read, organize, find, and store e-mail messages quickly.

You can choose to view your messages in a way that makes it easier for you to scan, read, and respond to them. You can organize your messages in folders, search for messages by category and other criteria, and archive your messages in Outlook or on your hard disk.

See Also Do you need only a quick refresher on the topics in this chapter? See the Quick Reference entries on pages xxxiii.

 Important Before you can use the practice files in this chapter, you need to install them from the book's companion CD to their default location. See "Using the Book's CD-ROM" on page xxi for more information.

Formatting Messages

E-mail messages are sent in one of three formats: HTML, Plain Text, or Outlook Rich Text Format (RTF). Outlook supports all three formats. Other e-mail programs might be able to work with only some of them.

■ *HTML* is the default Outlook message format. HTML supports text formatting, numbering, bullets, pictures and backgrounds in the message body, styles, and stationery. Most popular e-mail programs support HTML messages.

■   *Outlook Rich Text Format* supports a host of formatting options including text formatting, bullets, numbering, background colors, borders, and shading.

■   *Plain Text* is supported by all e-mail programs, but as the name implies, messages in Plain Text do not include any formatting.

For the most part, the HTML message format will meet your needs. When you send an HTML message to someone whose e-mail program doesn't support HTML format, the message is displayed as Plain Text in the recipient's e-mail program. Outlook automatically converts RTF messages you send over the Internet into HTML format. When you reply to or forward a message, Outlook uses the format of the original message by default. However, you can choose the format for any message you send.

When sending messages in HTML format, you can enhance the appearance of your messages using *stationery* and *themes*. When you use stationery, you can specify the background, fonts, bullets, images, and other elements you want to use in outgoing e-mail messages. You can choose from a collection of predefined stationery that comes with Outlook, customize one of the patterns, create new stationery, or download new patterns from the Web. If you use Microsoft Office Word as your e-mail editor, you can choose from additional patterns available as Word themes.

Important   The exercises in this book assume that you are using Word as your default e-mail editor. If Word is not your default e-mail editor and you would like it to be, on the Tools menu, click Options. Click the Mail Format tab, and select the "Use Microsoft Word to edit e-mail messages" check box. To turn off Word as your default e-mail editor, clear the check box.

In this exercise, you will format messages in HTML, Rich Text, and Plain Text formats, and then you will compose messages using stationery and themes.

BE SURE TO start Outlook before beginning this exercise.
OPEN your Inbox folder.

New Mail
Message

1   On the toolbar, click the **New Mail Message** button.

A blank Message form appears.

2   Click in the body of the message, and type Wow! Have you seen the new roses?

By default, the text is formatted in 10-point Arial (the Normal style).

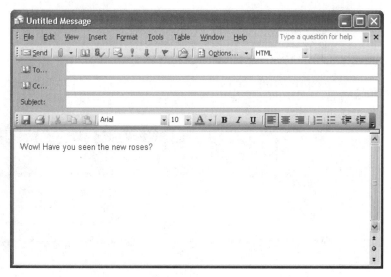

Font Size

3 Select the word *Wow!* (including the exclamation point), click the down arrow to the right of the **Font Size** box, and then click **16**.

Font Color

4 Click the down arrow to the right of the **Font Color** button, and then click the red square.

Message Format

5 Click the down arrow to the right of the **Message format** box, and then click **Plain Text**.

A message box appears, indicating that Plain Text format does not support some of the formatting in the message.

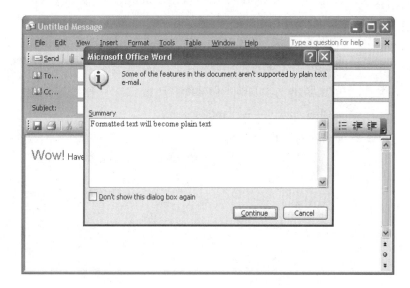

Tip   If you want to bypass this warning in the future, select the "Don't show this dialog box again" check box before continuing.

6   Click the **Continue** button.

The text is formatted in 10-point Courier New (the Plain Text style), and the formatting buttons on the E-mail toolbar become unavailable.

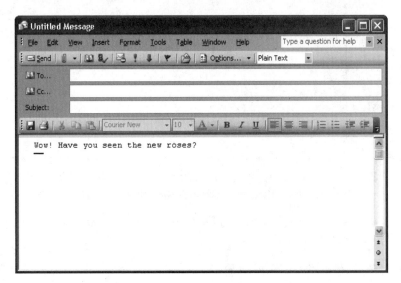

7   Click the down arrow to the right of the **Message format** box, and then click **Rich Text**.

The text formatting does not change, but the formatting buttons become available.

Close

8   Click the Message form's **Close** button, and when asked if you want to keep a draft of the message, click **No**.

The Message form closes.

9   On the **Tools** menu, click **Options**.

The Options dialog box appears.

10   Click the **Mail Format** tab.

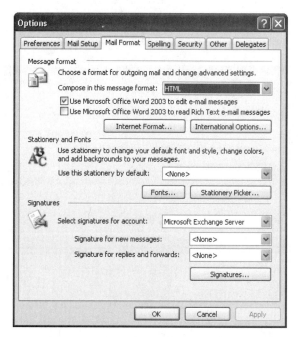

11　In the **Message format** area, click the down arrow to the right of the **Compose in this message format** box, click **Plain Text**, and then click **OK**.

The Options dialog box closes. The default message format for new messages is now set to Plain Text.

12　On the toolbar, click the **New Mail Message** button.

The Message form appears, with Plain Text format selected in the Message Format box.

13　Close the Message form.

14　On the **Tools** menu, click **Options**, and then click the **Mail Format** tab.

15　In the **Message format** area, click the down arrow to the right of the **Compose in this message format** box, and then click **HTML**.

16　In the **Stationery and Fonts** area, click the down arrow to the right of the **Use this stationery by default** box, click **Ivy**, and then click **OK**.

The Options dialog box closes. New messages will now be formatted in HTML format using the Ivy stationery.

17 On the toolbar, click the **New Mail Message** button.

The Message form appears, using the Ivy stationery.

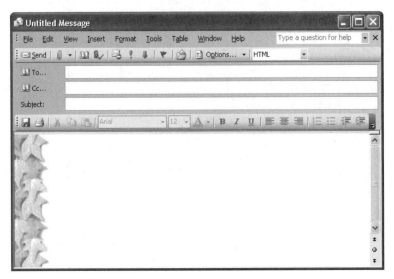

18 Click in the body of the message, and type Bring your family and come to.

By default, the text is formatted in green, 12-point Arial (the Normal style for this stationery).

Tip You can customize message stationery. On the Mail Format tab of the Options dialog box, click the Stationery Picker button. To edit existing stationery, click the stationery design you want, click the Edit button, apply the font, background, and color formatting you want, and then click OK. To create new stationery, click the New button in the Stationery Picker dialog box, and follow the directions in the wizard that appears.

19 On the **Format** menu, click **Theme**.

The Theme dialog box appears, with an extensive list of available formats.

20 In the **Choose a Theme** list, click **Compass**.

A preview of the Compass theme appears in the Theme dialog box.

21 Scroll down the **Choose a Theme** list, click **Papyrus**, and then click **OK**.

The Theme dialog box closes, and the Papyrus theme is applied to the message, replacing the Ivy stationery.

22 In the body of the message, press the ⌈Enter⌋ key, type **The Garden Company Summer Picnic**, press the ⌈Enter⌋ key, type **June 24th from 11:00 A.M. to 5:00 P.M.**, and then press the ⌈Enter⌋ key again.

Center

23 Click in the first line of text, and on the E-mail toolbar, click the **Center** button.

The line is now centered in the body of the message.

24 Click in the second line of text, and on the **Format** menu, click **Styles and Formatting**.

The Styles and Formatting pane appears at the right side of the message window.

Maximize

25 Click the **Maximize** button so you can see all the choices.

26 In the **Pick formatting to apply** area of the **Styles and Formatting** pane, click **Heading 1**.

The event title is now formatted with the Heading 1 style.

27   Click the third line of text, and in the **Pick formatting to apply** area of the **Styles and Formatting** pane, click **Heading 3**.

The time and date are now formatted with the Heading 3 style.

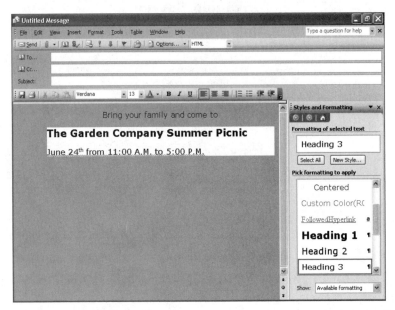

28   On the Message form, click the **Close** button, and when asked if you want to keep a draft of the message, click **No**.

The Message form closes, discarding the draft.

29   On the **Tools** menu, click **Options**, and then click the **Mail Format** tab.

30   In the **Stationery and Fonts** area, click the down arrow to the right of the **Use this stationery by default** box, click **<None>** at the top of the drop-down list, and then click **OK**.

The Options dialog box closes. New messages will now be formatted in HTML with no stationery applied.

BE SURE TO open a new message window, click the Restore Down button, and then close the window to restore the default size.

Changing Message Settings and Delivery Options

To help you manage your e-mail and convey the meaning of your messages more effectively, you can set the importance, sensitivity, and a number of delivery options for e-mail messages.

You can set a message to High, Normal, or Low *importance*. Messages sent with High importance are indicated by a red exclamation point. Messages sent with Normal importance have no special indicator. Messages sent with Low importance are indicated by a blue downward-pointing arrow. These indicators show up in the Importance column in the Inbox.

You can also set message *sensitivity* to Normal, Personal, Private, or Confidential. Messages marked as Private cannot be modified after they are sent.

To help you manage messages you receive, you can choose to have people's replies to your messages sent to another e-mail address. For example, you might have replies sent to a new e-mail address as you transition from one to another. To help you manage messages you send, you can choose whether to save copies of your sent messages and in which folder they should be saved. You can also specify when a message will be delivered and make a message unavailable after a certain date.

If your *e-mail server* is a Microsoft Exchange Server, you can use voting buttons to let e-mail recipients quickly respond to a question.

In this exercise, you will use voting buttons to respond to a message, set the importance of a message, and modify the delivery options for a message.

BE SURE TO start Outlook and display the Reading Pane before beginning this exercise.
USE the *SBSManaging* data file in the practice file folder for this topic. This practice file is located in the *My Documents\Microsoft Press\Office 2003 SBS\Managing* folder and can also be accessed by clicking *Start/All Programs/Microsoft Press/Microsoft Office System 2003 Step by Step*.
OPEN the *SBSManaging* data file from within Outlook.

1   In the practice file Inbox, click the **Saturday workshop** message from Karen Berg.

   The message appears in the Reading Pane. At the top of the message is an Infobar with instructions for voting.

2   Click the **Infobar**, and then click **Vote: Saturday**.

   Tip   If you open the message, you will see buttons corresponding to each of the voting options. In an open message, click the buttons rather than the Infobar to cast your vote.

A dialog box appears, giving you the options to send the response immediately or edit it first.

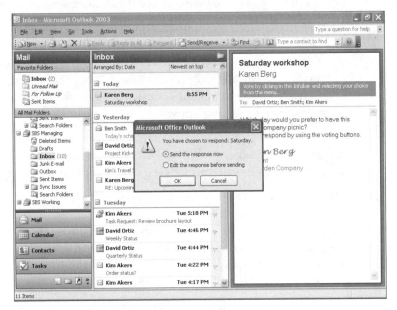

3   Leave the **Send the response now** option selected, and click **OK**.

The Infobar now shows that you have responded.

New Mail
Message

4   Click the **New Mail Message** button.

A new, blank e-mail message opens in its own window. If Word is your e-mail editor, Word's e-mail toolbar is displayed at the top of the window.

Options...

5   On the Message form's toolbar, click the **Options** button.

The Message Options dialog box appears.

6   In the **Message settings** area, click the down arrow to the right of the **Importance** box, and click **High** in the drop-down list.

7   In the **Delivery options** area, select the **Have replies sent to** check box, delete the text that appears in the adjacent box, and type te$t@gardenco.msn.com.

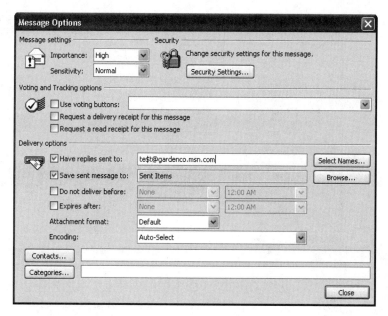

8   Click **Close**.

The Message Options dialog box closes, and you return to the Message form. The "Importance: High" button is selected.

9   In the **To** box, type your own e-mail address.

10   Click in the **Subject** box, type high importance, and then click the **Send** button.

The Message form closes, and the message is sent.

11   Click the **New Mail Message** button, and then click the **Options** button.

12   In the **Delivery options** area, click the **Browse** button.

The Select Folder dialog box appears.

13   In the **Folders** list, locate your own mailbox, click the *Drafts* folder underneath it, and then click **OK**.

When you send this message, a copy will be saved in your Drafts folder.

Tip   Saving frequently sent messages to your Drafts folder makes it easy for you to create and send new versions without entering the recipients and text every time.

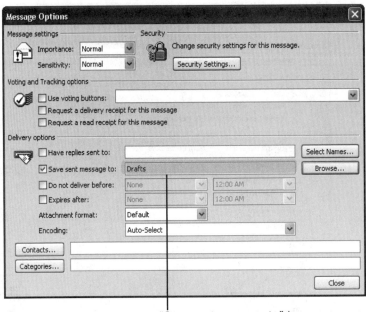

"Save sent message to" box

14 Click **Close**.

The Message Options dialog box closes, and you return to the Message form.

15 In the Message form, click the **Importance: Low** button.

Importance:
Low

16 In the **To** box, type your own e-mail address.

17 Click in the **Subject** box, type low importance, and click the **Send** button.

The Message form closes, and the message is sent.

18 Open your own Inbox.

Send/Receive

19 If the messages have not yet arrived in your Inbox, click the **Send/Receive** button.

When the messages arrive, the *high importance* message is marked with a red exclamation point and the *low importance* message is marked with a downward-pointing blue arrow. A corresponding message is displayed in the message header that is visible in the Reading Pane.

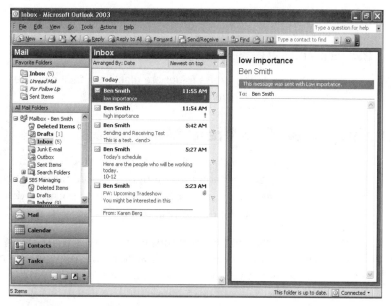

20 Click the *high importance* message, and then click the **Reply** button.

The Reply form appears. The To box contains the e-mail address you entered earlier, te$t@gardenco.msn.com.

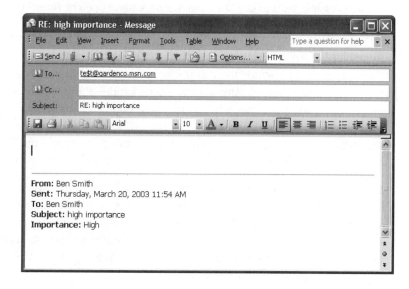

Close

21 Close the Reply form without saving the message, and then close the original message.

22 In the **Folder List**, click your *Drafts* folder.

The contents of the Drafts folder are displayed, including the copy of the message you sent with Low importance.

Customizing How You View Messages

As your Inbox gathers messages, it can be challenging to prioritize them. You can use Outlook to customize how you view, group, and sort messages. You can then quickly determine which are the most important, decide which can be deleted, and locate any messages that need an immediate response.

New in Office 2003
Arrangements

In addition to the Reading Pane and AutoPreview view options, you can choose to view only messages received in the last seven days, only unread messages, only messages sent to a certain person or distribution list, or a timeline of all your received messages. Outlook 2003 offers 13 pre-defined arrangements so you can see your messages the way you want. To experiment with the view options, on the View menu, point to Arrange By, point to Current View, and then click the view option you want.

See Also   For more information about viewing messages in the Reading Pane or by using the AutoPreview feature, see "Reading Messages and Opening Attachments" in Chapter 17, "Working with Outlook."

Regardless of the *view* you choose, you can group and sort your messages by any column simply by clicking the column heading. By default, messages in your Inbox are grouped by the received date in descending order—the most recent messages appear at the top of the list. Messages you received this week are grouped by day. Earlier messages are grouped by weeks or longer periods. But you can sort columns in either ascending or descending order. You can also group your messages by the contents of any column—by the sender of the message, for instance, or by the subject.

New in Office 2003
Arrange by Conversation

A new feature in Outlook 2003 is the ability to arrange messages by conversation. This is a grouped view similar to sorting messages by subject, but the conversations are displayed in order by date. For conversations with multiple messages, the unread or flagged messages are displayed by default. Additional messages are indicated by a small down arrow to the left of the conversation title. Click the down arrow to display all the messages in the conversation.

In this exercise, you will sort and group messages, select a defined message view, and customize your message view.

BE SURE TO start Outlook, open the *SBSManaging* data file, and turn the Reading Pane off before beginning this exercise.

USE the *SBSManaging* data file in the practice file folder for this topic. This practice file is located in the *My Documents\Microsoft Press\Office 2003 SBS\Managing* folder and can also be accessed by clicking *Start/All Programs/Microsoft Press/Microsoft Office System 2003 Step by Step.*

OPEN the practice file Inbox folder.

1   In the practice file *Inbox* folder, note the downward-pointing arrow in the **Received** column heading.

This indicates that the messages are currently sorted in descending order by receipt date.

2   Click the **From** column heading.

Outlook groups the messages in alphabetical order by sender. Within each group, the messages are still sorted by date received.

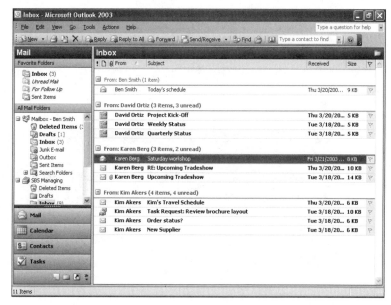

3   Click the **From** column heading again.

Outlook groups the messages in reverse alphabetical order.

4   Click the **Size** column heading.

Outlook groups the messages by size.

5   On the **View** menu, point to **Arrange By**, and then click **Subject**.

Outlook organizes the listed messages into message threads.

Note that the total number of items and the number of unread items in each group is indicated in parentheses following the conversation subject.

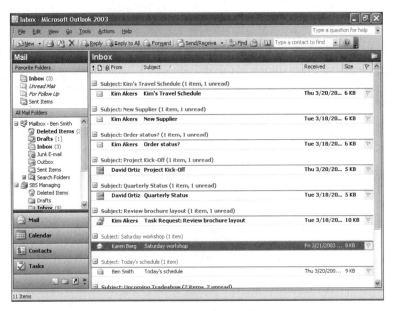

6   Scroll down, and click the minus sign to the left of the *Upcoming Tradeshow*
         subject line.

         The two messages with this subject are hidden, and the minus sign changes
         to a plus sign.

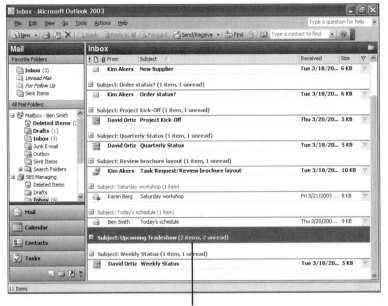

Messages indicator

7 On the **View** menu, point to **Arrange By**, and then click **Show In Groups** to turn this feature off.

Messages are no longer grouped; they are simply listed by subject.

Tip Unread items are distinguished from read items by their bold type and closed-envelope icons. For the purposes of this exercise, if you do not have any unread messages in the practice file Inbox, right-click a message, and click Mark as Unread on the shortcut menu. The message header in the Inbox will then change to bold, and its message icon will change from an open to a closed envelope.

8 On the **View** menu, point to **Arrange By**, point to **Current View**, and then click **Unread Messages in This Folder**.

Outlook filters the messages to show only unread messages.

Folder banner

The Folder banner indicates that a filter has been applied. (If you have no unread messages in your Inbox, it will appear to be empty.)

9 On the **View** menu, point to **Arrange By**, point to **Current View**, and then click **Messages**.

The messages are no longer filtered.

Tip You can also use the Ways to Organize pane to select a view for your messages. On the Tools menu, click Organize to open the pane. Then click Using Views, and click a view in the list.

10 On the **View** menu, point to **Arrange By**, point to **Current View**, and click **Customize Current View**.

The Customize View: Messages dialog box appears.

11 Click the **Fields** button.

The Show Fields dialog box appears.

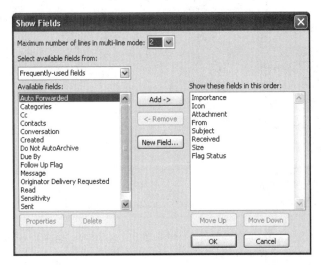

12 In the **Available fields** list, click **Sensitivity**, and then click the **Add** button.

The Sensitivity field is added to the list of columns to be shown in this view.

13   In the **Show these fields in this order** list, drag **Sensitivity** to appear just after **Importance**, and then click **OK**.

The Show Fields dialog box closes, and you return to the Customize View: Messages dialog box.

Tip   To change the order of columns in any view, simply drag the column headings to the locations you prefer. While you are dragging a column heading, red arrows indicate where the column will appear when you release the mouse button.

14   Click the **Other Settings** button.

The Other Settings dialog box appears.

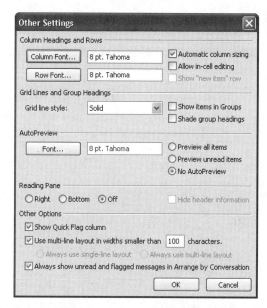

15   Click the down arrow to the right of the **Grid line style** box, click **Small dots**, and then click **OK**.

The Other Settings dialog box closes, and you return to the Customize View: Messages dialog box.

16   In the **Customize View: Messages** dialog box, click **OK**.

The Inbox is displayed with the new view settings.

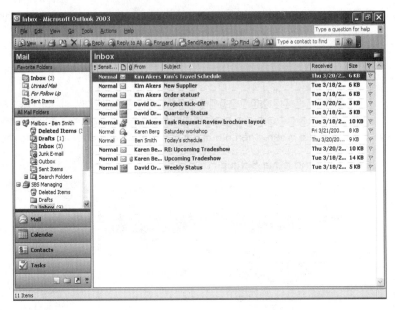

17   Drag the **Sensitivity** column heading downward, and release the mouse button when a large black X appears over the heading.

The Sensitivity column is removed from the view.

18   On the **View** menu, point to **Arrange By**, point to **Current View**, and then click **Define Views**.

The Define Views dialog box appears.

19   Click the **Reset** button, click **OK**, and then click **Close**.

The practice file Inbox display is restored to the default view settings.

Managing Messages with Color

Color-coding messages can help you easily distinguish messages received from certain people. For example, you might show all messages from your boss in red, and all messages from the finance department in green. You can also choose to have messages that were sent directly to you displayed in a different color than messages sent to a distribution list.

In this exercise, you will color-code messages.

BE SURE TO start Outlook and open the *SBSManaging* data file before beginning this exercise.

USE the *SBSManaging* data file in the practice file folder for this topic. This practice file is located in the *My Documents\Microsoft Press\Office 2003 SBS\Managing* folder and can also be accessed by clicking *Start/All Programs/Microsoft Press/Microsoft Office System 2003 Step by Step*.

OPEN the practice file Inbox folder.

1   On the **Tools** menu, click **Organize**.

The Ways to Organize pane appears.

2   In the **Ways to Organize** pane, click **Using Colors**.

The Using Colors tab is displayed with the sender of the currently selected message filled in.

3   Scroll to the bottom of the *Inbox* folder, and click the **Upcoming Tradeshow** message from Karen Berg.

4   In the **Color Messages** area, make sure *from* is selected in the first box, and *Karen Berg* appears in the second box.

5   In the third box, click **Fuchsia** in the drop-down list, and click the **Apply Color** button.

Messages from Karen Berg are now displayed in the selected color.

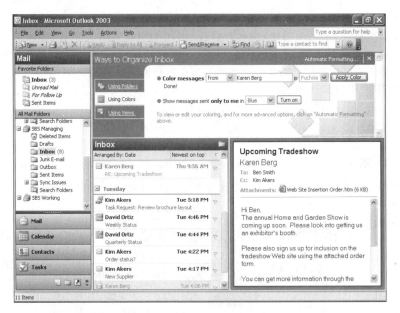

6   In the upper-right corner of the **Ways to Organize** pane, click **Automatic Formatting**.

The Automatic Formatting dialog box appears.

7   In the **Rules for this view** list, clear the **Mail received from Karen Berg** check box.

8   Click the **Delete** button.

The *Mail received from Karen Berg* rule is deleted.

9   In the **Automatic Formatting** dialog box, click **OK**.

The dialog box closes and the Inbox messages return to their normal color.

CLOSE the *Ways to Organize* pane and the *SBSManaging* data file.

Adding Signatures to Messages

By using a *signature*, you can personalize your messages and save time. A signature is a predefined block of text that can be inserted, manually or automatically, at the end of your messages. Signatures can include any text you like, but they typically include your name, title, and company name. Signatures can be formatted in the same ways that message text can be formatted.

New in Office 2003
Unique signature per account

In Outlook 2003, you can create a variety of signatures and assign a different signature to each of your Outlook accounts. If you like, you can create multiple signatures for different uses, such as formal business e-mail, casual business e-mail, and personal e-mail.

In this exercise, you will create a signature, and then instruct Outlook to insert the signature in all the new messages you create.

OPEN the practice file Inbox folder or your own Inbox.

1   On the **Tools** menu, click **Options**.

The Options dialog box appears.

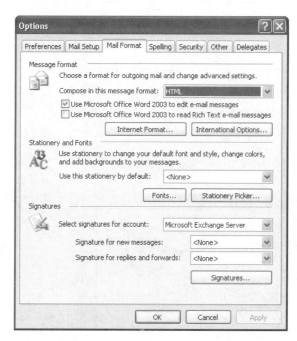

2   Click the **Mail Format** tab, and then click the **Signatures** button.

The Create Signature dialog box appears.

3   Click the **New** button.

The Create New Signature dialog box appears.

4   Type Professional as the name of your signature, and then click the **Next** button.

The Edit Signature dialog box appears.

5   In the **Signature text** box, type Regards and a comma, press the `Enter` key, and then type your name.

6   Select your name, and then click the **Font** button.

The Font dialog box appears.

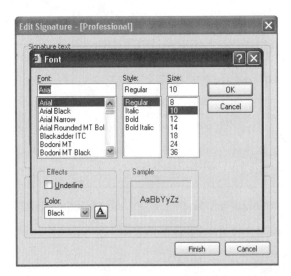

7   Change the font to **Arial Narrow**, the style to **Bold Italic**, and the size to **14**.

      The text shown in the Sample area reflects your changes.

8   Click **OK**.

9   Select both lines of text, and click the **Paragraph** button.

      The Paragraph dialog box appears.

10   Click **Center**, and then click **OK**.

11   Make any other changes you want, and then click **Finish**.

      Your newly created signature is now available in the Create Signature dialog box.

12 Click **OK**.

The Options dialog box appears. Note that the signature you just created is selected in the "Signature for new messages" list, and your default account is selected in the "Select signatures for account" list. Outlook will insert your signature into all new e-mail messages you send from this account.

Tip If you have more than one e-mail account set up in Outlook, you can use a different signature with each account. Follow the steps to create a new signature; then on the Mail Format tab of the Options dialog box, select the alternate account in the "Select signatures for account" list, select the signature you want to use with that account in the "Signature for new messages" list, and click Apply.

13 Click **OK**.

The Options dialog box closes.

New Mail
Message

14 On the toolbar, click the **New Mail Message** button.

A new message, containing your new signature, appears in the Message form.

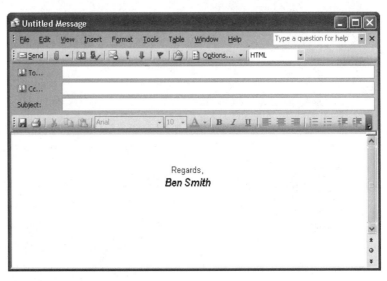

15 Close the message.

Tip To automatically insert your signature into forwarded messages and replies, on the Tools menu, click Options, and then click the Mail Format tab. Select the account in the "Select signatures for account" list, click the signature you want in the "Signature for replies and forwards" list, and click OK.

16 On the **Tools** menu, click **Options**, and then click the **Mail Format** tab.

17 In the **Signature for new messages** list, click **<None>**, and then click **OK**.

New messages will now appear without a signature.

BE SURE TO delete the *Professional* signature file if you don't want to keep it.

Flagging Messages for Follow-Up

You can't answer every message as soon as you read it, but you can mark messages that require response or action by attaching a *follow-up flag*. Flags come in six colors; you can use the different colors to indicate different types of follow-up, and you can set a *reminder* to pop up when the follow-up is due. You can quickly view your flagged messages by using the For Follow-up *search folder*.

Each message in your Inbox has a shaded Flag Status icon that indicates whether a message is flagged or completed. You can flag messages in any folder but the Flag Status icon appears only in active Inbox folders.

New in Office 2003
Quick Flags

FrontPage 2003 features Quick Flags, an easy way to flag a message. Simply click the shaded Flag Status icon to the right of a message, once to flag it for follow up, and again to mark it as completed. To change the current flag color, right-click the flag and click the color you want on the shortcut menu. To change the default flag color, right-click the flag, point to Set Default Flag, and then click the color you want. To remove a flag, right-click the flag and then click Clear Flag. You can also add a reminder to any flagged item.

Important   Because the Flag Status column does not appear in the practice file folders, this exercise is conducted in your own Inbox. The messages shown in your Inbox will vary from those shown here.

In this exercise, you will flag received messages, update flags, view messages by flag status, and flag a new outgoing message to bring it to the recipient's attention.

OPEN your own Inbox.

Flag Status

1 In your Inbox, click the **Flag Status** icon next to any message.

The icon and the flag turn red.

2 Click the **Flag Status** icon again.

The icon turns white and the flag changes to a check mark to indicate that the task is completed.

3 Right-click the **Flag Status** icon of another message (not a task or appointment), and then click **Add Reminder** on the shortcut menu.

The Flag for Follow Up dialog box appears.

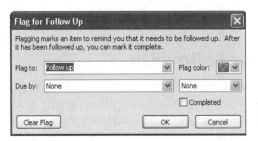

4 In the **Flag to** list, click **For Your Information**, in the **Flag color** list, click **Blue Flag**, and then click **OK**.

The message's Flag Status icon turns blue.

5 Click the message to display it in the Reading Pane.

The label *For Your Information* appears at the top of the message.

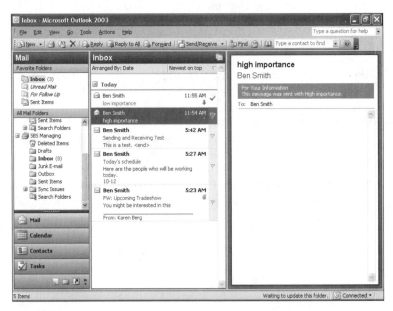

6 Open a different message.

7 On the message window's Standard toolbar click the **Follow Up** button.

Follow Up

The Flag for Follow Up dialog box appears.

8   Select the **Completed** check box, and then click **OK**.

The label at the top of the message shows the completed status.

9   Close the message.

In the Inbox, the Flag Status column now displays a check mark.

10   In the **Favorite Folders** list, click **For Follow Up.**

The message you flagged for follow up is displayed. If you have flagged multiple messages they are grouped by flag color.

New Mail
Message

11   Click the **New Mail Message** button.

A new message window appears.

12   On the message window's Standard toolbar, click the **Follow Up** button.

Tip   If Outlook alerts you that it is unable to open the For Follow Up folder, in the Navigation Pane, click the plus sign next to Search Folders, and then click the For Follow Up Search Folder.

13   The Flag for Follow Up dialog box appears.

14   In the **Flag to** box, type a custom label.

15   In the **Due By** list, click a date, and then click **OK**.

Your label text and deadline appear at the top of the message.

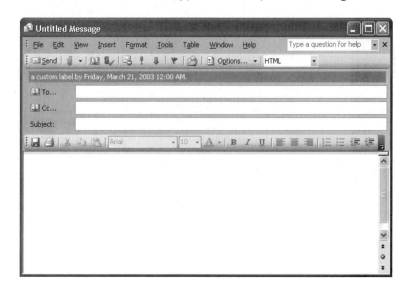

16 Close the message without saving it.

17 In the **Favorite Folders** list, click **Inbox**.

18 Right-click the **Flag Status** icon of each of the messages you flagged in this exercise, and then click **Clear Flag** to remove the flag.

Key Points

■   You can send messages in various formats. HTML messages support the most formatting, including stationary and themes.

■   You can create a signature for Outlook to add to new messages and/or forwarded messages and replies you send.

■   Messages can be grouped and sorted by sender, time, subject, size, or other fields.

■   You can create rules to display messages in particular colors depending on the sender, subject, contents, time, who else they were sent to, or almost any other criteria.

■   You can flag new and received messages for follow up at a later time. All your flagged messages appear in your For Follow Up folder, and Outlook can send you a reminder when the follow-up is due.

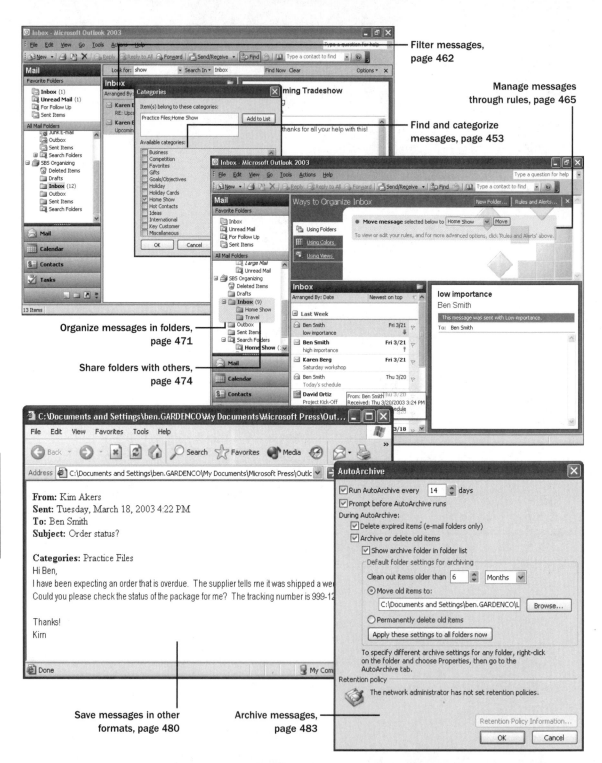

Filter messages, page 462

Manage messages through rules, page 465

Find and categorize messages, page 453

Organize messages in folders, page 471

Share folders with others, page 474

Save messages in other formats, page 480

Archive messages, page 483

Chapter 19 at a Glance

19 Finding and Organizing E-Mail Messages

In this chapter you will learn to:

✔ Find and categorize messages.

✔ Use Search Folders.

✔ Filter messages.

✔ Manage messages through rules.

✔ Organize messages in folders.

✔ Share folders with others.

✔ Save messages in other formats.

✔ Archive messages.

As you learn the fundamentals of sending, receiving, and managing *e-mail* messages, you will see how using e-mail can help you work more efficiently. Because you can customize the format of your messages, select from a number of message and delivery options, filter messages, and set up *personal folders* and *address books*, you can configure Microsoft Office Outlook 2003 to be as convenient and useful as possible. For example, if your company is working on a number of projects at the same time, you might ask each project team to use a particular phrase or keyword in the subject line of messages related to each project. Then when you need to focus on a particular project, you can filter messages to display only those items related to it.

See Also Do you need only a quick refresher on the topics in this chapter? See the Quick Reference entries on page xxxiii.

 Important Before you can use the practice files in this chapter, you need to install them from the book's companion CD to their default location. See "Using the Book's CD-ROM" on page xxi for more information.

Finding and Categorizing Messages

If you are having trouble locating a particular message in your *Inbox* or another message folder, you can search for it using Outlook's Find or Advanced Find features. You can look for messages in a single folder, a group of folders you select, or all your folders. You can instruct Outlook to search through the text of every message or only the Subject field.

To make finding messages easier, you can create *categories* and assign messages to them. With categories, you group messages by a common characteristic. Outlook includes a set of predefined categories, and you can create your own. For example, you might assign all messages about invoices and payments to the Finance category, or you might create a Payroll category for all messages related to timesheets and paychecks.

In this exercise, you will find a message using the Find feature, create a category, assign messages to it, and then find messages using the Advanced Find feature.

USE the *SBSOrganizing* data file in the practice file folder for this topic. This practice file is located in the *My Documents\Microsoft Press\Office 2003 SBS\Organizing* folder and can also be accessed by clicking *Start/All Programs/Microsoft Press/Microsoft Office System 2003 Step by Step*.
BE SURE TO start Outlook before beginning this exercise.
OPEN the *SBSOrganizing* data file from within Outlook, and then open the practice Inbox.

1   On the toolbar, click the **Find** button.

The Find pane appears above the practice Inbox.

2   In the **Look for** box in the **Find** pane, type show, a word that you know is contained within a message in your Inbox. Then click the **Find Now** button.

Outlook searches your messages and displays only those that contain the word you typed.

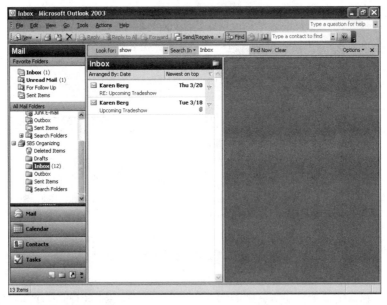

3   Press [Ctrl]+[A] to select both the found messages.

4 Right-click the selected messages, and click **Categories** on the shortcut menu.

The Categories dialog box appears.

Tip The messages in the practice file Inbox are categorized so they can easily be removed from your computer when you are finished with this course.

5 In the **Item(s) belong to these categories** box, after *Practice Files*, type ;Home Show to add a new category, and then click the **Add to List** button.

The category is added to the list and automatically selected for the messages.

6 In the **Categories** dialog box, click **OK**.

7 To redisplay all the messages, click the **Clear** button.

All your messages are displayed.

8 In the Inbox, click the **Today's schedule** message from Ben Smith once to select it.

9 On the **Edit** menu, click **Categories**.

10 In the **Available categories** list, select the **Home Show** check box, and then click **OK**.

The message is assigned to the category.

11 In the **Find** pane, click the **Options** button, and then click **Advanced Find** in the **Options** drop-down list.

The Advanced Find window appears.

12 In the **Advanced Find** window, click the **More Choices** tab, and then click the **Categories** button.

The Categories dialog box appears.

13 In the **Available categories** list, select the **Home Show** check box, and then click **OK**.

The Categories dialog box closes, and you return to the Advanced Find window. Your category appears in the Categories box.

14 Click the **Find Now** button.

Outlook searches your messages and displays the matching items in a list at the bottom of the Advanced Find window.

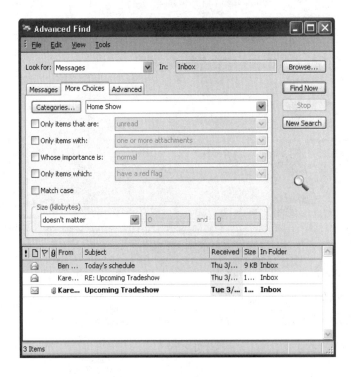

CLOSE the Advanced Find window and the Find pane.

Using Search Folders

Search Folders, like Outlook's Find feature, show all the files that match a set of search criteria, and can show files from different folders together in one place. Unlike Find, when you create a Search Folder, it becomes part of your mailbox and is always kept up to date.

New in Office 2003
Search Folders

The default Outlook 2003 installation includes three Search Folders: The For Follow Up folder displays messages flagged for follow-up, the Large Messages folder displays messages larger than 100 kilobytes (KB), and the Unread Mail folder displays messages that are marked as unread.

Search Folders are *virtual folders*. Each message in your mailbox is stored in only one Outlook folder (such as your Inbox), but it might appear in many Search Folders. Changing or deleting a message in a Search Folder changes or deletes the message in the Outlook folder where it is stored.

In this exercise, you will first experiment with the default Search Folders and then create and use a custom Search Folder.

USE the *SBSOrganizing* data file in the practice file folder for this topic. This practice file is located in the *My Documents\Microsoft Press\Office 2003 SBS\Organizing* folder and can also be accessed by clicking *Start/All Programs/Microsoft Press/Microsoft Office System 2003 Step by Step*.
BE SURE TO start Outlook and open the *SBSOrganizing* data file before beginning this exercise.
OPEN your own Outlook mailbox.

1   In the **All Mail Folders** list, click the plus sign next to *Search Folders* (in your own Outlook mailbox, not the *SBS Organizing* data file), and then click **Large Mail**.

In the content pane, the Large Mail Search Folder displays all your Outlook items that are larger than 100 kilobytes.

Troubleshooting   Depending on your previous use of Outlook, the default Search Folders might be empty.

2   Click the **Unread Mail** Search Folder.

In the content pane, the Unread Mail Search Folder displays the Outlook items that are marked as unread, from all your Outlook folders.

3   In the **All Mail Folders** list, expand the **SBS Organizing** data file.

The Search Folder provided as part of the SBS Organizing practice data file doesn't currently display any saved searches.

4 Right-click the practice *Search Folders* folder, and then click **New Search Folder** on the shortcut menu.

The New Search Folder dialog box appears.

5 In the **Select a Search Folder** list, under **Mail from People and Lists**, click **Mail from and to specific people**.

A browse box appears in the Customize Search Folder area at the bottom of the dialog box.

6 Click the **Choose** button.

The Select Names dialog box appears.

7 In the **Show Names from the** list, click **Contacts**. Then in the **Name** list, double-click **David Ortiz** and then **Kim Akers**, and then click **OK**.

In the New Search Folder dialog box, David Ortiz and Kim Akers are now listed in the "Show mail sent to and received from" box.

8   In the **Search mail in** drop-down list, click **SBS Organizing**. Then click **OK**.

9   If necessary, double-click the *Search Folders* folder to expand it, and then click the *David Ortiz* Search Folder.

The new Search Folder displays all the mail sent to or received from David Ortiz or Kim Akers.

10   Click the first message to display it in the Reading Pane.

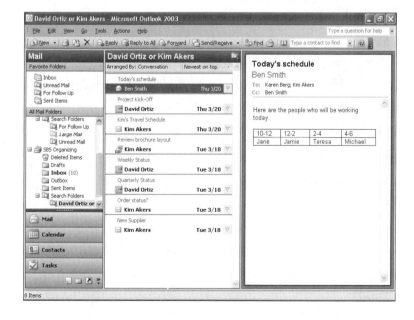

11 Right-click the new Search Folder, and then click **Rename** on the shortcut menu.

The name of the folder is selected for editing.

12 Type Marketing, and press the ⏎ Enter key.

The Search Folder is renamed.

13 On the **File** menu, point to **New**, and then click **Search Folder**.

The New Search Folder dialog box appears.

14 In the **Select a Search Folder** list, scroll to the **Custom** area, click **Create a custom Search Folder**, and then click the **Choose** button.

The Custom Search Folder dialog box appears.

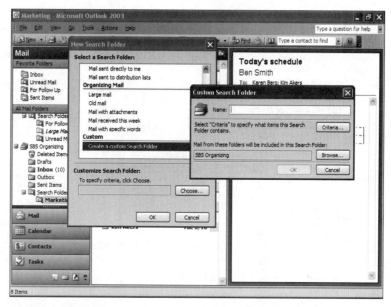

15 In the **Name** box, type Home Show, and then click **Criteria**.

The Search Folder Criteria dialog box appears.

16 Click the **More Choices** tab, and then click the **Categories** button.

The Categories dialog box appears.

17 In the **Available Categories** list, select the **Home Show** check box, and then click **OK**.

In the Search Folder Criteria dialog box, *Home Show* appears in the text box to the right of the Categories button.

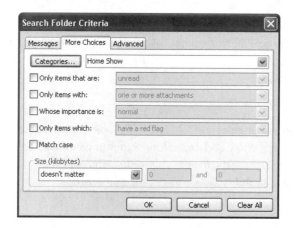

18   Click **OK** in each of the three open dialog boxes.

The new *Home Show* Search Folder appears in the Navigation Pane, and the content pane displays the items that are categorized as Home Show-related.

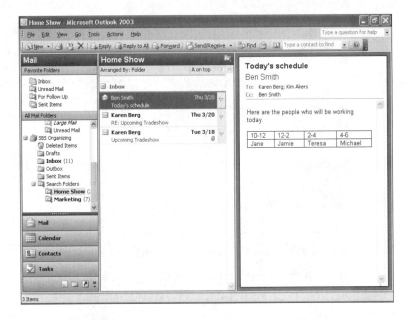

See Also   For more information about creating categories and assigning Outlook items to categories, see "Finding and Categorizing Messages" earlier in this chapter.

Filtering Messages

As messages accumulate in your Inbox, it can be a challenge to find specific messages or groups of messages. To help meet this challenge, you can *filter* your messages to display only those messages that meet common criteria, helping you identify a specific collection of messages.

In this exercise, you will define a view to filter messages.

USE the *SBSOrganizing* data file in the practice file folder for this topic. This practice file is located in the *My Documents\Microsoft Press\Office 2003 SBS\Organizing* folder and can also be accessed by clicking *Start/All Programs/Microsoft Press/Microsoft Office System 2003 Step by Step.*
BE SURE TO open the *SBSOrganizing* data file before beginning this exercise.
OPEN the practice file Inbox.

1   On the **View** menu, point to **Arrange By**, point to **Current View**, and then click **Define Views**.

The Custom View Organizer dialog box appears.

2   Click the **Copy** button.

The Copy View dialog box appears.

3   In the **Name of new view** box, type Filtered for Show, and click **OK**.

The Copy View dialog box closes, and the Customize View dialog box appears, showing the settings from the view you copied.

4   Click the **Filter** button.

The Filter dialog box appears.

5   In the **Search for the word(s)** box, type show, and click **OK**.

The Filter dialog box closes, and the Customize View dialog box shows the new filter settings.

6   In the **Customize View** dialog box, click **OK**.

The View Summary dialog box closes, and you are returned to the Custom View Organizer dialog box, which shows the new view in the View Name list.

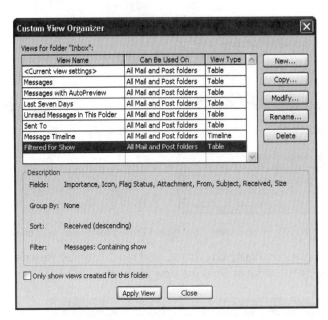

7   With **Filtered for Show** highlighted in the **View Name** list, click the **Apply View** button.

The Define Views for "Inbox" dialog box closes, and the Inbox is displayed, containing only the messages with the word *show* in the subject. The Folder banner indicates that a filter is applied.

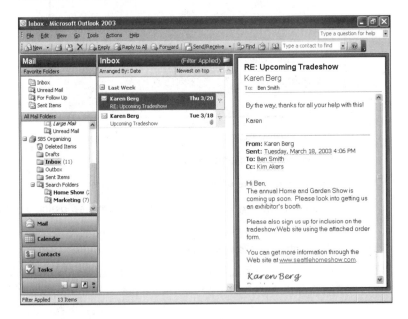

8 On the **View** menu, point to **Arrange By**, and then **Current View**.

The list of available views that appears includes the new *Filtered for Show* view.

9 On the **Current View** shortcut menu, click **Messages**.

The filter is removed, and the Inbox displays all the messages.

Managing Messages through Rules

You can instruct Outlook to evaluate your e-mail messages in the same way that you would evaluate them, and to make corresponding decisions about what to do with them. These instructions are called *rules*. You can create rules that process messages as they arrive or as you send them; checking for names, words, attachments, categories, or other message conditions on which you might base processing decisions. After the messages are evaluated, Outlook can automatically move, copy, delete, forward, redirect, reply to, or otherwise process messages that meet the criteria you set.

*New In
Office 2003*
New icon rules

In Outlook 2003, you can choose from a collection of standard rule or create your own by using the Outlook Rules Wizard. All your rules are summarized in a list, and differentiated by icons that indicate what they do.

Rules that are applied to messages as they are received or processed by the Exchange server are called *server rules*. Rules that are applied to messages stored on your computer are called *client rules*.

In this exercise, you will create a rule to manage messages that meet specific criteria.

USE the *SBSOrganizing* data file in the practice file folder for this topic. This practice file is located in the *My Documents\Microsoft Press\Office 2003 SBS\Organizing* folder and can also be accessed by clicking *Start/All Programs/Microsoft Press/Microsoft Office System 2003 Step by Step*.
BE SURE TO open the *SBSOrganizing* data file before beginning this exercise.
OPEN the practice file Inbox.

1 On the **Tools** menu, click **Rules and Alerts**.

The Rules and Alerts dialog box appears.

Troubleshooting You can set Outlook rules only when you are online.

Tip You cannot use Outlook rules to filter messages to an HTTP e-mail account.

2 Click the **New Rule** button.

The first page of the Rules Wizard appears, with the "Start creating a rule from a template" option selected. Take a moment to look over the types of rules you can create from a template.

3   In the **Select a template** list, click **Move messages from someone to a folder**, and then click the **Next** button.

4   In the **Select condition(s)** list, clear the **from people or distribution list** check box, and select the **with specific words in the subject** check box.

The "Edit the rule description" box is updated to reflect the change. The underlined words in the description are values that you must specify to complete the rule.

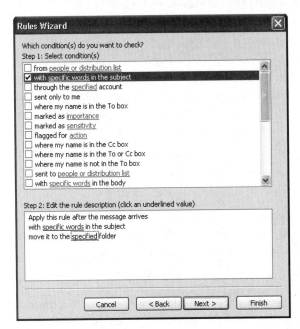

5   In the **Edit the rule description** box, click the underlined words **specific words**.

The Search Text dialog box appears.

6   In the **Specify words or phrases to search for in the subject** box, type Travel, click the **Add** button, and then click **OK**.

The "Rule description" box is updated to reflect the change.

7   In the **Edit the rule description** box, click the underlined word **specified**.

The Rules and Alerts dialog box appears, showing a list of folders for you to choose from.

8   Click the **New** button.

The Create New Folder dialog box appears.

9   In the **Name** box, type Travel.

10   In the **Select where to place the folder** list, scroll to and expand the SBS Organizing folder, and then click the **Inbox** folder.

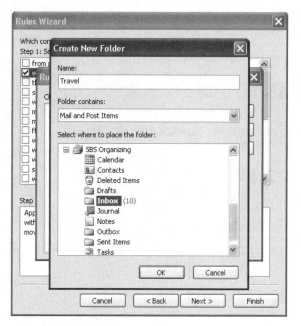

11   Click **OK**.

A new Travel folder appears as a subfolder of the practice Inbox.

12   In the **Rules and Alerts** dialog box, click **OK**.

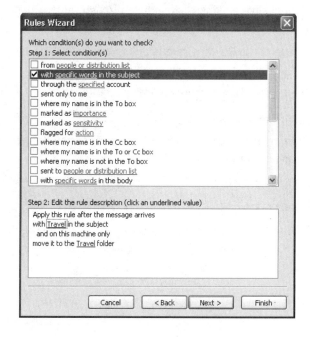

The dialog box closes, and the "Rule description" box is updated to reflect your folder selection.

13 Click the **Next** button.

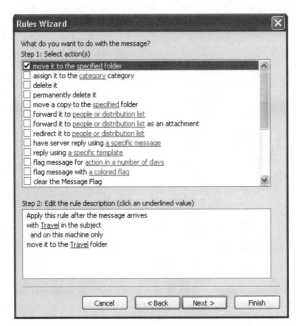

14 Review the possible actions you can take through Outlook rules, and then click the **Next** button.

The next page of the Rules Wizard is displayed.

15 In the **Select exception(s)** list, select the **except if it is flagged for action** check box, then in the **Edit the rule description** box, click the underlined word **action**.

The Flagged Message dialog box appears.

16 Click the down arrow to the right of the **Flag** box to see the available options, click **Any**, and click **OK**.

The "Edit the rule description" box is updated to reflect your selection.

17 Click the **Next** button.

The final page of the Rules Wizard is displayed, summarizing the parameters you have set for the Travel rule.

18 Select the **Run this rule now on messages already in "Inbox"** check box, and then click the **Finish** button.

Because this rule is created in an Outlook data file that is stored on your computer rather than on the server, Outlook warns you that this is a client-only rule.

19 In the warning box, click **OK**.

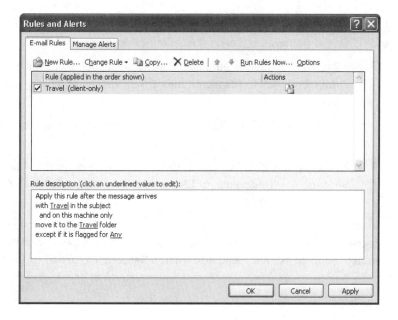

20 The rule is saved and is now listed in the Rules and Alerts dialog box.

21 Click **OK**.

The rule is now active, and Outlook applies it to the messages in the Inbox.

22 In the **All Mail Folders** list, expand the Inbox if necessary, and then click the **Travel** folder.

The contents of the Travel folder are displayed; in this case, the Kim's Travel Schedule message.

> **Tip** If you are using *Microsoft Exchange Server*, you can filter messages even when you are away from the office by using the *Out of Office Assistant*. You can explore this feature by clicking Out of Office Assistant on the Tools menu.

Filtering Junk E-Mail Messages

Outlook offers several options for managing junk e-mail messages (also called *spam*)—the unsolicited advertisements that can swamp your Inbox if your e-mail address finds its way into the hands of unscrupulous mailing list vendors. When enabled, the Junk E-mail filter will move messages that appear to be junk e-mail to a special folder, or it will delete them. You can specify a list of e-mail addresses or domains whose messages should always be treated as junk; you can also specify those that should never be treated as junk.

To filter junk e-mail:

1 On the **Actions** menu, point to **Junk E-mail**, and then click **Junk E-mail Options**.

The Junk E-mail Options dialog box appears.

2 On the **Options** tab, select a level of protection.

3 If you want Outlook to automatically delete suspected junk e-mail, select the **Permanently delete suspected Junk E-mail instead of moving it to the Junk E-mail folder** check box.

Do not select this check box if you set the protection level to High or Trusted Lists Only.

4 To specify an e-mail address or domain for inclusion in this filter, click the **Safe Senders**, **Safe Recipients**, or **Blocked Senders** tab, click **Add**, type the domain or e-mail address, and click **OK**.

To add the sender or recipient of a message to one of your Junk E-mail lists from your Inbox or other mail folder, right-click the message, point to Junk E-mail, and then click Add Sender to Junk Senders list, Add Sender to Trusted Senders list, or Add to Trusted Recipients list.

Organizing Messages in Folders

After you've read and responded to messages, you might want to keep some for future reference. With Outlook, you can organize your messages in a variety of ways.

Creating folders to organize your messages helps you avoid an accumulation of unrelated messages in your Inbox. For example, you can create a folder for each project you're working on and store all messages regarding a particular project in its own folder. Or you can create a folder to store all messages from your boss. You can move messages to the folders manually or have Outlook move them for you.

See Also   For more information about automatically moving messages, see "Managing Messages through Rules" earlier in this chapter.

Tip   If you are using a Microsoft Exchange Server account, the Out of Office Assistant can help you manage messages while you are away from the office. You can explore this feature by clicking Out of Office Assistant on the Tools menu.

In this exercise, you will organize messages by moving them to a new folder.

USE the *SBSOrganizing* data file in the practice file folder for this topic. This practice file is located in the *My Documents\Microsoft Press\Office 2003 SBS\Organizing* folder and can also be accessed by clicking *Start/All Programs/Microsoft Press/Microsoft Office System 2003 Step by Step*.
BE SURE TO open the *SBSOrganizing* data file before beginning this exercise.
OPEN the practice file Inbox.

1   On the **Tools** menu, click **Organize**.

The Ways to Organize pane appears.

See Also   For information about organizing messages with color, see "Managing Messages with Color" in Chapter 18, "Managing E-Mail Messages."

---

2   At the top of the **Ways to Organize** pane, click the **New Folder** button.

The Create New Folder dialog box appears.

Troubleshooting   If your default data store is a personal folder on your hard disk, the first item in the "Select where to place the folder" box is Personal Folders.

3   In the **Name** box, type **Home Show** as the name of your new folder.

4   In the **Select where to place the folder** list, click the SBS Organizing data file's **Inbox**, and then click **OK**.

The Create New Folder dialog box closes. The new Home Show folder appears as a subfolder of the Inbox folder. (You can scroll down the Navigation Pane to see the folder.)

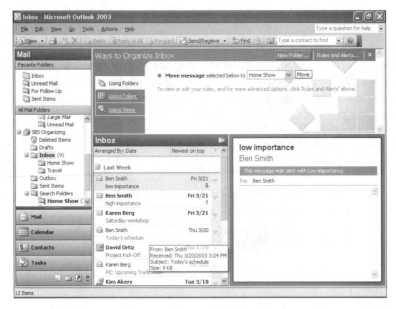

5   In the Inbox, click the **Upcoming Tradeshow** message from Karen Berg, and in the **Ways to Organize Inbox** pane, click the **Move** button.

The message is moved to the new folder.

6   Repeat step 5 to move the **RE: Upcoming Tradeshow** and **Today's schedule** messages to the new folder.

Tip   You can automatically move messages to another folder by creating a rule. To create a simple rule, such as moving all messages received from your boss to a separate folder, use the Using Folders tab of the Ways to Organize pane. For more complex rules, click the Rules Wizard button in the top right corner of the Ways to Organize pane.

7   In the **Navigation Pane**, click the **Home Show** folder.

The contents of the new folder are displayed.

8   In the **Navigation Pane**, drag the **Home Show** folder to the *SBS Organizing* folder.

The new folder is now listed at the same level in the folder structure as the Inbox and in alphabetical order with the other items at this level.

9   In the **Folder List**, right-click the **Home Show** folder, and then click **Rename** on the shortcut menu.

The folder name changes to an editable text box.

10   Type Garden Show, and press Enter .

The folder name changes.

11   In the **Folder List**, click the **Garden Show** folder to display its contents.

Move to Folder

12   Right-click the **Upcoming Tradeshow** message, and then click **Move to Folder** on the shortcut menu.

The Move Items dialog box appears.

13   Click the practice **Inbox**, and then click **OK**.

The message is moved to the Inbox.

Delete

14 Click the **RE: Upcoming Tradeshow** message, and then click the **Delete** button.

The message is deleted.

15 Drag the Today's schedule message to the practice Inbox in the **Navigation Pane**.

The message is moved to the Inbox, and the folder is now empty.

16 In the **Folder List**, click the **Garden Show** folder, and then press ⌊Del⌋.

17 When Outlook asks if you are sure you want to delete the folder, click **Yes**.

The folder is deleted. When you delete a folder, any messages contained within that folder are also deleted. (In this case, the folder is empty.)

CLOSE the Folder List.

Important   When you delete any item in Outlook, it is moved to the Deleted Items folder. You can view your deleted items by clicking that folder in the Folder List. You can tell Outlook to empty the Deleted Items folder every time you close the program by setting that option in the Options dialog box. On the Tools menu, click Options, click the Other tab, select the "Empty the Deleted Items folder upon exiting" check box, and then click OK. You can empty the Deleted Items folder at any time by right-clicking the folder in the Folder List and clicking Empty "Deleted Items" Folder on the shortcut menu.

Sharing Folders with Others

When you use Outlook, your messages, contacts, appointments, and other items are stored in folders. By default, the standard Outlook folders (Calendar, Contacts, Deleted Items, Drafts, Inbox, Journal, Junk E-mail, Notes, Outbox, Sent Items, Sync Issues, Tasks, and Search Folders) and the folders you create are private, meaning that only you can access them. However, if you are working on a network that uses Microsoft Exchange Server, you can choose to share private folders, allowing others to access them.

You can share folders with others in two ways. First you can give someone permission to access a folder. For example, you might have a collection of messages you want to share with a co-worker on a project. You can store those messages in a folder and give your co-worker access to that folder. You can select from a number of permission levels ranging from Owner (full access) to Reviewer (read-only access). When you select a permission level, Outlook indicates which actions will be allowed.

For example, you might grant Author access to your assistant who will help you manage incoming e-mail. As an author, your assistant can read items, create items, and edit and delete items that he or she creates, but those with Author permission level cannot create subfolders. Because permissions are defined as properties of an individual folder, you can grant someone Owner access to one folder and Reviewer access to another. You can also give more than one person permission to access a folder and select a different permission level for each person.

The second option for sharing folders is granting Delegate access. When you define someone as a *delegate*, you specify his or her access level to the Calendar, Tasks, Inbox, Contacts, Notes, or Journal as that of Editor, Author, or Reviewer. An editor can read, create, and modify items in the folder. An author can read and create items in the folder. A reviewer can read items in the folder. A delegate can be an editor in one folder and a reviewer in another. As an author or editor, a delegate can also send messages on your behalf. Recipients of messages sent by a delegate see both the manager's and the delegate's names on the message. Regardless of access level, a delegate cannot create subfolders. To allow someone to create subfolders, you must share the folder using permissions.

Important This exercise requires that you be connected to a Microsoft Exchange Server network.

In this exercise, you will copy a folder to your own mailbox and then practice different ways of sharing the folder.

USE the *SBSOrganizing* data file in the practice file folder for this topic. This practice file is located in the *My Documents\Microsoft Press\Office 2003 SBS\Organizing* folder and can also be accessed by clicking *Start/All Programs/Microsoft Press/Microsoft Office System 2003 Step by Step*.
BE SURE TO open the *SBSOrganizing* data file before beginning this exercise.

1 In the **Navigation Pane**, drag the button panel down so that all the buttons are minimized and you can see more mail folders.

2 Expand your own mailbox and the SBS Organizing data file so you can see their contents.

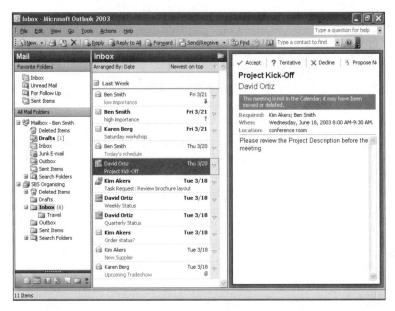

3 Right-click the practice Inbox, and on the shortcut menu, click **Copy**.

The Copy Folder dialog box appears.

4 Scroll to the top of the list and click your own mailbox.

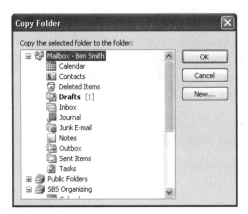

5 Click **OK**.

The practice Inbox folder is copied to your own mailbox as *Inbox1*.

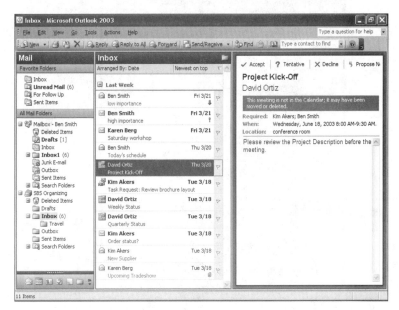

6   In your own mailbox, right-click the **Inbox1** folder, and on the shortcut menu, click **Sharing**.

The Inbox1 Properties dialog box appears, displaying the Permissions tab.

7   Click the **Add** button.

The Add Users dialog box appears.

8   Click the name of the co-worker with whom you want to share this folder, and then click the **Add** button.

The selected name appears in the Add Users box.

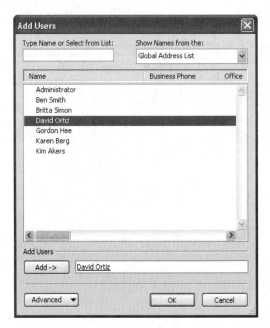

9   Click **OK**.

The Add Users dialog box closes. The Inbox1 Properties dialog box shows the selected co-worker's name in the list.

10   With your co-worker's name selected, in the **Permissions** area, click the down arrow to the right of the **Permission Level** box, and then click **Editor**.

The "Create items" and "Read items" check boxes are selected, and the All option is selected in the "Edit items" and "Delete items" areas.

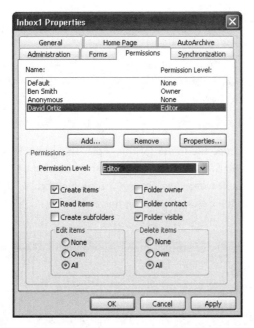

11 Click **OK**.

The new permission settings are applied to the Inbox1 folder. Your co-worker can now view the folder by opening it from within Outlook on his or her computer and can create, edit, and delete items within it.

Tip   To open another person's folder, on the File menu, point to Open, and then click Other User's Folder. Click the Name button, click the name of the person sharing the folder with you, and then click OK. In the Folder type drop-down list, click the folder you want to open, and then click OK.

12 If your co-worker is available, ask him or her to open your *Inbox1* folder to verify that the folder is shared as expected.

13 When you are finished, click the **Inbox1** folder, and on the toolbar, click the **Delete** button. When Outlook prompts you to confirm the deletion, click **Yes**.

The Inbox1 folder is deleted from your mailbox.

✕
Delete

BE SURE TO expand the Navigation buttons the way you want them.

Saving Messages in Other Formats

Sometimes a message will contain information that you want to use in another program. You can save a message as a plain text file, which most programs can open or import. Or you might save a message as an HTML document, which would make it easier to post it to a team portal or Web site.

In this exercise, you will save messages to your hard disk in different formats.

USE the *SBSOrganizing* data file in the practice file folder for this topic. This practice file is located in the *My Documents\Microsoft Press\Office 2003 SBS\Organizing* folder and can also be accessed by clicking *Start/All Programs/Microsoft Press/Microsoft Office System 2003 Step by Step*.
BE SURE TO open the *SBSOrganizing* data file before beginning this exercise.
OPEN the practice file Inbox.

1   In the Inbox, click the **Order status?** message from Kim Akers, and on the **File** menu, click **Save As**.

The Save As dialog box appears.

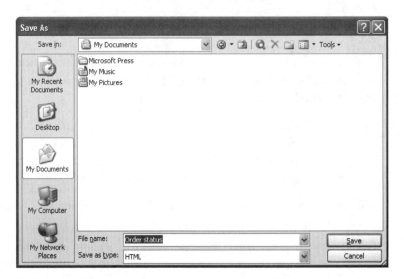

By default, Outlook saves e-mail messages as HTML files.

Tip   Your Save As dialog box will show your My Documents folder or the last folder in which you saved an Outlook item. If you have file extensions turned on, the name in the File Name box will be Order status.htm.

2   If the My Documents folder is not displayed in the **Save As** dialog box, click the **My Documents** icon.

3   Double-click *Microsoft Press*, *Office 2003 SBS*, *Organizing*, and then click **Save**.

The message is saved in the selected folder as *Order status.htm*.

4   In the Inbox, click the **Today's schedule** message, and on the **File** menu, click **Save As**.

The Save As dialog box appears, already open to the *My Documents\Microsoft Press \Office 2003 SBS\Organizing* folder.

5   Click the down arrow to the right of the **Save as type** box, click **Text Only** in the drop-down list, and then click **Save**.

The message is saved in the selected folder as *Saturday workshop.txt*.

6   On the **Start** menu, click **My Documents**. Double-click the *Microsoft Press*, *Office 2003 SBS*, and *Organizing* folders.

The folder contains the files you saved, along with the Outlook data file used in this chapter.

Web page

7   Double-click the *Order status* HTML file, which is indicated by a Web page icon.

The message opens in your default *Web browser*.

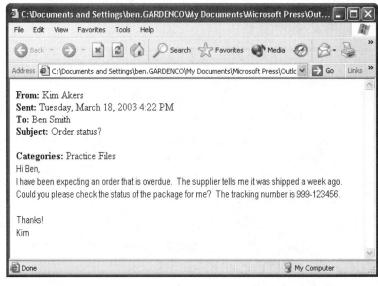

8 If the message contained any formatting, the HTML format preserves it.

Text page

9 In the *Organizing* folder, double-click the *Today's schedule* text file, which is indicated by a Text page icon.

The message opens in Notepad.

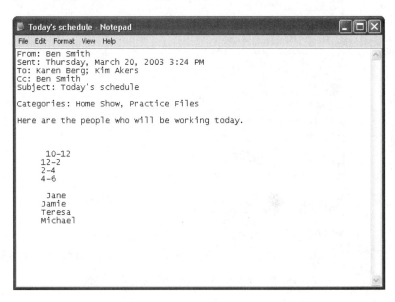

CLOSE the Notepad window, the browser window, and the Organizing folder.

Archiving Messages

As messages accumulate in your Inbox and other message folders, you might need to consider other ways to store them in order to cut down on the amount of storage space you're using. For example, you might want to *archive* all messages sent or received before a certain date. Archiving messages in a separate Outlook message file helps you manage clutter and the size of your primary message file, while still allowing easy access to archived messages from within Outlook.

You can archive messages manually or automatically. When archived messages are moved to a separate message file, the messages are removed from their original folder. By default, Outlook automatically archives messages in all folders at regular intervals to a location determined by your operating system. You can change the default global settings for the *AutoArchive* function and specify varying archive settings for specific folders. Archive settings selected for a specific folder override the global settings for that folder. If you don't specify AutoArchive settings for a folder, Outlook uses the global settings.

In this exercise, you will investigate your automatic archive options, and then archive messages manually.

USE the *SBSOrganizing* data file in the practice file folder for this topic. This practice file is located in the *My Documents\Microsoft Press\Office 2003 SBS\Organizing* folder and can also be accessed by clicking *Start/All Programs/Microsoft Press/Microsoft Office System 2003 Step by Step*.
BE SURE TO open the *SBSOrganizing* data file before beginning this exercise.
OPEN the practice file Inbox.

1 On the **Tools** menu, click **Options**.

The Options dialog box appears.

2 Click the **Other** tab, and then click the **AutoArchive** button.

The AutoArchive dialog box appears.

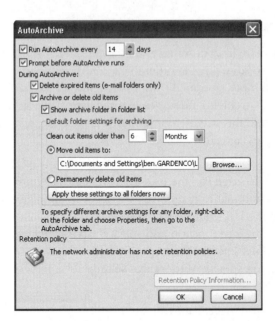

3 Review your AutoArchive default settings—particularly note the interval at which the archive will happen, the age at which items will be archived, and the location in the **Move old items to** box.

4 Click **Cancel** in each of the open dialog boxes.

The dialog boxes close without initiating any changes.

Tip You can use the Mailbox Cleanup feature to see the size of your mailbox, find and delete old items or items that are larger than a certain size, start AutoArchive, or view and empty your Deleted Items folder. To use this feature, on the Tools menu, click Mailbox Cleanup.

Folder List

5 In the **Navigation Pane**, click the **Folder List** icon.

The Folder List appears.

6 In the *SBS Organizing* data file, click the **Inbox** (not the Inbox in your mailbox).

7 On the **File** menu, point to **Folder**, and then click **Properties**.

The Inbox Properties dialog box appears.

8   Click the **AutoArchive** tab.

The AutoArchive options are displayed.

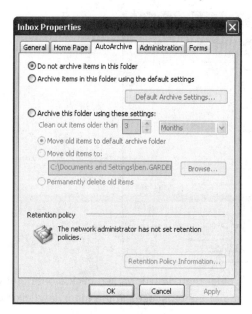

9   Select the **Archive this folder using these settings** option.

10   In the **Clean out items older than** box, select **1** and **Days**.

Important   You would usually stipulate a longer archive period, but for the purposes of this exercise you will archive all the messages in the practice Inbox.

11   Be sure the option to **Move old items to default archive folder** is selected, and click **OK**.

The Inbox Properties dialog box closes. Items in the Inbox will be archived according to the new settings. Items in all other folders will be archived according to the default settings.

12   On the **File** menu, click **Archive**.

The Archive dialog box appears.

13 With the **Archive this folder and all subfolders** option selected, click the **SBS Organizing** folder.

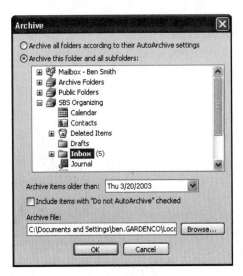

14 In the **Archive items older than** drop-down list, click a date that you know is later than the date of some of the messages in the Inbox, and click **OK**.

Outlook archives the messages in the practice Inbox according to your settings.

15 In the **Folder List**, double-click **Archive Folders** to expand it, and click the **Inbox** folder that appears within that folder.

The contents of the archived Inbox folder are displayed.

BE SURE TO close the *SBS Organizing* data file after completing this chapter.

Checking Addresses

By default, Outlook will check any e-mail address you type against the entries in the Outlook Address Book. If the address book does not contain an entry for a name that you type in the To, Cc, or Bcc boxes of a new message, when you send the message, Outlook will prompt you to select an address book entry or provide a full e-mail address.

To have Outlook check entries from your Personal Address Book:

1   On the **Tools** menu, click **Address Book**.

2   On the Address Book window's **Tools** menu, click **Options**.

3   In the **Addressing** dialog box, click the **Add** button.

4   In the **Add Address List** dialog box, click **Outlook Address Book**, and then click the **Add** button.

5   Click the **Close** button.

6   In the **Addressing** dialog box, click **OK**.

7   In the Address Book window, click the **Close** button.

Key Points

■   You can create folders to organize your mail. You can set up rules to move messages to folders based on the sender, other recipients, words in the subject or body of the message, and other factors.

■   You can use filters and Search Folders to view messages that meet certain search criteria.

■   Outlook can help you manage your mailbox by periodically archiving old items. Different folders can have different archiving schedules.

■   Using Microsoft Exchange Server, you can share folders in your mailbox with other members of your organization.

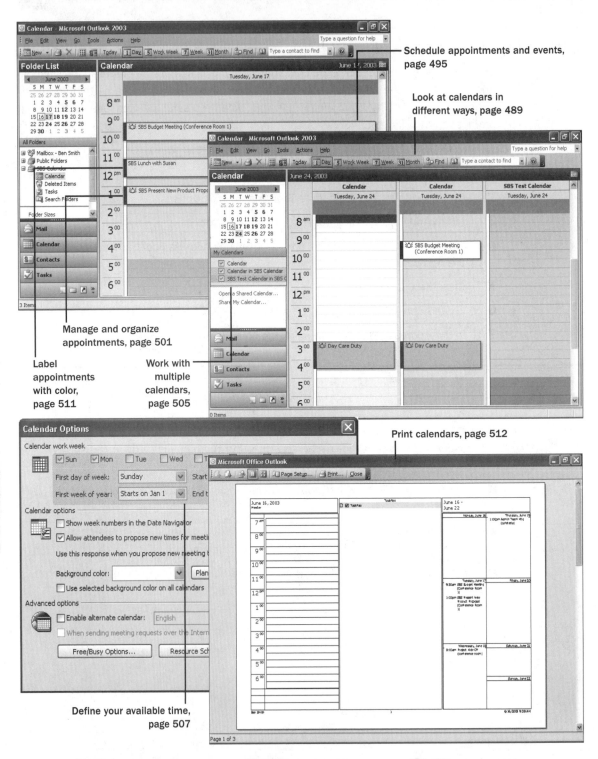

Schedule appointments and events, page 495

Look at calendars in different ways, page 489

Manage and organize appointments, page 501

Label appointments with color, page 511

Work with multiple calendars, page 505

Print calendars, page 512

Define your available time, page 507

Chapter 20 at a Glance

20 Managing Your Calendar

In this chapter you will learn to:

✔ Look at calendars in different ways.

✔ Schedule appointments and events.

✔ Manage and organize appointments.

✔ Work with multiple calendars.

✔ Define your available time.

✔ Label appointments with color.

✔ Print calendars.

Managing time effectively is a constant challenge for most people today. The Microsoft Office Outlook *Calendar* makes it easy for you to manage your schedule, including both appointments and events, as well as to view and print your schedule for a day, a week, or a month.

In this chapter, you will experiment with the Outlook Calendar and learn how to use its various features.

See Also Do you need only a quick refresher on the topics in this chapter? See the Quick Reference entries on page xxxiii.

 Important Before you can use the practice files in this chapter, you need to install them from the book's companion CD to their default location. See "Using the Book's CD-ROM" on page xxi for more information.

Looking at Calendars in Different Ways

To help you stay on top of your schedule, you can view your Calendar in a variety of ways:

■ *Day view* displays one day at a time, separated into half-hour increments.

■ *Work Week view* displays your work week in columnar format. By default, the work week is defined as 8:00 A.M. to 5:00 P.M. Monday through Friday. You can define your work week as whatever days and hours you want.

See Also For more information about defining your work week, see "Defining Your Available Time," later in this chapter.

■ *Week view* displays one calendar week at a time.

■ *Month view* displays five weeks at a time.

By default, your Calendar is displayed in Month view. To change the view setting, click the toolbar button for the view you want.

Outlook's default settings break the day into half-hour increments, with the *work week* defined as 8 A.M. to 5 P.M. Monday through Friday. You can change the Calendar's work week to reflect your own working hours, and you can schedule appointments for any time of any day.

The *Date Navigator* serves as a handy month calendar and an easy way to view your schedule for specific dates. To view your schedule for a particular date, simply click that date in the Date Navigator.

About Calendar Views

New in Office 2003

Calendar view

Outlook 2003 offers a streamlined Calendar view that now includes the Date Navigator, a day/time indicator, and the ability to view multiple calendars at once.

Outlook offers a number of ways to view your Calendar. To select the view, on the View menu, point to Arrange By, point to Current View, and then click the view you want.

Click this view	To see
Day/Week/Month	A calendar-like view of appointments, events, and meetings for the period of time you specify. This is the default view, and it includes the Date Navigator.
Day/Week/Month With AutoPreview	The Day/Week/Month view with the addition of the first line of comment text for each Calendar item.
Active Appointments	A list of appointments and meetings scheduled for today and in the future, showing details in columns.
Events	A list of events, showing details in columns.
Annual Events	A list of annual events, showing details in columns.
Recurring Appointments	A list of recurring appointments, showing details in columns.
By Category	A list of all items, grouped by category, showing details in columns.

In this exercise, you will experiment with the different ways to view and move around in your calendar.

Important   You can work through this exercise in your own Calendar or in the practice Calendar. If you use your own Calendar and don't already have appointments on it, you will not be able to see all the categories discussed here.

USE the *SBSCalendar* data file in the practice file folder for this topic. This practice file is located in the *My Documents\Microsoft Press\Office 2003 SBS\Calendar* folder and can also be accessed by clicking *Start/All Programs/Microsoft Press/Microsoft Office System 2003 Step by Step*.
BE SURE TO start Outlook before beginning this exercise.
OPEN the *SBSCalendar* data file from within Outlook.

Folder List

1   In the **Navigation Pane**, click the **Folder List** icon.

2   In the **Folder List**, expand the **SBS Calendar** data file, and then click the subordinate **Calendar**.

By default, the Calendar displays Day view. The current day is shaded in the Date Navigator.

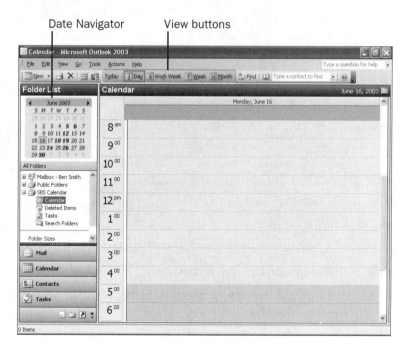

Date Navigator   View buttons

Tip You can increase the size of the Navigation Pane to display two months in the Date Navigator. With your Calendar displayed in Outlook, point to the vertical frame divider between the Navigation Pane and the Calendar. When the pointer changes to a double-headed arrow, drag the frame to the right.

3 In the Date Navigator, click the arrows to scroll to January 2004. Then click **8**.

The Calendar displays the schedule for January 8th, 2004.

4 On the toolbar, click the **Work Week** button.

The Calendar displays the schedule for your currently defined work week. The work week is shaded in the Date Navigator.

The bell indicates that a reminder
will appear before this meeting.

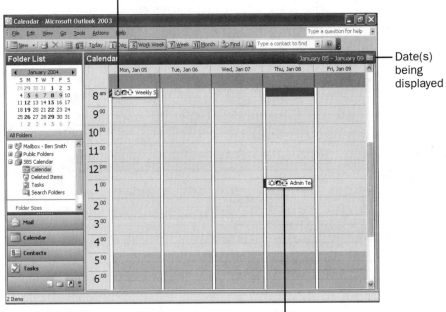

Circling arrows indicate a recurring appointment.

5 On the toolbar, click the **Week** button.

The Calendar displays the schedule for the seven-day week. The week is shaded in the Date Navigator.

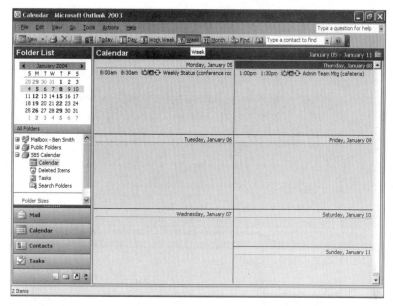

6 In the Date Navigator, click in the margin to the left of the week starting January 11.

The Calendar now shows the schedule for that week.

7 On the toolbar, click the **Month** button.

The Calendar shows the schedule for the current month. The month is shaded in the Date Navigator.

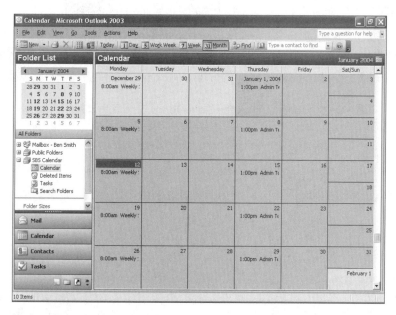

Notice that months are differentiated by alternating colors.

8 On the **View** menu, point to **Arrange By**, point to **Current View**, and then click **Active Appointments**.

The recurring and non-recurring appointments in the practice calendar are displayed. You can sort the appointments by clicking the column headers.

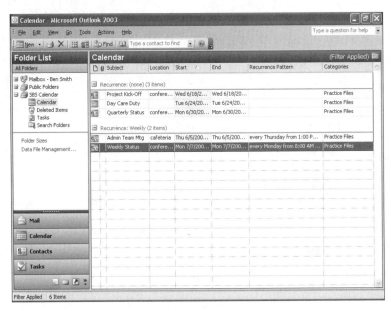

9 On the **View** menu, point to **Arrange By**, point to **Current View**, and click **By Category**.

Calendar items are displayed in a columnar list, grouped by category.

10 Investigate any other views that interest you. When you finish, on the **View** menu, point to **Arrange By**, point to **Current View**, and then click **Day/Week/Month**.

11 On the toolbar, click the **Day** button to display a one-day view.

Go to Today

12 On the toolbar, click the **Go to Today** button to display today's calendar page.

Scheduling Appointments and Events

Adding your time commitments to a calendar can help you manage your daily schedule. You can use Outlook's *Calendar* to schedule *appointments* (which typically last just part of a day) or *events* (which typically last all day long). For example, you might create an appointment in your Outlook Calendar for the time you will spend seeing your doctor, and you might schedule an event for an all-day seminar you plan to attend. Both appointments and events can be *recurring*, meaning they occur repeatedly at regular intervals—for example, daily, weekly, or monthly. You can specify a subject and location for each Calendar item as well as the date and time. You can indicate your availability as available, tentative, busy, or out of the office during the scheduled time, and you can choose to receive a *reminder* of an appointment or event. Reminders are displayed in a small dialog box that appears as the time of the appointment or event approaches. Outlook must be open for you to receive reminders.

In this exercise, you will schedule an appointment, schedule a recurring appointment, and schedule a multi-day event.

Important   You can work through this exercise in your own Calendar or in the practice Calendar. If you use your own Calendar, be sure to delete the appointments you create in the exercise. To make it easier to locate and identify the sample appointments, each appointment subject starts with the letters *SBS*.

USE the *SBSCalendar* data file in the practice file folder for this topic. This practice file is located in the *My Documents\Microsoft Press\Office 2003 SBS\Calendar* folder and can also be accessed by clicking *Start/All Programs/Microsoft Press/Microsoft Office System 2003 Step by Step*.
BE SURE TO start Outlook and open the *SBSCalendar* data file before beginning this exercise.

1   In the **Navigation Pane**, click the **Folder List** icon.

2   In the **Folder List**, expand the **SBS Calendar** data file, and then click the practice **Calendar**.

Calendar

Tip   If you want to work through this exercise in your own Calendar, simply click the Calendar icon in the Navigation Pane.

The Calendar appears, showing today's schedule.

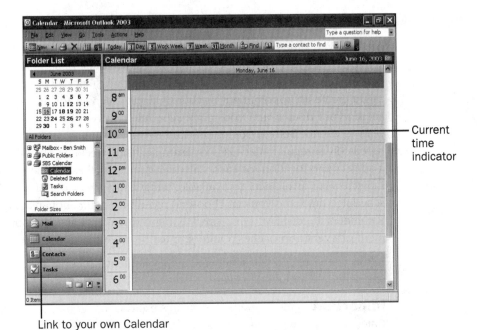

Current
time
indicator

Link to your own Calendar

Troubleshooting The default Calendar display is Day view. If your Calendar does not look like the one shown in this exercise, click the Day button on the toolbar.

3 In the Date Navigator, click tomorrow's date.

Tomorrow's schedule is displayed.

4 Double-click the 1:00 P.M. time slot.

A new Appointment form appears.

5 In the **Subject** box, type SBS Present New Product Proposal.

6 Press the [Tab] key, and in the **Location** box, type Conference Room 1.

7 Click the down arrow to the right of the second **End time** box (the one that displays the time, not the date), and in the drop-down list, click **2:00 PM** to set the meeting duration to one hour.

8 If necessary, select the **Reminder** check box to indicate that you want Outlook to remind you of this meeting. Click the down arrow to the right of the **Reminder** box, and in the drop-down list, click **30 minutes** to allow time to set up for your presentation.

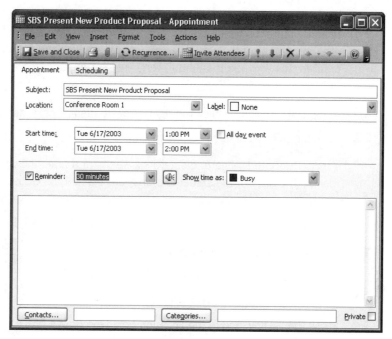

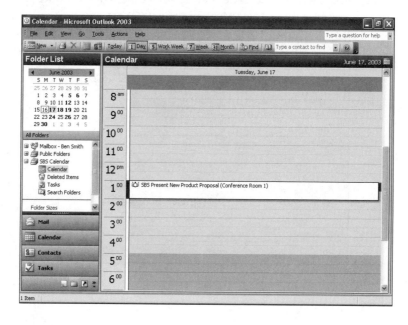

9   On the Appointment window toolbar, click the **Save and Close** button. If Outlook warns you that the reminder will not appear, click **Yes**.

The appointment is saved in the Calendar.

Tip You can quickly create an appointment by clicking the appropriate Calendar timeslot and then typing the appointment subject. To create a longer appointment, drag through the timeslots you want, and then type the subject. Appointments created this way use the default reminder setting and don't include a meeting location.

10 In the Date Navigator, click the right arrow to display next month.

11 Click the third Wednesday of the month.

Tip The Date Navigator displays six weeks at a time, including the selected month. The days of the selected month are black; days of the previous and next months are gray, but you can still select them in the Date Navigator.

The schedule for the selected day is displayed.

12 Double-click the 10:00 A.M. time slot.

A new Appointment form appears.

13 In the **Subject** box, type **SBS Status Report**.

14 Press the [Tab] key, and in the **Location** box, type **Boss's Office**.

15 Click the **Recurrence** button.

The Appointment Recurrence dialog box appears.

16 In the **Recurrence pattern** area, select the **Monthly** option, and then select the **The third Wednesday of every 1 month(s)** option.

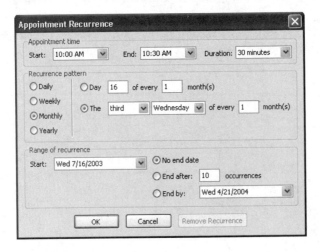

17 Click **OK**.

The recurrence settings are added to the Appointment form.

Create recurring appointments.

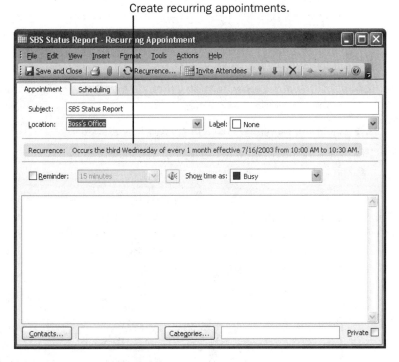

18 Click the **Save and Close** button.

The recurring appointment is added to your Calendar. Circling arrows indicate the recurrence.

19 In the Date Navigator, click the right arrow.

The Date Navigator shows the next month, with the third Wednesday appearing bold, indicating that an appointment is scheduled for that day.

20 On the **Go** menu, click **Go to Date**.

The Go To Date dialog box appears.

21 In the **Date** box, type 8/8/04, and then click **OK**.

The schedule for August 8th, 2004, is displayed.

22 Right-click the 9:00 A.M. time slot, and then click **New All Day Event** on the short-cut menu.

A new Event form appears.

23 In the **Subject** box, type SBS On Vacation.

24 Click the down arrow to the right of the **End time** box, and then click the 14th day of August on the drop-down calendar.

25 Clear the **Reminder** check box if it is selected.

26 Click the down arrow to the right of the **Show time as** box, and then click **Out of Office** in the drop-down list.

Tip   By default, Outlook adds the typical holidays for your country as Calendar events, but you can add the holidays of other countries. On the Tools menu, click Options. On the Preferences tab, click Calendar Options, and then click the Add Holidays button. Select the check boxes of the countries whose holidays you want to add, and then click OK in each open dialog box.

27 In the lower-right corner of the **Event** form, select the **Private** check box.

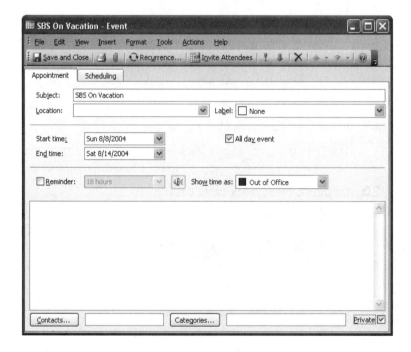

> **Tip** You can easily mark an existing appointment as *private* so that other Outlook users can't see its details. Simply right-click the appointment in the Calendar, and then click Private on the shortcut menu.

28 Click the **Save and Close** button. If Outlook warns you that the reminder will not appear, click **Yes**.

The new event is added to your Calendar. A key icon indicates that the appointment is private.

29 On the toolbar, click the **Go to Today** button.

Today's schedule appears.

BE SURE TO delete the SBS Present New Product Proposal, SBS Status Report, and SBS On Vacation appointments if you worked through this exercise in your own Calendar.

Managing and Organizing Appointments

You can use the Outlook Calendar to manage and organize your appointments in a variety of ways. You can enter details about an appointment to help you remember important information, such as the agenda for a meeting or directions to a client's office. And as with e-mail messages, you can assign meetings to categories and organize them in folders to help you sort your appointments. For example, you might assign a dentist appointment to the Personal category. Outlook includes a selection of useful categories, including Business, Personal, and Miscellaneous, but you can create additional categories to meet your needs. Or you might create a separate Personal calendar folder for your non-work-related appointments. When your schedule changes, you can also move, copy, and delete appointments.

> **See Also** For more information about categories, see "Finding and Categorizing Messages" in Chapter 19, "Finding and Organizing E-Mail Messages."

In this exercise, you will add details to an appointment and assign an appointment to a category. Then you will move, copy, and delete an appointment.

> **Important** You can work through this exercise in your own Calendar or in the practice Calendar. If you use your own Calendar, be sure to delete the appointments you create in the exercise. To make it easier to locate and identify the sample appointments, each appointment subject starts with the letters *SBS*.

USE the *SBSCalendar* data file in the practice file folder for this topic. This practice file is located in the *My Documents\Microsoft Press\Office 2003 SBS\Calendar* folder and can also be accessed by clicking *Start/All Programs/Microsoft Press/Microsoft Office System 2003 Step by Step*.
BE SURE TO open the *SBSCalendar* data file before beginning this exercise.

1 Click tomorrow's date in the Date Navigator.

Tomorrow's schedule is displayed.

2 Drag through the 9:30 and 10:00 time slots to select them.

3 Type **SBS Budget Meeting**, and press the Enter key.

The appointment is added to the Calendar.

4 With the appointment selected, press Enter again.

The Appointment form appears.

5 Click in the **Location** box, and type **Conference Room 1**.

Tip Outlook remembers the locations you type in the Location box. Instead of typing the location again, you can click the down arrow to the right of the Location box, and then click the location you want.

6 Be sure the **Reminder** check box is selected, and in the **Reminder** list, click **1 hour**.

7 Click the comments area below the reminder, and type a rough agenda for the meeting.

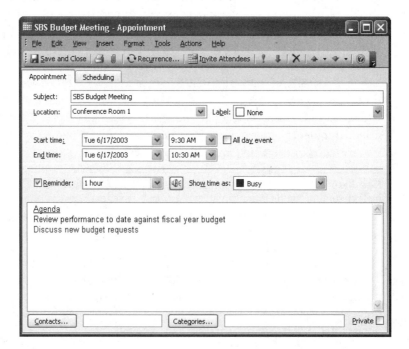

Tip To format the comment text, select the text to be formatted, click the Format menu, and then click Text or Paragraph.

8 At the bottom of the **Appointment** form, click the **Categories** button.

The Categories dialog box appears.

9   Click in the **Item(s) belong to these categories** box, type Finance, and click the **Add to List** button.

The Finance category is added to the list and is selected.

10   In the **Available categories** list, select the **Business** check box, and then click **OK**.

The selected categories are added to the Categories box in the Appointment form.

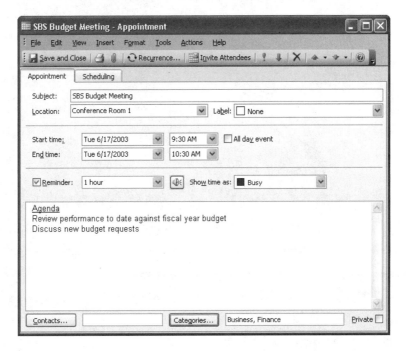

11 Click the **Save and Close** button.

12 If Outlook warns you that the reminder will not appear, click **Yes**.

The Calendar displays the updated appointment.

13 Click the 12:00 P.M. time slot, and type **SBS Lunch with Susan**.

14 Point to the bottom border of the appointment, and when the pointer changes to a vertical double-headed arrow, drag the bottom of the appointment to 1:00 P.M., and then press the [Enter] key.

The Calendar displays the updated appointment. In the Date Navigator, the selected date appears in bold, indicating that appointments are scheduled.

15 Point to the left border of the **SBS Lunch with Susan** appointment.

The pointer becomes a four-headed arrow.

16 Drag the appointment to the 11:30 A.M. time slot.

The lunch appointment is rescheduled for 11:30 A.M.

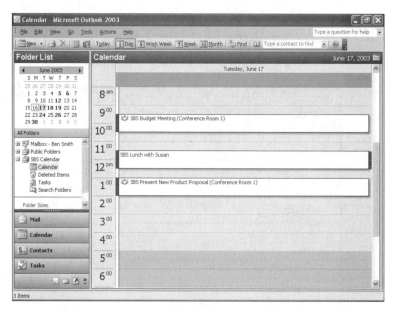

17 Point to the left border of the **SBS Budget Meeting** appointment.

The pointer becomes a four-headed arrow.

18 Using the right mouse button, drag the appointment to the same day of the following week in the Date Navigator.

A shortcut menu appears.

19   On the shortcut menu, click **Copy**.

Outlook displays the schedule for a week from tomorrow, showing the new Budget Meeting appointment.

20   In the Date Navigator, click tomorrow's date.

Tomorrow's schedule is displayed, showing the original Budget Meeting appointment.

21   Click the **SBS Lunch with Susan** appointment, and on the toolbar, click the **Delete** button.

Delete

The appointment is removed from your Calendar.

BE SURE TO delete the SBS Budget Meeting and SBS Budget Team appointments if you worked through this exercise in your own Calendar.

Working with Multiple Calendars

It is often handy to have more than one Calendar. For instance, you might want to maintain one Calendar for yourself, and one for a team project. Or you might want to have separate business and personal calendars. It is easy to create new Calendars.

New in Office 2003
Side-by-side calendars

With Outlook 2003, you can view several Calendars at the same time, and move or copy appointments and events between them. When you view and scroll multiple calendars, they all display the same date or time period.

In this exercise, you will create a new Calendar, and then view all the available Calendars at once.

USE the *SBSCalendar* data file in the practice file folder for this topic. This practice file is located in the *My Documents\Microsoft Press\Office 2003 SBS\Calendar* folder and can also be accessed by clicking *Start/All Programs/Microsoft Press/Microsoft Office System 2003 Step by Step.*
BE SURE TO open the *SBSCalendar* data file before beginning this exercise.

1   Display the practice Calendar.

2   Click the down arrow to the right of the **New** button, and then click **Folder** in the drop-down list.

The Create New Folder dialog box appears.

3   In the **Name** box, type SBS Test Calendar.

4   In the **Folder contains** drop-down list, click **Calendar Items**.

5   In the **Select where to place the folder** box, click the **SBS Calendar** folder.

6 Click **OK**.

The new Calendar appears in the SBS Calendar data file.

Calendar

7 In the **Navigation Pane**, click the **Calendar** icon.

The My Calendars list appears in the Navigation Pane, listing the available calendars. The *Calendar in SBS Calendar* check box is selected to indicate the calendar you are viewing.

8 In the **My Calendars** list, select the **Calendar** check box.

Outlook displays your main calendar and the practice calendar side by side.

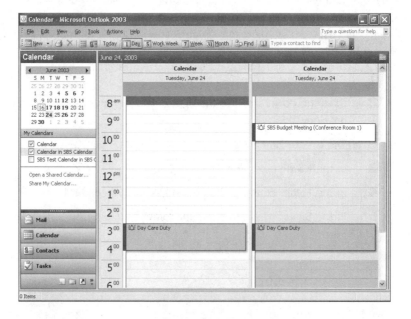

9   In the **My Calendars** list, select the **SBS Test Calendar in SBS Calendars** check box.

Outlook displays the three calendars side by side. Colored stripes across the calendar names match the colors on the displayed calendars so you can tell which is which.

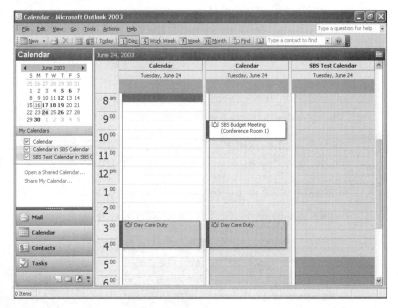

10   In the Date Navigator, click a bold date to find a day with a scheduled meeting or event.

11   Drag the event from one calendar to the next to move it. Right-click and drag the event, and then click **Copy** on the shortcut menu.

12   Clear the **Calendar** and **SBS Test Calendar in SBS Calendar** check boxes to display only the practice calendar.

BE SURE TO move any of your own appointments back to their original dates and times.

Defining Your Available Time

You can tell Outlook what your work schedule is so that other people can make appointments with you only during the times that you plan to be available. This defined time is called your *work week*. The work week is colored differently in your calendar, and by default is the only time displayed to other people on your network who look at your calendar.

By default, the work week is defined as Monday through Friday from 8:00 A.M. to 5:00 P.M. You can change this to suit your needs—for instance, if you work a late shift or weekends.

See Also   For more information about looking at other people's calendars, see "Viewing Other Users' Calendars" in Chapter 21, "Scheduling and Managing Meetings."

In this exercise, you will view and change your work week.

OPEN your own Calendar.

1   On the toolbar, click the **Work Week** button.

The calendar displays your current work week.

Troubleshooting   If your work week does not match the default days and times described here, work through this exercise using your own settings.

2   Scroll the calendar page so you can see the beginning and end of the work day.

Notice that the working hours are shaded differently from the rest of the day.

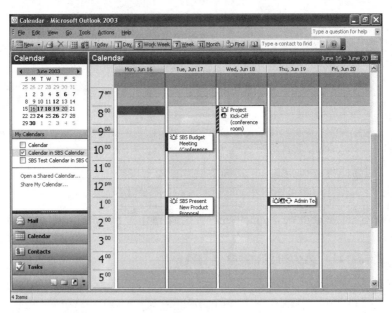

3   On the **Tools** menu, click **Options**.

The Options dialog box appears.

4   In the **Calendar** area of the **Preferences** tab, click **Calendar Options**.

The Calendar Options dialog box appears.

5   In the **Calendar work week** area, select the **Sun** and **Sat** check boxes, and clear the **Tue**, **Wed**, and **Thu** check boxes.

The work week is now set to Friday through Monday.

6   Click the down arrow to the right of the **Start time** box, and click **3:00 PM**. Then click the down arrow to the right of the **End time** box, and click **11:00 PM**.

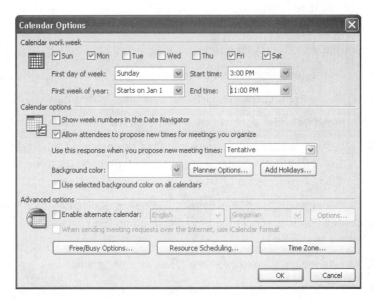

7   Click **OK**, and in the **Options** dialog box, click **OK** again.

Troubleshooting   Outlook doesn't allow you to define a workday that crosses midnight, or to define different start and end times for different days.

8   The Calendar displays your new default work week.

9   On the **Tools** menu, click **Options**, and then click the **Calendar Options** button.

10   Select the check boxes for your actual work days.

11   Set your actual start and end times.

12   Click **OK** to close each of the dialog boxes and set your default work week.

BE SURE TO set your default work week the way you want.

Working with Multiple Time Zones

If you frequently work with people from other countries or regularly travel internationally, you might want to change the time zone displayed in your Calendar or simultaneously view two time zones.

Each time zone is measured in reference to Greenwich Mean Time (GMT) or Universal Time (UTC). GMT is defined as the time at the Greenwich Observatory in England.

To change your current time zone:

1.   On the **Tools** menu, click **Options**.

2.   On the **Preferences** tab, click the **Calendar Options** button.

3.   In the **Calendar Options** dialog box, click the **Time Zone** button.

4.   In the **Time Zone** dialog box, click the down arrow to the right of the **Time zone** box, click the time zone you want, and then click **OK** three times to close all the dialog boxes.

Note that changing your time zone in Outlook is equivalent to changing your time zone in Control Panel. It affects the time displayed on the Windows taskbar and in any other Windows programs.

To simultaneously display two time zones in your Calendar:

1.   On the **Tools** menu, click **Options**.

2.   On the **Preferences** tab, click the **Calendar Options** button.

3.   In the **Calendar Options** dialog box, click the **Time Zone** button.

4.   In the **Time Zone** dialog box, select the **Show an additional time zone** check box.

5.   In both areas of the dialog box, click in the **Label** box, and type the label you want for the time zone. (For example, *home* or *office*.)

6.   Click the down arrow to the right of the second **Time zone** box, click the second time zone you want to display, and click **OK** three times to close all the dialog boxes and return to your Calendar.

You can use the Swap Time Zones button in the Time Zone dialog box to replace the current time zone with the second one. Swapping time zones changes all time-related fields, such as when messages are received or the time of appointments, to the new time zone.

Labeling Appointments with Color

To make important appointments stand out in your Calendar, you can color-code appointments and events, choosing from one of ten preset *labels* such as Important, Business, Personal, Vacation, Travel Required, and Phone Call, or editing the options to suit your needs. You can also mark an appointment as *private*. Private appointments appear in your Calendar, but the details are hidden from others.

In this exercise, you will change an appointment label and then learn how to change the preset labels.

USE the *SBSCalendar* data file in the practice file folder for this topic. This practice file is located in the *My Documents\Microsoft Press\Office 2003 SBS\Calendar* folder and can also be accessed by clicking *Start/All Programs/Microsoft Press/Microsoft Office System 2003 Step by Step*.
BE SURE TO open the *SBSCalendar* data file before beginning this exercise.

1 In the practice calendar, navigate to June 24, 2003.

Notice that the Day Care Duty appointment is colored green.

2 Double-click the *Day Care Duty* appointment.

The Appointment form appears. Notice that *Personal* is selected in the Label box.

3 Click the down arrow to the right of the **Label** box.

Note the preset options.

4 In the drop-down list, click **Must Attend**.

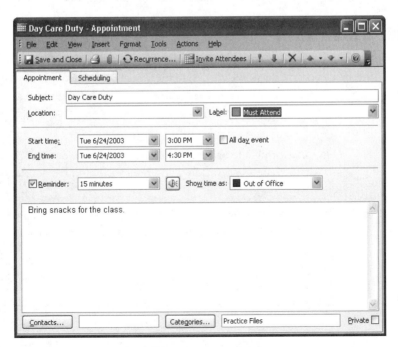

Save and Close

5 Click the **Save and Close** button. If Outlook warns you that the reminder will not appear, click **Yes**.

The updated appointment is saved in your Calendar and the color changes to orange, to indicate that this is a very important appointment.

Calendar
Coloring

6 On the toolbar, click the **Calendar Coloring** button, and then click **Edit Labels**.

The Edit Calendar Labels dialog box opens.

7 Review the preset options, and then click **Cancel** to close the dialog box without making any changes.

Printing Calendars

When your schedule is full and you find yourself running from one appointment to the next, you might not always be able to check your Outlook Calendar. By printing your Calendar, you can take your schedule with you. You can print your Calendar in a variety of formats, called *print styles*. You can select from the following pre-defined print styles:

- *Daily Style* prints the selected date range with one day per page. Printed elements include the date, day, TaskPad and reference month calendars, along with an area for notes.

- *Weekly Style* prints the selected date range with one calendar week per page, including reference calendars for the selected and following months.

■ *Monthly Style* prints a page for each month in the selected date range. Each page includes the six-week range surrounding the month, along with reference calendars for the selected and following months.

■ *Tri-fold Style* prints a page for each day in the selected date range. Each page includes the daily schedule, weekly schedule, and TaskPad.

■ *Calendar Details Style* lists your appointments for the selected date range, as well as the accompanying appointment details.

You select the date or range of dates to be printed each time you print.

In this exercise, you will print your Calendar in the Daily, Tri-fold, and Monthly styles.

Important To complete this exercise, you must have a printer installed. To install a printer, click the Start button and then click Control Panel. In Control Panel, click Printers and Other Hardware, and then click "Add a printer." If you are working on a network, your administrator can provide the information you need to install a printer.

BE SURE TO install a printer before beginning this exercise.

Go to Today

1 With your Calendar displayed in Outlook, on the toolbar, click the **Go to Today** button.

The Calendar displays your day's schedule.

Print

2 On the toolbar, click the **Print** button.

The Print dialog box appears, with the Daily Style format and today's date automatically selected.

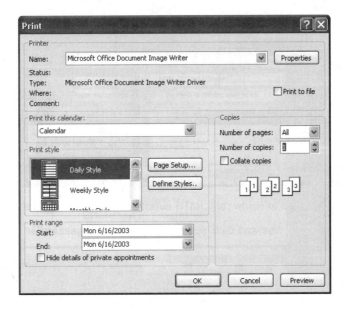

3 Click **OK**.

Outlook prints today's schedule in the Daily Style format, which approximates the Day view.

4 On the toolbar, click the **Print** button again.

The Print dialog box appears, with Daily Style and today's date as the default options.

5 In the **Print style** list, click **Tri-fold Style**.

6 In the **Print range** area, click the down arrow to the right of the **End** box, and click the date two days from today.

7 Click the **Preview** button.

The tri-fold calendar is displayed in Print Preview.

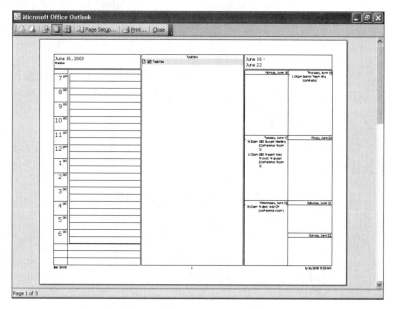

8 On the Print Preview window toolbar, click the **Print** button.

Outlook prints three pages—one page for each day of the selected date range—and closes the Print Preview window.

9   On the toolbar, click the **Print** button again.

Note that Outlook doesn't retain your settings from one print session to the next.

10   In the **Print style** list, click **Monthly Style**.

11   In the **Print range** area, click the down arrow to the right of the **Start** box, and in the drop-down list, click the last day of the current month.

12   Click the down arrow to the right of the **End** box, and in the drop-down list, click the first day of the next month.

13   Click the **Preview** button.

The monthly calendar is displayed in Print Preview.

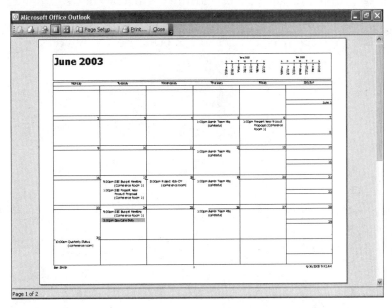

14   On the Print Preview window toolbar, click the **Print** button.

Outlook prints two pages—one page for each month in which the selected date range falls—and closes the Print Preview window.

CLOSE the *SBSCalendar* data file and exit Outlook.

Key Points

■ The Calendar tracks and organizes appointments. Appointments can be any length and can recur at any interval. Appointments can have a location and can contain notes.

■ You can further organize your appointments by assigning them to categories or folders. You can add color-coded labels to appointments and create rules for Outlook to label appointments for you.

■ You can view multiple calendars side by side. Calendars are color-coded for easy reference.

■ You can view your calendar by the day, work week, full week, or month. Your calendar can display times for multiple time zones.

■ You can print you calendar in predefined Daily, Weekly, or Monthly styles, or create your own print style.

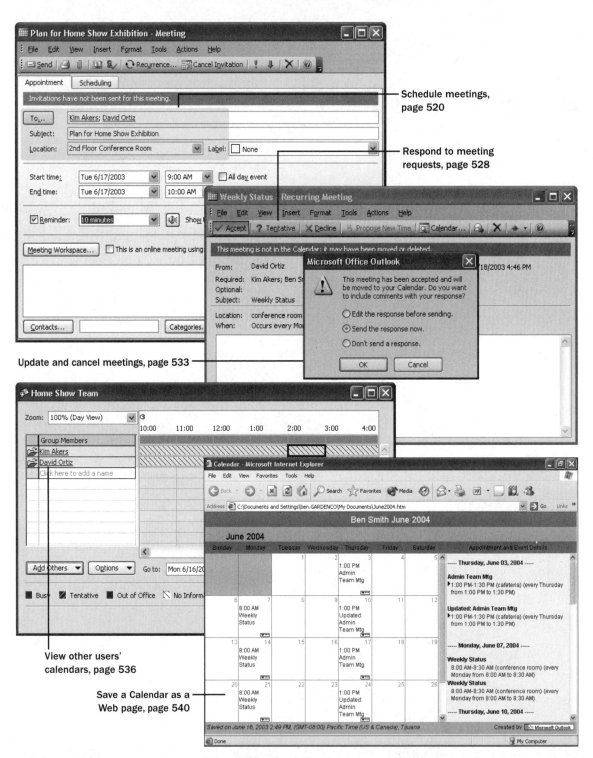

Schedule meetings, page 520

Respond to meeting requests, page 528

Update and cancel meetings, page 533

View other users' calendars, page 536

Save a Calendar as a Web page, page 540

21 Scheduling and Managing Meetings

In this chapter you will learn to:

✔ Schedule meetings.

✔ Respond to meeting requests.

✔ Update and cancel meetings.

✔ View other users' calendars.

✔ Save a Calendar as a Web page.

Microsoft Office Outlook 2003 can help you with the often onerous task of organizing meetings. You can organize meetings that happen in a particular place and meetings that happen online. You can view other attendees' *calendars* to check their availability. You can send meeting invitations and track attendee responses. And as schedules change, you can update or cancel scheduled meetings.

When another person organizes a meeting, you can respond to the meeting request manually or automatically; if the meeting time doesn't suit you, you can suggest a different time or date, while ensuring that all meeting attendees are kept up-to-date with the changes.

If you need to keep people other people informed of your schedule, you can publish your Outlook Calendar to the Internet and make it available to colleagues, friends, and family members who need the information. If you don't want to share all your calendar details, you can publish only information about when you are available and when you are busy.

See Also   Do you need only a quick refresher on the topics in this chapter? See the Quick Reference entries on page xxxiii.

Important   Before you can use the practice files in this chapter, you need to install them from the book's companion CD to their default location. See "Using the Book's CD-ROM" on page xxi for more information.

Scheduling Meetings

With Outlook, you can schedule meetings, invite attendees—both those who work for your organization and those who don't—and reserve resources such as conference rooms or equipment. To choose a date and time for your meeting, you can check the availability of attendees and resources by viewing their free/busy information. When inviting attendees from within your organization, you can automatically see their Outlook Calendar information. You can see free/busy information for people outside of your organization only if they make this information available over the Internet.

You also can have Outlook select the meeting time for you. You can indicate whether the attendance of each invitee is required or optional. Outlook uses this information when looking for available meeting times, prioritizing times that work for all required attendees and most optional attendees.

After you have selected a time, you send a *meeting request*—a type of e-mail message—to each invited attendee and requested resource. Responses from attendees and those responsible for scheduling the resources you requested are automatically tracked as you receive them.

In this exercise, you will plan a meeting, invite attendees, and set and then remove a meeting *reminder.*

USE the *SBSMeetings* data file in the practice file folder for this topic. This practice file is located in the *My Documents\Microsoft Press\Office 2003 SBS\Meetings* folder and can also be accessed by clicking *Start/All Programs/Microsoft Press/Microsoft Office System 2003 Step by Step.*
BE SURE TO start Outlook before beginning this exercise.
OPEN the *SBSMeetings* data file from within Outlook, and then open the practice Contacts in the *SBS Meetings* data file folder.

1   In the **Navigation Pane**, click the **Folder List** icon.

2   In the practice Contacts folder, hold down the ⌃Ctrl key and drag the **Kim Akers** contact to your own Contacts folder. Then hold down the ⌃Ctrl key and drag the **David Ortiz** contact to your own Contacts folder.

3   In the *SBS Meetings* data file folder, click the practice Calendar.

4   In the Date Navigator, scroll to June 2003, and then click **18**.

The Calendar displays the schedule for June 18, 2003.

5   On the **Actions** menu, click **Plan a Meeting**.

The Plan a Meeting form appears, listing you as the only attendee in the All Attendees list. The icon next to your name indicates that you are the meeting organizer. By default, the first available timeslot is selected for the meeting.

Meeting Organizer icon

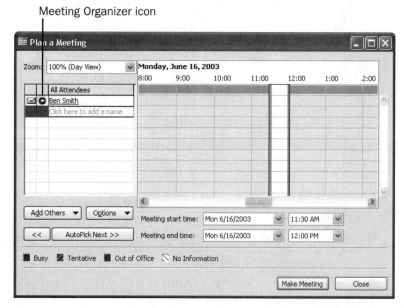

6   Click the **Add Others** button, and in the drop-down list, click **Add from Address Book**.

The Select Attendees and Resources dialog box appears, with your name in the Required box.

Important   In this exercise, you have been provided with contact information for fictitious employees of The Garden Company. If you want, you can use the names of your co-workers or other contacts to plan an actual meeting.

7   If you want to complete this exercise using the fictitious contacts, click the down arrow to the right of the **Show Names from the** box, and then click **Contacts**.

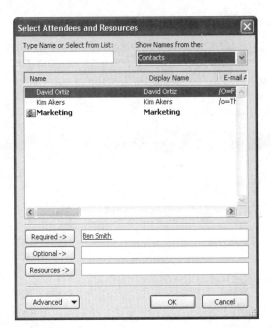

8   In the **Name** list, click **Kim Akers**, and then click the **Required** button.

The selected name is added to the Required Attendees box.

9   In the **Name** list, click **David Ortiz**, and then click the **Optional** button.

The selected name is added to the Optional Attendees box.

10   Click **OK**. If prompted to join the *Microsoft Office Internet Free/Busy Service*, click **Cancel**.

The attendees are added to the All Attendees list, with icons that indicate whether their attendance is required or optional.

Optional Attendee icon

Required Attendee icon

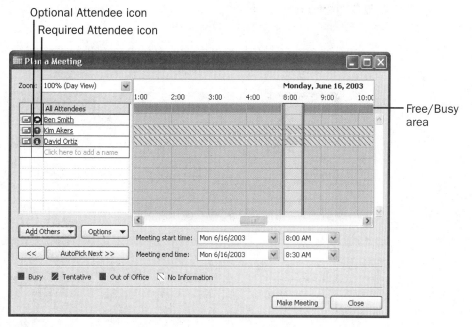

Free/Busy area

11 Use the horizontal scroll bar in the Free/Busy area to view attendee availability for Tuesday, June 17, 2003.

This area shows whether attendees are free, tentatively scheduled, busy, or out of the office. Busy time appears in blue, tentatively scheduled time in blue stripes, and time out of the office in purple. (If you are using fictitious names, free/busy information will not be available.)

12 In the Free/Busy area, click the 9:00 A.M. time slot to select that time.

The half-hour time slot you clicked appears as a vertical white bar. The "Meeting start time" and "Meeting end time" boxes change to reflect the date and time you selected.

Tip　To quickly find the next available free time for all attendees and resources, click the AutoPick Next button in the Plan a Meeting dialog box or on the Scheduling tab of the Meeting form.

13 In the Free/Busy area, click the red bar on the right edge of the selected meeting time, and drag it to 10:00 A.M.

The second "Meeting end time" setting reflects the change—the meeting is now scheduled to last for one hour.

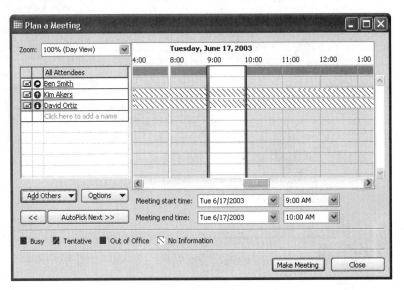

14 Click the **Make Meeting** button.

A new, untitled Meeting form appears with the attendees and meeting time information already set.

15 In the **Subject** box, type Plan for Home Show Exhibition, press the Tab key, and in the **Location** box, type 2nd Floor Conference Room.

16 Select the **Reminder** check box, click the down arrow to the right of the **Reminder** box, and then click **10 minutes**.

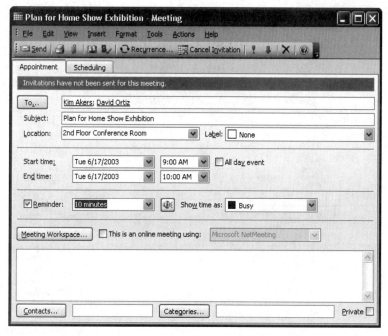

17 On the toolbar, click the **Send** button.

The meeting request is sent.

Important If the attendees you provided are fictitious, e-mail messages you send to them will be returned as undeliverable. You can delete the returned messages at any time.

Close

18 In the **Plan a Meeting** dialog box, click the **Close** button.

The Plan a Meeting form closes.

19 In the Calendar, navigate to June 17, 2003.

The meeting request appears in the 9:00 A.M. – 10:00 A.M. time slot.

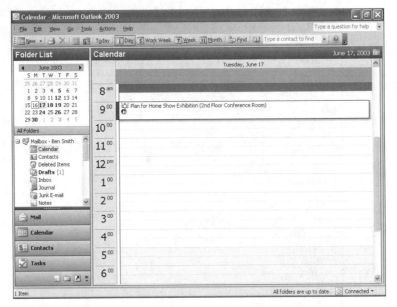

20 Double-click the **Plan for Home Show Exhibition** meeting.

The Meeting form opens.

21 Clear the **Reminder** check box.

22 On the toolbar, click the **Save and Close** button.

The updated meeting is saved. You will not receive a reminder for the meeting, but your meeting attendees will.

Scheduling Meeting Resources

If you are working on a network that uses *Microsoft Exchange Server* and your system administrator has added resources (such as conference rooms, audiovisual equipment, or meeting supplies) to the organization's *Global Address List*, you can reserve those resources for a specific meeting by inviting them to the meeting. Your meeting request is sent to the person designated by your administrator to manage the schedule for the resource. That person responds to your meeting request based on the availability of the resource at the time you requested.

To schedule a resource while creating a meeting request:

1 In the **Meeting** form, click the **Scheduling** tab.

2 Click the **Add Others** button, and then click **Add from Address Book**.

The Select Attendees and Resources dialog box appears.

3   In the **Name** list, select the resource or resources you want to add, click the **Resources** button, and then click **OK**.

4   Send the meeting request as usual.

To schedule a resource for an existing meeting:

1   Open the **Meeting** form.

2   On the **Scheduling** tab, add the resources you want.

3   Click the **Send Update** button.

Scheduling and Hosting Online Meetings

With *NetMeeting*, a program that comes with Microsoft Internet Explorer, you can conduct online meetings over the Internet. You can use NetMeeting to conduct audio and video conferences with one or more other people. NetMeeting conference participants can share applications, collaborate on documents, draw on a shared electronic whiteboard, or transfer files.

To take full advantage of NetMeeting's audio and video capabilities, you need an audio card, video card, speakers, microphone, and camera connected to your computer. Without a camera, you can view other people's video, but they cannot view yours.

To schedule a NetMeeting:

1   Create a new meeting request, including the attendees, subject, and meeting start and end times.

2   Select the **Reminder** check box.

3   Select the **This is an online meeting using** check box, and select **Microsoft NetMeeting** in the adjacent box. You might have to enlarge the window to see its entire contents.

4   Click in the **Directory Server** box, type logon.netmeeting.microsoft.com (the name of the Microsoft Internet Directory server).

5   Select the **Automatically start NetMeeting with Reminder** check box.

6   On the toolbar, click the **Send** button.

The meeting request is sent. When the meeting time arrives, NetMeeting starts automatically so that you and the other attendees can connect to the conference.

Your organization might use a *directory server* other than the one named above. Contact your system administrator or ISP for more information.

To host a meeting in NetMeeting, start NetMeeting, and on the Call menu, click Host Meeting. In the Host Meeting dialog box that appears, you can give the meeting a name and password, and set the options for the meeting, including who can place outgoing calls, accept incoming calls, and use NetMeeting features. You can also choose whether or not to require security for the meeting.

Find Someone
in a Directory

After the meeting has started, you can place calls to other meeting attendees by clicking New Call on the Call menu. If you don't know an attendee's address, you can find it by clicking the Find Someone in a Directory button and searching for the person's address in the directory.

Tip   For more information on using NetMeeting, start NetMeeting, and on the Help menu, click Help Topics. To start NetMeeting, click the Start button, point to Run, type **conf**, and click OK.

Responding to Meeting Requests

Just as you can send meeting requests, other people can send them to you. When you receive a meeting request, you can respond in one of four ways:

- You can accept the request and inform the requester that you will attend. Meetings that you accept are automatically entered in your Calendar.

- You can tentatively accept a request, indicating that you might be able to attend the meeting. Meetings that you accept tentatively are also entered in your Calendar, but your free/busy information will show you as only tentatively scheduled for that time.

- You can propose a new meeting time, in which case the request is referred to the meeting organizer for confirmation. Your Calendar shows the proposed new meeting time as tentatively scheduled.

- You can decline a meeting, in which case the request is deleted and no entry is made in your Calendar. When you decline a meeting, you can choose whether Outlook notifies the person who sent the request.

In this exercise, you will accept a meeting request, decline a meeting request, and propose a new meeting time in response to a meeting request.

USE the *SBSMeetings* data file in the practice file folder for this topic. This practice file is located in the *My Documents\Microsoft Press\Office 2003 SBS\Meetings* folder and can also be accessed by clicking *Start/All Programs/Microsoft Press/Microsoft Office System 2003 Step by Step*.
BE SURE TO start Outlook and open the *SBSMeetings* data file before beginning this exercise.
OPEN the practice Inbox in the *SBS Meetings* data file folder.

1   In the practice Inbox, double-click the **Weekly Status** meeting request.

The Meeting form appears.

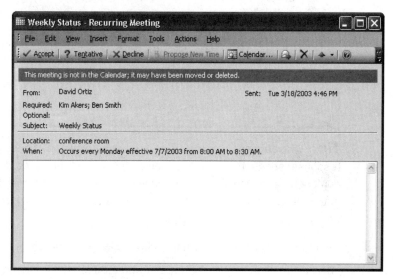

 2   To view the meeting in your Calendar before you respond, click the **Calendar** button on the toolbar.

Your Calendar appears in a new window, displaying the date of the requested meeting. For recurring meetings, the date of the first meeting is displayed. The requested meeting has a blue-striped bar at the left, which means it is tentatively scheduled.

Close

3   In the open Calendar window, click the **Close** button.

The Calendar closes.

4   On the **Meeting** form, click the **Accept** button.

A message box appears, prompting you to choose how you want to respond.

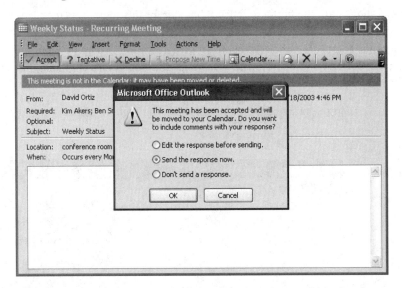

Tip   When accepting or declining a meeting, you can choose to send a standard response, send a response that you compose yourself, or send no response. If you don't send a response to the meeting organizer, your acceptance will not be tallied in the Meeting form. The organizer and other attendees will not know whether you are planning to attend the meeting.

5   With the **Send the response now** option selected, click **OK**.

Your response is sent to the person who requested the meeting, the Meeting form closes, and the meeting is entered in your Calendar.

6   In the Inbox, click the **Project Kick-Off** meeting request; then in the Reading Pane, click the **Decline** button.

A message box appears, prompting you to choose how you want to respond.

7   With the **Edit the response before sending** option selected, click **OK**.

The Meeting Response form appears. The status bar and Subject box indicate that you are declining the Project Kick-Off meeting request.

8   In the message body, type I will be out of the office on this day.

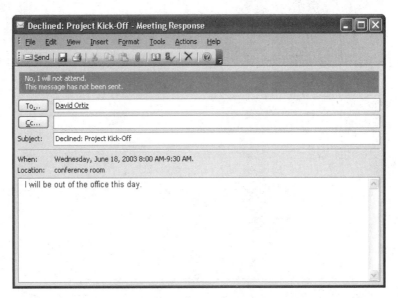

9 On the toolbar, click the **Send** button.

Your response is sent, and the Meeting form closes. The meeting is not added to your Calendar.

10 In the Inbox, right-click the **Quarterly Status** message, and on the shortcut menu, click **Propose New Time**. If prompted to join the Microsoft Office Internet Free/Busy Service, click **Cancel**.

The Propose New Time dialog box appears. The current meeting time is indicated in yellow.

11 In the Free/Busy area, click the **11:00** column, and drag the Meeting Time's right edge to 12:00. Then click the **10:00** column, and drag the Meeting Time's left edge to 11:00.

The meeting start and end times are updated to reflect your changes.

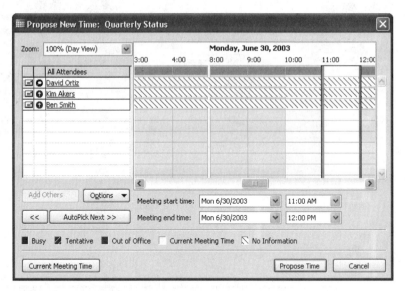

12 Click the **Propose Time** button.

The Propose New Time dialog box closes, and the Meeting Response form appears. The subject of the response indicates that you are proposing a new time for the meeting.

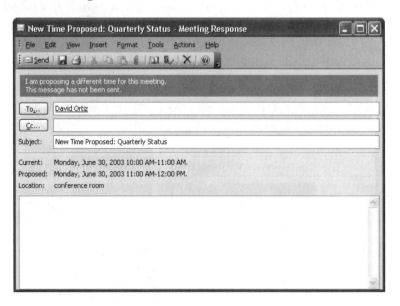

13 In the body of the message, type I will be out of the office on Monday morning., and on the toolbar, click the **Send** button.

Your response is sent, and the Meeting form closes. The meeting is added to your Calendar as tentatively scheduled for the original meeting time.

Automatically Responding to Meeting Requests

You can choose to respond to meeting requests automatically. Outlook will process meeting requests and cancellations as you receive them, responding to requests, adding new meetings to your calendar, and removing cancelled meetings from your calendar. If you choose, Outlook will automatically decline meeting requests that conflict with existing items on your calendar. You can also choose to automatically decline any request for a *recurring* meeting.

To instruct Outlook to automatically respond to meeting requests:

1 On the **Tools** menu, click **Options**.

The Options dialog box appears.

2 On the **Preferences** tab, click the **Calendar Options** button, and then click the **Resource Scheduling** button.

The Resource Scheduling dialog box appears.

3 Select the **Automatically accept meeting requests and process cancellations** check box.

4 Select the **Automatically decline conflicting meeting requests** and/or the **Automatically decline recurring meeting requests** check boxes if you want Outlook to do this.

5 Click **OK** to close each open dialog box.

Updating and Canceling Meetings

People's schedules can shift on a daily basis. Outlook makes it easy to update or cancel meetings as your needs change. For example, an important attendee might be sick or delayed, or have other plans come up that take precedence over your meeting. In this case, you can change the date or time of the meeting or cancel the meeting altogether. You can also add people to or remove people from the list of attendees.

In this exercise, you will create a meeting, reschedule the meeting, change the meeting attendees, and cancel the meeting.

BE SURE TO inform your practice meeting attendees that you are not scheduling a real meeting.
OPEN your Calendar.

Go to Today

1 In your Calendar, click the **Go to Today** button

Your schedule for today is displayed.

New
Appointment

2 On the toolbar, click the **New Appointment** button.

3 In the **Subject** box, type SBS Practice.

4 On the **Scheduling** tab, click the **Add Others** button, and then click **Add from Address Book**.

5 Invite two people from your address list to the meeting, and then click **OK**.

6 On the Meeting form toolbar, click the **Send** button.

You now have a meeting with which to work.

7 In the Calendar, double-click the **SBS Practice** meeting.

The Meeting form appears.

8 Click the **Scheduling** tab, and in the Free/Busy area, scroll to the next business day.

9 Click the **11:00 A.M.** time slot, and drag the right edge of the shaded area to **12:00 P.M.** to schedule the meeting to last for one hour.

The start and end times reflect the changes you made to the date and time.

10 In the **All Attendees** list, click the name of one of your invited attendees; press the [Del] key, and then press [Tab].

The attendee is removed from the list.

11 On the toolbar, click the **Send Update** button.

The updated Meeting form is sent. The removed attendee receives a meeting cancellation.

12 In the Date Navigator, click the next business day, and then double-click the **SBS Practice** meeting.

13 In the **Meeting** form, click the **Tracking** tab.

The Tracking tab displays the response received from each attendee.

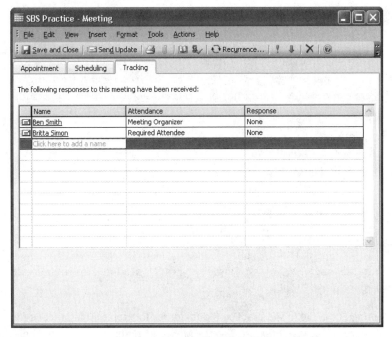

14 On the **Actions** menu, click **Cancel Meeting**.

A message box appears, prompting you to send a cancellation notice to the attendees.

15 With the **Send cancellation and delete meeting** option selected, click **OK**.

16 On the toolbar, click the **Send** button.

The cancellation notice is sent to all remaining attendees, the Meeting form closes, and the meeting is removed from your Calendar.

Tip You can easily send a new e-mail message to all attendees of a particular meeting. Simply open the meeting, and on the Actions menu, click New Message to Attendees. (This method works only on meetings for which attendees have already been invited.)

Viewing Other Users' Calendars

When organizing a meeting, it's helpful to be able to see when attendees are available without having to contact each person individually. With Outlook, you can see when people are free or busy by inviting them to a meeting, adding them to a group schedule, or viewing an Internet or intranet location where they publish their schedules.

A group schedule shows you the combined schedules of a number of people or resources at a glance. For example, you might create a group schedule containing all the people on your project team so you can quickly see when the entire team is available for a discussion.

If you are working on a network that uses Exchange Server, the free/busy information of other network users is available to you by default. In addition, if a person connected to your network has shared his or her Calendar, you can open that person's calendar directly.

In this exercise, you will create a group schedule and then create a meeting from that schedule.

USE the *SBSMeetings* data file in the practice file folder for this topic. This practice file is located in the *My Documents\Microsoft Press\Office 2003 SBS\Meetings* folder and can also be accessed by clicking *Start/All Programs/Microsoft Press/Microsoft Office System 2003 Step by Step*.
BE SURE TO open the *SBSMeetings* data file before beginning this exercise.
OPEN the practice Calendar in the *SBS Meetings* data file folder.

View Group
Schedules

1 With the Calendar displayed, on the toolbar, click the **View Group Schedules** button.

The Group Schedules dialog box appears.

2 Click the **New** button.

The Create New Group Schedule dialog box appears.

3 In the **Type a name for the new Group Schedule** box, type Home Show Team, and then click **OK**.

The Home Show Team group schedule appears, with the current date and time slot selected.

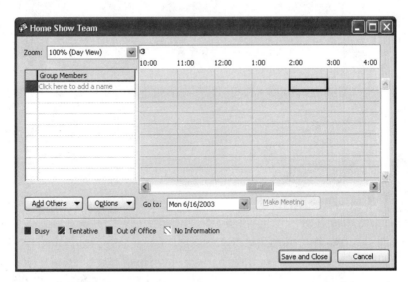

4 Click the **Add Others** button, and then in the drop-down list click **Add from Address Book**.

The Select Members dialog box appears.

5 To complete this exercise using the fictitious employees of The Garden Company, click the down arrow to the right of the **Show Names from the** list, and then click **Contacts**.

Tip You can complete this exercise with your own contacts. Simply select names from your Global Address List in place of the names given here.

6 In the **Name** box, click **Kim Akers**, hold down the ⌃ key, click **David Ortiz**, and then click the **To** button.

The names are added to the To list.

7 Click **OK**. If prompted to join the Microsoft Office Internet Free/Busy Service, click **Cancel**.

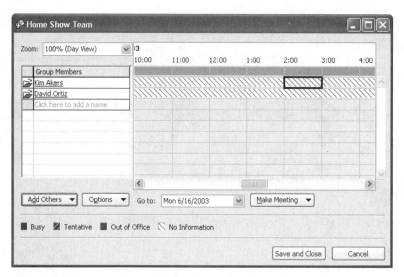

8 To see the most recent schedule information for the group members, click the **Options** button, and then click **Refresh Free/Busy**.

The Free/Busy area is updated. Outlook gathers information from wherever the free/busy information for your group members is stored—your Microsoft Exchange Server, the Microsoft Office Internet Free/Busy Service, or the Internet or Intranet locations selected by group members.

9 Click the down arrow to the right of the **Go to** box, and then click the next Monday.

The Free/Busy area shows the data for the date you selected. However, only half the day is visible.

10 Click the down arrow to the right of the **Zoom** box, and then click **50% (Week View)** on the drop-down list.

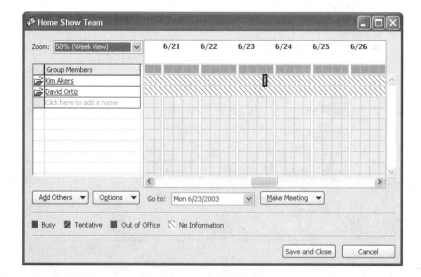

11 The Free/Busy area displays more of each person's schedule.

12 Click the **Make Meeting** button, and then click **New Meeting with All** in the drop-down list.

A new Meeting form appears, with the group members' names in the To box.

Close

13 Click the **Close** button, and when prompted to save your changes, click **No**.

The Meeting form closes, discarding the meeting request. If prompted to save your changes, click **No**.

14 In the **Home Show Team** group schedule, click the **Cancel** button.

The group schedule closes.

CLOSE the *SBS Meetings* data file and delete the Kim Akers and David Ortiz contacts from your Contacts folder.

Sharing Calendars

You can share your Calendar with other network users just as you would any other folder. To share your Calendar with another network user:

1 In the **Folder List**, right-click the **Calendar**, and then click **Sharing** on the shortcut menu.

2 On the **Permissions** tab of the **Calendar Properties** dialog box, click **Add**.

3 Select the person or people with whom you want to share your Calendar, and then click **OK**.

4 In the **Permissions** area, indicate the permissions you want to give the other network users, and then click **OK**.

If another network user shares his or her Calendar with you, you can open it on your own computer (for instance, to view it side by side with your own). To view a shared Calendar:

1 On the **File** menu, point to **Open**, and click **Other User's Folder**.

The Open Other User's Folder dialog box appears.

2 Click the **Name** button, click the name of a person who has shared his or her Calendar, and then click **OK**.

3 In the **Folder type** box, click **Calendar**, and then click **OK**.

The other user's calendar is displayed.

Saving a Calendar as a Web Page

To help you coordinate your plans with others, you can share your schedule over an intranet or the Internet. Your co-workers and clients can view your schedule even if they aren't using Microsoft Outlook. You can also share your schedule by saving your Calendar as a Web page or by publishing your free and busy times for others to see.

For example, you might post a calendar with important project dates on your company intranet, or you might publish to an Internet location, for your clients to view, the times that you are busy and the times when you are available. When you save your Calendar as a Web page, you can easily post it to any Web site to share it with colleagues, friends, or family members.

Tip   When you save your Calendar as a Web page, you can save it to your local computer or a network location. You might have to take additional steps to make that Web page available to others. Your network or ISP administrator can provide the information you need.

In this exercise, you will save your Calendar as a Web page that can be posted on an Internet or intranet site.

OPEN your own Calendar.

1   On the **File** menu, click **Save as Web Page**.

The Save as Web Page dialog box appears.

2   In the **Start date** box, type 6/1/04, press the ⌷Tab⌷ key, and in the **End date** box, type 6/30/04.

3   Click in the **Calendar title** box, delete any existing text, type your name followed by June 2004, and then click the **Browse** button.

The Calendar File Name dialog box appears.

4   On the **Places** bar, click **My Documents**.

5   In the **File name** box, type June2004, and then click the **Select** button.

The Calendar File Name dialog box closes, and the file name and the path to it are inserted into the "File name" box.

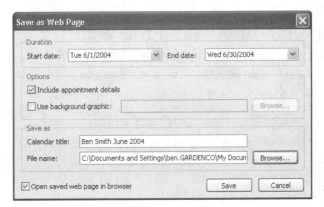

6 Be sure the **Open saved web page in browser** check box is selected, and then click the **Save** button.

The Save as Web Page dialog box closes, and the schedule is displayed in your Web browser. (The browser is loading the file from your computer, not the Internet—you haven't published the schedule to the Internet yet.)

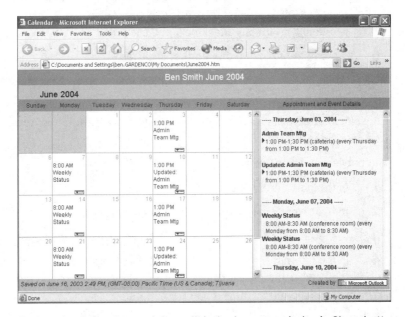

Close

7 Review the Calendar, and then click the browser window's **Close** button.

The Web browser window closes.

Sharing Schedule Information on the Web

Microsoft offers a Web-based service called the Microsoft Office Internet Free/Busy Service that you can use to publish information about your free and busy times to a designated, secure Internet location. If you and your colleagues don't have access to each other's calendars but do have access to the Internet, each of you can join this service and publish your free/busy information for others to view. Easy access to this information can save you a lot of time when you need to coordinate the schedules of a group of busy people.

To make your Calendar information available to other Office users:

1   On the **Tools** menu, click **Options**.

2   In the **Calendar** area, click the **Calendar Options** button, and then in the **Advanced options** area, click the **Free/Busy Options** button.

3   In the **Free/Busy Options** dialog box, select the **Publish and search using Microsoft Office Internet Free/Busy Service** check box.

4   If you want to request that other people make their schedules available through the Microsoft Office Internet Free/Busy Service, select the **Request free/busy information in meeting invitations** check box, and click **OK**.

5   If prompted to install the feature, click **Yes**.

6   When installation is complete, click **OK** to close the open dialog boxes.

You can also choose to publish your free/busy information to an intranet location you specify. Your administrator can provide you with the path to the appropriate location on your organization's intranet.

To publish your free/busy information to an intranet site:

1   In Outlook, on the **Tools** menu, click **Options**.

2   In the **Calendar** area, click the **Calendar Options** button.

3   In the **Advanced options** area, click the **Free/Busy Options** button.

4   In the **Internet Free/Busy** area, select the **Publish at my location** check box, click in the **Publish at my location** box, and type the server location provided by your administrator, followed by the file name you want.

5   Click **OK** to close each of the open dialog boxes.

     Your free/busy information is published to the specified location.

6   On the **Tools** menu, point to **Send/Receive**, and then click **Free/Busy Information** to publish your free/busy information to your server.

7   To view your published free/busy information, open your Web browser, and in the **Address** box, type the URL of the file on the server.

Your free/busy information appears as a text file in your browser window.

8   Review the information, and click the browser's **Close** button.

The Web browser window closes.

The contents of the "Publish at my location" box will typically be something like *server**share**username**June2002.vfb*. Include the full path and file name in the "Publish at my location" box.

The retrieval URL might not be the same as the path you entered in the "Publish at my location" box. Your administrator can provide you with the URL.

Key Points

- You can share your Calendar so that other members of your organization can see your appointments and meetings, or share just your free and busy times. You can also publish your Calendar on the Internet or your intranet.

- You can use Outlook to set up meetings, invite participants, and track their responses. If participants share their free and busy information, Outlook can choose a meeting time that best fits their schedules, or you can create a group schedule to show when everyone is free.

- Your organization can add conference rooms, projectors, and other resources to its address book and use Outlook to schedule their use.

- You can use Internet Explorer's NetMeeting feature to hold online meetings.

VI
Microsoft Office
FrontPage 2003

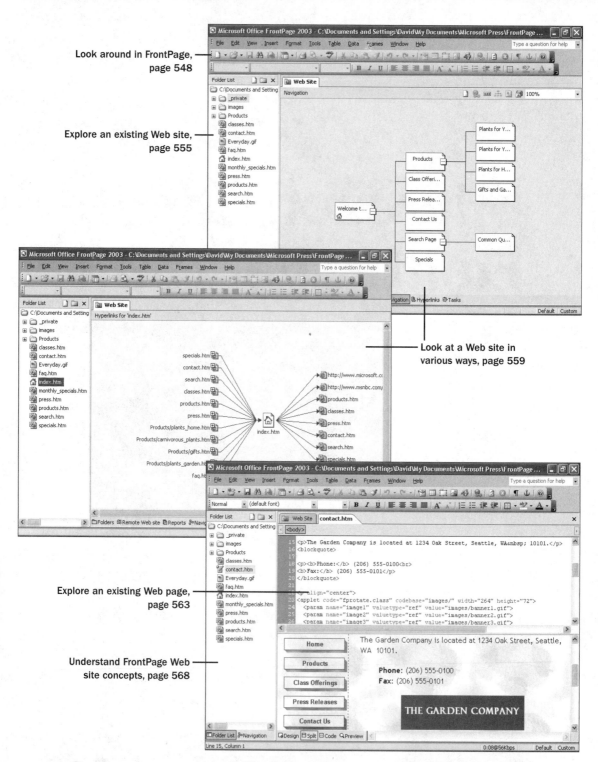

Look around in FrontPage, page 548

Explore an existing Web site, page 555

Look at a Web site in various ways, page 559

Explore an existing Web page, page 563

Understand FrontPage Web site concepts, page 568

Chapter 22 at a Glance

22 Understanding How FrontPage Works

In this chapter you will learn to:

✔ Look around in FrontPage.

✔ Explore an existing Web site.

✔ Look at a Web site in various ways.

✔ Explore an existing Web page.

✔ Understand FrontPage Web site concepts.

Microsoft Office FrontPage 2003 is a comprehensive application that you can use to develop Web sites. This sophisticated program includes everything you need to create Web sites ranging from a simple Web-based résumé to a complex Web-based retail store.

In spite of its sophistication, FrontPage is easy to use. As a member of *The Microsoft Office System 2003* suite of applications, it works pretty much the same way the other Office applications do. If you've avoided trying to create Web sites because you didn't want to learn how to program in *Hypertext Markup Language (HTML)*, FrontPage might well be the answer you've been waiting for. With FrontPage, you can easily create good-looking, interesting Web sites that incorporate complex elements, without typing a single line of programming code. But if you have some HTML programming experience or want to feel more in control, FrontPage gives you easy access to the code that it creates behind the scenes. You can view and edit the underlying HTML code at any time; but the great thing is that you don't have to. No programming experience is necessary to become a successful FrontPage developer.

This chapter introduces FrontPage and explains the concept of a FrontPage-based Web site. You will learn how to open an existing Web site, how to navigate between Web pages, and how to view the pages in different ways. You will then look at various ways of working in FrontPage and learn how to locate and control the FrontPage features you are likely to want to use in your own Web sites. In addition, you will learn how to view the underlying HTML code that makes all Web sites work. You will also get an overview of the different types of Web sites you can create with FrontPage and of the decision-making tools and resources that are necessary to create, manage, and maintain a personal or commercial Web site.

The exercises in this chapter and throughout the book are built around a Web site created for a fictitious garden and plant store called The Garden Company. The sample Web site, which is named *GardenCo*, contains realistic examples of content and structure that serve to demonstrate the concepts covered in each chapter.

See Also　Do you need only a quick refresher on the topics in this chapter? See the Quick Reference entries on page xxxiii.

Important　Before you can use the practice files in this chapter, you need to install them from the book's companion CD to their default location. See "Using the Book's CD-ROM" on page xxi for more information.

Looking Around in FrontPage

For those of you who don't have much experience with the other applications in the Office 2003 suite, here is a summary of some of the basic techniques you will use to work with FrontPage.

FrontPage 2003 commands are available from 11 *menus*. Office 2003 applications feature the same expanding, dynamic menus that were first made available in Office 2000. The menu commands used most often move to the top of each menu, making them easier to access. The menu commands you don't use are tucked out of sight, but can be easily accessed by clicking the double chevron at the bottom of the menu. Menu commands that are followed by an arrowhead have submenus. Menu commands that are followed by an ellipsis (...) open dialog boxes or task panes where you provide the information necessary to carry out the command.

Most of the menu commands are also represented graphically on 15 *toolbars*, all of which are customizable. The graphic on the toolbar buttons corresponds to the graphic next to the same command on the menu. Each of the buttons has a *ScreenTip* to tell you the name of the command.

Menu and toolbar options are unavailable when the option can't be applied either to the environment you're working in or to the specific object that is selected. Available menu commands are displayed in black; unavailable commands are *dimmed*, or displayed in a gray font.

In this exercise, you will learn to start and exit FrontPage. You will also look at the commands that are available on the FrontPage 2003 menus and toolbars, experiment with different ways of displaying the toolbars, and close a file.

BE SURE TO start your computer, but don't start FrontPage before beginning this exercise.

1   At the left end of the taskbar at the bottom of your screen, click the **Start** button. On the **Start** menu, point to **All Programs**, point to **Microsoft Office**, and then click **Microsoft Office FrontPage 2003**.

   Tip   Depending on your system resources, you might see a message box notifying you of additional system requirements for using certain Office 2003 features, such as Speech Recognition. If you see this message box, click OK to continue.

1   When FrontPage opens for the first time, you see a new file called *new_page_1.htm* in the Page view editing window.

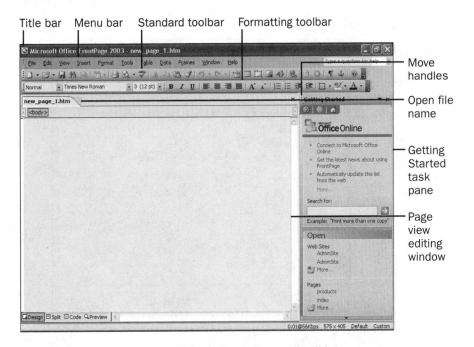

1   The Getting Started task pane is open. This task pane is displayed when FrontPage starts with no Web site open.

   Tip   If you don't want the task pane to be shown by default, click the Tools menu and then click Options. On the General tab of the Options dialog box, clear the Startup Task Pane check box, and then click OK.

2   Click the **File** menu to open it, and then click the double chevron at the bottom of the menu to expand the complete menu.

3 Study the commands available on the menu, and think about how you might use each one.

The Close Site, Publish Site, and Export commands are dimmed because they are unavailable at this time—in this case, because they apply to Web sites rather than Web pages, and no Web site is open at the moment. If you haven't previously used FrontPage, the Recent Files command is also dimmed.

Ellipses (...) follow the New, Open, Open Site, Save As, File Search, Publish Site, Import, Export, Page Setup, Print, Send, and Properties commands to indicate that each has an accompanying task pane or dialog box.

4 Click the **Properties** command to open the **Page Properties** dialog box for the current file.

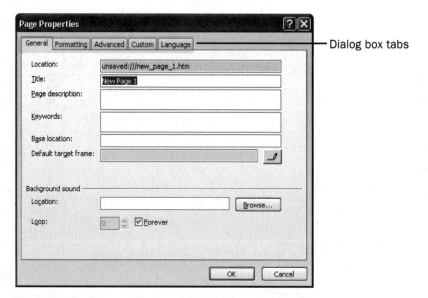

Dialog box tabs

5 Click each of the dialog box tabs to look at the available options. Then click **Cancel** to close the dialog box without effecting any changes.

6 Click the **File** menu to open it again.

Arrowheads follow the Preview in Browser, Recent Files, and Recent Sites commands to indicate that each has a submenu. Point to or click the Preview in Browser command to expand its submenu.

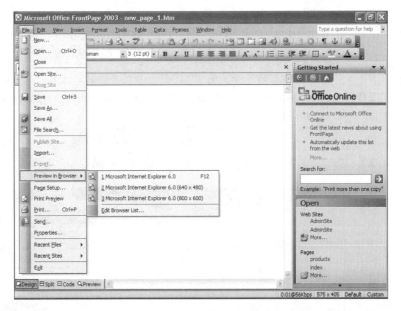

7   Repeat steps 2 through 6 for each of the remaining menus: **Edit**, **View**, **Insert**, **Format**, **Tools**, **Table**, **Data**, **Frames**, **Window**, and **Help**. Study the available and unavailable options, look at the dialog box options, and expand the submenus.

See Also   For more information about getting help with Microsoft FrontPage, refer to the "Getting Help" section at the beginning of this book.

---

8   Right-click anywhere in the menu and toolbar area at the top of the window to open the toolbar shortcut menu.

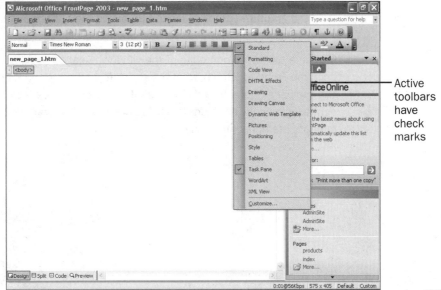

Active toolbars have check marks

Check marks indicate that the Standard and Formatting toolbars and a task pane are currently displayed. FrontPage automatically displays these two toolbars because they include buttons for the most commonly used page and file commands.

9   Press the [Esc] key to close the toolbar shortcut menu.

10 Point to each of the buttons on the Standard and Formatting toolbars to read their command names.

Each available button is highlighted as you point to it.

11 Drag the **Formatting** toolbar by its move handle to the center of the screen.

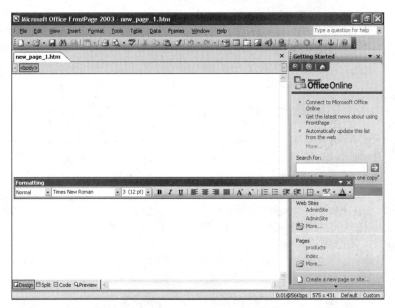

12 Drag the **Formatting** toolbar by its title bar to the left edge of the screen until it changes from horizontal to vertical orientation.

Moving a toolbar to one edge of the window is called *docking* the toolbar. You can dock the FrontPage toolbars at the top, left, bottom, or right edge of the window. The toolbar's orientation changes as it is moved. Toolbars docked on the left or right are vertically oriented; toolbars docked on the top or bottom and undocked toolbars are horizontally oriented.

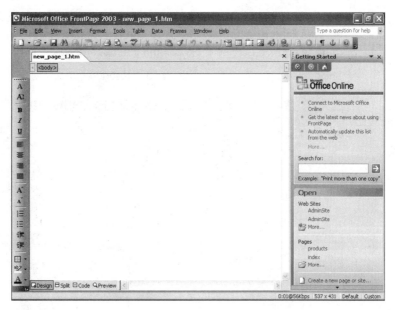

13 Right-click the Formatting toolbar to open the toolbar shortcut menu. On the toolbar shortcut menu, click **Drawing**.

The Drawing toolbar opens in its default location at the bottom of the screen.

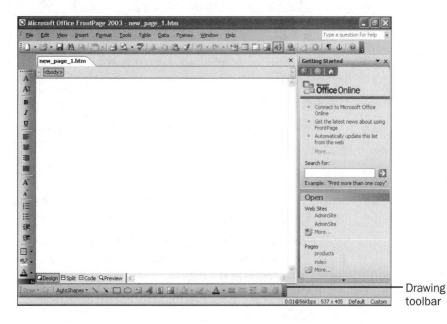

Drawing toolbar

14 Click the down arrow at the right end of the Drawing toolbar to display the **Add or Remove Buttons** command. Point to **Add or Remove Buttons**, and then point to **Drawing** to open the list of the commands that are available from the Drawing toolbar.

Check marks indicate the currently displayed commands.

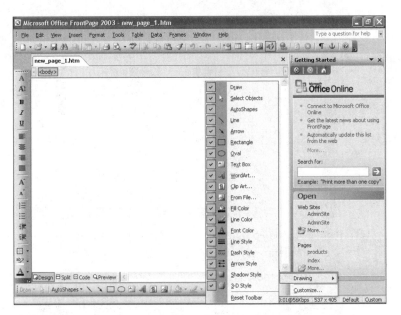

A similar list is available for each of the toolbars.

15 In the list, click the **AutoShapes**, **Line**, and **Arrow** buttons to remove them from the Drawing toolbar.

Notice that each button disappears from the toolbar as you click it.

16 Click **Reset Toolbar** to return the toolbar to its original state.

The list closes when you reset the toolbar.

Close

17 On the title bar, click the **Close** button to exit FrontPage.

18 Reopen FrontPage by clicking **Start**, pointing to **All Programs**, pointing to **Microsoft Office**, and then clicking **Microsoft Office FrontPage 2003**.

When FrontPage reopens, notice that the changes you made are still in effect; the Formatting toolbar is still docked at the left side of the window, and the Drawing toolbar is still open at the bottom.

19 Drag the Formatting toolbar by its move handle back to its original location below the Standard toolbar at the top of the window.

20   Right-click the Standard toolbar, and on the toolbar shortcut menu, click **Drawing** to close the Drawing toolbar.

21   On the **File** menu, click **Close** to close the *new_page_1.htm* file.

Exploring an Existing Web Site

When you work with other Office 2003 applications, you create self-contained documents that can be individually opened from within the application or from Microsoft Windows Explorer. When you work with FrontPage, you create a group of interconnected files that collectively make up a FrontPage-based Web site. As a result, Web sites must be opened from within FrontPage; clicking a single file name in Windows Explorer might open that file, but it won't open the Web site that the file belongs to.

After you open a Web site in FrontPage, you can look at the structure of the site in two views:

■   In *Folders view*, you can see and modify the *file structure* of a Web site. You can organize the files and folders that make up your Web site by using techniques similar to those you use to organize files and folders in Windows Explorer. You can add new folders, delete or move existing folders, and view the contents of folders.

■   In *Navigation view*, you can see or modify the *navigational structure* and hierarchical arrangement of the various pages on your Web site. In this view, you can click a page and drag it to another location in the Web site.

See Also   For information about FrontPage's other views, see "Looking at a Web Site in Various Ways" in this chapter.

In this exercise, you will open a sample FrontPage-based Web site and look at the file structure and navigational structure of the site.

USE the *GardenCo* Web site in the practice file folder for this topic. This practice file is located in the *My Documents\Microsoft Press\Office 2003 SBS\Understanding* folder and can also be accessed by clicking *Start/All Programs/Microsoft Press/Microsoft Office System 2003 Step By Step.*
BE SURE TO start FrontPage before beginning this exercise.

1   On the **File** menu, click **Open Site** (do not click **Open**).

2   In the **Open Site** dialog box, browse to the *My Documents\Microsoft Press \Office 2003 SBS\Understanding* folder.

Web site icon

3   A FrontPage-based Web site called *GardenCo* is located in this folder, indicated by the Web site icon preceding the name.

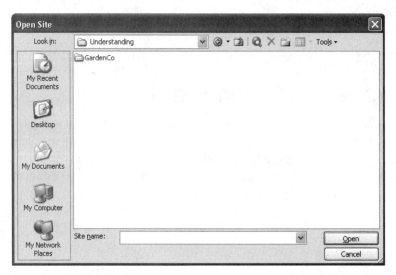

4 Click the **GardenCo** folder to select the Web site, and then click **Open**.

The open task pane closes and the Folder List opens, displaying in Folders view the accessible folders and files that make up the GardenCo Web site. You can double-click any file to open that file in FrontPage.

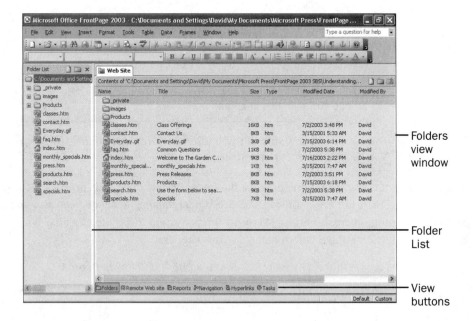

Important   A FrontPage-based Web site includes hidden folders and files generated by FrontPage for behind-the-scenes operations. Deleting or changing these files and folders might "break" the site by damaging the navigation structure, rendering links invalid, or worse; so FrontPage designates them as hidden. Provided your computer is not set to show hidden files and folders (this setting is on the View tab of the Microsoft Windows Folder Options dialog box), you will never see these files, and there will be no danger that you might accidentally delete them or alter them.

5   In the **Folder List**, click the plus sign preceding each of the folders to view the folder contents.

Webhome
pagepage
iconicon

6   Different icons designate the various types of files that make up this site. For example, the Web page icon precedes the *file name* of each page of the FrontPage-based Web site, and the home page icon indicates the *home page* of the site.

Close [Window]

7   Click the **Close** button to close the **Folder List**.

Toggle Pane

8   On the Standard toolbar, click the down arrow to the right of the **Toggle Pane** button, and then click **Folder List** in the drop-down list to redisplay the **Folder List**.

9   At the bottom of the **Folders view window**, click the **Navigation** button to switch to Navigation view.

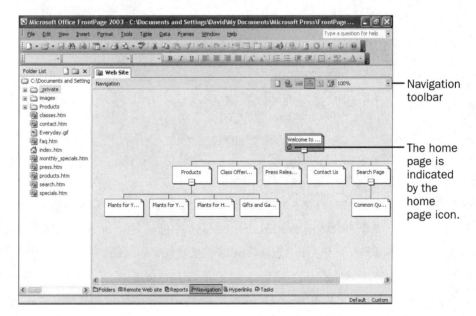

Navigation toolbar

The home page is indicated by the home page icon.

This view of the navigational structure is essentially a hierarchical map of how pages are connected within the site and what routes you can take to get from one page to another. As with the Folder List, you can open each of these files by double-clicking the page icon or title in the Navigation Pane.

10 Move the mouse pointer over each of the buttons on the Navigation toolbar to see the available commands.

Portrait/
Landscape

11 Click the **Portrait/Landscape** button to change the orientation of the Navigation view display.

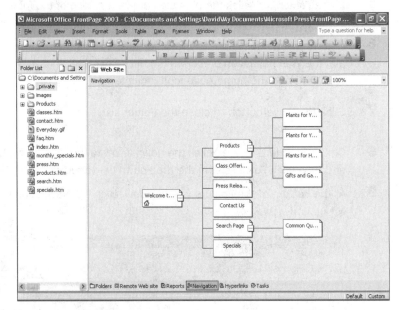

12 On the Navigation toolbar, click the down arrow to the right of the **Zoom** box, and then click **25%** in the drop-down list.

The drawing size changes.

13 In the **Zoom** drop-down list, click **Size To Fit** to optimize the navigation display within the current window.

14 Click the **Portrait/Landscape** button to return to the default navigational view.

15 Click the **Products** page (not the minus sign on its bottom edge) to select it.

16 On the Navigation toolbar, click the **View Subtree Only** button.

View
Subtree Only

If you are working with a particularly large Web site you can use this technique to single out one section of the navigation structure.

17 Click the **View Subtree Only** button again to see the entire *site map*.

18 On the **File** menu, click **Close Site** to close the Web site.

Looking at a Web Site in Various Ways

At the bottom of the working area, FrontPage 2003 provides six buttons for switching among different *views* of a Web site:

- *Folders view* displays the visible files and folders that are part of the open Web site. For each file, this view shows the file name, page title, file size, file type, the date the file was last modified and by whom, and any comments that have been added to the file information.

New in Office 2003
Remote Web Site view

- *Remote Web Site view* displays information about the published version of your Web site, so you can see the local and remote file structures simultaneously, similar to the view displayed by traditional *File Transfer Protocol (FTP)* programs. You can manipulate local and remote files and folders from this view.

- *Reports view* displays any of the 31 available basic reports about the open Web site. Reports view defaults to the last opened report. If no report has been open during the current FrontPage session, the default is a Site Summary report that collates the results of the other reports. To view one of the reports that make up the Site Summary, click the hyperlinked report name. The various reports can be chosen from the View menu or from the Reporting toolbar.

- *Navigation view* graphically displays a hierarchical view of all the files that have been added to the navigation structure of the open Web site. To add an existing file to the navigation structure, you simply drag the file into the Navigation view window, and drop it in the appropriate location. You can also create new files directly within Navigation view. To fit the site content into the window, you can switch between Portrait mode (vertical layout) and Landscape mode (horizontal layout) or zoom in or out using the buttons on the Navigation toolbar.

- *Hyperlinks view* displays the hyperlinks to and from any selected page in the open Web site. Internal hyperlinks are shown as well as external hyperlinks and e-mail hyperlinks. You select a file in the Folder List to see the hyperlinks to and from that file, and then select the plus sign next to any file name to further expand the view.

- *Tasks view* displays a list of *tasks* to be completed in the open Web site. FrontPage creates these tasks when you use a wizard to create a Web site, or you can create your own tasks. For each task, you see the status, name, and description. You can also see to whom the task is assigned; whether the task has been categorized as High, Medium, or Low priority; and when the task was last modified. Tasks are a useful way of tracking the readiness of a site.

You can switch between views by clicking the desired view on the View menu or by clicking the button for the view you want at the bottom of the working area.

Tip   The View menu also provides a Page View command. You will do most of your development work in Page view.

In this exercise, you will look at Web pages in each of the FrontPage views to get an idea of what information is available to you in each view.

USE the *GardenCo* Web site in the practice file folder for this topic. This practice file is located in the *My Documents\Microsoft Press\Office 2003 SBS\Understanding* folder and can also be accessed by clicking *Start/All Programs/Microsoft Press/Microsoft Office System 2003 Step By Step*.
BE SURE TO start FrontPage before beginning this exercise.
OPEN the *GardenCo* Web site in Folders view.

Remote Web
Site View

1   At the bottom of the window, click the **Remote Web site View** button.

Because this Web site has not yet been published, the view is blank.

2   Click the **Remote Web Site Properties** button.

3   In the **Remote Web Site Properties** dialog box, click each tab to see the publishing options you can set.

Optimize HTML

You can specify the location and server information of your published Web site. On the Optimize HTML tab, you can set options that decrease the size of your published file by removing elements such as authoring-specific comments, white space, and unnecessary tags and tag attributes from the published version.

4   When you finish looking at the options, click **Cancel**.

Reports View

5   At the bottom of the working area, click the **Reports View** button.

FrontPage opens the Reports toolbar and displays the Site Summary report for the open Web site.

To see the individual reports that are collated into the Site Summary report, you can click the hyperlinked report names in the Site Summary; or you can click the Reports down arrow at the left end of the Reports toolbar and then click the desired report in the drop-down list.

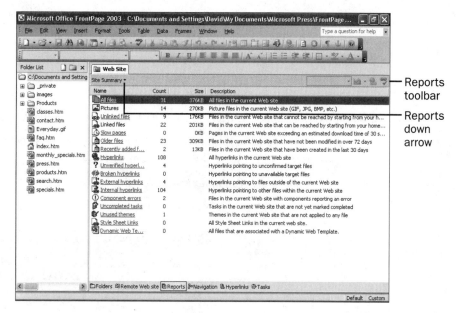

Reports toolbar

Reports down arrow

6 Move the mouse pointer over each of the buttons on the Reports toolbar to see the available commands.

7 In the Site Summary report, click the **Internal hyperlinks** link.

8 If a message box appears asking whether you want FrontPage to verify the hyperlinks, select the **Don't ask me this again** check box, and then click **Yes**.

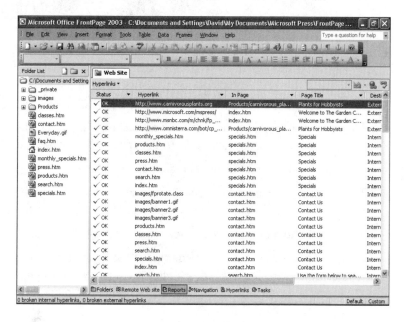

FrontPage tests each internal hyperlink and indicates whether it is good or bad by placing a green check mark or red X in front of the link.

9   At the far left end of the Reports toolbar, click the down arrow to the right of the **Report** box (which currently says **Hyperlinks**), and then click **Site Summary** in the drop-down list to return to the default report.

Hyperlinks
View

10   At the bottom of the working area, click the **Hyperlinks View** button.

Because no specific page is selected, the screen reads *Select a page from the Folder List to view hyperlinks to and from that page.*

11   In the **Folder List**, click **index.htm**, the home page.

All the hyperlinks to and from the home page are displayed.

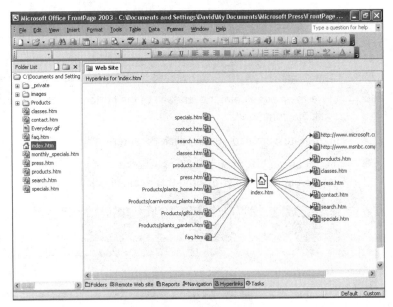

12   In the hyperlinks display, right-click **contact.htm**, and click **Move to Center** on the shortcut menu to move that file to the center point of the hyperlink structure.

Notice that different icons represent different types of links.

13   Click the plus sign next to any file icon to see the other hyperlinks from that file's page, and then click the minus sign to collapse the hyperlink view.

Tasks View

14   At the bottom of the working area, click the **Tasks View** button.

Tasks view shows you a reminder list of the things that need to be done in the open Web site. Tasks are automatically created when you use a FrontPage wizard to create a Web site. Tasks can also be created manually by anyone working on the Web site.

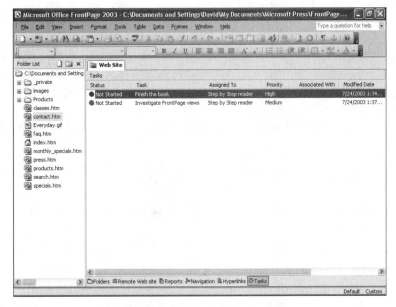

15 Double-click the task titled **Investigate FrontPage views** to open it.

16 In the **Assigned to** box, double-click or drag to select the current entry. Assign the task to yourself by typing your name, user name, or initials.

17 Read the description and study the task details, and then click **OK** to close the task.

18 Right-click the **Investigate FrontPage views** task, and click **Mark Complete** on the shortcut menu.

The task's Status setting changes from *Not Started* to *Completed*.

Important You can display previously completed tasks by right-clicking the background of the Tasks list, and then clicking Show History on the shortcut menu.

19 Double-click the task titled **Finish the book** to open it.

20 Read the description and study the task details, and then click **OK** to close the task.

CLOSE the *GardenCo* Web site.

Exploring an Existing Web Page

A Web site consists of one or more individual *Web pages*. When you develop a Web site, you work with the individual pages and the overall site structure. When you want to edit a Web page that is part of a FrontPage-based Web site, you first open the site in FrontPage, and then open the individual page. This avoids the possibility that you might make changes to a page and then disconnect it from the rest of the site.

It also ensures that changes made on an individual page are reflected across the entire site, as appropriate.

Important If FrontPage is your default HTML editor, you can open individual Web pages from outside FrontPage by double-clicking the page file in Windows Explorer. However, if FrontPage is not your default editor, accessing and changing files individually from outside FrontPage could result in damage to the Web site. To set FrontPage as your default HTML editor while starting FrontPage, click Yes when prompted to do so.

New In
Office 2003
Web Site tab

Page creation and editing tasks are done in *Page view*, which displays the open page or pages in the Page view editing window. At the top of the editing window is a tab for the current Web site and tabs for any open pages. You can open an existing page by double-clicking it on the Web Site tab. The tab at the top of each page shows the page's file name. If multiple pages are open, you can switch to another page by clicking its tab or by clicking its file name on the Window menu.

Tip To see information about an entire site and access the Folders view, Remote Web Site view, Reports view, Navigation view, and Hyperlinks view options, click the Web Site tab at the top of the Page view editing window.

Page view provides four different ways to view your Web page:

New In
Office 2003
Web page
views

- The *Design pane* displays the Web page as it will appear in a Web browser, except that additional design guides, such as shared border indicators and table and cell outlines, are also visible. You work primarily in this pane when creating Web pages.

- The *Code pane* displays the HTML code behind the Web page. Elements are color-coded to make it easier for you to discern text and content from the surrounding code. Each line of code is numbered. Error messages often refer to line numbers within the HTML code so you can quickly locate problems.

New In
Office 2003
Split view

- The *Split pane* simultaneously displays the design view and HTML code. Selecting a page element in the design view simultaneously selects the element in the code so you don't have to scroll through the code to find what you're looking for.

- The *Preview pane* displays the Web page as it will actually appear in a Web browser. Hyperlinks and most page elements are active in the Preview pane.

Most FrontPage users will do almost all page design work in the Design pane, which offers the simplest interface.

In this exercise, you will open an individual Web page in Page view and look at the page in the different Page view panes.

USE the *GardenCo* Web site in the practice file folder for this topic. This practice file is located in the *My Documents\Microsoft Press\Office 2003 SBS\Understanding* folder and can also be accessed by click-ing *Start/All Programs/Microsoft Press/Microsoft Office System 2003 Step By Step*.
BE SURE TO start FrontPage before beginning this exercise.

Open

1   On the Standard toolbar, click the down arrow to the right of the **Open** button, and then click **Open Site** in the drop-down list.

2   In the **Open Site** dialog box, browse to the *My Documents\Microsoft Press \Office 2003 SBS\Understanding* folder, click **GardenCo**, and then click **Open**.

The Web site opens in FrontPage with the Folder List displayed.

Tip   If the Folder List is not displayed, click Folder List on the View menu to display it.

3   In the **Folder List**, right-click the **contact.htm** file, and then click **Open** on the shortcut menu.

Open Web
page icon

The file icon changes to an open Web page icon, and the file opens in the *Page view editing window*. Folder List and Navigation buttons appear at the bottom of the Folder List; you can click these to switch between the Folder List and the Navigation Pane.

Web site tab   Web page tab

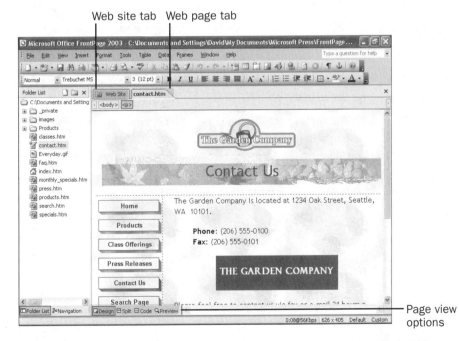

Page view options

At the top of the editing window, tabs appear for the current Web site and the open page. You can use the four buttons at the bottom to switch between different views of the open Web page.

4   Use the scroll bars to look at the entire page.

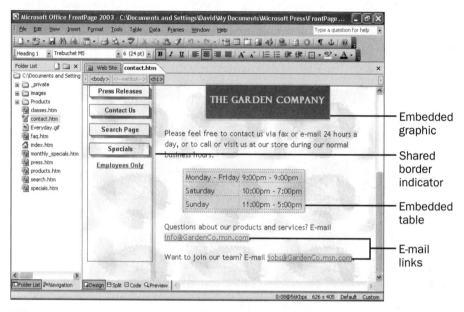

This page has *shared borders* at the top and left side of the page, delineated by dotted lines.

Shared borders appear on every page of the Web site and contain the same information, giving the site a consistent look. The top shared border of this site contains a corporate logo and the page title, or *page banner*. The left shared border contains a *link bar* displaying graphic *hyperlinks* that you can click to jump to other pages in the site.

The content area in the center of the page contains text, a graphic, a table, and two *e-mail links*.

5   At the bottom of the Page view editing window, click the **Show Code View** button to switch to the Code pane.

Show
Code View

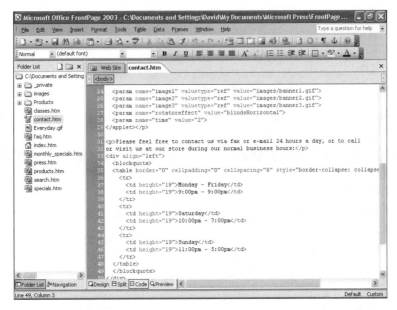

6 Find each section of text within the page code, and study the surrounding HTML code. Try to identify the code that creates each page element.

7 Click the **Show Split View** button to switch to the Split pane.

⊟ Split
Show
Split View

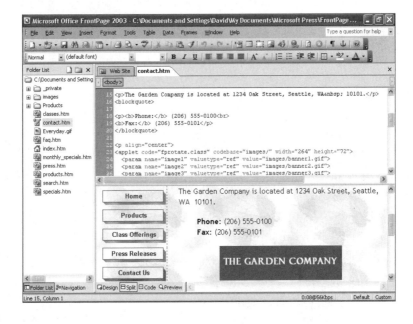

Show
Preview View

Close

8   Click the **Show Preview View** button to switch to the Preview pane.

9   Click the hyperlinked buttons on the link bar to switch to other pages.

10 When you're done looking at the page, click the **Close** button in the upper-right corner of the Page view editing window to close the file.

CLOSE the *GardenCo* Web site. If you are not continuing on to the next chapter, quit FrontPage.

Understanding FrontPage Web Site Concepts

This section discusses the types of sites that can be developed with FrontPage and the system requirements that are necessary to take full advantage of the FrontPage 2003 development environment.

There are two kinds of Web sites: *disk-based Web sites* and *server-based Web sites*. A disk-based Web site can be run on any kind of computer, or even from a floppy disk or CD-ROM. Disk-based Web sites support only basic HTML functionality. Many of the more interesting *Web components* that FrontPage supplies won't work on a disk-based site.

Server-based Web sites run on a Web server—a computer that is specifically configured to *host* Web sites. On a small scale, a Web server might be a local computer such as your own, or it might be an intranet server within your company. On a larger scale, Web servers that host corporate Internet sites are usually located at professional *server farms* run by an *Internet service provider (ISP)* or *Web hosting company*.

Most Web sites are initially developed as disk-based sites; that is, you develop them on your local computer. You then *publish* them to a Web server, either within your organization or at your hosted Web location.

- Some FrontPage *Web components*—ready-made elements that provide capabilities such as link bars and tables of contents—work only when they are placed on a page that is part of a FrontPage-based Web site.

- Some components require that the Web page or site be located on a Web server running Microsoft Windows SharePoint Services.

- Other common Web components work only in a server-based Web site located on a Web server running FrontPage Server Extensions.

- Some components pull their content directly from other Web sites, so they require an Internet connection to be visible.

- Server administration features are available only for server-based Web sites stored on Web servers running Windows SharePoint Services or FrontPage Server Extensions.

■   To display database information, your site must be hosted on a Web server that supports Active Server Pages (ASP) and ActiveX Data Objects (ADO).

FrontPage-based Web sites can run on any kind of Web server, but the full functionality of your Web site might not be available unless your site is hosted on a server with FrontPage Server Extensions installed. If you maintain your own Web server, installing the server extensions is a simple exercise; they are available on The Microsoft Office System 2003 installation CD-ROM. If you are looking for a company to host your Web site, or if you already have an ISP but you have never asked it to host a FrontPage–based Web site before, be sure to ask whether its servers have FrontPage Server Extensions installed.

Key Points

■   FrontPage is an easy-to-use program that provides all the tools you need to develop a simple or complex Web site.

■   FrontPage uses a menu and toolbar command structure like that of the other Microsoft Office System applications.

■   FrontPage Web sites consist of numerous files, some hidden, and should be opened for editing from within FrontPage rather than from Windows Explorer.

■   You can see and work with your Web site from several different viewpoints: Folders view, Remote Web Site view, Reports view, Navigation view, Hyperlinks view, and Tasks view.

■   A Web site consists of individual Web pages. The structure of each page is determined by the underlying HTML code. You can see and work with the HTML code in the Page view Code pane or Split pane, but you do most of your work in the Design pane. FrontPage makes it unnecessary for you to know how to create HTML code.

■   Web sites are initially developed on your local computer and then published to the Internet. Many features are not available for use until the Web site is published to a server running FrontPage Server Extensions.

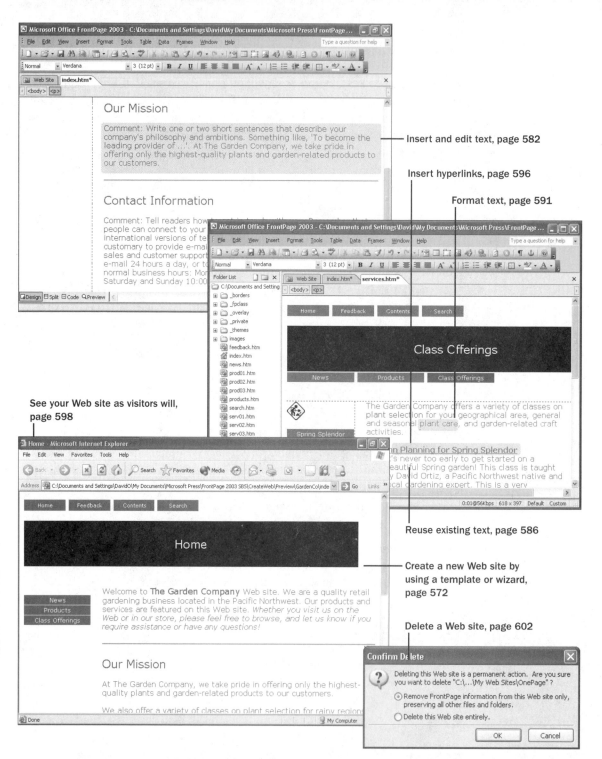

Insert and edit text, page 582

Insert hyperlinks, page 596

Format text, page 591

See your Web site as visitors will,
page 598

Reuse existing text, page 586

Create a new Web site by
using a template or wizard,
page 572

Delete a Web site, page 602

23 Creating a Web Site to Promote Yourself or Your Company

In this chapter you will learn to:

✔ Create a new Web site by using a template or wizard.

✔ Insert and edit text.

✔ Reuse existing text.

✔ Format text.

✔ Insert hyperlinks.

✔ See your Web site as visitors will.

✔ Delete a Web site.

All Microsoft Office System 2003 applications provide tools for jump-starting the creation of common types of files. Microsoft Office FrontPage 2003 includes templates and wizards you can use to set up the structure for basic types of Web pages and even entire Web sites. When you use one of these tools, FrontPage does most of the structural work for you, leaving you free to concentrate on the site's content.

You can use the FrontPage templates and wizards to create everything from a very basic Web page to a complex, multi-page, interactive site. These are great tools to use if you are new to Web design and want to explore the possibilities, or if you are looking for a quick way to get started on the creation of a real Web site.

In this chapter, you will walk through the steps for creating a couple of Web sites, including a corporate site that we will work with throughout most of the book. You will learn how to enter and format text, how to preview a Web site, and how to delete a site you no longer need.

See Also Do you need only a quick refresher on the topics in this chapter? See the Quick Reference entries on page xxxiii.

Important   Before you can use the practice files in this chapter, you need to install them from the book's companion CD to their default location. See "Using the Book's CD-ROM" on page xxi for more information.

Creating a New Web Site by Using a Template

The easiest way to create a new Web site is by using one of FrontPage's *templates*. Templates create the layout for a specific type of Web page or Web site, designating with placeholders the type of content you should put in each location. All you have to do is replace the placeholders with your own content, and you have a finished page or site to show off.

To create a Web site using a template, you simply select the template and specify the location where the site should be created. FrontPage then creates the new Web site and applies the template's structure to it, leaving it up to you to fill in the content and customize the look of the site to suit your needs.

In this exercise, you will create two different types of Web sites by using templates: a simple one-page site and a personal Web site.

BE SURE TO start FrontPage before beginning this exercise.

1   If the **New** task pane is not open, on the **File** menu, click **New**.

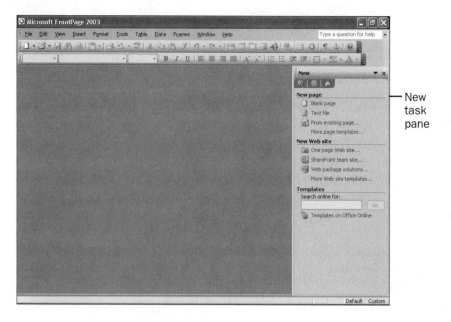

New task pane

2 In the **New Web site** area of the **New** task pane, click **More Web site templates**.

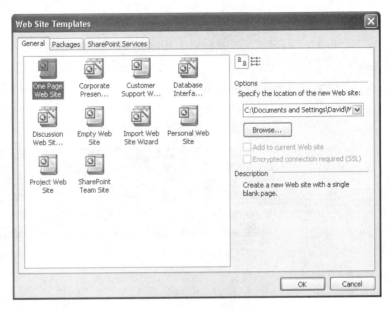

3 In the **Web Site Templates** dialog box, make sure the **One Page Web Site** icon is selected.

Tip You need to specify the location and name of the new Web site. FrontPage provides a special folder in which you can store your Web sites, called My Web Sites. This folder is located in your My Documents folder.

4 In the **Options** area, click the **Browse** button.

The New Web Site Location dialog box opens.

5 In the **New Web Site Location** dialog box, click the **My Documents** icon on the Places bar.

6 In the file list, double-click **My Web Sites**.

7 On the dialog box toolbar, click the **Create New Folder** button.

The New Folder dialog box opens.

Create
New Folder

8 In the **New Folder** dialog box, type **OnePage** in the **Name** text box, and then click **OK**.

9 In the **New Web Site Location** dialog box, click the **Open** button.

10 In the **Web Site Templates** dialog box, click **OK**.

In about three seconds, FrontPage displays the structure of your newly created one-page Web site.

Tip FrontPage opens your new Web site in the view that was last active. If your screen doesn't look like our graphic, check the Views bar and make any adjustments necessary to make your view the same as ours.

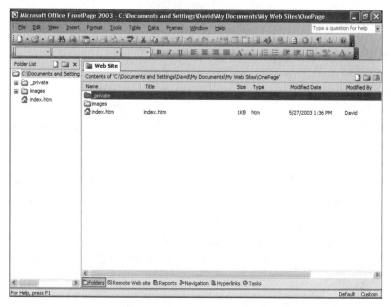

In FrontPage, it appears that your one-page Web site consists of a single file called *index.htm* and two empty folders called *_private* and *images*. However, if you look at the site's folder in Microsoft Windows Explorer, you will see that many folders and files (some of them hidden) support this single page.

Tip   If your Folder Options are not set to "Show hidden files and folders," you won't see all of the files and folders that support this page.

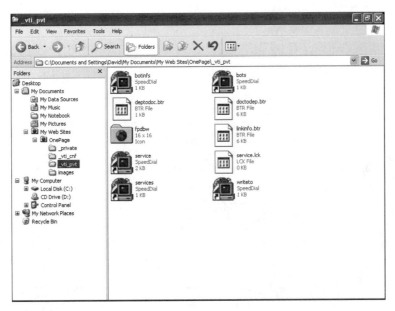

11   In the **Folder List**, double-click **index.htm** to open it in Page view.

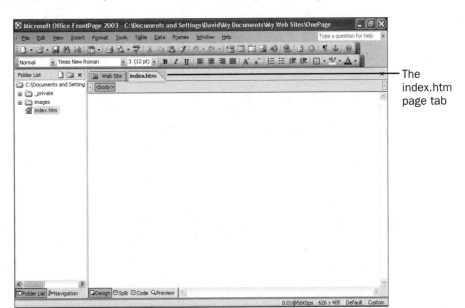

The index.htm page tab

When index.htm is displayed in Page view, the page is completely empty—a blank canvas upon which you can create a veritable work of art. By the time you finish this book, you will know how to create a fairly sophisticated page from scratch, but until then, it is a good idea to lean on FrontPage to give you a starting framework. Now you will test another template by creating a personal site to showcase your new skills.

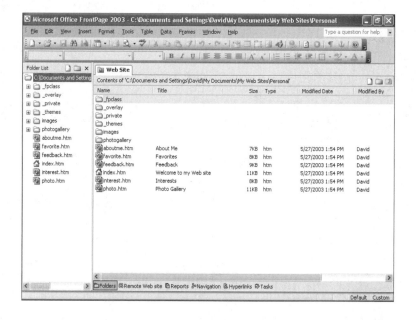

Create a new normal page

12 Click the down arrow to the right of the **Create a new normal page** button, and then click **Web Site**.

The Web Site Templates dialog box appears.

13 In the **Web Site Templates** dialog box, click (don't double-click) the **Personal Web Site** icon.

Tip   FrontPage suggests a location for your new Web site based on the location of the last Web site you created.

14 In the **Options** area, click the **Browse** button, and then navigate to the *My Web Sites* folder. Create a new folder named Personal, and click **Open**. In the **Web Site Templates** dialog box, click **OK**.

A second FrontPage window opens, displaying your newly created personal Web site. You now have two instances of FrontPage running on your computer at the same time.

15 In the **Folder List**, double-click the **index.htm** file to open the home page of the Web site in Page view.

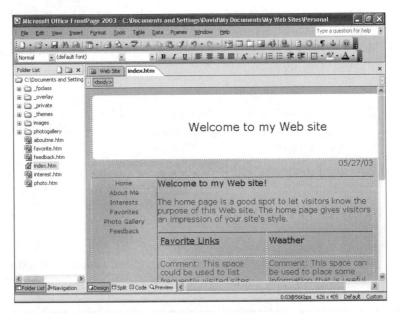

The home page provides placeholders for information about you and your interests, and links to your favorite Web sites. You can display photos of yourself, your family, your friends, your dog, and your vacations (real or imagined) in the photo gallery, and Web visitors can contact you by using the feedback page.

Placeholders currently represent all the information in this Web site. By replacing the placeholders with your own information, you can have an attractive site ready to publish in no time at all.

16 On the **File** menu, click **Close Site** to close the personal Web site.

Close

17 Click the FrontPage window's **Close** button to close the second instance of FrontPage and return to the first instance.

18 On the **File** menu, click **Close Site** to close the one-page Web site.

The New Task Pane

The New task pane contains convenient links to the Web sites and individual pages that you have created or worked with in FrontPage. It also contains links to templates and wizards you can use to create new Web pages or sites. If this task pane is not already open, you can open it using one of the following methods:

1 On the **File** menu, click **New**.

2 On the **View** menu, click **Task Pane**. If a different task pane is displayed, click the down arrow at the right end of the task pane's title bar, and click **New** in the drop-down list.

3 Right-click the toolbar, and click **Task Pane** on the toolbar shortcut menu. If a different task pane is displayed, click **New** in the task pane title bar's drop-down list.

4 Press Ctrl+F1.

To open the task pane every time you start FrontPage:

● On the **Tools** menu, click **Options**, and then on the **General** tab, select the **Startup Task Pane** check box.

Creating a New Web Site by Using a Wizard

In addition to using templates to create Web sites, you can create sites that are a little more complex by using one of FrontPage's *wizards*. Wizards are similar to templates, but even better. A wizard not only creates the layout of a page or site for you, it also leads you through the process of personalizing the content and the appearance of the final product.

For example, suppose that Karen Berg, the owner of a small, fictitious plant and garden store called The Garden Company, wants to communicate with her existing customers and expand her customer base by having a corporate presence on the Internet. If maintaining a Web site meets these modest goals, she might later choose to expand the site's capabilities to permit online retailing beyond the store's Seattle, Washington, location. However, to begin with, she wants to use FrontPage to create a good-looking Web site. This is a job for one of FrontPage's wizards.

In this exercise, you will use the Corporate Presence Web Wizard to create the basic corporate Web site.

Online Retailing

On the surface, expanding your business by selling goods or services over the Internet seems like a good idea. However, this decision should not be made without a good deal of analysis and planning. First, what you have to offer has to be so compelling that people will want to buy it, and second, you have to offer it under terms and conditions that will make people want to buy it from you, rather than from someone else. Unless you have an exclusive right to sell your particular product, you are going to be competing on many fronts, including price, cost and speed of delivery, and customer service. You must also consider how you will provide a secure environment for the handling of other people's money. All these topics are beyond the scope of this book, but if you are interested in learning more about online retailing, you might want to check out *Small Business Solutions for E-Commerce* by Brenda Kienan (Microsoft Press, 2000).

BE SURE TO start FrontPage before beginning this exercise.

Create a new normal page

1 Click the down arrow to the right of the **Create a new normal page** button, and then click **Web Site**.

The Web Site Templates dialog box appears.

2 In the **Web Site Templates** dialog box, click (don't double-click) the **Corporate Presence Wizard** icon.

3 In the **Options** area, click the **Browse** button, and browse to the *My Web Sites* folder.

Create New Folder

4 On the dialog box toolbar, click the **Create New Folder** button. Name the new folder CorpSite, and click **OK**.

5 Back in the **New Web Site Location** dialog box, click **Open** and then click **OK**.

The first of a series of Corporate Presence Web Wizard dialog boxes, called *pages*, appears. The wizard uses these pages to prompt you to make choices and enter basic corporate information.

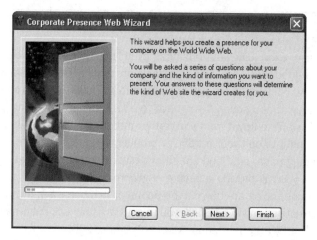

6 Read the information on the first page, and then click **Next** to move to the second page.

7 Continue reading the information and clicking **Next** to accept all the default selections in each of the **Corporate Presence Web Wizard** pages, until you come to the one that requests the name and address of the company.

8 Enter the information shown here (or your own personalized information), and then click **Next**:

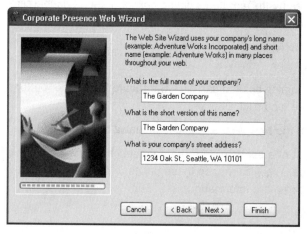

9 Enter the corporate contact information shown here (or your personalized information):

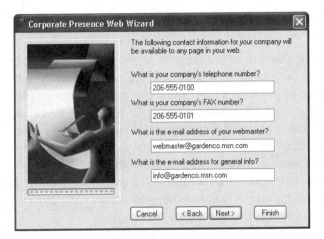

10 Click **Next**, and then click **Finish**.

FrontPage creates your site using the information you provided and then displays a list of the tasks that need to be completed to finish the site.

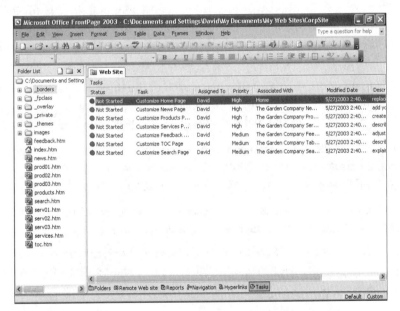

11 In the **Folder List**, double-click **index.htm** to open the home page in Page view.

12 Scroll to the bottom of the page, and notice the contact information you provided in the wizard.

CLOSE the *GardenCo* Web site.

E-Mail Aliases

When creating a Web site for a company or organization, it's wise to use generic e-mail addresses (called *aliases*) in your Web site contact information rather than addresses of individuals, so the address can stay the same no matter who is actually assigned to respond to the inquiry. For example, if The Garden Company listed its contact e-mail address as that of Karen Berg and then Karen was away for an extended period of time, messages might build up in her mailbox with no one to answer them. Similarly, if all Web site inquiries were directed to David Ortiz and then David left the company, valuable customer contacts could go unnoticed. Using an e-mail alias that automatically forwards received e-mail messages to one or more individuals ensures that customers' questions are always received by the appropriate person.

Inserting and Editing Text

You can enter new text in a Web page by typing it directly in each page. When you use a FrontPage wizard to create a new Web site, the wizard uses *comments* as place-holders for the text that you need to personalize. The comments inserted by the wizard suggest the type of information you should enter in each area.

In this exercise, you will replace each of the three main blocks of placeholder text on the home page of a Web site created by the Corporate Presence Web Wizard. Then you will add additional text and mark this task as complete.

USE the *GardenCo* Web site in the practice file folder for this topic. This practice file is located in the *My Documents\Microsoft Press\Office 2003 SBS\CreateWeb\InsertText* folder and can also be accessed by clicking *Start/All Programs/Microsoft Press/Microsoft Office System Step By Step*.

Open

1 On the Standard toolbar, click the down arrow to the right of the **Open** button, and then click **Open Site** in the drop-down list.

2 In the **Open Site** dialog box, browse to the *GardenCo* Web site that is located in the practice file folder, and click **Open** to open the Web site in FrontPage.

3 In the **Folder List**, double-click **index.htm** to open the home page in the Page view editing window.

Close

4   In the bar at the top of the **Folder List** pane, click the **Close** button to enlarge your work area by closing the Folder List.

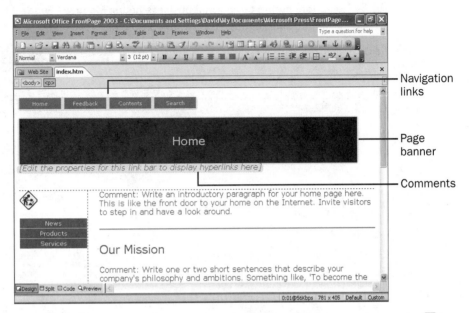

Navigation links

Page banner

Comments

5   In the body of the home page, click the introductory comment, and press the ⌷End⌷ key to position the insertion point at the end of the paragraph.

Tip   You can delete the comments before typing new text, but you don't have to. The comments will not be visible to your Web visitors.

6   Type the following text:
Welcome to The Garden Company. We are a quality retail gardening business located in the Pacific Northwest. Our products and services are featured on this Web site. Whether you visit us on the Web or in our store, please feel free to browse, and let us know if you require assistance or have any questions!

7   Position the insertion point at the end of the comment under the *Our Mission* heading, and then enter the following text:
At The Garden Company, we take pride in offering only the highest-quality plants and garden-related products to our customers.

8 After the comment under the *Contact Information* heading, enter the following text: **Please feel free to contact us via fax or e-mail 24 hours a day, or to call or visit us at our store during our normal business hours: Monday - Friday 9:00 a.m. - 9:00 p.m., Saturday and Sunday 10:00 a.m. - 5:00 p.m.**

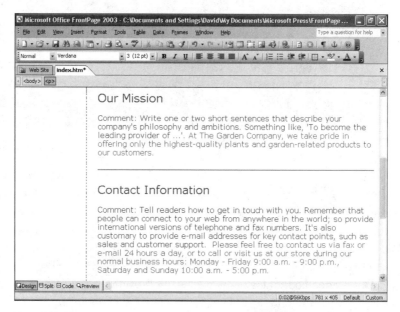

You can change the text that you've entered or add more text at any time.

9 Position the insertion point at the end of the paragraph under the *Our Mission* heading.

10 Press ⌈Enter⌋ to create a new paragraph, and then type the following text: **We also offer a variety of classes on plant selection for rainy regions, general and seasonal plant care, and garden-related craft activities.**

Show
Preview View

11 At the bottom of the Page view editing window, click the **Show Preview View** button.

Now you can see the page as your Web visitors will see it.

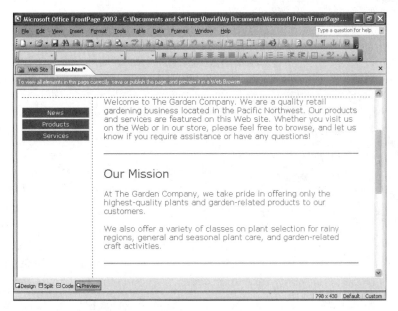

Save

12 On the Standard toolbar, click the **Save** button to save your Web page.

CLOSE the *GardenCo* Web site.

Making Comments in Web Pages

You can use comments to make notes to yourself or to communicate with other people working on a Web site. Comments don't show up in the published version of a Web page. You can insert, edit, and delete comments when you're working with a page in Design, Split, or Code view.

To insert a comment:

1 On the **Insert** menu, click **Comment**.

2 In the **Comment** text box, type your notes, and then click **OK**.

To edit a comment:

1 Double-click anywhere in the comment text block to open the **Comment** dialog box.

2 In the **Comment** text box, make your changes, and then click **OK**.

To delete a comment:

● Click the comment once to select it, and then press the Del key.

Reusing Existing Text

If you have already created material for another purpose, such as a press release or company brochure, you probably don't want to have to create it all over again in your Web site. And you don't have to.

FrontPage makes it simple to copy and paste text into a template-based Web site. You can insert chunks of text, graphics, spreadsheets, or drawings cut or copied from other Office applications. You can even insert entire files.

You can copy or cut multiple pieces of content from Microsoft Office System programs, and then paste the content into your Web pages. The Office Clipboard task pane stores text, tables, graphics, and other file elements in a convenient and accessible location and can archive up to 24 different elements across all The Microsoft Office System applications.

Each time you paste content from the Clipboard into FrontPage, the floating Paste Options button appears, which you use to apply the destination styles, keep the source formatting, or keep only the text for your pasted selection. You can ignore the Paste Options button if you want to keep the source formatting.

In this exercise, you will insert text from external files into the News and Services pages, and change the page banner. The text on the News page currently consists of a Web Changes heading and a discussion of site updates. Because you have decided that site updates won't be of interest to patrons of The Garden Company, you will change this page to one that contains press releases. You will also modify the three Services pages using text contained in a Microsoft Office Word document, and update the page titles to reflect their new content.

USE the *GardenCo* Web site and the *PR2* and *Classes* documents in the practice file folder for this topic. These practice files are located in the *My Documents\Microsoft Press\Office 2003 SBS\CreateWeb \InsertExist* folder and can also be accessed by clicking *Start/All Programs/Microsoft Press /Microsoft Office System 2003 Step By Step*.
OPEN the *GardenCo* Web site.

1   If the **Folder List** is not visible, on the **View** menu, click **Folder List**.

2   In the **Folder List**, double-click the **news.htm** file to open it in the Page view editing window.

3   Triple-click the **Web Changes** heading to select it, and type Press Releases.

The text of the heading is replaced, but its formatting is retained.

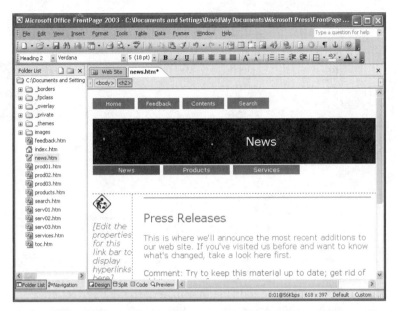

4   Replace the default opening paragraph, above the comment, with the following text: **Keep up with the news! Recent press releases and links to archived press releases are available here.**

5   Click the comment below the paragraph you just typed to select it.

6   On the **Insert** menu, click **File**.

The Select File dialog box appears.

7   Browse to the practice file folder for this exercise.

8   In the **Files of type** drop-down list, click **Word 97-2003** (*.doc).

9   Click **PR2** in the list of available files, and then click **Open** to insert the full text of the document in your Web page.

The text of the document is converted to rich text format and then to HTML and inserted into the News page, just as if you had created it there originally. The original formatting is retained.

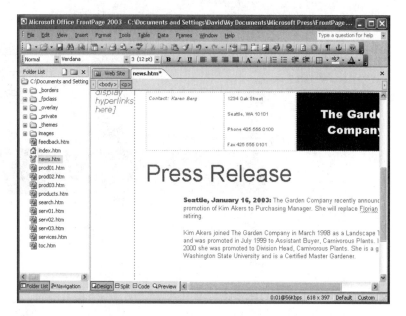

Tip Don't spend time making a document perfect before you import it. You can always make adjustments to the text of the document after it is imported into your Web page.

The contact information at the top of the imported text is contained in a table. The table cells are indicated by dotted lines.

10 Click anywhere in the table. On the **Table** menu, point to **Select**, and then click **Table**.

The table and its contents are selected.

11 Right-click the selection, and click **Delete Cells** on the shortcut menu to delete the table.

12 Triple-click the **Press Release** heading to select the entire paragraph, and press the ⌷Del⌷ key to remove it from the Web page.

13 Click the **Save** button to save your Web page.

Save

Your Web page is saved.

14 Click the **Close** button in the upper right corner of the work area to close the page file.

Close

15 Open the *Services* page.

16 Right-click the **Services** page banner, and click **Page Banner Properties** on the short-cut menu.

The Page Banner Properties dialog box appears.

17 In the **Page banner text** box, select and delete the current text, and then type Class Offerings.

18 Click **OK** to close the dialog box and change the page title.

This change affects the page title shown both on the page banner and in Navigation view.

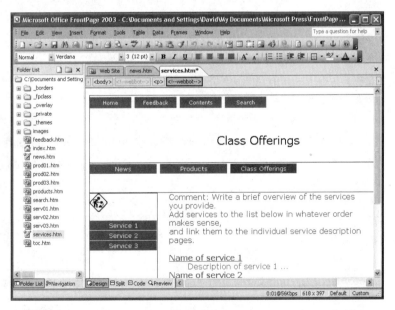

19 In Windows Explorer, browse to the *My Documents\Office 2003 SBS\CreateWeb \InsertExist* folder, and double-click **Classes** to open it in Word.

20 Triple-click anywhere in the introductory paragraph to select it, and press Ctrl+C to copy the text to the Office Clipboard.

21 Return to FrontPage. On the services.htm page, click the comment text to select it, and then press Ctrl+V to paste the overview text of the *Class Offerings* document from the Office Clipboard.

The copied text replaces the comment.

22 Select and delete the extra (empty) paragraph inserted with the text.

23 In the **Folder List**, open **serv01.htm**, **serv02.htm**, and **serv03.htm** (the three individual service files) for editing.

24 In each file, repeat steps 16 through 18 to change the page title to these short versions of the class names described in the *Class Offerings* document:

- Change *Service 1* to **Spring Splendor**.

- Change *Service 2* to **Carnivorous Plants**.

- Change *Service 3* to **Organic Byproducts**.

As you update each page banner, the navigational links under the page banners are updated simultaneously, as are the links on the services.htm page.

25 Return to the *services.htm* file, and note that the vertical navigation links along the left have also been updated to reflect the new page titles.

26 For each of the three *Name of service* links, double-click the link to select it, and type the full name of the corresponding course from the *Class Offerings* document, as follows:

- Replace *Name of service 1* with **Autumn Planning for Spring Splendor**.

- Replace *Name of service 2* with **Carnivorous Plants: Vicious or Delicious?**

- Replace *Name of service 3* with **Organic Byproducts: Use Them or Lose Them!**

Because these are hyperlinks, it is preferable to retype the link than to copy and paste it, to ensure that the link remains active.

See Also   For more information about hyperlinks, refer to "Inserting Hyperlinks," later in this chapter.

---

27 Copy and paste the first descriptive paragraph for each class from the *Class Offerings* document into *services.htm*, replacing the corresponding service description.

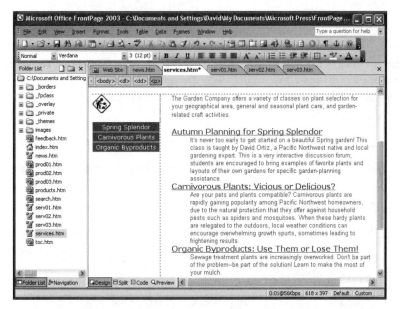

28 On each of the three individual class description pages (*serv01.htm*, *serv02.htm*, and *serv03.htm*), click anywhere in the body of the page, press `Ctrl`+`A` to select all the content, and then press the `Del` key.

29 In the *Class Offerings* document (the Word file), select and copy the descriptive text, learning objectives, and class schedule for each class, and then paste the information into the appropriate service page.

30 On the **File** menu, click **Save All** to save your changes to all the open files.

CLOSE the *GardenCo* Web site and the *Class Offerings* document, and quit Word.

Formatting Text

Web sites and Web pages created by FrontPage wizards are already formatted to look terrific without any additional effort from you. However, there are times when you will want to give a word or two a special look or make a paragraph stand out in some way. Most of the techniques you use in FrontPage to format text are the same as those you use in the other Microsoft Office System applications, so in this section, you will quickly review the types of formatting you are most likely to want to apply to your text, without much explanation.

In this exercise, you will format text and paragraphs using common Office formatting techniques.

USE the *GardenCo* Web site in the practice file folder for this topic. This practice file is located in the *My Documents\Microsoft Press\Office 2003 SBS\CreateWeb\FormatText* folder and can also be accessed by clicking *Start/All Programs/Microsoft Press/Microsoft Office System 2003 Step By Step*.
OPEN the *GardenCo* Web site.

1   Open **index.htm** (the home page) in the Page view editing window.

2   Select and delete the three comment blocks and the following spaces to make the page easier to read.

3   In the first paragraph, select the company name.

4   On the Formatting toolbar, click the **Increase Font Size** button.

Increase
Font Size

The font size shown in the Font Size box changes from *3 (12 pt)* to *4 (14 pt)* as the text size increases.

Tip   Font sizes are expressed in FrontPage in two ways: in points (as you are used to seeing in other applications, such as Microsoft Word and Microsoft Excel) and in sizes of 1 through 7. Eight options are available in the Font Size drop-down list: *Normal, 1 (8 pt), 2 (10 pt), 3 (12 pt), 4 (14 pt), 5 (18 pt), 6 (24 pt),* and *7 (36 pt)*.

5   Select the last sentence in the first paragraph (beginning with *Whether you visit us*), and click the **Italic** button to italicize the text.

I
Italic

6   Open **services.htm** (the Class Offerings page) in Page view.

Notice that the font used on this page is different from the default font on the home page.

7   Select the first paragraph.

Times New Roman ▾
Font

8   Click the down arrow to the right of the **Font** box, and click **Verdana** in the drop-down list.

Notice that the font size is still different from that on the home page.

9   With the first paragraph still selected, press ⌷Ctrl⌷+⌷ Space ⌷ to apply the default page formatting, which is 12-point Verdana. Repeat this step with each of the three class description paragraphs.

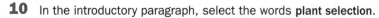

Font Color

10 In the introductory paragraph, select the words **plant selection**.

11 On the Formatting toolbar, click the down arrow to the right of the **Font Color** button, and change the font color to **Blue**. Repeat this procedure to change the words *plant care* to **Green** and *craft activities* to **Red**.

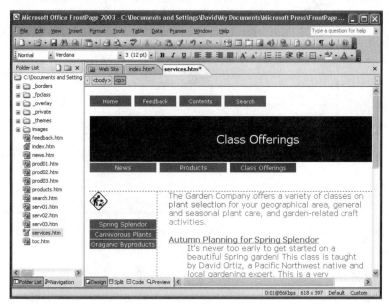

12 Open **serv01.htm** (the Spring Splendor page) in the Page view editing window.

Notice that the font on this page does not match the default site font on the home page.

13 Click Ctrl+A to select all the page content. In the **Font** drop-down list, click (**default font**).

The font of each of the page elements changes to the default element font.

14 Select the paragraph that gives details about the class location and size.

Borders

15 On the Formatting toolbar, click the down arrow to the right of the **Borders** button to display the **Borders** palette.

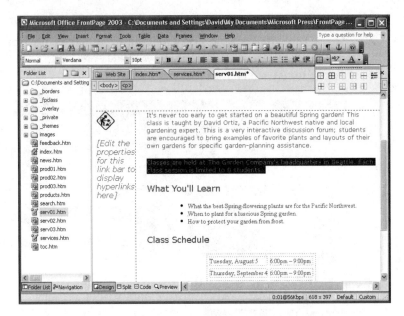

The Borders palette can be detached and docked elsewhere as a toolbar, or it can be detached and left as a floating toolbar.

Outside
Borders

16 Click the **Outside Borders** option to apply a border to the paragraph.

17 With the paragraph still selected, on the **Format** menu, click **Paragraph**.

The Paragraph dialog box appears.

18 In the **Paragraph** dialog box, do the following:

■ In the **Alignment** drop-down list, click **Center**.

■ In the **Indentation** section, set **Before text** and **After text** to 15.

■ In the **Spacing** section, set **Before** and **After** to 0.

Notice that your changes are reflected in the Preview area as you make them.

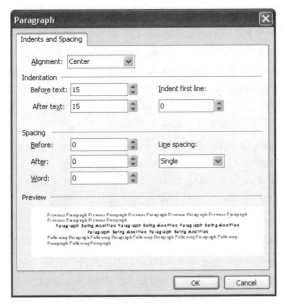

19 Click **OK** to apply the paragraph formatting.

20 Click an insertion point at the beginning of the second sentence in the bordered paragraph, and press ⇧Shift+↵Enter to insert a line break.

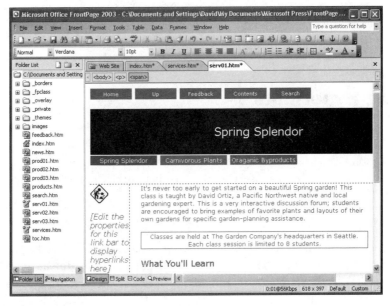

21 On the **File** menu, click **Save All** to save all the open files.

CLOSE the *GardenCo* Web site.

Cascading Style Sheets

Cascading style sheets (CSS) are documents that define formats and styles for page elements including headings, paragraphs, tables, lists, and so forth. The style sheet can be either an *embedded cascading style sheet* within a Web page, or as an *external cascading style sheet*. External style sheets can be referenced by multiple documents to provide a consistent look across pages and sites.

Web authors can also use cascading style sheets to stipulate how page elements are to be displayed by different browsers. Many Web sites utilize a *browser sniffer* that detects the Web browser and version used by each Web visitor and attaches the appropriate cascading style sheet to the site at that time.

To create an embedded cascading style sheet in FrontPage, click Style on the Format menu, and then define your own styles. The definitions are saved in the HTML code of the page.

To create an external cascading style sheet in FrontPage, select the CSS type from the options available on the Style Sheets tab of the Page Templates dialog box, click OK to create a CSS file, and then define your styles within the file.

To attach a style sheet in FrontPage, click Style Sheet Links on the Format menu, click Add, and browse to the CSS file on your computer or (if you have an Internet connection) anywhere on the Web.

The World Wide Web Consortium (W3C) originally developed cascading style sheets. For more information about current and future CSS specifications and how various browsers support CSS, visit their Web site at *www.w3c.org*.

Inserting Hyperlinks

When you use a wizard to generate a Web site, the wizard creates hyperlinks between the pages of the Web site. You can also add hyperlinks of your own. These hyperlinks might be to specific items of information on the same page or on a different page, to other Web sites, or to documents that are not part of any Web site.

In this exercise, you will create hyperlinks from the News page of the *GardenCo* Web site to important press releases that are stored in an external Word document.

USE the *GardenCo* Web site and the *PR1* document in the practice file folder for this topic. These practice files are located in the *My Documents\Microsoft Press\Office 2003 SBS\CreateWeb\InsertHype* folder and can also be accessed by clicking *Start/All Programs/Microsoft Press/Microsoft Office System 2003 Step By Step*. OPEN the *GardenCo* Web site.

1 Open **news.htm** in Page view.

2 Press Ctrl + End to move the insertion point to the end of the document.

3 Press Enter, type Archived Press Releases, and press Enter again.

4 On the **Insert** menu, click **Hyperlink**.

Browse for File

5 In the **Insert Hyperlink** dialog box, click the **Browse for File** button, browse to the *My Documents\Office 2003 SBS\CreateWeb\InsertHype* folder, click **PR1**, click **OK** to select the file, and then click **OK** again.

A hyperlink to the press release is inserted at the insertion point.

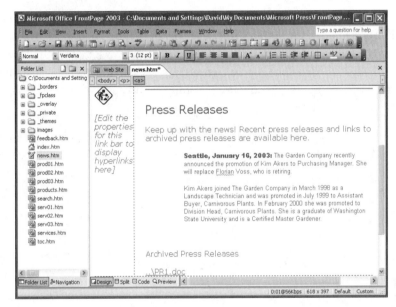

6 To view the contents of the linked file from within FrontPage, press the Ctrl key, and click the link.

A press release dated September 23, 2002 opens in Word.

7 Close the Word window to return to your Web site.

8 Save and close the *news.htm* file.

CLOSE the *GardenCo* Web site.

Making Your Site Accessible for Visitors

New in
Office 2003
Accessibility
checking

If you want your Web site to be comfortably viewed by the widest possible audience, you'll want to avoid including elements in your site that might affect its accessibility. For example, you will want to make navigation methods consistent throughout the site, and you'll want to group blocks of information so that they are more manageable. You can make your site accessible to viewers who have vision problems by using contrasting foreground and background colors and avoiding screen flicker. Paying attention to these and other issues while constructing your Web site will ensure that you do not inadvertently limit your audience.

FrontPage 2003 includes a new accessibility-checking feature that you can use to quickly check one or more pages of your Web site for potential accessibility problems. You can check your site against the World Wide Web Consortium's Web Content Accessibility Guidelines and the U.S. government Section 508 guidelines. The accessibility checker creates a list of errors, warnings, and suggestions for improving your Web site's accessibility.

To check the accessibility of a Web site:

1   Open the site that you want to check.

2   On the **Tools** menu, click **Accessibility**.

3   In the **Check where** area, select the **All pages** option.

4   Click the **Check** button.

5   When a message appears that FrontPage has finished searching the document, click **OK**.

6   When FrontPage displays a list of possible accessibility issues, click one of the problems to see a description in the **Problem Details** area, or double-click one of the problems to open the pertinent file to that location.

7   To create a printable problem report, click the **Generate HTML Report** button.

Seeing Your Web Site as Visitors Will

We've made a pretty good start at personalizing The Garden Company's Web site, and you are probably eager to see the results of your work. There are two ways to view a Web site created with FrontPage before it is published: in FrontPage or in a browser.

Previewing your Web site in FrontPage is a good way to look at the basic layout and evaluate the overall presentation of the site, but it doesn't always represent the site as a visitor will experience it. Apart from the fact that you probably can't see as much of the page as you intend your visitors to see, none of the advanced controls that you might choose to add later will work in this view.

To see an accurate preview of your Web site before it is published, you will want to preview it in a *Web browser*. Viewing the Web site in a browser is a great opportunity to test its usability and functionality before exposing it to the scrutiny of the real world. Always be sure to take the time to test your site before publishing it.

In this exercise, you will look at the *GardenCo* Web site in the Preview pane, preview it in your default Web browser, and then see how it looks to Web visitors using other screen resolutions.

USE the *GardenCo* Web site in the practice file folder for this topic. This practice file is located in the *My Documents\Microsoft Press\Office 2003 SBS\CreateWeb\Preview* folder and can also be accessed by clicking *Start/All Programs/Microsoft Press/Microsoft Office System 2003 Step By Step*.
OPEN the *GardenCo* Web site.

1 Open the home page in Design view.

Show
Preview View

2 At the bottom of the Page view editing window, click the **Show Preview View** button to switch to the Preview pane.

The Web page is displayed in FrontPage.

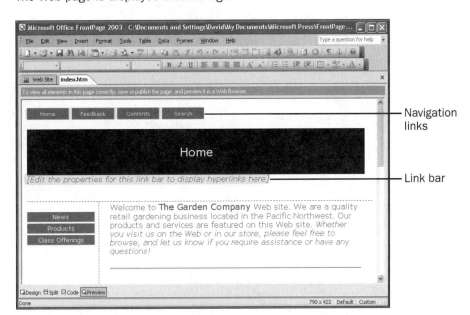

At the top of the screen, a message tells you the page contains elements that might need to be saved or published to be previewed correctly.

Important You can't preview a Web site in an Internet browser without first selecting a file.

Preview in Browser

3 On the Standard toolbar, click the **Preview in Browser** button to see how the site looks in your default Web browser.

Troubleshooting The Preview in Browser button's ScreenTip displays "Preview in (your default Web browser)".

Your default Web browser opens, displaying the *GardenCo* Web site home page.

Troubleshooting The Web site previews in this book are shown in Internet Explorer 6.0 with the default settings. If you are using another Internet browser or have made changes to your Internet Explorer settings, your display might be different.

4 Click each of the navigation links to view the different pages of the site.

Troubleshooting You cannot edit a file in FrontPage while you are previewing it in a browser. Attempting to do so causes an error called an *access violation*. Always close the browser, and then make any necessary changes to your site in FrontPage.

Close

5 When you're done, click the **Close** button to close the browser.

New in
Office 2003
Browser
and resolution
reconciliation

6   Click the down arrow to the right of the **Preview in Browser** button.

A drop-down list displays your browser viewing options, which might include multiple Internet browsers and/or multiple screen resolutions.

7   To see how the sample Web site appears at a screen resolution other than your own setting, click one of the commands that is different from your default setting.

8   Preview the site. When you're done, click the **Close** button to close the browser.

CLOSE the *GardenCo* Web site.

Optimizing Your Screen Display Properties

The width and height of your computer monitor display in pixels is called the *screen resolution*. When personal computers first became popular, most computer monitors were capable of displaying a screen resolution of only 640 pixels wide by 480 pixels high (more commonly known as *640 x 480*). Now most computer monitors can display at 800 x 600 pixels and 1024 x 768 pixels. Some monitors can even display a screen resolution of 1280 x 1024 pixels, or larger. Newer monitors no longer offer a 640 x 480 screen resolution.

Most computer users have the choice of at least two different screen area sizes. Some people prefer to work at an 800 x 600 screen resolution because everything on the screen appears larger. Others prefer being able to fit more information on their screen with a 1024 x 768 display.

When designing a Web page that consists of more than free-flowing text, it is important to consider the likely screen resolution of your Web visitors and design for the lowest common denominator. It is currently common practice to design Web sites to look their best when the visitor's screen area is set to 800 x 600 pixels. (This means that visitors who view your site with a 640 x 480 area will have to scroll to display the entire page.)

To check and change your screen resolution on a Windows XP computer:

1   At the left end of the Windows taskbar, click **Start**, and then click **Control Panel**.

2   In the Control Panel window, click **Appearance and Themes**, and then click **Display** to open the **Display Properties** dialog box.

3   On the **Settings** tab, look at the **Screen resolution** slider. The current screen resolution appears beneath the slider.

4   Drag the slider to change the screen resolution, and click **Apply** to apply your changes.

5   If a dialog box appears prompting you to confirm the change, click **Yes**.

6   When the screen resolution is the way you want, click **OK**.

Deleting a Web Site

When you first start creating Web sites with FrontPage, you will probably want to experiment. As a result, you will more than likely end up with Web sites on your hard disk drive that you no longer need. What's more, if you make a mess when creating a real Web site and decide to start over, because you already have a Web site with your chosen name stored on your hard disk drive, FrontPage will not allow you to overwrite the existing site with a new one. You must create a whole new set of files by appending a number to the name you want to use.

To solve these problems, you might be tempted to simply delete existing sites in Windows Explorer, but if you do, you risk leaving behind extraneous hidden files. Instead you must delete the sites from FrontPage. In this exercise, you will delete the two Web sites you created with templates at the beginning of the chapter.

Important If you did not create the *OnePage* and *Personal* Web sites in the first exercise of this chapter, skip this exercise.

USE the *OnePage* and *Personal* Web sites you created in the first exercise of this chapter.
OPEN the *OnePage* Web site.

1 In the **Folder List**, right-click the top-level folder of the site, and click **Delete** on the shortcut menu to open the **Confirm Delete** dialog box.

2 Select the **Delete this Web site entirely** option, and then click **OK** to delete the Web site.

The Web site is deleted and the Folder List closes because the displayed content no longer exists.

Open

3 Click the down arrow to the right of the **Open** button, and click **Open Site** in the drop-down list.

4 Browse to and open the *Personal* Web site created at the beginning of this chapter.

5 Repeat steps 1 and 2 to delete the *Personal* Web site.

BE SURE TO quit FrontPage if you are not continuing on to the next chapter.

Key Points

- You can quickly and easily create FrontPage Web sites by using a template or wizard. Both tools create and populate the basic Web site by using comments to suggest the types of text you can use to personalize the site. A wizard walks you through the process of personalizing the site.

- You can format text and paragraphs in FrontPage by using the same familiar commands as you do in other Office applications.

- To test the full functionality of a Web site, you must preview it in a Web browser. FrontPage 2003 makes it easy to preview your site in multiple browsers and screen resolutions.

- You should delete Web sites from within FrontPage rather than from Windows Explorer to ensure that all the hidden files and folders are correctly deleted.

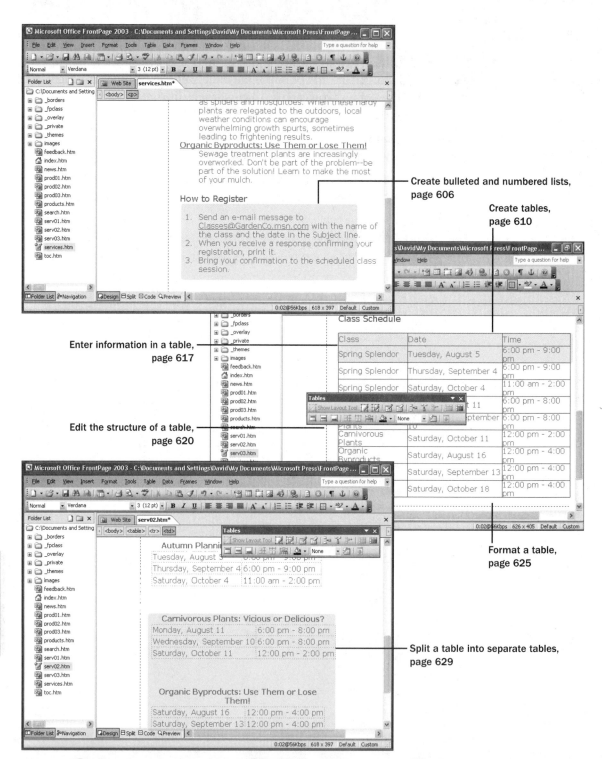

Create bulleted and numbered lists, page 606

Create tables, page 610

Enter information in a table, page 617

Edit the structure of a table, page 620

Format a table, page 625

Split a table into separate tables, page 629

24 Presenting Information in Lists and Tables

In this chapter you will learn to:

✔ Create bulleted and numbered lists.

✔ Create tables.

✔ Enter information in a table.

✔ Edit the structure of a table.

✔ Format a table.

✔ Split a table into separate tables.

You are probably familiar with the kinds of *lists* and *tables* you can create in applications such as Microsoft Office Word 2003 and Microsoft Office PowerPoint 2003. In Microsoft Office FrontPage 2003, you use similar techniques to create lists and most kinds of tables.

Lists and tables are traditionally used to present information in structured, easy-to-grasp formats. In addition, you can use tables to structure entire Web page layouts. Using tables to establish the look of an entire Web page minimizes browser display variations and gives you more control than if you depend on a non-structured presentation. For instance, you can use a table to create a Web page that is a specific height and width, and to lay out content in specific positions on the page.

In this chapter, you will learn how to create bulleted lists, numbered lists, and tables in a FrontPage Web page. First you will add lists to a few pages of The Garden Company's Web site. Then you will create tables by using three different methods:

■ By using the Insert Table button.

■ By using the Insert Table command.

■ By drawing lines to create the table's rows and columns.

By learning a variety of methods, you will be able to select the simplest method for creating your own tables in the future.

See Also   Do you need only a quick refresher on the topics in this chapter? See the Quick Reference entries on pages xxxiii.

Important   Before you can use the practice files in this chapter, you need to install them from the book's companion CD to their default location. See "Using the Book's CD-ROM" on page xxi for more information.

Creating Bulleted and Numbered Lists

You use lists to separate items of information that might otherwise be buried in a text paragraph. If the items don't have to appear in a particular order, they usually appear in *bulleted lists*; for example, a list of drought-tolerant plants would be presented in a bulleted list. If the items have to appear in a particular order, they usually appear in *numbered lists*; for example, instructions for repotting a particular houseplant would be presented in a numbered list.

To convert a series of regular paragraphs to a bulleted list, you select the paragraphs and on the Formatting toolbar, click the Bullets button. Similarly, to convert regular paragraphs to a numbered list, you select the paragraphs and on the Formatting toolbar, click the Numbering button. To convert bulleted or numbered items back to regular paragraphs, select the items, and click the corresponding button to toggle it off.

In this exercise, you will create a new bulleted list, add an item to an existing bulleted list, and create a numbered list.

USE the *GardenCo* Web site in the practice file folder for this topic. This practice file is located in the *My Documents\Microsoft Press\Office 2003 SBS\ListsTables\CreateList* folder and can also be accessed by clicking *Start/All Programs/Microsoft Press/Microsoft Office System 2003 Step By Step*.
BE SURE TO start FrontPage before beginning this exercise.
OPEN the *GardenCo* Web site.

Important   The exercises in this chapter build on the results of the previous exercise. If you work through all the exercises sequentially, you can continue working with your own file rather than closing and opening the sample Web sites from the practice file folders. When using the practice files, be sure to use the files from the correct practice file folder for each exercise.

1   If the **Folder List** is not already open, on the **View** menu, click **Folder List**.

2　　In the **Folder List**, double-click **serv01.htm** to open the Spring Splendor page in the Page view editing window.

3　　Position the insertion point on the blank line under the *What You'll Learn* heading.

4　　Type Which Spring-flowering plants are best for the Pacific Northwest.

5　　Press ⎡Enter⎤ to start a new line, and then type When to plant for a luscious Spring garden.

6　　Press ⎡Enter⎤, and then type How to protect your garden from frost.

7　　Select the three lines you just typed, and on the Formatting toolbar, click the **Bullets** button.

Bullets

The text is converted to a bulleted list.

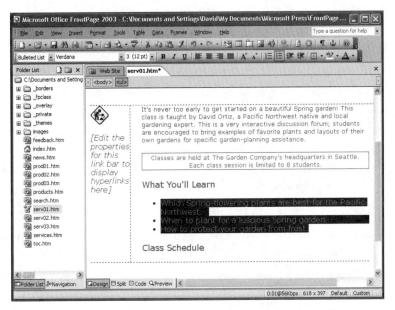

8　　Click the *serv01.htm* file's **Close** button to close the Spring Splendor page, saving your changes when prompted.

Close [Page]

9　　In the **Folder List**, double-click **serv03.htm** to open the Organic Byproducts page in the Page view editing window.

10　　To add a new bulleted item to the **What You'll Learn** list, position the insertion point at the end of the second item, and press ⎡Enter⎤.

A new, blank bulleted list line is created.

11 Type **When and where to use your mulch for maximum effectiveness.**

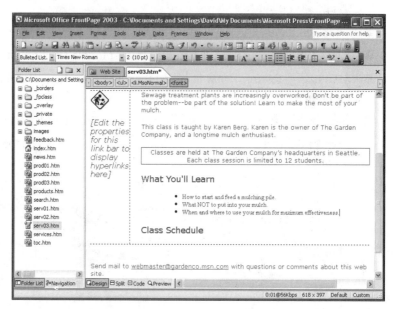

12 Close the Organic Byproducts page, saving your changes when prompted.

13 In the **Folder List**, double-click **services.htm** to open the Class Offerings page in the Page view editing window.

14 Press Ctrl + End to move the insertion point to the end of the page.

15 Press Enter to create a new line.

16 Type **Send an e-mail message to Classes@GardenCo.msn.com with the name of the class and the date in the Subject line.**

As you type, the e-mail address is automatically formatted as a hyperlink.

Numbering

17 On the Formatting toolbar, click the **Numbering** button to turn the paragraph into a numbered item.

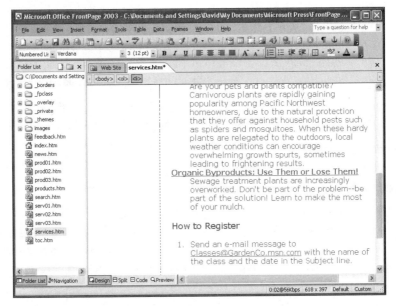

18   Press ⎡Enter⎤ to create a new numbered item.

19   Type When you receive a response confirming your registration, print it.

20   Press ⎡Enter⎤, and then type Bring your confirmation to the scheduled class session.

21   Press ⎡Enter⎤ to create a new line, and then click the **Numbering** button to turn off numbering and convert the new numbered item to a regular paragraph.

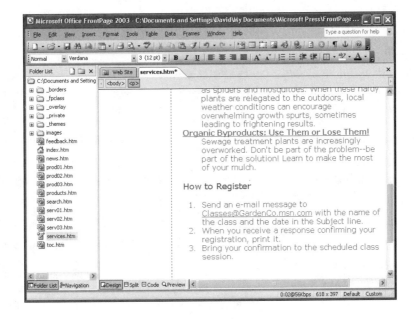

22 If you're interested, you might want to click the Code button to display the underlying source code for the numbered list in the Code pane. As you will see, FrontPage designates the entire list as an *ordered list* by enclosing it in <ol> and </ol> tags. Each list item is enclosed in <li> and </li> tags. A bulleted list has a similar structure, except that the entire list is designated as an *unordered list* by enclosing it in <ul> and </ul> tags.

23 Close the Class Offerings page, saving your changes when prompted.

CLOSE the *GardenCo* Web site.

Creating Tables

A *table* consists of vertical *columns* and horizontal *rows*. A table might have an overall *table title* that appears either as a separate paragraph above the body of the table or in the table's top row. It usually has a *header row*, which contains a title for each column, and it might have a *header column*, which contains a title for each row.

Tip Sometimes text or numbers would stand out better for your Web visitors if they were presented in columns and rows, but they don't need the structure of a table. In Word, you can use a tabular list—a set of pseudo columns and rows in which you use tabs to line everything up—instead of setting up a table structure. But FrontPage doesn't accommodate this type of list. When you want to put information in columns and rows, you need to create a real table.

In this exercise, you'll learn one way of creating a table as you set up the structure for a Class Schedules table. You will use this table to organize information about the gardening classes offered by The Garden Company.

USE the *GardenCo* Web site in the practice file folder for this topic. This practice file is located in the *My Documents\Microsoft Press\Office 2003 SBS\ListsTables\CreateTable* folder and can also be accessed by clicking *Start/All Programs/Microsoft Press/Microsoft Office System 2003 Step By Step*.
OPEN the *GardenCo* Web site.

1 In the **Folder List**, double-click the **serv01.htm** file to open the Spring Splendor page in the Page view editing window.

2 Press [Ctrl]+[End] to move the insertion point to the end of the page, and then press [Enter] to insert a blank line following the *Class Schedule* heading.

3 On the Standard toolbar, click the **Insert Table** button.

Insert Table

A grid drops down, on which you can indicate the size of your table.

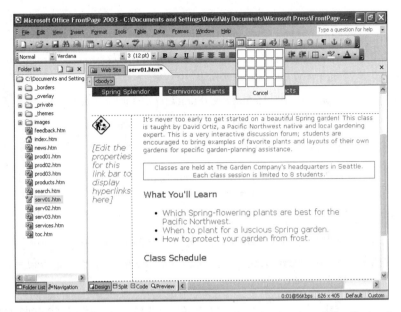

4   Point to the first *cell*—the intersection of the first row and the first column—and hold down the left mouse button. Drag the pointer until an area three cells wide by ten cells high is highlighted (the grid will expand as you drag the mouse to the edge), and then release the mouse button.

FrontPage inserts a table with the number of rows and columns you highlighted.

5   If necessary, scroll to the bottom of the page to see the entire table.

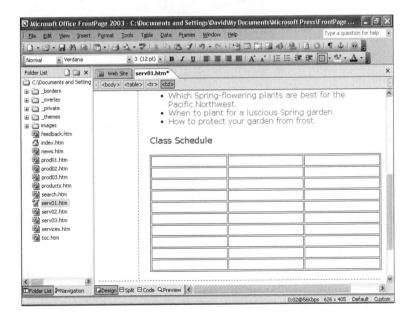

Close [Page]

6 Click the *serv01.htm* file's **Close** button to close the Spring Splendor page, saving your changes when prompted.

7 In the **Folder List**, double-click **serv02.htm** to open the Carnivorous Plants page in the Page view editing window.

8 Repeat step 2 to insert a blank line at the end of the page.

9 On the **Table** menu, point to **Insert**, and then click **Table**.

The Insert Table dialog box appears.

Tip   Unlike most corresponding menu commands and toolbar buttons in Microsoft Office 2003, the Insert Table menu command and the Insert Table button work differently. The command displays a dialog box, whereas the button displays a grid.

10 In the **Size** area, specify 9 rows and 4 columns for your table.

11 In the **Layout** area, set the **Cell padding** to 3, and verify that the width is set to 100 percent.

Tip   *Cell padding* is space between the borders of the cells and the text inside them. This padding is similar to the margins of a page.

12 In the **Borders** area, set the **Size** to 0.

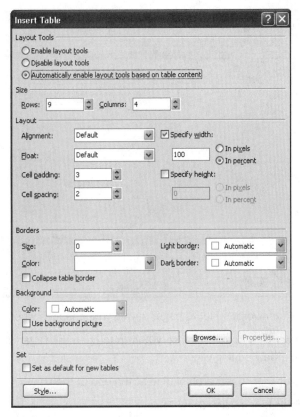

13 Click **OK** to create the table.

14 If necessary, scroll to the bottom of the page to see the entire table.

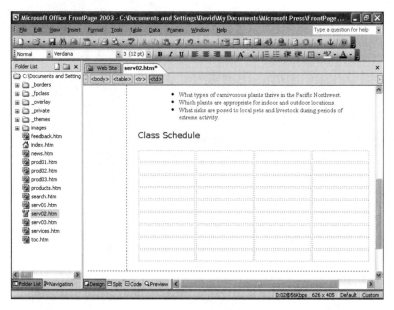

15 Close the Carnivorous Plants page, saving your changes when prompted.

16 In the **Folder List**, double-click **serv03.htm** to open the Organic Byproducts page in the Page view editing window.

17 Repeat step 2 to insert a blank line at the end of the page.

18 On the **Table** menu, click **Draw Table**.

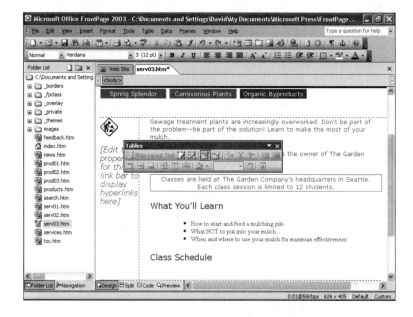

The Tables toolbar opens, and the mouse pointer changes to a pencil.

19 Scroll down so you can see the bottom of the page.

20 Click under the *Class Schedule* heading, and then drag the pencil pointer down and to the right, to create a table of approximately the same size as those you previously created in this exercise.

When you release the mouse button, FrontPage creates a single-cell table.

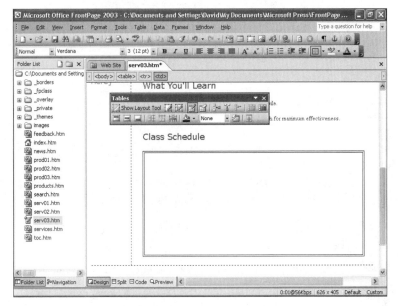

21 Using the pencil pointer, draw two vertical lines within the table to divide it into three columns.

22 Draw nine horizontal lines within the table to divide it into ten rows.

Tip   This will be easiest if you first divide the table into two rows, and then divide each row into five rows.

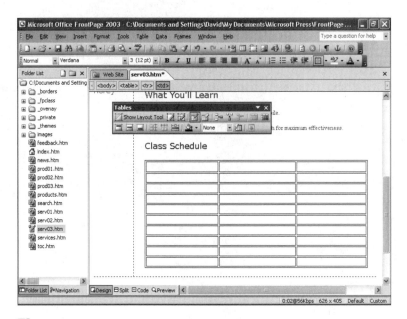

Tip   Experiment with the locations of the lines separating columns and rows; you will find that the table expands to meet your needs.

23   When you're done drawing the rough table, press the ⎡Esc⎤ key to change the pointer back to its original shape.

24   Drag through the table's cells to select them all.

25   On the **Tables** toolbar, click the **Distribute Rows Evenly** button to make all ten rows an equal height.

Distribute
Rows Evenly

26   On the **Tables** toolbar, click the **Distribute Columns Evenly** button to make all three columns an equal width.

Distribute
Columns
Evenly

27   Close the Organic Byproducts page, saving your changes when prompted.

28   At the right end of the **Tables** toolbar's title bar, click the **Close** button to close the toolbar.

Close (Toolbar)

CLOSE the *GardenCo* Web site.

Tip If you want to close a floating toolbar to reduce screen clutter, you can either click the Close button at the right end of the title bar of a floating toolbar, or right-click the toolbar, and click its name on the shortcut menu. To display a hidden toolbar, right-click any toolbar, and then click the name of the toolbar you want on the shortcut menu.

Converting Existing Text to a Table

If you have an existing block of text with items separated by commas, tabs, or paragraph marks, you can convert the text to a table.

To convert existing text:

1 Select the text you want to convert, and then on the **Table** menu, point to **Convert**, and click **Text to Table**.

The Convert Text To Table dialog box appears, in which you can tell FrontPage how the elements of the selected text are separated.

2 Make your selection, and click **OK**.

FrontPage converts the text to a table. You can use the Tables toolbar to make any necessary adjustments.

You can also convert a table to text by selecting the table, and on the Table menu, pointing to Convert and clicking Table to Text.

Entering Information in a Table

In the previous exercise, you created the structure for three tables on three separate pages of The Garden Company's Web site. Now you need to fill the tables with information to make them useful. You enter information in FrontPage tables the same way you enter it in Word tables.

In this exercise you will fill three existing tables with information. For The Garden Company's Web site, you'll place the same information in each table, but you would probably fill your own tables with different types of information.

USE the *GardenCo* Web site in the practice file folder for this topic. This practice file is located in the *My Documents\Microsoft Press\Office 2003 SBS\ListsTables\TableText* folder and can also be accessed by clicking *Start/All Programs/Microsoft Press/Microsoft Office System 2003 Step By Step*.
OPEN the *GardenCo* Web site.

1 In the **Folder List**, click the **serv01.htm** file to select it, and then hold down the [Ctrl] key, and click **serv02.htm** and **serv03.htm** so that all three files are selected.

2 Press ⌷Enter⌷ to open the three files in the Page view editing window.

3 On the Spring Splendor page, scroll down so you can see the entire table.

4 Position the insertion point in the first cell of the table, and then type Class.

> **Tip** If the Tables toolbar opens when you position the insertion point inside a table, you can drag it out of the way by its title bar, or you can close it by clicking the Close button at the right end of its title bar.

As you type, the table column widths adjust automatically to reflect the relationship between the contents of each column.

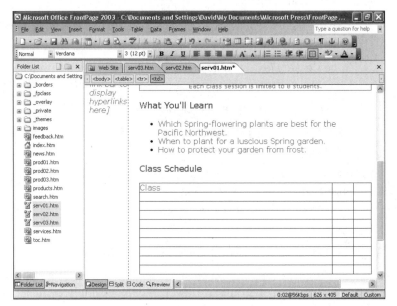

5 Press the ⌷Tab⌷ key to move the insertion point to the second cell, and then type Date.

The table column widths adjust automatically as you type each word.

6 Press ⌷Tab⌷ to move the insertion point to the third cell, and then type Time to complete the table's header row.

7 Enter the following information in the three columns of the table, under the respective headings:

Class	Date	Time
Spring Splendor	Tuesday, August 5	6:00 pm – 9:00 pm
Spring Splendor	Thursday, September 4	6:00 pm – 9:00 pm
Spring Splendor	Saturday, October 4	11:00 am – 2:00 pm
Carnivorous Plants	Monday, August 11	6:00 pm – 8:00 pm
Carnivorous Plants	Wednesday, September 10	6:00 pm – 8:00 pm
Carnivorous Plants	Saturday, October 11	12:00 pm – 2:00 pm
Organic Byproducts	Saturday, August 16	12:00 pm – 4:00 pm
Organic Byproducts	Saturday, September 13	12:00 pm – 4:00 pm
Organic Byproducts	Saturday, October 18	12:00 pm – 4:00 pm

Tip　If you don't feel like typing, you can copy and paste this information from the *ClassList* document stored in the practice file folder for this topic.

8　At the top of the Page view editing window, click the **serv03.htm** page tab to switch to that file.

9　On the Organic Byproducts page, fill the hand-drawn table with the same header row and the same three columns of information.

Note that the column widths do not adjust as you enter information into this table because you specified when creating it that the columns should be distributed evenly.

10　At the top of the Page view editing window, click the **serv02.htm** page tab to switch to that file.

11　The table on the Carnivorous Plants page has only nine rows, so this table will not have a header. Fill in the first two columns with the class and date information, and then fill in the fourth column with the time information.

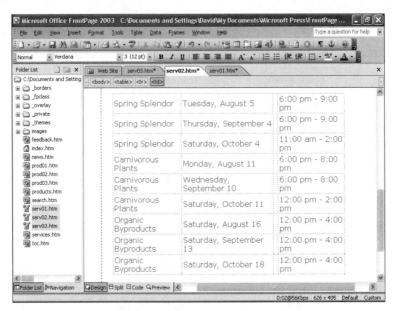

12 On the **File** menu, click **Save All** to save the open files.

CLOSE the *GardenCo* Web site.

Editing the Structure of a Table

Unless you are very skilled at creating tables, you will rarely create one that you don't have to later adjust in one way or another. Most likely, you will have to add or delete rows or columns and move information around until it is in the right place. Almost certainly, you will also have to adjust the size of rows and columns that are too big, too small, or unevenly spaced. Luckily, with FrontPage it is simple to fix all these structural problems.

Tip   When columns are much wider than the information they contain, your Web visitors might have to scroll from side to side to see all of the information in a table. When columns are too narrow, the text within will wrap, and your Web visitors might have to scroll up and down. Whenever possible, avoid these problems by resizing one or more of the rows or columns in a table as needed.

In this exercise, you will change the structure of an existing table to re-arrange the information it contains. On the Carnivorous Plants page of the sample Web site, the class schedule is currently presented in nine rows and four columns, one of which is blank. You will move information between columns, delete the unused column, and add a header row to this table.

USE the *GardenCo* Web site in the practice file folder for this topic. This practice file is located in the *My Documents\Microsoft Press\Office 2003 SBS\ListsTables\TableStruct* folder and can also be accessed by clicking *Start\All Programs\Microsoft Press\Microsoft Office System 2003 Step By Step*.
OPEN the *GardenCo* Web site.

1 In the **Folder List**, double-click **serv02.htm** to open the Carnivorous Plants page in the Page view editing window.

2 On the Carnivorous Plants page, click anywhere in the fourth column of the table.

The Tables toolbar opens.

Troubleshooting If the Tables toolbar does not open, right-click an open toolbar, and click Tables on the shortcut menu.

3 On the **Table** menu, point to **Select**, and then click **Column**.

4 Point to the upper-left corner of the selection, and drag the time information from the fourth column to the top cell of the third column.

Troubleshooting If you drag the selected cells to a cell other than the top cell of the column, the entire contents of the selection will be inserted in the cell to which you drag it.

5 Click anywhere in the top row of the table.

Insert Rows

6 On the **Tables** toolbar, click the **Insert Rows** button.

A new row is inserted at the top of the table.

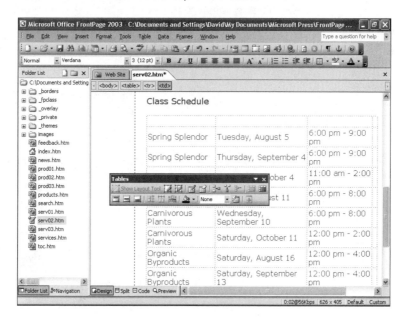

7 Click anywhere in the empty fourth column of the table.

8 On the **Table** menu, point to **Select**, and then click **Column**.

Delete Cells

9 On the **Tables** toolbar, click the **Delete Cells** button to delete the blank column from the right side of the table.

10 In the new header row, enter **Class**, **Date**, and **Time** as the column headings.

The table on the Carnivorous Plants page now looks like those on the Spring Splendor and Organic Byproducts pages.

Close [Page]

11 Click the *serv02.htm* file's **Close** button to close the Carnivorous Plants page, saving your changes when prompted.

12 In the **Folder List**, double-click **serv03.htm** to open the Organic Byproducts page in the Page view editing window.

13 Scroll down so you can see the entire table.

14 To adjust the size of the columns in the table on this page, start by pointing to the right border of the table's **Date** column.

The pointer changes to a double-headed arrow.

15 Double-click the border.

FrontPage resizes the column to exactly fit its contents.

AutoFit to Contents

16 Click anywhere in the table, and on the **Tables** toolbar, click the **AutoFit to Contents** button.

All the table columns adjust to the exact width of their contents.

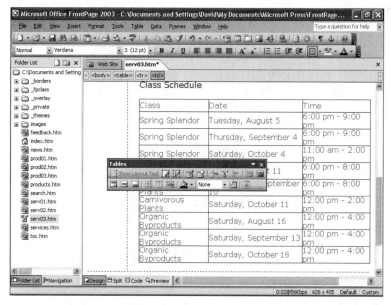

17 Right-click anywhere in the table, and then click **Table Properties** on the shortcut menu to display the **Table Properties** dialog box.

18 In the **Table Properties** dialog box, do the following:

- In the **Alignment** drop-down list, click **Left**.

- Set **Cell padding** to **3**.

- Select the **Specify width** check box.

- In the **Specify width** box, type **100**.

- Select the **In percent** option.

- In the **Borders** area, set **Size** to **0**.

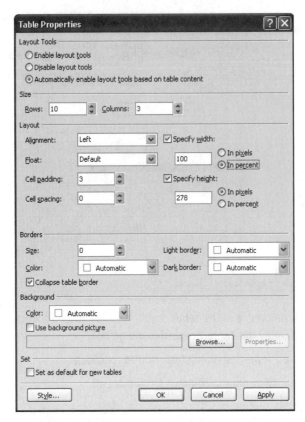

■   Click **OK** to close the dialog box and apply your changes.

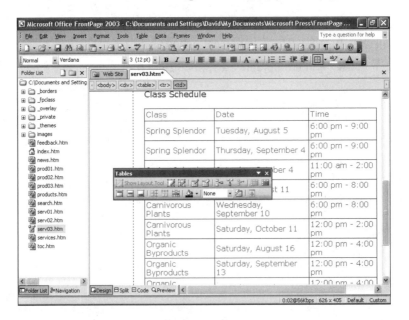

19   Move the mouse pointer to the top of the first column so that it changes to a down arrow. Hold down the left mouse button to select the column, and then drag to the right until all three columns are selected.

20   On the **Tables** toolbar, click the **Distribute Columns Evenly** button to make all the columns the same width.

Distribute
Columns
Evenly

21   Close the Organic Byproducts page, saving your changes when prompted.

CLOSE the *GardenCo* Web site.

Formatting a Table

In FrontPage, as in Word, you have several options for formatting tables. You can choose from a large variety of pre-formatted table styles or create your own look. You can even merge two or more cells into one cell so that a table entry spans several columns or rows.

FrontPage 2003 supports many of the standard Microsoft Office System table-formatting options, including the following:

- By using Fill Right and Fill Down, you can quickly copy content from one table cell to several others.

- By using AutoFormat, you can quickly create professional-looking tables by simply selecting a pre-formatted option from a list.

- By using the Borders button, you can format selected table and cell borders as easily as you can in Word and Excel, simply by clicking the type of border you want.

In this exercise, you'll format the tables in The Garden Company's Web site, first by doing things "the hard way"—and seeing just how easy that can be—and then by checking out a few of FrontPage's ready-made formats.

USE the *GardenCo* Web site in the practice file folder for this topic. This practice file is located in the *My Documents\Microsoft Press\Office 2003 SBS\ListsTables\FormatTable* folder and can also be accessed by clicking *Start/All Programs/Microsoft Press/Microsoft Office System 2003 Step By Step*.
OPEN the *GardenCo* Web site.

1   In the **Folder List**, double-click **serv02.htm** to open the Carnivorous Plants page in the Page view editing window.

2   Scroll down to the table, and select the three cells of the header row.

3   Right-click the selection, and click **Cell Properties** on the shortcut menu.

The Cell Properties dialog box appears.

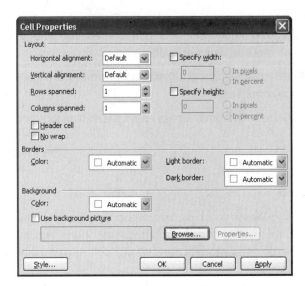

4   In the **Cell Properties** dialog box, select the **Header cell** check box.

5   In the **Background** area, click the down arrow to the right of the **Color** box to display the Standard and Theme color palettes.

     If you click More Colors, FrontPage displays a dialog box in which you can select from a palette of 127 colors or specify a custom color using the hexadecimal or RGB value. Your options are practically limitless!

6   Select your favorite color from the default set, and then click **OK** to close the **Cell Properties** dialog box and apply your changes.

     Tip   When a theme is attached to a Web page, the default colors include those used in the theme. It is generally best to select colors from the theme to maintain a consistent look and feel throughout your Web site.

     The background color is applied, and the words inside the header cells become bold and centered.

7   Because the cells are still selected, click away from the table to reveal the actual cell color.

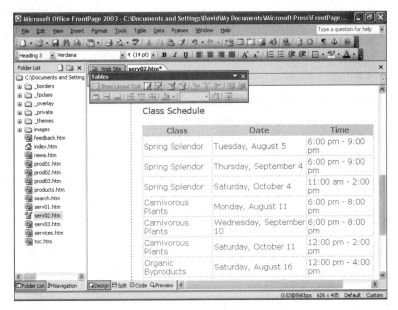

8 In the **Folder List**, double-click **serv01.htm** to open the Spring Splendor page in the Page view editing window.

9 Click anywhere in the table on that page.

Table
AutoFormat

10 On the **Tables** toolbar, click the **Table AutoFormat** button.

The Table AutoFormat dialog box appears.

11 In the **Table AutoFormat** dialog box, use the ⬇ key to scroll through the **Formats** list on the left.

When you select a format, a sample table with that format applied is displayed in the Preview window.

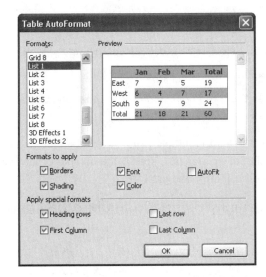

12 Select the **Subtle 1** format.

13 Because this table does not have a special first column, in the **Apply special formats** area, clear the **First Column** check box.

14 Click **OK** to apply the selected format to the table.

15 At the bottom of the Page view editing window, click the **Preview** button to switch to the Preview pane, then scroll down to see the table.

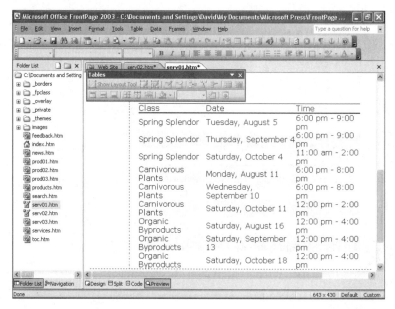

This table looks good, but notice that each class name in the first column is repeated three times. The table would look tidier if each class name appeared only once and spanned three rows.

16 At the bottom of the Page view editing window, click the **Show Design View** button to switch to the Design pane.

17 In the first column, select the three cells containing the words *Spring Splendor*.

18 On the **Tables** toolbar, click the **Merge Cells** button.

Merge Cells

FrontPage merges the three cells into one cell that still contains three instances of *Spring Splendor*.

Tip   To split one cell into multiple cells, select the cell, and click the Split Cells button. In the Split Cells dialog box, specify the number of rows or columns you want to split the merged cell into, and click OK.

19 Select and delete two instances of the class name, leaving just one.

The remaining class name is vertically centered within the cell.

20 Repeat steps 17 through 19 for the Carnivorous Plants and Organic Byproducts classes.

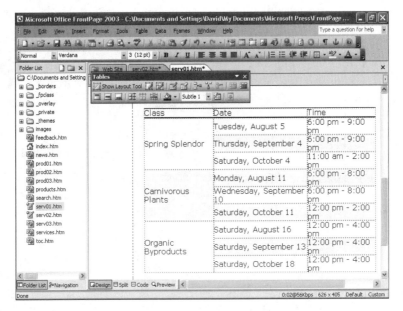

21 On the **File** menu, click **Save All** to save the open pages.

CLOSE the *GardenCo* Web site.

Splitting a Table into Separate Tables

In the same way that you can split and merge individual cells, you can split and merge entire tables. You can also nest one table within another. These options might seem pretty complex for presenting straightforward information, but they offer wonderful possibilities, particularly when you want to organize an entire Web page with one table.

In this exercise you will split the Class Schedule table into three separate tables, one for each class, with each class name as the table title.

USE the *GardenCo* Web site in the practice file folder for this topic. This practice file is located in the *My Documents\Microsoft Press\Office 2003 SBS\ListsTables\TableInTable* folder and can also be accessed by clicking *Start/All Programs/Microsoft Press/Microsoft Office System 2003 Step By Step.*
OPEN the *GardenCo* Web site.

1 In the **Folder List**, double-click **serv02.htm** to open the Carnivorous Plants page in the Page view editing window.

2   Scroll down to the table, and click in the first row containing the words *Carnivorous Plants*.

3   On the **Table** menu, click **Split Table**.

FrontPage splits the table into two tables.

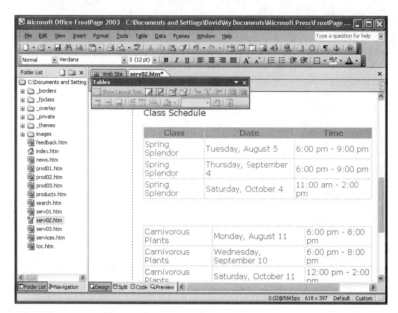

4   Click in the first row containing the words *Organic Byproducts*, and split the table again.

You now have three distinct tables.

5   Click in the row containing the words *Class*, *Date*, and *Time*.

6   On the **Table** menu, point to **Select**, and then click **Row**.

7   Right-click the selection, and click **Delete Rows** on the shortcut menu.

The header row is deleted.

8   With the insertion point in the **Spring Splendor** table, on the **Table** menu, point to **Insert**, and then click **Caption**.

A centered caption row is inserted at the top of the table.

9   Type **Autumn Planning for Spring Splendor** as the table caption.

Bold

10   Select the caption, and on the Formatting toolbar, click the **Bold** button.

11   Select the first column. Right-click the selection, and click **Delete Columns** on the shortcut menu.

The left column is deleted.

AutoFit to
Contents

12 On the **Tables** toolbar, click the **AutoFit to Contents** button.

13 Repeat steps 8 through 12 for the *Carnivorous Plants* and *Organic Byproducts* tables, using the following class titles as the table captions:

- **Carnivorous Plants: Vicious or Delicious?**

- **Organic Byproducts: Use Them or Lose Them!**

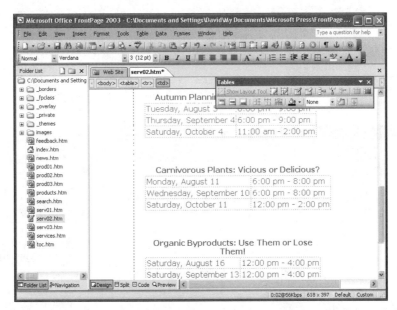

Close [Page]

14 Click the *serv02.htm* file's **Close** button to close the Carnivorous Plants page, saving your changes when prompted.

CLOSE the *GardenCo* Web site. If you are not continuing on to the next chapter, quit FrontPage.

Key Points

- You can format text as a bulleted or numbered list simply by clicking a button.

- You can convert text to a table, or convert a table to text.

- FrontPage 2003 supplies 38 predefined table formats from which you can choose, or you can format a table by hand.

- After creating a table, you can merge the contents of multiple cells or split individual cells into multiple cells. You can do the same with entire tables.

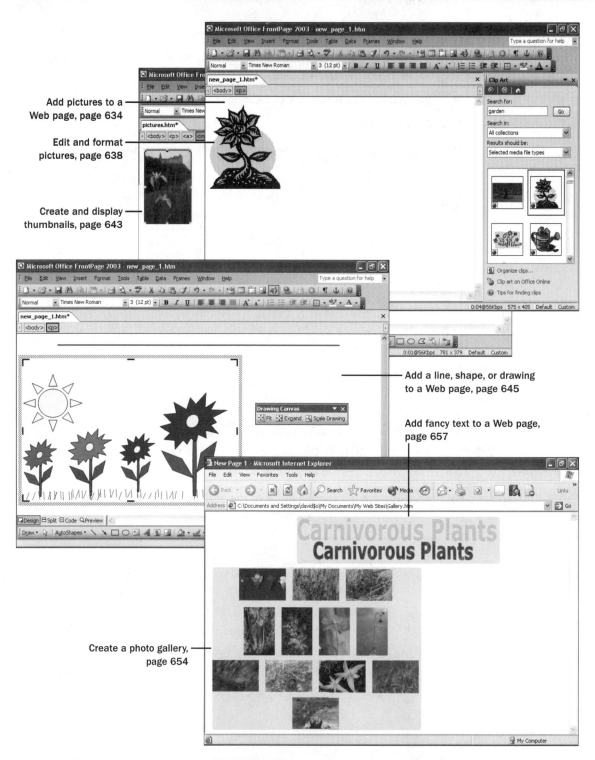

Add pictures to a
Web page, page 634

Edit and format
pictures, page 638

Create and display
thumbnails, page 643

Add a line, shape, or drawing
to a Web page, page 645

Add fancy text to a Web page,
page 657

Create a photo gallery,
page 654

25 Enhancing Your Web Site with Graphics

In this chapter you will learn to:

✔ Add pictures to a Web page.

✔ Edit and format pictures.

✔ Create and display thumbnails.

✔ Add a line, shape, or drawing to a Web page.

✔ Create a photo gallery.

✔ Add fancy text to a Web page.

You can do a lot to get your message across and increase the appeal of your Web pages by using well-crafted language and by formatting words and paragraphs to good effect. However, there are times when no matter how you format your text, it is not enough to grab the attention of your visitors and to make your Web site stand out from all the others.

At times like these, you need the pizzazz that pictures and other graphic images can add to your pages. With Microsoft Office FrontPage 2003, you can insert a variety of graphic elements, including clip art, picture files, scanned images, drawings, shapes, WordArt objects, and videos.

It is safe to assume that a large part of the appeal of The Garden Company's Web site, which is used as the example for most of the exercises in this book, would be pictures of plants, "idea" shots of gardens to provide inspiration, garden bed designs, and other visually enticing elements. No amount of text will do the trick for a Web site that is about things you have to see to appreciate, just as no amount of text can possibly substitute for a music clip on a site dedicated to a particular band or genre of music.

To make The Garden Company's Web site visually appealing, you would need to use graphics judiciously, carefully selecting an appropriate style and exercising some restraint to avoid a confusing effect. Because you will learn how to add a wide variety of graphic elements in this chapter, you will use the *GardenCo* Web site only when it's appropriate, practicing otherwise on a new page that you can discard when you're through with it.

See Also   Do you need only a quick refresher on the topics in this chapter? See the Quick Reference entries on page xxxiii.

Important   Before you can use the practice files in this chapter, you need to install them from the book's companion CD to their default location. See "Using the Book's CD-ROM" on page xxi for more information.

Adding Pictures to a Web Page

FrontPage makes it easy to add all kinds of *media*, including graphics, photos, videos, and even sound effects, into a Web page. When you're looking for a quick and simple graphic representation that won't cost you a licensing fee, an easy solution is to use *clip art*. A large library of clip art is included with The Microsoft Office System 2003, and a seemingly endless selection is available on the Microsoft Office Design Gallery Live Web site at *dgl.microsoft.com*. If neither of these sources has what you need, you can find hundreds of small clip art galleries on the Web. You can also purchase clip art CD-ROMs, many of which focus on particular themes or on particular styles of clip art.

The Clip Organizer

The Microsoft Office System 2003 stores various clip art elements in different folders, and all of them are available to you in FrontPage 2003.

You can use the Clip Organizer to access and organize media files through an easy-to-use task pane interface. The Clip Organizer contains hundreds of pieces of clip art and makes it easy to find additional digital art on the World Wide Web.

To organize your clips using the Clip Organizer:

1   In the **Clip Art** task pane, click **Organize clips**.

     The Add Clips to Organizer dialog box appears.

2   Click the **Now** button.

     The Microsoft Clip Organizer takes a few moments to create collections for you based on your media files, and then takes a few moments more to add keywords to your clips so that you can find them later using the keyword search feature.

You can find, access, and insert a variety of media files from the Clip Art task pane. In addition to traditional clip art, which usually consists of cartoon-like drawings, you can choose from photographs, movies, and sounds. This great resource area is a lot of fun to explore!

Where Web pages are concerned, it's worth keeping in mind the well-worn saying "A picture is worth a thousand words." You will often find it beneficial to add photographs to your Web pages to illustrate or enhance the text or to demonstrate a difficult concept. You can obtain Web-ready pictures in a variety of ways: by taking photographs with a digital camera, by scanning existing photographs to create digital files, by buying art files, or by downloading public-domain files from the Internet.

FrontPage 2003 can access picture files that are on your computer, on another computer on your network, or if you have an Internet connection, on a Web site.

For the highest display quality, you should use pictures that have been saved as *Graphics Interchange Format (GIF)* or *Joint Photographic Experts Group (JPG)* files. Both display well over the Web. The GIF file format supports up to 256 colors. The JPG file format was specifically developed for photographs and is the best format to use for photos and other graphics with more than 256 colors. When choosing a graphic format, it is important to remember that smaller files download faster. You might consider saving pictures in both GIF and JPG format to so you can compare file size and picture quality and select the format that best fits your needs.

Tip   When displaying a graphic in FrontPage's Design pane, you can easily convert it to GIF or JPG format. In Page view, right-click the graphic, and then click Picture Properties on the shortcut menu. Click the General tab, and then click the Picture File Type button. In the Picture File Type dialog box, select the GIF or JPG option. The original and changed sizes are shown at the top of the dialog box.

In this exercise, you will insert a piece of clip art and a photograph on a practice page.

USE the *GardenCo* picture in the practice file folder for this topic. This practice file is located in the *My Documents\Microsoft Press\Office 2003 SBS\Pictures\AddPicture* folder and can also be accessed by clicking *Start/All Programs/Microsoft Press/Microsoft Office System 2003 Step By Step*.
BE SURE TO start FrontPage before beginning this exercise.

Create a new
normal page

1   If a new page is not already open, on the Standard toolbar, click the **Create a new normal page** button to open a new blank page to use as a canvas for your artwork.

2   On the **Insert** menu, point to **Picture**, and then click **Clip Art**.

The Clip Art task pane opens.

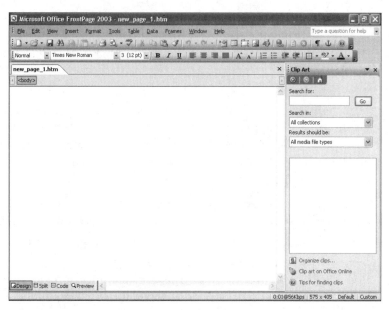

3   Click the down arrow to the right of the **Results should be** box. In the drop-down list, clear the **Photographs**, **Movies**, and **Sounds** check boxes. Make sure the **Clip Art** check box is selected. Then click away from the drop-down list to close it.

4   If you do not have an active Internet connection, click the down arrow to the right of the **Search in** box and clear the **Web Collections** check box. Then click away from the drop-down list to close it.

5   In the **Search for** box, type garden, and then click **Go**.

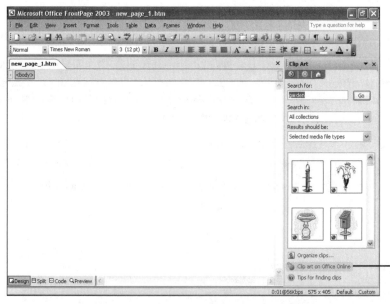

Office
Online Web
Collection
indicator

While FrontPage searches for clip art that matches your search term, the word *(Searching...)* appears above the Results box. When the search is complete, the results are displayed in the Results box.

6   Position the mouse pointer over the first graphic to display its keywords, dimensions, file size, and format.

Tip   A vertical bar with a down arrow appears when you position the mouse pointer over a graphic. Clicking the down arrow displays a list of options.

7   Scroll through the search results until you find a graphic you like.

8   Position the mouse pointer over the graphic, and click the down arrow that appears. In the drop-down list, click **Insert**.

FrontPage inserts the selected graphic in your page at the insertion point.

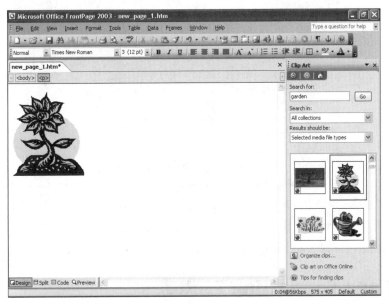

The inserted clip art might not be the right size for your page (sometimes it is very large). Later in the chapter, you will practice resizing graphics.

Close

9   Click the file's **Close** button to close the current file; click **No** when prompted to save your work.

10   On the Standard toolbar, click the **Create a new normal page** button to open a new page.

A new, blank page opens in the Page view editing window.

11 On the **Insert** menu, point to **Picture**, and then click **From File** to display the **Picture** dialog box.

12 In the **Picture** dialog box, browse to the practice file folder for this topic, and click (don't double-click) the **GardenCo** file.

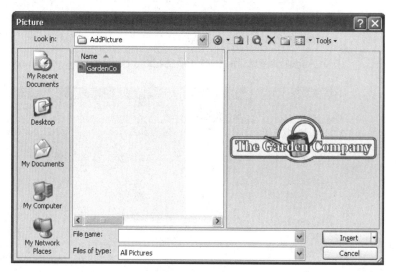

Views

13 If you don't see a preview of the picture in the dialog box, on the **Picture** dialog box's toolbar, click the down arrow to the right of the **Views** button, and then click **Preview**.

The dialog box displays a preview of the selected picture, which is The Garden Company's logo.

14 Click the **Insert** button to insert the logo on the Web page and close the Clip Art task pane.

CLOSE the practice file without saving your work.

Editing and Formatting Pictures

Sometimes the picture you add to a Web page won't produce exactly the result you are looking for—perhaps it's too large or too small, or perhaps it includes a variety of elements that distract from the thing you're trying to draw the visitor's attention to. For really drastic changes, you will need to manipulate the picture in a graphics-editing program before adding it to the Web page. But for small modifications like sizing, *cropping*, and adding a frame, you can do the job within FrontPage.

The commands used to edit and format pictures are contained on the Pictures toolbar.

- The Insert Picture From File command displays the Picture dialog box, where you can search for and insert a picture.

- The Text command creates a text box in the picture area into which you can insert your own text.

- The Auto Thumbnail command creates a small preview version of your picture, called a *thumbnail*, which is hyperlinked to the original. Viewers can click the thumbnail to view the full-size version.

- The Position Absolutely, Bring Forward, and Send Backward commands control the position of the picture on the page in relation to other elements; whether it is in front of or behind other objects; and whether it moves with the surrounding text.

- You can use the Rotate Left 90°, Rotate Right 90°, Flip Horizontal, and Flip Vertical commands to reverse and rotate your picture.

- You can use the More Contrast, Less Contrast, More Brightness, and Less Brightness commands to adjust the brightness and contrast of the selected picture.

- You can use the Crop command to cut the picture down to a smaller size. This will not shrink the picture, but will instead trim the edges of the picture as you indicate.

- You can use the Line Style command to display a menu of line widths and styles. By clicking More Lines on the menu, you can access the Format AutoShape dialog box, where you can change the width, length, color, and pattern of lines.

- You can use the Set Transparent Color command to select a particular color that will be transparent when the graphic is viewed on a Web page. This is ideal when you want to display an irregularly shaped object (one without straight borders).

- You can use the Color command to create a black and white, grayscale (black, white, and shades of gray), or washed out version of the original picture.

- You can use the Bevel command to apply a beveled edge to the selected picture, creating a self-framing effect.

- You can use the Resample command to refine the focus of a picture that has been enlarged or reduced.

■ You can use the Select command to change the insertion point to a pointer so that you can select a picture for editing. This button is selected by default when the Pictures toolbar is opened.

■ You can use the Rectangular Hotspot, Circular Hotspot, Polygonal Hotspot, and Highlight Hotspots commands to select and view hotspots, or image maps, on your picture. These are areas that can be hyperlinked to jump to other graphics, other Web pages, or other Web sites. They can even generate e-mail messages!

■ You can use the Restore command to undo all changes made to the picture since the Pictures toolbar was opened.

If the Pictures toolbar does not open automatically when you select a picture for editing, you can open it at any time by right-clicking the toolbar area and then clicking Pictures on the shortcut menu.

In this exercise, you will work with a photograph to practice using some of FrontPage's picture-editing and formatting capabilities. First you will size the picture and crop away the parts you don't want; then you will convert the picture to black-and-white and give it a beveled frame.

USE the *GardenView* picture in the practice file folder for this topic. This practice file is located in the *My Documents\Microsoft Press\Office 2003 SBS\Pictures\CropPicture* folder and can also be accessed by clicking *Start/All Programs/Microsoft Press/Microsoft Office System 2003 Step By Step*.

Create a new
normal page

1 On the Standard toolbar, click the **Create a new normal page** button to create a new page.

2 On the **Insert** menu, point to **Picture**, and then click **From File**.

The Picture dialog box appears.

3 Navigate to the **GardenView** image, select it, and click **Insert**.

The image is inserted into the Web page.

4 On the **View** menu, point to **Toolbars**, and then click **Pictures** to open the Pictures toolbar.

Tip   By default, the Pictures toolbar opens as a floating toolbar. If you prefer, you can dock it at the top, the bottom, or either side of the window.

5 Drag the Pictures toolbar to the bottom of the window to dock it out of the way.

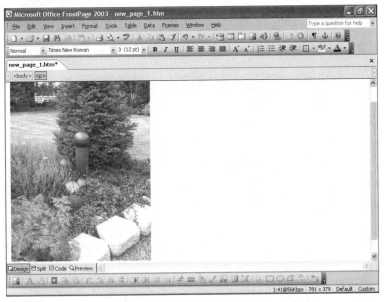

Crop

6   Click the picture to select it, and on the Pictures toolbar, click the **Crop** button.

A dashed box appears in the picture, defining the edges of the area to be cropped.

7   Drag the handles of the crop box until the box frames the collection of spheres.

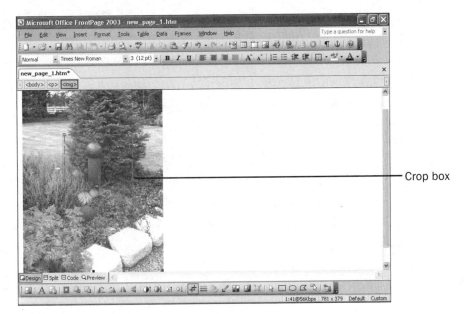

Crop box

8   Press ⟦Enter⟧ or click the **Crop** button again to crop the picture to the specified shape and size.

9   Double-click the picture to display the **Picture Properties** dialog box.

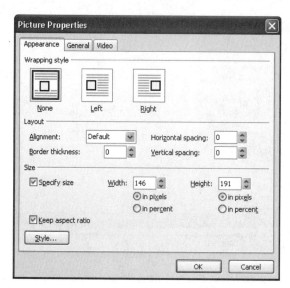

10   On the **Appearance** tab, make sure the **Specify size** check box is selected.

11   To prevent distortion, ensure that the **Keep aspect ratio** check box is selected.

12   Set the **Width** to **165** pixels.

The height setting automatically changes to match the new width.

13   Click **OK** to close the dialog box and apply your changes.

FrontPage resizes the graphic to your specified dimensions.

Color

14   On the Pictures toolbar, click the **Color** button.

15   In the **Color** drop-down list, click **Grayscale**.

The picture is converted to shades of gray, but retains the original quality of detail.

Bevel

16   On the Pictures toolbar, click the **Bevel** button.

The colors at the edges of the picture change to make it appear that the center is raised.

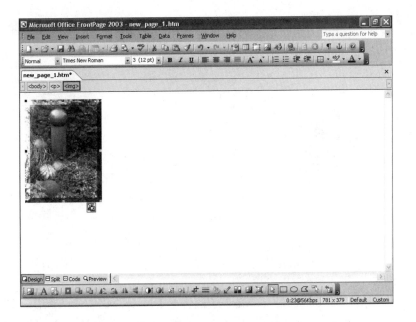

CLOSE the practice file without saving your work.

Creating and Displaying Thumbnails

Thumbnails are small versions of graphics that are hyperlinked to full-size versions. Thumbnails are often used on Web pages that contain many graphics that Web visitors might want to see (catalog items, for example). Because thumbnails are small, they download faster, so visitors are less likely to get impatient and move to another site.

In this exercise, you create a thumbnail of a picture and test it in FrontPage.

USE the *pictures* Web page in the practice file folder for this topic. This practice file is located in the *My Documents\Microsoft Press\Office 2003 SBS\Pictures\Thumbnail* folder and can also be accessed by clicking *Start/All Programs/Microsoft Press/Microsoft Office System 2003 Step By Step*.

1   On the **File** menu, click **Open**.

2   In the **Open File** dialog box, browse to the practice file folder for this topic, and double-click the **pictures** Web page.

3   Click the picture on the page to select it and activate the Pictures toolbar.

Auto Thumbnail

4   On the Pictures toolbar, click the **Auto Thumbnail** button.

The picture shrinks to thumbnail size and is surrounded by a blue border that indicates the presence of a hyperlink.

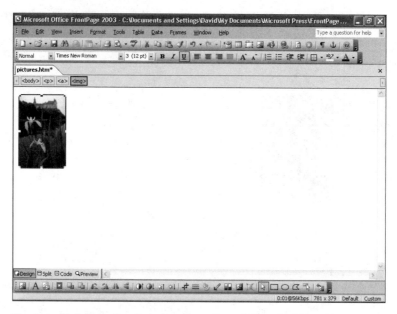

The hyperlink links the thumbnail version of the graphic to the original, which is no longer displayed on the page.

⊟ Split

Show
Split View

5 At the bottom of the Page view editing window, click the **Show Split View** button to display the HTML code that links the thumbnail to the original graphic.

The code looks something like this:

```
<p><a href="PH01245J[1].jpg">

<img border="2" src="file:///C:/Documents%20and%20Settings/Joan
/Local%20Settings/Temporary%20Internet%20Files/FrontPageTempDir
/PH01245J[1]_small.jpg" xthumbnail-orig-image="PH01245J[1].jpg"></a></p>
```

⚐Design

Show
Design View

6 At the bottom of the Page view editing window, click the **Show Design View** button to return to the Design pane.

7 Drag the handles surrounding the selected thumbnail to make it bigger.

The thumbnail becomes blurry and grainy when you make it bigger because it is not as detailed as the original picture.

Undo

8 After you have seen the effect of enlarging the thumbnail, on the Standard toolbar, click the **Undo** button to return the thumbnail to its original size.

Preview in
Browser

9 To experience the thumbnail link as your Web visitors will, on the Standard toolbar, click the **Preview in Browser** button. Save the page and embedded graphics when prompted to do so.

Your Web page opens in your browser, displaying the hyperlinked thumbnail.

10 Click the thumbnail to display the full-size graphic, and then click the browser's **Back** button to return to the thumbnail.

CLOSE the browser, and then close the practice file.
BE SURE TO close the Pictures toolbar if you don't want to display it.

Adding a Line, Shape, or Drawing to a Web Page

When it comes to dressing up your pages with graphic elements, you are not limited to clip art, pictures, and photographs. You can also create designs with lines, squares, circles, and other shapes, and if you are artistically inclined, you can even create entire drawings from within FrontPage. For professional-quality art, you should use a dedicated graphics program, but you can use FrontPage to turn out simple, Web-ready artwork.

FrontPage 2003 includes drawing tools that make it easy to incorporate specially formatted lines, a wide variety of preformed shapes, WordArt objects, text boxes, and shadows. These tools are similar to those in Microsoft Office Word and Microsoft Office PowerPoint. You can also copy drawings from other Microsoft Office System applications and paste them directly into your FrontPage-based Web site.

The commands you use to work with most graphics are represented as buttons on the Drawing toolbar and on the Drawing Canvas toolbar. Both of these toolbars can be opened at any time by right-clicking the toolbar area and clicking their names on the toolbar shortcut menu. The Drawing toolbar contains these commands:

■ The commands on the Draw menu control the grouping, position, and movement of objects.

■ You can use the Select Objects command to change the insertion point to a pointer so that you can select a drawing object for editing.

- You can use the AutoShapes command to display a menu from which you can choose any of 130 shapes, ranging from basic geometric shapes and arrows to fully formed weather indicators. Special flowchart, banner, and call-out symbols are also included. Clicking More AutoShapes at the bottom of the menu displays an additional 73 basic clip art items that you can build on. You can drag the AutoShapes menu or any of its submenus away from the Drawing toolbar so that they become floating toolbars.

- You can use the Line, Arrow, Rectangle, and Oval commands to draw these basic shapes in any size by clicking and dragging the shape onto the page.

- You can use the Text Box command to insert a text frame within a drawing.

- You can use the Insert WordArt, Insert Clip Art, and Insert Picture From File commands to insert existing graphic elements from your local computer or the Internet into your drawing.

- You can use the Fill Color, Line Color, and Font Color commands to control the colors of their respective elements.

- You can use the Line Style, Dash Style, and Arrow Style commands to format the thickness, color, solidity, and end caps of line elements.

- You can use the Shadow Style command to apply a variety of shadows to graphic elements. Clicking Shadow Settings opens a separate toolbar with which you can move an existing shadow or change its color.

- You can use the 3-D Style command to give graphic elements a three-dimensional look.

You can *group* several drawing elements together so that you can treat them as one. In this way, you can create a drawing out of several shapes, and then copy and paste the entire drawing, or reduce or enlarge it. If you want to treat the drawing as individual elements again, you can *ungroup* them at any time.

The "frame" in which drawings are created in FrontPage is called the *drawing canvas.* You can use the drawing canvas as an actual frame by formatting it with visible borders and background colors, but its main purpose is to contain all the elements of the drawing, so that the underlying HTML code for the drawing can be selected and treated as a unit. The formatting of the drawing canvas also determines the way in which text wraps around the drawing and the position of the drawing in relation to other objects on the page.

The Drawing Canvas toolbar opens when you insert a new drawing.

- You can use the Fit Drawing to Contents command to enlarge or shrink the drawing canvas to the same size as the drawing it contains.

- You can use the Expand Drawing command to stretch the drawing to the current size of the canvas.

- You can use the Scale Drawing command to enlarge the drawing to the current size of the canvas, but maintain its original height-to-width ratio.

In this exercise, you will first draw a horizontal line, create and insert a drawing that incorporates predefined shapes, and insert a shape directly into a Web page.

Create a new
normal page

1 On the Standard toolbar, click the **Create a new normal page** button to create a new page.

2 On the **Insert** menu, click **Horizontal Line** to draw a simple line across the top of the page.

3 Right-click the line, and then click **Horizontal Line Properties** on the shortcut menu.

The Horizontal Line Properties dialog box appears.

4 In the **Horizontal Line Properties** dialog box, do the following:

- Set the **Width** to **80** percent of the window.

- Set the **Height** to **3** pixels.

- In the **Color** drop-down box, click the **Green** square.

Tip Move the mouse over the colors in the Color drop-down list to see each color's name displayed as a ScreenTip.

- Click **OK** to close the dialog box and apply your settings, and then click anywhere on the page to deselect the horizontal line.

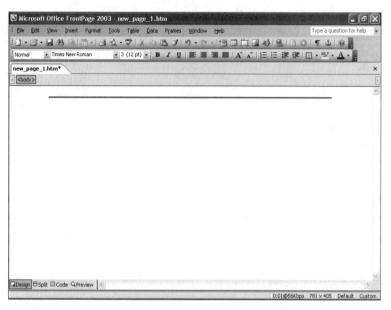

5 Press ⎡Ctrl⎤+⎡End⎤ to move the insertion point to the end of the page.

6 On the **Insert** menu, point to **Picture**, and then click **New Drawing**.

FrontPage displays an empty drawing canvas, the Drawing Canvas toolbar, and the Drawing toolbar.

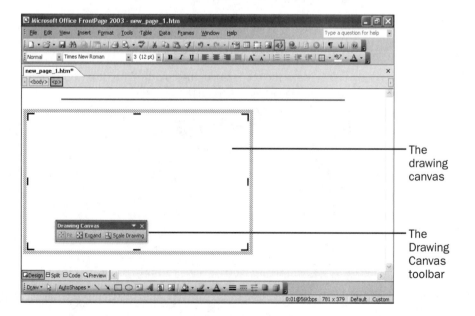

The drawing canvas

The Drawing Canvas toolbar

Tip   Depending on your previous actions, the Drawing toolbar might open as floating or docked. If it opens as a floating toolbar, you can dock it to keep it out of the way while you're working.

AutoShapes ▾

7   On the Drawing toolbar, click the **AutoShapes** button to display the menu of available shapes.

Tip   When you see a drop-down list with a "handle" on it (horizontal lines in a shaded stripe), you can drag the menu onto the work area, and it will float there as a toolbar until you click its Close button. Alternatively, you can dock it at the left, right, or bottom edge of the window.

8   Point to **Stars and Banners**, and then click the **Explosion 2** symbol (the second symbol in the top row).

Tip   Move the pointer over a symbol to see the symbol's name displayed as a ScreenTip.

9   Point to the upper-right corner of the drawing canvas, and drag downward to create a small "explosion" shape.

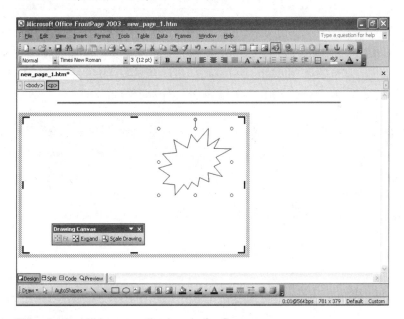

This shape will become the head of a flower.

10   Use the **Terminator** and **Decision** shapes available on the **AutoShapes Flowchart** menu to create a stem and leaves for your flower.

The Explosion 2 shape from the Stars and Banners menu

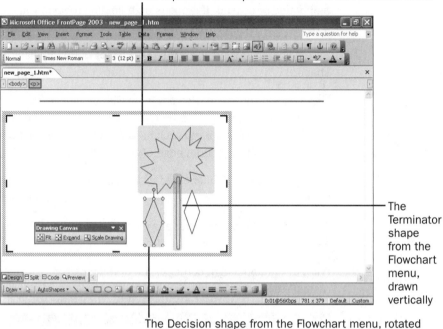

The Terminator shape from the Flowchart menu, drawn vertically

The Decision shape from the Flowchart menu, rotated

11   To rotate the "leaves" to appropriate angles, click each in turn, and drag its rotate handle (the green dot) in a clockwise or counterclockwise circle.

12   After the "leaves" are rotated, drag them into position against the "stem."

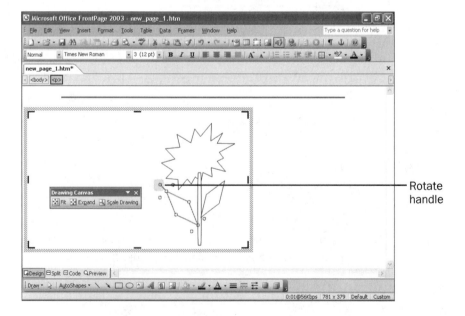

Rotate handle

13 Right-click the explosion, and on the shortcut menu, point to **Order**, and then click **Bring to Front**.

The head of the flower now appears in front of the stem. Depending on how closely you overlapped your stem and flower head, this repositioning might be difficult to see.

14 Experiment with the available shapes to create a garden scene.

The Sun shape from the Basic Shapes menu

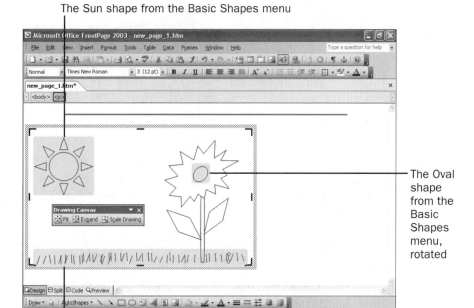

The Oval shape from the Basic Shapes menu, rotated

The Line shape from the Lines menu, copied and pasted several times

15 Click the head of the flower to select it, hold down the [Shift] key, and click the stem and each of the leaves so that they are all selected.

16 Right-click the selected elements, and on the shortcut menu, point to **Grouping**, and then click **Group**.

The elements are grouped so that you can work with the flower as a whole.

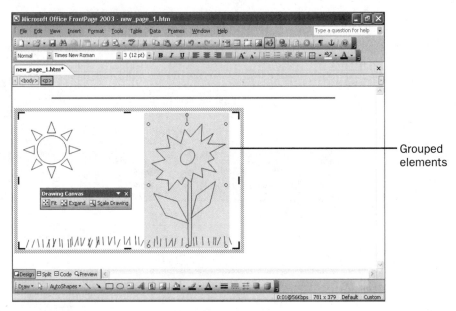

Grouped elements

Copy

17 On the Standard toolbar, click the **Copy** button to copy the picture to the Office Clipboard.

Paste

18 On the Standard toolbar, click the **Paste** button several times to paste multiple copies of the flower into your drawing to create an entire field.

Troubleshooting   If you find that you are pasting copies of the flower outside the drawing canvas, delete those flowers, click inside the drawing canvas, and paste again.

19 Drag each flower's sizing handles to move the flowers and make a field of flowers of different sizes.

20 Right-click each flower, point to **Grouping** on the shortcut menu, and click **Ungroup** to separate the elements so that they can be individually colored.

21 Right-click the sun in your picture, and click **Format AutoShape** on the shortcut menu to display the **Format AutoShape** dialog box.

22 In the **Format AutoShape** dialog box, do the following:

■   On the **Colors and Lines** tab, set the **Fill Color** to **Yellow**.

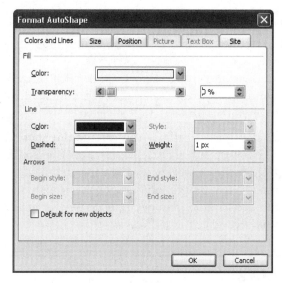

■ Click **OK** to close the dialog box and apply your settings.

23 Color the flower elements to create a cheerful garden scene.

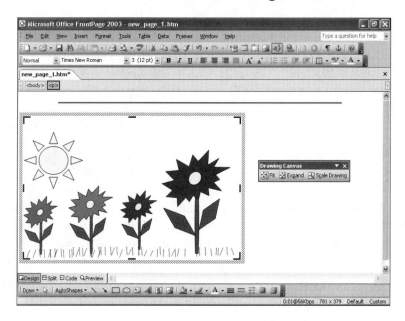

CLOSE the Drawing toolbar, and then close the practice file, saving your work if you want.

Creating a Photo Gallery

Companies like The Garden Company often want to include photo galleries in their Web sites—sometimes of products, sometimes of offices or other company buildings, or sometimes of key people whom Web visitors will deal with. To create a photo gallery by hand, you can simply add your pictures to a page, format them as thumbnails, and arrange them the way you want them.

FrontPage offers an even easier method. You can use the Photo Gallery Web component to quickly and easily create an attractive display of personal or business photos or images. You can choose from four styles, arranging your pictures either horizontally, vertically, in a tableau-style montage, or in a slideshow. With the Photo Gallery Web component, you can add captions and descriptions to your images and update the layout and content in seconds.

About Web Components

FrontPage 2003 offers many exciting, ready-made Web components that can be added to a Web page to give your site extra zing with very little effort.

FrontPage Web components range from decorative to informative to downright useful, and they are one of the most appealing aspects of the program. Any FrontPage-savvy designer can use Web components, such as *hit counters*, photo galleries, and link bars, to create a well-programmed, fully functional site without ever having to do any actual programming.

In this exercise, you will create a photo gallery in an existing Web site using the Photo Gallery Web component. The photos used in this exercise are from the Carnivorous Plant Database at *www.omnisterra.com/bot/cp_home.cgi* and are used by permission of the database owner.

USE the *plant1* through *plant12* photographs in the practice file folder for this topic. These practice files are located in the *My Documents\Microsoft Press\Office 2003 SBS\Pictures\PhotoGallery* folder and can also be accessed by clicking *Start/All Programs/Microsoft Press/Microsoft Office System 2003 Step By Step*. OPEN the *GardenCo* Web site.

Create a new
normal page

1   On the Standard toolbar, click the **Create a new normal page** button to open a new page.

2   On the **Insert** menu, click **Web Component**.

The Insert Web Component dialog box appears.

3   In the **Insert Web Component** dialog box, click **Photo Gallery**.

The photo gallery options appear in the display window.

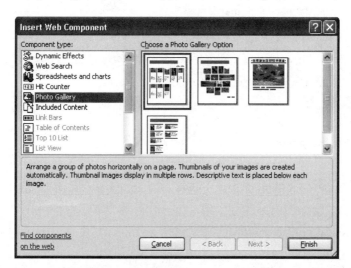

4   In the **Choose a Photo Gallery Option** box, click each of the four options, and read the description that appears in the pane.

5   Select the **Montage Layout** option (the second option in the top row), and click **Finish**.

The Photo Gallery Properties dialog box appears so you can add photos to the photo gallery.

Tip   If you later change your mind about the layout of your photo gallery, simply right-click the Photo Gallery Web component in Page view, and click Photo Gallery Properties on the shortcut menu to display the Photo Gallery Properties dialog box. On the Layout tab, select a different layout option, and click OK to reformat your photo gallery.

6   Click **Add**, and then click **Pictures from Files**.

7   Browse to the *My Documents\Microsoft Press\Office 2003 SBS\Pictures\PhotoGallery* folder, where you'll find 12 photos of carnivorous plants.

8   Click the **plant1** file, hold down the Shift key, and then click the **plant12** file.

All 12 photos are selected.

9 Click the **Open** button.

FrontPage imports the pictures into the photo gallery and displays them in the Photo Gallery Properties dialog box.

10 In the file list, click **plant1.jpg**.

11 In the **Caption** box, type Four Deadly Beauties.

12 Select the **Override and use custom font formatting** option.

13 Select the text in the **Caption** box.

Times New Roman

Font

14 In the **Font** drop-down list, click **Georgia**.

3 (12 pt)

Font Size

15 In the **Font Size** drop-down list, click **2 (10 pt)**.

Font Color

16 In the **Font Color** drop-down list, click the **Purple** square.

B

Bold

17 Click the **Bold** button.

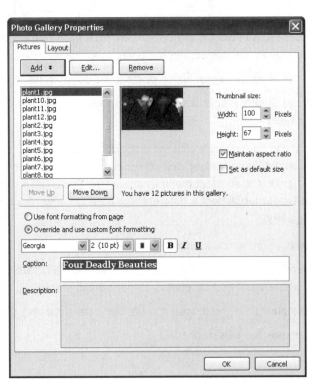

18 Click **OK** to close the **Photo Gallery Properties** dialog box and generate the photo gallery.

19 On the Standard toolbar, click the **Preview in Browser** button to preview the file in your default browser and window size. When prompted to do so, save the page file with the name Gallery.htm and the embedded graphics with their default names.

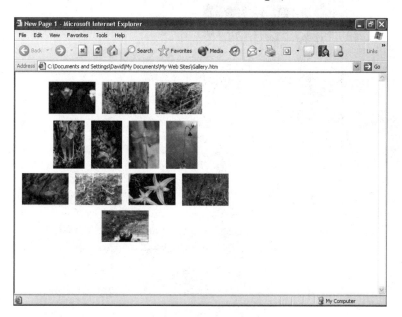

Pretty impressive for a few minutes' work!

20 Click the thumbnail graphics to open the full-size version, and then click the browser's **Back** button to return to the photo gallery.

21 When you're done admiring your work, close the browser to return to FrontPage.

CLOSE the practice file, saving your work if you want, and then close the *GardenCo* Web site.

Adding Fancy Text to a Web Page

WordArt objects are text objects with special formatting applied, for example to make them bend, slant, or appear in fancy colors. You can choose from 30 basic formatting options, and then make further changes from the WordArt toolbar. This toolbar opens automatically when you insert a WordArt object.

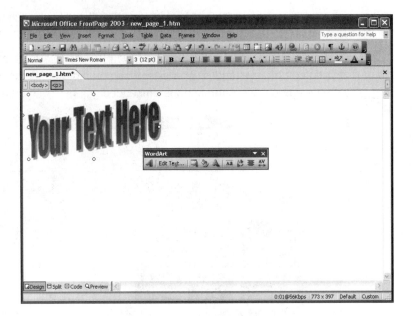

- You can use the Insert WordArt command to display the WordArt Gallery dialog box so that you can create a new WordArt object.

- You can use the Edit Text command to display the Edit WordArt Text dialog box, in which you can change the text, font, font size, and font formatting of your WordArt object.

- You can use the WordArt Gallery command to choose from 30 different WordArt styles.

- You can use the Format WordArt command to change the colors and lines, size, layout, and alternate Web text of your WordArt object.

- You can use the WordArt Shape command to build your WordArt around any of 40 basic shapes, curves, and angles.

- You can use the WordArt Same Letter Heights command to make uppercase and lowercase letters the same height.

- You can use the WordArt Vertical Text command to change text from the default horizontal alignment to vertical alignment.

- You can use the WordArt Alignment command to specify that the WordArt text is aligned to the left, center, or right within the available space, or that it be word-justified or stretched to fill the space.

- You can use the WordArt Character Spacing command to control the *kerning* between letters.

If you have already used WordArt to create fancy headings in Word documents, you know how easy it is to create effects that would be very hard, if not impossible, to replicate with regular formatting. For those times when ordinary formatting simply won't do the trick, you can use WordArt in FrontPage to create headings for your Web pages.

In this exercise, you will create an eye-catching WordArt page title.

Create a new
normal page

1   On the Standard toolbar, click the **Create a new normal page** button to create a new page.

A new page opens in the Page view editing window with the insertion point positioned at the top of the page.

2   On the **Insert** menu, point to **Picture**, and then click **WordArt**.

3   In the **Word Art Gallery** dialog box, click your favorite style.

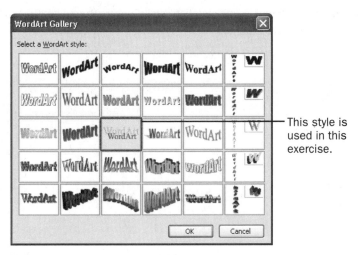

This style is used in this exercise.

4   After you select a style, click **OK**.

The Edit WordArt Text dialog box appears.

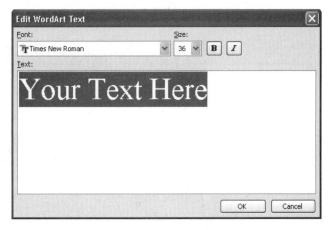

5   In the **Text** box, type Carnivorous Plants.

6 In the **Font** drop-down list, click **Verdana**.

7 In the **Size** drop-down list, click **24**.

8 Click the **Bold** button.

9 Click **OK** to close the dialog box and apply your settings.

FrontPage creates the page title according to your specifications, inserts it in the Web page at the insertion point, and displays the WordArt toolbar.

10 Click the WordArt toolbar's **Close** button to close the toolbar.

11 Click to the right of the WordArt object to deselect it.

12 On the **Format** menu, click **Paragraph**.

The Paragraph dialog box appears.

13 In the **Alignment** drop-down list, click **Center**. Then click **OK** to close the dialog box and apply your changes.

The WordArt title is centered on the page.

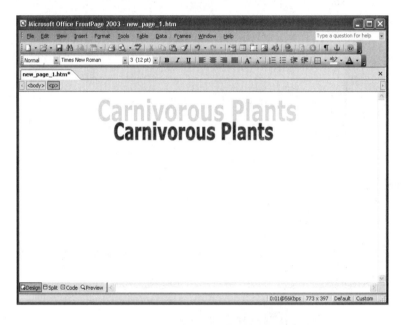

CLOSE the page file without saving your changes. If you are not continuing on to the next chapter, quit FrontPage.

Key Points

- You can add pictures of all kinds to your Web page. If you don't have a picture you want to use, you can select from the variety of clip art that comes with The Microsoft Office System 2003.

- If you have an active Internet connection, you can select from an extensive collection of clip art in the Office Online clip art gallery.

- You can create drawings from a variety of basic shapes directly in FrontPage, or paste in drawings from another Microsoft Office System application.

- You can easily create a functioning photo gallery by using the Photo Gallery Web component.

- You can add pizzazz to your Web page with fancy WordArt text.

VII
Microsoft Office
Publisher 2003

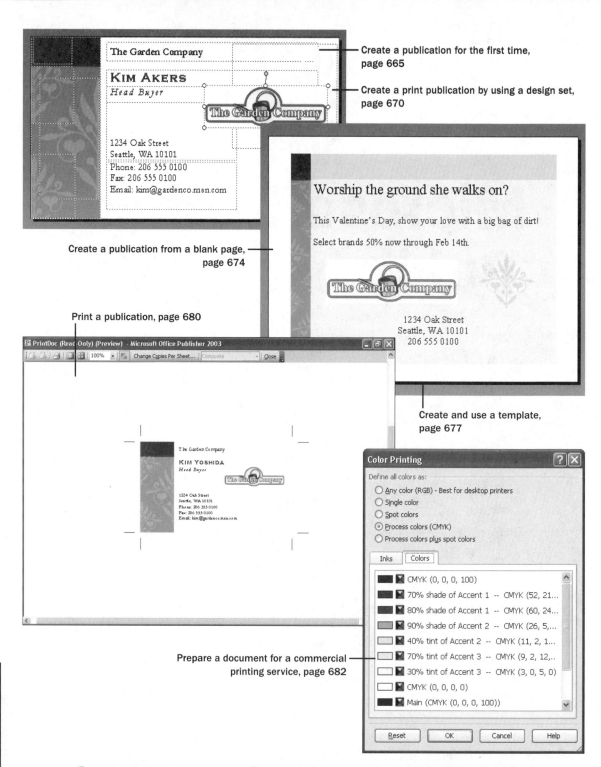

Create a publication for the first time, page 665

Create a print publication by using a design set, page 670

Create a publication from a blank page, page 674

Print a publication, page 680

Create and use a template, page 677

Prepare a document for a commercial printing service, page 682

Chapter 26 at a Glance

26 Creating and Printing Publications

In this chapter you will learn to:

✔ Create a publication for the first time.

✔ Create a print publication by using a design set.

✔ Create a publication from a blank page.

✔ Create and use a template.

✔ Print a publication.

✔ Prepare a document for a commercial printing service.

Microsoft Office Publisher 2003 makes it fun to create a variety of publications, from newsletters and flyers to complex brochures and catalogs. Because Publisher offers a broad variety of formats and printing options, you can use it at work (to produce marketing, sales, management, or other professional documents) or at home (to produce invitations, flyers, holiday letters, scrapbook pages, or just about anything you can think of).

See Also Do you need only a quick refresher on the topics in this chapter? See the Quick Reference entries on pages xxxiii.

 Important Before you can use the practice files in this chapter, you need to install them from the book's companion CD to their default location. See "Using the Book's CD-ROM" on page xxi for more information.

Creating a Publication for the First Time

The first time you create a publication, Publisher gathers information from you for its *personal information set.* Four different sets are available:

■ Primary Business

■ Secondary Business

■ Other Organization

■ Home/Family

After you provide the information for these sets, Publisher automatically plugs it into your documents, so you don't have to type it in more than once.

In this exercise, you will complete the Primary Business personal information set for The Garden Company while beginning work on the company's newsletter.

BE SURE TO start your computer, but don't start Publisher before beginning this exercise.

1 Click the **Start** button, point to **All Programs**, point to **Microsoft Office**, and click **Microsoft Office Publisher 2003**.

Publisher opens, showing the Start screen and the New Publication task pane.

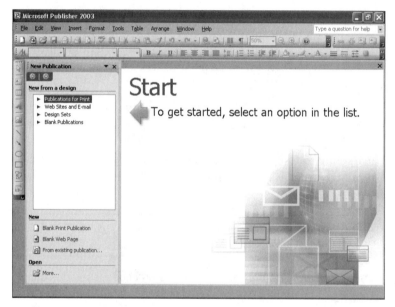

2 In the **New Publication** task pane, click **Publications for Print** to display the list of options.

3 In the **New from a design** list, click **Newsletters**.

The preview window shows the newsletter samples.

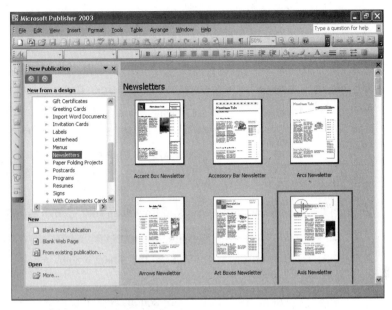

4   Scroll down the preview pane, and click the **Brocade** newsletter style.

Three things happen when you make your selection. First, the Newsletter Options task pane appears. Second, the Brocade newsletter's first page appears, ready for you to reformat it. And third, the Personal Information dialog box appears.

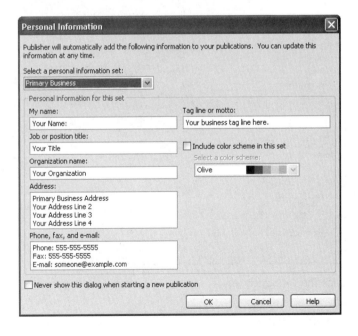

5   In the **Select a personal information set** list, click **Primary Business**.

6   In the **My name** box, type Kim Akers, and press [Tab] to move to the next field.

7   In the **Job or position title** box, type Head Buyer, and press [Tab].

8   In the **Organization name** box, type The Garden Company, and press [Tab].

9   In the **Address** box, type 1234 Oak Street, and press [Enter] to move to the next line. Then type Seattle, WA 10101, and press [Tab] to move to the next field.

10   In the **Phone, fax, and e-mail** box, type Phone: 206 555 0100, and press [Enter]. Type Fax: 206 555 0101, and press [Enter]. Then type Email: kim@gardenco.msn.com, and press [Tab].

11   In the **Tag line or motto** box, type How does your garden grow?

12   Select the **Include color scheme in this set** check box.

13   Click the down arrow to the right of the **Select a color scheme** box.

The default color scheme for this newsletter is Olive. When you click the down arrow, you see lots of other color scheme options.

14   Click **Moss**.

15   Click the **OK** button.

Troubleshooting   If you have entered personal information in Publisher before, click the Update button instead of the OK button.

The information you just typed is inserted into your newsletter, which uses the color scheme you selected.

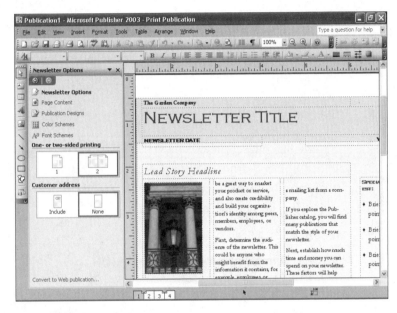

Troubleshooting   You might have to zoom in to see your information and color scheme clearly. On the Standard toolbar, click the down arrow to the right of the Zoom box, and click 100%.

Publisher retains the information and will insert it into any other document you create. You will not have to enter the information again; however, you can change it at any time.

Tip   To change the information you entered into a personal information set, on the Edit menu, click Personal Information.

Save

16   Click the **Save** button.

The Save As dialog box appears.

17   Navigate to the *My Documents\Microsoft Press\Office 2003 SBS\Creating* folder, and in the **File name** box, type TGC-NL. Then click **Save**.

18   On the **File** menu, click **Close**.

The newsletter closes, and Publisher displays the Start screen.

Creating a Print Publication by Using a Design Set

To help you create many different kinds of documents without having to labor over their design, Publisher includes several preformatted types of documents called *design sets*. These design sets include the following:

- Preformatted stationery (business cards, letterhead, envelopes, thank-you notes, "with compliments" cards, and postcards)

- Business forms (expense reports, fax cover sheets, inventory lists, invoices, purchase orders, job quotes, refund forms, billing statements, and weekly records)

- Calendars

- Catalogs

- Gift certificates and party invitiations

- Brochures, flyers, newsletters

- Shipping labels (for Avery 5164 labels)

- Web sites

- Microsoft Office Word documents

In this exercise, you will create a business card for Kim Akers, head buyer for The Garden Company.

USE the *Gardenco* graphic in the practice file folder for this topic. This practice file is located in the *My Documents\Microsoft Press\Office 2003 SBS\Creating* folder and can also be accessed by clicking *Start/All Programs/Microsoft Press/Microsoft Office System 2003 Step by Step.*

    1   In the **New Publication** task pane, click **Design Sets**.

           Troubleshooting   If the New Publication task pane is not displayed, on the View menu, click Task Pane. If a different task pane is displayed, click the down arrow at the top of the task pane, and then click New Publication.

The New Publication task pane displays the list of available design sets and samples of the first set, *Accent Box*.

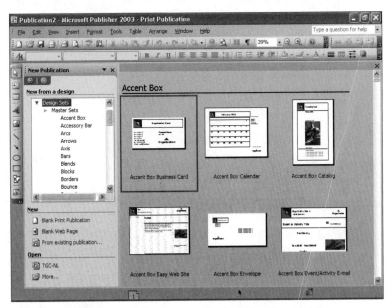

2   Under **Design Sets**, click **Master Sets** to expand the list, scroll down, and click **Brocade**.

The preview pane displays the samples available in the Brocade style.

3   In the preview pane, click **Brocade Business Card**.

Tip   It's a good idea to keep your publications consistent in format. The newsletter reflects a design that will match the business card you create here, as well as any other documents that you might create, from letterhead to shipping labels and everything in between.

Publisher opens a new business card using the Brocade format and inserts any personal information you have provided. You can change anything on the business card at this time.

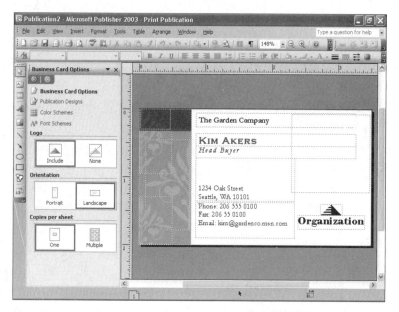

Troubleshooting If you haven't yet provided any personal information to Publisher, the Personal Information dialog box appears. In this box, you can specify your name, company address, and other pertinent information which Publisher will save so that you don't have to type it into each new publication.

4 Click the text box that contains the word *Organization*.

This is part of the default logo.

5 Hold down the ⎡Shift⎤ key, and click the pyramid portion of the default logo.

Both parts of the default logo are now selected.

6 Press the [Del] key.

A dialog box appears, prompting you to change the design to one that does not use a logo.

7 Click **No**.

The default logo disappears, leaving a blank spot so that you can insert The Garden Company's logo.

8 On the **Insert** menu, click **Picture**, and then click **From File**.

The Insert Picture dialog box appears.

9 Navigate to the *My Documents\Microsoft Press\Office 2003 SBS\Creating* folder, and click the **Gardenco.jpg** file.

10 Click **Insert**.

The Garden Company's logo appears.

Troubleshooting   The Garden Company logo might appear too large. In fact, it might completely cover the business card you're designing. If this happens, right-click the logo, and click Format Picture on the shortcut menu. Click the Size tab, and in the Scale area, change the height to a smaller percentage, such as 30. If the "Lock aspect ratio" check box is selected, the width will automatically change to match the height when you press Tab to move to the next field. After changing the height and width, click OK. Then the logo might not be positioned correctly. Drag it to any position that looks good to you.

Save

11 On the Standard toolbar, click the **Save** button.

The Save As dialog box appears.

12 Navigate to the *My Documents\Microsoft Press\Office 2003 SBS\Creating* folder, and in the **File name** box, type **BusCard-Kim**, and then click **Save**.

13 If Publisher prompts you to add the new logo to the Primary Business personal information set, click **Yes**.

Now your logo will also be automatically inserted into any document you create.

CLOSE the *BusCard-Kim* publication.

Creating a Publication from a Blank Page

Even though Publisher includes several easy-to-use publication types and design sets, sometimes it's easier to start from scratch. For example, you might have an idea about how you want the document to look, and none of the templates or pre-designed forms suit you. Or you might feel more creative when facing a blank sheet rather than one that illustrates someone else's ideas.

In this exercise, you will create a postcard advertising a Valentine's Day special on garden soil.

USE the *Gardenco* graphic in the practice file folder for this topic. This practice file is located in the *My Documents\Microsoft Press\Office 2003 SBS\Creating* folder and can also be accessed by clicking *Start/All Programs/Microsoft Press/Microsoft Office System 2003 Step by Step.*

1 On the **File** menu, click **New**.

Troubleshooting If the New Publication task pane is not open, on the View menu, click Task Pane. If a different task pane is displayed, click the down arrow at the top of the task pane, and click New Publication.

2 In the **New Publication** task pane, click **Blank Publications**.

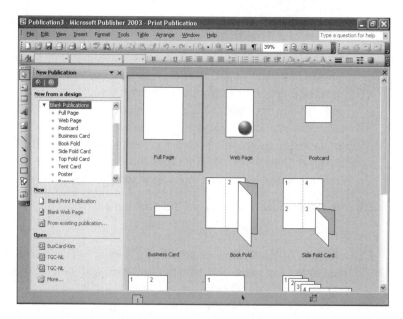

3   In the preview window, click **Postcard**.

A new, blank postcard opens.

4   In the **Apply a design** section of the task pane, scroll down until you see *Brocade*, and click it.

Publisher applies the Brocade design to the postcard.

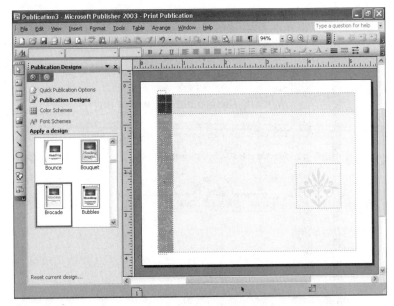

5   Click inside the postcard, and type Worship the ground she walks on?

6   Press [Enter] twice, and then type This Valentine's day, show your love with a big bag of dirt!

7   Press [Enter] twice, and then type Select brands 50% off through Feb 14th!

Font Size

8   Select the first line of text. Then on the Formatting toolbar, click the down arrow to the right of the **Font Size** box, and click **18**.

9   Select the remaining text. Then on the Formatting toolbar, click the down arrow to the right of the **Font Size** box, and click **12**.

10   On the **Insert** menu, click **Picture**, and then click **From File**.

The Insert Picture dialog box appears.

11   Navigate to the *My Documents\Microsoft Press\Office 2003 SBS\Creating* folder, click **Gardenco.jpg**, and then click **Insert**.

The Garden Company logo appears on the postcard.

Tip The Garden Company logo might appear too large. In fact, it might completely cover the business card you're designing. If this happens, right-click the logo, and click Format Picture. Click the Size tab and, in the Scale area, change the height to a smaller percentage, such as 50. If the "Lock aspect ratio" check box is selected, the width will automatically change to match the height when you press Tab to move to the next field. After changing the height and width, click OK.

12 Position the logo so that it is directly beneath the text.

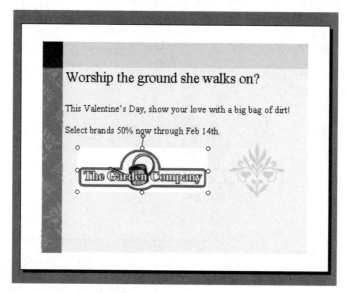

13 Click anywhere in the postcard to deselect the logo, and then position the insertion point at the end of the last sentence you typed.

14 Press Enter several times to move the insertion point to a position a little below the logo and the picture to its right.

15 Type **1234 Oak Street**, and press Enter.

16 Type **Seattle, WA 10101**, and press Enter.

17 Type **206 555 0100**.

Center

18 Select the three lines of text you just typed, and on the Formatting toolbar, click the **Center** button.

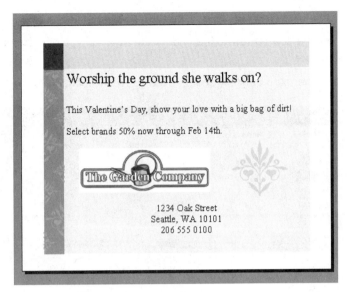

Save

19   On the Standard toolbar, click the **Save** button.

The Save As dialog box appears.

20   Navigate to the *My Documents\Microsoft Press\Office 2003 SBS\Creating* folder. Then in the **File name** box, type DirtSalePostcard, and click **Save**.

CLOSE the *DirtSalePostcard* publication.

Creating and Using a Template

Templates make life so much simpler. After you've labored over a document that you plan to use over and over again—like a business card or a newsletter—you can save it as a template. Then when it's time to create the next one, you need only open the template, replace existing text or images with new ones, and you're done.

In this exercise, you will save a postcard publication as a postcard template. You will then use the template to create a postcard for an upcoming spring sale.

USE the *SalePostcard* publication in the practice file folder for this topic. This practice file is located in the *My Documents\Microsoft Press\Office 2003 SBS\Creating* folder and can also be accessed by clicking *Start/All Programs/Microsoft Press/Microsoft Office System 2003 Step by Step*.
OPEN the *SalePostcard* publication.

1   On the **File** menu, click **Save As**.

The Save As dialog box appears.

2 In the **File name** box, type SaleCardTemplate.

3 Click the down arrow to the right of the **Save as type** box, and click **Publisher Template**.

Publisher automatically changes the "Save in" location to the Templates directory.

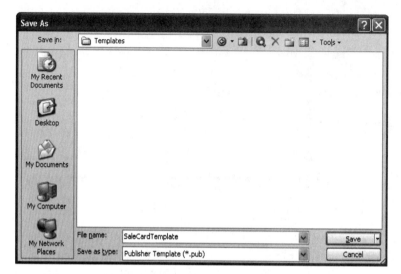

4 Click **Save**.

Publisher saves the postcard template.

5 On the **File** menu, click **Close**.

The template closes.

6 On the **File** menu, click **New**.

The New Publication task pane appears.

Troubleshooting   If the New Publication task pane is not open, on the View menu, click Task Pane. If a different task pane is displayed, click the down arrow at the top of the task pane, and click New Publication.

7 In the **New from a design** area of the **New Publication** task pane, click **Templates**.

Tip   If there were no templates in your Templates directory when you started Publisher, Templates does not appear in the "New from a design" area even though you created a template since you started Publisher. If this happens, exit and restart Publisher.

A list of available templates appears.

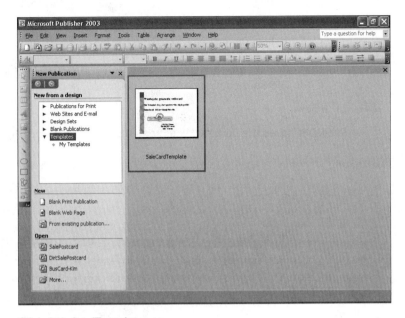

8 Click **SaleCardTemplate**.

A new publication based on the SaleCardTemplate template opens.

9 Select the first line of text, and type Spring is in the air!

10 Select the second and third lines of text, and type Find everything you need to make your garden bloom at our Spring sale extravaganza!

Fill Color

11 On the Formatting toolbar, click the down arrow to the right of the **Fill Color** button, and click **White**.

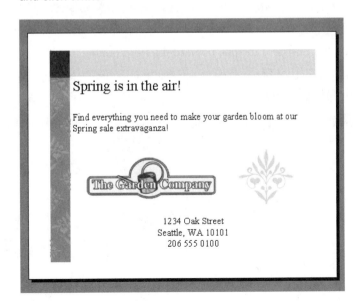

12 On the **File** menu, click **Save As**.

The Save As dialog box appears.

13 Navigate to the *My Documents\Microsoft Press\Office 2003 SBS\Creating* folder, and in the **File name** box, type *SpringSaleCard*.

14 Click **Save**.

Publisher saves the postcard you created based on SaleCardTemplate.

CLOSE the *SpringSaleCard* publication.

Printing a Publication

Most of the time, you'll print your publications on a standard printer. There are several ways to print a file. Publisher makes all of them easy—one method takes only one click of the mouse (assuming the file is already open). You can preview a file before printing it, choose the target printer, and set print options. When you preview, you can "eyeball" your publication to catch and correct any gross errors before actually printing it.

Tip   It's a good idea to preview a file before printing it so that you can avoid costly mistakes, especially if you are printing on a color inkjet printer whose color cartridges are expensive.

In this exercise, you'll print the same file twice.

USE the *PrintDoc* publication in the practice file folder for this topic. This practice file is located in the *My Documents\Microsoft Press\Office 2003 SBS\Creating* folder and can also be accessed by clicking *Start/All Programs/Microsoft Press/Microsoft Office System 2003 Step by Step*.
OPEN the *PrintDoc* publication.

Print

1 On the Standard toolbar, point to the **Print** button.

After a couple of seconds, a ScreenTip appears identifying the printer on which this file will be printed.

Tip   Verifying which printer will be used to print your publication is important if you have access to more than one printer.

ScreenTip identifying the current printer

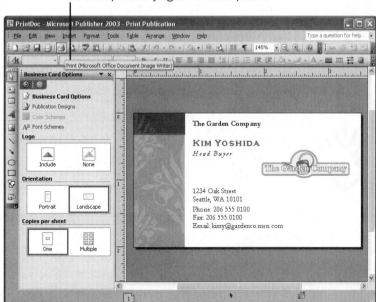

2   Click the **Print** button.

The designated printer prints the document.

Print Preview

3   On the Standard toolbar, click the **Print Preview** button.

The file appears in the Preview window, and the pointer turns into a little magnifying glass with a plus sign in it. You can click anywhere on the document to zoom in and see the targeted area enlarged.

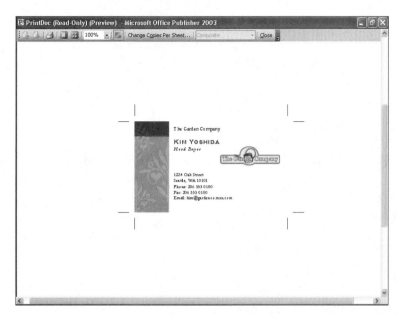

> **Tip**   If you detect any errors you want to correct, click the Close button on the Print Preview toolbar to return to the file.

4   On the Print Preview toolbar, click the **Print** button.

The Print dialog box appears.

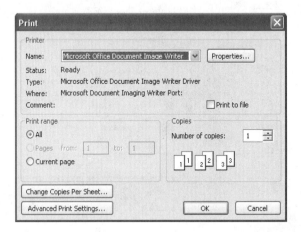

> **Tip**   You can access the Print dialog box without first going to Print Preview. On the File menu, click Print; or press [Ctrl]+[P] on your keyboard.

5   Click the down arrow to the right of the **Name** box.

If more than one printer is connected to your computer, you see a list of these printers. If only one printer is connected, only one printer is listed.

6   Click the printer on which you want to print this file.

7   In the **Print Range** area, verify that **All** is selected.

8   In the **Number of copies** box in the **Copies** area, type 2.

9   Click **OK**, and if prompted to save, click **No**.

Two copies of the file are printed on the designated printer.

CLOSE the *PrintDoc* publication.

Preparing a Document for a Commercial Printing Service

If you are going to print a large number of copies of a publication for wide distribution, you might want to use a commercial printing service. Standard computer printers are typically slow, printing only a few pages per minute, and they are expensive, especially if you're using a color inkjet. Both these factors sometimes make using a commercial printer an attractive alternative.

As you design your project, you should keep in mind the paper on which you plan to print it. Not all types of paper work in laser or inkjet printers. Heavy paper like cardstock is especially wearing on a standard printer. If you envision your document being printed on paper that is heavier than 20 to 28 pounds, you should consider setting it up for a commercial printer.

If you're planning to send a color publication to a commercial printer, you need to make a few decisions even before you begin designing it. You should consult with the commercial printer to determine which printing process is best for your document: *process color* (also called *CMYK*, which stands for the colors cyan, magenta, yellow, and black), *spot color*, or a combination of the two processes. After you've made that decision, you can use Publisher's Commercial Printing option to prepare the document for printing by a commercial printing service, and you can design your publication with a particular color printing process in mind.

Process-Color or Spot-Color Processing?

Commercial printers produce color publications using *printing plates*, with one plate used for each color in the job, as follows:

- Process-color printing uses four plates—one for each of the CYMK colors—to reproduce all the colors on a printed page. It is especially appropriate for printing documents that include full-color photographs, detailed and/or multi-colored graphics, or any illustrations that require exceptionally high-quality resolution. These types of documents might include catalogs, product flyers, or other marketing pieces in which the depiction of your product must be as accurate or high-quality as possible.

- Spot-color processing uses two or more plates—one for black and shades of gray, and one for each of the other colors used on the page. Spot colors are printed with semi-transparent, pre-mixed inks that usually come from standard color-matching guides. Your commercial printer should have a library of colors for you to look at. Be aware that the colors you see on your computer screen might not match the final outcome. You should discuss this with your commercial printer to ensure your satisfaction with the final product. Spot color is especially effective when you're printing a document with headings, borders, or logos that require emphasis, or line drawings or other graphics that require color matching. It's also the best choice when your document will use special inks or *varnish*. These types of documents might be newsletters or booklets (where the cover would be varnished).

Every color in a process-color job requires a separate color plate, so process-color printing is usually a more expensive choice. Spot-color processing is generally less expensive and more flexible in its pricing. Screen tints allow the commercial printer to create various shades without having to use separate plates. Also keep in mind that other elements contribute to the cost of a print job, such as paper choice, graphics, number of graphics, and final printed quantities.

In this exercise, you will prepare one publication for spot-color printing and another for process-color printing by a commercial printing service.

USE the *PrintDoc* and *PrintDoc2* publications in the practice file folder for this topic. These practice files are located in the *My Documents\Microsoft Press\Office 2003 SBS\Creating* folder and can also be accessed by clicking *Start/All Programs/Microsoft Press/Microsoft Office System 2003 Step by Step*. OPEN the *PrintDoc* publication.

1   On the **Tools** menu, point to **Commercial Printing Tools**, and then click **Color Printing**.

The Color Printing dialog box appears.

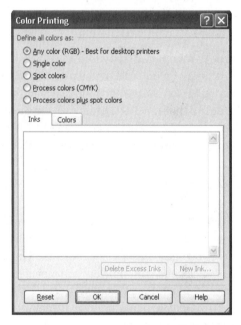

2   In the **Define all colors as** area, select the **Spot colors** option.

Publisher displays a message explaining that the colors in your publication will be converted to tints of spot colors.

Tip   When you select "Spot colors", Publisher 2003 automatically includes black as one of the colors in your document. The default number of colors is four, but you can add up to eight additional spot colors for a total of twelve. When you choose black and one spot color, Publisher automatically converts all non-black colors in your document to tints of the selected spot color. If you choose two spot colors in addition to black, Publisher changes all colors that match spot color #2 to 100% of that color, and all other colors (except black) to tints of spot color #1.

3   Read the message, and click **OK**.

Tip   If you don't want to see this message when printing spot color in the future, select the "Don't show this message again" check box, and click OK.

4   In the **Inks** list, click **Spot color 6: RGB (51, 102, 0)**, then click the down arrow that appears and click **Change**.

The Change Ink dialog box appears, displaying the Standard tab.

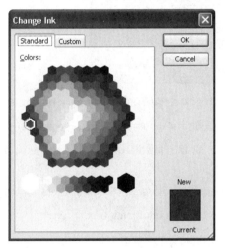

5   Click the **Custom** tab, and click the down arrow to the right of the **Color model** box.

A list of the available color models drops down.

Tip   A *color model* is a method of specifying color. Keep in mind that RGB (red-green-blue) and HSL (hue-saturation-luminance) are models for devices that transmit light, like your video monitor, whereas CMYK and PANTONE are for printed documents.

6   Click **PANTONE®**.

Tip   The first time you click PANTONE® , you will see a copyright notice. Read it, and then click OK to close the box. It will not appear again.

The PANTONE® Colors dialog box appears.

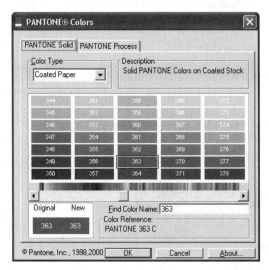

7   If the **PANTONE® Solid** tab of the **PANTONE® Colors** dialog box is not displayed, click it.

The PANTONE® Solid tab offers a number of paper type and color choices.

8   In the **Color Type** area, click the down arrow to display the color type options, and click **Uncoated Paper**.

9   Scroll to the right to see more colors, and click **5125** (a muted purple).

10 Click **OK** to return to the **Change Ink** dialog box.

11 Click **OK** to return to the **Color Printing** dialog box.

Notice that Spot Color 6, which was originally a deep green, is now the muted purple represented by PANTONE® 5125.

12 Click **OK** to close the **Color Printing** dialog box.

The changes are reflected in the document.

Tip   At this point in preparing a publication for commercial printing, you should inspect the document one more time before saving it. Publisher includes two tools to help you spot any issues before sending your publication to the printer:

■   The Graphics Manager, which you can use to locate any missing or modified pictures. On the Tools menu, click Graphics Manager.

■   The Design Checker, with which you can identify and resolve any potential design or layout problems. On the Tools menu, click Design Checker.

Save

13   On the Standard toolbar, click the **Save** button, and then close the *PrintDoc* publication.

Open

14   On the Standard toolbar, click the **Open** button, and in the **Open Publication** dialog box, navigate to the *My Documents\Microsoft Press\Office 2003 SBS\Creating* folder, and double-click the **PrintDoc2** file.

The *PrintDoc2* publication opens.

15   On the **Tools** menu, click **Commercial Printing Tools**, and then click **Color Printing**.

The Color Printing dialog box appears.

16   In the **Define all colors as** area, select the **Process color (CMYK)** option.

Publisher displays a message explaining that the colors in your publication will be converted to process colors.

17   Read the message, and click **OK**.

Tip   If you don't want to see this message when printing process color in the future, select the "Don't show this message again" check box, and click OK.

18   Click the **Colors** tab.

Publisher automatically identifies the colors used in the publication and lists them.

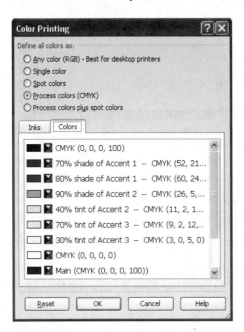

19   Click **OK** to close the **Color Printing** dialog box.

Tip   You should inspect the publication one more time, using the Graphics Manager and the Design Checker to help spot any issues, before saving the publication and sending it to the printer.

20   On the Standard toolbar, click the **Save** button.

Save

Publisher saves your changes.

CLOSE the *PrintDoc2* publication.

Key Points

- You can save personal and business information such as names, addresses, telephone numbers, logos, and color schemes to be automatically inserted into publications you create.

- You can create a new publication from a Publisher sample, a Publisher design set, your own template, or a blank page. You can apply a Publisher design set or a color scheme to a publication you create from a blank page.

- You can save your publication as a template to be used as the basis for future publications of the same type.

- You can print your publication to your own printer or you can prepare your publication for commercial printing.

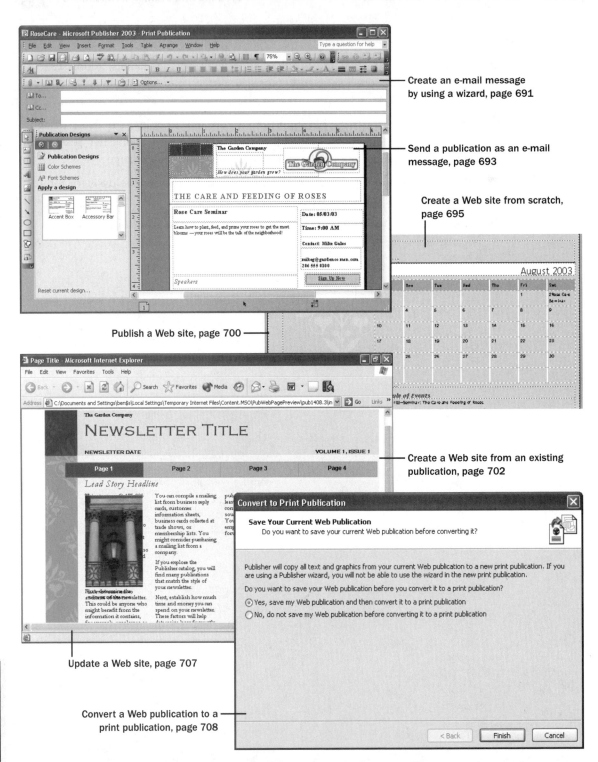

Create an e-mail message by using a wizard, page 691

Send a publication as an e-mail message, page 693

Create a Web site from scratch, page 695

Publish a Web site, page 700

Create a Web site from an existing publication, page 702

Update a Web site, page 707

Convert a Web publication to a print publication, page 708

Chapter 27 at a Glance

27 Creating Web Sites and E-mail Messages

In this chapter you will learn to:

✔ Create an e-mail message by using a wizard.

✔ Send a publication as an e-mail message.

✔ Create a Web site from scratch.

✔ Publish a Web site.

✔ Create a Web site from an existing publication.

✔ Update a Web site.

✔ Convert a Web publication to a print publication.

Microsoft Office Publisher 2003 helps you craft interesting newsletters, compelling brochures, professional business cards, fun greeting cards, and more. Now you can create Web sites and e-mail messages too!

With Publisher, you can quickly create a simple but effective Web site to promote your business, products, and services. You can also craft eye-catching e-mail messages for electronic newsletters, sales promotions, or event announcements.

See Also Do you need only a quick refresher on the topics in this chapter? See the Quick Reference entries on pages xxxiii.

 Important Before you can use the practice files in this chapter, you need to install them from the book's companion CD to their default location. See "Using the Book's CD-ROM" on page xxi for more information.

Creating an E-mail Message by Using a Wizard

Publisher helps you design effective e-mail messages for personal or business use. You might create a holiday newsletter to send to your family, or The Garden Company might feature a new product or announce upcoming events through e-mail.

In this exercise, you will create an e-mail message to be sent to The Garden Company customers announcing an upcoming workshop on caring for rose bushes.

BE SURE TO start Publisher before beginning this exercise.

1   In the **New Publication** task pane, click **Web Sites and E-mail**, and then click **E-mail**.

The E-mail list expands to show the types of pre-formatted messages available, and the preview pane shows samples.

2   In the list, click **Event/Speaker**, and in the preview pane, click **Brocade Event/ Speaker E-mail**.

Publisher opens and formats the new message.

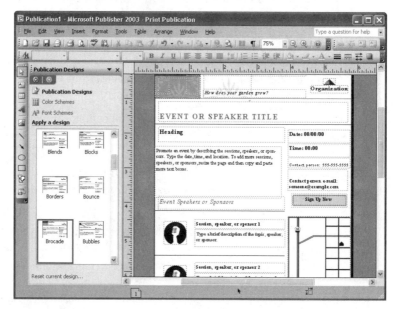

3   Click the text box containing the title, and type The Care and Feeding of Roses.

4   Click the date (00/00/00), and type the date of the first Saturday of next month.

5   Click the time, and type 9:00 AM.

6   Select the text that reads *Contact person: 555-555-5555*, and type Contact: Ben Smith.

7   Select the text in the box directly below the one you just typed in, and type ben@gardenco.msn.com. Press ⏎ Enter, and type 206 555 0100.

8   Right-click the box that reads *Sign Up Now*, and click **Hyperlink** on the shortcut menu.

9   In the **Address** box, type www.gardenco.msn.com, and click **OK**.

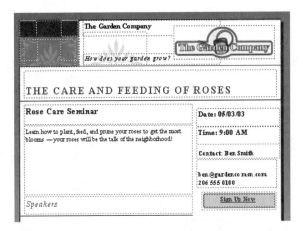

10   Edit the other text boxes as you want to describe the event. You might replace the map image with your own map, or delete the boxes for one of the three speaker events.

11   On the **File** menu, click **Close**.

12   When prompted, click **Yes** to save your publication.

13   In the **Save as** dialog box, browse to the *My Documents\Microsoft Press \Office 2003 SBS\Email* folder, and in the **File name** box, type **RoseWorkshop**. Then click **Save**.

Publisher saves and closes your e-mail message.

Sending a Publication as an E-mail Message

You can send documents created using Publisher as e-mail messages, whether or not you created the publication using an e-mail template. The contents of your Publisher document can be the message itself, or you can send publications as attachments to standard e-mail messages.

In this exercise, you will send the announcement for the upcoming rose care workshop as an e-mail message to the owner of The Garden Company for review.

USE the *RoseCare* publication in the practice file folder for this topic. This practice file is located in the *My Documents\Microsoft Press\Office 2003 SBS\Email* folder and can also be accessed by clicking *Start/All Programs/Microsoft Press/Microsoft Office System 2003 Step by Step*.
OPEN the *RoseCare* publication.

1   On the **File** menu, point to **Send E-Mail**, and click **E-mail Preview**.

Publisher displays your publication in a Web browser window to demonstrate how it will appear when viewed as an HTML e-mail message.

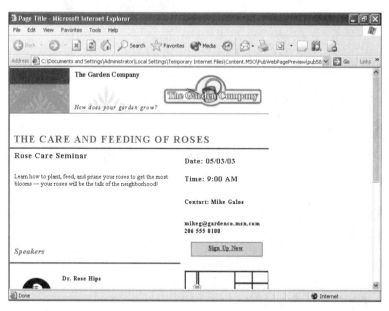

Close

2 In the upper-right corner of the preview window, click the **Close** button.

3 On the **File** menu, point to **Send E-mail**, and click **Send This Page as Message**.

The message header appears near the top of the Publisher window.

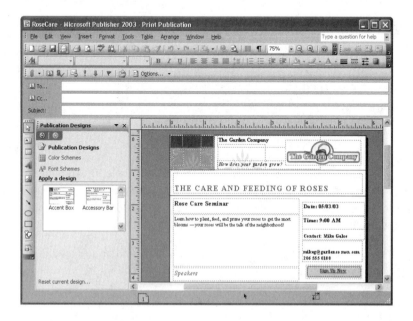

4　　In the **To** box, type Karen@gardenco.msn.com.

5　　In the **Cc** box, type your own e-mail address.

6　　In the **Subject** box, type For your review.

7　　On the E-mail toolbar, click **Send**.

Send

Publisher sends the message.

8　　On the **File** menu, click **Close**, and if prompted to save your publication, click **No**.

9　　Open your e-mail program, and check for new messages.

10　　Open the message you just sent to see how the publication looks.

CLOSE the *RoseCare* publication.

Creating a Web Site from Scratch

Publisher can help you create a great *Web site* for your small business or personal use. With the *Easy Web Site Builder*, you can quickly create a Web site from scratch—even if you've never done it before.

In this exercise, you will create a simple informational Web site for The Garden Company.

USE the *Daisies* graphic in the practice file folder for this topic. This practice file is located in the *My Documents\Microsoft Press\Office 2003 SBS\Email* folder and can also be accessed by clicking *Start/All Programs/Microsoft Press/Microsoft Office System 2003 Step by Step*.

1　　In the **New Publication** task pane, click **Web Sites and E-mail**.

Troubleshooting　　If the New Publication task pane is not visible, on the File menu, click New.

1　　The Preview pane shows the pre-made Web site layouts available for use. Scroll down to see the variety of options.

2　　Double-click **Brocade Easy Web Site**.

Publisher opens your new publication and displays the Easy Web Site Builder dialog box.

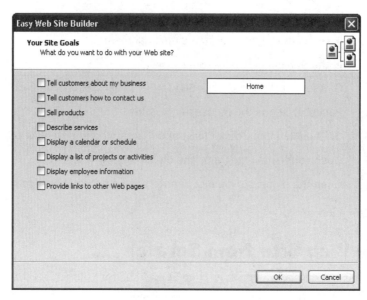

3   Select the **Tell customers how to contact us** and **Display a calendar or schedule** check boxes, and then click **OK**.

Publisher updates your publication to match your selections.

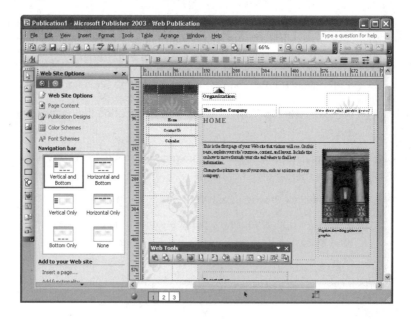

4   In the **Web Site Options** task pane, under the **Navigation Bar** heading, click **Horizontal Only**.

Troubleshooting   If the task pane is not visible, on the View menu, click Task Pane.

Publisher changes the layout of your publication to use a horizontal navigation scheme.

5   Click the text in the center of the Home page, and type a brief introduction to The Garden Company.

Tip   You can quickly change the overall look of your site by applying a font scheme. In the "Web Site Options" task pane, click "Font Schemes," and then in the "Apply a font scheme" list, click the scheme you want.

6   Right-click the picture of the lamppost, point to **Change Picture**, and click **From File**.

The Insert Picture dialog box appears.

7   Browse to *My Documents\Microsoft Press\Office 2003 SBS\Email*, and then open **Daisies**.

Publisher replaces the lamppost image with the photo of collection of daisies.

8   Click the text box below the image, and type Gerbera daisies and mums add vibrant color anywhere!

9   Right-click the logo containing the word *Organization* at the top of the page, and then click **Wizard For This Object**.

The Logo Designs task pane is displayed.

10   Click **Logo Options**, and then under **New or existing**, click **Inserted picture**. Then click the **Choose picture** button, browse to *My Documents\Microsoft Press \Office 2003 SBS\Creating*, and open **Gardenco**.

Publisher replaces the placeholder logo with The Garden Company's watering can logo.

Tip   If the logo is too large for the space, resize it. Point to the white circle near the upper-right corner of the logo, and when the mouse pointer turns into a double-headed arrow, drag up and to the right about an inch.

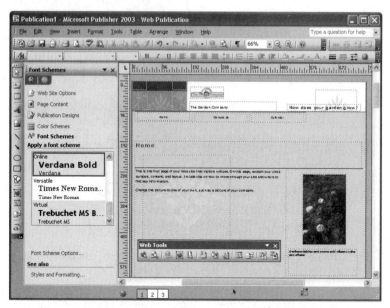

11 At the bottom of the window, click the number **2** to move to the second page.

Publisher displays the Contact Us page of your Web site.

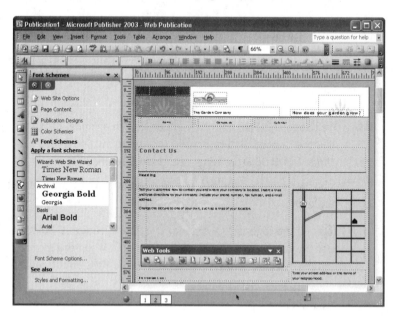

12 Click the text box that contains the word *Heading*, and type Getting to The Garden Company. Then click the text box directly below the heading, and type directions to your office.

13 Click the text box directly below the map, and type the hours that the store is open.

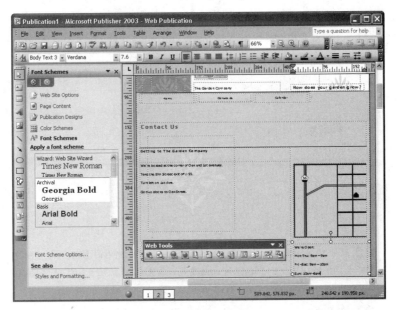

14 At the bottom of the window, click the number **3** to move to the third page.

Publisher displays the Calendar page, showing the current month.

15 Right-click the calendar, and click **Wizard for This Object** on the shortcut menu.

The Calendar Designs Wizard appears on the left side of the window. Note the available calendar design options.

16 Click the **Change Date Range** button near the bottom of the wizard pane.

The Change Calendar Dates dialog box appears.

17 In the **Start date** list, select next month, and click **OK**.

Publisher updates the calendar in your publication.

18 On the calendar, click the box for the first Saturday, and type Rose Care Seminar.

19 Click the text box below the heading **Schedule of Events**, and type the date of the first Saturday, followed by – Seminar: The Care and Feeding of Roses.

20 Right-click the text box directly below the one you just edited, and click **Hyperlink** on the shortcut menu.

The Insert Hyperlink dialog box appears.

21 In the **Address** box, type www.gardenco.msn.com, and click **OK**.

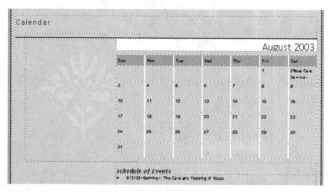

Save

22 On the Standard toolbar, click **Save**, and in the Save as dialog box, browse to the *My Documents\Microsoft Press\Office 2003 SBS\Email* folder. Then in the **File name** box, type TGC-Web, and click **Save**.

23 If Publisher asks whether you want to save the new logo as part of your Primary Business personal information set, click **Yes**.

Publisher saves your work. Now you're ready to publish it to the Web.

Publishing a Web Site

When you publish a publication to the Web, Publisher creates the *Hypertext Markup Language (HTML)* files and other files needed to view your publication as a series of Web pages in a *Web browser*. But the pages will not be available to Web users until you place them on a Web server. In other words, you need a place to host your Web site before people browsing the Internet can see your pages.

Web Hosting

Creating a Web site is great (and easy with Publisher), but you still need a place to put it. That's where *Web hosting* comes in. A Web hosting company stores your Web pages on a server that is "on the Internet," meaning that people browsing the Internet can access it. You create the pages and then upload them to the hosting company's server using tools they provide (typically a *File Transfer Protocol (FTP)* program).

Your *Internet service provider (ISP)* might provide Web hosting—in fact, your existing account might include some level of hosting service. Many other companies also provide hosting service—some catering to small businesses, others serving large companies and corporations. Some even provide the service free of charge, but there are usually restrictions or special terms for that service. Be sure to check the fine print!

When researching Web hosting service providers, consider the cost of the service, the space and transfer limits, and the file transfer and account management tools used.

In this exercise, you will publish your site so it can be displayed on the Web.

Web Page
Preview

1 On the Web Tools toolbar, click **Web Page Preview**.

Publisher prepares your Web page and displays it in a Web browser window.

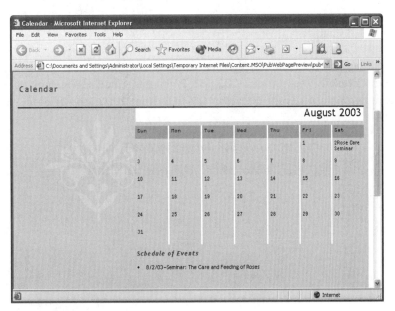

2 Close the Web browser.

Publish
to the Web

3   On the **Web Tools** toolbar, click **Publish to the Web**.

4   If Publisher displays a message about Web hosting service, read the message, and click **OK** to continue.

The Publish to the Web dialog box appears.

5   Browse to the *My Documents\Microsoft Press\Office 2003 SBS\Email* folder, and click **Save**.

6   If Publisher displays a message about how your HTML files were saved and how to update them in the future, read the message, and click **OK**.

Publisher saves the HTML and other files for your site to the selected folder. To post the site so that others can view it over the internet, copy those files to your Web server, following the instructions provided by your hosting service provider or system administrator.

CLOSE the *TGC Web* file.

Creating a Web Site from an Existing Publication

Publisher helps you get the most from work you've already done. By creating a Web site from an existing publication, you can leverage your existing promotional materials and present them online.

In this exercise, you will create a Web site from The Garden Company's monthly newsletter.

USE the *TGC-NL2* publication in the practice file folder for this topic. This practice file is located in the *My Documents\Microsoft Press\Office 2003 SBS\Email* folder and can also be accessed by clicking *Start/All Programs/Microsoft Press/Microsoft Office System 2003 Step by Step*.
OPEN the *TGC-NL2* publication.

1   On the **File** menu, click **Convert to Web Publication**.

The Convert to Web Publication Wizard appears.

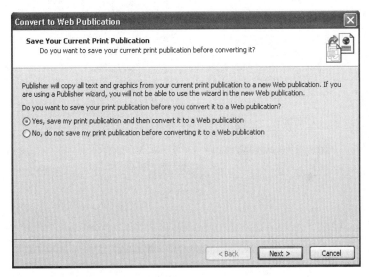

2   Select **Yes, save my print publication and then convert it to a Web publication,** and then click **Next**.

3   Select **Yes, add a navigation bar,** and click **Finish**.

Publisher displays the newsletter with a vertical navigation bar.

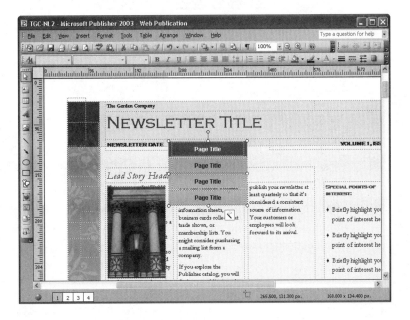

4 Right-click the navigation bar, and click **Wizard for this object** on the shortcut menu.

The Navigator Bar task pane disappears on the left side of the window.

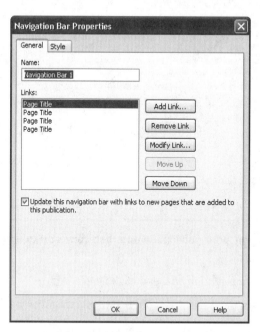

5 Under **Change navigation** bar, click **Add, remove, and reorder** links.

The Navigation Bar Properties dialog box appears.

6 Click the **Style** tab, and under **Orientation and alignment**, click **Horizontal** (row of hyperlinks).

7 In the **Hyperlink alignment** list, click **Center**, and then click **OK**.

Publisher reformats the navigation bar.

8 Drag the navigation bar to the blank area between the header of the newsletter and the first story.

Tip To fine-tune the position of an object (such as the navigation bar), click the object to select it, and then use the arrow keys on your keyboard to nudge it in the direction you want.

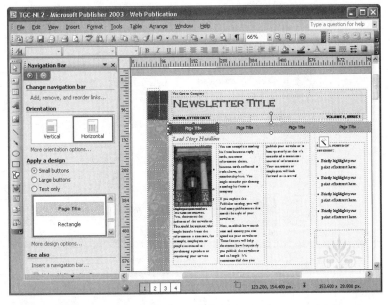

9   Click the first text box on the navigation bar, and type Page 1.

10   Click each of the other items on the navigation bar, and in turn type Page 2, Page 3, and Page 4.

11   At the bottom of the window, click the number **2**.

Publisher displays the second page of the newsletter.

12   Position the navigation bar. Repeat this process on pages 3 and 4.

13   At the bottom of the window, click the number **1**.

Publisher displays the first page of the newsletter.

Web Page
Preview

14   On the Web Tools toolbar, click **Web Page Preview**.

Publisher prepares your Web page, and displays it in a Web browser window.

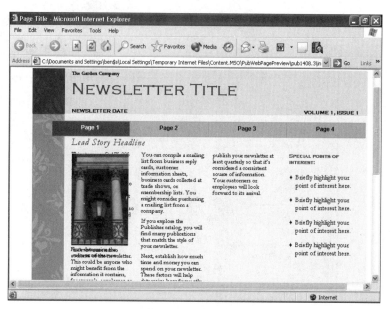

15 In the Web browser, click **Page 2** on the navigation bar.

The second page of the newsletter appears.

16 Close the Web browser.

17 On the Web Tools toolbar, click **Publish to the Web**.

18 If Publisher displays a message about Web hosting service, read the message, and click **OK** to continue.

> **Tip**   If you want to bypass this message in the future, select "Don't show me this message again" before clicking OK.

19 The Publish to the Web dialog box appears.

20 Browse to the *My Documents\Microsoft Press\Office 2003 SBS\Email* folder, and in the **File name** box, type TGC-NL2-Web, and click **Save**.

21 When Publisher displays a message about how your HTML files were saved and how to update them in the future, read the message, and click **OK**.

CLOSE the *TGC-NL2-Web* file.

Updating a Web Site

People are more likely to visit Web sites when the content changes regularly, offering them new, interesting information. Publisher can help you keep your Web pages fresh!

In this exercise, you will update The Garden Company's home page to announce an upcoming sale.

USE the *TGC-Web* publication in the practice file folder for this topic. This practice file is located in the *My Documents\Microsoft Press\Office 2003 SBS\Email* folder and can also be accessed by clicking *Start/All Programs/Microsoft Press/Microsoft Office System 2003 Step by Step.*
OPEN the *TGC-Web* publication.

1   At the bottom of the window, click the number **3** to display the third page of the site.

Publisher displays The Garden Company's calendar page.

2   On the calendar, click the last Saturday of the month, and type Clearance Sale.

3   Select *Clearance Sale*, and on the **Edit** menu, click **Copy**.

4   Click the next day (Sunday), and on the **Edit** menu, click **Paste**.

5   Below the calendar, under the heading *Schedule of Events*, click in the second event box, and type the dates of your sale followed by – Clearance Sale.

6   On the Web Tools toolbar, click **Web Page Preview**.

Web Page
Preview

Publisher prepares your Web page, and displays it in a Web browser window.

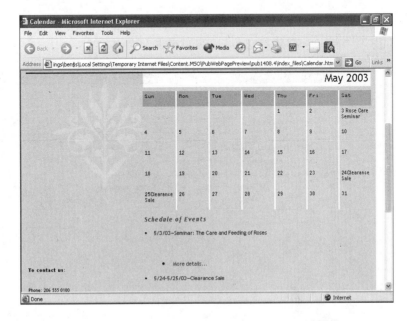

7 Close the Web browser.

8 On the Web Tools toolbar, click **Publish to the Web**.

Publish
to the Web

9 If Publisher displays a message about Web hosting service, read the message, and click **OK** to continue.

10 Browse to the *My Documents\Microsoft Press\Office 2003 SBS\Email* folder, and in the **File name** box, type TGC-Web, and click **Save**.

11 If Publisher displays a message about how your HTML files were saved and how to update them in the future, read the message, and click **OK**.

CLOSE the *TGC-Web* file.

Converting a Web Publication to a Print Publication

Just as you can quickly create Web publications from existing print publications, you can create print publications from existing Web publications. Your brochure Web site becomes your print brochure in minutes!

In this exercise, you will convert The Garden Company's Web site to a print brochure.

USE the *TGC-Web* publication in the practice file folder for this topic. This practice file is located in the *My Documents\Microsoft Press\Office 2003 SBS\Email* folder and can also be accessed by clicking *Start/All Programs/Microsoft Press/Microsoft Office System 2003 Step by Step*.
OPEN the *TGC-Web* publication.

1 On the **File** menu, click **Convert to Print Publication**.

The Convert to Print Publication dialog box appears.

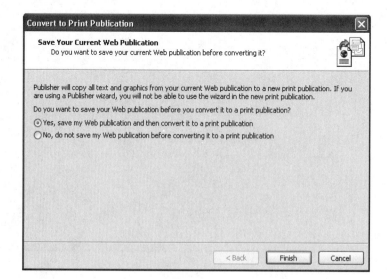

2 Select the **Yes, save my Web publication and then convert it to a print publication,** option and click **Finish.**

Publisher converts your Web publication to a print publication.

CLOSE the *TGC-Web* file.

Key Points

■ You can create rich e-mail messages using Publisher, and send them directly from Publisher. You can also send publications as attachments to an e-mail message.

■ You can create Web sites using a wizard, from a blank publication, or by converting an existing print publication. You can then publish HTML files based on the publication.

■ You can update Web publications and then publish new HTML files.

■ You can convert a Web publication for use as a printed document.

VIII
Microsoft Office
OneNote 2003

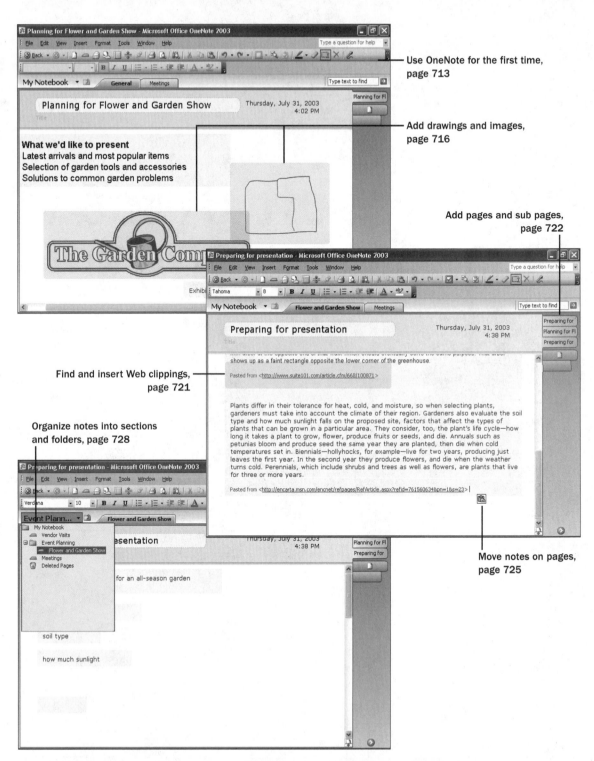

Use OneNote for the first time,
page 713

Add drawings and images,
page 716

Add pages and sub pages,
page 722

Find and insert Web clippings,
page 721

Organize notes into sections
and folders, page 728

Move notes on pages,
page 725

28 Taking Notes

In this chapter you will learn to:

✔ Use OneNote for the first time.

✔ Add drawings and images.

✔ Find and insert Web clippings.

✔ Add pages and sub pages.

✔ Move notes on pages.

✔ Organize notes into sections and folders.

Before creating almost any kind of document, presentation, or publication, you must gather information and organize your thoughts. You might even conduct research and interview experts. Microsoft Office OneNote 2003 helps you collect the results of all your preparation and planning in one consistent, convenient place—a virtual notebook!

With OneNote, you can jot down ideas generated in a brainstorming session, sketch your original vision, record your interviews, and assemble material from your online reference sources. You can enter original notes by typing on a keyboard, writing with a stylus on a Tablet PC, or drawing with a stylus or your mouse pointer. Your virtual notebook works much like a physical one—your notes are organized on pages and in sections. But you can also mark and highlight your notes as well as rearrange them, search them, and create Microsoft Outlook tasks from them—try that with a physical notebook!

For your convenience, OneNote automatically saves your notes at regular intervals, so you don't have to stop working to save. Simply close OneNote at the end of a session, and when you open it again, all your notes—in all the sections and all the pages—are there for you to continue your work.

See Also Do you need only a quick refresher on the topics in this chapter? See the Quick Reference entries on pages xxxiii.

 Important Before you can use the practice files in this chapter, you need to install them from the book's companion CD to their default location. See "Using the Book's CD-ROM" on page xxi for more information.

Using OneNote for the First Time

Getting started is easy: just open OneNote, and start typing, writing, drawing, inserting, or recording.

In this exercise, you will type some initial planning ideas for The Garden Company's presence in an upcoming flower and garden show.

BE SURE TO start your computer, but don't start OneNote before beginning this exercise.

1   Click the **Start** button, point to **All Programs**, point to **Microsoft Office**, and then click **Microsoft OneNote 2003**.

OneNote 2003 opens with two sections: *General*, on the blue tab, and *Meetings*, on the green tab.

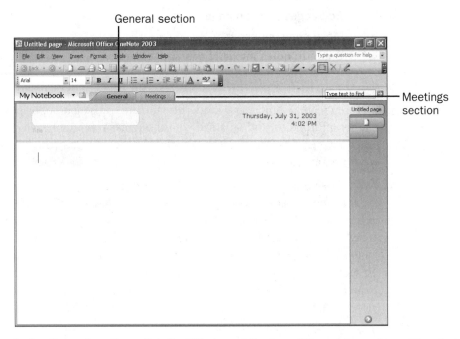

General section

Meetings section

2   In the *General* section, click the **Title** box at the top of the page, and type Planning for Flower and Garden Show.

3   In the body of the page, directly below the title, click the shaded area, and type What we'd like to present.

4   Press [Enter], and type Latest arrivals and most popular items.

5   Press [Enter], and type Selection of garden tools and accessories.

6   Press [Enter], and type Solutions to common garden problems.

B
Bold

7   Select the first line, *What we'd like to present*, and on the Formatting toolbar, click the **Bold** button.

Bullets

8   Select the remaining three lines of text on the page, and on the Formatting toolbar, click the **Bullets** button.

Tip   Click the down arrow to the right of the Bullets button to choose from a list of bullet styles.

9   Click any blank area of the note page, and type **Exhibition Theme: The All-season Garden**.

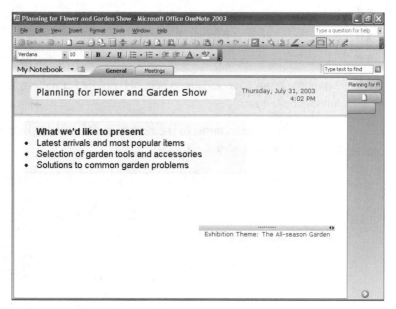

10   Near the top of the window, click the **Meetings** section tab.

OneNote 2003 displays the *Meetings* section of the notebook. This is where you'll record your notes during a meeting with the owner of The Garden Company.

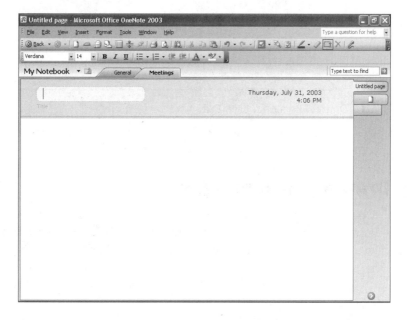

11 Click the **Title** box, and type Initial Planning Session.

12 Click in the body of the page, type Things we need, and press `Enter`.

Font Color

13 Select the text you just typed. Then on the Formatting toolbar, click the **Bold** button, click the down arrow to the right of the **Font Color** button, and click **Red**.

14 Press the ↓ key, and type Booth in exhibition hall.

15 Press `Enter`, and type Presentation slot.

16 Press `Enter` again, and type Advertising.

Numbering

17 Select the three lines you just typed, and on the Formatting toolbar, click the **Numbering** button.

Tip Click the down arrow to the right of the Numbering button to choose from a list of numbering styles.

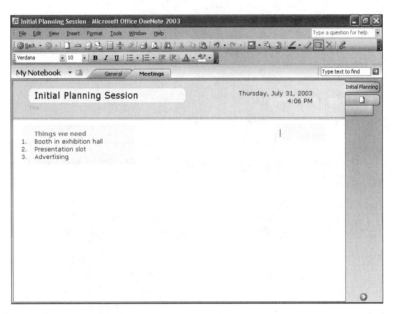

18 On the **File** menu, click **Exit**.

OneNote closes. Your notes are saved as you create them, so there's no need to save them when you close the program.

Adding Drawings and Images

Some of the best ideas were first jotted down as sketches on a napkin, and everyone knows that a picture is worth a thousand words. You can use OneNote to capture your idea as a sketch or diagram and to collect meaningful images in your notes.

In this exercise, you will add The Garden Company's logo, which will be used in promotion materials, to your notes. You will also sketch the layout of The Garden Company's booth in the exhibition hall at the flower and garden show.

USE the *Gardenco* graphic in the practice file folder for this topic. This practice file is located in the *My Documents\Microsoft Press\Office 2003 SBS\Notes* folder and can also be accessed by clicking *Start/All Programs/Microsoft Press/Microsoft Office System 2003 Step by Step*.
BE SURE TO start your computer, but don't start OneNote before beginning this exercise.

1   Click the **Start** button, point to **All Programs**, point to **Microsoft Office**, and then click **Microsoft OneNote 2003**.

OneNote opens, showing the *Meetings* section because that section was active when you closed OneNote.

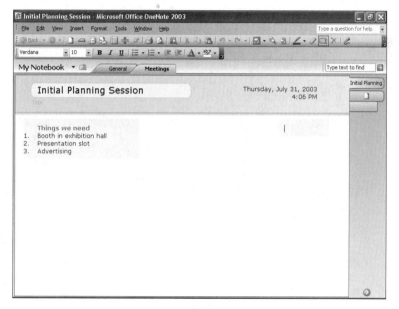

Tip   You can also open Microsoft OneNote from the system tray on the taskbar. Right-click the OneNote icon, and click Open OneNote on the shortcut menu.

2   Click the *General* section tab, and click the blank area below the text on the page.

3   On the **Insert** menu, click **Picture**.

The Insert Picture dialog box appears.

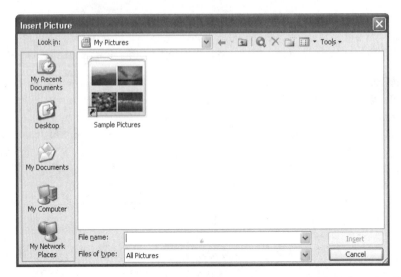

4 Browse to the *My Documents\Microsoft Press\Office 2003 SBS\Notes* folder, click **Gardenco.jpg**, and click **Insert**.

OneNote inserts the image into your notes.

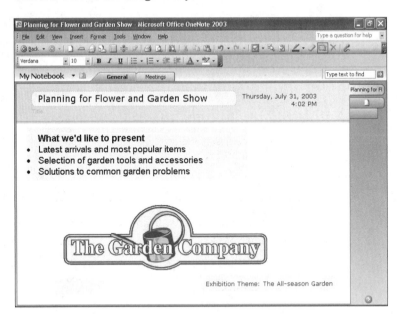

Tip You can also insert images from other documents or programs by copying and pasting them. Simply select and copy the image in the other program, and then paste it into your OneNote notebook.

Pen

5   On the Standard toolbar, click the **Pen** button, and move your mouse pointer over the note page.

Your mouse pointer becomes a small colored dot.

6   In any blank area of the note page, drag the shape of a square with mouse pointer.

Don't worry about making your lines straight—this is a rough sketch!

7   Click the down arrow to the right of the **Pen** button, and click another color.

8   Position the mouse pointer over one edge of the square you just drew, and drag the pointer to divide the square into two sections. The sections can be any size or shape you'd like—this will represent the layout for your exhibition booth.

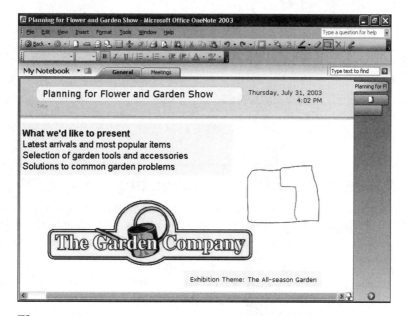

Tip   If you make a mistake while drawing, click the Eraser button on the Standard toolbar, and then click the portion of the drawing you want to erase.

Selection Tool

9   On the Standard toolbar, click the **Selection Tool** button.

10   Click in the larger portion of your exhibition booth drawing, and type main visitor area.

11   Click the smaller portion of the booth, and type demo area.

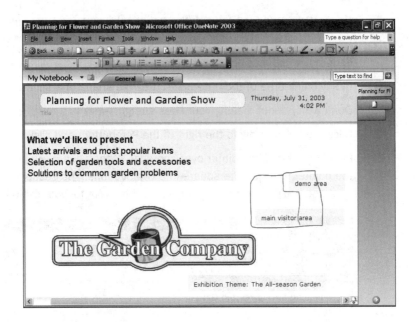

CLOSE OneNote.

Taking Notes in Your Own Handwriting

You can use your mouse or a stylus on a Tablet PC to add handwritten text and free-form drawings to pages in your virtual notebook. These notes are known as *ink*. If you use OneNote on a Tablet PC, you can keep your handwritten notes as ink or convert them to standard text.

To take handwritten notes, simply write the letters on the OneNote page with your pointing device. On a Tablet PC, OneNote recognizes your handwriting as text so that even if you don't convert the ink to text, you can search your handwritten notes.

Tip For the best results with handwriting recognition on a Tablet PC, create "lined paper" by tapping Rules Lines on the View menu, and then write between the lines. To verify that OneNote is recognizing your handwriting as text, tap Handwriting Feedback on the View menu.

Finding and Inserting Web Clippings

OneNote helps you conduct research online and collect the useful information you find in your virtual notebook. OneNote even records the source of the information—the URL of the Web page from which it came—in your notes.

In this exercise, you will find and insert excerpts from Web sites as you conduct research to develop a seminar to be presented by The Garden Company at the flower and garden show.

BE SURE TO start OneNote before beginning this exercise.

1 Open your Web browser, and go to one of your favorite Web sites. If you have a favorite site about gardening, go to that site.

2 Select a portion of the content of the page—pictures, text, links, or all of these—and on the **Edit** menu, click **Copy**.

3 Switch to OneNote, click a blank area of the page, and on the **Edit** menu, click **Paste**.

The Web page contents are inserted into your notes, with a citation indicating the source of the material.

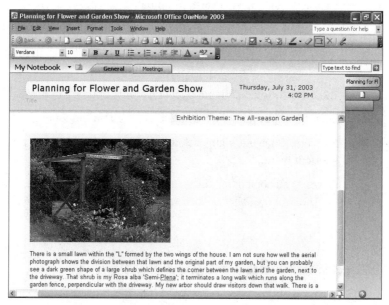

4 On the **Tools** menu, click **Research**.

The Research task pane appears on the right side of the OneNote window.

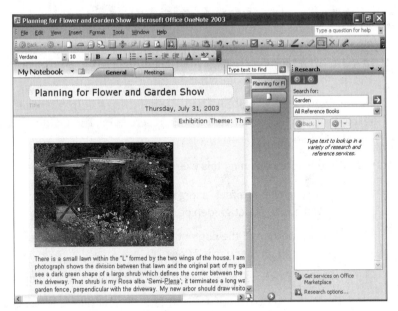

5   In the **Search for** box, type gardening, and in the drop-down list, click **Encarta Encyclopedia: English (North America)**.

The search starts, and then the results appear in the Research task pane.

6   Scroll through the search results list to see the variety of items found, and then near the top of the list, click **II. Selecting Plants**.

The Encarta topic entitled *Selecting Plants* appears in a Web browser window.

7   Select the first paragraph in the topic, and on the **Edit** menu, click **Copy**.

8   Switch to OneNote, right-click any blank area of the page, and click **Paste** on the shortcut menu.

The text you copied from Encarta is inserted into your notes, with a citation indicating the URL from which you obtained the material.

CLOSE OneNote.

Adding Pages and Sub Pages

A physical notebook contains a fixed number of pages. In OneNote, you add pages to your virtual notebook as you need them. In addition, you can create sub pages to group pages that contain notes about a single topic, or rearrange pages to organize your notes in a logical order.

In this exercise, you will add a page and sub page for notes you take while preparing a presentation for the upcoming flower and garden show.

BE SURE TO start OneNote before beginning this exercise.

New Page

1 On the upper-right side of the note page, click the **New Page** tab.

OneNote inserts a new blank page in the *General* section of your notebook.

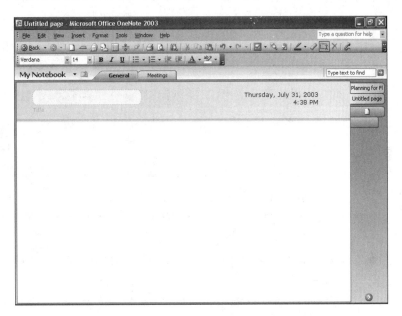

2 In the **Title** box, type Preparing for presentation.

3 Click anywhere on the blank note page, type 30 minutes, press `Enter`, and then type 50-80 people.

This page will contain notes about the logistics of developing and delivering the presentation.

New Sub page

4 On the upper-right side of the note page, click the **New subpage** tab.

OneNote adds a third page to your notebook and inserts the title from the second page because this page is a sub page to the second. The pages are now grouped together.

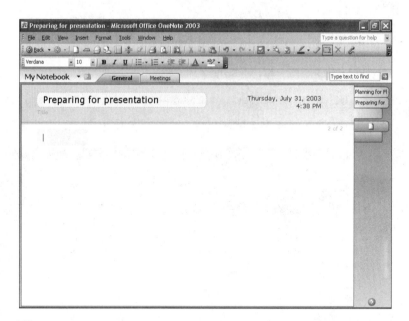

Tip To group existing pages, click the tab of the first page, hold down the [Ctrl] or [Shift] key while you click the tabs of the other pages, right-click the selected page tabs, and then click Group Pages on the shortcut menu.

5 Click anywhere on the blank note page, and type Topic: Selecting plants for an all-season garden.

This page will contain notes about the content of the presentation itself.

6 With your mouse, point to the tab for the first page in the *General* section of your notebook.

OneNote displays the number, the title, and the date the page was created in a ScreenTip.

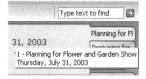

Tip To view a list of all the pages in your notebook, on the View menu, click Page List. From the Page List, you can view any page, sort the pages by section, title, or date, and filter the list to show only pages in the current section or folder.

7   Click the page tab, and drag it to the right until a small arrow appears indicating the location of the page. Then drag the page tab down until the arrow appears just below the second page tab.

The pages are reordered so that the second page is now the first page and what was the first page is now the second.

Tip   To move or copy a page or a group of pages to a new section or folder, on the Edit menu, click Move or Copy Pages.

8   Right-click the *General* section tab at the top of the notebook, and click **Rename** on the shortcut menu.

9   Type Flower and Garden Show, and press Enter.

OneNote applies the new name to the section.

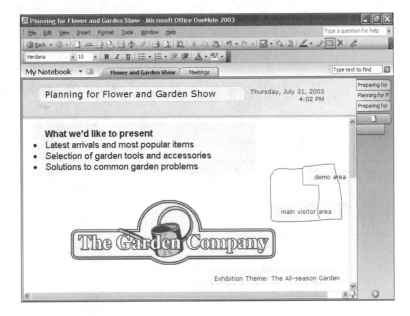

CLOSE OneNote.

Moving Notes on Pages

When taking notes, you are usually just gathering information without much regard for how they are organized. To make use of the information you've gathered, you typically need to organize your notes in a logical manner. With OneNote you can rearrange the notes in your virtual notebook—moving elements to any spot on a page or from one page to another.

In this exercise, you will move the Web clippings you gathered while doing research for the flower and garden show presentation to the page you've created for that work.

BE SURE TO start OneNote before beginning this exercise.

1 If the second page of the *Flower and Garden Show* section is not visible, click the tab for page 2 on the right side of the notebook.

2 On the Standard toolbar, click the **Selection Tool** button.

Selection Tool

3 Drag the mouse pointer across the page to select both Web clippings on the page.

The selected items are surrounded by dotted lines.

4 On the **Edit** menu, click **Cut**.

The selected items are copied to the clipboard and removed from the note page.

5 On the right side of the notebook, click the tab for page 3.

6 Click any blank area of the page, and on the **Edit** menu, click **Paste**.

The Web clippings are inserted into page 3.

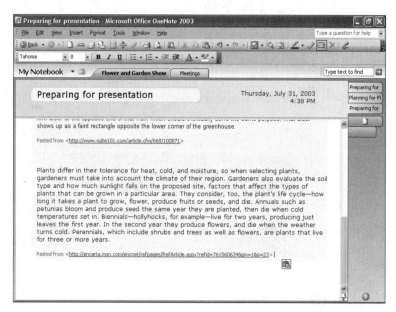

7 Scroll to the bottom of the page and click the down arrow at the bottom of the scroll bar.

8 Click a blank area of the page below the bottom Web clipping, and type any letter.

9 Scroll up to the first Web clipping, select all of it, and on the **Edit** menu, click **Cut**.

10 Scroll down to the box you added in step 8, select its text, and on the **Edit** menu, click **Paste**.

Tip By default, OneNote moves note elements through positions on a virtual grid on the page. As you drag elements on the page, you will see them snap from one grid location to the next. This feature is called *Snap to Grid* and can be very useful for lining up elements vertically or horizontally. If you want finer control when placing note elements, you can disable this feature. On the Edit menu, click Snap to Grid to toggle this feature on and off.

11 In the Web clipping from Encarta, select *climate of their region* at the end of the first sentence.

12 Drag the selected text to the blank area above the clipping.

The selected text is removed from the clipping and placed on its own as a separate note element.

13 Select other key phrases from the Encarta clipping—look for criteria gardeners might be interested in when selecting plants—and drag those phrases to the blank area above the clipping.

These phrases will help you create an outline for your presentation.

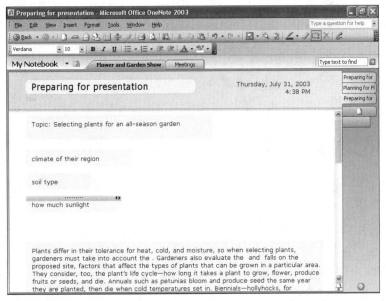

14 Click the dark gray horizontal bar at the top of the Encarta clipping, and press [Del].

The clipping is removed from the page.

CLOSE OneNote.

Organizing Notes into Sections and Folders

As you work with OneNote over time, you might collect notes about a wide variety of topics, and your virtual notebook could get disorganized. To help you keep track of them, you can divide your notebook into sections and folders. Sections can contain one or more pages or groups of pages. Folders can contain pages, sections, or other folders.

In this exercise, you will create a new section to record the notes you take while evaluating prospective vendors. You will also create a folder to store information related to the events you plan for The Garden Company.

BE SURE TO start OneNote before beginning this exercise.

1   On the **Insert** menu, click **New Section**.

OneNote creates a new section as a tab at the top of the note page, ready for you to name.

2   Type Vendor Visits as the section name, and press Enter .

3   Right-click the new section tab, point to **Section Color** on the shortcut menu, and click **Magenta**.

4   In the **Title** box, type Vendor Name Here.

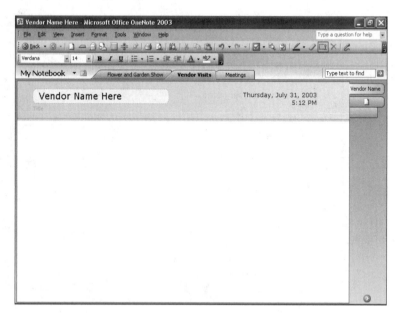

5   On the **Insert** menu, click **New Folder**.

OneNote creates a new folder as a tab at the top of the note page, ready for you to name.

Tip   The folder icon on the folder tabs helps you distinguish them from section tabs.

6   Type **Event Planning** as the folder name, and press Enter .

7   Right-click the **Flower and Garden Show** section tab, and click **Move** on the shortcut menu.

The Move Section To dialog box appears.

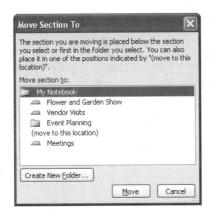

8   In the **Move section to** list, select the **Event Planning** folder, and click **Move**.

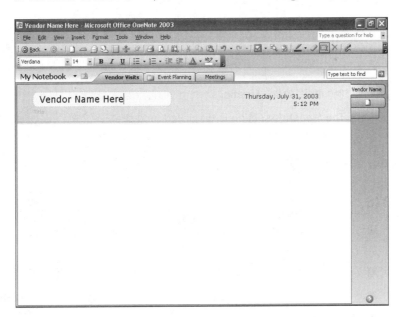

Tip   You can create a folder and move a section to your new folder in one process. Simply right-click the section tab, and click Move. In the Move Section To dialog box, click the Create New Folder button. When prompted, name the folder. Then select that folder in the Move Section To list, and click the Move button.

9 The *Flower and Garden Show* section is no longer visible because it is contained within the *Event Planning* folder.

10 Click the **Event Planning** tab.

The *Event Planning* folder opens, displaying the *Flower and Garden Show* tab.

11 Click the down arrow to the right of the folder name.

The drop-down list shows all the sections and folders in your notebook.

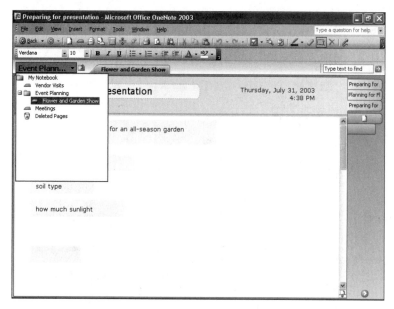

12 In the list, click **Meetings**.

The *Meetings* section is displayed, and the *Event Planning* folder again appears as a tab at the top of the page.

CLOSE OneNote.

Key Points

■ You can easily take notes made up of typed text, handwritten text, images, Web clippings, drawings, and sound recordings.

■ You take notes on pages and can group pages with related content.

■ You can organize pages into sections and sections into folders.

■ You can rearrange your notebook by moving notes and pages.

■ OneNote automatically saves your notebook at regular intervals and each time you close the program.

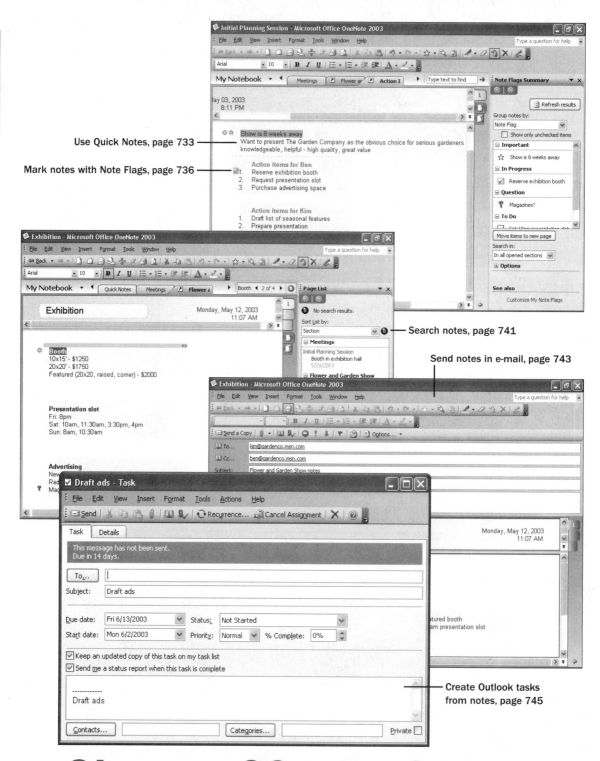

Use Quick Notes, page 733

Mark notes with Note Flags, page 736

Search notes, page 741

Send notes in e-mail, page 743

Create Outlook tasks from notes, page 745

Chapter 29 at a Glance

29 Working with Notes

In this chapter you will learn to:

✔ Use Quick Notes.

✔ Mark notes with Note Flags.

✔ Search notes.

✔ Send notes in e-mail.

✔ Create Outlook tasks from notes.

Microsoft Office OneNote 2003 makes the notes you take more useful by providing a number of ways to find them, mark them, and share them. With Quick Notes, you can jot down a great idea with minimal interruption to your current task. You can search your notes—no matter how many pages or sections there are. You can share your notes with colleagues and team members through e-mail and even create tasks for yourself or others using Microsoft Outlook.

See Also   Do you need only a quick refresher on the topics in this chapter? See the Quick Reference entries on pages xxxiii.

 Important   Before you can use the practice files in this chapter, you need to install them from the book's companion CD to their default location. See "Using the Book's CD-ROM" on page xxi for more information.

Using Quick Notes

Imagine that you are writing a critical report for your manager when a great idea for an unrelated project occurs to you. With a single click, you open Quick Notes—a miniature notes window—where you record the idea, and within seconds, you return to your report. When your report is finished, you get caught up in other tasks and forget about your great idea. But the next time you open your OneNote notebook, your Quick Note is there to remind you!

In this exercise, you will record your manager's answers to questions you've posed in a phone call. You plan to incorporate these notes with the others you've already taken while preparing for The Garden Company's presence at an upcoming flower and garden show.

USE the *Flower and Garden Show* notebook in the practice file folder for this topic. This practice file is located in the *My Documents\Microsoft Press\Office 2003 SBS\Mini* folder and can also be accessed by clicking *Start/All Programs/Microsoft Press/Microsoft Office System 2003 Step by Step*.

BE SURE TO start your computer, but don't start OneNote before beginning this exercise.

1   In the system tray on the Windows task bar (near the clock), click the **Microsoft OneNote** icon.

Troubleshooting   If the OneNote icon does not appear in your system tray, open OneNote from the Start menu, and then minimize the window. The icon will then appear in your system tray. You do not have to have OneNote open in order to take Side Notes, but opening OneNote places the icon in the system tray. The icon remains there until you specifically remove it—even when you close OneNote.

Microsoft Office OneNote 2003 opens.

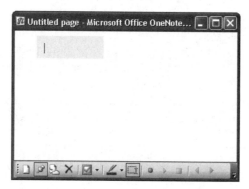

2   Type Get featured booth.

3   On the toolbar, click the **New Page** button.

New Page

A new blank page is added to your Quick Notes.

4   Type Join ad pool for Sunday and weekly papers and radio spots.

5   On the toolbar, click the **Previous Page** button.

Previous Page

6   Press [Enter], and type Sat 10am presentation slot.

7   On the toolbar, click the **Next Page** button.

Next Page

Close

8   In the upper-right corner of the Mini OneNote window, click the **Close** button.

Mini OneNote closes.

9   Click the **Start** button, point to **All Programs**, point to **Microsoft Office**, and then click **Microsoft OneNote 2003**.

OneNote 2003 opens, with a new section labeled *Side Notes*.

10   On the **File** menu, click **Open**, browse to the *My Documents\Microsoft Press \Office 2003 SBS\Mini* folder, click the **Flower and Garden Show** notebook, and click **Open**.

The Flower and Garden Show section is displayed and added to the tabs at the top of the notebook.

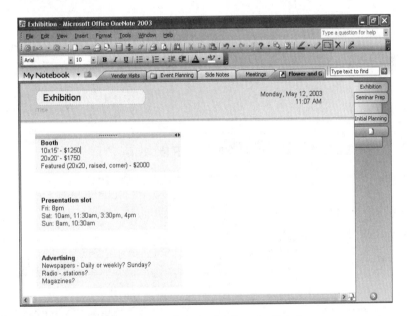

11   If the **Side Notes** tab is not already displayed, click it.

OneNote displays the notes you took using Side Notes.

12   In the **Side Notes** section, click the **Get Featured** tab.

13   Select the text on the page, and on the **Edit** menu, click **Cut**.

14   Click the *Flower and Garden Show* folder tab, right-click the blank area to the right of the notes about *Booth* and *Presentation slot*, and on the shortcut menu, click **Paste**.

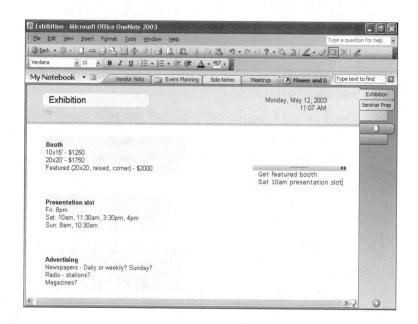

CLOSE OneNote.

Marking Notes with Note Flags

While reviewing notes in a paper notebook, people often mark various sections with stars or check marks, circle other items, or use a highlighter. Frequently, these markings are inconsistent and difficult or impossible to change later.

With Note Flags in OneNote, you can mark your notes with consistent flags—a check box for an action item, a star for important items, and so on. OneNote includes a few preset flags that you can customize, and you can create your own. You can also highlight parts of notes to draw attention to them.

In this exercise, you will update your notes to record the status of some action items and call attention to others.

USE the *Action Items* notebook in the practice file folder for this topic. This practice file is located in the *My Documents\Microsoft Press\Office 2003 SBS\Mini* folder and can also be accessed by clicking *Start/All Programs/Microsoft Press/Microsoft Office System 2003 Step by Step*.
BE SURE TO start OneNote before beginning this exercise.

NoteFlag

1　On the Standard toolbar, click the **Note Flag** button.

　　A small square appears to the left of the selected line of text.

Troubleshooting   The small square is a check box indicating a To Do item. This is the default selection for Note Flags. However, other flags are available to you. Because OneNote remembers which flag you used last, if you have already used Note Flags, you might see a different flag. To display the To Do indicator, click the down arrow to the right of the Note Flags button, and click To Do.

2   Press the ⬇ key, placing the insertion point in front of the line that reads *Sat 10am presentation slot*, and then click the **Note Flag** button again.

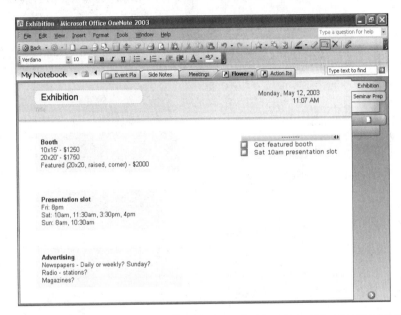

3   Click at the beginning of the line that reads *Magazines?* (under the heading of *Advertising*), and click the down arrow to the right of the **Note Flags** button.

The full list of available note flags appears.

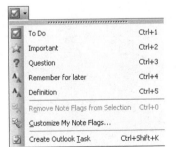

Troubleshooting   You might have to click the chevrons at the bottom of the menu to see the full menu.

4   In the drop-down list, click **Question**.

A small question mark icon appears to the left of the selected line of text.

5   On the Standard toolbar, click the down arrow to the right of the **Note Flags** button, and click **Customize My Note Flags**.

The Customize My Note Flags task pane appears on the right side of the window.

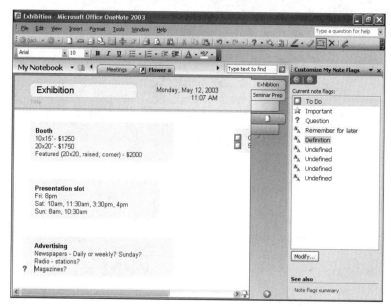

6   Click the first undefined item in the list, and click **Modify**.

The Modify Note Flag dialog box appears.

7   In the **Display name** box, type In Progress.

8   Click the down arrow to the right of the selected **Symbol**, and click the yellow check box.

9   Click **OK**.

The Modify Note Flag dialog box closes, and the new note flag appears in the Customize My Note Flags task pane.

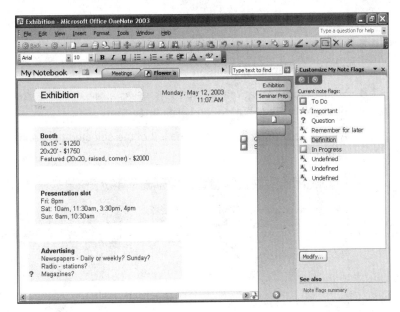

10   Double-click the **Important** note flag.

The Modify Note Flag dialog box appears.

11   Click the down arrow to the right of the selected **Highlight Color**, click **Sky Blue**, and then click **OK**.

The change is reflected in the list in the Customize My Note Flags task pane.

Close

12   In the **Customize My Note Flags** task pane, click the **Close** button.

The task pane closes.

13   On the **File** menu click **Open**, browse to *My Documents\Microsoft Press \Office 2003 SBS\Mini* folder, click the **Action Items** notebook, and click **Open**.

The Action Items section is displayed and added to the tabs at the top of the notebook.

14 Click the **Action Items** section tab, and click at the beginning of the line that reads *Reserve exhibition booth* in the *Action items for Ben*) area.

15 Click the down arrow to the right of the **Note Flags** button.

The menu now includes your customized note flag.

16 Click **In Progress**.

A small yellow check box appears next to the selected line of text.

17 Click the check box that you just inserted.

A red check mark appears in the box.

18 Select the text that reads *Show is 8 weeks away*, click the down arrow to the right of the **Note Flags** button, and click **Important**.

A small yellow star appears to the left of the selected text, and the text is highlighted in blue.

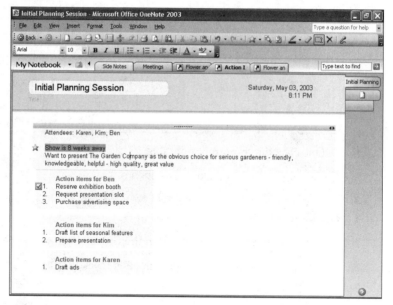

19 On the **View** menu, click **Note Flags Summary**.

The Note Flags Summary task pane appears on the right side of the window, summarizing the note flags in the current section.

20 In the **Search** list near the bottom of the task pane, click **My entire notebook**.

The list now includes note flags in other open sections.

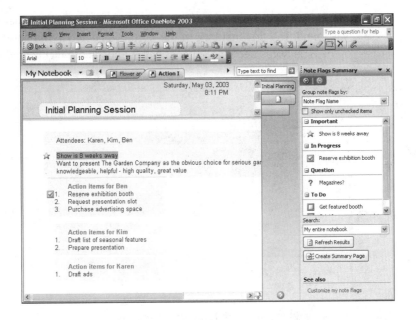

CLOSE OneNote.

Searching Notes

OneNote makes it easy to find your notes when you need them. Simply enter one or more keywords, and OneNote finds all references to that word, no matter where they are in your notebook.

In this exercise, you will find all notes related to the exhibition booth that The Garden Company will have at the flower and garden show.

USE the *Flower and Garden Show* and *Action Items* notebooks in the practice files folder for this topic. These practice files are located in the *My Documents\Microsoft Press\Office 2003 SBS\Mini* folder and can also be accessed by clicking *Start/All Programs/Microsoft Press/Microsoft Office System 2003 Step by Step*. BE SURE TO start OneNote before beginning this exercise.
OPEN the *Flower and Garden Show* and *Action Items* notebooks.

1   On the **Edit** menu, click **Find**.

OneNote prompts you to type the words you want to find in a box in the upper-right corner of the window.

> **Tip**   You can search your notes without using the menu commands. Simply type the words you want to find directly into the Search box, and click the Search button.

Find

2   Type booth in the box, and click the **Find** button.

The Search box is highlighted in yellow and indicates the number of times the word was found. The first instance of the word is selected in the notes on the first page of the *Side Notes* section. Subsequent instances are highlighted in yellow.

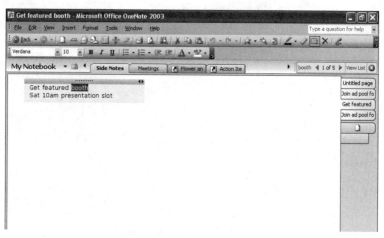

3   In the **Find** box, click the **Next Match** button.

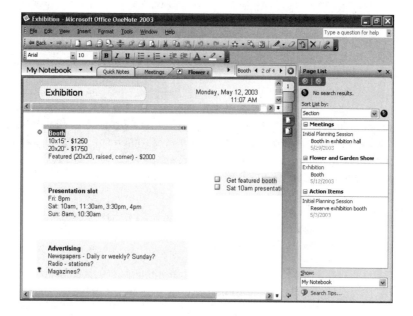

OneNote displays the page containing the next instance of the word, which is on the first page in the *Meetings* section.

4   In the **Find** box, click **2 of 4**.

Troubleshooting If your notebook contains other notes besides the ones used in this course, you might see *2 of 5* or some other number.

The Page List task pane appears, listing the pages that include the word *booth*.

5 Click **View List**, next to the **Find** box.

6 Under **Action items** in the **Page List** task pane, click **Initial Planning Session**.

OneNote displays the selected page with the matching words highlighted.

7 In the **Page List** task pane, click the **Close** button.

✕
Close

The Page List task pane closes.

8 In the **Find** box, click the **Clear Find Highlighting** button.

The Search box returns to its ready state, and the matching words are no longer highlighted.

CLOSE OneNote.

Sending Notes in E-mail

It's often helpful to share your notes with others—for example, when a co-worker is unable to attend a meeting, or when you are collaborating on a project. With OneNote and Outlook, you can easily send your notes through e-mail.

In this exercise, you will send the notes you've collected while doing research for a seminar to your co-presenter.

USE the *Flower and Garden Show* notebook in the practice file folder for this topic. This practice file is located in the *My Documents\Microsoft Press\Office 2003 SBS\Mini* folder and can also be accessed by clicking *Start/All Programs/Microsoft Press/Microsoft Office System 2003 Step by Step*.
BE SURE TO start OneNote before beginning this exercise.
OPEN the *Flower and Garden Show* notebook.

1 Click the **Flower and Garden Show** section tab.

2 Click the tab for **Seminar Prep** twice.

Both pages of the group are selected.

3 Hold down the Ctrl key, and click the tab for **Exhibition**.

All pages of the section are selected.

E-mail

4   On the Standard toolbar, click the **E-mail button**.

OneNote displays an e-mail message header at the top of the window.

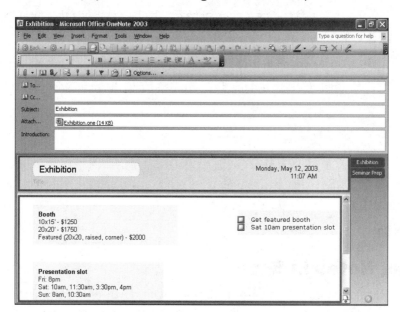

5   In the **To** box, type kim@gardenco.msn.com.

Tip   You can also select addresses from your Outlook Contacts instead of typing the address. Simply click the To, Cc, or Bcc button in the e-mail header to open the Select Names dialog box.

6   In the **Cc** box, type your e-mail address.

7   Select the text in the **Subject** box, and type Flower and Garden Show notes.

8   In the **Introduction** box, type Current status – please review.

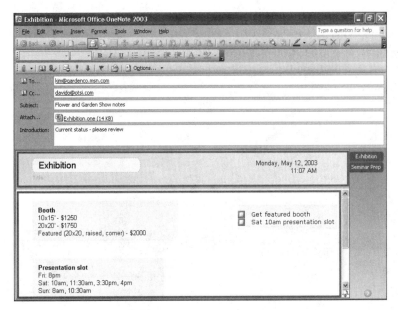

9 On the E-mail toolbar, click the **Send a Copy** button.

OneNote sends the message and closes the message header.

Tip To cancel a message before you've sent it, on the toolbar, click the E-mail button again to close the message header.

10 Open Microsoft Outlook, and check for new messages.

The e-mail message you sent from OneNote arrives. The pages you selected are the content of the message; scroll down the message to see that each page is displayed in succession. The notes are also contained in an attachment to the message called *Exhibition.one*.

CLOSE OneNote.

Creating Outlook Tasks from Notes

Frequently, your notes will be reminders of things you must do or things you must arrange for others to do. With OneNote, you can create Outlook tasks directly from your notes, and you can assign those tasks to yourself or others.

In this exercise, you will review your progress in planning for the upcoming flower and garden show and assign tasks as needed.

USE the *Action Items* notebook in the practice files folder for this topic. This practice file is located in the *My Documents\Microsoft Press\Office 2003 SBS\Mini* folder and can also be accessed by clicking *Start/All Programs/Microsoft Press/Microsoft Office System 2003 Step by Step*.
BE SURE TO start OneNote and Outlook before beginning this exercise.
OPEN the *Action Items* notebook.

1 If the *Action Items* section is not visible, click the **Action Items** section tab.

2 On the note page, under the heading *Action Items for Kim*, select the line that reads *Draft list of seasonal features*.

Create
Outlook Task

3 On the Standard toolbar, click the **Create Outlook Task** button.

An Outlook Task window appears, with the selected text showing as the subject.

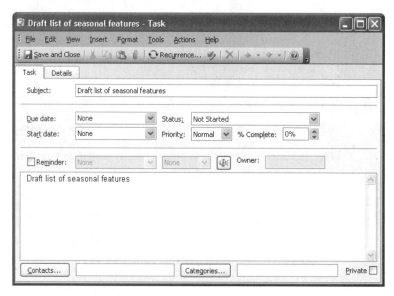

4 In the **Due date** list, select a date that is two weeks from today.

5 Select the **Reminder** check box.

Outlook automatically sets the reminder for the morning of the day the task is due.

Save and Close

6 Click the **Save and Close** button.

Outlook saves the task and adds it to your task list.

7 In OneNote, select the line that reads *Draft ads* under the heading *Action Items for Karen*.

8 On the Standard toolbar, click the **Create Outlook Task** button.

An Outlook Task window appears, with the selected text as the subject.

9   In the **Due date** list, select the date that is two weeks from today.

10 In the **Start date** list, select tomorrow's date, and clear the **Reminder** check box.

11 On the Standard toolbar, click the **Assign Task** button.

The Task window changes so that you can assign the task.

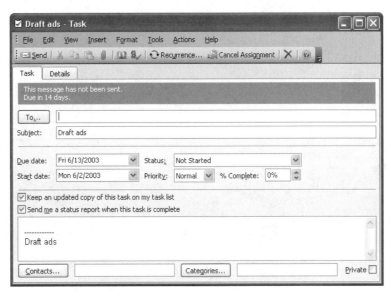

12 In the **To** box, type your e-mail address.

13 On the Standard toolbar, click the **Send** button.

The task request is sent.

Send

14 Switch to Microsoft Outlook, and check for new messages.

The task request arrives as a new message.

15 Select the task request.

The task request header includes Accept and Decline buttons.

16 Delete the message, and return to **OneNote**.

CLOSE OneNote.

Key Points

- You can take notes with one click using Quick Notes, and then incorporate them into your OneNote notebook later.

- You can mark your notes to indicate important concepts, questions, action items, and more. You can highlight your notes. You can also customize the flags you can set in your notes.

■ You can search your notes—through all the pages, sections, and folders—to find all references to a particular word or words.

■ You can share your notes with others by sending them in e-mail.

■ You can create Outlook tasks for yourself or others based on your notes.

IX
Microsoft Office
InfoPath 2003

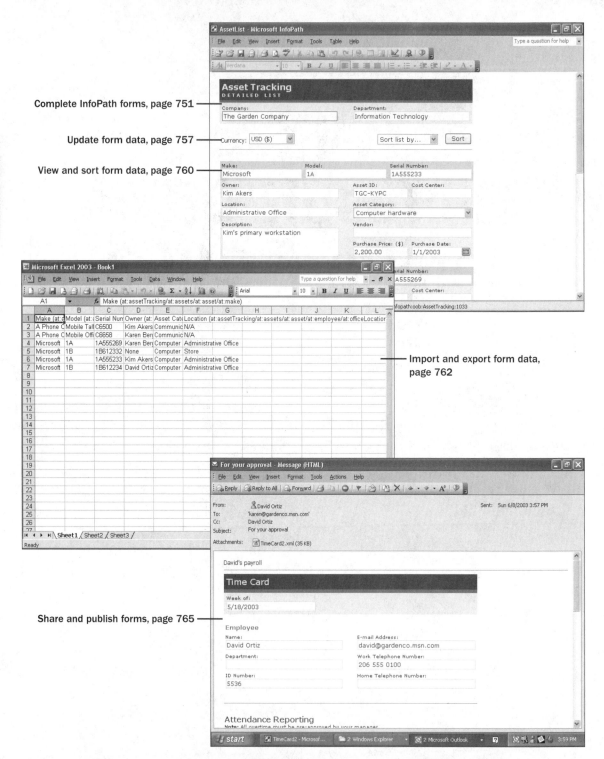

Complete InfoPath forms, page 751

Update form data, page 757

View and sort form data, page 760

Import and export form data, page 762

Share and publish forms, page 765

Chapter 30 at a Glance

30 Working with InfoPath Forms

In this chapter you will learn to:

✔ Complete InfoPath forms.

✔ Update form data.

✔ View and sort form data.

✔ Import and export form data.

✔ Share and publish forms.

Microsoft InfoPath—a new application in The Microsoft Office System 2003—helps you gather and use information through dynamic forms. The information collected through InfoPath forms can be shared with others, published to the Web, and easily reused, because the data is stored in industry-standard *Extensible Markup Language (XML)* files.

This chapter will introduce InfoPath forms, and show you how to complete, update, share, and publish forms. This chapter will also covers viewing, sorting, importing, and exporting form data.

See Also   Do you need only a quick refresher on the topics in this chapter? See the Quick Reference entries on pages xxxiii.

 Important   Before you can use the practice files in this chapter, you need to install them from the book's companion CD to their default location. See "Using the Book's CD-ROM" on page xxi for more information.

Completing InfoPath Forms

Because InfoPath uses familiar form *controls* such as text boxes, drop-down lists, and option buttons, completing InfoPath forms is easy. Simply open the blank form and go!

In this exercise, you will complete a time card form and then familiarize yourself with the travel itinerary form.

BE SURE TO start your computer, but don't start InfoPath before beginning this exercise.

1   Click **Start**, point to **All Programs**, point to **Microsoft Office**, and then click **Microsoft Office InfoPath 2003**.

InfoPath opens with the Fill Out a Form task pane displayed.

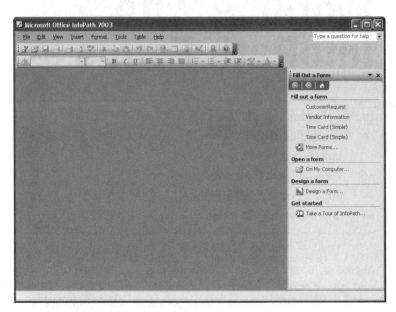

2 In the task pane, in the **Fill out a form** area, click **More Forms**.

The Forms dialog box appears.

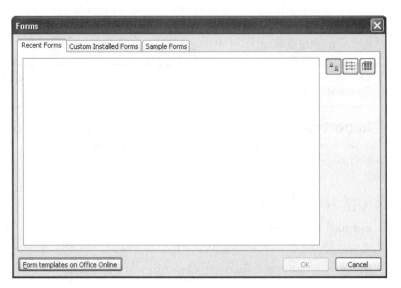

3 Click the **Sample Forms** tab.

The collection of sample forms is displayed on the tab.

Tip   More form templates are available on the Microsoft Web site. In the Forms dialog box, click the "Form templates on Microsoft.com" button.

4   Scroll down, click the **Time Card (Simple)** form, and then click **OK**.

The task pane closes, and the Time Card form opens.

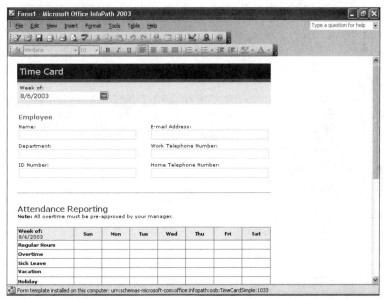

Week of

5   At the right end of the **Week of** box, click the **Week of** button.

A calendar appears, showing the current month.

6   Click the most recent Sunday.

The calendar disappears, and the date of the Sunday you selected appears in the "Week of" box.

7   In the **Name** box, type David Ortiz.

8   In the **E-mail Address** box, type david@gardenco.msn.com, and then press the Tab key.

9   In the **Work Telephone Number** box, type 206 555 0100, and press Tab twice.

10   Enter the following regular hours into the **Attendance Reporting** table: 4 on Sunday, 6 on Monday, 6 on Wednesday, 4 on Thursday, and 8 on Friday.

11   Enter the following vacation hours into the Attendance Reporting table: 4 on Tuesday.

The form calculates the totals for each day and the total for the week.

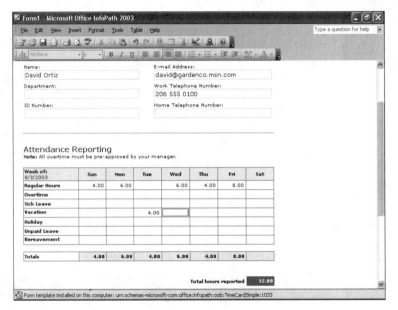

12   On the **File** menu, click **Close**.

13   When prompted to save the form, click **Yes**.

The Save As dialog box appears.

14   Browse to the *My Documents\Microsoft Press\Office 2003 SBS\InfoForms* folder. Then in the **File name** box, type DOTimeCard, and click **Save**.

InfoPath saves your form data and closes the form.

15   In the **Fill Out a Form** task pane, click **More Forms**.

Troubleshooting   If the Fill Out a Form task pane is not visible, on the File menu, click Fill Out a Form.

16 On the **Sample Forms** tab, click **Travel Itinerary**, and then click **OK**.

A travel itinerary form opens.

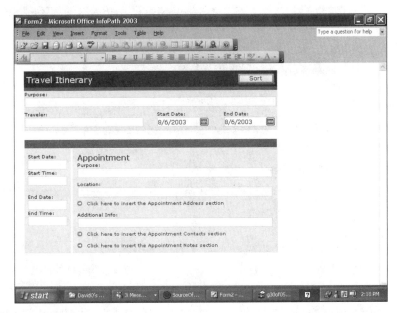

17 In the **Purpose** box, type Touring Vendor Grounds and Greenhouses.

18 In the **Traveler** box, type Kim Akers.

19 In the **Start date** box, type the date of the next Monday, and in the **End Date** box, type the date of the Friday following the start date you entered.

20 In the **Appointment** section, in the **Start Date** box, type the same start date you entered earlier, and in the **Start Time** box, type 3:00pm.

21 In the **Purpose** box, type Tour of Happy Horticulture, and in the **Location** box, type Happy Horticulture Greenhouses.

22 Click the right arrow below the **Location** box to insert the **Appointment Address** section.

Address fields are inserted into the form.

23 Point to the blue bar at the top of the **Appointment** section, which contains the start date of the appointment.

A dotted-line box appears around the section, and a down arrow appears to the left of the bar.

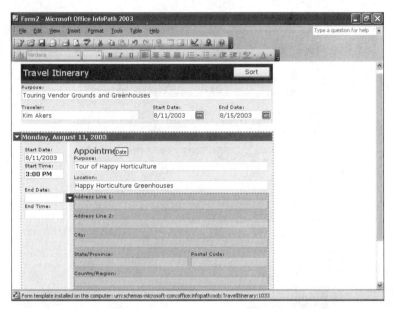

24   Click the down arrow, and in the drop-down list, click **Insert Appointment Entry Below**.

Tip   The drop-down list also includes options to insert sections for air and ground transportation, hotel accommodations, and comments.

A second appointment section is inserted into the form.

25   In the first **Appointment** section, point to any of the address fields.

A dotted-line box appears around the section, and a down arrow appears to the left of the first address field (Address Line 1).

26   Click the down arrow, and in the drop-down list, click **Remove Appointment Address**.

The address fields are removed from the form.

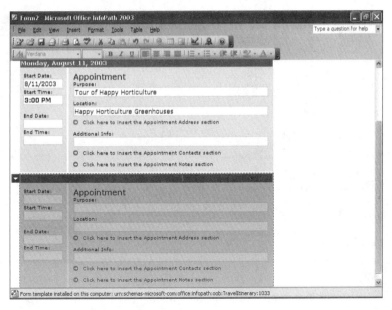

27 On the **File** menu, click **Close**.

28 When prompted to save the form, click **No**.

InfoPath discards your changes and closes the form.

Updating Form Data

InfoPath's forms can be designed to record the data needed for entire business process, such as processing payroll. An employee can complete a time card form, which is later updated by payroll personnel and approved by management.

Updating InfoPath forms is just as easy as completing one in the first place—simply open the form and edit!

In this exercise, you will update an employee's time card with payroll information.

USE the *TimeCard* form in the practice file folder for this topic. This practice file is located in the *My Documents\Microsoft Press\Office 2003 SBS\InfoForms* folder and can also be accessed by clicking *Start/All Programs/Microsoft Press/Microsoft Office System 2003 Step by Step*.

1 In the **Fill Out a Form** task pane, in the **Open a form** area, click **On My Computer**.

The Open dialog box appears.

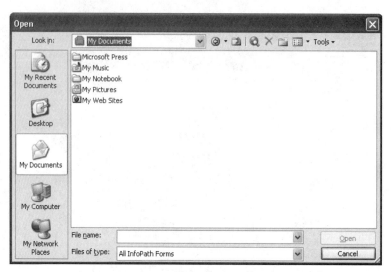

2 Browse to the *My Documents\Microsoft Press\Office 2003 SBS\InfoForms* folder, click **TimeCard**, and then click **Open**.

InfoPath opens the time card for David Ortiz.

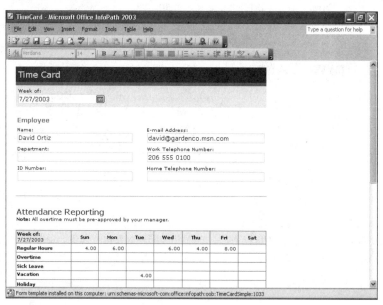

3 In the **ID Number** box, type 5536.

4 Below the **Attendance Reporting** section, click the
Information section.

The Payroll Information section is inserted into the form.

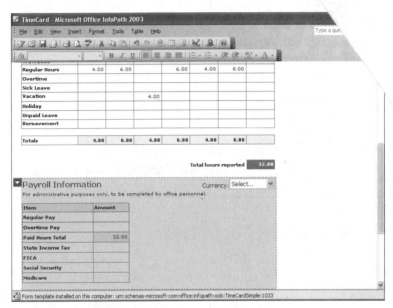

5 Click the down arrow to the right of the **Currency** box, and click **USD($)**.

The Amount column is formatted to accept entries in U.S. dollars.

6 In the **Regular Pay** box, type 400.

7 Press [Tab] three times, and in the **FICA** box, type 20.

8 Press [Tab] once, and in the **Social Security** box, type 28.

9 Press [Tab] once, and in the **Medicare** box, type 2.

InfoPath adds the decimal point and two decimal places to your entries to indicate
that they are dollar amounts.

Save

10 On the Standard toolbar, click **Save**.

InfoPath saves the changes to the form. The person doing payroll for The Garden
Company could now print the form to be signed and filed as a record of David Ortiz's
pay for the week. A copy of the form could then be included with David's paycheck.

CLOSE the *Timecard* form.

atures, in the form of digital certificates. You can get digital
.rcial certification authority, such as VeriSign, Inc., or from
administrator. You can also create your own certificate using a
_.indows, but these certificates are considered less secure than
_, from a third-party authority or provided by your system administrator.
, Help for more information on requesting digital certificates.

_.ly sign a form or to view the certificates of those who have already digitally
_,d the form:

1   Open the form.

2   On the **Tools** menu, click **Digital Signatures**.

Viewing and Sorting Form Data

InfoPath forms can be designed so that you can view and sort the data in various ways. For example, you might choose to view a summary of a list of items versus a list showing the detail of each item. Or you might sort data by categories, date, name, or any piece of data collected on the form.

In this exercise, you will manipulate a list of The Garden Company's computer assets by changing the view and sorting the data.

USE the *AssetList* form in the practice file folder for this topic. This practice file is located in the
My Documents\Microsoft Press\Office 2003 SBS\InfoForms folder and can also be accessed by clicking
Start/All Programs/Microsoft Press/Microsoft Office System 2003 Step by Step.
OPEN the *AssetList* form.

1   Click the down arrow to the right of the **Sort list by** box, click **Owner**, and then click
the **Sort** button.

The items in the list are presented in alphabetic order by the owner's first name.

2   Click the down arrow to the right of the **Sort list by** box, click **Serial Number**,
and then click the **Sort** button.

The items in the list are presented in ascending numeric order by the serial number.

3   At the right end of the row for the first asset, click the **Details** link.

The details for the selected assets are displayed.

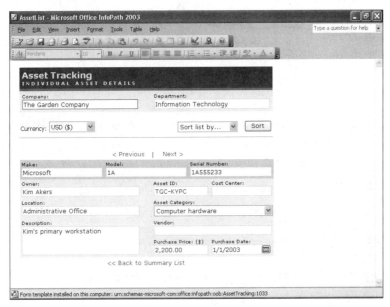

4   At the bottom of the form, click the **Back to Summary List** link.

The summary list is displayed.

5   On the **View** menu, click **Detailed List**.

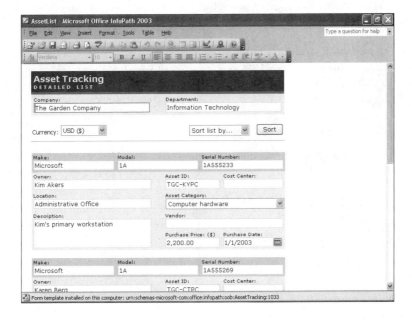

The assets are listed with their details.

6   Click the down arrow to the right of the **Sort list by** box, click **Purchase Date**, and then click the **Sort** button.

The items in the list are presented in order by the purchase date—the oldest items appear first.

7   Click the down arrow to the right of the **Sort list by** box, click **Asset ID**, and then click the **Sort** button.

The items in the list are presented in alphabetic order by the asset ID.

8   On the **View** menu, click **Summary List**.

The summary list is displayed again.

CLOSE the *AssetList* form without saving your changes.

Importing and Exporting Form Data

InfoPath helps you work with the data collected using its forms. You can import data from other forms that are based on the same form template by merging the forms. You can also export form data to Microsoft Excel.

In this exercise, you will merge the data from several lists by importing it into The Garden Company's asset list, and then export the data to a Microsoft Excel spreadsheet.

USE the *AssetList, PhoneList,* and *Fleet* forms in the practice file folder for this topic. These practice files are located in the *My Documents\Microsoft Press\Office 2003 SBS\InfoForms* folder and can also be accessed by clicking *Start/All Programs/Microsoft Press/Microsoft Office System 2003 Step by Step.* OPEN the *AssetList* file.

1   On the **File** menu, click **Merge Forms**.

The Merge Forms dialog box appears.

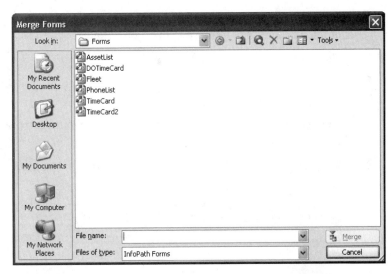

2   Browse to the *My Documents\Microsoft Press\Office 2003 SBS\InfoForms* folder.

3   Click the **Fleet** file, hold down the `Shift` key, click the **PhoneList** file, and then click the **Merge** button.

InfoPath merges the data from the three files and presents it in a single list.

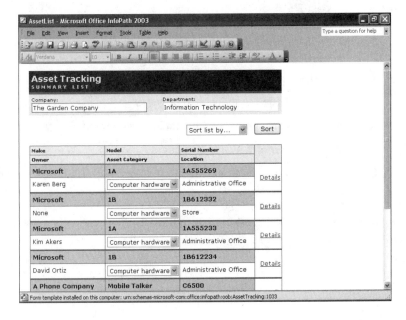

4 Point to the last item in the list (the blank row), click the down arrow to the left of the row, and click **Remove** in the drop-down list.

The item is deleted from the list.

5 Click the down arrow to the right of the **Sort list by** box, click **Asset Category**, and then click **Sort**.

The assets are grouped by category and the categories are presented in alphabetic order—Communications first and Vehicle last.

6 On the **File** menu, point to **Export To**, and then click **Microsoft Office Excel**.

The Export to Excel Wizard starts.

7 Click **Next**.

The second page of the wizard appears.

8 Select the **Form fields and this table or list** option, and then click **Next**.

The third page of the wizard appears.

9 Clear the **Company**, **Department**, and **Sort by** check boxes, and then click **Next**.

The fourth page of the wizard appears.

10 Verify that the **Export data from this form only** option is selected, and then click **Finish**.

InfoPath exports the form data to a spreadsheet. Microsoft Office Excel opens to display the spreadsheet. In Excel, you can manipulate the data as you would any spreadsheet and the original InfoPath forms remain intact.

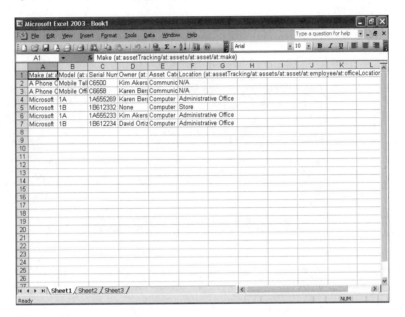

Tip Form data is exported in the view that was selected when you published it. You must export each view you want separately.

Close

11 At the right end of Excel's title bar, click the **Close** button, and when prompted to save the file, click **No**.

Excel closes, discarding the exported data.

CLOSE the *InfoPath* form without saving your changes.

Sharing and Publishing Forms

In most cases, the data collected in a form is only useful after it's shared with some-one other than the person completing the form. With InfoPath, you can send your completed form through e-mail, export your form to a Web page for easy viewing in a Web browser, or if the form is designed for it, submit the form data to a database or Web service.

In this exercise, you will send a completed time card through e-mail and publish it as a Web page for others to view.

USE the *TimeCard2* form in the practice file folder for this topic. This practice file is located in the *My Documents\Microsoft Press\Office 2003 SBS\InfoForms* folder and can also be accessed by clicking *Start/All Programs/Microsoft Press/Microsoft Office System 2003 Step by Step.*
OPEN the *TimeCard2* file.

1   On the **File** menu, click **Send to Mail Recipient**.

An e-mail address header is inserted at the top of the form.

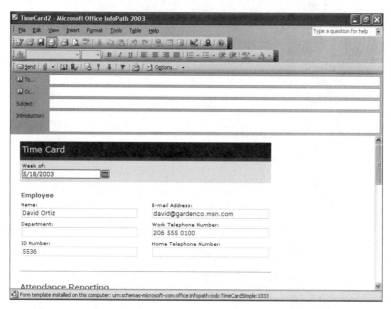

2   In the **To** box, type karen@gardenco.msn.com, and in the **CC** box, type your e-mail address.

3   In the **Subject** line, type For your approval, and in the **Introduction** box, type David's payroll.

4   On the E-mail toolbar, click the **Send** button.

InfoPath sends the form as an e-mail message.

5   Open Microsoft Outlook, and check for new messages.

The form arrives as a new message.

6   Double-click the message to open it and see how the form appears.

Send

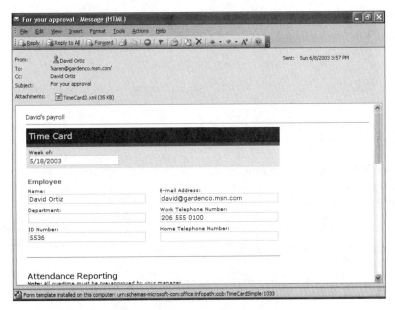

7 Close the e-mail message, and switch to InfoPath.

8 On the **File** menu, point to **Export To**, and then click **Web**.

The Export to Web dialog box appears.

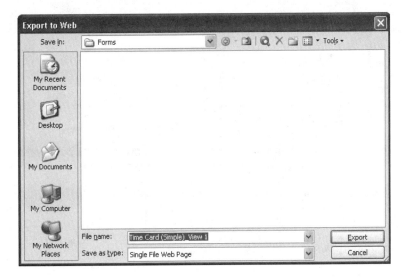

9 Browse to the *My Documents\Microsoft Press\Office 2003 SBS\InfoForms* folder.

10 In the **File name** box, type **DOPayroll**, and then click **Export**.

InfoPath saves the form as a single Web page.

11 Click **Start**, point to **All Programs**, point to **Accessories**, and then click **Windows Explorer**.

12 In the folder list on the left, browse to the *My Documents\Microsoft Press\Office 2003 SBS\InfoForms* folder.

13 In the file pane on the right, double-click **DOPayroll**.

An Internet Explorer window opens, displaying the time card.

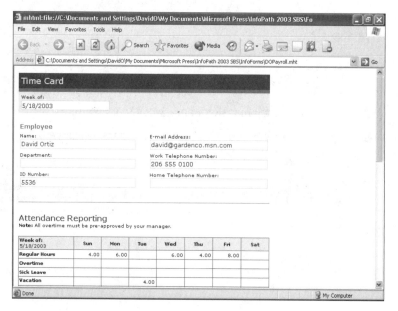

Tip   Form data is published in the view that was selected when you published it. You must publish each view you want separately.

Close

14 At the right end of Internet Explorer's title bar, click the **Close** button.

Internet Explorer closes.

CLOSE the *InfoPath* form without saving your changes.

Key Points

- You can complete rich, dynamic, electronic forms in the familiar Office application environment.

- You can update forms completed by you or by others.

- You can view and sort form data to best suit your needs.

- You can merge forms, importing the data from several forms into one.

- You can send forms via e-mail or publish them to the Web for others to see.

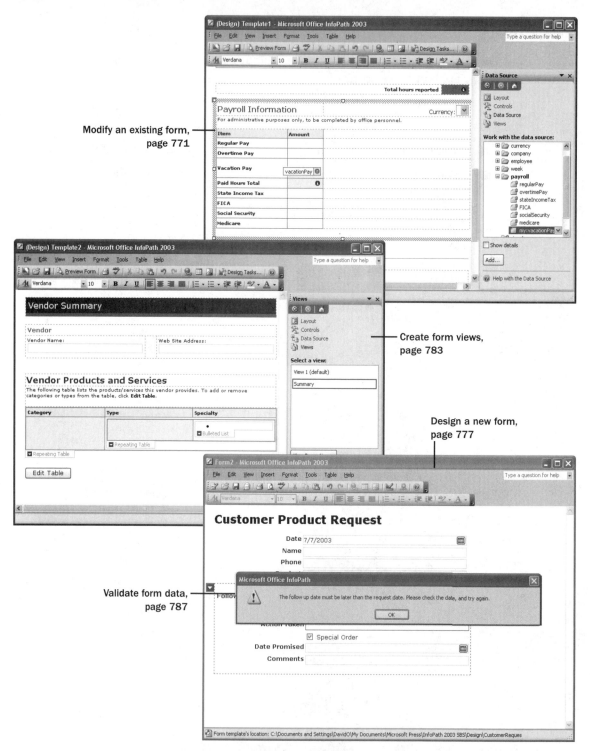

Modify an existing form, page 771

Create form views, page 783

Design a new form, page 777

Validate form data, page 787

Chapter 31 at a Glance

31 Designing InfoPath Forms

In this chapter you will learn to:

✔ Modify an existing form.

✔ Design a new form.

✔ Create form views.

✔ Validate form data.

With Microsoft InfoPath 2003, you have the power to create robust, dynamic forms. You can modify an existing form, customize a sample form, create a form from an existing XML data source or database, or design a new form from scratch. In each form, you determine its layout, the data fields and the controls for completing them, the data structure and rules for data validation, and the ways in which the form can be viewed. Your form can include rich text, tables, text boxes, drop-down lists, optional sections, repeating sections, links, and more.

See Also   Do you need only a quick refresher on the topics in this chapter? See the Quick Reference entries on pages xxxiii.

 Important   Before you can use the practice files in this chapter, you need to install them from the book's companion CD to their default location. See "Using the Book's CD-ROM" on page xxi for more information.

Modifying an Existing Form

By modifying an existing form (or customizing a sample form), you can easily create a form to meet your needs. For example, if a travel itinerary form created by one of your co-workers doesn't include space for additional comments at each stop, you can add a text field —you can even make the field optional or repeating.

When you are designing a form from scratch, InfoPath can create the form's *data source* for you. That option is not available when you are modifying an existing form, which uses an established data source. To modify the form, you must also modify the data source.

In this exercise, you will customize a simple time card sample to make it more useful for the payroll personnel at The Garden Company.

BE SURE TO start InfoPath before beginning this exercise.

1 In the **Fill Out a Form** task pane, click **Design a Form**.

The Design a Form task pane appears.

2 Click **Customize a Sample**.

The Customize a Sample dialog box opens.

3 Click the **Time Card (Simple)** sample, and click **OK**.

InfoPath displays the sample in design mode, and the Design Tasks task pane displays related tasks.

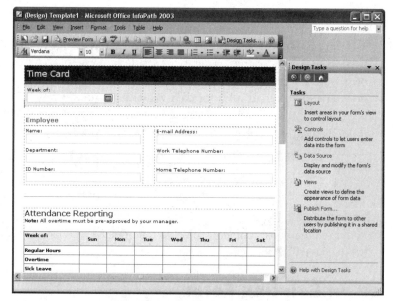

4 Scroll down to the **Payroll Information** section of the form, and click at the beginning of the table cell that contains the text *Overtime Pay*.

5 On the **Table** menu, point to **Insert**, and then click **Rows Below**.

InfoPath inserts a blank row between *Overtime Pay* and *Paid Hours Total*.

6 In the cell directly below *Overtime Pay*, type Vacation Pay.

7 In the task pane, click **Data Source**.

The task pane displays the data source structure.

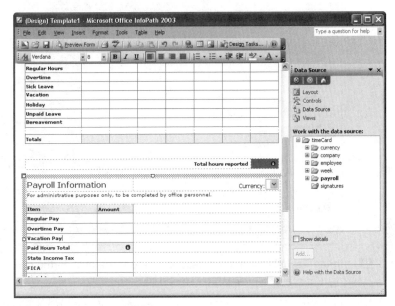

8 In the task pane, click **payroll**, click the down arrow that appears to the right of it, and in the drop-down list, click **Add**.

The Add Field or Group dialog box appears.

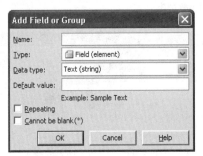

9 In the **Name** box, type vacationPay.

10 In the **Data type** list, click **Decimal (double)**, and then click **OK**.

The new field is added to the list of fields in the payroll group in the Data Source task pane.

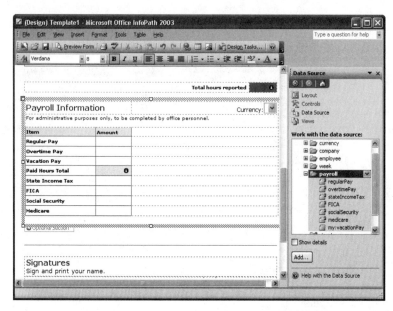

11 In the **Payroll Information** section of the form, click in the cell immediately to the right of the one in which you typed *Vacation Pay*.

12 In the task pane, drag the **my:vacationPay** field to the cell you just clicked.

InfoPath inserts a text box into the cell labelled *Vacation Pay*.

13 Select the **Vacation Pay:** label, and press ⌨Del.

14 Point to the text box you inserted.

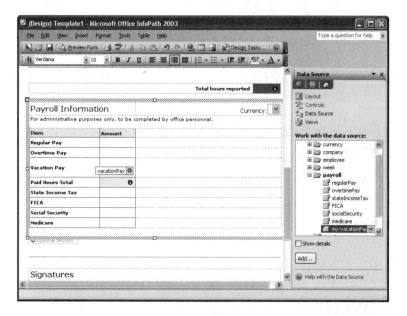

InfoPath indicates that the text box is configured to collect data for the field you created for vacation pay.

15 In the **Employee** section of the form, select the text *Home Telephone Number* and the text box after it, and press ⌦.

16 Select the text *ID Number* and the text box after it, and press ⌦.

The text boxes and their labels are removed from the form, and your mouse pointer is positioned at the end of the text box labelled *Department*.

17 In the **Data Source** task pane, click **employee**, click the down arrow that appears to the right of it, and in the drop-down list, click **Add**.

The Add Field or Group dialog box appears.

18 In the **Name** box, type preferences, in the **Type** list, click **Group**, and then click **OK**.

The new group is added to the data source list in the task pane.

19 Click **my:preferences**, click the down arrow that appears to the right of it, and in the drop-down list, click **Add**.

The Add Field or Group dialog box appears.

20 In the **Name** box, type mail, and in the **Data Type** list, click **True/False (boolean)**.

21 In the **Default Value** list, click **(Blank)**, and then click **OK**.

The data source list shows your new group and field.

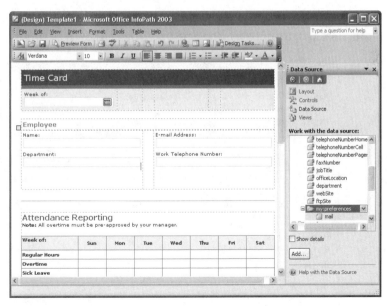

22 Near the top of the task pane, click **Controls**.

The Controls task pane appears.

23 Drag the **Check Box** control to the blank area below the *Department* text box in the **Employee** section of the form.

The Check Box Binding dialog box appears.

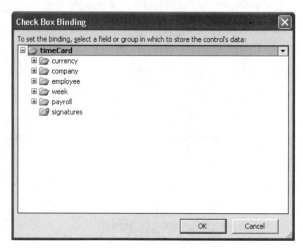

24 Click the plus (+) sign next to **employee**, and then click the plus (+) sign next to **my:preferences**.

25 Click the **mail** field, and then click **OK**.

InfoPath inserts a check box labelled *Mail* into the form.

26 Select the word *Mail*, and type Please mail my check to me.

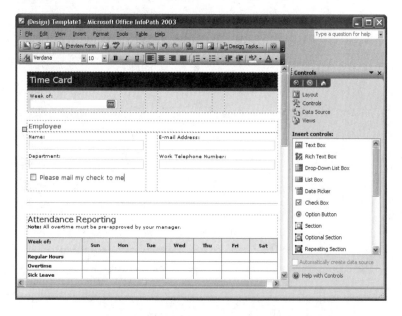

27   On the **File** menu, click **Close**, and when prompted to save the form, click **Yes**.

The Save As dialog box appears.

28   Browse to the *My Documents\Microsoft Press\Office 2003 SBS\Design* folder. Then in the **File name** box, type **RevisedTimeCard**, and click **Save**.

InfoPath saves your changes as a new form.

CLOSE the *RevisedTimeCard* template.

Tip   To complete a form based on a template saved on your computer, open the Fill Out a Form task pane, and click On My Computer. In the Open dialog box, browse to the location where the form template is saved, select it, and click Open. Form templates are saved with a file extension of *.xsn*.

Designing a New Form

If an existing form or sample isn't close to what you need, you can start with a blank form. When designing a new form, InfoPath will define your data source automatically as you work.

In this exercise, you will create a form for recording customer requests for products that are not immediately available from The Garden Company.

1   In the **Fill Out a Form** task pane, click **Design a Form**.

2   In the **Design Form** task pane, click **New Blank Form**.

InfoPath opens a new form and displays the Design Tasks task pane.

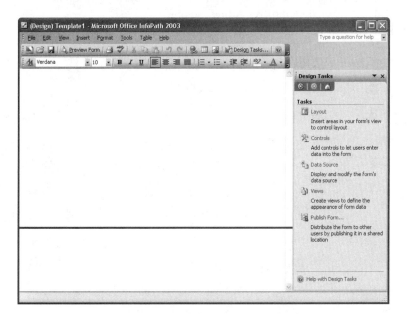

3 At the top of the form, type **Customer Product Request**. Then select the text you just typed, and on the **Format** menu, click **Font**.

The Font task pane appears.

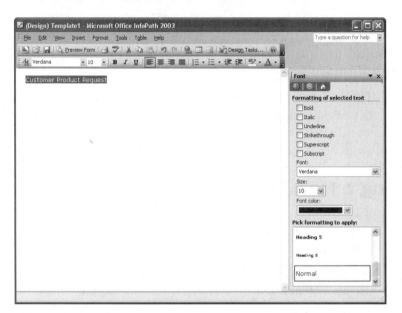

Tip You can also access the Font task pane by right-clicking selected text and clicking Font on the shortcut menu, or by clicking the title of the task pane and clicking Font in the Other Task Panes list. If you prefer, you can set font formatting directly on the Formatting toolbar.

4 In the task pane, select the **Bold** check box, and in the **Size** list, select **18**.

The appearance of the text reflects your formatting choices.

5 Press the → key, and press [Enter].

6 On the toolbar at the top of the task pane, click the **Back** button.

The Design Tasks task pane appears.

7 In the task pane, click **Layout**. Then in the **Insert layout tables** list, drag **Two Column Table** to the blank form, below the title.

The blank table is inserted into your form.

Back

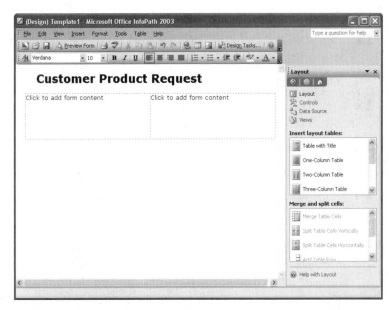

8   Drag the horizontal line at the bottom of the table up to make the row only tall enough to fit a single line of text.

9   Drag the vertical line between the two cells to the left until it is below the *d* in *Product* in the title.

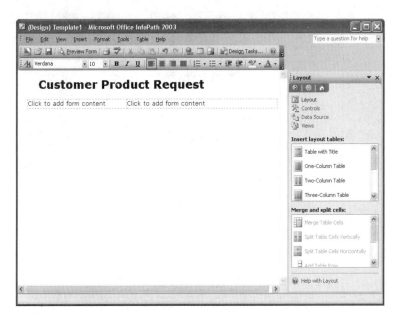

10 Click in the first cell, type Date, and then select the text you typed.

B ≣
Bold Align
Right

11 On the Formatting toolbar, click the **Bold** button, click the **Align Right** button, and then press ⟨Tab⟩ twice.

Your text is formatted, and a second row is added to the table.

12 Type Name, and press ⟨Tab⟩ twice. Then in the third row, type Phone, press ⟨Tab⟩ twice, and in the fourth row, type Product.

13 In the task pane, click **Controls**.

The Control task pane appears.

14 In the **Insert controls** list, drag the **Date Picker** control to the cell to the right of *Date*.

The new field is inserted into the cell.

Tip   By default, InfoPath automatically creates your data source when you design from a blank form. However, the field names are not meaningful—for example, *field1* or *field2* rather than *RequestDate* or *CustName*. To change a field name, right-click the control, and click Properties on the shortcut menu.

15 In the **Insert controls** list, drag the **Text Box** control to the cell to the right of *Name*.

16 Drag a **Text Box** control to the cell to the right of *Phone*, and then drag another **Text Box** control to the cell to the right of *Product*.

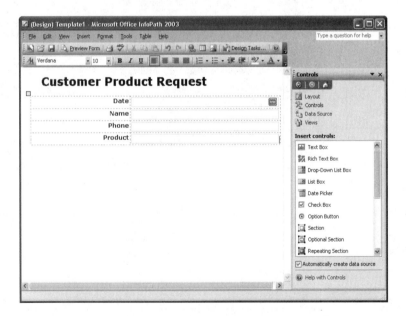

17 Press the ⬇, and in the task pane, click **Layout**. Then in the **Insert layout tables** list, under **Optional and Repeating**, click **Repeating Section**.

A blank repeating section is inserted at the end of the form.

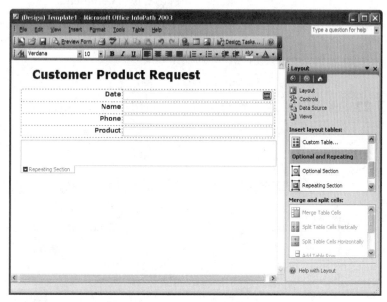

18 Click in the repeating section, and type Follow Up. Then select the text, on the Formatting toolbar, click the **Bold** button, press the ➡ key, and press ⏎.

19 Select the table at the top of the form (the one you created earlier in this exercise), and on the **Edit** menu, click **Copy**.

20 Click in the repeating section, and on the **Edit** menu, click **Paste**.

The table is inserted into the repeating section.

Tip A blue and white information icon appears in fields that store duplicate data—as do all the fields in your form at this time. Point to one of the fields to see how it is labelled.

21 In the repeating section, click the **Date Picker** box in the first row, and press ⑩.

22 In the task pane, click **Controls**. Then in the **Insert controls** list, click **Date Picker**.

A new date control that uses a different field name than the date field in the first table is inserted into the cell.

23 Press ⑨, and in the first cell of the second row, type Action Taken.

24 Press [Tab], press [Del], and in the **Insert controls** list, click **Text Box**. Then press [Tab], and in the first cell of the third row, type **Date Promised**.

25 Press [Tab], press [Del], and in the **Insert controls** list, click **Date Picker**. Then press [Tab], and in the first cell of the fourth row, type **Comments**.

26 Press [Tab], press [Del], and in the **Insert controls** list, click **Text Box**. Then click in front of *Date Promised* in the first cell of the third row of the table, and on the **Table** menu, point to **Insert**, then click **Rows Above**.

A blank row is inserted between *Action Taken* and *Date Promised*.

27 Click in the second cell of the new row, and in the **Insert controls** list, click **Check Box**.

A check box is inserted into the row, with a label of *Field 9*.

28 Select the label, and type **Special Order**.

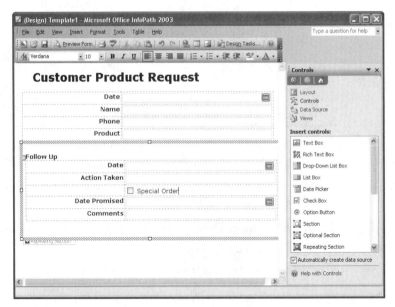

29 On the **File** menu, click **Close**. When prompted to save the form, click **Yes**.

The Save as dialog box appears.

30 Browse to the *My Documents\Microsoft Press\Office 2003 SBS\Design* folder. Then in the **File name** box, type **CustomerRequest**, and click **Save**.

InfoPath saves and closes your form.

Tip To fill out a form based on this template, click On My Computer in the Fill Out a Form task pane. Then browse to the location where the template is saved, click the template you want, and click Open.

Creating Form Views

When designing forms, you can specify multiple ways in which the form can be viewed. For example, you might define a view that summarizes a list of items in addition to the view that shows the detail of the items.

In this exercise, you will add a view to an existing form to provide a brief view of the products available from a particular vendor.

1   In the **Fill Out a Form** task pane, click **Design a Form**.

The Design a Form task pane appears.

2   Click **Customize a Sample**.

The Customize a Sample dialog box opens.

3   Click the **Vendor Information** sample, and click **OK**.

InfoPath opens the sample form in design mode.

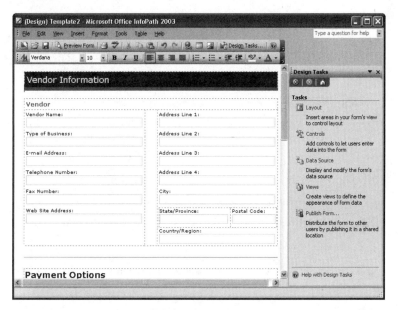

4   In the task pane, click **Views**.

The Views task pane appears.

5   In the **Actions** list, near the bottom of the task pane, click **Add a New View**.

The Add View dialog box appears, prompting you to enter a name for your view.

6   Type **Summary**, and click **OK**.

InfoPath adds your view to the Select a view list, and displays a blank page, which is your view for the time being.

7 In the **Select a view** list, click **View 1 (default)**.

InfoPath displays the original form view.

8 On the **Edit** menu, click **Select All**.

9 On the **Edit** menu, click **Copy**. Then in the **Select a view** list in the task pane, click **Summary**.

10 On the **Edit** menu, click **Paste**.

The contents of the original form view are inserted into your new view so that you can modify them.

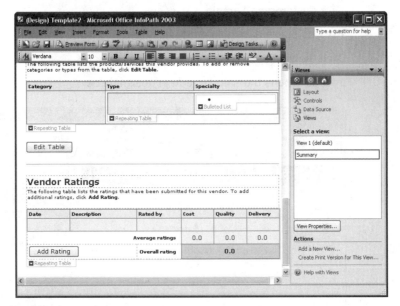

11 In the title at the top of the form, select the word **Information**, and type Summary.

12 In the **Vendor** table, select all the items in the second column, and press Del.

13 In the first column of the **Vendor** table, select the words *Web Site Address* and the text box following them.

14 Drag the selected items to the top of the second column.

15 In the first column, select everything except the words *Vendor Name* and the text box following it, and press Del.

Troubleshooting If there is extra white space at the bottom of the vendor table after you've removed most of the fields, there might be extra line breaks in the blank area. Click an insertion point at the very end of the table, and press Backspace to remove the extra lines.

16 Select everything between the **Vendor** table and the **Vendor Products and Services** section, and press [Del].

17 Select everything after the **Edit Table** button in the **Vendor Products and Services** section, and press [Del].

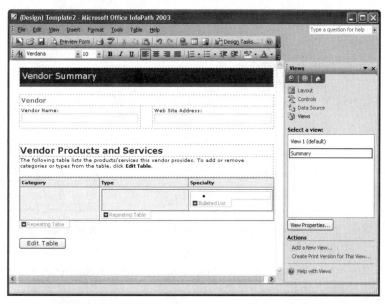

18 In the **Select a view** list, point to **Summary**, and then click the down arrow that appears to the right of it.

19 In the drop-down list, click **Set as Default**.

20 On the **File** menu, click **Close**, and when prompted to save the form, click **Yes**.

The Save As dialog box appears.

21 Browse to the *My Documents\Microsoft Press\Office 2003 SBS\Design* folder, and in the **File name** box, type VendorInfo, and click **Save**.

InfoPath saves and closes your form template.

22 In the task pane, click **Fill Out a Form**, and then click **On My Computer**.

The Open dialog box appears.

23 Browse to the *My Documents\Microsoft Press\Office 2003 SBS\Design* folder, click **VendorInfo**, and click **Open**.

InfoPath opens the form, showing the Vendor Summary view.

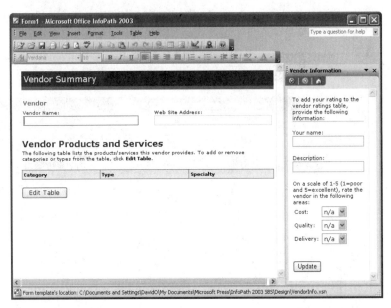

24 In the **Vendor Name** box, type A New Vendor, and at the end of the form, click **Edit Table**.

25 In the task pane, click **Inventory** in the drop-down list, select the **Seasonal** check box, and then click **Update**.

The category and type you selected are added to the Vendor Products and Services section.

26 In the **Specialty** column, type Annuals, press Enter, and then type Hanging Baskets.

27 On the **View** menu, click **View 1**.

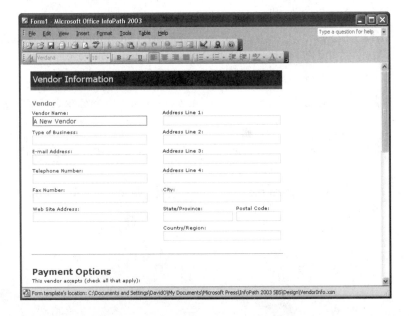

Your entries from the Summary view are carried over to the original, detailed form view. Scroll down to see your entries in the Vendor Products and Services section.

28 On the **File** menu, click **Close**, and when prompted to save the form, click **No**.

InfoPath discards your changes and closes the form.

Validating Form Data

To ensure that the data collected on your form is useful, you can define various rules for each field. You can set default values, specify which fields are required, and display instructional messages under conditions you specify.

In this exercise, you will modify a Customer Request form to validate the data that is entered into it.

USE the *CustRequest* form in the practice file folder for this topic. This practice file is located in the *My Documents\Microsoft Press\Office 2003 SBS\Design* folder and can also be accessed by clicking *Start/All Programs/Microsoft Press/Microsoft Office System 2003 SBS*.

1 In the **Fill Out a Form** task pane, click **Design a Form**, and then click **On My Computer**.

The Open in Design Mode dialog box opens.

2 Browse to the *My Documents\Microsoft Press\Office 2003 SBS\Design* folder, click **CustRequest**, and then click **Open**.

InfoPath opens the Customer Product Request form in design mode.

3 In the first row of the form, right-click the **Date Picker** control to the right of *Date*, and click **Date Picker Properties** on the shortcut menu.

The Date Picker Properties dialog box appears.

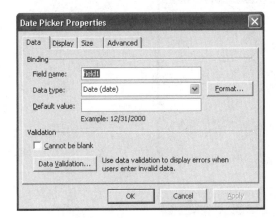

Tip　　The properties of a form control include the name of the data field. You can edit the name in this dialog box.

4   In the **Validation** area of the **Data** tab, select the **Cannot be blank** check box, and click **OK**.

5   In the first row of the **Follow Up** area, right-click the **Date Picker** control, and click **Date Picker Properties** on the shortcut menu.

The Date Picker Properties dialog box appears.

6   In the **Validation** area of the **Data** tab, click the **Data Validation** button.

The Data Validation dialog box appears.

7   Click the **Add** button.

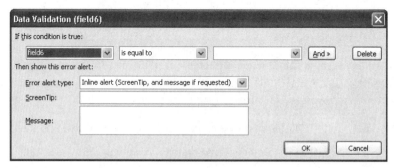

8   In the **If this condition is true** area, in the second drop-down list, click **is less than**. Then in the third drop-down list, click **Select a field or group**.

The Select a Field or Group dialog box appears, showing the list of fields used in the form. The first field, the date of the customer's request, is marked with a red asterisk, indicating that it is a required field.

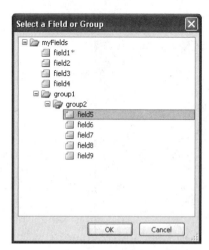

9   In the field list, click **field1**, and then click **OK**.

Your selection is added to the third drop-down list box, completing the condition statement.

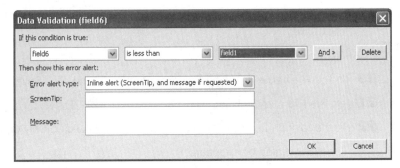

10 In the **Error alert type** box, click the down arrow and then click **Dialog box alert** (**immediately show message**).

11 In the **ScreenTip** box, type Invalid follow up date. Then in the **Message** box, type The follow up date must be later than the request date. Please check the date, and try again., and click **OK**.

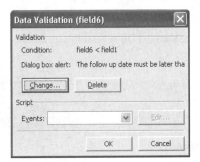

12 Your rule is summarized in the Data Validation dialog box.

13 Click **OK** twice to close both open dialog boxes, and then in the form, right-click the check box before *Special Order*, and click **Check Box Properties** on the shortcut menu.

14 In the **Default state** area of the **Data** tab, select the **Checked** option.

15 In the **Validation** area, click the **Data Validation** button, and in the **Data Validation** dialog box, click the **Add** button.

16 In the **If this condition is true** area, in the third drop-down list, click **FALSE**.

17 In the **ScreenTip** box, type Inventory item – place hold! Then in the **Message** box, type The customer has requested an item that is normally stocked in inventory. When additional stock arrives, hold the appropriate number of items for customer!, and click **OK**.

Your rule is summarized in the Data Validation dialog box.

18 Click **OK**, and then click **OK** again.

The Special Order check box is selected on the form.

19 On the **File** menu, click **Save As**. Then in the **Microsoft Office Infopath** dialog box, click **Save**.

The Save As dialog box appears.

20 In the **File name** box, type **CustomerRequest2**, and click **Save**.

21 On the **File** menu, click **Close**.

22 In the task pane, click **Fill Out a Form**, and then click **On My Computer**.

The Open dialog box appears.

23 Browse to the *My Documents\Microsoft Press\Office 2003 SBS\Design* folder, click **CustomerRequest2**, and then click **Open**.

The Customer Product Request form appears.

24 In the first **Date** box, type tomorrow's date, and press [Tab] four times.

25 In the second **Date** box, type today's date, and press [Tab].

A message box appears, containing the error message you specified. On the form behind the error message, the second Date field is surrounded by a red dotted line, indicating an error in the field.

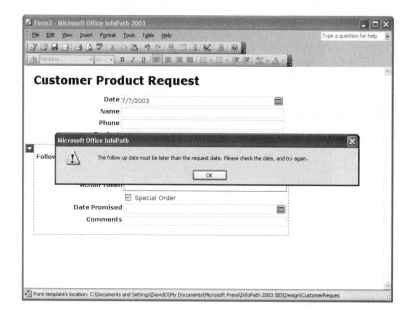

26 Click **OK**, and point to the field.

The ScreenTip you specified appears.

27 Clear the **Special Order** check box.

The check box is surrounded by a red dotted line, and the ScreenTip you specified appears.

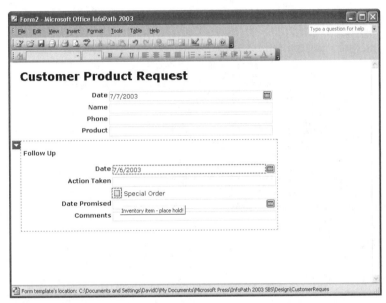

28 Right-click the check box, and click **Full error description** on the shortcut menu.

A message box appears, containing the error message you specified.

29 Click **OK**.

30 On the **File** menu, click **Close**, and when prompted to save the form, click **Yes**.

A message box indicates that there are errors on the form and asks whether you still want to save it.

31 Click **Yes**. Then in the **Save as** dialog box, browse to the *My Documents \Microsoft Press\Office 2003 SBS\Design* folder, type **CustReqError**, and click **Save**.

InfoPath saves and closes your form.

32 In the task pane, click **On My Computer**. Then in the **Open** dialog box, click **CustReqError**, and then click **Open**.

InfoPath opens the Customer Product Request form, indicating the errors on the check box and the second Date field.

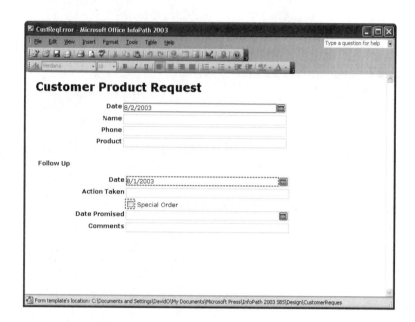

CLOSE the *Customer Product Request* form.

Key Points

- You can customize the sample forms provided with InfoPath or modify existing form templates.

- You can design your own form from scratch.

- When designing a form, you create the layout, add controls, define the data source and any data validation rules, and specify views. In some cases, InfoPath will define the data source for you automatically.

X
Collaborating with The Microsoft Office System

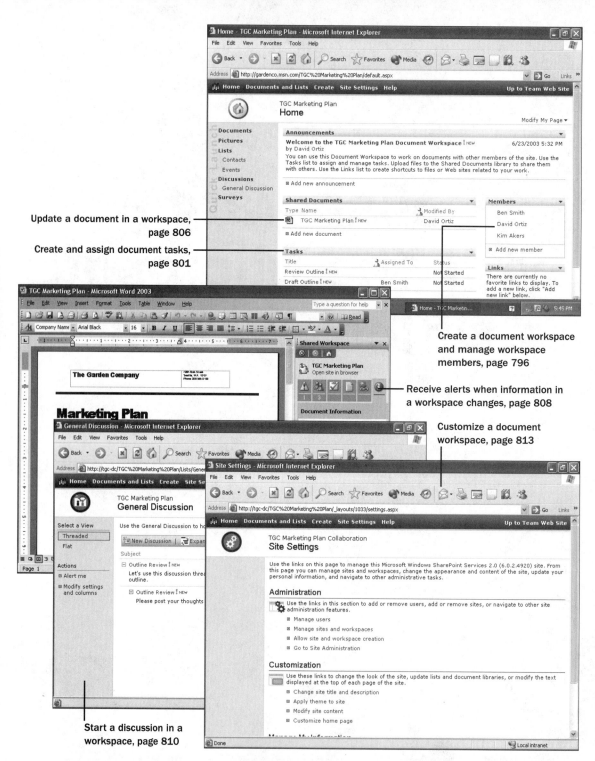

Update a document in a workspace, page 806

Create and assign document tasks, page 801

Create a document workspace and manage workspace members, page 796

Receive alerts when information in a workspace changes, page 808

Customize a document workspace, page 813

Start a discussion in a workspace, page 810

32 Working in a Document Workspace

In this chapter you will learn to:

✔ Create a document workspace and manage workspace members.

✔ Create and assign document tasks.

✔ Update a document in a workspace.

✔ Receive alerts when information in a workspace changes.

✔ Start a discussion in a workspace.

✔ Customize a document workspace.

Business documents are often created by several people working together. But that process can be difficult when you have to shuttle the file from one person to the next and then combine everyone's input. You might end up with multiple versions of the document, and communication can break down.

New in Office 2003

Dcoument workspace

A *document workspace* is a new feature in The Microsoft Office System 2003 that makes collaborating on Office documents much easier. A document workspace is a Microsoft Windows SharePoint Services site that contains your Microsoft Office Word, Microsoft Office Excel, Microsoft Office PowerPoint, or Microsoft Visio files, making them available to the people working on the document, called members, you specify.

With a document workspace, each member can edit the document directly in the workspace, or they can work on a local copy and synchronize their changes with the workspace periodically.

Because the document workspace is a SharePoint Web site, it includes several useful SharePoint features. You can define tasks and post announcements related to your document. You can also hold online conversations by using SharePoint's discussion board.

Creating, configuring, and working in a document workspace is simple. You can use your Web browser to access the SharePoint site or can you access the workspace through the Office application in which the document was created.

See Also Do you need only a quick refresher on the topics in this chapter? See the Quick Reference entries on page xxxiii.

> **Important** Before you can use the practice files in this chapter, you need to install them from the book's companion CD to their default location. See "Using the Book's CD-ROM" on page xxi for more information.

Creating a Document Workspace and Managing Workspace Members

When you have to generate a critical report and it is not feasible for your team to be in the same physical location at the same time, you need a document workspace.

To create a workspace, you start the document in Word, Excel, PowerPoint, or Visio. Then either e-mail the file to your team members or create the document workspace in your Office application and invite your team members to access the document from their location.

In this exercise, you will create a document workspace so that your team can work together to develop a marketing plan for The Garden Company.

> **Important** To complete this exercise, you must have access to a Microsoft Windows SharePoint Services server and permission to create workspace sites on it.

USE the *TGCMktgPlan* document in the practice file folder for this topic. This practice file is located in the *My Documents\Microsoft Press\Office 2003 SBS\Document* folder and can also be accessed by clicking *Start/All Programs/Microsoft Press/Microsoft Office System 2003 Step by Step*.
BE SURE TO start your computer and Word before beginning this exercise.
OPEN the *TGCMktgPlan* document.

1   On the **Tools** menu, click **Shared Workspace**.

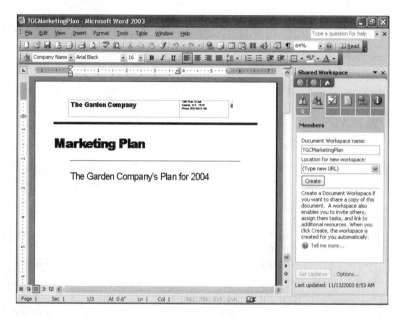

The Shared Workspace task pane opens.

2   Click the down arrow to the right of the **Location for new workspace** box, select a location for your workspace site, and then click **Create**. If no locations appear in the list, type the URL of the SharePoint Services Web site where you have permission to create document workspaces.

Troubleshooting   SharePoint Services Web sites that you have visited will automatically appear in this list of locations. If you can't create a workspace in the location you choose, the SharePoint administrator might not have enabled workspace creation for you or your user group. Contact your administrator for assistance.

Word uses SharePoint to create the new workspace and displays the updated Members tab.

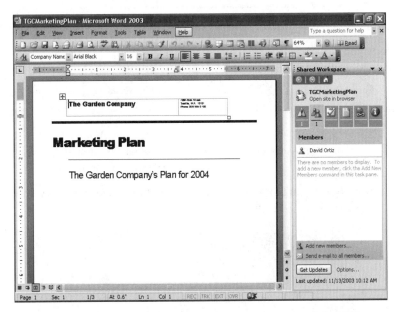

3   Near the bottom of the **Shared Workspace** task pane, click **Add new members**.

The Add New Members dialog box appears.

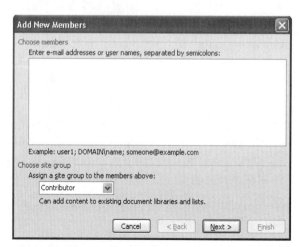

4 In the **Choose members** box, type the e-mail addresses of two of members of your domain separated by a semicolon (no spaces), and click **Next**.

For example, we typed *kim@gardenco.msn.com;ben@gardenco.msn.com*.

5 Check that the full names of your colleagues appear in the **Display Name** column, and then click **Finish**.

For example, the display names corresponding to the e-mail addresses we typed are *Kim Akers* and *Ben Smith* respectively. A message box appears, asking if you want to send an e-mail invitation to the new members.

6 Select the **Send an e-mail invitation to the new members** check box if necessary, and then click **OK**.

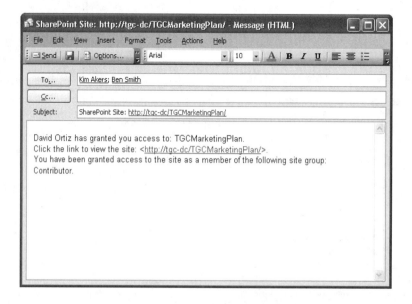

A new e-mail message form opens, addressed to your new members (Ben and Kim, in our case) and including the URL to the document workspace. You can edit the subject line and body of the message as needed.

7   In the **Cc** box, type your e-mail address, and on the Standard toolbar, click **Send**.

The e-mail message is sent. You can check your messages later to see the message that your members received. In Word, the Members tab lists the new members.

8   In the **Shared Workspace** task pane, click **Open site in browser**.

Microsoft Internet Explorer displays the TGCMarketingPlan home page. This is the entry point to your document workspace.

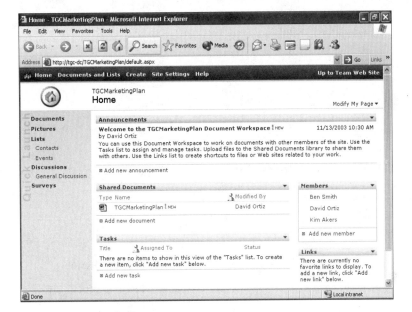

9   In the **Members** area, click **Add new member**.

Internet Explorer displays the Add Users page.

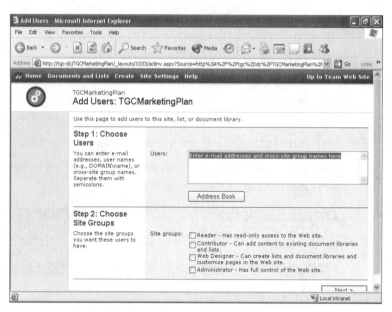

10 In **Step 1**, in the **Users** box, type britta@gardenco.msn.com.

Tip   When adding members from the document workspace site, you can choose contacts from your Outlook address book. On the Add Users page, click Address Book.

11 In **Step 2**, select the **Contributor** check box, and then click **Next**.

Internet Explorer displays the next page in the process of adding new members.

12 In **Step 3**, in the **Display Name** box, type Britta Simon.

13 In **Step 4**, in the **Body** box, type Join us in this effort!, and then click **Finish**.

Internet Explorer displays the TGCMarketingPlan home page, showing the new member.

14 Close Internet Explorer, and switch to Word.

15 In the **Shared Workspace** task pane, on the **Members** tab, click **Get Updates**.

The member information reflects the changes you made.

16 In the **Members** list, point to **Britta Simon**, and click the down arrow that appears to the right of the name.

Tip   From this drop-down list, you can also schedule a meeting with the selected member, add phone numbers for the member, or edit the member's user rights and information.

Tip   To quickly send e-mail messages to a member, simply click the name in the Members list. To quickly send e-mail messages to all members in the workspace, click E-mail All Members near the bottom of the Members tab.

17   In the drop-down list, click **Remove Member from Workspace**, and when prompted to confirm the action, click **Yes**.

18   On the **File** menu, click **Close**, and if prompted to save the changes, click **Yes**.

CLOSE Internet Explorer.

Creating and Assigning Document Tasks

After you've created the workspace, the collaboration can begin. To assure that progress is made, you can define a To Do list containing tasks that must be performed to complete the document. You can also assign tasks to workspace members. When members access the document workspace site or open the workspace document, they see the list and status of tasks.

In this exercise, you will create and assign specific tasks necessary to complete your marketing plan.

Important   To complete this task, you must have completed the first exercise in this chapter, "Creating a Document Workspace and Managing Workspace Members."

USE the *TGCMktgPlan* document in the practice file folder for this topic. This practice file is located in the *My Documents\Microsoft Press\Office 2003 SBS\Document* folder and can also be accessed by clicking *Start/All Programs/Microsoft Press/Microsoft Office System 2003 Step by Step*.
BE SURE TO start Word before beginning this exercise.

Open

1   On the Standard toolbar, click **Open**.

The Open dialog box appears.

2   Browse to the *My Documents\Microsoft Press\Office 2003 SBS* folder, and double-click the *Workspace* folder. Then click *TGCMktgPlan*, and click **Open**.

Word opens the marketing plan document and displays a message prompting you to get updates from the document workspace.

3   Click **Get Updates**.

Word displays the document with the Shared Workspace task pane open and displaying the current online status of the workspace members.

4   In the **Shared Workspace** task pane, click the **Tasks** tab.

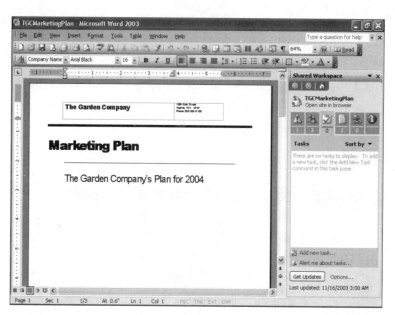

5 Near the bottom of the task pane, click **Add new task**.

The Task dialog box appears.

6 In the **Title** box, type Draft Outline.

7 In the **Assigned to** list, click your user name.

8 Click the down arrow to the right of the **Due Date** box, click a date one week from today, and then click **OK**.

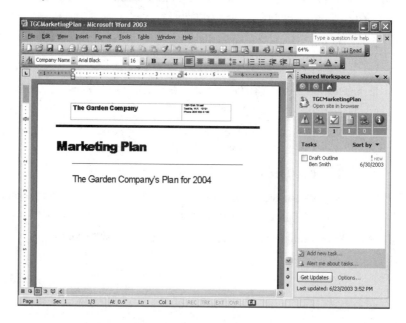

The task is added to the list in the Shared Workspace task pane.

9   In the **Shared Workspace** task pane, point to the new task, and then click the down arrow that appears to the right of it.

10   In the drop-down list, click **Alert Me About This Task**.

An Internet Explorer window opens, displaying the SharePoint page where you can configure a new alert for this task.

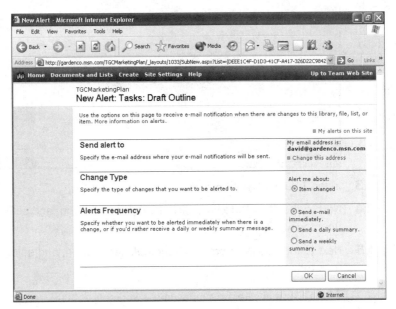

11   Review the default settings, and click **OK**.

The Tasks list in the document workspace is displayed in the Internet Explorer window.

12   At the top of the **Tasks** list, click the **New Item** button.

The Tasks: New Item page appears.

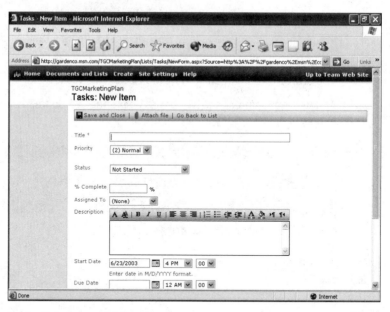

13 In the **Title** box, type Review Outline.

Calendar

14 Next to the **Start Date** box, click the **Calendar** button, and select a date one week from today.

15 Next to the **Due Date** box, click the **Calendar** button, and select a date two weeks from today.

Tip   Like many items in a document workspace, tasks are stored as items in a list. You can add other list items—announcements, links, events, and contacts—from the workspace home page. In the Announcements list, click "Add new announcements." In the Links list, click "Add new link." In the left navigation column, click Contacts or Events, and then click New Item.

16 Near the top of the page, click the **Save and Close** button.

The Tasks list appears, including the task you just created.

17 On the workspace menu bar, click **Home**.

The home page for the document workspace appears, summarizing the announcements, documents, members, tasks, and links in the workspace.

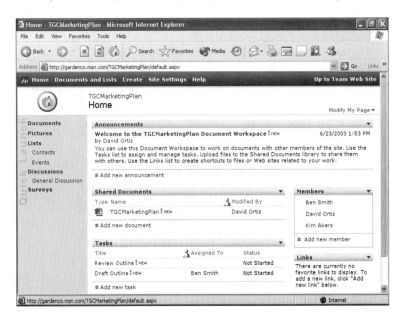

CLOSE Internet Explorer. Then close Word and save the document.

Updating a Document in a Workspace

While collaborating, each workspace member will presumably be adding to or editing the document and will need to update the document in the workspace so that other members can see the changes.

Tip   You can specify if or when you receive updates from the document workspace. In the Shared Workspace task pane, click Options.

In this exercise, you will update a the TGCMktgPlan document that is connected to a document workspace.

Important   To complete this task, you must have completed the first exercise in this chapter, "Creating a Document Workspace and Managing Workspace Members."

USE the *TGCMktgPlan* document in the practice file folder for this topic. This practice file is located in the *My Documents\Microsoft Press\Office 2003 SBS\Document* folder and can also be accessed by clicking *Start/All Programs/Microsoft Press/Microsoft Office System 2003 Step by Step*.
BE SURE TO start Word before beginning this exercise.
OPEN the TGCMktgPlan document, and click Get Updates.

1   Scroll down to the second page of the document, select the heading that reads *How to Modify This Report*, and type Introduction.

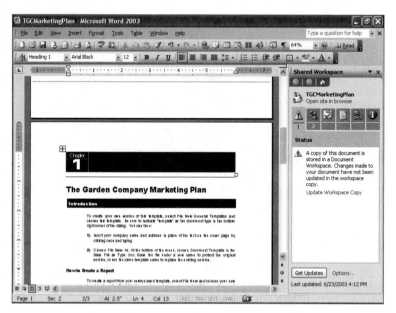

2   On the **File** menu, click **Close**, and when prompted to save the file, click **Yes**.

A message appears prompting you to update the document in the workspace.

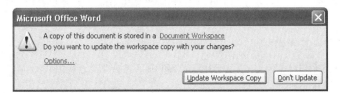

3   Click **Update Workspace Copy**.

The changes you made to your local copy of the document are integrated into the document in the workspace, and the document closes.

Tip   If you no longer want to receive updates from or add updates to the workspace, you can disconnect your local copy of the document from the workspace. In the Shared Workspace task pane, point to the title of the workspace, click the down arrow that appears to the right of it, and then click Disconnect from Workspace. You must save the document to complete the disconnection.

4   Open Internet Explorer, and go to your document workspace site.

The home page for the document workspace appears, summarizing the announcements, documents, members, tasks, and links in the workspace.

5   In the **Shared Documents** area, point to *TGCMktgPlan*, and then click the down arrow that appears to the right of it.

6   In the drop-down list, click **Edit in Microsoft Word**. If you see a message from Internet Explorer warning you that some files can harm your computer and asking you to confirm that you want to open the file, click **OK**.

The document opens.

7   Scroll down to the third page, select the *More Template Tips* heading, and type Our Brand.

8   On the **File** menu, click **Close**, and when prompted to save the changes, click **Yes**.

The updated document is saved to the workspace.

9   Switch to Internet Explorer, and in the **Shared Documents** area, click *TGCMktgPlan*. If you are prompted to confirm that you want to open the file, click **OK**.

The document opens in read-only mode.

10   Scroll down to confirm that your changes have been incorporated into the workspace document.

11   On the **File** menu, click **Close**.

The document closes.

CLOSE Internet Explorer.

Receiving Alerts When Information in a Workspace Changes

As work progresses, it can be helpful to know when certain milestones are reached. You might want to be notified as soon as a critical task is complete, or keep current as the document changes.

You can configure the workspace to alert you with an e-mail message when information in the workspace changes. You can specify which changes trigger alerts and whether you will be alerted immediately, daily, or weekly.

In this exercise, you will configure the document workspace so that you are alerted whenever information in the workspace changes.

Important   To complete this task, you must have completed the first exercise in this chapter, "Creating a Document Workspace and Managing Workspace Members."

USE the *TGCMktgPlan* document in the practice file folder for this topic. This practice file is located in the *My Documents\Microsoft Press\Office 2003 SBS\Document* folder and can also be accessed by clicking *Start/All Programs/Microsoft Press/Microsoft Office System 2003 Step by Step.*
BE SURE TO start Word before beginning this exercise.
OPEN the *TGCMktgPlan* document, and click Get Updates.

Troubleshooting   If the Status tab in the Shared Workspace task pane indicates that your changes are in conflict with the changes made to the workspace copy, click Document Updates, and then click Keep Workspace Copy. When working on your own document, be sure to merge or compare the copies before keeping one and discarding the other.

1   In the **Shared Workspace** task pane, click the **Document Information** tab.

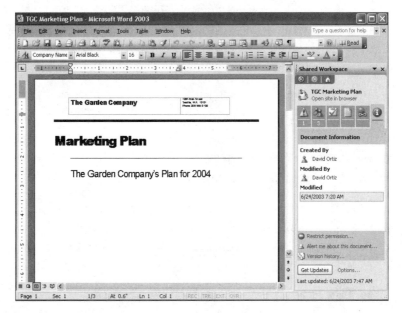

2   Near the bottom of the task pane, click **Alert me about this document**.

Internet Explorer displays the New Alert: Shared Documents: TGCMktgPlan page in the document workspace.

3   In the **Change Type** area, select the **Changed Items** option.

4   In the **Alert Frequency** area, select the **Send e-mail immediately** option, if necessary.

Tip   To see a list of all your alerts in this workspace, in the Alert Frequency area, click "View my existing alerts on this site."

5   Click **OK**.

Internet Explorer displays the Shared Documents list in the TGCMktgPlan document workspace. You will now receive an e-mail message, at the address associated with your SharePoint user account, whenever a change is made to the shared documents in the workspace.

6   Switch to Word, and in the **Shared Workspace** task pane, click the **Tasks** tab.

7   Near the bottom of the task pane, click **Alert me about tasks**.

Internet Explorer displays the New Alert: Tasks page in the TGCMktgPlan document workspace.

8   In the **Change Type** area, select the **All Changes** option, if necessary.

9   In the **Alert Frequency** area, select **Send a daily summary** option, and then click **OK**.

Internet Explorer displays the Tasks list in the TGCMktgPlan document workspace. You will now receive an e-mail message each day that summarizes any changes to tasks in the document workspace.

Tip   You can also set alerts from the workspace site. View the list that you want to receive alerts about—Shared Documents, Announcements, or Tasks—and in the left navigation column, click "Alert me."

10   Switch to Word, and in the **Shared Workspace** task pane, click the **Status** tab.

11   Near the bottom of the task pane, click **Get Updates**.

12   On the **File** menu, click **Close**. If prompted to save the file, click **Yes**.

Word closes.

CLOSE Internet Explorer.

Starting a Discussion in a Workspace

Discussing the contents of a document can help to resolve questions, pool knowledge, avoid conflicting edits and duplicated work, and facilitate the review and finalization process. Rather than scheduling meetings or conference calls to conduct your business, you can hold your discussions online, in the document workspace.

In this exercise, you will initiate a discussion board in your document workspace so your team can exchange ideas about the outline.

Important   To complete this task, you must have completed the first exercise in this chapter, "Creating a Document Workspace and Managing Workspace Members."

USE the *TGCMktgPlan* document in the practice file folder for this topic. This practice file is located in the *My Documents\Microsoft Press\Office 2003 SBS\Document* folder and can also be accessed by clicking *Start/All Programs/Microsoft Press/Microsoft Office System 2003 Step by Step.*
BE SURE TO start Word before beginning this exercise.
OPEN the *TGCMktgPlan* document, and click Get Updates.

1   In the **Shared Workspace** task pane, click **Open Site in Browser**.

Internet Explorer displays the TGCMktgPlan document workspace.

2   In the left navigation column, click **General Discussion**.

Internet Explorer displays the General Discussion page in the workspace.

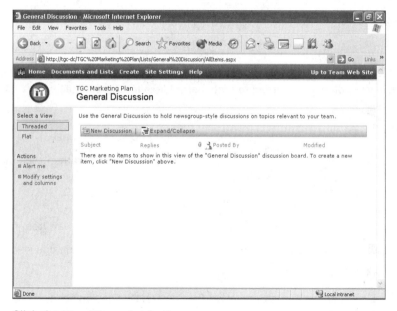

3   Click the **New Discussion** button.

Internet Explorer displays the General Discussion: New Item form.

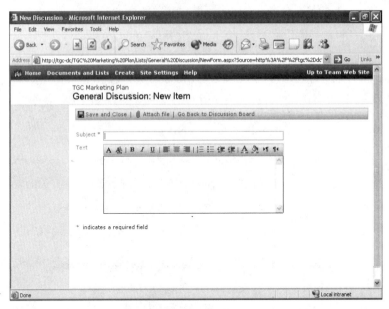

4   In the **Subject** box, type Outline Review, and in the **Text** box, type Let's use this discussion thread to brainstorm ideas for the outline.

5   Click the **Save and Close** button.

Internet Explorer displays the General Discussion page.

6   Point to the *Outline Review* discussion thread, and then click the down arrow that appears to the right of it.

7   In the drop-down list, click **Reply**.

Internet Explorer displays the General Discussion: New Item form.

8   In the **Text** box, type Please post your thoughts within one week.

9   Click the **Save and Close** button.

Internet Explorer displays the General Discussion page.

10   Click the plus (+) sign to the left of the *Outline Review* discussion thread.

The thread expands to show the content of the first message and your reply message.

Tip   To quickly expand or collapse all threads and messages in the discussion board, click the Expand/Collapse button.

11   Click the plus (+) sign to the left of your reply.

The message expands to show the content of your reply.

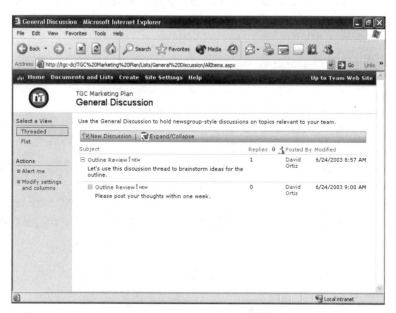

12   Click the minus (-) sign to the left of the first message in the thread.

The thread collapses, hiding its contents and your reply.

CLOSE Internet Explorer and Word.

Customizing a Document Workspace

As with any SharePoint site, you can tailor your document workspace to meet your needs. You can specify the title and write an informative description to introduce your workspace. You can modify the layout to be most useful for your team. You can also apply various color and visual themes to enhance the appearance of your site.

In this exercise, you will customize the appearance and layout of your document workspace.

Important   To complete this task, you must have completed the first exercise in this chapter, "Creating a Document Workspace and Managing Workspace Members."

USE the *TGCMktgPlan* document in the practice file folder for this topic. This practice file is located in the
My Documents\Microsoft Press\Office 2003 SBS\Document folder and can also be accessed by clicking
Start/All Programs/Microsoft Press/Microsoft Office System 2003 Step by Step.
BE SURE TO start Word before beginning this exercise.
OPEN the *TGCMktgPlan* document, and click Get Updates.

1   In the **Shared Workspace** task pane, click **Open Site in Browser**.

Internet Explorer displays the TGCMktgPlan document workspace.

2   On the workspace menu bar, click **Site Settings**.

Internet Explorer displays the Site Settings page in the workspace.

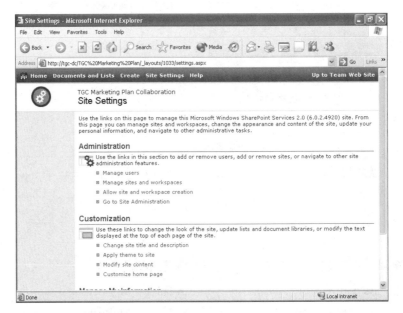

3   In the **Customization** area, click **Change site title and description**.

Internet Explorer displays the Change Site Title and Description form.

4   In the **Title** box, type TGC Marketing Plan Collaboration, and in the **Description** box,
type Let's make a great plan! Then click **OK**.

Internet Explorer displays the Site Settings page, reflecting the new title.

5   In the **Customization** area, click **Apply theme to site**.

Internet Explorer displays the Apply Theme to Web Site page.

6   In the list of themes, click **Iris**, and then click **Apply**.

Internet Explorer displays the Site Settings page, reflecting the new theme.

7   In the **Customization** area, click **Customize home page**.

Tip   You can also customize some aspects of individual lists like Announcements, Tasks, and so on. For example, you can change the order of the columns in the list. View the list you want to customize, and in the left navigation column, click "Modify settings and columns."

Internet Explorer displays the workspace home page with the Modify Shared Page task pane visible. The sections of the page are outlined and labelled as Top, Left, and Right.

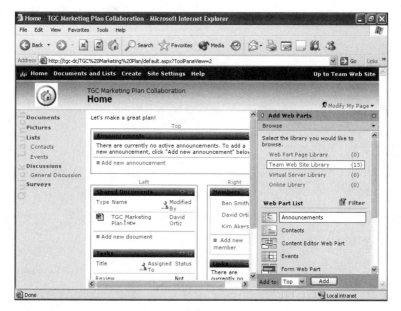

8   Drag the title bar of the **Shared Documents** list to the **Top** section, just below the **Announcements** description.

The Shared Documents list appears in the Top section.

9   In the **Modify My Page** task pane, under **Web Part List**, drag **General Discussion** to the **Left** section, just below the **Tasks** list.

10   On the workspace menu bar, click **Home**.

Internet Explorer displays the home page, reflecting your customization.

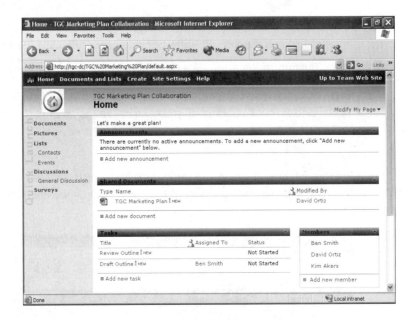

CLOSE Internet Explorer.

Key Points

- A document workspace is a SharePoint Web site that can be accessed by the team members who contribute to a shared document.

- You can create document workspaces for Word, Excel, PowerPoint, and Visio documents in two ways: by e-mailing the file as a *shared attachment*, or by using the Shared Workspace task pane in the Office application in which the document was created.

- You specify the workspace members who can access the workspace and contribute to the document.

- You can create tasks for completing the document and assign those tasks to yourself or others.

- You can be alerted by e-mail when information in the workspace changes.

- You and your team can discuss the document through an online discussion board in the workspace.

- You can customize the layout, content, and appearance of the document workspace to meet your needs.

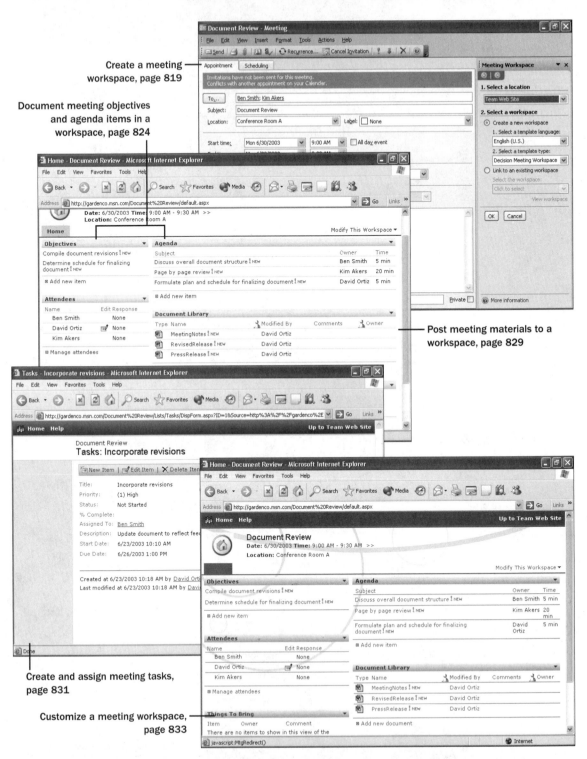

Create a meeting workspace, page 819

Document meeting objectives and agenda items in a workspace, page 824

Post meeting materials to a workspace, page 829

Create and assign meeting tasks, page 831

Customize a meeting workspace, page 833

Chapter 33 at a Glance

33 Teaming Up in a Meeting Workspace

In this chapter you will learn to:

✔ Create a meeting workspace.

✔ Document meeting objectives and agenda items in a workspace.

✔ Post meeting materials to a workspace.

✔ Create and assign meeting tasks.

✔ Customize a meeting workspace.

Scheduling is just the beginning of planning a meeting. The preparation tasks—including coordinating the agendas and background materials and distributing the information needed to run an effective meeting—can be a real challenge.

New in Office 2003
Meeting workspace

By using a *meeting workspace*, a new feature in The Microsoft Office System 2003, you can share all the information in one central location accessible to attendees through the Internet or your company's intranet. A meeting workspace is sub-site of a Microsoft Windows SharePoint Services Web site where you can publish your meeting agenda and objectives, post documents and files, track tasks, and more.

By centralizing this information, your meeting attendees always have access to the latest information, and you avoid sending large files through your e-mail system.

See Also Do you need only a quick refresher on the topics in this chapter? See the Quick Reference entries on pages xxxiii.

Important Before you can use the practice files in this chapter, you need to install them from the book's companion CD to their default location. See "Using the Book's CD-ROM" on page xxi for more information.

Creating a Meeting Workspace

When scheduling a meeting by using a meeting workspace, you include a link to the workspace in the meeting invitation and post all relevant information—objectives, agendas, documents, and so on—to the workspace. To access the workspace, meeting attendees click the link in the invitation they receive from you.

Whether the meeting takes place in person, over the phone, or through a conferencing program like Microsoft Windows NetMeeting, you can view the workspace and update it before, during, and after the meeting. You can allow attendees to update the workspace as well.

You can use Microsoft Office Outlook 2003 to create the meeting workspace while creating the meeting request, and a link to the workspace is automatically included in the body of the request. With other e-mail programs, the interaction between the meeting request and the meeting workspace might vary, but you can always create the workspace through the parent SharePoint Web site and then simply copy and paste the *URL* for the workspace into the meeting invitation.

In this exercise, you will create a meeting workspace in preparation for a group document review.

Important   To complete this exercise, you must have access to a Microsoft Windows SharePoint Services server and permission to create workspace sites on it.

BE SURE TO start Microsoft Outlook before beginning this exercise.

1   In the **Navigation Pane**, click **Calendar**.

Outlook displays your calendar for today.

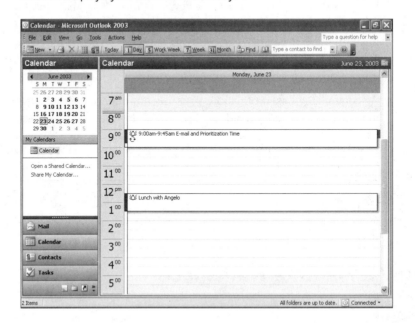

2   On the Standard toolbar, click **New**.

A new, untitled appointment form opens.

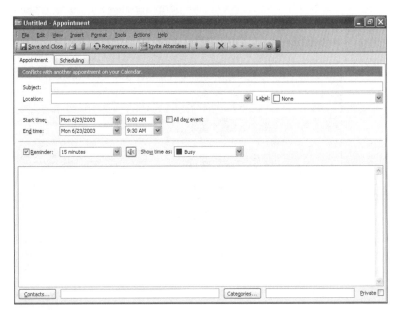

3   Click the down arrow to the right of the first **Start time** box, and click a date one week from today.

Outlook adjusts the end date.

4   On the Standard toolbar, click **Invite Attendees**.

The meeting form displays the controls you need to invite others to this meeting.

5   In the **To** box, type **ben@gardenco.msn.com; kim@gardenco.msn.com**, and in the **Subject** box, type **Document Review**.

Tip   To add or remove meeting attendees' names after creating the workspace, add them to or remove them from the meeting request in Outlook. When you send the invitation, Outlook will update the meeting workspace. You can also add or remove attendees' names through the meeting workspace by clicking "Manage attendees" in the Attendees area. However, you'll need to switch back to Outlook to update that information in the meeting request.

6 In the **Location** box, type Conference Room A, and then click the **Meeting Workspace** button.

The Meeting Workspace task pane appears on the right side of the window. If you have already visited a SharePoint Services site where you have permission to create workspace sites, a default location might appear in the "Create a workspace" area.

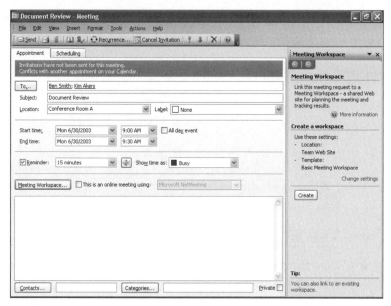

7 In the **Meeting Workspace** task pane, in the **Create a workspace** area, click **Change settings**.

The Meeting Workspace task pane displays the controls you need to select a location for your workspace and the type of workspace you want.

8 In the **Select a location** list, select the location you want. To enter a URL for a new site, click **Other**.

9 In the **Select a workspace** area, click the down arrow to the right of the **Select a template type** box, and click **Decision Meeting Workspace**.

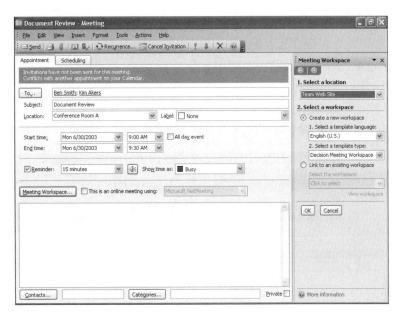

10   In the **Meeting Workspace** task pane, click **OK**, and then click **Create**.

Outlook connects to your SharePoint Web site and creates the workspace.
The meeting request window is updated to include the workspace information.

Tip   If you create the workspace in the wrong location, you can delete the work-space and create a new one. Open the meeting request, and in the Meeting Work-space task pane, click Remove. Then click Change Settings, select the location you want, and click Create.

11   On the Standard toolbar, click **Send**.

The meeting invitation is sent, and the meeting is added to your calendar.

Tip   If you change the information in the meeting request, Outlook will update the meeting workspace when you send the updates to your meeting attendees (To send a meeting update, on the Standard toolbar, click Send Update). If you change the meeting request and click "Save and Close" without sending the updates, your changes will not be sent to the workspace.

12   In the **Navigation Pane**, click the date of the meeting you just scheduled.
(It should be one week from today.)

Outlook displays your schedule for the selected day.

13 Double-click the **Document Review** meeting.

The meeting opens with the Meeting Workspace task pane visible.

14 In the **Meeting Workspace** task pane, click **Go to workspace**.

Internet Explorer opens to display the Document Review meeting workspace. The workspace summarizes the meeting date, time, and location, lists the meeting attendees, and includes space for meeting objectives, agenda items, and documents.

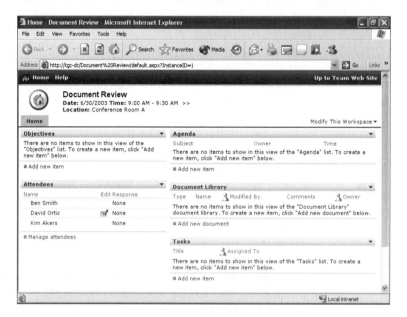

CLOSE Internet Explorer, the Document Review meeting, and Outlook.

Documenting Meeting Objectives and Agenda Items in a Workspace

Rather than typing meeting objectives and agenda items into one or more documents and distributing them by e-mail or bringing printouts of them to the meeting, you can list these items in the meeting workspace. Your attendees can then review these items in advance, which will help them be more prepared for the meeting. Also, if the objectives or agenda change, you can update them in the meeting workspace, and your attendees will see the latest information without your having to redistribute the information.

In this exercise, you will define meeting objectives and outline an agenda in the meeting workspace.

Important   To complete this task, you must have completed the first exercise in this chapter, "Creating a Meeting Workspace."

USE the *ReleaseSched* worksheet in the practice file folder for this topic. This practice file is located in the *My Documents\Microsoft Press\Office 2003 SBS\Meeting* folder and can also be accessed by clicking *Start/All Programs/Microsoft Press/Microsoft Office System 2003 Step by Step*.
BE SURE TO start Microsoft Outlook before beginning this exercise.

1   In the **Navigation Pane**, click **Calendar**.

Outlook displays your calendar for today.

2   In the **Navigation Pane**, click the date of the Document Review meeting.

Outlook displays your schedule for the selected day.

Tip   Calendar items that are linked to a meeting workspace are marked with a special icon.

3   Double-click the **Document Review** meeting.

The meeting opens with the Meeting Workspace task pane visible.

4   In the **Meeting Workspace** task pane, click **Go to workspace**.

Internet Explorer opens to display your Document Review meeting workspace.

5   In the **Objectives** area, click **Add new item**.

Internet Explorer displays the Objectives: New Item form.

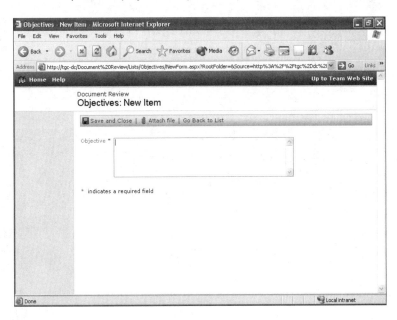

6 In the **Objective** box, type Compile document revisions, and then click **Save and Close**.

Internet Explorer displays the Document Review meeting workspace, including the new meeting objective.

Tip Editing list items such as objectives or agenda items in a workspace is easy. Simply click the item to view its details, and then click Edit Item.

7 In the **Objectives** area, click **Add new item**.

Internet Explorer displays the Objectives: New Item form.

8 In the **Objective** box, type Determine schedule for finalizing document, and then click **Save and Close**.

Internet Explorer displays the Document Review meeting workspace, including the new meeting objective.

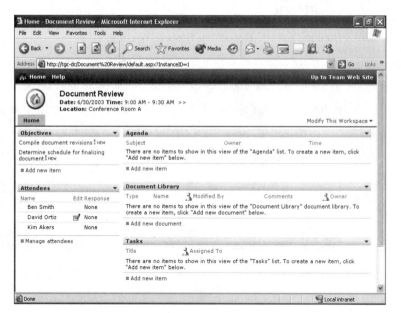

9 In the **Agenda** area, click **Add new item**.

Internet Explorer displays the Agenda: New Item form.

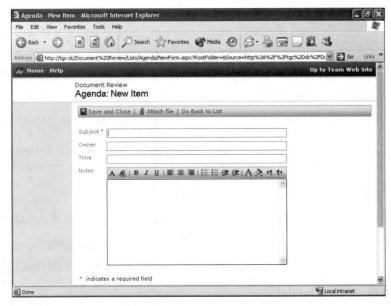

10 In the **Subject** box, type Discuss overall document structure.

11 In the **Owner** box, type Ben Smith, and in the **Time** box, type 5 min.

12 Click the **Save and Close** button.

Internet Explorer displays the Document Review meeting workspace, including the new agenda item.

13 In the **Agenda** area, click **Add new item**.

Internet Explorer displays the Agenda: New Item form.

14 In the **Subject** box, type Page by page review.

15 In the **Owner** box, type Kim Akers, and in the **Time** box, type 20 min.

16 Click the **Save and Close** button.

Internet Explorer displays the Document Review meeting workspace, including the new agenda item.

17 In the **Agenda** area, click **Add new item**.

Internet Explorer displays the Agenda: New Item form.

18 In the **Subject** box, type Formulate plan and schedule for finalizing document.

19 In the **Owner** box, type your name, and in the **Time** box, type 5 min.

20 In the **Notes** box, type Publication schedule attached, and then click **Attach File**.

Internet Explorer displays the controls you need to locate the file you want to attach.

21 Click the **Browse** button. In the **Choose file** dialog box, browse to the *My Documents \Microsoft Press\Office System 2003 SBS* folder, and double-click the *Meeting* folder. Then click *ReleaseSched*, and click **Open**.

The path to the ReleaseSched file is inserted into the Name box.

22 Click **OK**.

Internet Explorer displays the Agenda: New Item form, including the attachment.

Tip To delete an attachment from an agenda or objective item, click the item to view its details. Then click Edit Item, and next to the attachment, click Delete.

23 Click the **Save and Close** button.

Internet Explorer displays the Document Review meeting workspace, including the meeting objectives and agenda items.

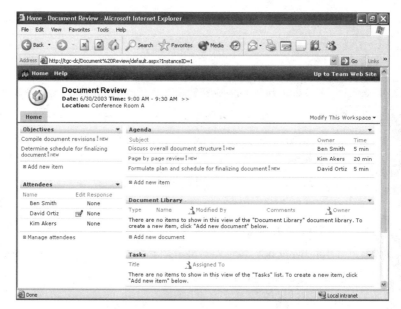

24 In the **Agenda** area, click **Formulate plan and schedule for finalizing document**.

Internet Explorer displays the detail for the agenda item.

25 Click *ReleaseSched*, and if prompted to confirm whether you want to open the file, click **OK**.

The schedule opens in Excel with the Shared Workspace task pane visible.

CLOSE Excel, Internet Explorer, the Document Review meeting, and Outlook.

Posting Meeting Materials to a Workspace

In the past, you might have sent background materials and notes for your meeting to your meeting attendees using e-mail. With a meeting workspace, you can post files in a document library that is accessible to your meeting attendees through the Web. You can post documents, spreadsheets, presentations—any kind of file that your attendees can open.

In this exercise, you will upload a key document to the meeting workspace.

Important   To complete this task, you must have completed the first exercise in this chapter, "Creating a Meeting Workspace."

USE the *PressRelease, MeetingNotes*, and *RevisedRelease* documents in the practice file folder for this topic. These practice files are located in the *My Documents\Microsoft Press\Office 2003 SBS \Meeting* folder and can also be accessed by clicking *Start/All Programs/Microsoft Press /Microsoft Office System 2003 Step by Step.*
BE SURE TO start your computer and Microsoft Outlook before beginning this exercise.

1   In the **Navigation Pane**, click **Calendar**.

Outlook displays your calendar for today.

2   In the **Navigation Pane**, click the date of the Document Review meeting.

Outlook displays your schedule for the selected day.

3   Double-click the **Document Review** meeting.

The meeting opens with the Meeting Workspace task pane visible.

4   In the **Meeting Workspace** task pane, click **Go to workspace**.

Internet Explorer opens to display your Document Review meeting workspace.

5   In the **Document Library** area, click **Add new document**.

Internet Explorer displays the Upload Document form.

6   Click **Browse**.

The Choose file dialog box appears.

7   .Browse to the *My Documents\Microsoft Press\Office System 2003 SBS\Meeting* folder, select *PressRelease*, and click **Open**.

The path to the selected file appears in the Name box.

8   Click the **Save and Close** button.

9   In the **Document Library** area, click **Add new document**.

Internet Explorer displays the Upload Document form.

10   Click **Upload Multiple Files**.

The Upload Document form displays a Windows Explorer-like interface where you can select multiple files at once.

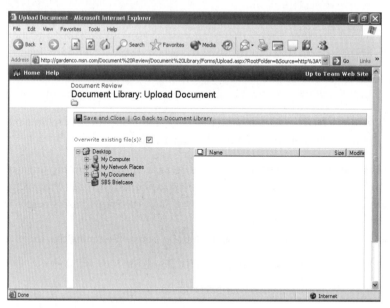

11 In the left column, browse to the *My Documents\Microsoft Press \Office System 2003 SBS\Meeting* folder.

The contents of the folder are listed in the right side of the window.

12 Select the **MeetingNotes** and **RevisedRelease** check boxes, and then click the **Save and Close** button. If you are prompted to confirm the action, click **Yes**.

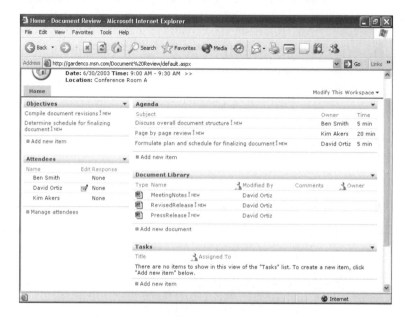

Internet Explorer displays the Document Review workspace, including the newly uploaded meeting notes and revised press release.

CLOSE Internet Explorer, the Document Review meeting, and Outlook.

Creating and Assigning Meeting Tasks

Typically, most meetings result in action items for attendees. Now you can easily track these tasks in the meeting workspace. You can create tasks, set their priority, assign them to attendees, and track their status to completion.

In this exercise, you will create and assign a task and then edit the task to indicate that it is complete.

Important   To complete this task, you must have completed the first exercise in this chapter, "Creating a Meeting Workspace."

BE SURE TO start Microsoft Outlook before beginning this exercise.

1   In the **Navigation Pane**, click **Calendar**.

Outlook displays your calendar for today.

2   In the **Navigation Pane**, click the date of the Document Review meeting.

Outlook displays your schedule for the selected day.

3   Double-click the **Document Review** meeting.

The meeting opens with the Meeting Workspace task pane visible.

4   In the **Meeting Workspace** task pane, click **Go to workspace**.

Internet Explorer opens to display your Document Review meeting workspace.

5   In the **Tasks** area, click **Add new item**.

Internet Explorer displays the Tasks: New Item form.

6   In the **Title** box, type Incorporate revisions, click the down arrow to the right of the **Priority** list, and click **(1) High**.

7   Click the down arrow to the right of the **Assigned To** box, click **Ben Smith**, and in the **Description** box, type Update document to reflect feedback from review meeting.

Calendar

8   Next to the **Due Date** box, click the **Calendar** button, and select a date three business days from today.

9   Click the down arrow to the right of the second **Due Date** box, click **1 PM**, click the down arrow to right of the third **Due Date** box, and click **00**.

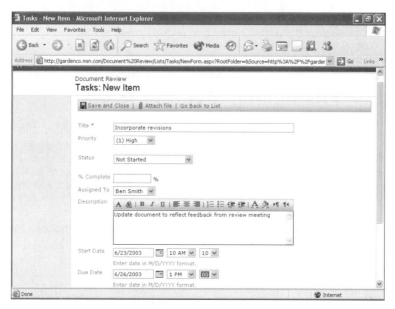

10 Click the **Save and Close** button.

Internet Explorer displays the Document Review workspace, including the new task.

11 In the **Tasks area**, click **Incorporate revisions**.

Internet Explorer shows the detail for the task.

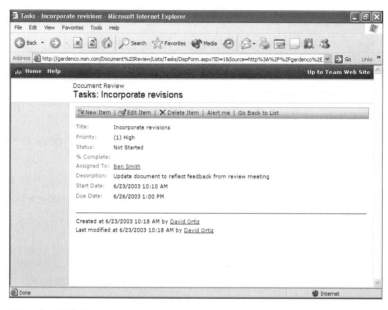

12 Click the **Edit Item** button.

Internet Explorer displays the Tasks: Incorporate revisions form.

Tip   You can attach files as well as agenda or objective items to tasks. When creating or editing the task, click Attach File.

To delete an attachment from a task, click the item to view its details. Then click Edit Item, and to the right of the attachment, click the Delete link.

13   In the **Status** list, click **Completed**, and then click the **Save and Close** button.

Internet Explorer displays the Document Review workspace. The Tasks list no longer includes the completed task.

14   Click the **Tasks** page's title bar.

Internet Explorer displays the Tasks page, which indicates that the task is complete.

CLOSE Internet Explorer, the Document Review meeting, and Outlook.

Customizing a Meeting Workspace

Because a meeting workspace is a special kind of SharePoint Web site, you can use a number of SharePoint features to customize the workspace to meet your needs. You can add or remove sections of the page, called *Web parts*. The lists of tasks, objectives, or agenda items are examples of Web parts. You can rearrange the Web parts to be most useful to you and your team. You can even add pages to your site, which you would then fill with Web parts. You can also choose from a number of themes that change the color scheme and visual style of your site.

In this exercise, you will add, remove, and rearrange Web parts in your meeting workspace, and then apply a theme to the site.

Important   To complete this task, you must have completed the first exercise in this chapter, "Creating a Meeting Workspace."

BE SURE TO start Microsoft Outlook before beginning this exercise.

1   In the **Navigation Pane**, click **Calendar**.

Outlook displays your calendar for today.

2   In the **Navigation Pane**, click the date of the Document Review meeting.

Outlook displays your schedule for the selected day.

3   Double-click the **Document Review** meeting.

The meeting opens with the Meeting Workspace task pane visible.

4   In the **Meeting Workspace** task pane, click **Go to workspace**.

Internet Explorer opens to display your Document Review meeting workspace.

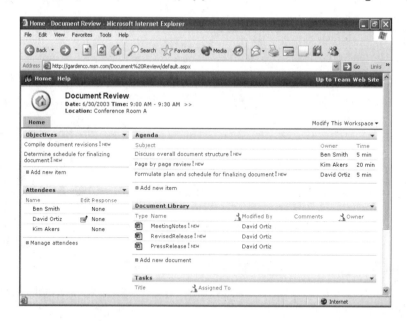

5   In the upper-right corner of the page, click the down arrow to the right of the **Modify This Workspace** button, and click **Design This Page**.

Internet Explorer displays the workspace in design mode.

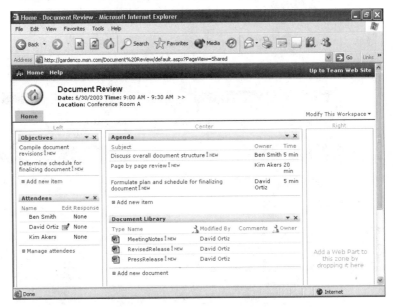

Close

6   Scroll down, and in the blue title bar for the **Decisions** list, click the **Close** button.

The Decisions list is removed from the page.

7   In the upper-right corner of the page, click the down arrow to the right of the **Modify This Workspace** button, and click **Add Web Parts**.

Internet Explorer displays the workspace in design mode and displays the Add Web Parts task pane on the right side of the window.

8   In the **Web Parts** list, drag the **Things to Bring** Web part to the first column, under the **Attendees** Web part.

The Things to Bring list is added to the first column.

9   In the upper-left corner, click **Home**.

Internet Explorer displays the Document Review meeting workspace, reflecting your layout changes.

10 In the upper-right corner of the page, click the down arrow to the right of the **Modify This Workspace** button, and click **Site Settings**.

Internet Explorer displays the Site Settings page.

11 In the **Customization** area, click **Apply theme to site**.

Internet Explorer displays the Apply Theme to Web Site page.

12 In the list of themes, click **Compass**, and then click **Apply**.

Internet Explorer displays the Site Settings page, reflecting the new theme.

13 In the upper-left corner, click **Home**.

Internet Explorer displays the Document Review meeting workspace.

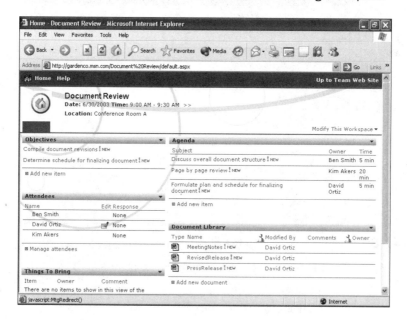

CLOSE Internet Explorer.

Key Points

- You can use a meeting workspace to communicate important information such as agendas, reference materials, tasks, and so on with meeting attendees, before, during, and after the meeting.

- You can list the meeting objectives and agenda items in the meeting workspace.

- You can post meeting materials such as background information or meeting notes to a document library in the meeting workspace.

- You can create and assign tasks related to the meeting.

- You can customize the appearance and layout of the meeting workspace.

Glossary

absolutely   The designation of a picture whose position is determined by measurements you set. See also *relatively*.

absolute path   A designation of the location of a file including the root directory and the descending series of subdirectories leading to the end file. See also *relative path*.

access violation   A type of error caused by attempting to access a page or site that is not allowed.

action button   Navigation buttons that can be added to slides.

action query   A type of query that updates or makes changes to multiple records in one operation.

active cell   A selected cell.

Active Directory   A network service that stores information about resources, such as computers and printers.

Active Server Pages (ASP)   Pages stored on a server that generate different views of the data in response to choices users make on a Web page.

add-ins   Supplemental programs that extend a program's capabilities.

address book   A collection of names, e-mail addresses, and distribution lists used to address messages. An address book might be provided by Microsoft Outlook, Microsoft Exchange Server, or Internet directory services.

address card   Contact information displayed in a block that looks like a paper business card.

adjustable objects   Objects with an adjustment handle (a small yellow diamond) that allows you to alter their appearance without changing their size.

adjustment handle   A small yellow diamond you can use to alter the appearance of the shape without changing its size.

agenda slide   A slide used at the beginning of a presentation that outlines in bulleted points the presentation's material.

aggregate function   A function that groups and performs calculations on multiple fields.

alias   An alternate name used for identification. Using a generic e-mail alias that automatically forwards received e-mail messages to one or more individuals ensures that messages are always received by the appropriate person.

alignment   The manner in which a cell's contents are arranged within that cell (for example, centered).

All Mail Folders   The list that displays the folders available in your mailbox. If the Folder List is not visible, on the Navigation Pane, click Folder List.

anchor tag   Code in an HTML document that defines a bookmark or a link to a bookmark, Web page, Web site, or e-mail address.

animated pictures   GIF (Graphics Interchange Format) or digital video files that you can insert into a slide presentation as a movie.

animation scheme   A set of professionally designed animations divided into three categories: Subtle, Moderate, and Exciting.

anonymous user   A members of the general public who views a Web site.

append query   A query that adds a group of records from one or more tables to the end of one or more tables.

appointment   An entry in your Outlook Calendar that does not involve inviting other people or resources.

arc   A curved line whose angle you can change by dragging an adjustment handle.

archiving   Moving old or expired items out of your Inbox and other message folders to an alternate location for storage.

arguments   Specific data a function requires to calculate a value.

arithmetic operator   An operator that performs an arithmetic operation: + (addition), – (subtraction), * (multiplication), or / (division).

article   A message posted to a Discussion Web site.

ASCII   Acronym for *American Standard Code for Information Interchange*, a coding scheme for text characters developed in 1968. ASCII files have the extension *.asc*.

ASP   See *Active Server Pages*.

aspect ratio   The relationship between a graphic's height and width.

attachment   A file that accompanies an e-mail message.

attribute   A changeable characteristic of a shape—such as fill, line, and shadow—or of text—such as style, font, color, embossment, and shadow.

auditing   The process of examining a worksheet for errors.

AutoArchive   An Outlook feature that archives messages automatically at scheduled intervals, clearing out old and expired items from folders. AutoArchive is active by default.

AutoContent Wizard   A wizard that takes you through a step-by-step process to create a presentation, prompting you for presentation information as you go.

AutoCorrect A feature that corrects common capitalization and spelling errors (such as changing as *teh* to *the*) as you type them.

AutoFilter A Microsoft Excel tool you can use to created filters. See also *filter*.

AutoForm A feature that efficiently creates forms using all the available fields and minimal formatting.

AutoFormats Predefined formats that can be applied to a worksheet.

automatic layout behavior A feature that recognizes when you insert an object onto a slide and changes the layout to fit the objects on the slide.

AutoPreview A view which displays the first three lines of each message in your Inbox, making it easy to scan for your most important messages.

AutoSummarize This feature in Word identifies the main points in a document and sets them apart for quick reference.

AutoText A feature similar to AutoCorrect that makes corrections as you tell it to, rather than automatically.

axis A common element in a chart. The x-axis (usually horizontal) plots the categories, and the y-axis (usually vertical) plots the values.

back-end database The part of a split database that is stored on a server for security reasons, and which usually consists of the tables and other objects that you don't want people to be able to modify. See also *front-end database*.

background The underlying colors, shading, texture, and style of the color scheme.

binary file A file coded so that its data can be read by a computer.

bookmark A location in a document that is marked so that you, or your reader, can return to it quickly.

Boolean A data type that can hold either of two mutually exclusive values, often expressed as *yes/no, 1/10, on/off,* or *true/false.*

Boolean query A True or False query that utilizes logical operators including AND, OR, IF THEN, EXCEPT, and NOT.

border The edge or visible frame surrounding a workspace, window, document, table, cell, or graphic.

bound Linked, as when a form used to view table information is linked to the table.

Briefcase A replication folder that you use to keep files in sync when you work on different computers in different locations.

browser sniffer A program that detects the Web browser and version used by each Web visitor.

bullet A small graphic, such as a dot, that introduces a line or paragraph in a list.

bullet points   A list of items in which each item is preceded by a symbol.

bulleted lists   An unordered list of concepts, items, or options.

button   A graphical image or text box that executes a command. Buttons appear on toolbars, in dialog boxes, and in other display elements.

Cached Exchange Mode   A feature of Outlook that creates local copies of your mailbox and address book on your computer and keeps them synchronized. Cached Exchange Mode monitors your connection status and speed and optimizes data transfer accordingly.

Calendar   The scheduling component of Outlook that is fully integrated with e-mail, contacts, and other Outlook features.

caption   The expository text associated with a graphic or other type of figure.

case   The capitalization (uppercase or lowercase) of a word or phrase. Title case has the first letter of all important words capitalized. Sentence case has only the first letter of the first word capitalized. *ZIP* is all uppercase, and *zip* is all lowercase. Toggle case changes uppercase to lowercase and vice versa.

category   A keyword or phrase that you assign to Outlook items so that you can easily find, sort, filter, or group them.

cell address   A combination of the column letter and the row number at the intersection where the cell is located.

cell   The intersection of a row and a column in a table or spreadsheet. A cell is displayed as a rectangular space that can hold text, a value, or a formula.

cell padding   The space between the borders of a cell and the text inside it.

change markers   Icons that indicate where reviewers have made a revision to a slide.

character formatting   Collectively, a font and the attributes used to vary its look.

character spacing   The space between letters and other characters in words and sentences. Character spacing can be adjusted so the characters are closer together or farther apart.

character style   A set of attributes that can be applied to selected characters by selecting the style from a list.

chart   A graphic that uses lines, bars, columns, pie slices, or other markers to represent numbers and other values.

chart area   The entire area within the frame displayed when you click a chart.

check-box form field   A form field that enables you to provide several options, which users can click to indicate their choices.

child page   A Web page that is subordinate to another Web page, known as the parent page.

class module   One of two types of modules in Microsoft Visual Basic for Applications (VBA). A class module is associated with a specific form or report. See also *standard module*.

Click and Type   A way to insert text, graphics, or other items in a blank area of a document. When you double-click in a blank area, Click and Type will automatically apply the paragraph formatting to position the item where you double-clicked.

client rules   Rules that are applied to messages stored on your computer.

clip art   A ready-made graphic that can be copied and incorporated into other documents or presentations.

code   VBA programs; also called *procedures*, referred to in Access as modules. See also *class module*; *standard module*.

Code pane   One of the four panes in FrontPage Page view. This pane displays the HTML code behind the Web page.

collaboration site   A Web site for team use. See also *SharePoint team Web sites*.

collate   To assemble or print in order.

color menu   The color palette associated with Drawing toolbar buttons, such as Fill Color, Line Color, or Font Color.

color model   A method of specifying color, such as RGB (red-green-blue) and HSL (hue-saturation-luminance) for monitors and CMYK (cyan-magenta-yellow-black) and PANTONE® for printers.

color scheme   A set of eight complementary colors available for designing your PowerPoint slides. A color scheme consists of a background color, a color for lines and text, and six additional colors balanced to provide a professional look to a presentation.

column   One of the vertical sections or stacks of information in a table or spreadsheet.

column headings   The gray buttons (A, B, C, etc.) across the top of a datasheet. See also *row headings*.

combo box   A control in which you can either select from a drop-down list or type an option.

comma-delimited text file   A data file consisting of fields and records, stored as text, in which the fields are separated from each other by commas.

command button   A control shaped like a button to which you can attach code that runs when the button is clicked.

comment   A note embedded in a document, Web page, or code segment that can be hidden or displayed as needed.

comment balloon   In Word's Track Changes feature, a text box that appears in the margin of the document.

comparison operator   An operator that compares values, such as < (less than), > (greater than), and = (equal to).

component   A part of a database that is used to store and organize information. Also known as a *database object*.

compress   To reduce the file size of an image. Sometimes picture quality is compromised for smaller file size.

compression   A means of compacting information for more efficient transportation.

conditional formats   Formats that are applied only when cell contents meet certain criteria.

conditional formula   A formula that calculates a value using one of two different expressions, depending on whether a third expression is true or false.

connection pointer   A small box pointer with which you drag a connection line between two connection points.

connection points   Small blue handles on each side of a shape that you use to add a connection line between two shapes.

constant   A named item that retains a constant value throughout the execution of a program, as opposed to a variable, whose value can change during execution.

contact   A person, inside or outside of your organization, about whom you can save information, such as street and e-mail addresses, telephone and fax numbers, and Web page URLs, in an entry in your Contacts folder in Outlook.

control   An object such as a label, text box, option button, or check box in a form or report that allows you to view or manipulate information stored in tables or queries.

control boxes   The gray boxes at the beginning of a row or column in a datasheet that correspond to the different data series.

control property   A setting that determines the appearance of a control, what data it displays, and how that data looks. A control's properties can be viewed and changed in its Properties dialog box.

control source   The source of a control's data—the field, table or query whose data will be displayed in the control.

criteria   The specifications you give to Access so that it can find matching fields and records. Criteria can be simple, such as all the records with a postal code of 98052, or complex, such as the phone numbers of all customers who have placed orders for over $500 worth of live plants within the last two weeks.

cropping   Cutting off the top, bottom, or sides of a graphic to trim it to a smaller size.

cross-reference   An entry that refers the reader to another entry.

crosstab query   A query that calculates and restructures data for easier analysis. See also *select query*; *parameter query*; *action query*.

data access page   A dynamic Web page that allows users to directly manipulate data in a database via the Internet.

data marker   A graphical representation in a chart of each data point in a data series. The data is plotted against an x-axis, a y-axis, and—in three-dimensional charts—a z-axis.

data point   The value in a datasheet's cell that, together with other data points, comprise a data series.

data series   A group of related data points in a datasheet.

data series marker   A graphical representation of the information in a data series.

data source   A database or file from which information is drawn for another purpose, such as a mail merge document or data access page.

data table   A grid attached to a chart that shows the data used to create the chart.

data type   The type of data that can be entered in a field: text, memo, number, date/time, currency, AutoNumber, Boolean (Yes/No), OLE object, and hyperlink. You set the data type by displaying the table in Design view.

data warehouse   A company that serves as a data repository for a variety of data and that may make use of replication to keep each database synchronized when more than one version of the database is updated in more than one remote location.

database application   A database that is refined and made simpler for the user by the sophisticated use of queries, forms, reports, a switchboard, and various other tools.

database program   A program that stores data. Programs range from those that can store one table per file (referred to as a *flat database*) to those that can store many related tables per file (referred to as a *relational database*).

database security   The protection of database information from accidental damage, destruction, or theft through the use of encryption, passwords, access permissions, replication, and other security measures.

database window   The window from which all database objects can be manipulated or accessed.

datasheet   A numerical representation of data in cells that form rows and columns.

Datasheet view   In Access, the view in which the information in a table or query can be viewed and manipulated. See also *views*.

date and time fields   These fields supply the date and time from your computer's internal calendar and clock, so that you don't have to look them up.

Date Navigator   The small calendar that appears next to the appointment area in the Outlook Calendar. The Date Navigator provides a quick and easy way to change and view dates.

Day view   The Calendar view displaying one day at a time, separated into half-hour increments.

decrypting   "Unscrambling" a database that has been encrypted for security reasons.

delegate   A person given permission to read, reply to and delete your messages in one or more folders.

delete query   A query that deletes a group of records from one or more tables.

delimited text file   A type of text file format in which each record and each field is separated from the next by a known character called a *delimiter*.

delimiter   A character such as a comma (,), semicolon (;), or backslash (\), or pairs of characters such as quotation marks (" ") or braces ({}), that are used to separate records and fields in a delimited text file.

demote   In an outline, to change a heading to body text or to a lower-level heading; to indent a title or bulleted item on a slide, moving it down in the outline to a lower-level item (a bullet item or sub-point).

dependents   The cells with formulas that use the value from a particular cell.

design grid   The name given to the structure used in Design view to manually construct and modify advanced filters and queries.

Design Master   In replication, the version of the database from which replicas are made and where changes made to replicas are copied and synchronized.

Design pane   One of the four panes in FrontPage Page view. This pane displays your page much as it will appear in a Web browser.

design template   A presentation with a designed format and color scheme.

Design view   The view in which the structure of a table or query can be viewed and manipulated. See also *views*.

desktop alert   A notification that appears on your desktop when a new e-mail message, meeting request, or task request appears in your Inbox.

desktop publishing   A process that combines text and graphics in an appealing and easy to read format, such as a report, newsletter, or book.

destination file   A file into which you are inserting information created in another program.

DHTML Acronym for *Dynamic Hypertext Markup Language*.

diagram A relational representation of information, such as an organization chart.

dial-up networking A component of Windows with which you can connect your computer to a network server through a modem.

digital ID A private key that stays on the sender's computer and a certificate that contains a public key. The certificate is sent with digitally signed messages.

digital signature An electronic, secure stamp of authentication on a document.

digitally signing Proving one's identity by attaching a digital certificate to an e-mail message. The certificate is part of the sender's digital ID.

dimmed In reference to menu commands, unavailable and displayed in gray font.

directory server A computer on which a directory is stored.

discussion Web site A Web site where people communicate by submitting, or posting, messages, or articles. Discussion Web sites include the following features:

disk-based Web site A Web site that is located on a floppy disk, CD-ROM, or a computer that is not configured as a Web server.

distribution list A collection of e-mail addresses combined into a single list name. All members of the list receive the e-mail message sent to the list name.

docked toolbar A toolbar that is attached to the edge of a window.

docking Attaching a toolbar to one edge of the window.

Document Map A pane on the left side of the screen that displays the document's headings. You can click a heading in the Document Map to move to that heading in the document.

document properties Information about a document, including details about the document's creation and modification, size and location, author and subject of the document, and more.

document workspace A Microsoft Windows SharePoint Services site that contains your Microsoft Office Word, Microsoft Office Excel, Microsoft Office PowerPoint, or Microsoft Visio files, making them available to the people working on the document, called members, you specify.

document window The part of a Word program where you enter and edit text.

domain name The unique name that identifies an Internet site. A domain name has two or more parts, separated by periods, as in *my.domain.name*.

dotted selection box The border of a selected object that indicates that you can manipulate the entire object.

downloading   Moving or copying items from a server to a local computer.

draft   A message that has not yet been sent.

drag-and-drop editing   A method for quickly moving or copying selected text by dragging it to a new location. To copy selected text, you hold down the [Ctrl] key as you drag.

drawing canvas   An area that contains drawing objects.

drawing object   An image created within Word—an AutoShape, a diagram, a line, or a WordArt object.

drop-down form field   A form field with which you can provide predefined answers so that users are limited to specified choices.

duplicate query   A form of select query that locates records that have the same information in one or more fields that you specify.

dynamic effect   A Web component, such as a banner ad or marquee, that adds motion to a Web page.

Dynamic Hypertext Markup Language (DHTML)   A new version of the standard authoring language, HTML, that includes codes for dynamic Web page elements.

dynamic Web page   A page whose content is created in response to some action on the part of a user who is viewing the page over the Internet. See also *static HTML page*.

e-mail   Electronic mail.

e-mail address   The information that identifies the e-mail account of a message recipient, including the user name and domain name separated by the @ sign. For example, *someone@microsoft.com*.

e-mail links   A hyperlink that initiates a new e-mail message window.

e-mail server   A computer, on a network, that routes and stores e-mail messages.

embedded cascading style sheet   A document embedded within a Web page that defines formats and styles for different page elements.

embedded object   An object that becomes part of the destination file and is no longer a part of its source file.

encrypted   Encoded for privacy protection.

encrypting   Encoding data to prevent unauthorized access. An encrypted message is unreadable to all but the recipient, who has a public key that will decrypt it.

endnote   A note or citation that appears at the end of a document to explain, comment on, or provide references for text in a document. See also *footnote*.

error code   A brief message that occurs in a worksheet cell, describing a problem with a formula or function.

event   In Access, an action performed by a user or by Access, to which a programmed response can be attached. Common user events include Click, Double Click, Mouse Down, Mouse Move, and Mouse Up.

exclusive use   A setting used when you want to be the only person who currently has a database open. You must open a database for exclusive use when setting or removing a password that limits database access.

exporting   The process of converting and saving a file format to be used in another program.

expression   A combination of functions, field values, constants, and operators that yield a result. Expressions can be simple, such as *>100*, or complex, such as *((ProductPrice*Quantity)*.90)+(Shipping+Handling)*.

Expression Builder   A feature used to create formulas (expressions) used in query criteria, form and report properties, and table validation rules.

Extensible Markup Language (XML)   A refined language developed for Web documents that describes document structure rather than appearance.

extension   A period followed by a three-letter program identifier. Examples of extensions are *.doc* for Word and *.xls* for Excel.

external cascading style sheet   A document outside of a Web page that defines formats and styles for different page elements. External style sheets can be referenced by multiple documents to provide a consistent look across pages and sites.

field   An individual item of the information that is the same type across all records. See also *records*.

field name   A first-row cell in a datasheet that indicates the type of information in the column below it.

file   Information, such as a document, that a program saves with a unique name.

file format   The way that a program stores a file so that the program can open the file later.

file name   The name of a file.

file structure   A description of a file or group of files that are to be treated together for some purpose. Such a description includes file layout and location for each file under consideration.

File Transfer Protocol (FTP)   A protocol that allows users to copy files between their local system and any system they can reach on the network.

Files report   A FrontPage report providing information about all the files in a Web site or about specific groups of files, such as those most recently added or modified.

filter   To exclude records from a data list in a mail merge.

filtering   A way to view only those items or files that meet conditions you specify.

First Line Indent marker   In Word, the small upper triangle on the horizontal ruler that controls the first line of the paragraph.

fixed-width text file   A common text file format that is often used to transfer data from older applications. Each record is always the same number of characters long, and the same field within the records is always the same number of characters. Any characters not occupied by real data are filled with zeros.

flag   A marker that can be set to true or false to indicate the state of an object.

flat database   A simple database consisting of one table. See also *relational database*.

floating toolbar   A toolbar that is not attached to an edge of a window.

folder   An icon signifying a place on a hard disk for organizing documents and programs. Folders can contain files and subfolders.

Folder List   In Outlook, the list that displays the folders available in your mailbox.

Folders view   The FrontPage view that displays the visible files and folders that are part of the open Web site.

follow-up flag   An icon associated with a message indicating a need for action.

font   A complete set of characters that all have the same design.

font color   One of a range of colors that can be applied to text from a standard or customized palette.

font effect   An attribute, such as superscript, small capital letters, or shadow, that can be applied to a font.

font size   The size of text, usually expressed in points.

font style   An attribute that changes the look of text. The most common font styles are regular (or plain), italic, bold, and bold italic.

footer   A region at the bottom of a page whose text can be applied to all or some of the pages in a document.

footnote   A note or citation that appears at the bottom of a page to explain, comment on, or provide references for text in a document. See also *endnote*.

form   A printed or online document with instructions, questions, and fields (blanks) where users can enter their responses. In Access, a database object used to enter, edit, and manipulate information in a database table. A form gives you a simple view of some or all of the fields of one record at a time.

form field   A predefined place where users enter their answers to the questions on a form.

form field properties   Settings with which you can change form field attributes, such as text field length or the check box default setting.

Form view   The view in which you can enter and modify the information in a record. See also *views*.

formula   A mathematical expression that performs calculations, such as adding or averaging values.

frame   A division of a Web page that contains either content or a link to content from another source.

frames page   A special page for viewing multiple elements, including Web documents.

frameset   The single shell page of a frames page that contains individual frames of information drawn together from multiple sources.

freeze   To assign cells that will remain at the top of a worksheet regardless of how far down the worksheet a user scrolls.

friendly name   A simple name that translates into a more complex one; friendly names used to identify Web locations are translated by the computer to more complex IP addresses.

front-end database   The part of a split database that is distributed to the people who analyze and enter data. The actual data tables are stored on a server for security reasons. See also *back-end database.*

FTP   See *File Transfer Protocol.*

function   A named procedure or routine in a program, often used for mathematical or financial calculations.

function procedure   In VBA, a procedure that is enclosed in Function and End Function statements and returns a value. See also *sub procedure.*

Global Address List   An address book, provided by Microsoft Exchange Server, that contains all user and distribution list e-mail addresses in your organization. The Exchange administrator creates and maintains this address book.

graphic   A picture or a drawing object.

Graphics Interchange Format (GIF)   A file format for saving pictures that displays well over the Web.

grayscale   A black and white image that displays shades of gray.

gridlines   Lines that appear in a chart to make it easier to view the data.

group One of four elements—the other three being object, permission, and user—on which the Access user-level security model is based.

grouping An action that allows a set of elements to be moved, sized, or otherwise changed as a single unit. See also *ungrouping*.

grouping level The level by which records are grouped in a report. For example, records might be grouped by state (first level), then by city (second level), and then by postal code (third level).

guillemets The « and » characters that surround each merge field in a main document.

Handout Master In PowerPoint, the part of a template that controls the characteristics (background color, text color, font, and font size) of the handouts in a presentation. To make uniform changes to the handouts, you change the Handout Master.

Hanging Indent marker In Word, the small lower triangle on the horizontal ruler that controls all lines in a paragraph except the first.

hanging indent Paragraph formatting adjusted by small triangles on the horizontal ruler where the first line of text is indented less than the subsequent lines.

header A region at the top of a page whose text can be applied to all or some of the pages in a document.

header column The column in a table that contains the title of each row.

header row The row in a table that contains the title of each column.

hit counter A feature on a Web site, usually on the home page, that counts the number of "visits" to the site.

home page The starting page for a set of Web pages in a Web site. The home page includes links to other pages and often provides an overview of the entire Web site.

hosting The process or service of storing a Web site on a configured Web server and serving it to the intended audience.

hotspot A defined area on an image map that is hyperlinked to a bookmark, Web page, Web site, or e-mail address.

hovering Pausing the pointer over an object for a second or two to display more information, such as a submenu or ScreenTip.

HTML See *Hypertext Markup Language*.

HTML format The default format for Outlook e-mail messages. This format supports text formatting, numbering, bullets, alignment, horizontal lines, pictures (including backgrounds), HTML styles, stationery, signatures, and Web pages.

HTML tag   An HTML command that determines how the tagged information looks and acts.

HTTP   See *Hypertext Transfer Protocol.*

hyperlink   The text or graphic that users click to go to a file, a location in a file, an Internet or intranet site, page, location, and so on. Hyperlinks usually appear underlined and in color, but sometimes the only indication is that the pointer changes to a hand.

Hyperlinks view   The FrontPage view that displays the hyperlinks to and from any selected page in the open Web site.

Hypertext Markup Language (HTML)   A tagging system used to code documents so that they can be published on the World Wide Web and viewed with a browser.

Hypertext Transfer Protocol (HTTP)   The client/server protocol used to access information on the World Wide Web.

image map   A graphic element containing hotspots.

IMAP   Internet Message Access Protocol, a protocol that organizes messages on the server and you choose messages to download by viewing their headers.

import   The process of converting a file format created in another program.

importance   The urgency of a message. Messages can be of High, Normal, or Low importance.

Inbox   The default message folder in Outlook. Typically, incoming messages are delivered to the Inbox.

Included Content components   A set of Web components that you can use to create links to the text or graphics you want to display on a Web page, rather than inserting them directly.

indent markers   Markers shown along the horizontal ruler that are used to control how text is indented on the left or right side of a document.

indented index   An index that uses subentries on separate lines below the main entries.

index   A list of the topics, names, and terms used in a document along with the page numbers where they are found. An index typically appears at the end of a document.

index entry   An entry in the body of a document that tags terms to be included in the Word's automated construction of an index. See also *XE.*

input mask   A field property that determines what data can be entered in the field, how the data looks, and the format in which it is stored.

insertion point   The blinking vertical line that appears in the document or presentation window, indicating where text or objects will appear when you type or insert an object.

instant messaging   A method of communication in which you send electronic messages that appear on the recipient's screen immediately.

Internet mail   A type of e-mail account that requires that you connect to the e-mail server over the Internet. POP3, IMAP, and HTTP (for example, Hotmail) are examples of Internet mail accounts.

Internet Protocol (IP) address   The number that uniquely identifies a specific computer on the Internet.

Internet Service Provider (ISP)   A company that provides individuals or organizations with the necessary software and information to get access to the Internet, and with the Internet connection itself. Many ISPs also serve as Web hosts. See also *Web hosting company.*

intranet   A secure, proprietary Web-based network used within a company or group and accessible only to its members.

IP address   See *Internet Protocol address,*

Joint Photographic Experts Group (JPG)   A graphics format used for photos and other graphics with more than 256 colors.

Journal entry   An item in the Journal folder that acts as a shortcut to an activity that has been recorded. You can distinguish a Journal entry from other items by the clock that appears in the lower left corner of the icon.

kerning   The distance between letters in a word.

key combination   Two or more keys that perform an action when pressed together.

keyword   A word that is part of the VBA programming language.

label   In Outlook, a color and short text description you can apply to meetings and appointments to organize your Calendar. In Access, text that identifies what each data series represents.

label control   An area on a form containing text displayed on the form in Form view.

LAN   See *local area network.*

landscape   Horizontal orientation in which the page is wider than it is tall.

landscape mode   A display and printing mode whereby columns run parallel to the short edge of a sheet of paper.

launching   Publishing a Web site to the Internet for the first time.

Layout Preview   A view of a report that shows you how each element will look but without all the detail of Print Preview.

Left Indent marker   In Word, the small square on the horizontal ruler that controls how far the entire paragraph sits from the edge of the text object. The Left Indent marker moves the First Line Indent marker and the Hanging Indent marker, maintaining their relationship.

legend   A chart element that identifies patterns or colors assigned to data; a list that identifies each data series in a datasheet.

line break   A manual break that forces the text that follows it to the next line. Also called a *text wrapping break*.

link   A hyperlink. Text that is a link is usually colored and underlined to distinguish it from surrounding text.

link bar   A hyperlinked list of Web pages within a Web site, providing access to the specified pages.

linked object   An object created in another program that maintains a connection to its source. A linked object is stored in its source document, where it was created. You update a linked object within its source program.

linking   The process of connecting to data in other applications.

lists   Items of information, either numbered or bulleted, set off from a paragraph.

live attachments   See *shared attachments*.

lobby page   An information page that appears on the server before the beginning of broadcast.

local area network (LAN)   A network that connects computers in a relatively small area, typically a single building or groups of buildings. Generally, all computers in an organization are connected to a LAN.

localhost   An example of a friendly name for an IP address. See also *friendly name*.

logical operator   One of the Boolean operators: AND, OR and NOT.

Lookup Wizard   The wizard in Access that simplifies the creation of a Lookup list.

lowercase   Small letters, as opposed to capital, or uppercase, letters.

macro   A command or series of commands (keystrokes and instructions) that are treated as a single command and used to automate repetitive or complicated tasks.

macro project   A group of components, including code, that constitute a macro.

mail merge   A process used to personalize individual documents in a mass production.

main document   The document that is combined with the data source in the mail merge process.

main form   One form that is linked to one or more tables. See also *subform*.

main report   One report that displays records from one or more tables. See also *subreport*.

make-table query   A query that creates a new table from all or part of the data in one or more tables. Make-table queries are helpful for creating a table to export to other Microsoft Access databases.

manual page break   A page break that you insert in a document. A manual page break appears as a dotted line across the page with the label *Page Break*.

many-to-many relationship   A relationship formed between two tables that each have a one-to-many relationship with a third table. See also *one-to-many relationship*; *one-to-one relationship*.

mapped network drive   A drive to which you have assigned a drive letter. Used for quickly accessing files stored in locations that are not likely to change. See also *UNC path*.

margin markers   Small squares on the ruler that move both the upper and lower indent markers.

mask   A field property that determines what data can be entered in a field, how the data looks, and the format in which it is stored.

master   A design pattern that is applied to slides, handouts, and speaker notes.

master document   A document that contains a set of subdocuments.

MDE   See *Microsoft Database Executable*.

media   Graphics, videos, sound effects, or other material that can be inserted into a Web page.

meeting request   An e-mail message inviting its recipients to a meeting.

meeting workspace   A central location where meeting attendees can access information through the Internet or a company's intranet.

menu   A list of commands or options a user can select to perform a desired action.

merge fields   Placeholders that indicate where Word inserts personalized information from a data source.

message header   Summary information that you download to your computer to determine whether to download, copy, or delete an entire message from the server. The header can include the subject, the sender's name, the received date, the importance, the attachment flag, and the size of the message.

Microsoft Clip Organizer   A tool that enables you to collect and organize clip art images, pictures, sounds, and motion clips.

Microsoft Database Executable (MDE)   A compiled version of a database. Saving a database as an MDE file compiles all modules, removes all editable source code, and compacts the destination database.

Microsoft Exchange Server   An enterprise-level e-mail and collaboration server.

Microsoft Office 2003   The Microsoft suite of applications for personal and professional use, updated for 2003.

Microsoft Office Internet Free/Busy Service   A Web-based service that you can use to publish your schedule to a shared Internet location.

Microsoft Visual Basic for Applications (VBA)   A programming language developed in 1990 that uses a visual environment to simplify the development of the user interface (the commands used to communicate with a computer).

module   A location within a Visual Basic project where a macro is stored.

Month view   In Outlook, the Calendar view displaying five weeks at a time.

more colors   Additional colors that you can add to each color menu.

move handle   The four vertical dots at the left end of a toolbar by which you can move the toolbar around.

named range   A group of cells in an Excel spreadsheet.

native format   The file format an application uses to produce its own files.

navigation button   One of the buttons found on a form or navigation bar that helps users display specific records.

navigation frame   A graphical panel used for navigating from slide to slide in a PowerPoint presentation on the Web.

navigation structure   A hierarchical map of how Web pages are connected within a Web site and what routes the user can take to get from one page to another.

Navigation view   In FrontPage, a view of all the files that have been added to the navigational structure of the open Web site.

nesting   Embedding one element inside another.

NetMeeting   A program that enables Internet teleconferencing.

network security   Technologies to protect your network connections to the Internet or other public networks.

network server   A central computer that stores files and programs and manages system functions for a network.

news server   A computer, in your organization or at your Internet service provider (ISP), which is set up specifically to host newsgroups.

newsgroup   A collection of messages related to a particular topic posted to a news server.

newsreader   A program used to read messages posted to a newsgroup.

Normal style   Word's default predefined paragraph style.

Normal template   Word's default document template.

Normal view   In Word, a view in which you write and edit documents. In PowerPoint, a view that contains all three panes: Outline/Slides, Slide, and Notes.

Note Flag   An icon used to assign a given meaning to a section of notes. Among other things, note flags may indicate that a note is important, raises a question, or requires action.

note separator   The line that divides the notes from the body of the document.

note text   The contents of a footnote or endnote.

notes   Outlook items that are the electronic equivalent of paper sticky notes.

Notes Page view   In PowerPoint, a view in which you can add speaker notes and related graphics.

Notes Pages Master   In PowerPoint, the part of a template that controls the characteristics (background color, text color, font, and font size) of the speaker notes in a presentation. To make uniform changes to the speaker notes, you change the Notes Pages Master.

Notes pane   In PowerPoint, an area in Normal view where you can add speaker notes.

numbered list   An ordered list of concepts, items, or options.

object   An item, such as a graphic, video or sound file, or worksheet, that can be inserted in a Word document and then selected and modified. In Access, one of the components of an Access database, such as a table, form, or report. In PowerPoint, any element that you can manipulate.

Office Assistant   A tool that answers questions, offers tips, and provides access to the Help system for Microsoft Office 2003 features.

Office Clipboard   A storage area shared by all Office programs where multiple pieces of information from one or more sources are stored.

Office drawings   The specially formatted lines, shapes, WordArt objects, text boxes, and shadowing that can be incorporated into Microsoft Office documents.

Office Online   A clip art gallery that Microsoft maintains on its Web site. To access Office Online, you click the "Clip Art on Office Online" link at the bottom of the Clip Art task pane.

offline folder   A folder you use to access the contents of a server folder when you are not connected to the network. It is important to update the folder and its corresponding server folder to make the contents of both identical.

offset   The direction and distance in which a shadow falls from an object.

OLE Linking and Embedding   A feature that allows you to insert a file created in one program into a document created in another program.

one-to-many relationship   A relationship formed between two tables in which each record in one table has more than one related record in the other table. See also *many-to-many relationship*; *one- to-one relationship*.

one-to-one relationship   A relationship formed between two tables in which each record in one table has only one related record in the other table. See also *many-to-many relationship*; *one- to-many relationship*.

operator   See *arithmetic operator*; *comparison operator*; *logical operator*.

optimistic locking   Locking a record only for the brief time that Access is saving changes to it.

option button   A control on a form that allows users to select preferred settings.

ordered list   The Hypertext Markup Language (HTML) term for a numbered list.

orientation   The direction—vertical or horizontal—in which a page is laid out in a printed document.

orphan   The first line of a paragraph printed by itself at the bottom of a page.

Out of Office Assistant   An Outlook feature that helps you manage your Inbox when you're out of the office. The Out of Office Assistant can respond to incoming messages automatically, and it enables you to create rules for managing incoming messages.

Outline view   A view that shows the structure of a document, which consists of headings and body text.

Outline/Slides pane   In PowerPoint, an area in Normal view where you can organize and develop presentation content in text or slide miniature form.

Outlook Rich Text Format (RTF)   A format for Outlook e-mail messages that supports a host of formatting options including text formatting, bullets, numbering, background colors, borders, and shading. Rich Text Format is supported by some Microsoft e-mail clients, including Outlook 97, Outlook 2000, Outlook 2002, and Outlook 2003.

Package for CD   A feature that helps you ensure that you have all the presentation components you need when you have to transport a PowerPoint presentation for use on a different computer.

page   See *data access page*.

page banner   A textual or graphic image that displays the title of a Web page.

Page Based On Schedule component   A FrontPage component that displays the contents of a file for a limited period of time.

Page component   A FrontPage component that displays the contents of a file wherever it is inserted.

page hits   The number of visits a Web page or site receives.

page title   The text that is displayed on the page banner of a Web page and in the title bar of a Web browser.

Page view editing window   The FrontPage window in which a Web page is edited.

Page view   The FrontPage view from which page creation and editing tasks are done. This view displays the open page or pages in the Page view editing window.

PANTONE®   A color model that defines hundreds of spot-color inks or process colors by combining CMYK inks.

paper stock   Paper of a particular weight and texture.

paragraph   In word processing, any amount of text that ends when you press the Enter key.

paragraph formatting   Collectively, the settings used to vary the look of paragraphs.

paragraph style   A set of formatting that can be applied to the paragraph containing the insertion point by selecting the style from a list.

parameter query   A query that prompts for the information to be used in the query, such as a range of dates.

parsing   In Access, the process of analyzing a document and identifying anything that looks like structured data.

password   A unique set of letters and characters used to allow access to files or processes.

permission   An attribute that specifies how a user can access data or objects in a database.

permissions   Authorization status that allows access to designated documents or programs.

Personal Address Book   An address book for personal contacts and distribution lists, rather than work-related contacts. The e-mail addresses and distributions lists in this address book are stored in a file with a *.pab* extension.

Personal Folders file   A data file in which Microsoft Outlook saves messages, appointments, tasks, and journal entries on your computer.

Personal Web Server (PWS)   An application that transmits information in Hypertext Markup Language (HTML) pages by using the Hypertext Transport Protocol (HTTP). It provides the ability to: publish Web pages on the Internet or over a local area network (LAN) on an intranet.

pessimistic locking   Locking a record for the entire time it is being edited.

photo album   A personal collection of digital images to use in presentations.

picture   A scanned photograph, clip art, or another type of image created with a program other than Word.

Picture Based On Schedule component   The component that displays the contents of designated graphics files for a specified period of time.

PivotChart   An interactive chart that is linked to a database.

PivotTable   An interactive table that is linked to a database.

pixel   Short for picture element. One pixel is a measurement representing the smallest amount of information displayed graphically on the screen as a single dot.

Places bar   A bar on the left side of the Save As and Open dialog boxes that provides quick access to commonly used locations in which to store and open files.

Plain Text   A format for Outlook e-mail messages that does not support any text formatting but is supported by all e-mail programs.

plot area   The area that includes the data markers and the category (x) and value (y) axes in a chart.

point   A measurement for the size of text. A point is equal to about 1/72 of an inch.

POP3   A common protocol used to retrieve e-mail messages from and Internet e-mail server.

populate   To fill a table or other object with data.

portrait   Vertical orientation in which the page is taller than it is wide.

portrait mode   A display and printing mode whereby columns run parallel to the long edge of a sheet of paper.

posting   Transferring files or messages to a Web site or server.

PowerPoint Viewer   A program that allows you to show a slide show on a computer that does not have PowerPoint installed.

precedents   The cells that are used in a formula.

presentation window   The electronic canvas on which you type text, draw shapes, create graphs, add color, and insert objects.

Preview pane   The FrontPage window in which Web pages can be viewed before they are published.

primary key   One or more fields that determine the uniqueness of each record in a database.

Print Layout view   A view that shows a document as it will appear on the printed page.

Print Preview   A view of a report that allows users to see exactly how the report will look when printed.

print style   A combination of paper and page settings that determines the way items are printed. For most items, Outlook provides a set of built-in print styles, and you can create your own.

Printing plate   A prepared surface from which printing is done.

private   A property of an appointment or meeting that prevents other users from seeing its details even if they have permission to view your calendar.

private store   A database for storing public folders in an Exchange sever.

privileges   Access rights that enable or restrict a user in viewing or modifying a Web site.

Problems report   A FrontPage report that contains information about broken or slow links and errors.

procedure   VBA code that performs a specific task or set of tasks.

Process color   A method of commercial printing that can produce all the required colors on a printed page.

profile   A group of e-mail accounts and address books configured to work together in Outlook.

program window   The main window in a program that includes many of the menus, tools, and other features found in all Microsoft Office program windows, as well as some features that are unique to a specific program or version.

promote   In an outline, to change body text to a heading, or to change a heading to a higher-level heading. To remove an indent on a bulleted item or sub-point of a slide, moving it up in the outline to it a higher-level item (a bulleted item or title).

properties   Information about a PowerPoint presentation such as the subject, author, presentation title, and so on.

property   A setting that determines the content and appearance of the object to which it applies.

publishing   Copying your Web site files to a Web server to display the site to the intended audience.

pure black and white A black and white image that displays only black and white without any shades of gray.

query A database object that locates information so that the information can be viewed, changed, or analyzed in various ways. The results of a query can be used as the basis for forms, reports, and data access pages. In Word, a set of selection criteria that indicate how to filter recipients in a mail merge.

Quick Notes Notes taken in the Mini OneNote window. Quick Notes are automatically added to your OneNote notebook for later use.

range A block of cells in a worksheet or datasheet.

readability statistics Information about the reading level of a document determined by the average number of syllables per word and words per sentence in relation to various U.S. reading scales.

Reading Layout view In Word, a view that shows a document as it will appear on a handheld reading device.

Reading Pane In Outlook, a pane in which you can view a message without opening it.

read-only The designation of a file that can be opened and viewed but not modified.

record selector The gray bar along the left edge of a table or form.

record source The place from which information derives between two bound objects, such as a field that pulls information from a table. See also *control source*.

records All the items of information (fields) that pertain to one particular entity, such as a customer, employee, or project. See also *field*.

recurring Describes items that occur repeatedly. For example, an appointment or task that occurs on a regular basis, such as a weekly status meeting or a monthly haircut, can be designated as recurring.

reference mark A number or character in the main text of a document that indicates additional information is included in a footnote or endnote.

referential integrity The system of rules Access uses to ensure that relationships between tables are valid and that data cannot be changed in one table without also being changed in all related tables.

relational database A sophisticated type of database in which data is organized in multiple related tables. Data can be pulled from the tables just as if they were stored in a single table.

relationship An association between common fields in two tables.

relative path A designation of the location of a file in relation to the current working directory. See also *absolute path*.

relative reference A cell reference in a formula, such as =B3, that refers to a cell that is a specific distance away from the cell that contains the formula. For example, if the formula =B3 were in cell C3, copying the formula to cell C4 would cause the formula to change to =B4.

relatively The designation of a picture whose position is determined by its relation to another element of a document, such as a margin, page, column, or character. See also *absolutely*.

reminder A message that appears at a specified interval before an appointment, meeting, or task, announcing when the activity is set to occur. Reminders appear any time Outlook is running, even if it isn't your active program.

Remote Web Site view A view of information about the published version of your Web site that you use to see the local and remote file structures simultaneously. You can manipulate local and remote files and folders from this view.

replica A copy of the Design Master of a database.

replicating The process of creating a Design Master so that multiple copies of a database can be sent to multiple locations for editing. The copies can then be synchronized with the Design Master so that it reflects all the changes.

report A database object used to display a table or tables in a formatted, easily accessible manner, either on the screen or on paper.

Reports view The FrontPage view that displays the available reports about the open Web site.

Research service A feature that enables you to access the reference material included in Word, materials you add to the service, and Internet resources.

revision marks Underlines, strike-through marks, and colored text that distinguishes revised text from original text.

RGB (Red, Green, and Blue) values The visible spectrum represented by mixing red, green, and blue colors.

rich media The combined use of motion and sound in media.

Rich Text Format (RTF) A common text format that many programs can open.

Rich Text See *Outlook Rich Text Format*.

role A named set of permissions to which specific users can be assigned.

root Web A Web site that contains a subweb.

rotating handle A small green handle around a shape used to adjust the angle of rotation of the shape.

row A horizontal line of cells in a spreadsheet or table.

row headings   The gray buttons (1, 2, 3, etc.) along the left side of a datasheet. See also *column headings*.

row selector   The gray box at the left end of a row in a table that, when clicked, selects all the cells in the row.

rules   A set of conditions, actions, and exceptions that process and organize messages.

run-in index   An index that lists subentries on the same line as the main entries in an index.

running a query   The process of telling Access to search the specified table or tables for records that match the criteria you have specified in the query and to display the designated fields from those records in a datasheet (table). See also *criteria*; *query*.

saving   The process of storing the current state of a database or database object for later retrieval. In Access, new records and changes to existing records are saved when you move to a different record; you don't have to do anything to save them. You do have to save new objects and changes to existing objects.

scalable font   A font that can be represented in different sizes without distortion.

scaling   Sizing an entire object by a set percentage.

schema   A description of the structure of XML data, as opposed to the content of the data. Applications that export to XML might combine the content and schema in one *.xml* file or might create an *.xml* file to hold the content and an *.xsd* file to hold the schema.

screen real estate   A term for the amount of space a designer has in which to present the information in a Web page.

screen resolution   The width and height of a computer monitor display in pixels.

ScreenTip   A pop-up box that tells you the name of or more information about a button, icon, or other item on the screen when you place the pointer over the item.

scripts   A list of commands executed without user interaction.

search folder   A virtual folder that contains a view of all e-mail items matching specific search criteria.

section break   A portion of a document that you can format with unique page settings, such as different margins. A section break appears as a double-dotted line across the page with the words *Section Break* and the type of section break in the middle.

Secure Multipurpose Internet Mail extensions (S/MIME)   A standard specification for authenticating and encrypting e-mail.

security level   A setting that determines whether presentations that contain macros can be opened on your computer.

security zone   A feature that you can use assign a Web site to a zone with a suitable security level.

select   To highlight an item in preparation for making some change to it.

select query   A query that retrieves data matching specified criteria from one or more tables and displays the results in a datasheet.

selection area   A blank area to the left of a document's left margin that you can click to select parts of the document.

selection box   A gray slanted line or dotted outline around an object.

selector   A small box attached to an object that you click to select the object.

sensitivity   A security setting of an e-mail message that indicates whether a message should be treated as normal, personal, private, or confidential.

server farms   Large-scale operations for hosting corporate or organizational Web sites.

Server Health   A FrontPage feature used to detect and repair potential problems with links on a server.

server rules   Rules that are applied to messages that are received or processed by the Exchange server.

server-based Web site   A Web site that is located on a computer that is configured as a Web server. See also *disk-based Web sites*.

server-side applications   Programs, run on the Web server rather than on a Web visitor's own computer, that enable you to post and modify content on a Web site.

SGML   See *Standard Generalized Markup Language*.

shading   Background and foreground colors or pictures the designer places on the Web page.

shape   An object that can be drawn free-form or created using tools provided by PowerPoint. Shapes can be sized, moved, copied, and formatted in a variety of ways to suit your needs.

shared attachments   Attachments saved on a SharePoint Document Workspace Web site, where a group can collaborate to work on files and discuss a project. Also called *live attachments*.

shared border   The areas at the top, bottom, left, or right of all or some of the pages in a Web site, in which common elements are displayed. Shared borders give the site a consistent look.

SharePoint team Web sites   A collaboration site for team use that consists of a Home page, a Document Libraries page, a Discussion Boards page, a Lists page, a Create Page page, and a Site Settings page.

sharing a database   Providing access to a database so more that one person can access it to add or alter its information.

signature   Text and/or pictures that are automatically added to the end of an outgoing e-mail message.

site map   A graphical depiction of the locations of Web pages in a Web site.

Site Summary report   A FrontPage report that summarizes statistics for the entire Web site.

sizing handle   A white circle on each corner and side of a shape that you can drag to change the shape's size. To preserve the shape's proportions, you can hold down the Shift key while resizing a shape.

slanted-line selection box   The border of a selected object that indicates that you can edit the object's content.

Slide Master   The part of a template that controls the characteristics (background color, text color, font, and font size) of the slides in a presentation. To make uniform changes to the slides, you change the Slide Master.

Slide Master view   In PowerPoint, the view from which you make changes to slides, using the Slide Master View toolbar. You switch to Slide Master view by pointing first to Master and then to Slide Master on the View menu.

Slide pane   Area in Normal view where you can view a slide and add text, graphics, and other items to the slide.

Slide Show view   In PowerPoint, a view where you can preview slides as an electronic presentation.

Slide Sorter view   In PowerPoint, a view where you can see all slides in a presentation in miniature.

slide timing   The length of time that a slide appears on the screen.

slide transition   The visual effect when moving from slide to slide in presentation.

Smart Tag   A flag that helps you control the result of certain actions, such as automatic text correction, automatic layout behavior, or copying and pasting.

soft page break   A page break that Word inserts in a document when the text reaches the bottom of the specified text column. In Normal view, a soft page break appears as a dotted line across the page.

source control   A feature that ensures that only one person at a time can edit a particular file.

source document   The original document, created in the source program, to which an object is linked.

source file   A file created in a source program that you are inserting in a destination file.

source program   The program that created the document that has been linked to a slide object.

spam   Electronic junk mail.

Spelling and Grammar   A feature that finds errors and suggests and makes corrections.

splash screen   An introductory screen containing useful or entertaining information. Often used to divert the user's attention while data is loading.

split bar   A line the defines which cells have been frozen at the top of a worksheet.

Split pane   One of the four panes in Page view. This pane simultaneously displays the design view and HTML code.

Spot color   A method of printing that creates color by mixing a limited number of colors with shades of black.

SQL   See *Structured Query Language*.

SQL database   A database that supports SQL and that can be accessed simultaneously by several users on a LAN.

Standard Generalized Markup Language (SGML)   A comprehensive system for coding the structure of text documents and other forms of data so that they can be used in a variety of environments.

standard module   A VBA program that contains general procedures that are not associated with any object.

static HTML page   A Web page that provides a snapshot of some portion of the database contents at one point in time.

static page   A Web page with hard-coded content.

stationery   A preset or automatic format for e-mail messages that specifies fonts, bullets, background color, horizontal lines, images, and other design elements.

status bar   The bar at the bottom of the presentation window that displays messages about the current state of PowerPoint.

string   A series of characters enclosed in quotation marks.

Structured Query Language (SQL)   A database sublanguage used in querying, updating, and managing relational databases—the de facto standard for database products.

style   A set of character and paragraph formatting that can be applied by selecting the style from a list.

stylus   A pen-shaped input device that is used to write, draw, or point and click to items on a touch screen.

sub procedure   A series of VBA statements enclosed by Sub and End Sub statements.

subdatasheet   A datasheet that is embedded in another datasheet.

subdocument   A subordinate document that is used in master documents.

subentry   A subtopic index listing.

subfolder   A folder within a folder.

subform   A form inserted in a control that is embedded in another form.

subpoints   Indented items below a bulleted item.

subreport   A report inserted in a control that is embedded in another report.

Substitution component   A component in FrontPage that associates names, or variables, with text. See also *variable*.

subweb   A stand-alone Web site that is nested inside another Web site; subwebs can have a unique set of permissions.

summary slide   A slide that lists titles of slides in a presentation and which can be used as a home page or an agenda slide.

switchboard   A form used to navigate among the objects of a database application so that users don't have to be familiar with the actual database.

synchronizing   The process of comparing and updating information between two versions so that both are up-to-date.

syntax   The format that expressions must conform to in order for Access to be able to process them.

tab leader   A repeating character (usually a dot or dash) that separates an entry from the page number associated with it. Tab leaders are often found in a table of contents and can be dotted, dashed, or solid lines.

tab stops   Locations across a page that you use to align text.

table   A structured presentation of information organized in vertical columns (records) and horizontal rows (fields).

Table AutoFormat   A set of 18 predefined table formats that include a variety of borders, colors, and attributes.

table of authorities   A table used in legal papers and other types of official documents that lists statutes, citations, case numbers, and similar information.

table of contents   A list of the main headings and subheadings in a document along with corresponding page numbers, which typically appears at the beginning of a document.

table of figures   A list of graphics, pictures, or figures and their corresponding captions in a document.

table title   The overall name of a table that appears either as a separate paragraph above the body of the table or in the table's top row.

Table Wizard   In Access, a tool that helps users construct tables.

Tablet PC   A Microsoft computer that is used exclusively through a touch screen. Tablet PCs run Windows XP.

tag   A command inserted in a document that specifies how the document, or a portion of the document, should be formatted.

task list   A list of tasks that appears in the Tasks folder and in the TaskPad in Calendar.

task pane   A pane that enables you to quickly access commands related to a specific task without having to use menus and toolbars.

TaskPad   The list of tasks that appears on the right side of the Outlook Calendar window.

tasks   Personal or work-related activities you want to track through to completion.

Tasks view   The FrontPage view that displays a list of tasks to be completed in the open Web site.

teams   Groups of users who work in collaboration to accomplish a task.

template   In Word, a document that stores text, styles, formatting, macros, and page information for use in other documents. In FrontPage, A predefined layout and design for specific types of Web pages and sites. In Access, a ready-made database application that users can tailor to fit their needs. In PowerPoint, an applied pattern used in creating the slides, handouts, and speaker notes in a PowerPoint presentation.

text animation   An effect applied to text that makes it appear on a slide in increments: one letter, word, or section at a time.

text box control   A control on a form or report where data from a table can be entered or edited.

text form field   A form field with which you can provide several types of text boxes so that users can enter text.

text label   A text object used primarily for short phrases or notes.

text object   A box that contains text in a slide and is handled as a unit.

text placeholder   A dotted-lined box that you can click to add text.

text wrapping break   A manual break that forces the text that follows it to the next line. Also called a *line break*.

theme   A set of unified design elements and color schemes.

Thesaurus   A Word feature that looks up alternative words or synonyms for a word.

thumbnail   A small version of a graphic or slide that is hyperlinked to the full-size version. In Word, a small image that represents a page in a document and that you can click to navigate to that page.

tick-mark labels   The labels that identify the data plotted in a chart.

Title Master   The part of a template that controls the characteristics (background color, text color, font, and font size) of the title slides in a presentation. To make uniform changes to the title slides, you change the Title Master.

title slide   The first slide in a presentation.

title text   Text that identifies the name or purpose of a slide.

TOC   The group of navigation links to each page of a Web site. Abbreviation for Table of Contents.

toggle   An on/off button or command that is activated when you click it and deactivated when you click it again.

toolbar   A graphical bar containing groupings of commands represented by buttons or icons.

Toolbar Options button   The button at the right end of a toolbar that provides access to hidden buttons and other toolbar options.

transaction record   The written record of transactions.

transparency film   Clear sheets for use in overhead projectors that can be written or printed on like paper.

unbound   Not linked, as when a control is used to calculate values from two or more fields and is therefore not bound to any particular field. See also *bound*.

UNC   See *universal naming convention*.

ungrouping   Separating a drawing into its individual elements so that they can be moved, sized, or otherwise edited one at a time. See also *grouping*.

Uniform Resource Locator (URL)   A unique address for a page on the World Wide Web, such as *http://www.microsoft.com*.

universal naming convention (UNC) path   A path format that includes the computer name, drive letter, and nested folder names. See also *mapped network drive*.

unmatched query   A form of select query that locates records in one table that don't have related records in another table.

unordered list   The Hypertext Markup Language (HTML) term for a bulleted list.

update query   A select query that changes the query's results in some way, such as by changing a field.

uppercase   Capital letters, as opposed to lowercase letters.

URL   See *Uniform Resource Locator*.

Usage report   A report that helps you count, track, analyze, and summarize the activity on your Web site.

user   A person authorized to access a database but who generally is not involved in establishing its structure.

validation rule   A field property that tests entries to ensure that only the correct types of information become part of a table.

variable   A named object that can assume any set of values.

VBA   See *Microsoft Visual Basic for Applications*.

VBA procedure   A VBA program.

vCard   A standard text-based format for storing contact information.

version   A document that has been altered from the original; Word records changes from version to version to help you track the editing history of a document.

view   The display of information from a specific perspective.

virtual folders   Folders that look like and link to an original folder.

Visual Basic Editor   The environment in which VBA programs are written and edited.

Visual Basic Integrated Development Environment (IDE)   See *Visual Basic Editor*.

watermark   A picture or text that appears faintly in the background of a printed document.

Web browser   A program such as Microsoft Internet Explorer that is used to locate and display web pages.

Web component   A ready-made programmatic element that adds capabilities such as link bars and tables of contents.

Web hosting company   A business that provides server space for Web sites. Many ISPs provide Web hosting as one of their services. See also *server-based Web sites*.

Web Layout view   A view that shows a document as it will appear as a Web page.

Web page   The document or one of multiple documents that make up a Web site. See also *file name*.

Web parts   Sections of a Web page.

Web server   A computer that is specifically configured to host Web sites.

Web site   A collection of Web pages with navigation tools and a designed theme.

Week view   In Outlook, the Calendar view displaying one full week at a time.

widow   The last line of a paragraph printed by itself at the top of a page.

WIF   See *workgroup information file.*

wildcard characters   Placeholders for unknown characters or characters in search criteria. When using the Find and Replace dialog box, characters can as place-holders for a single character, such as *?ffect* for *affect* and *effect*, or multiple characters.

Windows SharePoint team Services   Microsoft's server application for team Web sites that are used for information sharing and document collaboration.

wizard   A helpful tool that guides users through the steps for completing a specific task.

Word document window   A window that displays a document, along with the tools most frequently used when creating, editing, and formatting a document.

word processing   A process by which you create, edit, and format text documents.

word processing box   A text object used primarily for longer text.

word wrap   The movement of text to the next line when typing goes beyond the right margin.

WordArt   Text objects with special formatting applied to add bend, slope, color, or shadow.

work week   The days you are available for work-related appointments and meetings each week. Outlook displays the days outside your selected work week as shaded, to indicate that you are normally not available on those days.

Work Week view   In Outlook, the Calendar view displaying only the work days of one week in columnar format. You can define your work week as whatever days and hours you want.

Workflow report   A FrontPage report that gives site administrators an idea of the current status of a site that is under development. You can review the status of files, see to whom their development is assigned, see whether or not files have been published, and see whether files are currently checked out to anyone.

workgroup   A group of users in a multiuser environment who share data and the same workgroup information file. When you install Access, the setup program creates a default workgroup and sets up two groups, Admins and Users, within that workgroup.

workgroup information file (WIF)   The file where information about the objects, permissions, users, and groups that comprise a specific workgroup is stored.

workgroup template   A template that is stored in a central location so that it can be used by people working on a network.

worksheet   A page in a Microsoft Excel spreadsheet.

World Wide Web (WWW)   A network of servers on the Internet that support HTML-formatted documents.

wrapping   The breaking of lines of text to fit the width of the cell or text box.

WWW   See *World Wide Web*.

x-axis   The horizontal plane in a chart on which data is graphically represented. Also called the *category axis*.

XE   An index entry field code that defines the text and page number for an index entry and other options, such as a subentry text. See also *index entry*.

XML   See *Extensible Markup Language*.

XML schema   A description of a document's structure.

y-axis   The vertical plane in a chart on which data is graphically represented. Also called the *value axis*.

Index

Numerics

3-D drawings, 646

A

C

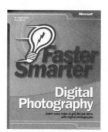

Learning solutions for every software user

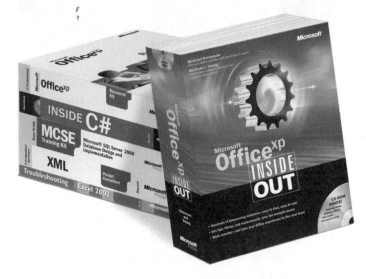

Microsoft Press learning solutions are ideal for every software user—from business users to developers to IT professionals

Microsoft Press® creates comprehensive learning solutions that empower everyone from business professionals and decision makers to software developers and IT professionals to work more productively with Microsoft® software. We design books for every business computer user, from beginners up to tech-savvy power users. We produce in-depth learning and reference titles to help developers work more productively with Microsoft programming tools and technologies. And we give IT professionals the training and technical resources they need to deploy, install, and support Microsoft products during all phases of the software adoption cycle. Whatever technology you're working with and no matter what your skill level, we have a learning tool to help you.

The tools you need to put technology to work.

***Microsoft*®**

microsoft.com/mspress